Mr Scott Mitchell
3502 SE Pinehurst Ave
Milwaukie, OR 97267

AF327337

SOARING ON WINGS LIKE

Eagles

A History of Oklahoma Christian University

Dr. Stafford North

Oklahoma Christian University
Oklahoma City, Oklahoma 73136
2008

Published by Oklahoma Christian University
Box 11000
Oklahoma City, Oklahoma 73136

Printed by Sheridan Books, Inc.
Ann Arbor, Michigan 48103

Editing by Heidi Gabrielle Nobles
Cover design and page layout by Kim Walden

Dust jacket. On the right: the mansion, with its tower, served as the primary
building on the Central Christian College campus in Bartlesville from 1950 to
1958. On the left: the Freede Centennial Tower, built as the centerpiece of the
Oklahoma City campus in 2008, and marking the Oklahoma centennial.

Library of Congress Control Number: 2008936402
ISBN: 978-0-615-24819-6

TABLE OF CONTENTS

PREFACE

The story of Oklahoma Christian University began in 1946, when discussions started among members of Churches of Christ in Oklahoma about establishing a college designed primarily to serve their needs. While this fellowship had a college in Cordell, Oklahoma, from 1908 to 1931, no such institution had existed for fifteen years.

After four years of meetings, fundraising, purchasing a campus, and hiring administrators, faculty, and staff, Central Christian College opened for students in 1950 at Bartlesville. Its beginning with 97 students and a campus of three buildings was hardly auspicious, but it was a start. From those seeds has grown the Oklahoma Christian University of today, with 2,500 students on its two campuses in Oklahoma City, Oklahoma, and Portland, Oregon.

A multitude of people have played a part in this remarkable venture: faculty and staff, the Board of Trustees, donors, students, parents of students, a host of friends, and even those associated with other institutions of higher education.

Those of us at Oklahoma Christian also believe God has had a hand in this development. Since the institution is dedicated to His glory and to the development of students to serve His purposes throughout the world, we believe He has providentially led and blessed this effort.

President Mike O'Neal and Vice President of Academic Affairs Jeanine Varner came to me in the spring of 2006 asking that I compose this history of Oklahoma Christian. They believed that after more than fifty years, the time had come for the story to be written so it could be known more widely. They also said, as nicely as they could, that if this history were not written soon, those of us who had lived through the early years of it would not be around to help. It was with some reluctance that I accepted this challenging task. It would mean giving up some of my normal teaching load for two years, and that was hard, since teaching is what I most love to do. They convinced me, however, that in the long run, the greater good would come from making this story available.

Why does this story need to be told? Because it relates the struggle, often against great odds, of those who have believed strongly in the primary purpose of the university to educate children from families of Churches of Christ. Because it tells how often heroic, sacrificial efforts have brought this university to its present success. Because it tells of the students whose training at this university has prepared them for service to their communities, to their countries, to the world, and especially, to the kingdom of God. Because it reveals the determination of those connected with the university to achieve excellence in all they do. In short, a history of Oklahoma Christian University provides a story to inspire those who serve and attend this university so they will recognize its heritage of purpose, sacrificial effort, and remarkable achievement. This account also will be of interest to those in the higher education community who want to observe the development of a private institution of higher education from its beginning to one of international recognition.

Two earlier histories of Oklahoma Christian have been written. The first was *Central Christian College: From Dream to Reality*, written and published in 1970 by W. O. Beeman, who served for ten years as the business manager of Oklahoma Christian College. Beeman's work has been very helpful in tracking much of what happened to that point in the history of the college, especially in the areas of finances and facilities.

For Oklahoma Christian's 50th Anniversary, Dr. Terry Johnson, then chancellor of the university, compiled an outstanding pictorial history called *Jubilee*. Johnson's book presents a beautiful array of pictures with accompanying text to portray the first fifty years. Neither of these works, as useful as they are, however, provides a detailed, comprehensive history of the university from its beginning until now. Such is the aim of this current endeavor. I have written the book to provide both an interesting narrative about the many facets of the university and a factual account for those needing a ready reference for information about Oklahoma Christian.

President O'Neal also asked that, in the process of writing this history, effort be given to upgrading the archives of the university held in the Library. JJ Compton is our archivist and has worked hard to get many items about the history of the university into usable status. She and I have gathered other materials for the archives, including a number of videotaped interviews with those who have played vital roles in the university's development. We also have gathered via email recollections of many who were students and faculty during earlier years. In 2008, the archives moved into much better space in the OC library to allow for better presentation and preservation of items recounting the history of the university.

To guide in the process of writing this history, President O'Neal established an oversight committee composed of himself, Dr. Bailey McBride, Dr. John Maple, Dr. Lynn McMillon, Ron Frost, Tamie Willis, and Dr. Jeanine Varner. Dr. Varner was chair of the committee until her departure from the university in the summer of 2007 and, since that time, Dr. Maple has served as chair. Committee members have read drafts of the chapters to provide guidance, advice, and editorial assistance to make the final outcome more useful. They also have helped in making decisions about the content and format of the book. The committee employed OC alumnus Heidi Gabrielle Nobles (2002), a professional editor now living in Columbia, South Carolina, to serve as principal editor of this work, and alumnus Kim Walden (1998) of Oklahoma City as the graphic artist to do the final layout and paging. Both of these have made major contributions to the success of this effort. My wife, Jo Anne, has also helped with many useful suggestions as we have discussed this project over the past two years.

Many on campus have provided assistance—too many, of course, to name them all. Three, however, have given special help: Dr. Mickey Banister, registrar; Jeff Bingham, vice president for financial affairs; and Micah Wooten of the Marketing department.

My greatest concern in writing this history is what I have left out. Obviously, because of space limitations, many who have played important roles in the work of Oklahoma Christian University will not even be mentioned. Some will read this book hoping to see a reference to a parent or favorite teacher and will be disappointed. Faculty members over the years, for example, would number in the hundreds and staff members would reach a similar total. So if your favorite person or story is not included, please know this does not mean I do not consider that person or moment significant. There is just too much to tell it all. I hope what is told, however, will reveal the story of what the Lord has done for His kingdom through those He has brought together for the work of Oklahoma Christian University for more than fifty years. By the time you finish this account of the founding and development of Oklahoma Christian, I hope you will agree that the title is fitting: *Soaring On Wings Like Eagles*.

—Stafford North
September, 2008

Chapter 1
THE BEGINNING

A Surprise Offer

The year was 1946. World War II had just ended, and the U.S. government was making many military properties available for civilian use. One of these was an abandoned ordnance plant six miles south of Pryor, Oklahoma, and twenty-five miles northeast of Tulsa. The Dupont Corporation had used part of this property to manufacture explosives during the war, and there were a large number of buildings to house workers.[1] From October 1944 through March 1945, the government had used some of these buildings to house prisoners of war, mostly German officers, so the facility was sometimes called "The Prisoner of War Camp." City officials in Pryor, population 4,500, sought a good tenant to boost the local economy. They thought an educational institution would meet the qualifications the government had established, and a college would be a great addition to the Pryor community.

As the Chamber of Commerce scanned the Oklahoma collegiate scene, they saw that the Baptists had Oklahoma Baptist University; the Methodists, Oklahoma City University; the Presbyterians, the University of Tulsa; the Catholics, St. Gregory's College; the Disciples of Christ, Phillips University; and the Nazarenes, Bethany Nazarene College. The Churches of Christ, with some 628 congregations throughout the state, did not have a college. In view of this, the local superintendent of schools, Garland Godfrey, proposed that the Pryor Chamber of Commerce contact Churches of Christ about starting a college in the former ordnance plant.[2]

On an afternoon late in May of 1946, Richard Ealen, editor of the *Pryor Daily Times-Democrat,* acting on behalf of the Chamber, called A. H. Bryant, preacher for the Church of Christ in Pryor, inviting

A.H. Bryant

him to his office immediately. Bryant arrived shortly and Ealen told him the City of Pryor was proposing to purchase the nearby 340-acre government site along with its buildings, equipment, furniture, and appliances to donate to Churches of Christ if they would operate a college there. Bryant said he was "floored" because establishing such a college was a completely new idea to him. Quickly, however, he saw the possibilities and visited with other church members about the proposal.[3]

A May 27 article in the *Pryor Daily Times-Democrat* detailed the offer the city was making to Churches of Christ. The article explained there were "65 dormitories, each with 28 rooms and four baths. . . . Each of the buildings is 29 x 104 feet with two full stories." The article quoted Bryant as saying that the college would not need "a considerable number of the 86 buildings and these might be disposed of in a manner which would aid in raising funds."[4]

Having received a favorable response from local brethren, Bryant and Joe Pollard, also of Pryor, sent invitations to all Churches of Christ in Oklahoma and to some in surrounding states asking members of the church to meet on June 4 "to discuss the possibility of establishing a college."[5] Bryant, Ray Rayburn, and George T. Jones, all members of a temporary committee calling the meeting, toured Oklahoma to encourage members of the church to attend.[6]

On June 4, eighty-three preachers, elders, and interested members assembled in Pryor: sixty-six from Oklahoma, nine from Arkansas, six from Kansas, and one each from Missouri and Texas.[7] Bryant informed these men of the possibility of acquiring property from the government "for the purpose of establishing and operating a college."[8] In a tour of the facilities, the group selected eleven buildings suitable for student housing and six other buildings appropriate for other uses.[9] This property was estimated to be worth "several hundred thousand dollars."[10]

Those present authorized Bryant to release the following statement to the newspaper: "Definite decision was made at a meeting of representatives of the churches of Christ Tuesday, June 4, 46, and plans are being made to receive dormitory city to be used for college purposes, if and when same is tendered to said churches of Christ, by the city of Pryor and the chamber of commerce."[11] While the majority at the meeting agreed to accept the property if officially offered, some were reluctant about using the surplus army buildings available in Pryor.[12]

At this June 4 meeting, no doubt some remembered a college serving Churches of Christ in the Oklahoma area that had existed in Cordell. This school had operated from 1908 to 1931 under three different names[13] with a peak college-level enrollment of seventy-six. While the school had gone bankrupt during the early years of the Depression, it had served students and churches well and had produced many preachers.

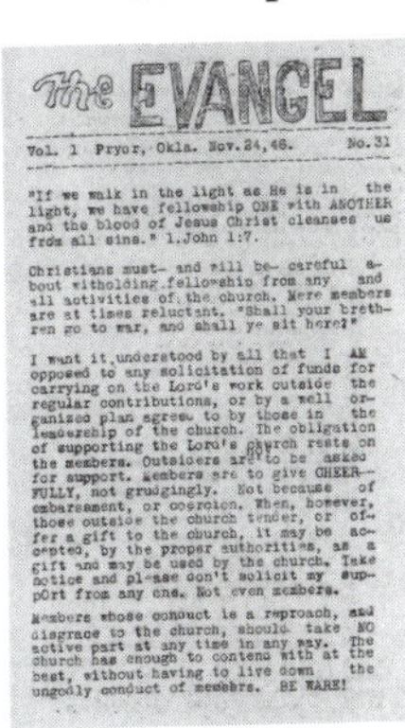

Vol. 1 Pryor, Okla. Nov. 24, 46.   No. 31

"If we walk in the light as He is in the light, we have fellowship ONE with ANOTHER and the blood of Jesus Christ cleanses us from all sins." 1 John 1:7.

Christians must- and will be- careful about witholding fellowship from any and all activities of the church. Mere members are at times reluctant. "Shall your brethren go to war, and shall ye sit here?"

I want it understood by all that I AM opposed to any solicitation of funds for carrying on the Lord's work outside the regular contributions, or by a well organized plan agreed to by those in the leadership of the church. The obligation of supporting the Lord's church rests on the members. Outsiders are to be asked for support. Members are to give CHEER-FULLY, not grudgingly. Not because of embarassment, or coercion. When, however, those outside the church tender, or offer a gift to the church, it may be accepted, by the proper authorities, as a gift and may be used by the church. Take notice and please don't solicit my support from any one. Not even members.

Members whose conduct is a reproach, and disgrace to the church, should take NO active part at any time in any way. The church has enough to contend with at the best, without having to live down the ungodly conduct of members. BE WARE!

The Evangel

Those assembled at the meeting also knew that churches tended to grow in the area around Christian colleges; they had seen that happen in such cities as Abilene, Nashville, and Searcy. So the prospect of building a Christian college in Oklahoma to serve youth from Churches of Christ and to foster growth in the church caught the interest of many. Perhaps this prospective gift of land and buildings would allow a college serving these purposes again to find a home in Oklahoma.

Since the response on June 4, 1946, was generally favorable, the group nominated fourteen prospective Board members from Oklahoma, Texas, Kansas, and Missouri. Sixty-four returned the mail ballots electing L. O. Sanderson of Tulsa, Frank Winters of Oklahoma City, Rue Porter of Neosho, Otis Broadus of Wichita, and C. E. Parker of Tulsa.[14] Only Rue Porter, however, agreed to serve.[15] After this discouraging development, the group apparently did not act over the next two months.

On September 22, the *Evangel*, weekly bulletin for the Pryor Church of Christ, carried a letter Frank Winters had written to the Pryor Chamber of Commerce. Winters, an elder for the Culbertson Heights Church of Christ in Oklahoma City, had been elected to the Board of Trustees, but had chosen not to serve. He thanked the Chamber, but speaking for himself, he said, "In my opinion, we are not in position to approve the establishment of the college at this time, and this letter is written, hoping that you will not obligate yourselves until we know more about whether or not it is a practical undertaking. All the people I have talked with seem to be doubtful of it being a practical proposition."[16]

A Name, a Charter, and a Plan

Even with these discouraging developments, some remained convinced of the need for a college to serve Churches of Christ in Oklahoma, and thought the Pryor opportunity worth pursuing. These supporters persevered, convening a meeting in Pryor on September 25, and those coming appointed a temporary board, instructing them to continue negotiations and to seek a charter.[17]   The group even chose a name for the new college—Mid-States Christian College. By the meeting's end, it seemed a college would indeed be established at Pryor.[18]   Bryant took the documents to the Secretary of State in Oklahoma City on September 26, and the charter for Mid-States Christian College was issued that day.

Now on a fast track to meet the deadline Pryor officials had set, the temporary Board of Trustees met at the office of the Chamber of Commerce in Pryor on September 27. At this first official meeting, the Board chose officers, adopted a seal, and appointed a committee to draw up by-laws. Those assembled also instructed Bryant and Pollard to continue negotiating with Pryor officials for the government property.[19]

The Board next met October 25, and Chairman Bryant shared the news that he had been asked to come as soon as possible to a meeting in Fort Worth with the Federal Public Housing Authority. He was to bring evidence of his authority to represent the corporation in negotiations and proof of the need for a college in Pryor to meet the needs of servicemen and women entitled to attend college under the GI Bill. The government also said the college would have to agree to provide the streets, sidewalks, landscaping, and utilities for the property even if the college was given the land, buildings, and furnishings. In a resolution dated October 25, the Board named Bryant as its agent for dealing with the government.[20]

The offer now did not seem quite as promising as it had in the beginning. The federal government was not going to deliver a fully prepared campus, and the college would have to raise a large amount of money to ready the site for use. With no money on hand and no prospect of any in the near future, the project might have ended. Undaunted, however, the five-man Board proceeded, passing a resolution about the need for a college in Pryor and authorizing Bryant to enter an agreement with the government for the property.[21] The perseverance of these pioneers for Christian education demonstrated their strong desire to have a college in Oklahoma for members of Churches of Christ, and their unwillingness to let slip through their fingers what they perceived to be an unusual opportunity.

A Contract and Further Negotiations

On October 28, 1946, Bryant signed a contract with the Federal Public Housing Authority for eleven buildings "to be converted into 406 dormitory accommodations and 60 family dwelling units and utility facilities necessary to furnish services to such buildings."

On the basis of this contract, on November 3, Bryant wrote:

> Papers transferring eighteen buildings have been executed. Eleven of these Dormitory style buildings have been transferred to the Mid-States Christian College for housing purposes only. The additional six buildings are to be used by the government in assembling in college style such buildings as are to be used by the college for other than housing purposes. All building material needed by the college for other than housing purposes will be furnished by the government. . . . All college buildings other than housing units are to be furnished completely with all necessary installations and equipments. Buildings to be delivered to the Mid-States Christian College as soon as all necessary plans are properly executed.[22]

In this same bulletin, Bryant wrote that the Federal National Bank of Wichita, Kansas, "was not in a position to negotiate with college representatives in the final consummation of real estate." He did not, however, see this as an insurmountable problem and said, "Our hopes are that this school will afford hundreds of boys and girls—the finest in the land—christian education and training. To this end we willingly, and wholeheartedly commit ourselves and our purpose."

Just five days later, on November 8, Bryant reported: "Plans for a Christian College at Pryor are now in the last, or final stages. We must decide to leave it to some other religious institution that will operate it, or go to work in earnest." He now spoke not only of the eleven dormitories, but of fifteen other buildings the government would erect, equip, and furnish.[23]

On November 17, Bryant, acting in his capacity as chair of the temporary Board, stated in the *Evangel* he had called a meeting of the Board for November 19 and reported the government was ready to deed to Mid-States Christian College the land, eleven dormitories, and fifteen other buildings for an administration building, gymnasium, cafeteria, classrooms, science laboratories, music practice rooms, and a small auditorium. The Board issued a call for a general meeting of "brethren of the Churches of Christ" from the states of Oklahoma, Arkansas, Kansas, and Missouri on December 10. The invitation for this meeting read, "plans will be inaugurated for promoting and furthering the interests of Mid-States Christian."[24]

The December 10 meeting was well attended, and among those present was Abilene Christian Vice President W. R. Smith. His account of the meeting appeared in the *Christian Chronicle*, a newspaper begun in 1943 to report news among Churches of Christ. Smith explained that starting a Christian college in Oklahoma was

> an opportunity which ought to be seized and prosecuted with vigor. In fact, if our brethren fail to institute and perpetuate a school on this property, some other group will. No Christian school has ever been started with so much property as a free gift. Surely the brethren in the State of Oklahoma and adjacent states will rally to this golden opportunity and build a school which will rank with the best.[25]

Smith's report confirmed the gift of the property, announced widely the prospect of starting a Christian college in Oklahoma, and showed support from Abilene Christian College even though that school, undoubtedly, would lose some students and financial support from the area. If the cause of Christian education would be expanded, the administration in Abilene would give its support.

At this December 10 meeting, the group chose a permanent Board of Trustees. They selected as chair Byron Fullerton, who had been a minister at the Culbertson Heights congregation in Oklahoma City, but had recently moved to Norman to assist in establishing the University Church of Christ. The group also chose other members to the Board: Cline Mansur of Vinita, Rue Porter of Neosho, J. E. Wright of Tulsa, Warren Kelly of Muskogee, G.

Byron Fullerton

W. Roberts of Bartlesville, Ray Kellogg of Wichita, Frank Winters of Oklahoma City, and T. E. Burch of Wewoka. The new permanent Board, comprised wholly of preachers and elders among Churches of Christ,[26] sprang quickly into action. Following Chairman Fullerton's visit with government officials in Ft. Worth, he notified Board members about the progress. J. E. Wright responded, "I think you are doing good work. . . . With these accomplishments and a few others that I believe will eventually come our way, I think we will be in position to go ahead."[27]

Problems Arise

Problems, however, soon began to surface. On December 18, Frank Winters wrote Joe Pollard, rejecting another request that he serve on the Board. This influential elder from Oklahoma City said, "I have probably talked with a score or more of our leading brethren in this section of the country, all of whom are doubtful about the practicability and advisability of trying to build a Christian college at Pryor under all the circumstances." He then referred to the Christian college at Cordell which had failed, in part, he said, because it was "handicapped by having a location which was not easily accessible." Winters explained that "Oklahoma probably needs a Christian college," but "in order to succeed, the college should be located in a practical place."[28]

Winters wasn't the only person with concerns about the location: Board member Cline Mansur, a civil engineer, wrote Fullerton on December 29: "I wish we could talk the government into remodeling the barracks buildings which they are giving us, as we connect to necessary utilities the additional buildings which they 'may' give us. Otherwise, we shall have to put out a huge sum at the outset."[29] Another trustee, G. M. Roberts, principal of College High School in Bartlesville, wrote Fullerton on January 10: "I am open to convictions but still have to be convinced that we are getting the property that we need for a permanent college plant."[30] A more concrete blow came at the next Board meeting in Pryor on January 21. Richard Ealen, representing the Pryor Chamber of Commerce, reported that "Pryor has had a set-back." The Federal Land Bank in Wichita had stated that they "would not allow a municipality to exercise its priority to obtain real property if such property is to be donated to an educational institution." Representatives from Pryor, he explained, would be going to Wichita to "straighten out the matter."[31]

An even more serious problem arising in that January 21 meeting regarded the Board itself. Fullerton said, "Kellogg won't serve; Winters won't serve; Burch wants to be relieved; Porter is in California; Roberts didn't arrive for reasons unknown." The Board did not have a quorum. "Considerable discussion then ensued: are we for the project at Pryor? can we sell it?" Fullerton explained that as soon as Pryor officials reported about the land, "a meeting of representatives of all congregations will be called. At that time the board will submit its findings and opinions; if the group then wants to continue the project as contemplated at Pryor the present Board can either carry on, or resign."[32]

In a January 28 letter to Fullerton, Wright shared his concerns:

> I have been thinking considerably concerning the project at Pryor and the meeting you are going to call soon. It seems to me that we have tried from every angle to find a workable solution to the problems which have presented themselves and have investigated every phase of the offer of land and equipment with its requirements and stipulations and that

after doing so with open minds the entire board is still unsold on the advisability of proceeding further. However after making this thorough investigation we will never regret asking the brethren to abandon the project. Nevertheless we do not want the abandonment of the project at Pryor to blight any prospects of a college in Oklahoma and it is, I am sure, our desire to seek other possibilities and locations that might be more enhancing.[33]

While sentiment was increasing for a college in Oklahoma to serve Churches of Christ, interest in the Pryor location was declining.

An End and a Beginning

Despite the strong efforts and the great investment of time and travel on the part of many, the project to start a Christian college in Pryor was unraveling. On February 20, 1947, Byron Fullerton, on behalf of the Board of Mid-States Christian College, issued the following "IMPORTANT ANNOUNCEMENT FOR CHURCHES OF CHRIST":

We have held meetings; we made a trip to Fort Worth; we have conferred with brethren experienced in the problems of Christian education. We have tried to make ourselves believe the proposal would be a good thing, but we have not been able to do so. We think it would probably be a 'White elephant.' Here are our reasons: (1) The land and buildings are seven miles out of Pryor. (2) The buildings are of wood construction, and even now are in need of paint. (3) The land is not suitable for agricultural purposes. (4) Jobs would not be available for students who have to work. (5) The situation is such that we do not believe we would want to send our own children there to school. (6) We do not think this is the place for a permanent school which we all desire. (7) What we would get from the Federal Government is very indefinite. (8) Even when remodeled the buildings would not be very suitable for class room buildings.

We are asking the brethren to help us make the final decision on the matter. There might be enough who disagree with us to go ahead. Because of this, and because we have a lot of sentiment for a Christian College in Oklahoma we are calling a meeting of <u>all brethren who will come</u>. The meeting will be held in the building of the <u>Southwest Church of Christ,</u>

<u>2600 So. Agnew Street in Oklahoma City</u> on February 28, 1947. The meeting will begin at 10:30 a.m. on that date. . . .

We will, also, discuss the matter of establishing a Christian College elsewhere. Everybody will be given an opportunity to express themselves.[34]

At the February 28 meeting, after a report of the situation and general discussion, Board member L. O. Sanderson moved that the Board of Trustees of Mid-States Christian College be dissolved. The next sentence of the minutes states definitively: "Discussions of Mid-States Christian College concluded."[35]

Board of Trustees meeting in 1947. First row L to R, Lloyd Smith, unknown, Bob Tinius, unknown, L.O. Sanderson, John Banister, G.R. Tinius. Byron Fullerton and J.E. Wright are behind Sanderson to the left.

Chairman Fullerton then called for discussion of the future possibilities of Christian higher education in Oklahoma. A. S. Croom recommended the appointment of a steering committee, the employment of a president and a fundraising campaign of from $250,000 to $500,000 before approaching any city for a possible location. The assembled group accepted this recommendation and named a steering committee of eight. They chose as chairman G. R. Tinius, who was operating a leather wholesale company in Tulsa and who had been an elder at both 10th and Rockford and East Side in Tulsa.[36] Other members were J. E. Wright of Tulsa, secretary; A. S. Croom of Enid; L. O. Sanderson of Norman; Frank Winters of Oklahoma City; Byron Fullerton of Norman; Lloyd Smith of Lawton; and Warren Kelly of Muskogee. The group had a good geographic spread and now that the prospective location was no longer in Pryor, Winters agreed to serve.

This meeting closed the door on any possibility of a Christian college in Pryor, but opened the door to other more promising possibilities. W. O. Beeman, summarizing the significance of this meeting, explained:

> With this meeting came an end to the movement started in Pryor on May 26, 1946. It had been an epic struggle. Many good and capable men had spent days and hours of their time . . . and while in the end nothing tangible was left, there was created the desire and determination to establish a Christian college in Oklahoma. The charter of Mid-States Christian College was surrendered; the Board of Trustees was disbanded; so there is no connection legal or otherwise between it and [the later] Oklahoma Christian College, but the same men are involved, the purposes are the same. So in every real sense, Mid-States Christian College and the activity which started in Pryor on May 26, 1946, has never ended; the dissolution of Mid-States Christian College corporation and the formation of a steering committee to make a new start was merely a shifting of gears, because the new steering committee plunged into its work with renewed vigor and determination.[37]

The decision not to proceed with the proposal to start a Christian college in Pryor after so much work could easily have discouraged any further efforts to establish such a college in Oklahoma. The fact that those ending the Pryor opportunity were the very group which continued the effort for a college in Oklahoma to serve Churches of Christ shows their strong commitment to this purpose. So convinced were they, however, that the time was right for a Christian college in Oklahoma, they did not give up.

The new steering committee moved quickly, meeting in Oklahoma City on March 11, 1947. The committee held six regional meetings to determine whether sufficient interest existed among church members to support establishing a Christian college in Oklahoma.[38] The Board minutes of April 22, 1947, report the outcome of those six meetings. In Wichita at the West Side Church of Christ, L. O. Sanderson spoke with 114 present. At Lawton, thirty-six heard Robert Alexander from Abilene Christian College who spoke in place of the scheduled president of Abilene Christian, Don Morris. In Ada, where Sanderson also spoke, 125 attended. Norvel Young spoke in Tulsa on April 14 at the Mainstreet Church of Christ on April 14, drawing 500 from Tulsa and twelve other cities, and at Muskogee the sentiment was "good." In Oklahoma City, John Banister spoke at the Culbertson Heights Church of Christ on May 5 where there was "much sentiment" in favor of starting a college and "no opposition to it."[39]

The Growing Board, the Relationship to the Church, and the First Employee

As a result of these regional meetings, the Steering Committee concluded on April 22 that "the brethren are very favorable towards the establishment of a christian college." They decided, therefore, to select additional members to serve with them.[40]

At a meeting on May 5 prior to the Oklahoma City public event, the Steering Committee proposed to add nine to their number and for these seventeen to serve as the Board of Trustees. On May 19, at a meeting in the Oklahoma City YMCA, three more were added to make twenty. This new, self-perpetuating Board elected G. R. Tinius, president; Rex Westerfield, vice president, Calvin Proctor, secretary, and J. D. Fine, treasurer. At this same meeting, the Board employed G. R. Tinius, its own president, to begin on June 1 to raise the $250,000 deemed necessary as a beginning amount. The Board also decided that the name and location of the new college would be determined later, but immediately appointed an executive committee and a committee to determine the legal requirements for chartering a college in Oklahoma.

G.R. Tinius

The last action of the meeting that day was to adopt the following resolution about the relationship of the new college to local congregations of the Churches of Christ.

> Whereas, a group of individuals, interested in Christian Education has begun the work of endeavoring to build a Christian College in this section of the country, and
>
> Whereas, we believe that such an institution should be kept separate and apart from the church;
>
> Therefore be it resolved, that such an institution shall be organized as a business corporation and that no funds shall be solicited or accepted from any congregation of the Lord's Church, but that contributions be confined to individual Christians and those interested in Christian Education.[41]

In this action, the Board was placing itself on the conservative side of an issue Churches of Christ were then debating as to whether congregations should contribute directly to colleges or whether donations should come from individual church members.

The new college now had its first employee, G. R. Tinius, who would begin the task of raising $250,000 for a school that had no location and no name, and existed only as a Board of Trustees.

A New Name

A month later, at a meeting on June 3, J. E. Novak suggested that the new school bear the name Central Christian College, and the motion passed.[42] A mail ballot of the other members of the Board led to the unanimous adoption of that name.[43]

Tinius soon established a "temporary" office for Central Christian College in his own business office in Tulsa which, he said, would not cost the college anything and would give him a convenient place from which to operate. Until the spring of 1949, communications about Central Christian College bore the address of 228 East Third Street in Tulsa.

At a meeting on July 31, the Board approved by-laws and Articles of Incorporation. In this process, the Board also adopted qualifications for members of the Board:

> The said college and institution of learning shall be under the management, direction, and control of a Board of Trustees to be composed of not less than twenty (20) nor more than thirty (30) persons, each of whom shall be a member of a congregation of the Church of Christ, which takes the New Testament as its only and sufficient rule of faith, worship, and practice, and rejects from its faith, worship, and practice everything not required by either precedent or example, and which does not introduce into the faith, worship, and practice as a part of the same or as adjuncts thereto any supplemental organization or anything else not clearly and directly authorized in the New Testament either by precept or example; and no person shall be qualified to act as a trustee whose religious belief, faith, or practice is not in conformity with the provisions and qualifications set out in this paragraph.[44]

The intent of the statement was clear. The new college was to have close ties to Churches of Christ. All of its Board members would not only be members of this church, but must be personally committed to believe and practice only those things "clearly and directly authorized in the New Testament by precept or example." The new Board had already achieved an interesting balance: no money would be accepted directly from congregations of Churches of Christ, but all members of the Board would be members of congregations fully subscribing to the beliefs common among these churches.

It is interesting to note that the Board's statement for the qualifications of its members was taken almost verbatim from the charter of Abilene Christian College,[45] and that statement was taken entirely from the charter of Gunter Bible College, founded in 1903 near Sherman, Texas. Jesse P. Sewell, later president of Abilene Christian College, and William B. Gano (who, as a matter of trivia, was the grandfather of wealthy industrialist and movie-maker Howard Hughes) wrote the statement for Gunter in 1901.[46]

The statement demonstrates that colleges among Churches of Christ sought to be closely tied to their church constituency and to reflect the views of that fellowship. They knew that without such ties, they would neither fulfill their mission or raise the support to continue.

Fundraising Efforts Expanded

In July, Tinius published the first *Bulletin* for Central Christian College, which he sent to as many church members as possible. In one article he gave a brief history of the situation in Pryor and listed the names of the twenty Board members. Another article explained that the Board had chosen Tinius to direct the effort to raise $250,000. The center and back page of the four-page bulletin contained an article by L. O. Sanderson entitled "A School—and the Best for the Central West." The article provides a carefully stated rationale for a Christian college in Oklahoma. "A Christian school offers the best known means of combining the finest influence with our secular pursuits in training." To explain, Sanderson continued, "Public schools are crowded, both with students and with many activities in which Christian children cannot participate. In these crowded, limited, political, and worldly environments, our children are molded—for better or worse, with the odds against the desirable." He contrasts this with a college having Christian teachers for students from Christian homes, that teaches them the Bible and sets high moral standards, and that, along with this, teaches the secular subjects they need. He closes with an appeal for those who desire such a school to send their contributions, whether large or small. "It has been done; it can be done! Christian people of the central West should rise to the occasion and help make 'Central Christian College' the school of real worth, the school that lives up to its purposes, that maintains its balance, that stays in its place, and that will live on and on to accomplish its great work."[47]

Sanderson's article stated clearly the rationale of Central Christian's founders. They sought to establish an institution of higher learning where students could prepare for their careers, but within a strong framework of Christian beliefs, morals, and examples. They were not seeking merely to shelter their children from the dangers they saw in other types of institutions, but to provide the foundation for the higher calling to which they hoped their children would aspire.

To create interest in the new college, between October 1947 and late summer 1948, supporters held "mass meetings" in Tulsa, Oklahoma City, Ada, Wichita, and Muskogee. Some of the best known preachers in the brotherhood spoke: E. R. Harper, minister from Little Rock, L. R. Wilson, president of Florida Christian College, Delmar Owens, minister from Tulsa, Norvel Young, minister from Lubbock, and Cleon Liles, minister from Little Rock. G. R. Tinius reported at the 1947 Abilene Christian Lectureship about the developing Christian college in Oklahoma.[48]

In November, Tinius published a second issue of the Central Christian College *Bulletin*, again emphasizing the need for a Christian college in Oklahoma. In this issue, Byron Fullerton argued that "state schools" often lead Christian young people into false ideas. He stated that a Christian college could "save most of our youth, and give them the training that would enable them to be efficient leaders of the Lord's church in the future." Fullerton noted that at both the University of Oklahoma and Oklahoma State University there are about 350 students who indicate membership in the Church of Christ or give it as their preference. He also stated that many attend other state colleges in Oklahoma and Kansas and some even attend colleges of various denominations. So he believed there were enough students to attend Central Christian College, and after all, "[if] we should begin with an enrollment of only two hundred we would feel that we had made a wonderful start."[49]

In articles in the first two bulletins for Central Christian College, Sanderson and Fullerton had made the case for establishing a new Christian college in Oklahoma. They believed such a college could serve Christian young people by training them for their occupations in an environment that would preserve and enhance their spiritual life, and, along with this, prepare them for leadership in the church. Such a vision has, of course, remained a major goal of Oklahoma Christian University.

A key meeting of the Board came on December 4, 1947. In a November 11 letter to call the meeting, Tinius reported he had raised $17,000 in cash and pledges. Even though this amount was still far short of the $250,000 goal, the Board believed the time had come to establish a college in Oklahoma because, in a bold move, the Board authorized Chairman Tinius to search for a man "to head the college."[50]

Bartlesville

December of 1947 and a dramatic new development! In a memorandum to Board Members, dated December 26, 1947, Tinius wrote: "An exceptionally fine piece of property has been offered us at a reasonable price." The Executive

The Foster Mansion in Bartlesville

Committee of the Board had inspected a site in Bartlesville and called a meeting for January 15, 1948, to give other members an opportunity to see it.[51]

At that meeting, Board members toured the previous home of H. V. Foster, a Bartlesville oil millionaire. Foster had died, and his widow had married C. E. Burlingame, another oil millionaire. For seven years, the American Military Academy had rented this mansion and currently had a student body of fifty-five.[52] As Board members toured the site, they would have seen a 152-acre property, on rolling hills. The central feature was a Spanish-style mansion of thirty-two rooms named La Quinta, built in 1932 at a cost of $500,000.[53] The Board surely would have recognized its possibilities. Its first-floor guest bedrooms could become administrative offices, its dining room and kitchen could feed the students, its library could serve for the college library, its second-story family living quarters could be used for student housing, and its living room could serve as a student gathering place. Out-buildings could serve other purposes. And the landscaping was beautiful. Minutes of this meeting indicate that the group was interested and voted to place an option on the property.[54]

Eleven days later, on January 26, the Board met again, this time in the Skirvin Tower in Oklahoma City. The asking price on the Bartlesville property was $150,000 and the City of Bartlesville promised to contribute $100,000 to the college's building fund once college officials had obtained the property and started construction on other buildings.[55] The property certainly had greater possibilities than the location in Pryor. It was permanent construction and far more attractive. The location was in one of Oklahoma's larger and better-known cities, and local support appeared strong. After negotiations, the Board and the Burlingames agreed on a price of $125,000 with a $25,000 down payment and a ten year loan on the remainder.[56]

At a March 1 meeting at the Tulsa Hotel in Tulsa, the Board engaged G. R. Tinius to head a campaign to raise money for the proposed Central Christian College. The Board gave Tinius the "authority to organize the campaign and employ sufficient men or manpower to conduct a campaign under [the] direction of [the] Executive Committee."[57] On April 12, Tinius reported $44,243 in the building fund and that he had published a twelve-page brochure which included an artist's drawing of a new campus plan. He hoped the college could open in September of 1949.[58] In that same memorandum, Tinius reported to Board members that on Friday, April 16, Bartlesville civic leaders would meet to announce the establishment of Central Christian College and to kick off a fundraising campaign for the new college. George Benson, president of Harding College, would be the speaker.

By May 19, Tinius reported, "The tempo of our campaign is gradually picking up." He said two brethren would begin work in fundraising on June 1, one of whom was John Stevens of Bentonville, Arkansas. Stevens, he noted, was a graduate of Abilene Christian College who was completing work on a master's degree at the University of Arkansas in Fayetteville. Tinius reported that Stevens "wishes a permanent connection on the faculty of our school. He has an invitation now to join the faculty at Denver University and Abilene Christian College."[59] John Stevens went on to teach for and eventually become president of Abilene Christian University

The same memo to the Board provides a list of the members of the committee to raise funds in Bartlesville. Tinius said, "if this Committee can't get the money, it just can't be done. We are fortunate that such men are taking an interest in our school. . . . I am asking them for $250,000." The committee included A. W. Ambrose, president of Cities Service Oil Company; K. S. Adams, president of Phillips Petroleum Company; W. C. Smoot, president of the First National Bank; William Doenges of the Ford Motor Company; and many other prominent Bartlesville citizens.[60]

In May, Tinius began using a picture of the Bartlesville mansion on college letterhead. By August 2, however, he appeared discouraged. "Very little progress has been made in the past sixty (60) days on our Campaign for funds, total subscriptions to date approximately $65,000.00." He also reported that Stevens "has worked faithfully the past seven weeks" but with "only fair results in contributions." Tinius also said the drive in Bartlesville had "made some progress," and he hoped for a report by August 15.[61] In the months since his May report, with both Tinius and Stevens raising funds, only $10,000 more in cash and pledges had been raised, and payments on the Bartlesville property soon would be expected.

On September 13, Tinius wrote to the Board that Mr. Burlingame had granted a thirty-day extension on the option and the Bartlesville campaign was underway with a goal of $225,000; on September 30, Tinius reported that Mr. Burlingame had further extended the option to November 18 at the request of the businessmen in Bartlesville "due to their inability to complete their financial drive by October 8th."[62] Tinius expressed some frustration that matters had not moved more rapidly, saying, "I have been in Bartlesville almost every day since our meeting in Oklahoma City."

At a meeting at the Jens-Marie Hotel in Ponca City on November 5, the Board voted to ask the City of Bartlesville to apply half of the $100,000 the city was pledging to the initial property cost with the other half to be placed in escrow to be released when another building project was begun. If this could be done, Board members believed the college could start classes in September of 1949. On November 11, the Board met again in Ponca City and voted to finalize the purchase of the Bartlesville property.[63]

On January 7, 1949, in Oklahoma City, the Board received a financial report from Tinius indicating that $27,515.30 in cash had been contributed, with more pledged. This report also indicated that $15,000 had been paid on the Bartlesville property.

At this meeting, the Board unanimously voted to extend to Eldon A. Sanders, superintendent of the Tipton Orphans Home in Tipton, Oklahoma, an offer to become president of the college. Sanders, with an M.A. degree from the University of Southern California, had served fourteen years as superintendent of schools at Quanah, and had preached for twenty-eight years.[64] According to a March 2 Tinius memorandum, however, Sanders turned down the offer.[65] The college was still without a president.

About this time, G. R. Tinius sent to supporters an undated public letter announcing that Central Christian College was "a reality." The letter indicated that the contract had been signed to purchase the Foster property in Bartlesville and that classes would begin in September of 1949. Tinius emphasized that "a college, where constant influence and guidance of Christian men and women will assist young people in acquiring an academic education and in development of Christian character, should challenge every member of the Church in Oklahoma, Kansas, Missouri, and Arkansas." [66]

The letter indicates the Board saw a guiding hand working behind the scenes: In the letter, Tinius reports he had traveled 30,000 miles "interviewing individuals and groups relative to support for the school," and that the Burlingames had "saved the day" by offering a liberal financing plan and by contributing $50,000 in furnishings which were in the Bartlesville mansion. "Acquiring this property was no 'accident,'" the letter states, "It was planned that way."

A President Chosen

L.R. Wilson

Still without a president, the Board pursued the possibility of employing L. R. Wilson in the role. A very well-known Texas preacher, Wilson had spent the last three and a half years as founding president of Florida Christian College, but had submitted his resignation from that position effective July 1, 1949. While in Florida, he had published a book of radio sermons he had preached in Texas, Oklahoma, and Florida called *The Never Failing Scriptures*. As a writer for the *Firm Foundation*, one of the best known publications among Churches of Christ, and having been a local minister for churches in Tulsa and Ada, Wilson was widely known and respected among Oklahoma churches. If Wilson would accept the presidency, he would bring both his solid reputation as a preacher and his experience with starting a college. Tinius contacted Board members, and in February, with their approval, visited Wilson in Florida to see if he would have interest in taking the lead in starting another Christian college. Wilson was not particularly receptive to the idea but agreed to consider it. When Tinius reported Wilson's response, the Board, nonetheless, voted unanimously to seek to get Wilson to take the job,[67] and invited him to meet with them at the Skirvin Hotel in Oklahoma City on March 4-5, 1949. At this meeting, the Board offered Wilson the job.[68]

Tinius shared with the Board in a March 19 memorandum that the Executive Committee had met with Wilson on March 9 in Bartlesville and showed him the property there. He had made suggestions about what would be needed in addition to the existing buildings—a boys dormitory, a girls dormitory, a gymnasium, a dining room/assembly hall, equipment, some re-modeling, and an operating fund. Addressing these needs, he said, would require at least $500,000.[69] But Wilson had just finished more than three grueling years as the founding president of a Christian college and wanted to return "to my first love: that of preaching the gospel."[70] If he came, he would be taking the leadership of a fundraising effort which, so far, had not had great success. While taking on this daunting task, he would also have to start from zero in assembling a faculty and staff and recruiting a student body. After this meeting, Wilson had said he would give a final word after visiting with his wife in Florida. In that same memo, Tinius reported to the Board, "I received a call from Brother Wilson Thursday evening the 17th, stating that he had decided to work with us and I am sure all will rejoice in his decision."[71] Wilson later wrote in a memoir about his presidency that he had accepted "reluctantly" but "had a feeling that God would hold me responsible if I did not help them to get started—when they needed me most."[72] The Board had found in Wilson a man whose reputation would be an asset, whose Oklahoma connections were strong, and whose presidential experience would be valuable.

Losing no time, Wilson met with the funding committee from Bartlesville on March 15 to "reveal our plans" and to encourage them "to increase their proposed offering to the school."[73] Wilson would officially begin as president on September 1, 1949, obviously too late for the college to start that September but, at least, there was now a president who had proven himself by starting another Christian college and who would become, at that date, a full-time president of the new college.

Chester Grimes, speaking to the first Central Christian College Lectureship in 1951, said that when the Board chose Wilson as president, they "came through with flying colors." He was "one who had the courage, fortitude and determination to do it. And one who had the confidence of the entire brotherhood as to his ability, integrity, soundness and tenacity; an unbeatable combination."[74]

In his first move, Wilson asked the Board for permission to employ several who had worked with him at Florida Christian, including Elvin Higgins to be vice president, and Elwood Whitacre as business manager. These two came to the Bartlesville campus in July 1949 to begin full-time work and continued for several more years.[75]

On May 4, Tinius reported to all Board members on the substance of a Board meeting the previous Friday where Wilson had outlined a fundraising plan in which each member of the Board would assume responsibility for a certain geographic area. In his area, the Board member was to solicit "every church member" for a pledge to be paid over eighteen months. He had also suggested that the elders and preacher in each congregation be contacted first so they would understand about the fundraising to be done among their members. Elvin Higgins would arrive in Bartlesville on July 1 and would begin working with Board members on their solicitation.[76]

As the plans for a college in Oklahoma were moving forward, Wilson and Board members were seeking to develop strong contact with church members and gain their financial support, but they did not want to offend church leaders by contacting their members for contributions without their knowledge. On June 1, Tinius wrote churches to explain the fundraising plan and request that they send their church directories or membership rolls so the college could make contact with the members.[77]

Funding, however, was slow to come. On July 13, Wilson wrote members of the Board: "We need $1,000 right now. In fact, this is a 'must'—and I'm counting on you to see that we have this not later than the middle of next week." He mentioned that the caretaker, vice president, and secretary were already on the payroll and that "incidentals are already being paid out of private funds which will have to be replaced immediately. Be sure to get what you can here by the first of the week, and get started on the pledge cards and collection of funds for the overall program without delay."[78]

The Board met on August 26. G. R. Tinius, who had labored so hard to get the college started, reported that he had borrowed $4,500 personally for the down payment on a home for the president in downtown Bartlesville and that he would forego $2,000 the college owed him in salary.[79] The Board agreed to meet in thirty days and, if the situation were not improved, to make further decisions about the future of the college. Because funds were slow to come in, Wilson sensed that church members' interest in the new college was low and asked the Board for thoughts about the problem.

One of the means President Wilson developed to create interest in the new college was a fifteen minute religious radio program that broadcast in Tulsa, Oklahoma City, Miami, Wichita Falls, and Wichita. He asked church members to support this program and to announce it in their churches.[80]

Wilson and those working with him were making progress and were working hard, but much remained to be done before they were ready to open a college.

Preparations for Opening in September, 1950

The faith and determination of the Board and early employees of the fledgling college were strong and eventually proven worthwhile. At a meeting on September 30, 1949, at the Skirvin Hotel in Oklahoma City, Wilson reported that while on August 26 the college had a deficit of $2,375, by September 30 he had cash on hand of $6,185 and pledges of $32,039. The Board inspected preliminary architectural drawings for three proposed new buildings on the campus, estimated to cost $300,000, and passed a resolution authorizing the employment of an engineer to draw up a campus masterplan to include locations of buildings, roads, and utilities.[81]

During the fall of 1949, President Wilson met with members of the Churches of Christ throughout Oklahoma and Kansas. Fundraising had improved, but it still was not going well enough, and the date for starting classes in September of 1950 was moving ever nearer. He requested a meeting of the Board on January 6, 1950. At this meeting Wilson, known to be plain-spoken and bold in his manner, made a strong statement to Board members:

> You selected me as your servant to head this institution. I am directly amenable to you. If I am unable to do the job expected of me, then you should not feel under any obligation to retain me in the position I now occupy. Whatever it takes to make a success of the school should be your first consideration. This school was not begun to create a job for anybody. It was started for the service we may render to boys and girls, and whatever it takes to accomplish this work we should see that it is done.
>
> You were chosen by the people, and are directly responsible to the people. It is up to you to see that the job is done which you were selected to do. If you cannot do it, then you should be replaced with men who can. In brief, the people are looking to you first of all, and to me only as your servant, to establish Central Christian College for the benefit of our young people. If we are not able to do it, then we have no business wasting the time and means we are in an effort to do so. I believe we can, and urge you to give the very best you have to this effort to see that it is done.[82]

Wilson hoped his challenge to the Board would keep them engaged and motivated, and suggests the strong role Board members played in getting the college started.

At that same meeting, Wilson reported that since September 1, he personally had raised $26,314 in cash and about $45,000 in pledges. But three new buildings were needed: two dormitories and a combination cafeteria and gymnasium. These, he said, would cost about $250,000. If classes were to begin in September of 1950, construction on the buildings would have to begin very soon and funds were not on hand to do so. At the meeting, Wilson and the Board decided that Wilson should meet with preachers, elders, and board members in various locations to find people who would agree to raise $1,000 each.[83]

As if the operational and construction needs were not bad enough, Louis McKinney and N. D. Welty, representatives from the City of Bartlesville, came to the January 6 meeting to report that only

$40,000 of the promised $100,000 had been raised. They further stated that this amount was all they would be able to get. The Board responded with a letter to the Bartlesville committee stating that on the basis of their $100,000 promise the Board had purchased the property in Bartlesville and was moving forward with plans to start construction on additional buildings. The letter closed with these words: "In view of the foregoing, we cannot accept the committee's report as final, nor in fulfillment of the pledge made. Therefore, we respectfully ask that your committee continue its campaign and make another report to the Board of Trustees within sixty days." But Bartlesville raised no additional funds, nor was any other report ever given.[84] This failure of the Bartlesville community to make good on its initial promise for a much larger amount indicated their interest in Central Christian was not as great as had first been thought.

Still believing in the importance of establishing a Christian college in Oklahoma, however, the Board moved ahead. In the January 6 meeting, Cline Mansur, engineer, and Leman Wilson, architect, both members of the Church of Christ in Tulsa, presented their plan for the location of future buildings, sewers, and roads on the Bartlesville campus. The sites for the two dormitories were accepted and, with a small adjustment, so was the cafeteria-gymnasium location.

To a March 24 meeting of the Board, President Wilson made a number of recommendations, including: (1) that fundraising be continued with increased vigor, (2) that each Board member contact a reliable builder in his community to see if lower bids on the new construction could be obtained, and (3) that negotiations be started immediately to see if a loan could be obtained to make payments on the buildings.[85]

At this meeting, Wilson also asked Board approval for his first four faculty appointments. For dean, Wilson recommended Dr. James O. Baird, who had been teaching at David Lipscomb for six years. Baird, who held a doctorate in higher education from Peabody College, had read in the *Gospel Advocate*, a widely read journal among Churches of Christ, about the start of a new Christian college in Oklahoma and had contacted Wilson.[86] Since he was an excellent teacher and preacher with outstanding educational training and credentials, Wilson chose him to lead the academic side of the institution.

Dr. James O. Baird

He also recommended Roy H. Lanier, Sr., to chair the Bible Department. Lanier was a very well-known minister who had held meetings at many congregations in the Oklahoma area and had

Roy Lanier, Sr.

often spoken at college lectureships. He had written widely for brotherhood publications and was an effective teacher. Lanier held a bachelor's degree from Abilene Christian and was completing a master's degree from Hardin Simmons University in preparation for his work at Central Christian. His coming would signal to church members that the college was going to have quality people on its faculty and that its Bible teachings would be doctrinally sound.

Wilson also recommended the employment of Harold Fletcher to teach music, direct the chorus, and provide other musical activities. Fletcher, a graduate of Abilene Christian, was completing a master of music degree from Hardin Simmons. Since Fletcher had taught one year at Florida Christian, Wilson knew of his outstanding capabilities as both a musician and a teacher.

Harold Fletcher

The fourth faculty member Wilson proposed for Board approval was Winnie Clayton, who would be the college librarian. She held a B. S. and M. S. from Oklahoma A&M College as well as a bachelor's degree in library science from George Peabody College.

Wilson also submitted at this meeting a faculty salary schedule: those with a bachelor's degree would receive $2,250 a year, those with a master's degree would be paid $2,750 a year and those with a doctor's degree would receive $3,300 a year. These salaries were far below standard for college faculty but were the most Wilson thought the college could afford to pay. That he could get such a high quality faculty for these amounts demonstrates that these professors had a sacrificial spirit and a deep commitment to Christian education in Oklahoma. They agreed to come even before there were students to teach and classrooms in which to teach them.[87]

In an April 6 meeting, the Board agreed to proceed with building a dormitory to house seventy women. To finance the $75,000 dormitory, the college would borrow $25,000 from L. B. Clayton, a member of the Board, use $25,000 from the Bartlesville fund, and raise the other $25,000. Construction began a few days later. The dormitory was a two-story brick building with thirty-five, two-student rooms, and an apartment for the supervisor.[88]

In their next meeting on May 30, the Board authorized

construction of a frame building containing eight classrooms and an assembly hall which would accommodate two hundred in folding chairs. This building would provide most of the college's classroom space as well as a meeting place for daily chapel and special events.[89]

The college published its first catalog in May, announcing the starting date for classes as Wednesday, September 27, 1950. Tuition for one semester would be $125 and 123 different courses were listed. Under the heading "A Brief History," the catalog expressed the need for more colleges among Churches of Christ because "the schools we now have were all running over, and [there was] the need for more."[90] The post-World War II student boom had filled these institutions, often pushing to them to the limit. This situation clearly was part of the stimulus for a new college in Oklahoma.

Professors began arriving in late summer and these faculty members, with administrators and family members, helped in getting buildings and grounds ready for classes to begin. The dream of a Christian college that had begun in May of 1946 to obtain excess government buildings in Pryor was now about to become a reality in Bartlesville.

Already becoming evident were qualities which would be hallmarks of Oklahoma Christian University: the dedicated work both of volunteers and employees, a willingness to confront and overcome obstacles, excellence as a goal toward which all would strive, close ties with Churches of Christ, and a faith in God's direction and answer to prayer. The decision not to start a college in temporary buildings on an abandoned government facility, but to wait for a quality location, proved to be wise. The leadership chose a president who was well-known and respected among Churches of Christ and who had experience in establishing a Christian college. The volunteer Board's determination to work through many obstacles at great personal sacrifice set the pattern for years to come. Without the perseverance of Board chairmen Bryant, Fullerton, and Tinius, the college would never have become a reality. The selection of faculty members who were well prepared both academically and spiritually and who would teach effectively showed a commitment to academic excellence which has characterized the institution throughout its history.

The process had been arduous, but many members of Churches of Christ in Oklahoma and Kansas were strongly committed to having a college for their children. Not only did they feel the need because other colleges in their fellowship were filled from the post-war student boom, but they wanted an institution closer to home which would encourage more of their children to attend. They also thought such a college would be a stimulus for church growth in the area.

Chester Grimes, involved from the beginning in Pryor, expressed well the sentiments of those so determined to establish a

Christian college in Oklahoma. He said he thought of the college as one "where our children could be trained in secular things of earth and at the same time retain their faith in God and the Bible. A place where they could have their associates and associations among those of kindred interests, and under a wholesome environment."[91]

More than four years after the dream first began to take shape in the office of Richard Ealen in May of 1946, a college in Oklahoma to serve Churches of Christ was now ready to receive students. For the Board, donors, early employees, and many church members who had participated, the process of giving birth to a new college had been difficult and long.   Believing strongly in the need for such an institution, they looked forward to its opening with great anticipation.

Chapter 1, Endnotes

[1] G. R. Tinius, "An Early History of Oklahoma Christian College," Unpublished Essay, 1965, OC Archives, 1; "Report of the Original Proceedings in the Acquisition of the College Project at Pryor," Unpublished report following meeting of June 4, 1946, on letterhead of Mid-States Christian College, OC Archives, 1.

[2] Tinius, History, 1.

[3] A. H. Bryant, Letter to James O. Baird, April 9, 1963, OC Archives.

[4] "College at Dormitory City Endorsed by Leaders in City Conference Here," *Pryor Daily Times-Democrat*, May 27, 1946, 1.

[5] "Representatives of Church of Christ from 628 Churches of State to Meet Here June 4-5 to Discuss College Plans," *Pryor Daily Times-Democrat*, about June 1, 1946.

[6] E. Ray Rayburn, Letter to W. R. Smith, May 31, 1946, OC Archives.

[7] Chester A. Grimes, "The Beginning of Central Christian College," First Annual Central Christian College Lectureship, March 27, 1951, OC Archives.

[8] "Report," 1.

[9] A. H. Bryant, "Report on College Prospects," *Evangel*, November 17, 1946, OC Archives.

[10] W. R. Smith, "Mid-States Christian College Organized at Pryor, Okla., To open With Large Plant as Gift," *Christian Chronicle*, January 8, 1947.

[11] Bryant, "Report," 2.

[12] Grimes, 2.

[13] The school operated from 1908 to 1919 as Cordell Christian College, from 1920 to 1924 as Western Oklahoma Christian College, and from 1925 to 1931 as Oklahoma Christian College.

[14] Grimes, 2.

[15] Minutes, September 25, 1946, OC Archives.

[16] A. H. Bryant, "Present Status of the Proposed College," *Evangel*, September 22, 1946, OC Archives.

[17] Minutes, September 25.

[18] Ibid.

[19] Minutes, Board of Trustees, September 27, 1946, OC Archives. In the early years, sometimes the controlling board is called "Board of Directors" and sometimes "Board of Trustees." After a time, the practice was always to call the group "Board of Trustees." In this book and in the references, the term "Board of Trustees" is used throughout.

[20] Resolution Number Two, 1946, October 25, 1946, OC Archives.

[21] Ibid.

[22] A. S. Bryant, Bulletin #28, Report of College Prospects, November 3, 1946, OC Archives.

[23] A. S. Bryant, Bulletin #29, A Brief Report of College Proceedings, November 8, 1946, OC Archives.

[24] A. H. Bryant, "Report on College Proceedings," *Evangel*, November 17, 1946, OC Archives.

[25] Smith, *Christian Chronicle*.

[26] Minutes, Board of Trustees, December 10, 1946, OC Archives.

[27] J. E. Wright, Letter to Byron Fullerton, January 8, 1947, OC Archives.

[28] Frank Winters, Letter to Joe Pollard, December 18, 1946, OC Archives.

[29] Cline Mansur, Letter to Byron Fullerton, December 29, 1946, OC Archives.

[30] G. M. Roberts, Letter to Byron Fullerton, January 10, 1947, OC Archives.

[31] Minutes, Board of Trustees, January 21, 1947, OC Archives.

[32] Ibid.

[33] J. E. Wright, Letter to Byron Fullerton, January 28, 1947, OC Archives.

[34] Byron Fullerton, "Important Announcement for Churches of Christ, February 20, 1947, OC Archives.

[35] Minutes, Board of Trustees, February 28, 1947, OC Archives.

[36] "The Legion of Honor," *Central Christian College Bulletin*, September 1954, OC Archives.

37 W. O. Beeman, *Oklahoma Christian College: Dream to Reality*, (Delight, Arkansas: Gospel Light Publishing Company, 1970), 25-26.
38 Minutes, Board of Trustees, March 11, 1947, OC Archives.
39 Minutes, Board of Trustees, April 22, 1947, OC Archives.
40 Ibid.
41 Minutes, Board of Trustees, May 19, 1947, OC Archives.
42 Tinius, History, 4.
43 Minutes, Board of Trustees, June 3, 1947, OC Archives.
44 Minutes, Board of Trustees, July 31, 1947, OC Archives. These Articles of Incorporation were filed on January 22, 1948.
45 John C. Stevens, *No Ordinary University* (Abilene, Texas: Abilene Christian University Press, 1998), 489.
46 Ibid., 3, 448.
47 L. O. Sanderson, "A School—and the Best for the Central West," *Central Christian College Bulletin*, July 1947, OC Archives.
48 Tinius, History, 5.
49 Byron Fullerton, "Another Christian College," *Central Christian College Bulletin*, NovemΣber 1947, OC Archives.
50 Minutes, Board of Trustees, December 4, 1947, OC Archives.
51 G. R. Tinius, Memorandum to Board Members, December 26, 1947, OC Archives.
52 "City to Benefit By Establishment of College Here," *Bartlesville Examiner-Enterprise*, April 18, 1948, 3.
53 Jack Jones, "College in a Mansion," *Bartlesville Examiner-Enterprise*, March 12, 1950, 15.
54 Minutes, Board of Trustees, January 15, 1948, OC Archives.
55 Minutes, Board of Trustees, January 26, 1948, OC Archives.
56 G. R. Tinius, Letter to Byron Fullerton, February 6, 1948, OC Archives.
57 Minutes, Board of Trustees, March 1, 1948, OC Archives.
58 G. R. Tinius, Memorandum to Board Members, April 12, 1948, OC Archives.
59 G. R. Tinius, Memorandum to Board Members, May 19, 1948, OC Archives.
60 Ibid.
61 G. R. Tinuis, Memorandum to Board Members, August 2, 1948, OC Archives.
62 G. R. Tinius, Memorandum to Board Members, September 30, 1948, OC Archives.
63 Minutes, Board of Trustees, November 11, 1948, OC Archives.
64 Minutes, Board of Trustees, January 7, 1949, OC Archives; Batsell Barrett Baxter and M. Norvel Young, *Preachers of Today*, Vol. 2 (Nashville: Gospel Advocate Company, 1970), 383-384.
65 G. R. Tinius, Memorandum to Board Members, March 2, 1949, OC Archives.
66 G. R. Tinius, Announcement to the Public, n.d., OC Archives.
67 Tinius, History, 7.
68 Minutes, Board of Trustees, March 4, 1949, OC Archives.
69 G. R. Tinius, Memorandum to Board Members, March 19, 1949, OC Archives.
70 L. R. Wilson, "I Resign as President," Unpublished Manuscript, January 4, 1967, OC Archives.
71 Ibid.
72 Wilson, "I Resign."
73 G. R. Tinius, Memorandum, March 19, 1949.
74 Grimes, 4.
75 Tinius, "History," 7.
76 G. R. Tinius, Memorandum to Board Members, May 4, 1949, OC Archives.
77 G. R. Tinius, Letter to University Church of Christ, June 1, 1949, OC Archives.
78 L. R. Wilson, Letter to Board Members, July 13, 1949, OC Archives.
79 Minutes, Board of Trustees, August 26, 1949, OC Archives.
80 L. R. Wilson, Announcement to the Public. n.d. OC Archives.
81 Minutes, Board of Trustees, September 30, 1949, OC Archives.

[82] Minutes, Board of Trustees, January 6, 1950, OC Archives.
[83] Ibid.
[84] Ibid.
[85] Minutes, Board of Trustees, March 24, 1950, OC Archives.
[86] James O. Baird. Interview on audiotape with the author on November 2, 1989, and subsequent days, Tape 1, OC Archives.
[87] Minutes, March 24.
[88] Minutes, Board of Trustees, April 6, 1950, OC Archives.
[89] Minutes, Board of Trustees, May 30, 1950, OC Archives
[90] *Central Christian College,* 1950, OC Archives, 5.
[91] Grimes, Introduction.

Chapter 2
THE FOUNDATION YEARS IN BARTLESVILLE

Laying Cornerstones

Summer, 1950! After four years of dedicated efforts, members of Churches of Christ in Oklahoma were excited to see September almost at hand. The first *Central Christian College Catalog*, published in May, reveals qualities that would characterize the new institution throughout future years.

The new two-year institution would be a liberal arts college, the typical model among Churches of Christ. Since the early days of the Restoration Movement, colleges among these churches had offered a broad educational curriculum. In his history of these colleges, Norvel Young says, "All of these schools have studiously avoided being known as theological seminaries or 'preacher factories.'"[1] Courses listed in this first catalog were divided among fourteen departments: art, Bible, business, education and psychology, physical education, English, industrial arts, home economics, languages, mathematics, music, natural science, social science, and speech.[2]

This course list reflects the purpose of the institution as stated in the Articles of Incorporation: "to establish, maintain and operate a collegiate institution of learning which shall be for the advancement of education in which the arts, sciences, languages and Holy Scriptures shall always be taught, together with such courses of instruction as shall be deemed advisable by the Board of Directors."[3]

To graduate, each student had to complete sixty-four hours, including twelve in a major field and twenty in electives, along with twelve in Bible, six in American history and government, twelve in English, and two in physical education. Students could receive a junior college certificate or an associate degree in arts, science, or commerce.[4] In a speech to the Bartlesville Rotarians, President L. R. Wilson assured his hearers that Central Christian College is not a "junior college," although it is at first offering only two years of college work. The third and fourth year classes will be added as demand develops, he said. He expressed the hope that the additions might be made in three or four years, but said it might be "five or ten" because of extensive laboratory and library facilities that would be demanded, and because the college was determined to maintain the highest academic standards.[5]

In addition to outlining the curriculum, the first catalog laid another cornerstone: a thirty-minute daily chapel period, "at which time hymns are sung, the Bible is read, prayers are offered, and talks are made. Occasionally plays are given, or other wholesome entertainment offered. . . . All students and teachers are required to attend chapel, except when properly excused."[6] And daily required chapel is still the standard at Oklahoma Christian University.

The catalog explained that

> Central Christian College was founded primarily for the purpose of providing a school where young people may continue their education under Christian environment and influence. It was not intended as a 'preacher factory' in any sense. Regardless of what a student plans to be in life, he (or she) should be a Christian first of all. . . . The greatest service [the college] can render is that of strengthening young people in character and preparing them for Christian service, regardless of their calling in life.[7]

In keeping with this vision, the catalog also announced another foundational tenet: "All students are expected to take some course in the Bible every semester."[8]

For the 1950–1951 year, a student would pay $125 for 12 to 18 hours; meals were $35 a month, and the room charge $12 a month. Students also paid a $10 activity fee to cover library use, mailing services, a yearbook, and a student newspaper.[9] The first students at Central Christian, thus, paid a total of $350 a semester, about $20 less than the equivalent cost for attending Abilene Christian College.[10] Keeping the cost affordable was another basic element of the college's plan. To attract the students the college was founded to serve, the price would have to be kept low.

Opening Faculty and Staff

Among the first employees, President Wilson brought Dr. James Baird to teach Bible and education and serve as dean. This administrative role, in reality, combined the work of academic dean, student life dean, and registrar. To fill the key position of head of the Bible Department, Wilson chose Roy Lanier, Sr., who would teach Bible and Greek. Wilson brought four professors with him from Florida Christian: Elvin Higgins to teach math and physics and be vice president; his wife, Myrtle Higgins, to teach English and speech; Harold Fletcher to teach music; and Joy Henshall, the Laniers' daughter, to teach secretarial science and be secretary for the president.

Elvin R. Higgins

To these, Wilson and Baird added six more faculty. Joe Spaulding, a coach and teacher at Harding College, came to teach history and physical education. Howard Longley would teach business; Lucian Bagnetto would teach science; and Joan Fergus instructed in both art and home economics. Winnie Clayton was librarian. Elwood Whitacre came with Wilson from Florida to be business manager. Eldy Davis directed maintenance, and Anna Bell Ward served as an administrative secretary.

Elwood Whitacre

For a small first-year school, the faculty was remarkable. As junior college professors, they were well-prepared academically, with most holding a master's degree from a major university, and they took special interest in students individually and served as Christian role models. All were all members of the Church of Christ. These qualities would guide in faculty selection from that time forward. Wilson later wrote he had chosen Baird as the dean because he "was qualified not only academically" but also spiritually, understanding "the real meaning of Christian education."[11] Lanier, well known in the brotherhood, was a careful student of the Bible, having preached, taught, and written widely. Fletcher, as time would show, was not only an excellent teacher but a highly capable musician. Spaulding would later teach for seventeen years at Abilene Christian University. Henshall would eventually be associate dean of the Graduate School at Tennessee State University in Cookeville, Tennessee.

Why did they come? With the average professor's salary at less than $2,700 a year, they certainly could have drawn larger salaries elsewhere. Primarily they came because they believed strongly in the college's mission to provide a Christian education for families among Churches of Christ, and their pioneering spirits led them to want to help begin a new institution.[12] They were excited to think this could be the start of something big. Many of the early students shared in that same spirit of idealism and saw attending Central Christian as a way both to get a strong education and to help start a new Christian college.

Important Contacts with Higher Education

Early in September, soon after Baird arrived but before classes began, Wilson suggested that the two of them call on the chancellor of the Oklahoma State Regents for Higher Education in Oklahoma City. The State Regents were responsible for determining whether credit from a new college in Oklahoma would be accepted at state institutions. Wilson and Baird met with Chancellor Mel A. Nash and showed him a list of the college faculty with their academic preparation and a schedule of classes. The only suggestion Nash made, Baird commented later, was that typing class did not have to meet every day. Nash agreed to send someone from a well-established Oklahoma junior college for a visit after classes began. This person would

Dean James Baird shows students the letter of accreditation from the Oklahoma State Regents for Higher Education.

report findings to him. About two months into the school year, Dr. Loren Brown of Northern Junior College in Tonkawa visited Central Christian, and before the first semester had ended, Chancellor Nash wrote that work done at Central Christian would be transferable to other colleges and universities.[13] This contact with the State Regents before classes ever began was important not only for initial state accreditation, but also for laying a foundation for excellent future relationships with the State Regents and other academic institutions in the state.

On that same September day, Wilson and Baird visited President George Cross at the University of Oklahoma. He received them cordially and put them in contact with the university's registrar, Dr. James E. Fellows. Fellows was an officer in the American Association of Registrars and Admissions Officers and was responsible for

Oklahoma's information in their publication going to all colleges and universities in the country about acceptance of credit. Contact with Fellows, which continued through the sixties, enabled Central Christian to be included in this nationally circulated *Report of Credit Given* as an institution from which academic work was transferable.[14] By the end of the first year, the college had also been approved by the Veteran's Administration for students to attend on the GI Bill.[15]

In establishing solid academic credentials from the first, Wilson and Baird laid an important foundation that continues to pay valuable dividends to students.

Facilities

The institution opened with modest but adequate academic facilities. Although construction on the classroom building had not started until June, it was ready by the start of school in September. This "L-shaped," frame building, constructed for $15,000,[16] provided eight rooms for classes and faculty offices, four on either side of a long hallway. Daily chapel took place in the building's assembly hall, which could seat about two hundred. The hall also served for chorus rehearsals and for public events. On

At the lower right is the classroom building, in the center is The Mansion, at the lower left is the bookstore, added after the first year, and at the upper left is the Women's Dormitory.

one end, a speaker's platform was elevated by nine inches, but there were no stage facilities. The building, painted white on the outside, had an open gas heater in each room and no restrooms. Even with its limitations, this classroom building served for all the years the college operated in Bartlesville.

The Mansion was fully utilized, providing space on the first floor for administrative offices, the library, the cafeteria, and on the second floor for men's housing. In addition, Fletcher had two rooms in the former maid's quarters for music, a classroom and a studio.

Both rooms had pianos that, Harold Fletcher recalls, the Laniers had bought and shipped from Abilene as a contribution. Art and home economics classes also met in former maid's quarters. Bagnetto set up a chemistry lab in what had been a garage. A large basement room in The Mansion served for biology. Clayton started the library in two rooms that had been The Mansion's library. The larger, twenty-six by eighteen feet with built-in bookshelves, served as a reading area, while the smaller was the library workroom.

The Library in The Mansion

The large living room, forty by twenty feet with a huge imported rug covering the wood floor, served for group meetings, and a lounge. Faculty members and their spouses, in addition to getting their own housing ready, spent many hours preparing The Mansion for the opening. Since it had not been used for a year, cleaning the thirty-two room building was a huge task.

Opening Day

Students began arriving Saturday, September 23, and, after two days of registration, classes began at 7:40 a.m. on Wednesday, September 27. President Wilson officially opened the college at the 10 a.m. chapel services. Harold Fletcher led the opening song, "I'm Not Ashamed to Own My Lord," which has been sung at every opening-day chapel since that time.

The 1950–1951 yearbook, called *La Quinta*, showed pictures of twenty sophomores and seventy-four freshmen, a total of ninety-four, with a male-female ratio of 2 to 1. Most of the students came from Oklahoma, but there were also students from Kansas, California, Texas, New Mexico, Arizona, Missouri, and Indiana. Elvin Higgins had worked hard at recruiting, and so had President Wilson and the faculty. They visited churches, showed people the campus, and wrote letters to those whose names they had collected from churches. Ruth Wilson, the president's wife, was in charge of mailing, using primarily an "addressograph machine" to make plates for addresses.

As students came, they were struck with the beauty of the campus. One wrote, "Upon entering the mansion for the first time, I stood very still for a few minutes, being completely spellbound by its elegance and splendor."[17]

Classes and Chapel

Grade reports from the first semester show thirty-seven courses offered, not including chorus and private lessons in voice and piano. Elvin Higgins had only one student in both zoology and physics. The largest course, Lucian Bagnetto's beginning chemistry, included twenty-six students. With the average class size at 10.7, students felt close to faculty members and received individual attention.[18]

Virtually everyone on campus attended daily chapel in the assembly hall. President Wilson spoke often, many of his addresses being like Bible class lectures. His lessons ranged from discussions of a passage of Scripture to pronunciation of Bible place names to

Singing in chapel at Central Christian College in 1953. Elvin Higgins and L. R. Wilson sit on the front row.

lectures on smoking, against which he often railed. Preachers from local congregations, preachers coming to the area for meetings, and faculty members also spoke. With a ceiling height in the room of only eight feet, singing in chapel had an excellent sound.

Sometimes after the chapel devotional, speakers dealt with secular topics. Bob Kurland was one such early speaker. A prominent All-American basketball player with Oklahoma A&M, he was then playing for the Phillips Sixty-Sixers. Kurland was seven feet tall and, with only seven feet three inches from the floor of the speaker's platform to the ceiling, he chose to avoid the platform.

A Dormitory and "The Mule Barn"

The men were housed primarily in three locations. About twenty lived on the second floor of The Mansion in its three large bedrooms, which the students named "The Mule Barn," "The Blue Room," and "The Pink Room." Normally six to eight men lived in each of the large rooms.[19] A dressing room and bath adjoined each bedroom. The college also leased a house at 1111 Johnstone in downtown Bartlesville, where twenty other men stayed with a supervisor, and eight more lived in the Freeman Vaughn home at 413 Delaware. The remaining men resided in other homes in town.[20] Many students depended on the bus service that ran from downtown to the campus.

At the start of classes in 1950, the women's dormitory was still under construction, so during the fall, the young women stayed in homes of church members. After Christmas however, the residence hall, designed for seventy women, was completed

Women's dormitory on Bartlesville campus

and women moved on campus. The rooms had three color schemes: solid blue, canary yellow with one grey wall, and pastel pink with one grey wall.[21]

Students ate meals in the elegant formal dining room of The Mansion, a beautifully paneled room, thirty-one by eighteen feet, with a majestic carved fireplace. Adjoining rooms provided a serving area and the kitchen, where Elvie Armstrong, Helen Davis, and Rubye Vaughn prepared the meals.

First Year Finances

As classes began in September of 1950, President Wilson was starting his second year as president. His first year had been a monumental struggle to obtain finances, facilities, and faculty. Now with students on the campus, more employees to be paid, and a dean to handle academic matters and student conduct, Wilson gave his major attention to fundraising. At a meeting of the Board on November 2–3, 1950, Wilson reported that the college owed $45,667. He recommended the sale of $100,000 in bonds bearing 4 percent annual interest, with 10 percent to be paid off each year. Such financing would give Wilson more time

Board of Trustees in 1951. Front row left to right: G. R. Tinius, L. R. Wilson, Loyd L. Smith, J. S. Maple. Second row: Floyd Perry, L. B. Clayton, J. D. Fine, Floyd Lawson, Glenn Durrill, Rowland Roberts. Third row: J. E. Wright, Warren Kelly, Ted Norton, O. T. Lowry, A. R., Wallace.

First Lectureship at Central Christian College in 1951

to raise the money and allow him to make timely payments of debt and salaries.[22]

By the end of the school year in May 1951, even though some bonds had been sold, the situation was serious enough for Wilson to ask each Board member personally to sign a note on a $10,000 loan from the First National Bank in Bartlesville. He also asked each Board member to declare how many bonds he would buy.[23] Each meeting of the Board seemed to bring a new financial crisis, calling on the members to make personal contributions to keep the college in operation. And each time, they rose to the challenge. Again at the August meeting, Board members personally signed on a note, this time for $20,000.[24] Unlike the situation in the early days of many private colleges, however, employees at Central Christian never went without their paychecks.

President Wilson started the Central Christian Lectures on March 26–29, 1951, in the spring term of the first year. Raymond Kelcy was the first speaker with a lesson on "New Testament Faith." Other speakers included Ted Norton, Homer Hailey, Norvel Young, Jack Meyer, J. B. Kinney, Ernest Highers, L. L. Gieger, G. K. Wallace, Walter Bryan, A. V. Isbel, James W. Nichols, and Charles Tinius. Chester Grimes gave a lecture on "The Beginning of Central Christian College," in which he said, "Today we see a dream come true."[25]

Student Activities Begin

Sometime early in the first school year, student devotionals began. On Thursday nights, the students gathered outside, either on the west terrace of The Mansion or around the well in the front circle. When the weather was bad, they worshipped in The Mansion's living room. Many students and some faculty attended the weekly event, which featured singing, Scripture reading, prayers, and an occasional talk

Evening devotional on the west terrace of The Mansion

by a student or professor. These devotionals continued throughout the years in Bartlesville and have remained an important part of the spiritual fabric of the university.

Students also began meeting on Monday nights in the parlor of The Mansion for spiritual training. Both men and women attended and, as part of the activity, young men had the opportunity to lead singing, read Scripture, lead prayer, and deliver talks. Sometimes, guest speakers would come, particularly missionaries who had returned from the field. This activity laid a foundation for such later groups as the Harvesters, the Gleaners, and Outreach.

At the very beginning of the first year, Harold Fletcher started the chorus, which quickly became one of the most important groups on campus. In the first semester, the choral group had twelve women and sixteen men. Out of a total student body of ninety-seven, nearly a third sang in the chorus. Fletcher, an e x c e l l e n t musician who knew how to get the most out of his singers, produced a group that James Baird

First chorus at Central Christian College pictured in the living room of The Mansion

called "first class."[26] The chorus sang locally at civic clubs, at the Bartlesville Musical Research Society, and at congregations in the area. Annually, they took a week-long tour throughout Oklahoma and surrounding states, staying in church members' homes and singing at church buildings. Fletcher's repertoire for the chorus included hymns, choral arrangements of many religious works, and secular pieces. A reporter who heard the chorus in concert in the fall of

1951 complimented the group, saying that "purity of vowel sounds, splendid enunciation and clearness of final consonants made the work of the group stand out."[27]

Students in the chorus developed very close ties with each other and with Harold and Mary Helon Fletcher, both of whom traveled with them. In those early years, the chorus provided one of the primary windows through which the public could view the college, and its high quality brought great good will. The chorus sang at every major college event and served as the college's "calling card" in many places.

In the spring of that first year, Fletcher also directed the college's first musical production: Kurt Weill's one-act folk opera *Down in the Valley*. The students presented it outside on the west terrace of The Mansion, which offered a "stage area" eighteen feet deep and seventy feet wide, with seven arches framing it behind. The audience sat in folding chairs on the lawn in front of the terrace. Jesse Wiseman sang the male lead and Barbara McFarland the female lead, with her brother, Bud McFarland, and Lew Meeks rounding out the soloists in the cast.[28]

Early faculty reception in the reception area of The Mansion

As part of that same event, the thirty-one-member chorus also performed "a varied program of religious and secular music" that emphasized "American works in the choral field." Also "included in the purely choral program . . . [were] works by Palestrina, Heinrich, Schultz, Greig, and others."[29] Director Fletcher clearly set high standards for the first-year choral group.

A social highlight, beginning the first year in Bartlesville, was the faculty-staff reception for students. On an evening early in the year, the employees and spouses, with the women in formals and men in dress suits, formed a receiving line for students in the reception room of The Mansion. The room was elegant with its dragon-motif, carved teakwood table and chairs, imported tapestries, handmade rugs designed especially for the room by craftsmen in Austria and Spain, beautiful classical pictures on the wall, and a curved staircase leading to the second floor.[30] Students came to meet their professors, administrators and other employees. For most of the students, such an event was a new social experience. This opening reception for students continued as a tradition through many years, even after the school moved to Oklahoma City.

In December 1950, students had their first Christmas banquet, a tradition that has continued throughout the years of the university. "In keeping with the Christmas spirit, the teachers donned aprons and waiters' cloths. The students got a chance to tell the instructors what they wanted and how it should be done instead of the regular process of the professor telling the pupil."[31] Later, there were freshman-sophomore banquets as well.

In October of the first year at Bartlesville, students began a newspaper called the *Tower*, named after the imposing tower on top of La Quinta. Typically nine and a half by twelve inches and four pages long, the paper was issued biweekly. Also in that first year, students created the first yearbook, named *La Quinta* after The Mansion. Mildred Webb edited this annual, which had forty-six pages of copy and twelve pages of advertisements.

Joe Spaulding

Intramural sports also began that first year, with contests between students in touch football, track, softball, and volleyball. And a college basketball team played nine games, winning five. Not intercollegiate yet, they played primarily company teams in a city league.[32] Joe Spaulding coached.

During the first semester in Bartlesville, Harold Fletcher composed the words and music for an alma mater titled "Central Christian, Hail to Thee!"

> Central Christian, Tower of Truth, Alma Mater, Hail to Thee!
> Built to teach the power of truth; thus thy purpose ever be.
> Lift your voices, anthems raise! Swell the chorus in her praise.
> We will love and honor Thee, Central Christian, Hail to Thee.

A quartet of Barbara McFarland, Eva Jean Foster, Bud McFarland, and Lew Meeks was the first to sing the new song. Even though the later change of name to Oklahoma Christian required some adjustment in wording, this anthem remains the cherished song students sing weekly in chapel and at basketball games.

At the beginning, regulations on student conduct were strict, but generally in keeping with standards of other Christian colleges. On weeknights, women were to go to their dorm rooms after supper, and men were to be in their rooms by 7:15. Students could sign out after that time to go to campus activities or to the library. Administrators believed it was their responsibility to know where students were in the evenings. There was to be no public display of affection. Date night was on Fridays from 7 to 10:30 p.m. and was regulated rather carefully: dating students were either to have a chaperon or to double-date. They could go on dates to church on Sundays and Wednesdays, but were to return to the campus as soon as church was over. Women were not to wear slacks or blue jeans except when participating in active sports. Large, swinging gates at the two entrances to the campus were locked at 9:30 on weeknights and at 10:45 on date night to keep intruders off the campus. Another effect, however, was to encourage students not to be late or they would have to leave their cars by the road overnight. Over the years in Bartlesville, some of these rules were loosened a bit but not by very much.[33]

At the end of the first year, six graduated: Galen Groves, Eva Jean Foster, Sarah Parker, Corine Willett, Bill Henshall, and Barbara McFarland. Dr. Athens Clay Pullias, president of David Lipscomb College in Nashville, spoke at the baccalaureate ceremony on Sunday afternoon,

Some of Central Christian's first graduates: Galen Groves, Eva Jean Foster, Sarah Parker, pictured here with Duane Eggleston, who graduated the following year

June 3, at the 6th and Dewey Church of Christ. Dr. Adron Doran, an educator and member of the Kentucky House of Representatives, spoke at the graduation ceremonies held on the west terrace of The Mansion at 8 p.m. on Friday, June 8.[34]

Successful First Year

The first year of operation in Bartlesville was clearly a success. The first faculty was well qualified, and ninety-seven students were enough to start a solid academic program and a good range of quality extracurricular activities. Before the end of the first semester, the State Regents had granted a very important accreditation so academic work would transfer to other collegiate institutions. With the small number of students and most of them engaging in the activities available, the students developed extremely close ties. Even fifty years later, students from "Bartlesville days" speak fondly of the bonds they formed.

Students were well impressed with their first year, and freshmen wanted to return. Chapel, devotionals, and Bible classes had built a spiritual foundation. Chorus and musical activities were a huge success for a beginning college, and students had produced a yearbook and school paper. And while the men had not fared so well in housing, the women had spent the last half of the year in a well-designed new dormitory.

Financially, Wilson had kept the school going. He had paid salaries and bills even though he had been forced to sell bonds and borrow. Yet, considering the situation in January of 1948, just two and a half years before, the progress was outstanding: a campus had been located and bought, although not yet fully paid for; a deeply committed Board of Trustees, willing to make personal sacrifices, was in place; a dedicated faculty and staff was at work; and members of Churches of Christ in the area were becoming aware they had their own college in Oklahoma.

All in all, the first year must be considered a success. There was, however, no time to rest. In three months, the second year would begin and getting ready for that would require everyone's full effort.

Debt Retired on Bartlesville Campus

Some good financial news came in December of 1951. Cities Service and Phillips, both headquartered in Bartlesville, gave $12,500 each,[35] and the following March brought even more good news: $78,385 in bonds had been sold, and $10,000 in bonds had already been retired.

With this good progress came a very important opportunity. The Burlingames offered a discount on paying the remaining debt on the property. They would cut $25,000 from the total due and all further interest on the loan if the remaining $69,500 could be paid in sixty days. Having the property free of debt would take away payments on that loan and would be a big step forward in public perception about the permanence of the college.[36]

The April *CCC Bulletin* announced a special drive to pay off the property. An article entitled "A $30,000.00 Gift to Central Christian College," said,

There is every reason to believe some new buildings may be financed by outside sources when once the mortgage has been retired. But large business concerns simply cannot be induced to erect buildings on mortgaged property. There is a great deal of money in Bartlesville, and these business people are interested in the success of this school. But they want to know that it is going to be a success. The surest guarantee to them is the retirement of the school's indebtedness. Once this is done, the future of the school is assured.[37]

The article continued, "**Get out your check book or your billfold and send in that contribution today.**"

By a May 13 Board meeting, Wilson reported that the Burlingames, after two days of conferences, had agreed to reduce the payment to $60,000 and had extended the time to June 30. He also reported that Phillips had given $10,000 on the project.[38] At the June 26 meeting of the Board, Wilson reported that $30,482 had been raised plus $14,459 from the Board for a total of $44,941 toward the debt. Enough more was in prospect to set the date of July 4 as the time to burn the mortgage, and officials planned a large celebration.[39]

The big event took place, as scheduled, at 12 noon on July 4. The group gathered first in the assembly hall for a prayer and a rededication service. Harold Fletcher led the summer camp chorus in several selections. Then Raymond Kelcy and G. R. Tinius spoke to the large audience "on the many known difficulties encountered in starting the college." L. B. Clayton, chairman of the Board of Trustees, voiced appreciation to

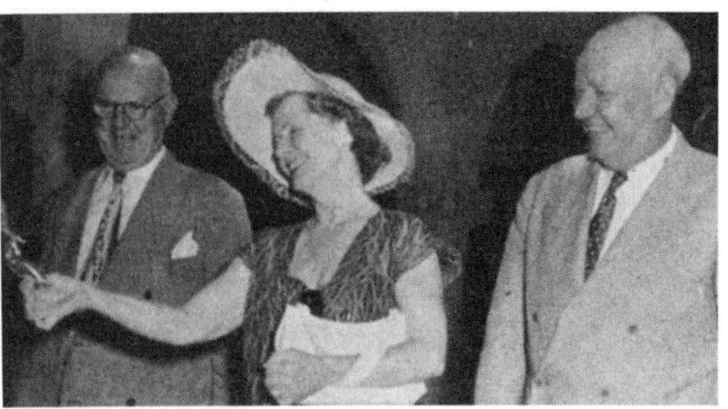

Mrs. Burlingame holds the burning mortgage as her husband, left, and G. R. Tinius, right, look on.

all who had helped, both from the Bartlesville community and from Churches of Christ. President Wilson gave a brief financial report, following which "the audience expressed its thanks to Wilson for his large part in making a success of the educational and financial program." The crowd then moved to the west terrace of The Mansion, "where Mrs. Burlingame held the mortgage and G. R. Tinius, who had done so much over the years to raise money for the college, struck the match on the sole of his shoe and set fire to the mortgage paper."[40]

Wilson wrote in the July *Bulletin*, "We are encouraged by what has been accomplished in the three years we have been working at this job. With a total of five buildings, 152 acres of land, and two years of successful school work behind us, the future is very bright."[41]

Faculty and Academics in Other Bartlesville Years

The second year saw a few changes in the faculty. Bagnetto was gone, and Gerald McCoy came to teach science. Marguerite Orr replaced Henshall in secretarial science. Zelma Lawyer came to teach English and oversee the women's dormitory. She had been a

Stafford North

missionary in Africa and had lost her husband there. Frank Pounders, who worked for a local law firm, taught speech, but had to be replaced in midyear. James Baird recalled that when he realized he would need a new speech teacher in January of 1952, he had called Don Morris, president of Abilene Christian, and asked for a recommendation. Morris suggested Stafford North, who had finished at ACC in 1950 and was near completion of a master's degree in speech at Louisiana State.[42] North was twenty-one and single when he came. In addition to teaching speech, he also taught Greek and tennis and was with students in many other ways, singing with them in the chorus, participating in intramural sports, and directing many extracurricular activities.

Other long-term teachers came a little later. David Howton taught business from 1952 to 1956 and Sarajane Brandon secretarial science from 1953 to 1955. Also in 1953, Taylor Carter joined the faculty in business and Bible, and his wife, Oma, became librarian.[43] She reported 2,228 books in the library when she came in the fall of 1953,[44] and doubled that number during the remaining years in Bartlesville. Another significant addition to the staff in 1953 was "Miss Nancy" Wallingford to run the school store, constructed by September 1951. At "Miss Nancy's Bookstore," students could get mail, buy books and cokes, and get a smile from Miss Nancy.[45] W. C. Whiteside came in 1953 to teach science and math and later served for two years as acting dean. Sara Gillespie taught home economics from 1953 to 1956 and Joyce Edmondson from 1956 to 1958. Paul Phillips taught social science from 1953 to 1955. Dr. Duane Slaughter, the first full-time faculty member with a doctorate, taught physical education during the 1954–1955 year. After the Laniers left in 1953, Baird, Carter, and Hugo McCord taught the Bible classes. In addition to teaching some college courses, McCord was the preacher for the 6th and Dewey Church of Christ in Bartlesville. In 1954, he became vice president of the college.[46] Lawyer taught a Bible course for women and North taught homiletics. Bill Carmack replaced North during the two years of 1954–1956 while North was on leave for doctoral work. Raymond Kelcy started teaching in 1956, but only on a part-time basis, driving from Tulsa, where he preached at 10th and Rockford. In 1956, Darvin Keck joined the science faculty, coming from Eastern Oklahoma A&M in Wilburton, where he also had been preaching.[47] Elvin and Myrtle Higgins left after the spring term of 1956, and the following fall, Bailey McBride returned to Bartlesville to teach English, having graduated from CCC in 1954 and then from David Lipscomb in 1956. He had already begun graduate work at the University of Tennessee. Alumnus Tommy Webb taught in 1956-1957, but stayed only one year. Joseph Jones arrived in 1956 primarily to teach history, but he also served as dean for a time. Earle H. West was academic dean during 1957–1958, also teaching science. Clarence Buller became director of maintenance in 1957, and his wife, Wilma, worked in the mail room.

Each of these faculty and staff members played a significant role in the founding years. They counted their jobs as a ministry to help start Christian education in the Oklahoma area and accepted heavy loads and low pay in making their contribution to the cause.

The curriculum for later years at Bartlesville was similar to that of the first year, but the number of students was always growing. In the fall of 1951, there were 130 students, and by 1957–1958, the last year in Bartlesville, the number had risen to 191. A survey of alumni indicated that 47 percent of CCC students came from farms, 25 percent from small towns, and 28 percent from cities.[48]

Since the very beginning in 1950 and throughout the Bartlesville years, teachers encouraged a serious attitude about academic studies. James Cail, a student in 1956–1958, remembers that teachers gave their courses a sense of importance and used class time and assignments to encourage students to see value in intellectual pursuits. He also recalls that they saw Central Christian as a part of a larger academic picture and wanted to prepare students well for studies elsewhere.[49]

Important educational figures also visited the campus. In May of 1952, Guy Snavely, president of the Association of American Colleges, conducted a seminar on the Central Christian campus for presidents and deans of Oklahoma colleges and universities. He also addressed the eighteen-member second graduating class on the topic of "preparedness."[50] Dr. C. I. Pontius, president of the University of Tulsa, spoke at the third commencement, which had twenty graduates.[51] In 1954, Dr. Oliver S. Willham, president of Oklahoma A&M, spoke at the fourth commencement exercises, when over thirty students graduated.[52] Dr. Mel Nash, chancellor of the Oklahoma Board of Regents for Higher Education, spoke at commencement in 1956.[53]

Students looked favorably on their academic work at Central Christian. A survey of alumni, probably taken in 1956, showed 56 percent of the students said they received higher grades at their transfer institution than at CCC, indicating they had been well prepared.[54] Dr. Baird reported at the end of the third year that the Central Christian faculty's preparation placed them in the top 7 percent of the nation's junior colleges.[55]

Spiritual Activities in Other Bartlesville Years

Many among the Bartlesville faculty and students preached every Sunday. In January of 1952 an article in the *Bulletin* listed places where professors and students preached, which included at least ten cities in Oklahoma and several in Kansas.[56] The presence of the

Preacher's Club in 1953

college was having a large impact on the churches of the area, and having so many preachers on the campus provided a good spiritual influence. In 1952, the Preacher's Club had twenty members, and by the next year, it had reached forty-nine.[57]

The missionary spirit on campus was strong during all the years in Bartlesville, and many students became long-term missionaries. Roy Lanier, Sr. encouraged missions, as did Dr. Baird and others. Mrs. Lawyer, the only one on campus who had actually lived as a missionary abroad, promoted missions by what she said as well as by the life she lived. She had spent four years as a missionary in Africa, her time there cut short by the loss of her husband and a son. She had written a book, *I Married a Missionary*, published in 1943, about a woman going as a missionary to Africa, the story based largely on her own experiences. On campus, then, she was one who had lived the missionary life and who encouraged others to go to far-away places to spread the message of Christ.

Zelma Lawyer

A mission study class focused on mission fields, and returning missionaries often came to speak to the mission group and to chapel. As a result, the Bartlesville student body produced many missionaries. Earl Edwards married Gwen Hall, and they went to Italy as missionaries. Mitchell Greer married Lois Summers, and they did mission work in Sweden. John Beckloff spent his life in missions, primarily in Nigeria, and for a few years, he worked to revive the *Christian Chronicle* with its strong missions emphasis. His brother, James Beckloff, after a career in education, worked as a missionary in China and Nigeria. Barbara McFarland later went to Harding, where she met and married Wendell Key, and, after stateside mission work for several years, they spent time in Nigeria and twenty-five years in Cameroon. Loy Mitchell married Donna Taylor and they served forty years in Africa at Nhowe Mission. His brother, Scott Mitchell, along with Mary Mason, his wife, were also missionaries in Africa. Keith Robinson married Mary Ann Cornelius and together they served for many years in Italy. Gene Cloer, a CCC alumnus and a long-time professor at Harding University, has served in many missionary roles over the years. Charles Moore and his wife, Carolyn James, served in Italy, as did Don Shackelford and his wife, Joyce Brewer. Jerry Campbell was a missionary in Brazil. Leon Clymore and Mark Legg were missionaries to Africa, and Frank Buck and his wife Opal Brewer served in Italy. Many others were preachers, and still others spent a lifetime teaching at a Christian college.

Well-known preachers visited campus to speak in chapel, at the Lectureship, or at evening student meetings. Close ties with Churches of Christ were evident because the list reads like a Who's Who among Churches of Christ of the fifties: Melvin Wise, Jim Bill McInteer, Trine Starns, Hershel Dyer, Alan Bryan, John Stevens, E. W. McMillon, A. R. Holton, W. B. West, N. B. Hardeman, John Banister, Delmar Owens, James Bales, Harvey Scott, C. E. McGaughey, Bill Humble, Don Morris, L. O. Sanderson, Eldred Stevens, Willard Collins, Mac Layton, Perry Cotham, B. C. Goodpasture, Mack Lyon, C. R. Nichol, Ira North, Norvel Young, Roy Lanier, Jr., George Benson, George Bailey, Batsell B. Baxter, Reuel Lemmons, Frank Pack, Homer Hailey, and many more.

Student Organizations

Bill Gosnell

Student government began near the end of the first year, when students developed a constitution and elected officers for the 1951–1952 school year. Bill Gosnell of Bartlesville was chosen as the first president with Larry Riley as vice president, Mildred Webb as secretary, and Peggy Hall as reporter.[58] There was a student advisory council of another four students and a student council of fifteen. Joe Spaulding served as faculty advisor.

Over the years, many student clubs emerged: a drama club called La Quinta Players, a Future Homemakers Club, Mission Study Club, Christian Workers, Pep Club, Harvesters and Worthy Women, and a service club called Criados de la Quinta. As the 1955–1956 school year was drawing to a close, the college announced plans to start new social clubs the following year. They would be designed after Harding's plan: every student would be invited to be a member of a club, students would indicate their top three choices, no student would receive more than one invitation, and initiation activities would be carefully screened. Each club would conduct two major social functions a year. The clubs would have four purposes: to develop leadership, to encourage scholarship, to teach Christian conduct, and to instill Christian attitudes.[59] The clubs took Greek city names. The 1958 *La Quinta* shows four clubs, all of which included both men and women: Spartans, Dorians, Trojans, and Olympians. There were also clubs by states: the K-Klub for Kansans, Sooner Club for Oklahomans, Razorback Club for Arkansans, and Cosmopolitan Club for those from east of the Mississippi. Other geographic clubs came later.

Joan Woods (Sikes) remembers that in 1952 she and others were on a committee to choose a mascot for the college. She suggested "eagles" and this became the committee recommendation.[60] The eagle was approved and has remained the mascot since that time. Dean Baird proposed the colors of maroon and grey because he had seen them at Montgomery Bell Academy in Nashville and thought they looked attractive on athletic uniforms. His suggestion was adopted.[61]

Musicals

Stafford North arrived in January of 1952, and he and Harold Fletcher teamed up that spring for their first joint production: two one-act operas, *Amahl and the Night Visitors* and *The Telephone*, both by Gian

Carlo Mennoti. *Amahl*, which first appeared on television in 1951, was brand new, and CCC became one of the very first colleges to perform it. The leading character is a boy who encounters the wise men on their way to visit the Christ-child. Among the students that year was Bobby Miller, a young man whose voice had not changed and who was small in stature—a perfect fit to play Amahl. Fletcher, directing the musical elements, and North, the staging, prepared the two operas for outdoor performance on the west terrace. At dress rehearsal on May 15, it was clear that Miller had a serious case of laryngitis. That night, Fletcher and North took Miller to see a throat specialist, who indicated there was no way his voice would improve enough to sing anytime soon. Late that night, the directors visited with Marcia Martin, who had the female lead in the other opera, asking if she would spend the next day studying the part and sing it from the pit while Miller played the part and "mouthed" the words on stage. She agreed.

On the afternoon of the performance came another problem: the weather. It was spring in Oklahoma, and the forecast called for storms and possible tornados that night. At four in the afternoon, the directors decided to move the performance to Bartlesville's College High Auditorium. North mobilized the stage crew and began moving sets and erecting them in the auditorium for which they were not designed.

By curtain time, actors and stage were ready, and the performance began—Fletcher directing the singers, Mary Helon Fletcher and student Claudette Robertson accompanying on two pianos, and North backstage helping students adjust to a stage on which they had never even practiced.

The next day, the *Bartlesville Examiner* carried a long story about the performance, reporting, "the courageous directors and performers conquered the difficulties and came through with a splendid performance." The reviewer continued, "Marcia Martin spent the entire day learning the music and the talented lad [Miller] enacted his role so skillfully that, had an announcement not been made prior to the performance, no one would have known that he was not doing all the singing."[62]

One of the most far-reaching developments of the early years came at Thanksgiving in 1952: the first production of *Songs America Sings*. Fletcher and North had pondered how they could have a full-scale musical to showcase the abundant student talent and, at the same time, draw a large crowd. The young college needed something spectacular. A Broadway musical was beyond their resources and would not be unique to Central Christian. What could fill this need? The determined pair decided to write a musical themselves and have students perform it at Bartlesville's Central High School auditorium on a real stage and with ample seating. They would, of course, use "songs America sings" from many sources but put them into a musical revue that would be special for Central Christian. They could add a few original songs along the way when they desired, collaborating on the words and

Students perform the theme song from Songs America Sings in 1952.

Fletcher composing the music. The show opened, in fact, with an original theme song that set the stage for the show:

> These are the songs America sings;
> Songs filled with laughter, and romance, and things.
> Songs from the southland, songs from out west.
> Songs to remind you of the one you love best.
> Some like it hot; some like it cold.
> Some like it fresh and some like it old.
> These are your choices; give ear to our voices
> In Songs America Sings.

The two-hour show, in several acts, featured a wide range of American music: barbershop, blues, hillbilly, and popular. It had comedy sketches and satire. Harold and Mary Helon Fletcher accompanied on two pianos.

The show was a great hit! Over a thousand people saw the two performances built into the college's homecoming activities. Students had sold tickets throughout Bartlesville, so many townspeople came, as well as family and church members. James Baird recalled his reaction to

*Robin Hoodlum and his Merry Ragtime Band.
Robin, played by James Cail, sits in the center.*

the first performance: "When I sat in the audience the first time it was shown, I was amazed. It had glitz and was wonderful fun. When the curtain rang down, I knew we had a winner." He said it gave the college a "rallying point" and made people realize "we could do well."[63] A review in the *Bartlesville Examiner-Enterprise* the day after the first performance said: "The reaction of the audience was one of tumultuous approval."[64] With a student body of only 130, nearly every student was involved on stage, in building sets, or in one of the operating crews.

A new version of *Songs America Sings* came as a highlight in each of the five additional years the college was in Bartlesville. There were scenes of romance, political satire, and nostalgia, with lots of popular songs and even a spoof of Elvis Presley. The Russian space program got into the act when a cave man named "Sputnik" went into orbit. Robin Hoodlum, played by James Cail, and his Merry Ragtime Band were featured in another act. An act in another show featured a Western scene that portrayed façades of "The Lost National Bank," which robbers actually "stole," taking it off the stage, the "Wells Gofar Agency" and—horrors—a "Salooon." Even though everybody came out of the salooon drinking milk, Dr. Baird received a letter criticizing the college for featuring a saloon on stage. In the future, whenever one of the writers suggested doing something to which there might be some possible objection, the other would squelch the suggestion simply by saying, "Dear Brother Baird."

The Western scene with the Salooon

Fletcher, of course, helped write and gave musical direction to all six Bartlesville shows. North worked on four, and while he was away in graduate school, Bill Carmack filled his role on the other two. Bailey McBride, who had performed in the show as a student, joined the writing staff when he returned to teach. Over the time in Bartlesville, attendance rose to nearly 2,000 a year, quite a crowd for an original musical by a college with fewer than 200 students.

Drama and Forensics

Students also performed one-act plays, presenting them both on campus and at the state junior college tournament. In the spring of 1954, North directed students in *Queens of France*, by Thornton Wilder, and won first place, bringing home the first trophy of any kind for Central Christian. Tommy Webb portrayed the conniving lawyer, with Marilyn Cotner, Dayne Bentley, and Doris Myers playing the duped "queens." In other years, North also directed such one-act plays as the "wall scene" from Shakespeare's *Midsummer Nights Dream* (1953) and *The Princess Marries the Page* by Edna St. Vincent Millay (1957).

Lanier, Spaulding, North, Higgins, and Fletcher at the piano

Sometimes the faculty entertained the students. At a get-acquainted party early in the fall of 1952, a faculty quartet of Elvin Higgins, Joe Spaulding, Stafford North, and Roy Lanier sang a rendition of "Too Old to Cut the Mustard Anymore" with personal applications to themselves—Harold Fletcher had revised the words to fit the singers and accompanied on the piano.

Students also participated in debate and forensics. Frank Pounders began the program in the fall of 1951, when the students competed in a tournament at East Central Teachers College in Ada. There Gene Talbert and Allen Yowell won four out of six debates in the "A" division and tied for third place. After North arrived in the middle of that year, the debate and forensic teams continued under his leadership. Bill Carmack coached debate and forensics in North's absence during the 1954–1955 and 1955–1956 school years, and on December 17, 1954, the *Tower* reported that Clyde Wilson and Leon Clymore had won an excellent rating at a tournament in Ada in which thirty-five colleges were entered.[65] In Spring 1957, after North returned, James Cail and Charles McCord took first place in the Oklahoma Junior College Speech League's annual tournament, with Cail taking honors for best debater. Rose Mansur and Barbara Anthony placed second. Certainly a strong showing for the smallest junior college in the state! That year, the college won first overall in the tournament.[66] Cail and McCord repeated as winners in 1958.

In the spring of 1952, North initiated an intramural speech tournament in which more than forty students, a third of the student body, participated. Both men and women competed in Bible reading, poetry reading, extemporaneous speaking, radio speaking, and prepared speaking. This contest became an annual event, continuing through all the Bartlesville years, and for a time in Oklahoma City, with both club and individual competition.

Intercollegiate Sports Begin

Intercollegiate sports began in the fall of 1956. The college had a basketball team from the first year, but had played primarily company teams at the YMCA. Now, under Coach Gerald McCoy, the team would play other junior colleges. The previous year, the Eagles had "played four such games on an experimental basis, winning two of the four." In 1956–1957, they planned a full slate of games against such schools as Northern Oklahoma Junior College, Conners State, Eastern Oklahoma A&M, Okmulgee Tech, and the Tulsa University freshmen. Some athletic scholarships were given to the eight-man squad that included Frank Daniels, Jerrel Thompson, Mark Legg, Bill Witt, Richard Kerns, Bobby Vaughn, James Weatherwax, and David Leonard.[67] Unfortunately, the team lost all its games in the first semester.[68] On top of that, the schedule for the second semester was cancelled because four of the eight players became academically ineligible. At CCC, intercollegiate sports had gotten a start, but a rather inauspicious one.

First intercollegiate basketball team

Darvin Keck coached basketball in the 1957–1958 year. The squad won four of fourteen games, losing seven of the others by fewer than ten points. New players on this team included Robert Hutchison, Dave Harvill, Gary Gregory, Jim Evans, Joe Eddie McCormack, Richard Blankenship, Ralph Hunter, Carroll Lee, Wayne Springer, and George Larson.[69] The Eagles even had cheerleaders: three men and two women in 1956–1957, and six women in 1957–1958.

Campus Life

In 1955, the college purchased a bus for $7,000 to be used for chorus trips, basketball trips, transportation to church for students and other

Students load for a chorus trip on the first CCC bus called "The Beast."

needs. Van Barnes was the official driver of what the students called "The Beast."[70]

Also in 1955, the college purchased an army barracks from Tinker Field, moved it to the Bartlesville campus, renovated it, and put brick veneer around the lower outside wall. The new facility could house twenty-two men, which raised to over forty the number of men who could live on campus. While most men still lived in Bartlesville homes, doubling the men living on campus was an improvement.[71]

As with most colleges, students played pranks. The guys of the "Mule Barn" would slip in the new men's dorm and put "rotten egg" chemicals near the coke machine. Sometimes they pushed cars off the regular parking lot into a muddy area. The men on the second floor of La Quinta occasionally climbed down an outside wall to go into town for a Coke at the Hilltop Café.[72] Perhaps the most notable prank was on Halloween night in 1957. In the center of the circular drive in front of The Mansion stood a beautiful, Italian marble well. There was no actual well, but the beautiful "well top" was there, pulley and all. A few students thought starting a fire in the well would be a good Halloween prank. It was far from any building. "What could be the harm in that?" they thought. The following morning, as people began to move around the campus, much to the dismay of every one, they found the beautiful marble well was cracked. The group overseeing student conduct, the Welfare Committee, sprang into action to locate the culprits and mete out appropriate punishment. From then on, however, the Welfare Committee was known as the Well Fire Committee.

Student discipline took various forms. Students were often "campused," meaning they were denied their date night privileges. Serious violations such as drinking meant dismissal. For some infractions, men on the second floor of The Mansion had to "run the stairs," meaning they would have to run up and down the circular stairs to the tower several times, a total of forty-nine steps to the top.

Even with all the activities for a small student body to carry on, many students still found time to work. An article in the *Tower* in 1954 reported that Central Christian College had the "workingest" student body among those Oklahoma colleges with under a thousand in enrollment. "Sixty-seven percent of the student body is employed in some type of outside work with nineteen percent working at least forty hours a week." "Students are employed," the article continued, "by over thirty diverse concerns, including oil companies, service stations, grocery stores, construction companies, accounting offices, department stores, and manufacturing companies."[73] Several students, over the years, also drove school buses.

The first international student came to Central Christian in September 1952, when Kurt Blum arrived from Switzerland. He had spent time in Frankfurt, where missionaries told him of the college. Wanting to prepare to serve the Lord in Switzerland, Blum spent all the funds he had getting to Bartlesville, and through bulletin articles and other contacts, the college raised the funds for his education. In 1957, Yoriko Ofusa came from Japan and was a campus favorite.

The college had no summer school, but during the summer months the campus hosted camps. Several hundred campers, from sixth through twelfth grades, came from several states each summer to sing in chorus with Harold Fletcher, have Bible classes with Roy Lanier, take trips to Woolaroc Museum, and participate in a variety of crafts and sports. Many other faculty and students helped over the years with the summer camps.[74]

Bartlesville Students Who Returned

From Bartlesville students came six who would return as long-term professors at the college. Bailey McBride, the first to return, came back to teach English in 1956 through 1958, went away for more schoolwork and returned in 1966 to chair the Division of Language and Literature. From 1975 to 1996, he served as chief academic officer; from 1996 to 2006, he was editor of the *Christian Chronicle*; and today he continues to serve as director of the Honors Program. Joe McCormack returned in 1967 and taught English for thirty-five years. James Cail, who finished a bachelor's degree at Abilene Christian, came from 1963 to 1968 to work in student recruitment and as director of admissions. After a doctoral program at Baylor, Cail returned in 1972 to teach psychology and sociology, retiring in 2003. Dr. Gene Talbert chaired the Education Division from 1974 to 1980. Cherry Pyron (Tredway) taught home economics and later, after receiving a doctorate from OSU, taught interior design, serving from 1987 to 2002. Dr. Robert McMillan was professor of mathematics for thirty-two years, from 1969 until his death in 2001. Rita Payne (McGinnis) returned to serve as secretary to Stafford North from 1967 to 1975 and Duane Eggleston served as director of admissions from 1987 to 1995.

Wilson and the Board

L. B. Clayton

On March 2, 1951, L. B. Clayton, an elder at the 10th and Francis Church of Christ and owner of a lumber yard in Oklahoma City, was elected chairman of the Board to replace G. R. Tinius, who had served since February 28, 1947. In that same meeting, in response to a question Clayton raised, the Board voted unanimously that "we amend our constitution and bylaws to prevent solicitation or acceptance of contributions from the treasury of a congregation."[75] This matter was a major issue in the brotherhood at the time and the Central Christian Board wanted to make clear where it stood on this issue. Abilene Christian College had created some controversy by starting to take contributions "from the church treasury," and the Central Christian Board wanted to steer clear of a similar situation.[76]

At a meeting of the Board on May 13, 1952, Chairman Clayton introduced the subject of "securing Professional help to raise finances for the school." President Wilson reported that other Christian colleges had been using such help, and the Board instructed Wilson and Clayton to investigate. On October 13, 1953, the Board employed the John Price Jones Company to raise capital funds for the expansion of the campus.[77] The company prepared an elaborate twenty-eight-page brochure requesting $475,000 to construct two buildings as immediate needs: a men's dormitory and an auditorium-classroom building. The brochure listed an additional $775,000 in "deferred needs" for a cafeteria-gymnasium, library, science building, furnishings and equipment, and repairs on The Mansion and grounds. The sponsoring committee listed in the brochure was most impressive: Oklahoma Governor Johnston Murray; Dr. G. L. Cross, president of the University of Oklahoma; Dr. Oliver S. Willham, president of Oklahoma A&M; Dr. C. I. Pontius, president of the University of Tulsa; Dr. M. A. Nash, chancellor of the Oklahoma State Regents for Higher Education; as well as several well-known ministers among Churches of Christ and a number of businessmen.[78]

In a memoir about his resignation, however, President Wilson said the man the Jones Company "sent to help us to implement our plans on a day-to-day basis" was "comparatively new at the job, and did not give to us the sense of direction we needed." At a luncheon of Bartlesville leaders, Wilson presented the expansion plan. Mike Irelan, president of Cities Service Company, was favorable, but, Wilson said, Kenneth Adams, chairman of the Board of Directors of Phillips Petroleum Company, "refused to go along with us. When he turned thumbs down, the others with business concerns in Bartlesville felt that they simply could not give us the support we needed without a substantial commitment from Phillips Petroleum Company."[79] While considerable effort and expense went into trying to use the Jones company, the effort overall was not successful and resulted in each party's placing some blame on the other. The failure of this plan began to create uneasy feelings between Wilson and some members of the Board.

On March 3, 1953, the Board decided to employ Truman Moore of Oklahoma City, a friend of Chairman Clayton, as a "field representative" to add more help in fundraising. A year later, at a Board meeting on May 6, 1954, "Brother Clayton suggested that Brother Truman Moore had not received the cooperation he should have in his work. Brother Wilson took sharp issue with him on this matter and insisted that he had done everything he knew to do."[80] As Wilson later explained:

> This, however, brought on some differences between Brother Clayton and myself. Hence, it was but natural that I would want to be relieved of my responsibilities, so as to give the Board a free hand to choose someone who could pick up and go forward with the work, which I believed to be so vitally important to the cause of truth and right."[81]

An additional matter before the Board at the May 6 meeting was Dean James Baird's request for a two-year leave of absence. Howard Horton, his long-time friend, had requested the Baird family to replace him in the mission work he had been doing in Nigeria. Horton had gone there to nurture an indigenous effort in New Testament Christianity. The Bairds had long wanted to do missionary work and saw this as a welcome opportunity, and the Lawrence Avenue Church of Christ in Nashville, sponsors of the Hortons, had agreed to support the Bairds. The Board agreed to Baird's two-year leave.[82]

A Change in the Presidency

Wilson now faced a difficult dilemma. He thought the time had come for him to resign, but the man he had hoped would take his place was now to be gone for two years.[83] The Bairds, with their three small girls, were preparing to leave as soon as the school year was over. They had taken their shots and were packing barrels with what they would take.[84] Wilson moved quickly, requesting a special meeting of the Board on May 28, 1954, at the Skirvin Hotel in Oklahoma City. At this meeting, he later wrote, "I tendered my resignation, effective September 1, 1954, with the suggestion that even though Brother Baird was planning to leave the country in less than two weeks, it might not be too late to offer him the presidency, if the Board wished to do so."[85] No minutes remain of this meeting—a fact that Wilson said was "just as well"—but the Board decided to accept Wilson's resignation and to ask Baird to become president.[86]

President Wilson had not told Dean Baird of his resignation plan in advance but there had been some signals. Chairman Clayton had given Baird a hint of what he thought was coming, and Raymond Kelcy, a preacher in Tulsa, had called him to express the hope that, if Wilson resigned, Baird would consider being his successor. By the time the Board called to offer him the presidency of the college, the Bairds had already decided they would accept if the offer came, and they did. He later said, "I was a young Turk and I wanted to see what I could do." Although he said he had "little inkling" of what it would be like to be president, he loved Christian education and had the dream to help provide others the opportunity he had received at Freed Hardeman.[87]

Wilson and Baird spent the summer of 1954 working through the transition. W. C. Whiteside had already been selected to be acting dean and teach math during the time the Bairds were to be in Nigeria.

Wilson's final day at Central Christian came August 31, when he met with the faculty as they prepared to open the new school year. He emphasized that "the most important part of the school day" is not any academic class hour "but is the Chapel period.

Dean James Baird in his office in The Mansion

Christian schools are founded to help in shaping and forming Christian character. It has been found in the experience of thousands that the daily chapel in Christian schools is most effective and far reaching in developing strong, devoted Christian boys and girls." His emphasis on the importance of chapel helped make it a foundation stone for all future years. As the final act in his presidency, he "handed to the incoming president, James Baird, a parting gift: A box of aspirin." [88]

All expressed statements of support and good wishes. Wilson wrote in the July *Bulletin*, "The Board of Directors made a wise decision in selecting Brother James O. Baird to head Central Christian College upon my retirement. . . . He knows the school both inside and out, and is eminently qualified to take up the reins and go forward in this work."[91] In the same issue of the *Bulletin*, the Board of Trustees provided a statement of appreciation to Wilson:

> It was with regret that the Board accepted the resignation of Brother Wilson as president of Central Christian College. However, we know that he has devoted five of the best years of his life to the school . . . five arduous, busy, strenuous years, and that he has done for Central Christian College a work that will live on through the years and that will continue to be felt in eternity.[92]

The August *Bulletin* recorded a statement of appreciation from Wilson to the Board: "Perhaps no one makes greater sacrifices for a Christian college—and with less thanks—than the Board of Directors. This is certainly true of the Directors of Central Christian College." He admitted, "We do not always agree on the best methods of financing the College when we meet together. We sometimes have some heated discussions. But all of these discussions are carried on as Christian brethren." Wilson continued, saying, "I count each and every one a close personal friend, and want to express my heartfelt gratitude and sincere appreciation to each and every one for the hard work and sacrifices made during my administration."[93] Wilson went to preach at the Central Church of Christ in Amarillo,[89] and, in 1956, he became editor of *The Voice of Freedom* periodical. He died on May 31, 1968.[90]

Baird Begins His Presidency

Dr. Baird had known the school from its opening and had seen the struggles Wilson had confronted. He was convinced, however, that Central Christian had an important place to fill and was determined to help the young school rise to a higher level.

Baird immediately faced serious financial problems as the 1954–1955 school year was about to open. He called a special meeting of the Board on August 13, 1954, to reveal a "financial emergency of $18,000—$8,000 in bills to pay, $4,000 in payroll, and $6,000 due at the Fourth National Bank in Tulsa." Again, Board members came to the rescue, as the Board minutes show: "In the light of the situation, it was proposed that each board member give $1,000 to the school immediately. Then let brother Baird or others of the School work with each member to raise as much of the amount as possible." Thirteen were thought to be willing to do this, with another two willing to give $500 each.[94]

Hugo McCord

As he began as president, Baird made some changes in his administrative staff. He appointed Hugo McCord, widely known as an outstanding gospel preacher, as his vice president. He believed this move would give the college a stronger standing in the brotherhood since the Laniers had left a year earlier. Elvin Higgins, who had been vice president, was shifted to assistant to the president. McCord helped publicize college events, edited the college *Bulletin,* worked with the Lectureship, and helped with summer events on the campus. He continued to preach in Bartlesville and in other places as invited.[95] H. E. Whitacre continued as business manager, and W. C. Whiteside was acting dean. Higgins continued to teach and raise money but left after one year, at which point Baird felt the need for someone to handle more administrative details and asked Stafford North, returning in September of 1956 after two years of doctoral work at the University of Florida, to become assistant to the president. When North arrived, now married to Jo Anne Boswell, he helped Baird both with public relations and administrative details, but continued to teach speech, help write and direct *Songs America Sings*, and work with speech and drama activities.

W. O. Beeman

Whitacre also left after a year and, to replace him, Baird brought W. O. Beeman, a spry sixty-one year old with a distinguished career in business. He served in the role for ten years and was an excellent link to financial institutions with which the college had to deal. Baird also brought Loyd Smith on staff to assist with fundraising.

Almost immediately, President Baird began to implement plans for improving the financial situation. In the *Bulletin* for September 1954, he reported to the college's constituency that the accumulated debt was $130,000, with $60,000 of that on the women's dormitory. The college's most immediate need, however, was to raise $64,000 during the coming school year to meet the difference between projected costs and income from students. So here was Baird's appeal:

Large monied men of the church in the area of Central Christian College have helped but have not endowed the college. Even if they did, still the College would be on a firmer foundation if ten thousand poor Christians would each buy a stake in Central Christian each month. We want ten thousand partners who will not subtract one penny from their regular church offerings, but who will forego a dollar's worth of ice cream or pie each month to keep Central Christian out of the red. Ten thousand helping partners, each with a stake in the college, each offering prayers for its welfare, each advertising the College to young boys and girls, each giving a dollar a month, will not only take care of the annual deficit but will be in other ways a mighty force for spiritual good.[96]

Baird said both Higgins and Smith would work full-time to find these donors, each of which would be called a "stepping stone." He further reported that of 852 pledges the college held, 712 were inactive and that the expansion drive for the men's dormitory resulted in only $64,178, of which $16,001 was in cash.

By July 1955, over a thousand had signed on to give a dollar a month. In the late fall of the year, President Baird asked the wives of Tulsa Board members "to plan a city-wide picnic for the purpose of introducing the Stepping Stone Program in Tulsa." To create a greater interest in Christian education and further the Stepping Stone Program, these women decided to plan regular monthly meetings of women in Tulsa and surrounding areas.[97] These meetings brought such speakers as Avanelle Baird, Zelma Lawyer, Oma Carter, and George Benson. Thus began the women's support group for the college that at first was called "Stepping Stones" and later "Oklahoma Christian Women's Association." By May of 1958, women in other cities had begun to organize groups.

The January 1956 *Bulletin* reported the number of "$1 a month" contributors was 2,215 and announced a goal of 5,000 by August 31. "If this goal can be reached, it will be the equivalent of an endowment of 1 ½ million dollars."[98] By November 1956, the number of these donors had risen to 3,301.[99] By September 1957, with the number above 5,000, a drive for 10,000 donors was launched.[100] The *Bulletin* article urged each current Stepping Stone to sign up someone else and reported that this method of giving was meeting half of the operational deficit. The 10,000 goal was never reached, partly because other fundraising methods were introduced, but the Stepping Stone plan served well for many years and started the women's association that continues to be an effective tool for the university. Over the years, these women have contributed more than $2 million dollars to the university.

Soon after becoming president, Baird requested permission

from the Board of Trustees to start an Associate Board. While this group would have no decision-making authority, its members would meet with the Board once a year for discussions about the college, would be asked to contribute at least $500 a year, and would help share information about the college in their local areas. Many who later became members of the Board of Trustees got their early connection with the college through this Associate Board.[101]

In June of 1955, the Board discussed the possibility of a government loan to build another women's dorm and to remake the existing "carriage house" into a cafeteria. Before starting more construction in Bartlesville, however, particularly since the City of Bartlesville had not contributed as much as had been expected, President Baird thought the Board should study the possibility of moving the college to another city in Oklahoma. While the details of this decision and subsequent move await the next chapter, it should be noted that Dr. Baird took a strong position to consider this possibility. After the decision to move was made, much of his work was directed toward that transition.

On one of his visits to Oklahoma City, President Baird visited R. C. Moss, an Oklahoma City church leader. As they discussed the future of Central Christian, Moss suggested that having Dr. George Benson connected with the college would be a great asset. At first, Baird says, he thought such an action would "be a reflection on my inadequacy to lead and build the institution." But as Baird thought about and discussed with others the decisions that would have to be made in planning to move the college to Oklahoma City and the fundraising required to make that a reality, he decided to ask Benson to help. First, Baird sent W. O. Beeman, the Central Christian business manager and a good friend of Benson's, to prepare the way.[102] After a favorable initial response, Baird visited Benson in his Searcy office and asked, "Would you come and help us in the development of [Central] Christian in some official capacity?" Immediately Benson replied that he would.[103] Benson, who would continue as president of Harding College, was a native Oklahoman and had many contacts in the state. Many Oklahoma business leaders held Dr. Benson in high regard because he was known nationwide as a strong advocate for free enterprise and citizenship education.

Dr. George S. Benson

At first, the Board discussed asking Benson to serve as a "special advisor" because "having a formal connection with Dr. Benson would benefit the school tremendously in the light of the forthcoming drive among the Oklahoma City business men."[104] Two months later, however, they decided that the best course would be to appoint Dr. Benson as chancellor, a role in which he would devote a third of his time to Oklahoma Christian and for which he would receive the annual salary of $5,000. In this role he would be the chief executive officer of the college.[105] This position would give Benson a strong connection with the college, thus giving him more leverage in fundraising. It would also mean, of course, that President Baird was subject to him and would seek his approval on major decisions. Baird had proposed this plan and, to his credit, was quite willing to accept it because he believed Benson's help in moving the college to Oklahoma City would be invaluable. Perhaps even more interesting is the fact that the Harding Board was agreeable to this arrangement in which Benson would have less time for that college and would, indeed, transfer some of the major contacts he had cultivated in Oklahoma from possible Harding donors to Central Christian. This agreement must be regarded as one of the most generous arrangements any Christian college has made in helping another one to grow in its early years. The plan began in 1956 and lasted for more than ten years.

In 1957, President Baird made another important personnel decision. He asked both Hugo McCord and Raymond Kelcy to study for doctorates in theology, an undertaking that prepared them for long-term service to the college in the Bible department. McCord went to New Orleans Baptist Theological Seminary to study Old Testament, while Kelcy attended Southwest Baptist Theological Seminary in Ft. Worth for New Testament studies.[106] Both eventually returned and anchored the Bible department for many years.

L. B. Clayton of Oklahoma City served as chairman of the Board until March 31, 1955. At that time, the Board elected G. R. Tinius of Tulsa to that post, but he served only until October 28, when he resigned from the Board due to "ill health." Then Van Martin of Ponca City, who had been vice chairman, became temporary chairman for the remainder of the year.[107] At the Board meeting in March of 1956, Martin was elected chair and served until April 1, 1958, when Dean Smith of Tulsa became chairman.[108]

Observations on the Bartlesville Years

Not everything went smoothly in those early years. The enrollment was lower than had been initially hoped, there were discipline problems, and a limited curriculum caused some students to have to make up courses after they transferred. Science facilities were below college standards, and The Mansion was showing signs of wear and was not entirely suitable as the key building on a college campus.

Most of the men had to live off campus for the years in Bartlesville, and campus athletic facilities were only makeshift. The budget was extremely tight, thus seriously limiting expenditures for teaching materials, equipment, and library.

Still, the progress over the eight years in Bartlesville was remarkable. The full-time student body grew from 97 in the fall of 1950 to 191 in the fall of 1958. For each of those years, the college had been accredited by the Oklahoma State Regents, allowing academic work to transfer and raising the school's prestige. Although the administration had sold bonds and borrowed from banks to help with cash flow, the college's operating income had exceeded operating expenses in all eight years.[109] The initial expense of $125,000 on the Bartlesville campus had been paid off, partly by money raised and partly through the generosity of the Burlingames who had reduced the repayment required. A classroom building, a women's dormitory, and a men's dormitory had been constructed and largely paid for. There had been times of financial crisis when the Board of Trustees had come to the rescue with personal donations and signatures on bank notes, but, all in all, the Bartlesville years saw a successful start in finances and facilities.

Most importantly, however, the Bartlesville years laid the foundation for what was to come. Fundamental qualities that would characterize the institution for decades to come were set in place during those eight years. Academic standards were demanding, and student learning, as demonstrated by the success of graduates attending other colleges, was outstanding. Ties between faculty and students were strong because faculty members were available to students and took a special interest in their success. High quality became the hallmark of student forensic, musical, and dramatic activities as seen in the chorus, one-act operas and plays, debate, and *Songs America Sings*. A strong intramural athletic program began and flourished at Bartlesville, and intercollegiate competition in basketball got a start. Social life was active, and the affection among students was particularly strong. Students had frequent banquets, picnics, and dates, and many students found lifetime mates.

Students were expected to live by high moral standards, and daily chapel was an integral part of campus life. Students attended weekly evening devotionals and had a wide range of religious activities such as Harvesters, Worthy Women, and Mission Study. A strong interest in missions pervaded the campus, leading many to devote a lifetime to taking the message of Christ to distant lands. Through all of these years, ties between the college and its Christian community were strong, with most of the funds, most of the students, and all of the teachers and administrators coming from Churches of Christ.

Those involved in Central Christian frequently prayed for

God's blessing on their work and believed they had received it. The above description will sound familiar to anyone who has attended Oklahoma Christian University at any stage of its existence, because the foundation for these qualities laid at Bartlesville has continued to characterize the institution through all the years since.

Chapter 2, Endnotes

1   M. Norvel Young, *A History of Colleges Established and Controlled by Churches of Christ* (Kansas City, Missouri: Old Paths Book Club, 1949), 27.

2   *Central Christian College Catalog*, 1950, 11-21, OC Archives.

3   Articles of Incorporation, Dated January 22, 1948, Office of President, Oklahoma Christian University.

4   *Catalog*, 1950, 10.

5   "Character Building Looms Large as Goal of College," *Bartlesville Examiner-Enterprise*, 1950, Ruth Wilson Scrapbook, 17, OC Archives.

6   *Catalog*, 1950, 6.

7   Ibid.

8   Ibid.

9   Ibid., 8-9.

10   *Catalog*, Abilene Christian College, 1950-51, 29-30.

11   L. R. Wilson, "I Resign as President," Unpublished Manuscript, January 4,1967, 2, OC Archives.

12   Interviews with Harold Fletcher, Bailey McBride, and recollections of the author.

13   James O. Baird, Interview on audiotape with the author on November 2, 1989, and subsequent days, Tape 1, OC Archives.

14   Ibid.

15   Minutes, Board of Trustees, May 22, 1951, OC Archives.

16   "Work Report Is Made By College Head," *Bartlesville Examiner-Enterprise*, December 30, 1950, 10.

17   "Students Give First Impressions of School," *Central Christian College, Bulletin,* October 1951, OC Archives.

18   Grade reports from Fall, 1950, Registrar's Office, OC.

19   Joe McCormack, Interview on video with the author, June 9, 2006, OC Archives.

20   Minutes, Board of Trustees, September 19, 1952, OC Archives.

21   "Real Home Away from Home Is Provided By CC College," *Bartlesville Examiner-Enterprise*, Summer, 1950, Ruth Wilson Scrapbook, 16, OC Archives.

22   Minutes, May 22, 1951, OC Archives.

23   Ibid.

24   Minutes, Board of Trustees, August 14, 1951, OC Archives.

25   Lectureship Program, 1951, OC Archives.

26   Baird, Interview, Tape 1.

27   Qtd. in "A Cappella Chorus is Being Received Enthusiastically," *Central Christian College Bulletin*, January 1952, OC Archives.

28   "Production By Chorus Rehearsed," *Bartlesville Examiner-Enterprise*, April 22, 1951, 8.

29   "College Chorus Rehearsing for American Folk Opera," *Bartlesville Examiner-Enterprise*, April 15, 1951, Ruth Wilson Scrapbook, 16, OC Archives.

30   "$100,000 in Furnishings part of Gift to College," *Bartlesville Examiner-Enterprise*, Probably Spring 1950, Ruth Wilson Scrapbook, 16, OC Archives.

31   "Central High (sic) Holds Annual Banquet Party," *Bartlesville Examiner-Enterprise,* December 19, 1951, Ruth Wilson Scrapbook, 60, OC Archives.

32   "796th Clips Central Christian By 56-47," *Bartlesville Examiner-Enterprise,* January 15, 1952, 5.

33   Student Handbooks, OC Archives.

34   "Kentuckian To Speak at Exercises," *Bartlesville Examiner-Enterprise,* June 3, 1951, 20; "First Class Graduates at College," *Bartlesville Examiner-Enterprise,* June 8, 1952, 10; "College Head to Address Graduates," *Bartlesville Examiner-Enterprise*, June 1, 1951, 23.

35   Minutes, Board of Trustees, December 11, 1951, OC Archives.

36   Minutes, Board of Trustees, March 14, 1952, OC Archives.

37 "A $30,000 Gift to Central Christian College," *Central Christian College Bulletin*, April 1952, OC Archives.

38 Minutes, Board of Trustees, May 13, 1952, OC Archives. "Will It Be Too Little, Too Late?" *Central Christian College Bulletin*, June 1952, OC Archives.

39 Minutes, Board of Trustees, June 26, 1952, OC Archives.

40 "Christian College Realizes a Dream," *Bartlesville Examiner-Enterprise,* July 5, 1952, 1; "Mrs. Burlingame Burns Mortgage on College," *Bartlesville Examiner-Enterprise*, July 5, 1952, Ruth Wilson Scrapbook, 49, OC Archives.

41 "Thanks a Million to You," *Central Christian College Bulletin*, July 1952, OC Archives.

42 Baird, Interview, Tape 1.

43 *La Quinta*, 1954.

44 "Numerous Gifts Catalogued," *Tower*, October 30, 1953, OC Archives.

45 "Central Christian College Opens 2nd Year With Added Facilities," *Bartlesville Examiner-Enterprise*, August 26, 1951, 6.

46 "Vice President of Central Christian," *Central Christian College Bulletin*, September 1954, OC Archives.

47 "New Faculty Members," *Central Christian College Bulletin*, June 1956, OC Archives.

48 Survey of 130 Alumni Responses taken about 1956, CCC Enrollment file, OC Archives.

49 James Cail, phone conversation with author, November 2, 2006.

50 "Dr. Guy Snavely Will Speak At Seminar Here," *Bartlesville Examiner-Enterprise*, May 9, 1952, 24; "Presidents Award to Three Frosh," *Bartlesville Examiner-Enterprise*, May 25, 1952, 5.

51 "C. I Pontius to Address C.C. College Graduates," *Bartlesville Examiner-Enterprise*, May 1953; Ruth Wilson Scrapbook, 60, OC Archives.

52 "A.&M. President Graduation Speaker," *Central Christian College Bulletin*, May 1954, OC Archives.

53 "Sixth Annual Graduation Exercises," *Central Christian College Bulletin*, May 1956, OC Archives.

54 Survey.

55 "Central Christian College Completes 3rd Year of Work," *Bartlesville Examiner-Enterprise*, June 1954, Ruth Wilson Scrapbook, 61, OC Archives.

56 "Faculty Members and Students are Sounding Out the Word," *Central Christian College Bulletin*, January 1952, OC Archives.

57 "Forty-nine Students Plan to Preach," *Tower*, October 30, 1953, OC Archives.

58 *La Quinta,* 1952, 16.

59 "Harding Plan Is Explained," *Tower*, April 13, 1956, OC Archives.

60 Joan Woods Sikes, "First Two Years in Bartlesville," Online OC History Project.

61 James O. Baird, "Oklahoma Christian University 1950-1974," Unpublished Manuscript, 4-5, OC Archives.

62 "College Operas Given Through Difficulties," *Bartlesville Examiner-Enterprise,* May 17, 1952, Ruth Wilson Scrapbook, 27, OC Archives.

63 Baird, Interview, Tape 1.

64 "College Show Gets Plaudits of Audience," *Bartlesville Examiner-Enterprise*, November 28, 1952, 10.

65 "Debaters Win honors at Ada," *Tower*, December 17, 1954, OC Archives.

66 "Students Take Top Honors at State Tourney," *Tower*, March 26, 1957, OC Archives.

67 "CCC Begins Inter-Collegiate Basketball," *Central Christian College Bulletin*, November 1956, OC Archives; *La Quinta*, 1957, 39.

68 "Eagle Quintet, Okmulgee Five Clash Tonight," *Tower*, January 18, 1957, OC Archives; "CCC Cancels Basketball," *Tower*, February 8, 1957, OC Archives.

69 *La Quinta*, 1958, 74-75.

70 "New Bus for CCC," *Central Christian College Bulletin*, November 1955, OC Archives.

[71] "New Boy's Dormitory," *Central Christian College Bulletin*, November 1955.

[72] McCormack.

[73] "C.C.C. High in Student Employment," *Tower*, March 5, 1954, OC Archives.

[74] "US is Well Represented at CC Camp," *Bartlesville Examiner-Enterprise*, Summer 1952, Ruth Wilson Scrapbook, 46, OC Archives.

[75] Minutes, Board of Trustees, March 2, 1951. OC Archives.

[76] Owen Cosgrove, *Morris* (Ft. Worth: Star Bible Publications, 1993), 76-81.

[77] Minutes, Board of Trustees, October 13, 1953, OC Archives.

[78] "A Growing College for a Growing Region," John Price Jones Expansion Brochure, n.d., OC Archives.

[79] Wilson, "Resign," 4.

[80] Minutes, Board of Trustees, May 6, 1954, OC Archives.

[81] Wilson, "Resign," 6.

[82] Minutes, Board of Trustees, May 6, 1954, OC Archives.

[83] Wilson, "Resign," 6-7.

[84] Baird, Interview, Tape 3.

[85] L. R. Wilson, Letter to W. O. Beeman, January 4, 1967, OC Archives.

[86] Wilson, "Resign," 7.

[87] Baird, Interview, Tape 3.

[88] "Wilson's Last Words on Retiring," *Central Christian College Bulletin*, September 1954, OC Archives.

[89] "President Wilson Announces Resignation," *Central Christian College Bulletin*, June 1954, OC Archives.

[90] "L. R. Wilson Dies; Dedicated Life Draws Praise of Many," *Central Christian College Bulletin*, July 1968, OC Archives.

[91] "Wilson Commends President-Elect Baird," *Central Christian College Bulletin*, July 1954, OC Archives.

[92] "A Statement of Appreciation by the Board of Directors," *Central Christian College Bulletin*, April 1952, OC Archives.

[93] L. R. Wilson, "Many Thanks to the Board of Directors," *Central Christian College Bulletin*, August 1954, OC Archives.

[94] Minutes, Board of Trustees, August 13, 1954, OC Archives.

[95] Earl I. West, *The Enchanted Knight: The Life Story of Hugo McCord* (Germantown, Tennessee: Religious Book Service, 1999), 56.

[96] "Campaign Launched for 10,000 Donors to Give $12 a Year," *Central Christian College Bulletin*, September 1954, OC Archives.

[97] "Tulsa Stepping Stones to Work on '2 for 1,'" *Central Christian College Bulletin*, September 1957, OC Archives.

[98] "Goal of 5000 Stepping Stones," *Central Christian College Bulletin*, January 1956, OC Archives.

[99] "Stepping Stones Reach New High," *Central Christian College Bulletin*, November 1956, OC Archives.

[100] "Drive for 10,000 Stepping Stones Begun," *Central Christian College Bulletin*, September 1957, OC Archives.

[101] Minutes, Board of Trustees, October 1, 1954, OC Archives.

[102] W. O. Beeman, *Oklahoma Christian College: Dream to Reality* (Delight, Arkansas: Gospel Light Publishing Company, 1970), 84.

[103] Baird, "Oklahoma Christian University," 11.

[104] Minutes, Board of Trustees, September 25, 1956, OC Archives.

[105] Minutes, Board of Trustees, November 16, 1956, OC Archives.

[106] "Kelcy on Leave," *Central Christian College Bulletin*, November 1957, OC Archives.

[107] Minutes, Board of Trustees, March 31, 1955, OC Archives; Minutes, Board of Trustees, October 28, 1955, OC Archives.

[108] Minutes, Board of Trustees, March 27, 1956, OC Archives; Minutes, Board of Trustees, April 1, 1958, OC Archives.

[109] Comparative Statement, Income and Expense; *Report of a Self Study*, Oklahoma Christian College, September 1960, OC Archives.

Chapter 3
THE MOVE

The Background

The Central Christian Board believed they had made an excellent choice in locating the college in Bartlesville, one of Oklahoma's best smaller cities. The Mansion was strikingly beautiful, the 152 acres gave plenty of space for future growth, and the business community had promised strong support. And in Bartlesville, Central Christian started well.

Early on, however, it was clear that not everything was entirely satisfactory. Of the $100,000 initially promised for construction of new buildings, the City of Bartlesville only raised $40,000.[1] Another negative indication came in 1953 when the Board employed the John Price Jones Company of New York to help in a capital fundraising campaign. President Wilson and company representatives developed a long-range plan designed to raise $1,250,000. When Wilson presented the plan to key leaders in Bartlesville, however, Kenneth Adams, chairman of the Phillips Petroleum Board, "turned thumbs down," and "the other business concerns in Bartlesville felt that they simply could not give us the support we needed" without help from Phillips.[2] Wilson wrote in his resignation memoir of another problem: "Many of the business men in Bartlesville were disappointed by my resignation, and refused to give Brother Baird any help, either financially or otherwise."[3]

The February 1955 Board minutes reflect more concerns about the college's relationship with the Bartlesville community. This meeting was called to "discuss with Brother Tinius the possibility of his coming to Bartlesville to make special contacts in order to definitely determine whether or not the School will receive any support from Bartlesville."[4] Board minutes quote Tinius as saying that "the major reason we have not received better support from Bartlesville is that we have not been a part of Bartlesville." Tinius continued: "we need a man to sit in on the Chamber of Commerce meetings and serve on some committees—in other words, just be one of them." The Board asked Tinius to check into the matter, come up with a plan, and report back. Further Board minutes do not mention any report from Tinius on the Bartlesville situation, but the following month, he was elected chairman of the Board,[5] and on June 18, the Board hired him "to direct fund raising for the college on a full time basis."[6] At the same meeting in June, President Baird reported that the Bartlesville Campaign for $30,000 had raised only $15,000. "The discussion following by the Board was focused on the mistake of anticipating too much support from Bartlesville due to religious prejudice."[7]

Loyd L. Smith

One Saturday morning in the spring of 1955, President Baird and Loyd L. Smith, a fundraiser for the college, were on campus in their weekly meeting to discuss their work, when "Out of the clear blue," according to Baird, Smith stated, "We ought to move this college to Oklahoma City."[8] "That idea grabbed me," Baird said, and he began to give it thought. At the next Board meeting on June 18, Baird proposed that the Board study the possibility of moving the college. He later said, "The idea caught them off balance" because he had not laid the groundwork. The suggestion, according to Baird, was "inflammatory."[9] The Board chose not to give this matter any consideration.[10]

The Compromise

Baird requested a special meeting of the Board on July 4, three weeks later. Fifteen members of the Board met in the Library of The Mansion and Baird told them, "I'd like for us to consider moving the school, but if this is beyond consideration, then you can accept my resignation."[11] For this action, Baird gave two reasons: First, some Board members were not living up to their agreement to give or raise $1,000 a year for the college, and second, "the major reason for [the] resignation was the Board's unwillingness at the June 18 meeting to even study the possibility of moving the School to Oklahoma City."[12] Baird then left the room while the Board discussed his resignation and the reasons for it. They rejected his resignation and developed a plan to appoint a special committee to study the advisability of moving the college. This three-man committee from outside the Board would study the matter and report on October 28: "one man to be selected by Brother Tinius, one by Brother Baird, and these two to select a third to make investigation as to the feasibility of moving the School to a larger city."[13] Baird appointed Dr. George Benson as his representative.[14] Tinius selected Dalton Voss of Ponca City. These two selected Dr. Ralph Owens of Oklahoma City.[15]

The committee prepared a thorough report entitled "The Comparative Merits of a Smaller City versus a Larger City as the Location for a Christian College." They had studied six aspects of the question and presented information on each.[16] First, on the question of "moral life," they commented that in earlier years, each Christian college had been located in a "relatively isolated place" to provide a buffer from the world. Now, however, they concluded, with cars, radio, television, and the theatre, there was not much difference in the moral climate in larger or smaller cities, and since more students would be coming from and going back to larger city life, it was better to prepare them in that environment.[17]

On the second issue, "the student aspect," their conclusion was that more students would attend if the college were located in a larger city. Students from smaller places would go to the city, but those from the city were less likely to go to a smaller place.[18] The third issue was the faculty. On this point, likewise, the committee concluded that well-prepared faculty more likely would want to live in a city environment than in a smaller location.[19] Fourth was "the clientele," by which they meant "students, alumni, parents of students, parents of prospective students, and others who may have a reason to be especially interested in the institution." In a larger city, more of the clientele could be close to the institution and thus, in a larger city, more would be willing to help the college.[20] Fifth, from the "service" aspect, the committee determined that the larger city, again, would have advantages. With more people close by, the college could be of greater service. The report mentioned that Oklahoma City had five main railroad lines, nine bus lines, four airlines, and nine federal highway outlets, plus seven state highway outlets. Oklahoma City also had "24 churches, and a membership of 6,500" and was "the center of the Church of Christ population for the general area."[21] So with more people close by and better access to transportation, the committee agreed that the college could serve its constituency more effectively in a larger city.[22]

Finally, the committee looked at the financial aspect. "Some twenty Christian colleges have been started by our brethren during the last fifty years, and . . . with few exceptions only those in average or larger cities have survived."[23] Of the four senior colleges among Churches of Christ at that time, three were in larger cities and only one, Harding, was in a smaller city. The report then detailed what financial assistance these colleges were receiving from their local communities and also provided similar information on colleges associated with other religious groups. The data showed that the amount of support from the local community was proportional to its size.[24] Thus, a college located in a larger city likely would receive more in local support than if it were in a smaller community.

The committee summarized that there might be some room for debate on the moral aspect, "But with regard to the next five the committee feels that the advantages are clearly in favor of the larger city."[25]

The report then addressed the question of whether a college already located in a smaller place would gain or lose more by moving. Their conclusion was that, over time, the financial advantages of the city would far outweigh even a loss in selling a present campus. "Should a college in a smaller location desire to move to a city, it would probably be good for a special committee to be very carefully selected for the purpose of canvassing the larger cities in the desired area to see which one would be the more friendly to the move, which one would make the larger financial offer, and which one might have the better transportation facilities and which was nearer the center of the clientele to be served. Then a wise decision could likely be made."[26]

The Decision to Move

Voss and Owens were present at the Board meeting on October 28 to present the committee's findings. Their report actually made no recommendation as to whether Central Christian College should move. They had only studied the question of whether a larger or smaller city was preferable as a college location. At the same time, however, according to President Baird, the evidence in the report was quite convincing.[27] After the committee presented its report, the Board unanimously passed the following resolution:

(1) The same committee which made the study be requested to serve as a committee to secure an offer from Tulsa or Oklahoma City.
(2) If an offer of $250,000 plus a suitable site of at least 20 acres be procured that the College would accept it. (This amount was established in consideration of the fact that our present property is valued at $350,000.)
(3) An effort be made, in light of pending governmental loan [for a men's dormitory], to make the approach to Tulsa and Oklahoma City within 60 days.[28]

By October, then, the Board, which had refused even to consider moving the college at a meeting in June, not only had studied the question, but had agreed to move if certain provisions were met. The committee's report had been quite persuasive. As difficult as it had been for the Board to decide to move the college, however, more hard questions lay ahead. Would Oklahoma City or Tulsa make an offer to move the college to their city? Could church members who had supported the college in Bartlesville be convinced this was a good move? Could the funds be raised to start over on a new campus?

The study committee agreed to help with the next step and, along with President Baird, decided that the civic community in a prospective city would have to provide $200,000, the church members in that community would have to provide another $100,000, and the church members throughout the rest of Oklahoma would be asked to contribute another $100,000.

Since Bartlesville was about fifty miles from Tulsa, college ties there were stronger than in Oklahoma City. It was in Tulsa that the first women's association group had been formed, and many Central Christian teachers often had preached there. After initial visits with church leaders along with civic and business leaders in both Tulsa and Oklahoma City, however, the scale began to tilt toward Oklahoma City.[29] Benson had close ties with leaders in Oklahoma City[30]; it was the capitol city and was more in the center of both Oklahoma's population and of members of Churches of Christ. And the response of Oklahoma City leadership was more positive. On November 18, 1955, the Board, after hearing a report on developments in Oklahoma City, set December 8 as the date for a meeting with "active church leaders" in the city to see if the members of the church were willing to raise $100,000. "Following this dinner meeting on the 8th Brother Benson is to approach the civic leaders."[31] While Benson would not become chancellor of Central Christian for another year, and even with his duties continuing as president of Harding College, he was already beginning to play a significant role at Oklahoma Christian.

During January of 1956, working with a local committee composed of Dr. Ralph Owens, Rex Westerfield, G. A. Hale, R. C. Moss, and Frank Winters, Dr. Benson raised $100,000 from members of Churches of Christ in Oklahoma City, the first of the three goals to be met if the college were to move.[32] By the January 28 Board meeting, Benson had also secured a promise from the Oklahoma City Chamber of Commerce to give $150,000 plus the site.

With this success, college officials next sought support from members of the church across the state. To launch this effort, with Owens as chairman and Westerfield as vice chairman, Benson and Baird decided to have a mass meeting of church members at the Zebra Room in the Oklahoma City Municipal Auditorium on March 5.

Meeting in the Zebra Room of the Municipal Auditorium

The primary speakers were Dr. George Benson, president of Harding College, and Don Morris, president of Abilene Christian College, both of whom would speak in support of a Christian college in Oklahoma.[33] Of course, Dr. Baird would speak for Central Christian.

The turnout was huge: "Over 1,200 Christians were present for the dinner meeting, and it was said at the time that it was the largest assembly of members of the church in the history of the state."[34] Those present, representing every county in Oklahoma, were excited and supportive about the move to Oklahoma City and the future prospects of the college.[35] On March 22, the college sponsored a rally among church members in Wichita Falls. Berry Brown, "one of the greatest names in golf" and an elder at the 10th and Broad Street Church of Christ, was general chairman of the meeting, and Bryon Nelson, another great name in golf who was also a member of the church, served as master of ceremonies. Again, Benson, Morris, and Baird spoke, and the choruses from Harding, ACC, and Central Christian all sang.[36]

By midsummer, the college had raised $155,000 from church members throughout the state to go with the nearly $100,000 church members in Oklahoma City already had contributed.

The third and final requirement to make the move was actually to receive the funds that the Oklahoma City business community had promised. Bartlesville had not delivered on its original promise. Would Oklahoma City? E. K. Gaylord, publisher of the *Daily Oklahoman* and one of the key business leaders of the city, wrote Dr. Benson on June 21, saying: "Oklahoma City has accepted your challenge to raise $200,000 for Central Christian College." He reported $49,500 in hand and thought the amount would reach $60,000 in a few days. "This is merely earnest money to prove that the city will finish its

E. K Gaylord and James Baird

obligation next November."[37] Dr. Baird recalled that Mr. Gaylord took a personal interest in this campaign. He not only made a generous contribution himself, but he also "personally walked the streets of Oklahoma City carrying cards of prospective donors."[38] This first connection with the Gaylord family was the beginning of one of the most important relationships in the history of Oklahoma Christian.

With the three criteria assured, the Board began the process of looking for a site in Oklahoma City. On March 27, the Board gave members L. B. Clayton, J. E. Wright, T. E. Burch, and Jesse Stratton the authority to "make the final decision on the selection of a site for the School at Oklahoma City."[39] Later, G. A. Hale, R. C. Moss, Frank Winters, and Amon Wright were added to this group. At that same meeting, a three-person committee of Glenn Durrill, Leon Lugar, and Cline Mansur were to "investigate possibilities of sale of the Bartlesville property."[40]

Dr. Ralph Owens

At the June 26 Board meeting, Dr. Ralph Owens reported that the drives among Oklahoma and Oklahoma City members of the church had been successful, and that Oklahoma City leaders had assured him that their drive would also reach its goal. On the basis of this information, Dr. R. E. Cogswell moved and Jesse Stratton seconded that "the college move to Oklahoma City." The motion carried unanimously.[41] Also at the June 26 meeting, the Board authorized the firm of Owen, Mansur, Steele, and Nusbaum to do preliminary work on the site and master plan.

The Announcement, the Site, and More Fundraising

The die was now cast. The Board was charging "full speed ahead" to prepare for moving the college. The Board did not, by any means, have enough money to build and furnish the necessary buildings on a new campus, but it had met the targets for making the decision to move.

In September of 1956, Central Christian College made the official public announcement when the *CCC Bulletin* carried this headline: "College to Move to Oklahoma City." The article said operations would begin there in 1957 (although operations actually did not begin there until 1958) and outlined the successful fund drives that had made the decision possible.[42]

The next step was to choose the location in Oklahoma City. The site committee looked at a location in Moore and later took an option on seventy acres near Lake Hefner at the intersection of Northwest Highway and Northwest 63rd Street. This site offered good space and an excellent connection to major roads. But Cline Mansur, consulting engineer, pointed out that a $36,000 sewer lift station would have to be installed, and with the slope toward the lake, a large amount of grading would be required.[43] While the committee was studying this location, the Oklahoma City Chamber of Commerce offered a different site, two hundred acres near the corner of Eastern and Memorial Road, northeast of the city. E. K. Gaylord favored this location[44] and took Frank Winters and R. C. Moss to lunch to encourage this choice.[45] It combined three adjoining tracts: two of eighty acres each and one of forty. The Chamber had

From atop a downtown building, Benson, with Baird watching, points to the northeast to indicate the campus site.

already put together a deal from the three owners to sell at $500 an acre—a total of $100,000. At the time, the site seemed to be "in the country," eleven miles from downtown Oklahoma City and not even within the city limits. The two hundred acres, however, was located near an intersection of two major roads and was totally clear of any buildings, thus allowing complete freedom in planning its use. Having open space all around the campus also meant that control could be exercised on the development of the area nearby. So, on September 1, 1956, Central Christian officials signed the contract for this property.[46]

In the fall of 1956, Central Christian prepared a brochure to use for finishing the fund drive in Oklahoma City. The sponsoring committee was impressive: E. K. Gaylord, publisher of the *Daily Oklahoman*; federal judge Stephen Chandler; C. A. Vose, president of the First National Bank; Donald Kennedy, president of OG&E;

D. W. Hogan, Sr., president of City National Bank; H. B. Groh, general manager of Southwestern Bell Telephone Company; B. D. Eddie, president of Superior Feed Mills; retired admiral John E. Kirkpatrick, Kirkpatrick Oil Company; Roland V. Rodman, president of Anderson-Prichard Oil, and others. With such backing, gained largely through connections Dr. Benson had with many leaders of business, Central Christian College was coming to Oklahoma City through the front door. The brochure, in fact, made the point that the college would follow the lead of Harding College "for its accent on citizenship, Americanism and individual responsibility."[47] The brochure revealed the general plan for the new campus: an administration-classroom building at $500,000, two dormitories at $400,000, a cafeteria-kitchen-student center at $100,000, a gymnasium at $150,000, and equipment at $100,000. The total cost for these buildings and equipment was listed at $1,250,000.[48]

The brochure, for use among Oklahoma City business firms, outlined the plan for raising this $1,250,000. Churches of Christ in Oklahoma City had already donated $100,000; members of Churches of Christ from outside Oklahoma City were well on their way to raising an additional $250,000. Government loans for the dormitories would provide $400,000, and the sale of Bartlesville property would add $250,000 more. The college hoped to raise the remaining $200,000 to $250,000 from the Oklahoma City business community. The program was certainly ambitious and good progress had been made already, especially among church members.

By July 1959, after the first year of operation in Oklahoma City, college officials reported they were near $300,000 in contributions in cash and pledges from Oklahoma members of Churches of Christ—actually $87,110 from Oklahoma City and $181,204 from across the state. They hoped an additional $30,000 would come soon. The drive had been a real grassroots effort: "The county chairmen have worked diligently, and over 1200 workers have been enlisted to help in this work."[49] For a college that had failed in several of its campaigns to raise funds for new buildings in Bartlesville, the success of the campaign to build an entirely new campus in Oklahoma City was highly satisfying and shows that interest and support had risen to a new level. The wisdom of the move certainly was verified.

Planning for the New Campus

Along with fundraising, college officials and the Board were also seeking a master plan for the buildings and roads on the new campus. In their meeting on September 25, 1956, Jack Nusbaum showed a proposed plan and the architectural drawing for the first building, two hundred feet long and sixty feet wide. About half of this building's 26,000 square feet would provide space for seventeen classrooms of twenty-four by thirty-two feet, while the other half would serve administrative and faculty offices.[50]

Dr. Benson, who was present for the meeting but who would not be appointed chancellor for another six weeks, suggested that these architects "consult with architects who have specialized in building college campuses."[51] As Dr. Baird reported years later, Dr. Benson had recently attended an educational conference where the nationally known firm of Caudill, Rowlett, and Scott presented a session on campus design.[52] Since the firm had an office in Oklahoma City, Benson thought it would be important to use these designers as consultants.[53] This suggestion, in effect, turned down the Nusbaum master plan and design for the first building and delayed the start of any construction. It was, however, a suggestion destined to have a profound effect on the eventual look and layout of the campus.

Cline Mansur also reported on expected engineering costs for the property: $7,500 in paved roads, $21,000 for a water well and pumps, $4,000 for a thousand feet of distribution lines, and $11,000 for sewage disposal. In addition, there would be some costs for campus grading.[54]

At a special meeting of the Board on March 15, 1957, the firm of Caudill, Rowlett, and Scott, along with Nusbaum, Owen, Mansur, and Steele, presented a 125-page report. First, this study assembled quotations from many sources on the importance of careful campus planning. It emphasized the need to look fifty years into the future, to provide flexibility since building usage certainly would change, and to keep the needs of students foremost. The designers, who viewed a college campus as a small city, said the campus should be "zoned," much like a city would be. They proposed a living zone on the west side, an academic zone on the east side, and, between these, an intermediate activity zone for library, food service, and a gymnasium. Thus students, needing to access these central services from both the housing and the academic areas, would find these conveniently in the center of the campus. Using this concept, the new college

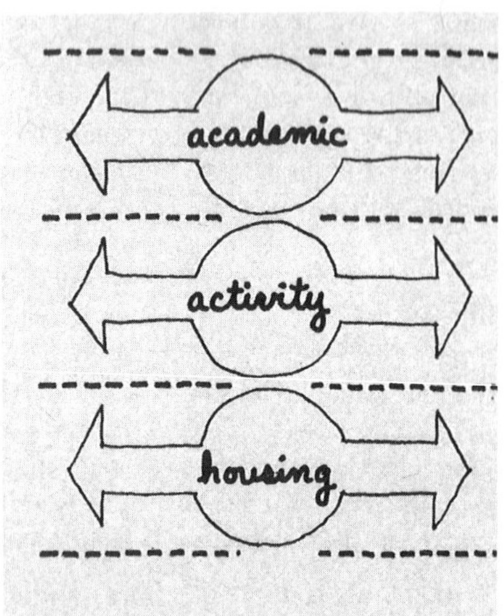

Drawing from report of Caudill, Rowlett, and Scott. West is toward the bottom of the chart and north is on the left.

would arrange buildings of like purpose along the axis of an east-west mall. As additional buildings of each type were added, they would be placed in the proper zone by expanding each zone to the north and south. This plan assured that from the very beginning, there would be "the feeling of a campus" and, as expansion came, the design would preserve an orderly arrangement. The plan also provided that no roads would cross the central mall, thus giving students unhindered pedestrian access to all parts of the campus.[55]

The report's second foundational concept was "the modular approach," which proposed that a space the size of eight classrooms become the "building block module." Designers, then, could place two of these together, stack one on top of the other or make other arrangements of them and, in so doing, create a harmony of design that was both aesthetically pleasing and highly flexible. The designers also recommended generally one-story buildings at first, both to use space efficiently and to create more buildings to give a "campus" feel. All interior walls would be movable to accommodate future changes in need.[56] The report emphasized the importance of "vistas" so that from any point on campus there would be a good view both internally and externally.[57]

As a result of extensive research, discussions, and focus groups, the designers offered a master plan for the campus, which at first would accommodate up to 500 students, then expand to 1,500 students, and eventually serve 5,000 students.

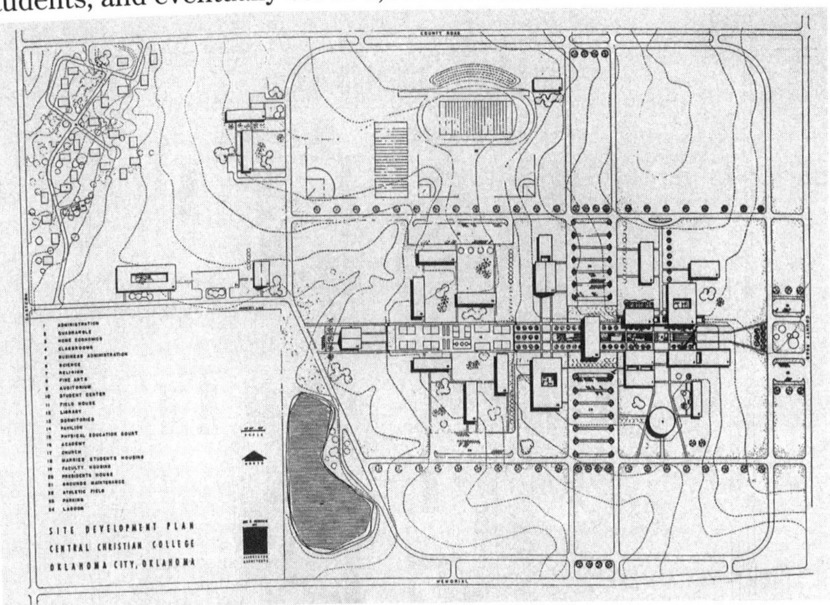

Master plan from Caudill, Rowlett, and Scott for the 200-acre Central Christian College campus, with the housing zone on the left (west), the activity zone in the center, and the academic zone on the right

They recommended eight buildings as stage one: for the academic zone, four buildings—two for classrooms, a library-auditorium, and another for administrative offices; for the housing zone, two dormitories, one for men and one for women; and for the activity zone, a cafeteria-student center and a gymnasium.[58]

For the Board meeting, Caudill, Rowlett, and Scott presented not only an extensive written report of their findings, but also drawings of the proposed campus layout and an architectural model of buildings for the 1500-student plan. Although waiting for this report had brought a six-month delay, Board members were impressed with the plan and approved it unanimously.

This master plan became the basis for articles in *College and University Business, American School and University,* and the *Junior College Newsletter* which praised the new campus, even calling it "America's most modern college campus."[59]

With these important decisions made, work on the new campus could now proceed. Fundraising continued while the architects developed plans for individual buildings. At the October 4 Board meeting, W. O. Beeman reported that L. E. Scott had offered $185,000 for the Bartlesville property, and the Board accepted the offer. Scott would create a housing development on parts of the property, and he would seek to sell to another college the portion where the CCC buildings had been. While the Board had hoped to get more for the property, they realized that the market for it was limited.[60]

The Groundbreaking

As part of the overall plan for raising funds, Benson and Baird decided there should be a formal groundbreaking. Such an event would create more interest, show progress, and get the name of the college before more people. The college *Bulletin* for May, 1957, announced the date of May 11, at 2 p.m., for the groundbreaking and listed those to be featured on the program: Dr. George Benson; Oklahoma Governor Raymond

Sign erected on the site of the new Central Christian College campus in Oklahoma City

Gary; E. K. Gaylord; M. A. Nash, chancellor for the Oklahoma Board of Regents for Higher Education; Delmar Owens, minister of the Eastside Church of Christ in Tulsa; Donald Kennedy, president of OG&E; J. G. Puterbaugh, president of McAlester Fuel Company; and Cecil Webb, district vice president of Oklahoma Natural Gas Company. Between 1 and 4 p.m., college personnel would be on hand to provide guided tours of the yet-to-be constructed campus.[61]

People began arriving by 10:00 a.m. to be part of this great occasion, but to no avail. Rain poured all day, and those who came had to be sent home without seeing anything but the future site of the campus.[62] College officials set a second date for May 25, and again publicized the event. This time, however, they offered an alternative in case of rain: the downtown Municipal Auditorium. Again, rain poured, and groundbreaking for the new campus took place eleven miles from the actual site. A box of dirt from the campus sat on the stage, and those designated turned a shovel full of dirt in the box. While the groundbreaking had not achieved all that was hoped, it did bring a considerable amount of attention to the college and its new site.

Souvenir ribbon for guests at the groundbreaking

Construction Begins

By the fall of 1957, plans for the four academic buildings were complete, and on October 24, the Board contracted with Lippert Brothers Construction Company to build, agreeing to costs plus $20,000. Since Lippert made a $10,000 contribution to the college, his fee would actually be only $10,000, certainly a modest sum. The four buildings were expected to cost $650,000 plus $50,000 for water, electric power, gas, and sewer. The college had about a third of this amount in cash and nearly half once remaining pledges were received. While the fundraisers would continue working, finishing the buildings would require borrowing. Dr. Benson, Dr. Baird, and W. O. Beeman worked out an arrangement with C. A. Vose, president of the First National Bank in Oklahoma City, for a line of credit up to $300,000, and the amount was later increased as more was required. This arrangement allowed construction to proceed as quickly as possible, and the four academic buildings were substantially ready when school began in the third week of September in 1958. Beeman reported

Students observe the progress on the Arts and Science buildings on the Oklahoma City campus

that Dr. Ralph Owens and G. A. Hale, both Oklahoma City Board members, handled many of the details until college offices moved to Oklahoma City during the summer of 1958.[63]

But what of the other four buildings Caudill, Rowlett, and Scott had proposed? The two dormitories and the student center-cafeteria would be "revenue producing" and could, therefore, be built through a U.S. government program that allowed low-cost, self-liquidating loans to colleges for such facilities. The gym, which didn't qualify for such a loan, would have to wait. In their meeting on February 28, 1958, the Board approved the legal documents to request the loan. The government, however, required the college to prove that it would have sufficient students to warrant the housing facilities and that it had the funds available to finish the rest of the campus. By May, the college had met the requirements, so the government granted a $600,000 loan on the three buildings, and construction could begin. Lippert Brothers would build these facilities also.[64]

As the campus buildings began taking shape, excitement began to rise. The July 1958 *Bulletin* reported,

> Comments from all those who have seen the new buildings at Eastern and Memorial Road in Oklahoma City have one thing in common: an exclamation of joy. There is no doubt but the new Central Christian College campus will be a real showplace as an educational plant. The classrooms will be well equipped and the library, auditorium and offices much improved over the Bartlesville facilities. The new dormitories and student center are uniquely designed and will be a real credit to the school.[65]

No doubt, the facilities would be much better than those at Bartlesville. While The Mansion had beauty and charm, it was aging and had not been designed as an educational facility, and the classroom building was clearly "second rate." In the new buildings, the classes and laboratories would have first-class collegiate facilities. Science, music, and home economics would especially have great improvements.

The new campus had a two-hundred seat auditorium with theater seats and a stage. The library would be in much larger facilities, more conducive to study. The student center-cafeteria would offer more and better space, and the dormitories would allow all boarding students to live on campus.

Aesthetically, the new campus would have something special. All the buildings were contemporary in design, made of red brick with a white band at the top, giving a sense of harmony to the campus. While the dormitories at first seemed a little far away from the other buildings, their placement was in keeping with the zoned concept that would serve so well for many years ahead.

Moving and Getting Ready to Open

The physical move came in stages. The college first rented space in the Longfellow School building in Oklahoma City so administrators could office there to oversee the final work on the campus, get ready to open school at a new location, and continue with fundraising and public relations. President Baird moved there on June 10; W. O. Beeman, the business manager along with his staff, and Dr. North, now dean of instruction, came in July.[66] These administrators were engaged in all that goes with getting ready for a new school year, and were preparing for an enrollment that for the first time would go above two hundred.

In addition, the administrators were involved in moving to the new campus all those things that were still useful. The special furnishings and works of art in The Mansion stayed there and were reclaimed by the Burlingames, from whom the college had purchased the Bartlesville campus.[67] Much, however, remained to move: office furnishings, files, two hundred tablet arm chairs, some dorm furnishings, a limited amount of science equipment and supplies, tools and equipment for maintenance including an Allis Chalmers tractor and a large sixty-inch mower, and, of course, library books—over four thousand of them.[68]

Hiring professional movers to do this work was beyond the college's financial capacity, so college personnel moved everything themselves. Sidney Roper had just moved to Bartlesville from Canada and had a one-and-a-half ton pickup. The college borrowed it and Clarence Buller, with his son Jerry, moved most of the items to Oklahoma City in that black pickup truck. Unfortunately, the truck was not in the best condition. It blew tires

Clarence Buller

and overheated, and when the voltage regulator quit, the generator overcharged and melted the battery. On top of all that, it was hard to drive, moving down the road about ten degrees off-center. In spite of all this, however, the Bullers and their helpers managed. L. D. Danner of Sayre sent two of his trucks to help with the large items, and by the end of August, everything had been moved.[69]

The small administrative staff also had another major project: ordering the furniture and equipment for the new buildings. The college had never before had the luxury of getting so many new and matching items for classrooms and laboratories. The science faculty especially was excited to be able to purchase top quality lab tables for chemistry and biology, along with equipment and supplies that would greatly improve the college's capacity to teach science. The new library furnishings allowed many more students to use the library at the same time, and the new shelving and seating were of excellent quality. Home economics would have new stoves and refrigerators and sewing machines. The cafeteria would get all new kitchen equipment and seating. Although the dormitories would not open until the second semester, the administrators were busy getting those furnished, as well.

Of course, as five buildings were being finished and two dormitories were under construction, there were many details to handle, including landscaping. Since the new campus had been primarily farm land, there were no trees in the main area of the buildings. Tommy Roberts, a nationally known landscape architect and a member of the Mayfair Church of Christ, provided assistance. He recommended honey locusts, rapid-growing trees, to be planted on each side of the mall, and ascending elms, which would eventually become taller trees, to be planted along the entrance drive and other locations on campus. To help with getting grass started, Oklahoma City friends of the college had several Saturday grass planting "parties."

Joseph Jones

In August, the new administration building was ready to be occupied, so Baird, Beeman, North, and Joseph Jones, dean of students, moved into the building to get ready for the start of classes, set for late in September. Among their problems was that the parking lots had not been paved and sidewalks were not yet completed. When it rained, as it did several days in late August and September, they had to remove their shoes in their cars, wade in mud to the building, and clean up in the restroom before coming, spick and span, to their offices.

The College Opens in Oklahoma City

Classes began on the new campus on September 22, 1958, with 207 students enrolled, a growth of 8.4 percent over the previous year. The two classroom buildings, the library-auditorium, and the administration building were finished. The cafeteria building was

*Completed Arts building on the mall of the new Central
Christian College campus in Oklahoma City*

complete, but some of the cooking equipment was not yet installed. Glenn Nance, the new food service manager, could heat food in ovens but did not yet have stoves for cooking. So for the first week, he fed the students on paper plates with precooked food and frozen TV dinners. After that, he was able to provide regular meals.[70]

Since the two dorms were not yet finished, special arrangements had to be made for housing. The college leased a large residence at 636 N. E. 14th Street in Oklahoma City to house thirty women, supervised by Gene Embry, a new science teacher, and his wife, Betty. The college rented a motel at 7100 North Kelly to house thirty more women, supervised by new Bible teacher Howard Horton and his wife, Mildred. Dean Jones found places for all the men and the remainder of the women in homes of Christians in Oklahoma City, Midwest City, Bethany, and Edmond.[71]

A New College

The move was complete, but the difference was much more than just a change of location from Bartlesville to Oklahoma City. While the eight years in Bartlesville had been good in many ways and had served students well, great new opportunities were now apparent. The young college had a completely new campus with buildings all designed for college use. Its campus zoning concept was new and forward-looking. The two-hundred acre site provided great opportunities for expansion. Its administration came largely intact from Bartlesville, and some key teachers had come, but most of its faculty members were new. In many ways, Central Christian College had not only a new location but a new life and new horizons. The move, with its fundraising efforts, had given the college a much higher profile and support among members of Churches of Christ in Oklahoma and surrounding states. As a result, these Christians developed a strong sense of ownership in the college.

Beeman wrote of this moment:

> It was almost as if the institution had gone to sleep in Bartlesville and awakened three months later in a new world. None of the old apathy, frustration, and vague feelings of being in a hostile environment were transferred to Oklahoma City. New life; new enthusiasm; new visions of success animated the new campus. . . . [T]he warmth and friendliness of the Oklahoma City welcome transformed the college almost overnight . . . into an aggressive, optimistic, success-oriented institution.[72]

While the Bartlesville years had made a great impact for good on many students, it had become clear that the success many had dreamed of for Central Christian College was not likely to happen there. Starting its ninth year in Oklahoma City, Central Christian had been reborn—a new city, a new campus, many new faculty members, a stronger tie with its church constituency, and a new hope for the future.

Chapter 3, Endnotes

1 Minutes, Board of Trustees, January 6, 1950, OC Archives.
2 L. R. Wilson, "I Resign as President," Unpublished Manuscript, January 4, 1967, 4, OC Archives.
3 Ibid., 7–8.
4 Minutes, Board of Trustees, February 12, 1955, OC Archives.
5 Minutes, Board of Trustees, March 31, 1955, OC Archives.
6 Minutes, Board of Trustees, June 18, 1955, OC Archives.
7 Ibid.
8 James O. Baird, Interview on audiotape with author on November 2, 1989, and subsequent days, Tape 3, OC Archives.
9 Ibid.
10 Minutes, Board of Trustees, July 4, 1955, OC Archives.
11 Baird, Interview, Tape 3.
12 Minutes, July 4.
13 Ibid.
14 Baird, Interview, Tape 3.
15 Ibid.; James O. Baird, "Oklahoma Christian University, 1950–1974," Personal Memoir, OC Archives.
16 George Benson, Ralph Owens, and Dalton Voss, "The Comparative Merits of a Smaller City versus a Larger City as the Location for a Christian College," Unpublished Manuscript, OC Archives, 2–3.
17 Ibid., 3–4.
18 Ibid., 4–6.
19 Ibid., 6.
20 Ibid., 6–7.
21 Ibid., 8.
22 Ibid., 7–8.
23 Ibid., 9.
24 Ibid., 9–13.
25 Ibid., 13.
26 Ibid., 15.
27 Baird, Interview, Tape 3.
28 Minutes, Board of Trustees, October 28, 1955, OC Archives.
29 W. O. Beeman, *Oklahoma Christian College: From Dream to Reality* (Delight, Arkansas: Gospel Light Publishing Company, 1970), 75.
30 Baird, Interview, Tape 3.
31 Minutes, Board of Trustees, November 19, 1955, OC Archives.
32 "College to Move to Oklahoma City," *Central Christian College Bulletin*, September 1955, OC Archives; "Largest Gathering of State Brethren Meets in Behalf of Central Christian College," *Central Christian College Bulletin*, June 1956, OC Archives.
33 "Oklahoma City Luncheon Will Launch Statewide Campaign," *Tower*, March 2, 1956, OC Archives.
34 Beeman, 76.
35 Baird, Interview, Tape 3.
36 "Wichita Falls is Scene of Christian Education Rally," *Tower*, March 16, 1956, OC Archives.
37 E. K. Gaylord, Unpublished Letter, June 21, 1956, in file with Board Minutes, OC Archives.
38 Baird, Oklahoma Christian, 12.
39 Minutes, Board of Trustees, March 27, 1956, OC Archives.
40 Minutes, Board of Trustees, June 26, 1956, OC Archives.
41 Ibid.
42 "College to Move."
43 Beeman, 78.
44 Baird, "Oklahoma Christian University," 13.
45 Ruth Winters, Personal Interview with author, September 27, 2006.

46   Beeman, 78.
47   "Upon These Broad Shoulders Rests the Future of America," Oklahoma City Campaign Brochure, 1956, 12, OC Archives.
48   Ibid., 10.
49   "$300,000 Drive Nears Goal as 5,000 Give," *Central Christian College Bulletin*, July 1959, OC Archives.
50   Minutes, Board of Trustees, September 25, 1956, OC Archives.
51   Ibid.
52   Baird, "Oklahoma Christian University," 13.
53   Baird, Interview, Tape 4.
54   Minutes, September 25.
55   Caudill, Rowlett, and Scott, "An Approach to College Design," presented to the Board of Trustees on March 15, 1957, OC Archives.
56   Ibid.
57   Baird, Interview, Tape 4.
58   Caudill, Rowlett, and Scott.
59   "Campus Receives National Recognition," *Central Christian College Bulletin*, January 1959, OC Archives.
60   Meeting, Board of Trustees, October 4, 1957, OC Archives.
61   "Preparations Underway for Groundbreaking," *Central Christian College Bulletin*, May 1957, OC Archives.
62   Beeman, 86.
63   Ibid., 86–89.
64   *Central Christian College Bulletin*, July 1958, OC Archives.; Minutes, Board of Trustees, February 28, 1958, OC Archives; Minutes, Board of Trustees, June 23, 1958, OC Archives.
65   *Central Christian College Bulletin*, July 1958, OC Archives.
66   Beeman, 97.
67   Ibid., 94.
68   Ibid., 98.
69   Ibid.
70   Ibid., 102.
71   Ibid., *Focus*, 1959, 5, OC Archives.
72   Beeman, 99–100.

Chapter 4
THE PRESIDENTS

Through its first fifty-eight years, five presidents have led Oklahoma Christian University. The first was a minister, the second primarily an educator, and the last three were lawyers. Two served for five years, two for twenty or more, and the current president has been in office for six years. What background did each bring to his office? What administrative team did each assemble? What administrative style did each use? How well did the institution fare under each? A review of the work of these five men reveals the importance of their contributions to the institution.

The First President: L. R. Wilson
1949–1954

Personal Background

Lawrence Ray Wilson was born in Cord, Arkansas, December 23, 1896.[1] Wilson lost his father when he was but eleven, and his mother when he was fourteen. His father was Presbyterian, his mother Methodist, and he attributed to them his "strong faith in God" and "a high regard for His word."[2] After the deaths of his parents, he stayed for a time with relatives, but not being comfortable with them, early in life he became responsible for himself. In 1915, he was baptized into Christ at a gospel meeting in Tupelo, Arkansas, where he had gone for a job. Soon thereafter, he began delivering sermons.[3]

Wilson enlisted in the army during World War I, serving in the Quartermaster Corps of the Third Cavalry. After the war he sought more education and moved to Henderson, Tennessee, where, at age twenty-three, he started as a freshman in Freed-Hardeman High

School. For five of his six years in Henderson, he lived in the home of N. B. Hardeman, who was his mentor. While there, he married Ruth Johnson, also a student, who became a lifelong partner in all his varying roles.

After graduating from the two-year college program at Freed-Hardeman, he moved to Jackson, Tennessee, to complete a B.A. degree in Greek from Union University. Wilson then moved to Jasper, Alabama, to earn an M.A. in history at Birmingham Southern College. During all of these years in school, he was also preaching.[4]

Wilson later served as minister for churches in Tennessee, Oklahoma, and Texas. He was well known for his successful religious radio program and had four public debates, two with Baptists and two with Pentecostals.[5] He wrote the front-page article for the *Firm Foundation* from 1939 to 1946 and, during those same years, authored the *Firm Foundation Adult Quarterly*, widely used in classes among Churches of Christ. As he became better known, he was called to conduct gospel meetings in many states.[6]

In November 1945, Wilson was preaching for the Denver Heights Church of Christ in San Antonio, Texas. At that time, members of Churches of Christ in Florida formed a board of trustees to start a Christian college in that state. This board contacted Wilson about becoming president of the new school. While Wilson had taught a few college classes at a Bible chair when preaching in Knoxville, Tennessee, he had little experience in college teaching or administration.

On the other hand, Wilson was a very hard worker, of strong character and determination, and well-known and highly respected throughout the brotherhood of Churches of Christ. The Board of the new Florida Christian College saw him as one who could help them start the new school, but Wilson was reluctant, not really wanting to leave the pulpit. Since, however, he believed strongly in Christian education and since the Florida brethren convinced him he was the best person for the job, he accepted.[7] With property already purchased for a campus in Temple Terrace, Wilson set to work to open the college in September of 1946, just ten months away.[8] He had to employ a staff, hire ten teachers, recruit students, and refit the buildings for college purposes. And he had to raise a large amount of money.

Wilson was successful at Florida Christian College, serving as its president through its third year of operation. By then, however, he believed the time was right for him to return to preaching, and for the college to find someone else to provide leadership. At that moment in 1949, however, another board was seeking a president to establish a Christian college, this time in Oklahoma. When they learned Wilson was leaving Florida Christian, they contacted him immediately.

Since he was well-known in Oklahoma through his local work in both Ada and Tulsa and was experienced in starting a Christian college, he seemed ideal. The Board sent G. R. Tinius to Florida to contact him about becoming president of Central Christian. Wilson did not jump at the opportunity. He loved to preach and wanted to return to that work. In the end, however, he said, "I finally decided that I did not want to face God in the judgment while trying to run away from a duty that I was asked to perform."[9] He began his work with Central Christian College in September 1949.

*Wilson with his wife,
Ruth, and two children,
Ray and Elizabeth*

Wilson's Administrative Team

Dean Baird

President Wilson put together an effective administrative team. He chose Dr. James O. Baird to be dean. With years of preaching and college teaching experience, along with a doctorate from George Peabody College, Baird was well prepared for college administration, and, having attended Freed-Hardeman College, he was a strong proponent of Christian education.

For vice president, Wilson chose Elvin Higgins, who had worked with him at Florida Christian. Higgins had begun his career in education in 1931 as principal of the county school system in Murray and Garvin counties of Oklahoma. He held a bachelor's degree from East Central State College at Ada, and later, obtained an M.S. degree from Oklahoma A&M. While in the Army Air Corps during World War II, Higgins was stationed in San Antonio and there attended the church where Wilson preached. When Wilson went to Florida Christian as president, he asked Higgins to go with him to teach math and physics.[10]

*E. R. Higgins in his
office at The Mansion*

As vice president, Higgins directed public relations, led student recruiting, helped students find jobs, and assisted with fundraising. In addition, he taught classes in math and physics. Higgins was an energetic man with a very outgoing personality who knew students personally and took a special interest in them.

For business manager, Wilson chose another from Florida Christian: Elwood Whitacre. Born in Harrisburg, Pennsylvania, in 1921, Whitacre had served in the Army Air Corps during World War II. Educated as an accountant, he was assigned to a financial office and, following his release from service, continued to work for the government in Tampa, Florida. Whitacre became the first business manager of Florida College, and when Wilson came to Central Christian, he brought Whitacre with him to serve Central Christian in the same capacity. In this role, he was responsible for financial records, expenditures, and campus property. His integrity, sound judgment, and hard work allowed him to serve well as part of Central Christian's first administrative team.[11]

Elwood Whitacre

Wilson's Administrative Leadership

L. R. Wilson was a man of dogged determination and hard work, having developed early in life the quality of never giving up. He was somewhat stern but also had a good sense of humor when the time was right. Wilson was a man of strong integrity, whose character was beyond reproach. His contact with students came primarily through chapel and his presence at student events. A man of strong spiritual commitment, he took special interest in campus religious life, particularly the Preacher's Club. By leaving academic matters and student life primarily to his dean, Wilson focused on major policies and fundraising.

Wilson worked diligently to connect Central Christian College with members of the Churches of Christ in Oklahoma and the surrounding area. He knew this relationship was essential for the college's survival, and in this mission, he was very successful. He preached often in churches and worked with members of the Board to make calls on church members. He traveled often throughout the area seeking support, often sleeping in his own car to save money.[12] One of Wilson's primary means of contact with the church constituency was a weekly radio program primarily on two Oklahoma radio stations: KGLC of Miami and KRMG of Tulsa. He began the fifteen-minute religious broadcast in 1949, when he came to be president, and continued it until his resignation in 1954. Wilson would sometimes mention the college on the broadcast, and even when he did not, he was connecting with church members around the state.[13]

While the college had been born through the efforts of church leaders in the state, Wilson knew this sense of ownership needed to be spread to as many church members as possible. To attain this goal, he started a religious lectureship in the spring of the college's very first year. In the second year, he began summer camps on the campus for children of church members. More than two hundred young people from sixth through twelfth grade attended the first year, and there were even more in subsequent years. CCC faculty conducted the camps.[14] To connect with alumni, Wilson created the annual homecoming in the college's second year.

Much of Wilson's work was with the Board of Trustees. He sometimes had to call them into special session to request their personal donations to meet a crisis. Twice he asked them to sign personally on bank notes.[15] And, although he occasionally had differences with them, their teamwork in these early days was critical to the progress of the institution.

Wilson's fierce determination to start a successful Christian college in Oklahoma was the driving force behind the college in its early days. Many others contributed, but he deserves much credit for giving the college a successful start.

Upon Wilson's leaving Central Christian, Dr. Baird wrote a tribute revealing much about his work as president:

> For five years, Brother Wilson has spent himself for the College. They have been grinding and demanding years. They have been years intermingled with despair and triumph. But through them there has been wrought the heroic achievement of a college being built on a solid foundation scripturally and spiritually, as well as financially and academically. No matter how long the College may exist and what personnel it may attract, no one will ever make the contribution to it and in quite the same way as the one who had enough faith and courage to come when the school was only a dream and to work until that dream was a living, growing reality.[16]

Summary of the Wilson Years

Of course, when President Wilson came to start Central Christian, the college had virtually nothing. The Board had purchased the Bartlesville campus, but most of the funding for it was yet to be raised and the net worth of the college when he came was small. According to a report when the college first applied for membership in the North Central Association of Colleges and Schools, contributions in the college's first year of operation totaled $60,352, with academic and auxiliary income bringing the total income to $86,011. Operating expenses were $78,709, leaving a balance of $7,302. His last year, 1954, showed contributions of $64,355, with academic and auxiliary income bringing the total to $133,231. With operating expenses at $111,589, the balance was $21,643.[17]

In addition, Wilson raised enough to finish paying off $95,000 on The Mansion and persuaded the Burlingames, from whom the college bought the property, to forgive the other $30,000. He built a $15,000 classroom building and paid off about half the debt on the women's dormitory. When Wilson left office on September 1, 1954, the college had assets of $338,645, liabilities of $135,675, and net worth of $202,970. The liabilities included $16,143 in bills, $33,400 in borrowed money to repay, and $62,405 in bonds to retire.[18]

The Wilson era saw the college begin with a student population of 97, which by 1953, had grown to 175. Under Wilson's leadership, many of the foundations of the institution were established: required daily chapel, a required Bible class each term, outstanding musical programs, student devotionals, student publications, intramural athletics, student clubs, a high moral expectation of students and faculty, and a level of academic excellence unusual for a new college.

One of two gates into the Bartlesville campus

It is difficult to imagine the magnitude of the task of starting a college. While such an undertaking must be a group effort involving many, the burden falls primarily on the shoulders of the person in the lead—the president. The record of the first years clearly demonstrates that Wilson deserves credit for bringing to reality the vision of the founders for a Christian college in Oklahoma. Those associated with Oklahoma Christian University in later years owe him a great debt for starting Central Christian College and setting it on the right course. While he had been reluctant at first to take the responsibility of becoming the founding president of a second Christian college, once he accepted the task, he pursued it vigorously and successfully.

Second President: Dr. James O. Baird
1954–1974

Personal Background

James and Avanelle Baird with their children Lynn, Harriet, Frances, Jim, and Morrow Beth, with the clock given for twenty-five years of service

James Oscar Baird was born in Lebanon, Tennessee, on January 16, 1920. After graduating from Castle Heights Military Academy, he and his cousin, Norvel Young, toured the world for six months, visiting most of Europe, Egypt, Palestine, Iraq, Iran, and even China and Japan. Baird attended Freed-Hardeman College during the two years of 1938–40, and then received a bachelor's and a master's degree from George Peabody College. He began preaching while attending Freed Hardeman, and during his time at George Peabody, he preached for the Grandview Avenue Church of Christ in Nashville. During 1943–1944, Baird attended the Princeton Seminary and preached for the church in Trenton, New Jersey.[19]

Baird began college teaching at David Lipscomb College in 1944 as a professor in sociology and in 1945–1946 took leave to complete his doctorate at George Peabody. In 1949 at David Lipscomb, he began teaching Bible. While at Lipscomb, Baird met and married Avanelle Elliott of Pine Bluff, Arkansas, who had a master's degree and was serving as secretary to Lipscomb president Batsell Barrett Baxter.[20]

While President Wilson was putting together his staff, Baird contacted him, and Wilson thought him ideal to serve as dean for the new college. So James and Avanelle with their two daughters, Harriet and Lynn, moved from Nashville to Bartlesville in the summer of 1950. Later, they had three more children: Frances, Jim, and Morrow Beth.

When Wilson resigned as president, he recommended Baird to the Board as the best qualified candidate for the presidency because he had served well as dean, was well acquainted with all elements of the operation, and knew those associated with the college, both on and off the campus.

During the Baird years, great changes took place. The college changed its location from Bartlesville to Oklahoma City, built an entirely new campus, changed the name from Central Christian College to Oklahoma Christian College, and grew from a junior college with 181 students to a senior college with 1,236. Momentous years indeed!

Baird's Administrative Team

Hugo McCord

When James Baird became president of Central Christian College in September 1954, he made a change in the role of vice president. Elvin Higgins was re-assigned as assistant to the president, and Baird named Hugo McCord as vice president. Since Roy Lanier, Sr. had left in June of 1953, Baird believed he needed a person in a prominent role who was well-known among Churches of Christ as solid in the faith and an able proclaimer of the Word. He found that person in Hugo McCord, who had been teaching part-time at the college and preaching at the 6th and Dewey Church of Christ in Bartlesville. As vice president, McCord represented the college to the brotherhood, worked with the Lectureship, produced the bimonthly bulletin, and taught Bible classes. He served as vice president through the 1961–1962 school year, although part of that time he was away in graduate study.

Higgins continued to play an important role, especially in fundraising, but left after a year. Elwood Whitacre continued as business manager for a year, but left at the same time as Higgins. To replace Whitacre, Baird brought W. O. Beeman to serve as business manager. At age sixty-one, Beeman had worked in key management roles in several businesses, most recently as business manager of WHBQ-TV in Memphis. Since 1937, he had been a member of the Board of Trustees of Harding College, and had served as an elder in three different congregations.[21]

W. O. Beeman

Stafford North

Baird did not replace Higgins for a year, but then chose Stafford North, returning from doctoral work at the University of Florida, to be assistant to the president. In this role, North worked with publications, public events, recruitment of students, and public relations, and also continued to teach. Joseph Jones, who taught history, and

Earle West, who taught chemistry, each served a year in the dean's role during the last two years in Bartlesville. In the spring of 1958, the year of the move to Oklahoma City, Baird asked North to become dean of instruction. Jones became dean of students and served in that role through 1962.

Following Jones, Bill Kirk was dean of students for three years, followed by Howard Horton for two years, Dr. Joe Schubert for two, and Dr. Lawrence Rhodes for five. The role of business manager also experienced changes. Beeman served until 1965 and then became director of student financial aid until 1973. Elwood Whitacre returned for the 1965–1966 year as business manager, followed by Junius Bailey for a year. Then in 1967, Gary Fields took that position, serving for twenty-nine years, through the remainder of the Baird administration and through all the Johnson years. Jack McElroy was director of data processing from 1967 to 1990, starting with an accounting machine using key punch cards[22] and then with an IBM 1130 added in 1969.[23]

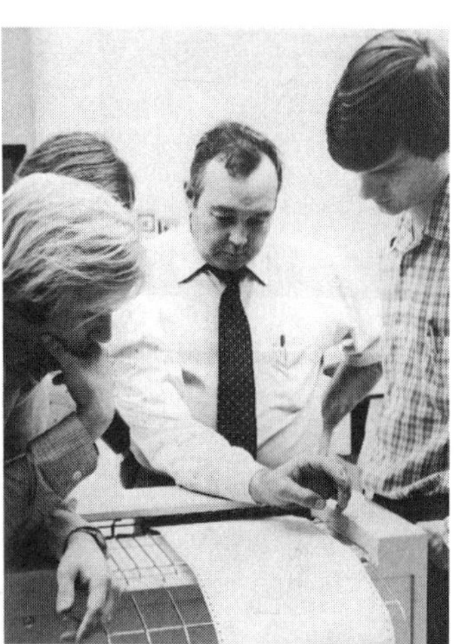

Jack McElroy and students

Dr. O. B. Stamper was North's associate dean from 1965 to 1967. Bob Smith served as assistant dean for curriculum and records in 1968–1969 and then as dean of admissions and registrar. Dr. Marshall Gunselman became associate dean for learning resources in 1969. North served as dean of instruction until 1971.

In 1969, Stafford and Jo Anne North began inviting all OCC employees and their families to their backyard for a 4th of July picnic, a tradition that continued until he stepped out of administration in May 1994. The number coming to the picnic was usually above 150 and provided an important time of association among all those who worked at the college. In 1970, North started the *Campus Community*, a weekly newsletter to bring campus news to all employees.

In 1971, Baird designated North as dean of the college, a role to coordinate all internal aspects of the institution. Baird had decided that having someone to lead internally would enable him to serve more effectively in external matters of public relations and fundraising. Dr. Bailey McBride, who had returned to teach English in 1966, became associate dean of the college in 1971, working mainly in academic matters.

During the Baird years, the internal administrators, a faculty member, and a student representative served as the Administrative

Council. This group made decisions about many internal matters and responded to student and faculty questions, suggestions, and complaints. Faculty and students also had representatives on all standing committees such as Academic Affairs, Religious Life, Student Life, Library, Student Guidance, Faculty Rank, Campus Life, Athletics, and Learning Center.

In addition to internal administration, North's role included responsibility for all campus construction. As new buildings were added, he served as the liaison between faculty and staff on campus who presented their needs and the architects who were designing the building. He also served as the owner's representative to work with the architects and contractors as buildings were under construction.

In 1958, to help with fundraising, Dr. Baird employed Bob Hunt as vice president for development, a role he filled for three years. Then in 1962, Baird employed Phil Watson for that position and he continued until July of 1967. In the latter part of his administration, Baird used Dr. Terry Johnson as staff counsel and then as vice president and, in the last year of his presidency, as executive vice president. Guy Ross became part of the team in 1970, when he became assistant to the president.

Baird, Benson, and Watson congratulate each other on a fundraising success

Dr. Benson served as chancellor for eleven years, starting in 1956, when Dr. Baird suggested the role and the Board appointed him to that office. With the move to Oklahoma City in sight and the many decisions and heavy fundraising that would require, Baird wanted the extra help Benson could bring. They worked closely together in fundraising and on projects to give the college greater visibility. In the role of chancellor, Benson had the top administrative leadership position, but concerned himself primarily with financial affairs. In a letter dated February 8, 1966, Benson wrote to the Board of Trustees:

> I am enjoying very much my work at Oklahoma Christian College and the very fine association with Doctor Baird, Doctor North, Phil Watson and others. . . . I am not allowing myself to become involved in the day to day administration of the College. . . . I have the impression, however, that Doctor Baird, Doctor North, the Dean of Men and others are doing a very excellent job in maintaining a good wholesome Christian atmosphere, in maintaining reasonable discipline, and in maintaining

a high level of academic efficiency.[24]

Benson traveled frequently in a small private plane, with his own pilot, and often was seen landing on a strip running north and south

Benson and his plane on the landing strip. The original science building is in the background.

along the east side of the campus, parallel with Benson Road. He presided at many of the college's public events, spoke in chapel, and sometimes even taught a one-day-a-week Bible class. His connection with the college during the important transitional years from 1956 to 1967 was vital. He helped in planning the move to Oklahoma City, assisted in devising the funding plan for the new campus, connected the college to many of its major donors such as the Gaylords and the Davissons, provided guidance in the administration of the college, and, by lending his well-known name, enabled many to see the college in a favorable light.

Baird's Administrative Leadership

Dr. Baird was president for twenty years and during that time showed himself as a very capable administrator. He pushed himself and others hard. Often out of town during the week contacting prospective donors and building relationships to help the college, he would meet with his administrative staff on Saturday mornings. During the later years of his administration, he came to rely more on the internal team to care for operational details.

As student numbers were growing rapidly during the Baird administration, so was the curriculum. In 1960, the junior college announced the addition of two more years of collegiate work, allowing the college to graduate its first four-year class in 1962. The new senior college offered bachelor's degrees in Bible, business, science, and elementary and secondary education. Within two more years, the college added degrees in English, speech, mathematics, and physical education.

As an administrator, Baird was creative and visionary. He was concerned, for example, about the appearance of the campus and determined that the master plan laid out originally by Caudill, Rowlett, and Scott would be maintained, even if that meant waiting longer to build a facility. In 1963, when starting the process of building a new auditorium, architects from Hudgins, Thompson, and Ball came with a first proposal. He thought the style did not sufficiently match that of the other buildings on the campus, and so asked the architects to redo the design. Similarly, as the details were being developed

Hardeman Auditorium in 1965

for the new auditorium, he at first opposed having a fly loft above the stage because he thought it would create an unsightly extension on top of the building. North, working with the music and drama faculty and architects on plans for the building, finally arranged a compromise in which there would be a fly loft to allow for raising and lowering curtains and sets, but its height would be kept to a minimum.

Baird's creativity is evident in his development of the Oklahoma Christian Investment Corporation, a business venture to provide revenue for the college. He obtained enough capital to begin investments that eventually would create a substantial revenue stream for the college. More details of this plan follow in the chapter on Key Decisions.

Another instance of Baird's leadership came in 1962, when he determined the college should embark on its first major effort at long-range planning. He had read Dr. Sidney Tickton's model for long-range college planning, and when Tickton was to speak in Dallas, Baird took his administrative team to the session. Wanting to glean the most from their being together at the conference, Baird asked them all to sit together during lunch to discuss what they were hearing and, following lunch, that they go back to the meeting in the same elevator so as not to lose a minute.

When they returned to the campus, Baird formed a steering committee, with North as chair, and with five subcommittees to generate a projection from 1963 to 1972. The ninety-five page report, called the Decade of Progress Study, analyzed input from faculty, administration, students, Board, alumni, and community representatives. The process also included input from church members around the state, as well as a written survey mailed to alumni and supporters. Continuing the concept of long-range planning, Baird called for another projection for 1970–1979 which was called Design for Progress. Those directing this study conducted thirteen area meetings attended by 329 persons.[25] Their input, along with information from many on campus, provided a good base for the study. This 115-page report offered a comprehensive blueprint with directions for the school's academic program, spiritual life, personnel, facilities, and finances.[26]

Student listening to audiotapes in the Learning Center

Baird's visionary leadership was also evident in the development of the Learning Center. In 1964, when the original library on the Oklahoma City campus was out of space, Baird wanted to do more than simply build another library building. He insisted that North and Oma Carter, librarian, study college libraries around the country. When they found that some libraries were beginning to use study carrels equipped with dial-access systems to audiotapes, he asked North and others to investigate that concept more thoroughly. The result was the development of a learning center unique in higher education that brought great attention to the college and effectively served the college's academic program. This decision, too, is chronicled in the chapter on Key Decisions.

Baird was known for frugality. He kept a tight rein on expenditures, and in this, Beeman was his close ally. All expenditures had to be directly approved by the business manager. Since money was hard to raise, Baird insisted that it be used carefully. When he and North, for example, traveled to Chicago to attend the annual meeting of the North Central Association in which the college was seeking membership, they would go by overnight train on a clergy discount, stay together in one room at the YMCA, and walk several blocks through the "red light district" to the upscale Palmer House where the meetings were conducted. Faculty and staff were added very carefully and only when their salaries were justified by growth in tuition and revenue. Baird sought ways to enable the student-faculty ratio to increase so the academic program could be more cost efficient, and during his tenure, the ratio rose above thirty to one.

A significant event during the Baird years happened on Wednesday, September 11, 1963, the day prior to the start of fall classes. Phil Watson, vice president for development, was also the preacher at Harrah, about twenty-five miles east of the campus. He was away that Wednesday night, but his wife, Jackie, and their infant daughter, Angie, along with four OCC students, drove to Harrah for services. On the return trip to the campus, they came to a railroad crossing unaware a train was rapidly approaching. The resulting crash killed them all. The students were senior Jerry Wheeler, roommate of Terry Johnson, junior Janice Novak, sophomore Karen Hetrick, and freshman Sharon Stewart. The tragic event, of course, brought great sadness to the campus as the school year opened, and the entire campus mourned this great loss. The 1964 *Aerie* described opening day:

Classes began without the normal gaiety and vivacity characteristic of the opening day of school. Sadness lay in the air; the flag floated at half-mast; and tears streaked many cheeks. In the morning hours, chapel met and everyone turned to God for comfort and understanding, for only He could know the purpose of death in such young lives.[27]

A memorial to these six, built at the east end of the mall, remains today.

A major advancement during the Baird years was achieving accreditation from the North Central Association. The college had sought such recognition for many years and first applied for admission to the North Central Association as a junior college. Before the Association took action on the application, however, the Board decided to expand to a senior college, graduating the first class in 1962. The college withdrew the application and began the process of applying as a senior college. The North Central Association granted accreditation in 1966.

During his presidency, Dr. Baird was a strong disciplinarian. Students were expected to obey the rules, and the stated punishment for failure to do so was strictly applied. Students were dismissed on the first infraction for drinking intoxicants, for staying out of the dorm overnight in suspicious circumstances, or for sexual misconduct. The college had a strict dress code which students were expected to follow.

The most notable application of Baird discipline occurred in 1969. Students at other colleges and universities had been occupying campus buildings by sitting on the floor until some grievance had been addressed to their satisfaction. Dr. Baird wanted to prevent any sit-ins on the OCC campus and in 1967 initiated, with Board approval, a policy of campus communication that outlined various ways students could seek to solve a problem or be heard on an issue. Along with acceptable ways listed, however, the policy stated that a sit-in was not acceptable behavior and any students involved in such action would be dismissed.

In March 1969, an issue arose about conduct at a party after a basketball game. The primary charge against students participating was a violation of the regulation forbidding them to be out of their residence hall overnight. There were also indications of drinking alcoholic beverages. This behavior, if true, subjected students to dismissal. After discipline committee deliberations, fourteen students were dismissed including some who were African American. Some students considered the action racially biased, and one, Ron Wright, though not involved in the discipline, took a lead in supporting their cause. As Dean Mock saw trouble brewing, he reminded Wright of the policy forbidding sit-ins and encouraged him not to use this approach. On March 6, the next day, twenty students who felt their concerns had not been satisfied, went to the Benson Administration Building with their list of grievances. They presented a document which began, "We will continue to occupy this building until . . . ." President Baird was summoned from a meeting and, when he read the document and sized up the situation, considered their action a violation of the stated policy. He then went to each student individually, saying, "I am President James O. Baird. What is your name?" Someone with Baird wrote down each name. Then he told that student, "You have five minutes to leave the building or you will be dismissed from school and be arrested for trespassing." Two of the students left; eighteen stayed. Seven of those who stayed were among those previously dismissed, and sixteen of those who stayed were African Americans. Baird called the police and the eighteen protesters were taken to jail. Students and faculty helped the students make bail, so they did not stay there long. Two weeks later the trial came, and the eighteen pled guilty. They did not have to pay a fine or do any more time, but they were not allowed back in school that term. In an interesting turn, Ron Wright, who has had a distinguished career in education, later served for a year on the OC Board of Trustees.[28] In Fall 2002, he spoke at the OC chapel service and in introducing him, Dr. Bailey McBride expressed his regrets about the incident over thirty years earlier.

The sit-in received wide publicity. Those who opposed student sit-ins, including "numerous daily newspapers and religious periodicals,"[29] praised Baird for his action, while those who favored allowing students this means of expression opposed Baird for his handling of the situation. For those on both sides of the dispute, the incident illustrated Baird's view of enforcing the rules as they were written.

Another characteristic of the Baird presidency was attention to citizenship education. Dr. Benson had developed such a program at Harding, and they both believed something similar would be good at Oklahoma Christian. The first event the college sponsored in Oklahoma City after announcing its forthcoming move to the city was a three-day "Freedom Forum," held in early 1958 at the downtown Skirvin Hotel. Senator John McClellan from Arkansas, along with Dr. Benson and Dr. Clifton L Ganus, Jr., from Harding were among the speakers.[30]

In 1959, Benson and Baird established at OCC the American Citizenship Training Center to provide educational materials for high school teachers, offer summer seminars for both teachers and students, publish a monthly newsletter for the business community, and bring speakers for public events. The Center achieved two

Bob Rowland

results: It filled what Benson and Baird considered to be a gap in the economic and political education of youth, and at the same time, it presented Oklahoma Christian in a role many prospective donors saw as positive. Gifts for the Center were solicited separately from college funding, and Beeman reported that from 1959 through 1966, citizenship gifts produced $110,800 above the program's expenses, thus yielding this sum for the general budget of the college.[31] Its larger benefit, of course, was in laying a foundation to seek donations directly for the institution from those appreciating the college for providing such a program. Marion Hickingbottom directed the American Citizenship Center in the early sixties. After others who served shorter terms, Bob Rowland came to direct the Center in 1972. Frank Davis later became his assistant. Pen Woods came in 1969 to develop the Living Legends Oral History Project for Oklahoma. Partnering with the Oklahoma Historical Society, Woods was responsible for some two thousand oral interviews with people who have lived through important events in Oklahoma history. He also worked with OCC's citizenship education program and continues to do so today.

One of the strongest characteristics of the Baird style was his determination to maintain and strengthen the strong connection between the college and its church constituency. Wilson had laid the foundation, but Baird took this relationship to a higher level. He preached at congregations often, and once each year, he and Avanelle invited area preachers and wives to their home for dinner.

From 1963, Dr. Raymond Kelcy was chair of the Bible Department, and he, along with Dr. Hugo McCord and Dr. Bill Jones, formed the base of the Bible faculty during the Baird years. These three had all done local preaching for many years and

McCord and Kelcy having fun on Western Day

Bill Jones

related well with preachers in the area. They were respected for their doctrinal soundness and appreciated for their handling of questions at the annual Open Forum during the Lectureship. Their Bible teaching not only produced many ministers and other workers in the church, but also promoted much goodwill for the college during the Baird years.

Early in his presidency, Baird started a fundraising plan that sought ten thousand Christians to give a dollar a month to Central Christian. The number making such a contribution eventually rose to more than five thousand, meaning that every month a host of members of Churches of Christ were thinking about the institution. Another of Baird's effective fundraising techniques was to divide Oklahoma and surrounding areas into districts, then into counties, and then into congregations within the county. College officials used this system to try to contact every church member in the area to request a donation. This approach not only raised funds, but also heightened the sense of ownership church members felt for the college.

Another means of developing strong relationships with the church constituency came through campus public events. Baird continued the Lectureship Wilson had begun, giving it high visibility. There were also annual Labor Day rallies that brought large numbers of supporters to the campus. The most notable of these took place in 1961, when Pat Boone, then the best-known public person among Churches of Christ, came to campus. The weather that day was typical of

Pat Boone leading a student devotional while on the campus for the Labor Day Rally

Oklahoma. It rained in the morning, causing President Baird to move the scheduled evening barbeque to the National Guard Armory in Edmond, where standby arrangements had been made. By 1 p.m., however, the sky cleared, and the event was moved back to campus. People began arriving about 3 p.m., and the crowd was huge—seven thousand as estimated by the Oklahoma Highway Patrol.[32] The paved parking was soon filled, as were the sides of streets, so cars began pulling onto the grassy surface to the west of the main entrance.

The event proceeded as planned, with Dr. Benson presiding. As the program was about to begin, he needed $10,000 more to reach the goal for the "Progress Appeal" campaign for which this rally was the climax. So, never missing a chance, Dr. Benson turned to his famous guest before starting the program and asked Pat Boone to make up the difference, which he did. Benson and Baird spoke about the future of the college. Boone led singing and addressed the crowd. "No one seemed to mind that the food ran out, the cars were stuck in the mud, and nearly everybody had to stand."[33]

When the program was over, Clarence Buller, using two tractors, pulled many cars to solid ground so they could leave. The following morning, the campus looked terrible with trash and ruts everywhere, but it had been a great day for publicizing the college and for connecting with its constituency.

Baird congratulates Beeman on his book.

In 1970, near the end of the Baird years, W. O. Beeman, who had served as business manager and then was director of student financial aid, published *Oklahoma Christian College: From Dream to Reality,* a history of the college's first twenty years. Since Beeman had been involved for most of those twenty years, his data collection and own recollections were invaluable. Beeman died in 1973.

Summary of the Baird Years

Since the 1975 *Report to the North Central Association* was filed the year after Dr. Baird left the presidency and was based on the preceding ten years, it provides a good source for analyzing conditions at the close of his presidency. This report discloses that the curriculum was tightly controlled with departments offering no more than 50 percent more hours than were required for a degree. This plan allowed some choice in courses, but held the offerings, and therefore costs, to a minimum. The report also mentions arrangements for students to enroll at Central State University for courses they wanted or needed, but which were not available at Oklahoma Christian. Registration was simple for this dual enrollment, and shuttle-bus service was available between the two campuses.[34]

This same North Central report indicates that the student-faculty ratio was close to one to thirty during the previous five years,[35] that the average class size was twenty-six,[36] and that the average number of advisees was thirty per faculty member.[37] The total number of faculty that year was thirty-seven full-time and twenty-seven part-time, [38] more than triple the number in 1955, Baird's first year.[39] In 1955, there were no full-time faculty with earned doctorates,[40] but by 1975, that percentage among full-time professors had increased to 62 percent.[41] During the twenty years Dr. Baird was president, library holdings grew from 3,745[42] to 80,000.[43]

While Baird was president, the Oklahoma Christian campus expanded rapidly. From the five buildings on the Bartlesville campus in 1954, the Oklahoma City campus in 1974 had nineteen totally new buildings, including an administration building, eight dormitories, one apartment building for married students, a student center-cafeteria, a gymnasium, and eight academic buildings: the original three plus Hardeman Auditorium, Mabee Learning

Mabee Learning Center

Center, Payne Physical Education Building, Davisson American Heritage Building, and Herold Science Hall.

When Dr. Baird became president, the net worth of the institution was $202,970. When he left, twenty years later, the net worth had grown to $10,287,716. There had been virtually no endowment when he came, but he had begun an endowment valued at $1,294,397. Annual operating expense of the college had risen from $111,589 to $3,078,138, and in Baird's last year, net operating income exceeded the expenses by $1,351,015.

Clearly, the Baird years showed remarkable progress. The move to Oklahoma City proved to be highly successful and there can be little doubt that the college would never have developed so well had it stayed in Bartlesville. The Baird presidency was indeed the time of "the great leap forward."

In 1973, Baird had complicated heart surgery and came very close to death. Although he recovered satisfactorily, he believed the time had come for him to pass the stressful work of the presidency to someone else. He had groomed Terry Johnson for that responsibility, and the Board of Trustees, after investigating the options, decided that Johnson was the best choice for the new president. Baird continued to serve the college as chancellor and taught some Bible classes over the next fifteen years. From 1981 to 1993, he wrote a monthly column for the *Christian Chronicle*.[44] Dr. Baird died in 1998.

The Third President: J. Terry Johnson
1974 to 1995

James Terence Johnson was born in Springfield, Missouri, on October 25, 1942. He attended Parkview High School and then Southern Methodist University. While Johnson was in his first year at SMU,

Dr. J. Terry Johnson

President James Baird came to speak at Skillman Avenue Church of Christ, and Johnson attended. They talked, and when Baird, always on the lookout for students, returned to campus, he wrote Johnson with the offer of a fifty dollar scholarship to come to Oklahoma Christian the following year. Johnson accepted, never even having seen the campus.

While a student, Johnson was a starter at second base on the baseball team and majored in English as preparation for law school. He worked in admissions, contacting prospective students, and worked with the youth at the Village Church of Christ. He also met Martha (Marty) Mitchell during his OCC years, and they were married on May 2, 1964, three weeks before his graduation, with Dr. Darvin Keck of the OCC faculty performing the ceremony. Their first child, Jennifer, was born in 1968, and their second, Jill, in 1970. After graduating from OCC, Johnson returned to Southern Methodist for law school and worked at the Walnut Hill Church of Christ as associate minister.

After Johnson finished law school in 1967, he continued working for Walnut Hill. President Baird offered him the position of staff legal counsel and assistant professor of business, which he accepted, beginning at OCC in August 1968. In 1970, he took on the additional role of president of the Oklahoma Christian College Investment Corporation. Two years later Baird named Johnson vice president, and the next year, executive vice president. Baird had seen in him qualities he believed would make a good president of the college and so enabled him to have the experiences that would prepare him for that role.

When President Baird retired from the presidency in 1974, the Board of Trustees named thirty-one-year-old Johnson as president, and in so doing made him the youngest college president in the United States. Johnson was the first alumnus of Oklahoma Christian to become president. Though young, he was well prepared.

Johnson's Administrative Team

When Terry Johnson became president, he elevated Guy Ross, a long-time friend who had been assistant to the president, to the role of vice president. The Johnson-Ross team had significant help from Alan Phillips, Bruce Kerr, James DuBoise, Andy Benton, David Owens, Ray Warlick, and Kevin Jacobs. Johnson and Ross often traveled together to make calls. One memorable incident in New York City came when they were standing on the street corner

Guy Ross

trying to decide how to get to their next call. A man coming alongside heard them talking and gave directions. When they arrived at the office they sought, that same man was sitting behind the desk.

At the beginning of his presidency, Johnson named Stafford North as executive vice president, a position he filled until a year before Johnson left office. In this role, he coordinated all internal functions as he had during the closing years of the Baird administration. Gary Fields continued as business manager. In 1975, Johnson appointed Bailey McBride as academic dean. Richard Mock served as dean of campus

McBride, North, and Fields

life and Bob Smith as dean of admissions and registrar. The internal team of North, McBride, Mock, Smith, and Fields worked together for many years, providing stability in the internal administration of the college. They met weekly for coffee as a time to share insights, solve problems, and provide internal communication. Along with a student and faculty representative, they also constituted the Administrative Council, continued from the Baird years. The Council met monthly to coordinate registration procedures, the school calendar, many budgetary matters,

Richard Mock

the orientation of new students, matters pertaining to the physical plant, decisions on the standards for student conduct, and much more. This team worked together through most of the Johnson years, handling the majority of campus operational matters. On important policy matters and development of the budget, of course,

Smith and Eggleston

the president was directly involved. Duane Eggleston served as director of admissions from 1987 to 1995 and in this role was also part of this internal team.

After North's retirement from administration to return to teaching, President Johnson named Dr. Bailey McBride as provost, Joe Watson as vice president for administration, Tom Clark as vice president for admissions and marketing, and Guy Ross as senior vice president.

Johnson's Administrative Leadership

Terry Johnson brought great energy to the role of president. Dr. Baird moved to the role of chancellor, and they worked together on many fundraising calls, particularly to see those with whom Baird already had a strong relationship. The transition was remarkable for its smoothness and cooperation between the two.

Being younger, Johnson connected more with students and sought more openness in his administration. He and his wife Marty often hosted officers of the Student Senate for dinner at their home. In fact, the Johnsons actually lived in a presidential home on the campus and used it frequently for entertaining campus guests,

Terry Johnson as Elvis

Lectureship speakers, student groups, and prospective donors. One day, for example, Mrs. Johnson prepared lunch for Sam and Helen Walton, Ed and Thelma Gaylord, Carrie Lou Little, Eleanor Foster, and a few other major donors.[45]

One of Johnson's ways to connect with students was performing annually in *First Week Follies*. In 1979, Bob Lashley, then alumni director, began producing a program for the opening week of classes in which faculty and staff entertained the students. An excellent singer, Lashley performed with a backup instrumental group, providing some of the songs himself. He also involved members of the faculty and staff, sometimes in comedy skits and sometimes with musical numbers. Johnson, who sang well, performed each year, imitating well-known singers such as Elvis Presley, Buddy Holly, Garth Brooks, Al Jolson, Pat Boone, and Kenny Rogers. As Willie Nelson, he and Stafford North, as Julio Iglesias, sang "To All the Girls I've Loved Before."

The 1995 *Report to the North Central Association*, prepared after Johnson had resigned but before his replacement was named, made the following comment on Johnson's administrative style:

> The team management approach established by Dr. Johnson is a notably different approach from the administrative approach of the university in previous years. It is, however, an approach which appears to be highly effective and to provide a strong administrative leadership which will be critical during the period of transition into a new presidency.[46]

Like Baird, Johnson was firm in his enforcement of campus rules. During his years, for example, college policies did not permit beards or long hair for men because, during the years of the Vietnam War, these were considered signs of rebellion. Drinking continued to be an offense meriting dismissal, but some flexibility was introduced allowing some first-time violators to participate in a drug and alcohol education program. During his term, Johnson strengthened the health care program for students and, in 1981, added Dr. Arlis Wood as a full-time counseling psychologist.

Enterprise Square, USA

Johnson continued the emphasis on citizenship education which Benson and Baird had begun. The American Citizenship Center hosted many student seminars and other programs, and Bob Rowland served as director of this program until 1991. The high point in citizenship education at Oklahoma Christian came during the Johnson years with the opening of Enterprise Square, USA, in 1982. This 60,000 square foot, $10 million major exhibition hall used high tech displays to teach the American system of government and free enterprise economics. At its peak, it brought 60,000 visitors a year to the campus. The story of Enterprise Square is covered fully in the chapter on Key Decisions.

When the Garvey Center opened in 1978, with its additional facilities for music, art, and communications, Dr. Johnson sought a way to highlight these areas. In connection with the faculty in those departments, he began Gala Week. During a week in the fall term, the college brought to campus nationally known figures from the performing arts, the media, and the visual arts. These met with students, exhibited their work, and gave public performances or lectures. As concert performers, the college brought Robert Merrill and Roberta Peters of the Metropolitan Opera Company; Eugene Fodor, acclaimed violinist; actor James Whitmore; and pianist Peter Nero. From the media came Howard K. Smith, Edwin Newman, Douglas Edwards, Douglas Kiker, and Bill Monroe, all on the major television networks. To represent the visual arts, the college brought Charles Banks Wilson, Robert Peak, Ray Harm, James Boren, and Leonard McMurry.[47] The five-year Gala Week run was an exciting time for students and off-campus guests alike. Students had important learning experiences and the events placed the college in a favorable light.

The most widely publicized public event of the Johnson years was the visit of President George H. W. Bush to the Oklahoma Christian campus. In March of 1992, Bush was campaigning for reelection and wanted a stop in Oklahoma City. The Republican Party decided the Thelma Gaylord Forum, just north of the Bible Building, would be the best place for the rally. It had a large, protected standing area bounded by a brick wall, which would help with security. The sponsors of the event built a platform from which Bush could be seen, even by those standing outside the Forum itself. They built another platform in the rear to accommodate the video cameras of news organizations and the nearly one hundred journalists covering the event. The crowd, estimated at eight thousand, overflowed the Forum and spilled on to the surrounding areas.[48]

Security was tight. The Bible building was closed for the morning, and entrance to the Forum required passing through metal detectors. The Secret Service checked every angle and was much in evidence. The crowd began gathering at 6:30 a.m. on the morning of Friday, March 6, which turned out to be a beautiful day, with the Bradford pears around the Forum showing their white blooms. OC athletic teams lined the stairways on the north side of the Bible building. The OC Band and Chorale and others entertained the crowd until Bush arrived about 10 a.m.

President Bush (41) speaking at Oklahoma Christian in 1992

with many well-known Republican office holders. Bush spoke on his familiar theme of "traditional family values," and the next day, "a front-page photograph of President Bush on Oklahoma Christian's campus appeared in newspapers from Oklahoma City to New York to Tokyo."[49]

Having a sitting president of the United States appear on the campus was quite an exciting event for faculty, students, and friends of the university, regardless of their political views, and the public relations value was huge. Bush returned in November of 1994 to speak in the OC gymnasium at a Republican political rally.

President Johnson had a strong interest in broadening the scope of educational opportunities available to students at Oklahoma Christian. One of the major additions during his administration came in 1985 with the offering of degrees in electrical and mechanical engineering. As detailed in the chapter on curriculum, the addition of these degrees required a $3 million dollar building, another $1 million for equipment, a $3 million endowment, and attracting qualified faculty who would teach for far less than they could make as professional engineers.

In 1986, the college began a plan to encourage students to spend the fall term abroad, traveling in Europe with their stay centered in Vienna. The program became very successful, with a faculty sponsor and about thirty students going abroad each fall.

Another important academic advancement during the Johnson years came in 1988 when the college added its first graduate program. Under the leadership of Dr. Howard Norton, the Division of Bible added a master of arts degree requiring thirty-six graduate hours in a combination of practical and scholarly courses. Dr. Lynn McMillon served as the first chair of the graduate program from its beginning to 2001. For six of those years, the degree was also available in connection with the Institute of Practical Ministry, associated with the Highland Oaks congregation in Dallas. The program has attracted many area ministers in Churches of Christ and so has provided both a service to them and a good connection with congregations in Oklahoma.

Being an alumnus, Johnson was particularly interested in strengthening ties with alumni. In 1975, the alumni office began an annual callout to ask former OCC students for financial support. That year, the total pledged was $104,660 and met a matching gift of $75,000.[50] In 1995, Johnson's last year, this callout brought in $362,589 in pledges.[51]

One of the major events of the Johnson administration was the change from "college" to "university." Many institutions similar to Oklahoma Christian had already made the change, including other colleges among Churches of Christ. In the fall of 1990, Oklahoma Christian College became Oklahoma Christian University of Science and Arts. The eight academic divisions were reorganized into five colleges: Bible, Business, Education, Liberal Arts, and Science and Engineering. Each of the colleges had its own dean and some had departmental chairs working with the dean. Additional details on this change are reported in the chapter on Key Decisions.

The first half of the Johnson years saw the continuation of the Kelcy, McCord, Jones foundation for the Bible program. As

Howard Norton

the number of students grew, however, more Bible teachers were needed. In the fall of 1972, Dr. Lynn McMillon, an OCC alumnus, obtained a Ph.D. degree from Baylor University. For a time he divided his teaching between Bible and history, but in 1976 began teaching full-time in Bible. Howard Norton joined the Bible faculty in 1977, Johnny Pennisi came in 1981, Dr. Loren Gieger in 1984, Dr. Don Vinzant in 1989, and Dr. Jim Baird in 1992. McCord, however, retired after the 1979–80 year, and Kelcy died on August 26, 1986. Bill Jones continued to teach through the Johnson years. After Kelcy's death, Johnson appointed Dr. Howard Norton as chair of the Bible Division, and he continued in that role through the remainder of the Johnson term. Norton was a former missionary to Brazil and supported a strong missions emphasis.

Johnson also sought, as had President Baird, to keep strong ties and communication with the college's church constituency. Johnson preached at churches and, in 1975, started taking a group of faculty members to fill pulpits in major metropolitan areas on specified Sundays.[52] The group went to such cities as Tulsa, Wichita, Kansas City, Dallas/Ft. Worth, San Antonio, Denver, Houston, and Oklahoma City. Often an evening event at a high school or other public venue would finish the day with an activity to promote the college among Christian high school students and parents. Bob Rowley led in making arrangements for these events. Johnson also used the Lectureship and other public events for church members as ways to connect the college with its church constituency.[53]

Another Johnson initiative to serve the church constituency came in 1981 when Oklahoma Christian College began publishing the *Christian Chronicle.* Started in the 1943 by Olan Hicks, the *Chronicle* had long been the international newspaper among Churches of Christ, sharing news about churches from all over the world. While at times it had ceased publication, since 1976 John and Dottie Beckloff, long-time missionaries, had worked to revive it. An alumnus of Central Christian in Bartlesville, John approached the college about assuming publication of the paper.

In the *Chronicle,* Johnson and his staff saw an opportunity to provide a much-needed information service to members of Churches of Christ and a way to gain goodwill by making the service available. Raymond Kelcy encouraged the plan, saying that taking ownership of the *Chronicle* would be one of the most significant decisions the college would ever make.[54]

At a March 31 luncheon, Johnson announced, "We are dedicated to serving the brotherhood in many effective and practical ways.

Publishing a Christian newspaper is an appropriate way in which the College can broaden its outreach program."[55] Howard Norton became the editor and James Baird the publisher. The OCC Board and administration gave the new team a "mandate that it not be a house publication for OCC and that it reflect the highest quality of journalism."[56] Oklahoma Christian published its first issue of the *Chronicle*, a sixteen-page tabloid, in September, 1981, and in that first issue stated this goal: "to tell good news about Churches of Christ around the world and to support the evangelization of the entire world."[57]

From 1984 to 1989, two OCC alumni served in major roles, Joy McMillon as managing editor and Scott LaMascus as staff writer. In those early years, the *Chronicle* emphasized professional journalistic standards in news gathering and reporting. By 1986, the paper had increased its size to twenty-eight pages and had 60,000 subscribers.

After Howard Norton's years as editor, 1981 to 1996, Bailey McBride served as editor until 2006, and his column, which he has written for twenty-six years, continues to be one of the *Chronicle's* most popular features. Glover Shipp became managing editor in 1989, serving in that role until 1999 and as senior editor until 2001. In 1996, Lynn McMillon became general manager. Scott LaMascus replaced Shipp as managing editor in 1999, filling that role until 2006. In that year, McMillon became the editor, Bobby Ross, another OCC alumnus, came from the Associated Press to be managing editor, and Tamie Ross, an OC mass communications major, joined the staff to develop the *Chronicle* online.

In its early OCC years, the *Chronicle's* operating costs were above its income from advertising, subscriptions, and donations. In 1996, when President Jacobs named Lynn McMillon the new general manager, he charged him with a mandate to operate the *Chronicle* within its income. Since 1997, the newspaper has more than covered its expenses both by increased subscriptions and by an aggressive effort to raise donations through mailing campaigns. By 2007, the *Chronicle* was not only covering its costs, but had refunded to the university almost all of the nearly $900,000 deficit accumulated earlier.[58] Since 2003, the OC Board of Trustees has delegated oversight of the *Chronicle* to a separate Board chaired by Dale Brown of Midland, Texas.

As a newspaper, the *Chronicle* has reported on a wide range of events taking place within the brotherhood of Churches of Christ. Over the years, some have criticized the *Chronicle's* coverage and/or editorial comments, but the response has been largely favorable. A professional market survey in 1999, for example, showed that 92 percent of the readers were either satisfied or very satisfied. By the 2006 survey, the number of those in these categories had risen to 94 percent.[59] In 2007, the *Chronicle* placed third in the Associated

Church Press competition for national or international newspapers.

The decision to publish the *Chronicle* proved to be a good one; certainly it has been a valuable and appreciated service. By 2007, the monthly publication had grown to forty pages with a circulation of 105,000, the number of actual readers being estimated at nearly two and a half times that number. Even its advertising, which occupies about 40 percent of its space, helps inform the brotherhood about books, materials, services, and institutions within Churches of Christ. In deciding to publish this newspaper, Johnson again demonstrated his strong desire to find opportunities to serve and build ties with Churches of Christ.

In 1992, when the Board of Columbia Christian College in Portland, Oregon, saw the college was losing accreditation because of financial problems and would, therefore, not be able to continue operation, they sought a way to develop some alternative plan for keeping Christian education alive on their campus. They contacted sister institutions among Churches of Christ asking for assistance, but Oklahoma Christian was the only one that showed significant interest in coming to their aid. Under Dr. Johnson's leadership in September 1994, the university opened a four-year institution called Cascade College on the former campus of Columbia Christian. Johnson's primary motivation for this effort was to keep a college led by members of Churches of Christ operating in the Northwest. He hoped, too, that students from that area would know Oklahoma Christian better so that in those cases where Cascade did not fit their needs, they might decide to attend OC. While the Columbia Board took responsibility for existing debt and agreed to assist with operating expenses, Oklahoma Christian took the primary responsibility for funding and operations. A fuller account of this development appears in the chapter on Key Decisions.

Summary of the Johnson Years

Terry Johnson served as president of Oklahoma Christian for twenty-one years, from September of 1974 to December of 1995, the longest term anyone has served in this office. During his tenure, the college excelled in many ways. It moved from a college to a university, began offering graduate work, and opened Cascade College as a branch campus in Portland, Oregon. Another major academic expansion came with the development of degrees in electrical and mechanical engineering, the first among colleges associated with Churches of Christ. In 1981, Oklahoma Christian began publishing the *Christian Chronicle,* in 1982, Enterprise Square opened, and in 1986, the Vienna Studies Program began. In all of these moves, Johnson showed an entrepreneurial spirit in his willingness to take some risk, but in the end, all these moves served to advance the standing and service of the university.

During Johnson's term of office, the university not only continued its accreditation with the North Central Association and NCATE, but gained accreditation from the Accrediting Board for Engineering and Technology, from the National Association of Schools of Music, and from the Association of Collegiate Business Schools and Programs.

The Learning Center received a major renovation and expansion in 1985. That same year, the library

Biblical Studies building and Thelma Gaylord Forum

made the transition to an online catalog and added connections to many databases. The Biblical Studies building and the adjoining Thelma Gaylord Forum were completed in 1987. To serve the newly developed engineering programs, the Prince Engineering Center was completed in 1988. More seating and another playing court were added to the Payne Field House in 1991. During the nineties, Johnson expanded campus computing services and upgraded student housing.

During the twenty-one years Johnson served as president, overall enrollment increased, although it declined during five of his last six years. In President Baird's last year, 1974, enrollment stood at 1,236. By 1990, total enrollment had grown to 1,700, but by Johnson's last year, it had declined to 1,456 with 237 additional students that year at Cascade. During the Johnson years, the number of faculty grew from thirty-seven full-time faculty and twenty-seven adjuncts to seventy-seven full-time faculty and thirty-four adjuncts, and the percentage of full-time faculty with doctorates rose to 68 percent. In the Johnson years, the full-time faculty teaching load was reduced from fifteen to twelve semester hours, thus allowing more time for professors to prepare for classes and connect with students. The student-faculty ratio decreased from thirty to one to fourteen to one, which allowed for more specialization and student-faculty interaction but resulted in a substantial increase in operating costs.[60] Also during the Johnson years, in 1995, Oklahoma Christian was first named to the list of Best Colleges, published by *U.S. News and World Report.*

Three administrators from the Johnson era were inducted into the Oklahoma Higher Education Hall of Fame. Dr. Stafford North was the first, in 1997, then Dr. Johnson in 2000, and Dr. Bailey McBride in 2004.

Financially, the college prospered in many ways during the

Johnson years. The net worth grew from $10,287,716 to $44,449,403 with assets at $88,828,029 and liabilities at $44,378,526. Endowment increased from $1,294,387 to $21,394,586, and operating expenses climbed from $3,078,138 a year to $22,464,958. In Johnson's last two years taken together, however, operational income was $504,835 less than expenses. Other financial problems were developing, as well. Some of the pledges on the Engineering Building and the Bible Building had not materialized, so the buildings required loans. In addition, some of the auxiliary enterprises that were supposed to break even were not doing so—Cascade College, the *Christian Chronicle*, and Enterprise Square—and these were a financial drain. And, of course, the decrease in enrollment also meant a decrease in income. The next president would have some financial challenges to meet, but would also have years of progress on which to build.

Overall, the twenty-one Johnson years were a time of great growth and progress. President Johnson provided creative leadership and extraordinary capacity in fundraising. He led a team of effective administrators to whom he delegated most internal matters. The Johnson years saw the advancement from college to university and the addition of Cascade College. He strengthened ties between the university and both the local civic community and the church constituency. He also was responsible for important additions to the physical plant and a remarkable increase in endowment and net worth. By adding substantially more faculty and several new degree programs, he strengthened the academic program. Those well-known among Churches of Christ came to speak in chapel and on the Lectureship. Outstanding public events on campus characterized the Johnson years including visits from the president of the United States, governors, business leaders, and those famous in the arts and media. The Johnson years were truly extraordinary.

The Fourth President: Dr. Kevin Jacobs
1996 to 2001

Personal Background

Kevin Eugene Jacobs was born on March 31, 1960, in Shawnee, Oklahoma, and attended Shawnee High School, where he was senior class president and lettered in football, basketball, and baseball. In 1978, he enrolled in Oklahoma Christian College, majoring in accounting and minoring in Bible. As a student, he won the Outstanding Business Student Award and participated in business

Kevin Jacobs

games. In 1980, while still a student at OCC, he married Morrow Beth Baird, the daughter of former president James O. Baird. They had four children: Jami, Jacey, Kaleb, and Kade.

After graduating from Oklahoma Christian, Jacobs moved to Nashville where he attended Vanderbilt University to study for a law degree, which he received in 1985. He then returned to Oklahoma Christian to teach business and to be staff counsel. From 1986 to 1994, he served as vice president of the Oklahoma Christian College Investment Corporation. He led in the construction of Tealridge Manor, a retirement center adjacent to the campus, and in 1990 was named vice president and general counsel of the university. In 1993, as Cascade College was beginning in Portland, Jacobs was chosen as its inaugural president.

Terry Johnson announced his resignation from the presidency of Oklahoma Christian in May of 1995. The Board selected Jacobs as his replacement, believing his experience both at the Oklahoma City campus and at Cascade provided good preparation. He took office in January of 1996 and served until May of 2001.

Jacobs' Administrative Team

Soon after Kevin Jacobs took office, he began putting together his own administrative team. Bailey McBride, who had been serving as provost, became editor of the *Chronicle* and director of the Honors Program. Jacobs then named Dr. Jeanine Varner, who had been dean of the College of Liberal Arts, as vice president for academic affairs. Dr. Arlis Wood, who had been

Jeanine Varner

a counselor at OC and later dean of students at Cascade, returned to OC as dean of students. Jacobs also brought Dr. Mickey Banister, who had been academic dean with him at Cascade, to serve as administrative vice president. Joe Watson was named vice president for operations, and Mark Hager came as chief financial officer. After a year, Hager left and was replaced by Jay Jones. In June of 1999, Jacobs employed Alfred Branch as executive vice president, a role in which he oversaw all nonacademic activities of the campus and led the Oklahoma Christian Investment Corporation. When Branch began serving, Joe Watson was shifted to vice president of special projects, a role in which he worked primarily on building construction. Terry Johnson served as chancellor, usually on a part-time basis, for most of the Jacobs years.

When Jacobs began his term as president in 1996, the financial picture was tight, and enrollment had been in decline for several years. He decided, therefore, to reduce the number of faculty by at least seven positions before the next school year. Among the ways he sought to achieve this reduction was to offer an early retirement package. Dr. Howard Norton, dean of the College of Biblical Studies and editor of the *Christian Chronicle*, who did not favor some of Jacob's plans, was one who accepted this offer. To replace Norton as dean of the College of Biblical Studies, Jacobs selected Dr. Lynn McMillon. An OCC alumnus, McMillon had been on the OC faculty since 1966 and, since 1988, had served as chair of the Bible graduate program. He was also well-known for

Lynn McMillon

his work both in Restoration history and in marriage and family relations. Other long-term faculty accepting the early retirement package were Dr. Darrel Alexander, Dr. Bill Jones, Dr. Howard Leftwich, Dr. Elmo Hall, Dr. Roland Schultz, Dr. Ron Bever, and John Pennisi.[61]

Jacobs' Administrative Leadership

Jacobs came to the office of president believing some changes would best serve the institution. He not only placed new personnel in each of the key administrative roles but clearly sought to make changes in the style of administration. Jacobs wanted to be "student oriented." In an interview with the *Talon*, shortly after the announcement of his new role, Jacobs commented, "I want to engage in the life of the campus and be close to what is happening on campus."[62] A staff editorial in the *Talon* stated,

> We expect Jacobs to be a harbinger of change. Administration unfortunately is comprised of good people in an outdated and, in many ways, contrary system. We expect President Jacobs to do what he can to improve that.
>
> We expect Jacobs to work to improve the relationship between the student body, the faculty and administration, so that it is less a parent-child one, and more a co-worker relationship.[63]

To demonstrate this intent, Jacobs moved the president's office from the Learning Center to the Student Center and put large windows in his outside office wall so those passing by could see him at work. He worked closely with the Student Senate officers and accepted their suggestions about changing some of the rules, dropping the rule against long hair for men and allowing students to wear shorts to class and chapel. He also changed the curfew policy to permit qualified students to have a "curfew waiver."[64] Jacobs dropped the Administrative Council and, in its place, put in a President's Advisory Council. This group had more faculty representatives than the previous plan but had less authority. He met regularly with his administrative team to deal with internal matters. Faculty members and students continued to serve on standing committees.

One of Jacobs' major goals as he took office was to get enrollment rising again. He believed this essential for the financial health of the institution, for campus morale, for the public image, and for achieving the mission of the university. Along with changes in the recruiting plan, Jacobs also authorized increases in student scholarships. For the fall of 1996, enrollment was up significantly, from 1,456 to 1,562, and the number of full-time freshman rose impressively from 438 to 545. By the fall of 1998, total headcount had risen to 1,690. As enrollment increased, Jacobs restored faculty positions previously cut, which provided improvement in the academic offerings, but which also increased expenses.

Another of Jacobs' goals was to improve campus facilities. He wanted not only to add needed space, but also to upgrade the quality.

McIntosh Conservatory

In 1996–97, he completed the expansion of the Gaylord Student Center with increased space for serving and seating and included a spacious new office for Student Senate. Wood paneling, higher quality carpet, and more attractive lighting fixtures improved the look of the whole facility.

In 1997, a fire in the Garvey Center brought the opportunity for other changes. With the insurance money and other funds, the entire area was expanded and remodeled. Suggestions from faculty members in music, art, and communication brought important improvements to the facility. An elegant new recital hall seating two hundred was added, as was the McIntosh Conservatory, a large open space which could serve for exhibits, receptions, weddings, dinners, and a host of other events. Jacobs also improved the campus entrance on Memorial Road, adding curved brick walls and planting areas to greet those coming to the campus.

There was, however, a downside to these improvements. Not enough funds were raised to cover all of the costs, and the university borrowed to make up the deficit. This debt, added to obligations the university already had from previous construction, began to weigh heavily.

In addition to the improvement of physical facilities, another significant development of the Jacobs years was the addition of a wireless network to cover the entire campus. This wireless system allowed each student to have a laptop computer and to use it in classes, in the residence halls, in the library, or anywhere else on campus. While it was in fall of 2001, after Jacobs had left, before each student had his or her own laptop, the decision for this development took place during Jacobs' years as president.

Another important development during the years of the Jacobs' presidency came in 2000, when Oklahoma Christian began the MBA degree. The program began with twenty-nine students and by 2007 had grown to 227.[65]

Like all previous presidents, President Jacobs wanted the goodwill of the church constituency. Early in his presidency, he preached at churches and sought to foster good relations. Unfortunately, the departure of key personnel who had served as liaisons with churches, his unsuccessful effort to reshape the lectureship program into a series of smaller events, and other situations which arose strained those relationships during much of his presidency.

Summary of the Jacobs Years

The Jacobs years saw important steps forward. Enrollment increased from 1,456 in 1995 to 1,808 in 2000, with another 321 at Cascade.[66] Campus appearance and facilities improved with important additions in landscaping and in both space and quality at the Gaylord Student Center and the Garvey Center. Total assets increased from $88,828,029 to $92,660,818.

Another major achievement during the Jacobs years was a major gift from Ed Gaylord. Terry Johnson had cultivated this relationship during his presidency and continued those ties as chancellor. In 1999, Edward L. Gaylord committed to a significant Charitable Lead Trust, which, together with subsequent commitments from the E. L. and Thelma Gaylord Foundation, have resulted in one of the largest gifts in the history of the university.

Not all the financial numbers during the Jacobs years, however, were favorable. The net worth declined slightly, from $44,449,503 to $43,639,908, primarily because of borrowings to fund shortfalls in capital projects and operations. Funds invested as endowment also decreased from $21,394,586 to $19,197,122. The capital debt load, which began in Johnson's last years and increased from capital projects during Jacob's years, was creating a heavy burden on the university's financial resources.[67]

The 1999–2000 year saw a good increase in gift income but the 2000–2001 year did not go so well, ending with an operating deficit of $3,060,286.[68] Although on February 23, 2001, the Board expressed its confidence in Jacobs, problems continued to mount.[69] As Jacobs weighed these factors, he asked for a meeting on May 10 with Board Chair Ralph Chain at Roman Nose State Park. There he gave Chain his letter of resignation, effective immediately. In a conference-call meeting the next day, Chain shared with the Board that Jacobs had told him, "This is the way I want to do this—it is best for the school and my family. It is time for me to resign and let the school go forward."[70]

Alfred Branch, Acting President
2001–2002

Alfred Branch

Since Jacobs' resignation came rather suddenly, the Board had no time to select a replacement before he left office. Having served as executive vice president for two years, Alfred Branch was the natural choice to step in as acting president to give the Board of Trustees time to select a new president. He was an alumnus who had left a successful career in real estate management with Trammel Crow to return to his alma mater. He had been part of the president's cabinet and had served as general administrator over fiscal matters and the campus plant. He was well liked and respected on campus. The Board asked him to serve as chief executive officer until the permanent choice could be made.

Those serving in various administrative capacities continued in their roles, and the team worked together. Academic programs and student activities continued much as they had, and the wireless campus plan was completed, thus allowing each student to have his or her own computer to use anywhere on campus.

Branch saw the necessity of making substantial budget cuts to

Bill Goad and Al Branch officially cutting the wire to make the campus wireless

reduce the drain on financial resources. In all, he initiated budget cuts of about $1.5 million, including the decision to drop the baseball program, which he believed could not be justified financially in the existing situation. During the Branch year, there was still an operational deficit, but offsetting this loss during that year, the college received one of the most important gifts in its history when alumni Richard and Pat Lawson, on January 24, 2002, donated four million shares of stock in Lawson Software. During the year Branch was acting president, the university received $10 million from the sale of some of the Lawson stock. For the 2001–2002 year, then, total assets for the university grew from $92,660,818 to $99,667,588, with total liabilities increasing only $974,239. Later sales of the Lawson stock yielded additional millions.[71]

Branch was among those considered to be the next president, but the choice went to Dr. Mike O'Neal, who took office in June 2002. Branch deserves credit for courageous and effective leadership during a difficult year and for continuing to work as Executive Vice President with the new administration.

The Fifth President: Dr. Mike E. O'Neal
2002–Present

Personal Background

Mike Elkins O'Neal was born in Paris, Texas, on February 6, 1946, although his family was living in Hugo, Oklahoma, at the time. When he was four, the family moved to Colorado but after four years returned to Hugo. After his freshman year in high school, his family moved to Antlers, Oklahoma, where he finished high school. His father's sister was married to Jim Maple, Sr., long-time member of the Oklahoma Christian Board of Trustees. The O'Neal side of the family also had strong ties to Oklahoma Christian, his older brother, Foy, and several cousins having attended. [72]

Mike and Nancy O'Neal

In 1964, Mike O'Neal enrolled in Oklahoma Christian. In addition to attaining an excellent academic record, he took part in many campus activities: intramural basketball, softball, and football, playing drums occasionally with the band, serving as vice president of the sophomore class, and participating in the first international studies program to Heidelberg, Germany, from January to May 1966. After two years at OCC, O'Neal transferred to Harding University so he could major in accounting. There he was president of the Student Government Association in his senior year. After graduating from Harding, he served in the U.S. Navy from 1968 to 1970, reaching the rank of lieutenant and receiving a Bronze Star for Meritorious Service in Vietnam. While in the Navy, he passed the CPA exam with the highest score in Oklahoma and seventeenth highest in the nation. He earned his juris doctorate degree in 1974 from Stanford University with a concentration in business and tax law. For two years, 1974–1976, he taught on the business faculty at Harding and served in the planned giving office. In 1976, he joined the staff at Pepperdine University as general counsel, then became vice president for finance and administration, and was named vice chancellor in 1991. In these roles, O'Neal assisted in raising funds for the university and, as chief financial officer, overseeing the operating budget, the university endowment, construction, facilities, information technology, and other administrative functions.[73]

A member of the Church of Christ from his youth, O'Neal has served as a Bible class teacher, preacher, song leader, and elder. O'Neal and his wife Nancy have two children, Michael and Amanda, both of whom have graduated from Oklahoma Christian.

In choosing the successor to Kevin Jacobs, the Board of Trustees had narrowed the search for president to three: Alfred Branch, who was serving as acting president; Dr. Phil Lewis, dean of the College of Business; and O'Neal. They chose O'Neal because of his many years of experience in administration at a Christian university, particularly in fundraising and financial management. He also had been active in the Church of Christ as an elder, and the Board concluded he understood and supported the spiritual mission of the university.

O'Neal's Administrative Team

John deSteiguer

Dr. O'Neal chose to continue into his administration several who had been part of the Jacobs team. Alfred Branch returned to his post as executive vice president. Dr. Jeanine Varner continued to serve as vice president of academic affairs until 2007, when she left to become dean of the College of Arts and Sciences at Abilene Christian University. She was replaced by Dr. Allison Garrett, an OC alumna with a J. D. and a master's degree in law and who had been teaching at the Faulkner University School of Law. Jay Jones was moved to vice president for human resources and university services, and Jeff Bingham was advanced from controller to chief financial officer. Dr. Mickey Banister was shifted to registrar, and Joe Watson returned to the classroom to teach in engineering. O'Neal brought Dr. John deSteiguer, who had been vice president for development at Northeastern Oklahoma State

Neil Arter

University, to fill the role of vice president for advancement at OC and also appointed Neil Arter as dean of campus life. In O'Neal's first two years, Kyle Wray served as vice president for admissions and marketing. After he left, Risa Forrester became the dean of enrollment and marketing.

O'Neal's Administrative Leadership

Dr. O'Neal came to the office of president knowing that several areas would need immediate attention. First, he knew he must get a balanced budget, and quickly embarked on a number of cost-saving measures. He eliminated some faculty and staff positions and consolidated the university's five colleges to three to reduce overhead. These and other cuts allowed O'Neal and his staff to trim the operating budget by about $2.5 million. Their goal was to achieve what they termed "a sustainable model," which meant they would have to raise no more than $1 million each year to fund the deficit in operational expenses. This concept also included recovering depreciation on the physical plant, covering debt service, and operating on a balanced budget. Thus, the unrestricted $1 million a year, along with income from endowment, student tuition, and other sources would cover all operational expenses. By holding operational fundraising to this level, the fundraising team could give more attention to securing endowment gifts, fundraising for capital improvements, and working with long-term gift prospects. The continuing payout of the Gaylord Charitable Trust and the income from the Lawson gift, of course, were great benefits during the O'Neal years. These gifts largely were placed in endowment.

Another need O'Neal addressed early was Board membership. Don Millican became chair of the Board at the time O'Neal became president. A substantial number of the Board, however, were advancing in years to the point where they would move to life membership, an attending but nonvoting status. During his early years, O'Neal added twenty-one new members to bring Board membership to thirty-three.

O'Neal, with input from other administrators, faculty, staff, and students, developed written documents that stated clearly the mission and values of the university. One such document was a statement of core values: faith, scholarship, integrity, stewardship, and liberty. Another was the university's mission statement: "Oklahoma Christian University is a higher learning community which transforms lives for Christian faith, leadership, and service." Based on this mission statement, the O'Neal team developed a "covenant," which all associated with the university are asked to support. This document states that the university's "foundation" is a belief in God and in the

Bible as His word. The covenant calls for all associated with the university to submit both to God's will and to one another in love, and to do their best in everything as service to God. The covenant asks for all to live in respect for others and to accept the community's standards. In addition to these, O'Neal, with input from the campus, has developed "The OC Graduate," a document that identifies the characteristics, skills, and knowledge of those who complete a degree at the university.[74]

President O'Neal inaugurated an annual dinner for donors giving $1,000 or more a year for unrestricted scholarships to recognize their gift and to develop stronger ties with them. To these dinners, O'Neal invited as speakers some well-known individuals such as Art Linkletter, Michael Medved, Dinesh D'Souza, Gene Stallings, and Ken Blanchard.

O'Neal also sought to strengthen relations with the church constituency. He often preached at churches, spoke at preachers' meetings, and made himself available to preachers who wanted to visit. To strengthen the spiritual dimension on campus as well as to seek to improve relationships with churches, he employed OC alumnus Shon Smith as vice president for church relations. In this role, Smith directed chapel and the Lectureship and in other ways promoted spiritual activity on campus.

Noting that there was some increase in diversity among Churches of Christ, Smith and O'Neal decided to use a few speakers on the 2004 Lectureship from a wider range of views than had been the practice on previous lectureships. Some were pleased with this move, while others interpreted it as a change in position for the university. During the Lectureship at an Open Forum period, O'Neal read a seven-page statement in which he reaffirmed the university's spiritual commitment to truths that had characterized it from its beginning. O'Neal also invited all who wished to come to a meeting on February 13 to present their views about the Lectureship situation with the promise that he would hear them but would not respond immediately. The meeting drew about three hundred, some speaking in favor of what had been done while others spoke in opposition. In 2007 O'Neal substituted for the Lectureship a new annual program called Quest, scheduled near the end of May. Led initially by Dr. John Harrison of the OC Bible faculty and Dr. Don Vinzant, minister at the Edmond Church of Christ, this three day program offered speakers with Biblical insights and practical suggestions about the work of the church.

One of O'Neal's most important early moves was to encourage the development of a Faculty Association. Up to this point, faculty members had participated on various committees and administrative groups that made decisions about academic, student, and spiritual matters.   Previous presidents, however, had resisted the idea of faculty members meeting without administrative presence to propose policies and suggest changes. With O'Neal's willingness to accept a faculty senate, the faculty spent about a year under the leadership of Dr. Ken Adams, Department of Music, in setting up the structure for the senate. After some negotiation, the plan was accepted and went into effect in 2003.

In another change in administrative pattern, O'Neal established a Strategic Vision Committee. This group, composed of key administrators, four faculty representatives and three staff representatives, seeks to set priorities for the university, direct resources toward those priorities, approve the general budget, decide about major internal initiatives, and assure annual assessment of the university's programs. O'Neal's emphasis on strategic planning has clearly been a strength.

To promote communication on campus and provide a sense of openness, O'Neal began monthly campus briefings to which any employee is welcome. These information sessions provide a forum for various administrators to report on enrollment, finances, special events, policies, or other matters of interest. An opportunity for questions allows for interaction. O'Neal has also had some similar sessions with students.

University House—two residence halls joined by a common lobby

One of the major initiatives of the O'Neal years has been to improve student housing. The condition and amount of housing was clearly a hindrance to enrollment, and improvements were needed badly. In 2005–2006, three residence halls underwent major renovations. In addition, in Fall 2005, University House opened with separate wings for 108 men and 98 women. This upscale residence hall includes laundry rooms, fitness centers, and areas for study, meetings, and lounging. The housing plan also included additional apartments to serve both upperclassmen and married students, opening in 2005 and 2006. The total cost for renovation, furnishings, and new construction in these housing units was $34.9 million, including a new mechanical plant to serve much of the campus. These additions were financed almost entirely through loans to be repaid through student rental income. This housing initiative provided major renovation of dormitory rooms and added 216 new residence hall beds, as well as space for 378 students in new apartments. While not all the new space was filled immediately, it provided room for growth and a greater attraction for students.[75]

O'Neal also sought to maintain useful contact with students. He occasionally attended the annual freshman retreat at the beginning of each school year, asked for student input on policies being developed, and responded directly to student questions and criticisms.

During the O'Neal years, there have been four major curricular expansions. The MBA program, begun under President Jacobs, has grown rapidly under O'Neal's presidency to provide a significant source of revenue for the university. In 2005, the Bible graduate program was expanded to include a master of divinity degree, both because the M.A. program alone was expected to decline in numbers and because of the additional service the M.Div. program could offer to ministers in the area. The program has provided a substantial increase in Bible graduate students, from forty-four in 2004 to fifty-six in 2006. In 2006, the university began offering a nursing program, which was approved by the Oklahoma Board of Nursing. By 2007, the total number of nursing students had grown to 109. In April 2008, O'Neal announced the addition of a master's degree in engineering which would begin the following fall.

Another O'Neal innovation has been a summer conference that brings together Board, faculty, and staff. The first of these was held on the Cascade College campus in Portland, Oregon, and involved the OC Board, representatives from the Cascade Board, staff, and spouses. "Faith and Learning" was the topic. In July of 2005, the event, held on the OC campus, was built around the book by David Dockery called *Taking Every Thought Captive*. About 150 attended, representing faculty, staff, trustees, and spouses. Another similar conference on the OC campus came in July 2006, when the group studied the topic of "Starting Strong, Finishing Stronger." The 153 present probed the question of retention at Oklahoma Christian.

One of the most interesting developments under President O'Neal's leadership involves the African nation of Rwanda. In November of 1994, Rwandan President Paul Kagame invited Board Member Richard Lawson and his wife Pat to come to Rwanda because Kagame had visited Lawson Software in Milwaukee. The Lawsons insisted that Mike and Nancy O'Neal accompany them, and they also took along Dave Jenkins, who was serving as a visiting missionary at OC. All of these visitors were well impressed with the progress President Kagame was bringing to this strife-torn nation and were determined to be of help.

As a result of this trip, a number of interesting developments ensued. Dave Jenkins and his family have moved to Rwanda as missionaries with governmental recognition for Churches of Christ. President Kagame and some members of his cabinet visited the Oklahoma Christian campus on April 26, 2006, the first foreign head of state to come to the university. Oklahoma Christian entered into an agreement with the government of Rwanda to provide major scholarship assistance for ten new Rwandan students a year to begin studies at Oklahoma Christian starting in the fall of 2006. These students are selected by a very careful screening process overseen by Bryan and Holly Hixson, who left their employment at OC to become missionaries in Rwanda. Several OC students have also chosen to go to Rwanda to serve. By the academic year of 2009–2010, there will be forty Rwandan students attending the university. The government of Rwanda has offered, for an excellent price, a very attractive building for the church to purchase for their use, and Dr. O'Neal helped raise funds for the purchase. In addition, OC students have undertaken a program called "Wishing Well" through which they are raising the funds to dig wells in Rwanda to improve the water supply in remote locations. The Rwandan connection provides a good example of how OC's outreach can connect with distant places for the advancement of the Lord's kingdom as well as improving the conditions of all humankind.[76] In April 2008, Dr. O'Neal attended a conference at the United Nations in New York to share the OC plan with others interested in similar work in underdeveloped nations.

O'Neal, as Presidents Johnson and Jacobs before him, worked to continue the operation of Cascade College in Portland. Under his leadership, Cascade reached the point not only of paying its own way but of repaying most of the deficit it had created. Dr. Bill Goad, OC alumnus and former professor and administrator at Oklahoma Christian, became president at Cascade in 2006.

Summary of the O'Neal Years

President O'Neal came at a critical time in the history of Oklahoma Christian. Financial problems were clearly in evidence and the relationship with the university's church constituency needed improvement. He attacked these matters head-on, making progress in both areas.

In the year ending in 2007, the university's annual operating expenses had increased to $47,501,215, but operating income was above this amount by $2,749,752. Also by 2007, total assets were $157,049,679 with liabilities at $88,866,887; thus, the net worth was $68,182,792. The largest piece of current liability is for student housing, which will be repaid by income from the housing facilities. By 2007, funds invested as endowment had risen to $68,051,000, an increase from the $35,025,000 in 2002, primarily because of the Lawson gift. These endowment numbers now also include some properties held by the university that, in previous years, were not counted in endowment. The endowment comparisons within the O'Neal years, therefore, are accurate, but may not be compared exactly with the numbers from preceding years. O'Neal has put the budget back in order and restored confidence among the university's constituencies in the university's financial standing. In 2007, his team also provided $2,835,000 for debt reduction and campus improvements.[77]

O'Neal gathered an effective advancement team led by Dr. John deSteiguer. This team has not only raised sizable amounts of money, but has built good relationships with prospective donors and with alumni, the church constituency, and the local community.

Enrollment has grown significantly in the O'Neal years, from 1,760 in 2002 to 2,258 in 2007. The number of full-time faculty has grown correspondingly, from 90 to 104, and the number of adjunct instructors has increased from 73 to 109, partly due to the growth in the MBA program and the addition of nursing. Important academic developments include the expansion of the graduate offerings and the addition of the nursing program. In Spring 2006, the university received a ten-year unconditional reaccreditation by the Higher Learning Commission of the North Central Association.

One of the most significant developments of the O'Neal years has been the improvement in both residence halls and apartments. These additions have laid the foundation for growth in the coming years.

The first six years of O'Neal's presidency have seen vital improvements in the financial status of the university, strong increases in enrollment, restatement and publicizing of the Christian mission of the university, and strengthening of the academic program.

The Five Presidents

Five individuals have served as president of Oklahoma Christian University. Each has had to meet challenges, and each has led the university to significant improvements. L. R. Wilson had the particular challenge of starting the college—making the college known and assembling faculty, students, donors, and facilities. James Baird led in the move to a new campus and expansion into a well-known and respected institution. Terry Johnson's leadership brought Oklahoma Christian to university status, with more students, more endowment, more facilities, and a broader curriculum. Kevin Jacobs led the university to growth in enrollment and improvement in campus facilities. Mike O'Neal has brought financial stability, improved student housing, more growth in enrollment, and improvements in the academic program.

All of these presidents have sought to fulfill the mission for which the university was founded: to provide a strong Christian education, while preparing students for a lifetime of service to community, family, and church. Serving as the person with ultimate responsibility for the progress of an institution like Oklahoma Christian is difficult and demanding, and the university has been blessed by having leaders who have devoted themselves to the task.

Chapter 4, Endnotes

1 Loyd L. Smith, *Gospel Preachers of Yesteryear* (Allen, Texas: Loyd L. Smith, 1986), 430.

2 L. R. Wilson, "A Beggar," *Central Christian College Bulletin*, September 1951, OC Archives.

3 Smith, 430.

4 Ibid.

5 Ibid.

6 C. G. "Colly" Caldwell, "Introduction," *Making a Difference: Florida College—The First Fifty Years* (Temple Terrace, Florida College, 1996), 18; Smith, 431; James O. Baird, "L. R. Wilson—Twice President," *Central Christian College Bulletin*, 1951, OC Archives; Batsell Barrett Baxter and M. Norvel Young, *Preachers of Today* (Nashville: The Christian Press, 1952), I, 374.

7 Roland and Olive Lewis, "Profile of a President," *Making a Difference: Florida College—The First Fifty Years* (Temple Terrace: Florida College, 1996), 17. At the beginning, the college was called Florida Christian College, but in later years the name was changed to Florida College.

8 Ibid., Caldwell, 8.

9 Lewis, 19.

10 "E. R. Higgins—Vice President," *Central Christian College Bulletin*, October 1951, OC Archives.

11 "H. E. Whitacre—Business Manager," *Central Christian College Bulletin*, December 1951, OC Archives; "Our Loss," *Central Christian College Bulletin*, July 1955, OC Archives.

12 Terry Johnson, Email to the author, December 9, 2007.

13 "Radio Work on Independent Basis," *Central Christian College Bulletin*, September 1953, OC Archives.

14 "US Is Well Represented at CC Camp," *Bartlesville Examiner-Enterprise*, July, 1952, Ruth Wilson Scrapbook, OC Archives, 46.

15 Minutes, Board of Trustees, May 22, 1951, OC Archives; Minutes, Board of Trustees, August 14, 1951, OC Archives.

16 James O. Baird, "A Good-by with Gratitude," *Central Christian College Bulletin*, July 1954, OC Archives.

17 *Report of a Self-Study: Oklahoma Christian College*, September 1960, OC Archives.

18 W. O. Beeman, *Oklahoma Christian College: From Dream to Reality* (Delight, Arkansas: Gospel Light Publishing Company, 1970), 64.

19 "James O. Baird, Dean," *Central Christian College Bulletin,* November 1951, OC Archives.

20 Ibid.

21 "Our Gain," *Central Christian College Bulletin,* July 1955, OC Archives.

22 *President's Report, 1966,* OC Archives.

23 *President's Report, 1969,* 16, OC Archives.

24 Beeman, 160.

25 *Design for Progress Through the Seventies*, A Planning Report for 1970–1979, 114, OC Archives.

26 Ibid, *passim.*

27 "In Memoriam," *Aerie*, 1964, 4, OC Archives.

28 Richard Mock, Interview audiotaped with the author, September 28, 2006, OC Archives.

29 "Dr. Baird's Stand Applauded," *Oklahoma Christian College Bulletin*, April 1969, OC Archives.

30 Pendleton Woods, Letter to author, September 29, 2006, OC Archives.

31 Beeman, 147–148.

32 Beeman, 146.

33 Ibid.

34 *Report of a Self-Study: Oklahoma Christian College*, December 1, 1975, OC Archives, 37.

[35] Ibid., 53.
[36] Ibid.
[37] Ibid., 44.
[38] Ibid., 51.
[39] *Report, 1960*, 22.
[40] Ibid.
[41] *Report, 1975*, 51.
[42] *Report, 1960*, 27.
[43] *Report, 1975*, 58.
[44] James O. Baird, *Perspectives* (Delight, Arkansas; Gospel Light Publishing Company, 1999), 11.
[45] Terry Johnson, Videotaped interview with author, June 16, 2006, OC Archives.
[46] *Report of a Self-Study: Oklahoma Christian University of Science and Arts*, September 1995, OC Archives, 35.
[47] Files of the Office of the President under Gala Week.
[48] "Institutional Growth, Achievements and Performance," *President's Report, 1991–1992*, OC Archives.
[49] J. Terry Johnson, *Jubilee: Oklahoma Christian University 1950–2000*, 125.
[50] "Alumni Callout Exceeds Goal," *Oklahoma Christian College Reporter*, December 1975, OC Archives.
[51] *Report from the President, 1994–95*.
[52] Minutes, Board of Trustees, December 8, 1974, OC Archives.
[53] Bob Rowley, Email to author, October 4, 2006, OC Archives.
[54] Information from Lynn McMillon, March 12, 2008.
[55] "OCC to Publish Christian Chronicle," *OCC Reporter*, April 1981, 1, OC Archives.
[56] Bailey McBride, "Chronicle affirms mission of former editor," *Christian Chronicle*, September, 1981, 9, OC Archives.
[57] "The purpose," *Christian Chronicle*, September, 1981, 2, OC Archives.
[58] Lynn McMillon, Written memo, August 13, 2007.
[59] Readership Study by Insight Market Research, James Bost, Director, Oklahoma City, March 2006, 8.
[60] *Report, 1995*, 6.
[61] Christy Robinson, "Faculty Accept Early Retirement Package," *Talon*, March 1,1996, 1, OC Archives.
[62] Allison Ogle, "Jacobs Takes Reigns as Johnson Resigns," *Talon*, October 6, 1995, 1, OC Archives.
[63] "High Dreams for New President," *Talon*, January 12, 1996, 3, OC Archives.
[64] Tonna Condict, "Hair, Curfew Changes Approved by Jacobs," *Talon*, March 1, 1996, 1, OC Archives.
[65] Enrollment Data, Office of the Registrar, OC.
[66] Ibid.
[67] Financial Data, Office of the Vice President for Finance, OC.
[68] Ibid.
[69] Minutes, Board of Trustees, March 6, 2001, OC Archives.
[70] Minutes, Board of Trustees, May 11, 2001, OC Archives.
[71] Financial Data.
[72] Information from Dr. Mike O'Neal.
[73] Files on Dr. Mike O'Neal, Office of the President, Oklahoma Christian University.
[74] Documents available on the OC Web site.
[75] Information from the Office of the Executive Vice President, Oklahoma Christian University.
[76] Information from Dr. Mike O'Neal.
[77] Financial Data.

Chapter 5
THE BOARD OF TRUSTEES

At the first Central Christian College Lectureship, on March 27, 1951, speaker Chester Grimes related how the college began. Deeply involved in the four-year saga that led to the college's opening in September 1950, he said, "Central Christian College has had a glorious beginning and we all hope for a glorious future." He further observed:

> The bringing of this vision into reality was no small task. It took courage and persistence on the part of those who served on the board of directors. It took more than that—hard work, long hours of driving, driving hundreds of miles at night after their own business. It meant neglecting their own affairs—absence from families—and at great expense to themselves. All of this and more was the price that had to be paid by someone in order to bring us to the point where we stand today."[1]

These words describe well the sacrificial spirit of all who have served on the Board of Trustees through more than sixty years. All have been volunteers who received no pay for their Board service, who traveled at their own expense, and who gave freely of their time and judgment to help the institution succeed. They have contributed generously, sometimes out of necessity, to keep the institution alive. They have solicited funds, agonized over decisions, and suffered when things went badly. They have also enjoyed the camaraderie of their associates and the fruits of their success.

When L. R. Wilson retired after five years of working with the Board, he wrote:

Perhaps no one makes greater sacrifices for a Christian college—
and with less thanks—than the Board of Directors. This is
certainly true of the Directors of Central Christian College.

They have never received one cent for their time, their
services, or for their many sacrifices. They give several
days of their time each year to the College, they sign their
names to notes, bonds, and to personal checks to help keep
the college going.

All of this they do without any thought of personal glory, or
any special thanks from anyone. They do it for the glory of
God and the good of our young people.[2]

This commitment of Board members to the institution grows from
their passion to see the university's mission fulfilled. All have
believed in the value of Christian education and wanted to see young
people, especially from Churches of Christ, prepare for occupations
in an institution where they could find both academic excellence and
spiritual development. And for this goal, they have given much.

The Function of the Board of Trustees

The most basic function of the Board of Trustees is to be "trustees,"
that is, to hold the institution in trust, to be faithful to its mission
and thus to honor the wishes of its founders and supporters. If the
Board does not steer a firm course toward achieving the institution's
fundamental mission, then no matter what else the university may
achieve, the trustees have failed. Over the first half-century of its
existence, Board members of Oklahoma Christian have consistently
held this function of the Board to be primary. They have maintained
this focus by setting policies and selecting a president committed to
the mission.

Since the first efforts to start a Christian college in Oklahoma
through early 2007, 145 different individuals have served on the
Board of Trustees. As stated in the bylaws, all of these have been
members of the Church of Christ, all have been deeply involved
as members of their local congregations, and all have had a strong
interest in the spiritual development of young people. Every meeting
of the Board begins with prayer for their work and for those directing
the institution, and Board members often have expressed their belief
that God has been at work among them and through them.

At various stages of the development of the university, of course,
the Board has focused on different matters, and has worked under

different styles of leadership. A review of Board activities under each of the twelve men who have served as chair reveals both the way the Board has worked and the issues it has faced. These chairs have included two preachers, a rancher, five businessmen, a podiatrist, two lawyers, and an accountant.

The Twelve Chairmen

A. J. Bryant

A. J. Bryant

A. J. Bryant, minister of the Church of Christ in Pryor, Oklahoma, was the first chairman of the Board. He received an offer from the Pryor Chamber of Commerce to donate land and government buildings so members of the Churches of Christ could start a college there. As a board was formed to consider this offer and to bring such a college into being, the members chose Bryant, sixty-two and with twelve years in the pulpit, as chairman. During the four months he served, from September 25 to December 10, 1946, the Board's primary focus was on two things: building support for a Christian college in Oklahoma, and negotiating with the government to obtain the property in Pryor. During Bryant's leadership, the Board adopted the name of Mid-States Christian College for the school they hoped to found.

Byron Fullerton

Byron Fullerton, minister for the University Church of Christ in Norman, and who later served as superintendent of the Tipton Home, replaced Bryant. He served just over two months, until February 28, 1947. By this time, it had become evident that the plan to start a college in Pryor would not succeed. There were problems with getting the property and buildings from the government, and there was considerable doubt among church members that Pryor was the place to put a Christian

Byron Fullerton

college even if the government delivered on its promise. This early effort, then, with two chairmen of a Board who worked very hard, did not bring the college they hoped would materialize. Their efforts, however, stirred strong interest in Oklahoma for establishing such a college somewhere in the state and laid a foundation for reaching that goal.

G. R. Tinius

Even as the Mid-States Christian College Board of Trustees passed out of existence, a new Board was formed. G. R. Tinius, an elder at 10th and Rockford Church of Christ and a businessman from Tulsa, became chairman of a new Board on February 28, 1947. He served until March 2, 1951, near the end of the college's first year of operation.

G. R. Tinius

Tinius, whose son, Bob, at the time was attending Abilene Christian College, filled a very unusual role. He was not only chairman of the Board, but the Board also chose him as the college's first employee. He was charged with raising money on behalf of a new college without a campus, without students, and without employees other than himself. The exact amount he raised is not recorded, but under his leadership, the Board held meetings around Oklahoma to encourage interest in starting a Christian college, purchased property in Bartlesville, and selected the first president, L. R. Wilson. Tinius deserves much credit for keeping alive the movement to start a college in Oklahoma. Without his perseverance, the whole effort might have foundered. A men's residence hall on the Oklahoma Christian campus is named in his memory.

While Tinius was chair, the Board adopted the policy that set the qualifications for membership on the Board of Trustees,

> each of whom shall be a member of a congregation of the Church of Christ, which takes the New Testament as its only and sufficient rule of faith, worship, and practice, and rejects from its faith, worship, and practice everything not required by either precedent or example, and which does not introduce into the faith, worship, and practice as a part of the same or as adjuncts thereto any supplemental organization or anything else not clearly and directly authorized in the New Testament either by precept or example; and no person shall be qualified to act as a trustee whose religious belief, faith, or practice is not in conformity with the provisions and qualifications set out in this paragraph.[3]

Tinius usually called Board meetings in hotels around Oklahoma, but after the Bartlesville property was secured, they typically met there. They had to deal with one financial crisis after another, sometimes even having called meetings to ask for their personal contributions or to sign their names on a bank note. But they kept the dream alive and succeeded in getting the college started.

L. B. Clayton

On March 2, 1951, as the first year of operation for Central Christian was nearing its end, the Board chose L. B. Clayton, on the Board since 1947, and vice chairman since March 4, 1949, as its new chairman. Clayton was an elder of the 10th and Francis Church of Christ in Oklahoma City and owned a lumber company. He, like Tinius, had a son, Joe, who attended Abilene Christian College. Clayton served until March 31, 1955. During his years, Board minutes reflect primary attention to the financial needs of the college and to facilities. They approved the budget, agreed to faculty salary increases, and initiated regional meetings to increase interest in the college. They also dealt with rather detailed matters for a board,

L. B. Clayton

such as the purchase of a pickup truck and a bus and problems regarding a septic tank. They also raised the number of possible Board members from twenty to thirty.

G. R. Tinius for a Second Term

After Clayton's term, G. R. Tinius was chosen for a second term as chairman, but served only seven months. On October 28, 1955, he resigned from the Board for ill health. During this period, the Board first refused to discuss moving the campus from Bartlesville, then agreed to study the question, and finally, at the October 28 meeting, agreed to move if a city would provide sufficient funding. Tinius, who had worked so hard to get the college started in Bartlesville, had, at first, opposed the move. So, while Tinius' second term was short, it was eventful.

Van Martin

Van Martin, vice chairman under Tinius, filled out the year as temporary chair and then was elected chairman. An automobile dealer from Ponca City, Martin served almost three years, until April 1, 1958. During these years, the Board began receiving reports from the dean and business manager, approved the start of intercollegiate basketball, and agreed to the start of social clubs for students. Their

Van Martin

main attention during this time, of course, was on the move from Bartlesville. They agreed on Oklahoma City as the new location, selected the site on which the campus would be built, and employed Dr. Benson as chancellor. The Board selected architects and designers and agreed to the contracts and loans for constructing the new buildings. They appointed a building committee of their own members, which handled many of the details about the new campus on behalf of the Board. The Martin years saw great advancement from a college of limited potential in Bartlesville to the location in Oklahoma City with much greater opportunities before it.

Dean Smith

Dean Smith, a lawyer from Tulsa and member at the 29th and Yale congregation, became chairman on April 1, 1958. He served until October 27, 1961. These were years of getting the new college program started in Oklahoma City. On March 31, 1959, the Board agreed to change the name from Central Christian College to Oklahoma Christian College, primarily because the new Oklahoma City location put the college just three miles from Central State College, and two "Centrals" so close together was confusing.[4]

Dean Smith

In the meeting on March 31, the Board approved an amended set of bylaws which included the following statement about the Board:

> The governing body of this institution shall be a Board of Trustees to be composed of not less than twenty (20) and not more than thirty (30) persons, each of whom shall be of legal adult age, a member of the Church of Christ in good standing, who believes in and adheres to a strict construction of the Bible as set forth in the Articles of Incorporation.[5]

On April 19, 1959, the Board approved the expansion from a junior college to a senior college, offering bachelor's degrees in Bible, science, business, and education.[6] During the Smith years, the Board not only approved the curricular expansion, but also approved a new salary plan, benefits, and an evaluation policy for faculty. They also discussed the need for personal contact between faculty members and students having academic problems. This Board approved the building of "The Barn" to provide space for physical education and

Photo of the Board of Trustees from the 1958 La Quinta. Front row from right to left: Dr. James O. Baird, L. B. Clayton, Glenn Durrill, Van Martin, Roland Roberts, Dr. George S. Benson. Second row: J. H. Maple, Elmer Shackelford, Jack Evans, J. E. Wright, S. Beach Maple, G. A. Hale, Harl Mansur, Sr., Dee Cummings, Dr. Harl Mansur, Jr. Third row: Jesse Stratton, James S. Maple, T. E. Burch, Elwood Whitacre, T. E. Milholland, Henry Oldham, Roland Beustring, Bob Steele, Taft Milford, W. O. Beeman, L. E. Mitchell, Dr. Ralph Owens, Jim Bills, Floyd Lawson.

intercollegiate basketball.[7] They also approved additional dormitories for a growing student body[8] and expansion of the student center.

One of the most difficult issues the Board faced during Smith's term of office was the integration question. Although President Wilson had said before the college began that the institution would be open to "any student regardless of race, creed, or background,"[9] no minority students, apparently, sought to attend during his term of office. On October 28, 1955, the Board appointed a committee "to investigate the feasibility of taking negro students in at CCC,"[10] but no results from that study were ever reported in Board minutes. The matter arose again in 1959, when a letter came from the Stillwater Church of Christ asking whether Central Christian accepted black students. The Board replied that they would place the matter "under advisement," but no later reply was recorded.[11] About this time, some black students and their families inquired about attending Oklahoma Christian and were told they could not enroll.

In 1954, the United States Supreme Court decision in Brown vs. Board of Education had required public schools to integrate, and this ruling eventually was applied to public colleges and universities. Public institutions of higher education in Oklahoma, therefore, had begun admitting undergraduate black students in 1955.[12] Feelings about the issue were running high around the nation with marches and sit-ins and opposition. Many private colleges and universities in the South, not being under this decree, had not yet decided to integrate.

At a meeting on March 31, 1960, the Board appointed G. A. Hale, Jack Burton, and Glenn Durrill as a committee on "desegregation" to investigate the matter.[13] The committee made its recommendation "in favor of admitting Negros,"[14] and the Board discussed the report on March 28, 1961. At that Board meeting, President Baird reported that the faculty and administration thought the time had come to admit black students. This proposal raised lengthy and sometimes heated discussion. Those in favor thought it improper and unnecessary to exclude these students, while those opposed were afraid that admitting them would cause some white families to send their children to other colleges. At that time, none of the previously segregated colleges among Churches of Christ had, as yet, allowed black students to come. Abilene Christian College admitted black students at the graduate level in 1961, as junior and senior students in 1962, and students at any level in 1963. Freed-Hardeman College and David Lipscomb College did not integrate until 1965 and Harding after that. Some in the church thought it was better for black students to go to Southwestern Christian College, an institution operated primarily by black church members for a black student body.[15]

After lengthy discussion, by a vote of twelve to seven, the Board passed the following resolution: "Beginning with the 1961–62 term, the administration be empowered to admit qualified students regardless of race or color." By the same vote, they defeated a subsequent proposal that black students be admitted only as day students.[16] The Board is due considerable credit for a courageous decision to integrate before it was required by the government and before any other previously segregated colleges among Churches of Christ had decided to do so.

In the fall of 1961, three female black students became the first of their race to attend Oklahoma Christian: Gloria Johnson from Spencer, Oklahoma, along with Ruth Robinson and Cheryl Maynard, both from Oklahoma City. Two of these students remained only one year while the third continued for two years. All three were members of the Dorian Club social service club.[17] The number of African American students increased gradually and the integration process went well. In an effort to avoid problems, parents could request notification about whom their children were dating, and black and white students were not placed as roommates without prior agreement. The "sit-in" incident in 1969, reported in Chapter 4, was the most serious problem encountered in campus race relations. In 1978, John Thompson, a popular black student from Chickasha, Oklahoma, was elected president of the student body.

So the three Smith years saw many very important decisions that affected the long-range future of the institution.

G. A. Hale

On October 27, 1961, G. A. Hale, who had served as vice chairman since April 1, 1958, succeeded Dean Smith as chairman of the OCC Board. Hale was an Oklahoma City businessman generally credited

G. A. Hale

with inventing the parking meter. He was a quiet but effective man. His six-year term as chair saw many important developments. Oklahoma Christian became the permanent depository for the academic records of Cordell Christian College, the University of Oklahoma having agreed to transfer them. The Board adopted the TIAA-CREF retirement program for its employees.[18] Hardeman Auditorium and the Mabee Learning Center were planned and built, the Building Committee of the Board being very active in these projects. The Board approved more residence halls and an expansion of the student center because during these six years, the enrollment almost tripled, from 379 to 1,005. In 1964, the Board approved the addition of summer school classes when the administration believed it feasible,[19] and in 1965, the first overseas student program was approved to allow students to individualize a semester abroad within provided guidelines.[20] In 1967, the Board approved the adoption of the trimester plan for dividing the year into three equal four-month periods.[21]

Hale's term, then, included many key decisions. He stepped down as chairman for ill health in February and died a few months later in August of 1967. President James Baird said that Hale had been "one of the major forces behind the growth of Oklahoma Christian College," having served both as "chairman of the board and as chairman of the building committee."[22]

J. E. Wright

J. E. Wright, who had been on the Board since 1947 and vice chairman since February 12, 1963, was appointed chair on February 8, 1967. Wright owned and operated Sentinel Manufacturing Company in Tulsa and served as an elder at the Brookside Church of Christ. He was a Bible teacher and had written a book summarizing the Bible called *God's Progressive Plan*. He later wrote commentaries on Acts and Hebrews. Wright served only one year as chairman and during that period the

J. E. Wright

Board authorized the building of a gymnasium[23] and two additional residence halls.[24] They also authorized the college to purchase property in Emporia, Kansas, which would be leased to TG&Y.[25] This development became the prototype for other similar activities, which brought about the Oklahoma Christian Investment Corporation.

Ralph Owens

On February 6, 1968, Dr. Ralph Owens became chairman of the Board. He served in this role for twelve years, through the end of President Baird's tenure and into the early years of President Johnson's. Owens had attended Abilene Christian College, where he played football, and there he gained a favorable view of Christian education. He was a podiatrist by profession and an elder of the Southwest Church of Christ in Oklahoma City.

Owens became directly connected with the college when Dr. Benson and Dalton Voss chose him as the third member of the committee to study moving the college from Bartlesville. He then became a major force in that move by leading both the Oklahoma City and the statewide church drives for funds to make the relocation possible. He was added to the Board in November, 1956, and served as treasurer of the Board from 1958 until he became chairman ten years later. Owens' strong commitment to Christian education grew not only from his own experience at Abilene Christian, but also from his great interest in working with youth. His wife, Roma Hailey, whom he met at Abilene and who was from a family long involved in Christian education, became a leader in the Oklahoma Christian Women's Association.

Dr. Ralph Owens

Owens' twelve years as chair spanned from 1968 through 1980. All the other officers of the Board remained in place during those years: Jess Stratton as vice chairman, Leon Lugar as treasurer, and C. A. Buchanan as secretary. These four, plus J. E. Wright and Deryl Gotcher as members-at-large, composed the executive committee that often met between Board meetings and that prepared the agendas for meetings of the full Board.

These twelve years were certainly momentous ones for the college, and under Owens' leadership, the Board of Trustees played a major part. From 1968 to 1980, enrollment grew from 1,135 to 1,522, and during his term, major additions came to campus facilities: the Davisson American Heritage Building, the Payne Physical Education Center, the Herold Science Hall,[26] new dormitories and married student apartments, expansions of the Learning Center and the Student Center, and buildings for Fine Arts and Mass Communications. The initial plans for Enterprise Square, USA were also laid during this period, although the facility was not completed until later.

With the addition of six major academic facilities during these years, the academic strength of the institution grew significantly. Faculty and students had more and better classrooms and improved specialized space for science laboratories, art and music studios, a campus radio station, and courts for physical education. More and larger faculty offices also helped the academic program. In addition, the Board adopted a new faculty salary scale, standards for faculty rank, and a plan for tenure called "continuous employment."

During the Owens years, the Board did much of its work through a committee structure. The Corporate Affairs Committee dealt with matters pertaining to the Board itself and recommended sixteen new members for the Board, who were added during that time. The Building and Grounds Committee was especially active in making decisions about new facilities. They helped decide on the architects, approved the plans, analyzed the bids, and made decisions during the construction. Vernon Newell, who owned Southwestern Roofing Company in Oklahoma City, was chairman of the Building Committee during those years, and, as a local builder, was much involved in the college's construction activities.

The Board's Development Committee directly assisted in planning fund drives among both the church and the business constituencies, many Board members even being part of the solicitation teams. The Finance Committee kept watch on the budget and expenditures, reporting to each Board session on how well the college was meeting its financial obligations. Since enrollment was about level from 1968 to 1973, the administration frequently provided information on how they were cutting the budget to keep it in balance with growing costs but not a growing student body. To the credit of the Board and administration, during the Owens years there was a faculty-staff salary increase almost every year. An Endowment Committee kept watch on the college's endowment funds, sometimes

Seated left to right : Walter Smith, Carrie Lou Little, Charles Floyd, Leon Lugar, C. A. Buchanan, Ralph Owens, Jess Stratton, Dr. Joe Stafford, Ralph Fails, L. E. Mitchell, O. B. Saunders. Standing left to right: Jim Maple, Bill Bonebreak, Allen Reese, W. A. Henderson, Riley Cavin, Bill Beeman, Deryl Gotcher, Dr. John Sudbury, Dr. Joe Kelsey, Vernon Newell, Ralph Chain, Kent Nowlin, J. E. Wright, Dr. Jack Stephenson, Glenn Hetrick.

recommending the type of investments to make, sometimes even the specific investments to buy or sell.

When Judge William Davisson left his estate to the college, it included several ranch properties. Some of these were sold, but the college continued to own others. Since the Board had several ranchers among its members, they formed a Ranch Committee, and for several years, this committee oversaw the operation of the ranches. They employed the services of ranch specialists from the First National Bank in Oklahoma City to do the actual ranch management, but they kept in very close touch. Board minutes during those years show frequent discussions about the price of cattle, the amount of sales, and improvements on the ranches.

When the Board met, the committees typically had their sessions on Friday afternoons, each with an administrator present to provide information, and then the committees reported at the Saturday morning meeting of the full Board. This committee structure was a vital part of the Board's operation during the Owens years.

While Owens was chair, the Board added its first female member, Carrie Lou Little, in 1978, and its first alumnus, Charles Floyd, in 1979.

One of the key decisions of the Owens years, of course, was the replacement of President James O. Baird. When Baird resigned in 1974, the Board formed a selection committee that brought the recommendation for J. Terry Johnson to become the next president of the college.

Owens was not a strong public speaker, but his example of dedication and hard work provided a strong base for his leadership. The twelve years of his chairmanship certainly rank among the most important in the institution's history. At the beginning of that period, OCC's net worth was $3,647,545 and, by the end of Owens' term, net worth had grown to $27,742,445.

Deryl Gotcher

Deryl Gotcher

At the November 10, 1979, meeting of the Board, Owens, Lugar, and Buchanan asked to be relieved of their leadership roles on the Board at the next meeting on February 23, 1980. The Board complied with their request, electing a new slate of officers: Deryl Gotcher as chair, Jess Stratton continuing as vice chair, Riley Cavin as secretary, Bill Beeman as treasurer, and Joe Stafford as member of the executive committee at large. Ralph Owens continued on the executive committee as past chair and J. E. Wright served as an honorary member.

The remarkable twelve-year longevity of the Owens chairmanship was exceeded by the Gotcher years, which lasted from 1980 until 1997. Thus, Gotcher would serve during the last fifteen years of the Johnson presidency and through the first two years of Kevin Jacobs' term. Gotcher, a lawyer who at one time served as president of the Oklahoma Bar Association, was an elder of the Park Plaza Church of Christ in Tulsa.

As during the Owens years before him, Board officers stayed much the same throughout Gotcher's term. Jess Stratton served as vice chairman until his death in 1990 when Bill Beeman took that role. Riley Cavin served as secretary until his death in 1989. Beeman was treasurer until his appointment as vice chairman to replace Stratton. Other members of the executive committee during the Gotcher years were Dr. Ralph Owens, as past chairman, and Dr. Joe Stafford. Stafford became secretary after Cavin's death, and Lyle Harms replaced Beeman as treasurer. In 1989, Ralph Chain became a member-at-large on the executive committee.

Gotcher's meetings were carefully planned and moved effectively. He continued to use the committee structure that had served well in previous years. During this time, the Board began the practice of having one of its meetings each year away from the campus, the first of which was in 1985 at Western Hills Lodge near Wagoner, Oklahoma.[27]

The Gotcher term saw great changes at Oklahoma Christian. During those years, the college became a university, and the institution added the Biblical Studies Center, the Thelma Gaylord Forum, and the Prince Engineering Center. It also expanded the Gaylord Student Center, the Mabee Learning Center, and the Garvey Center. Not all of these projects, however, were fully funded at the time of their construction, thus creating financial stresses later on. Two additional residence halls and married student apartments provided better and additional student housing.

These years certainly had their highs and lows. During those seventeen years from 1980 to 1997, total headcount of students on the Oklahoma City campus grew some from the 1,657 in 1980, but then fell as low as 1,430 in 1995. The number increased back to 1,631 after Kevin Jacobs' first two years. During the Gotcher years, the Board made many important decisions about the academic program: the addition of engineering degrees, the first offering of a graduate degree with the master of arts in Ministry, the addition of Cascade College in Portland, Oregon, and the change from college to university.

While the Enterprise Square project was begun during the Owens years, it opened during Gotcher's term in 1982 and provided the college with an outstanding opportunity for service and great publicity. Along with these benefits, however, came a financial burden, because endowment for Enterprise Square was never enough to cover all its operating expense.

Many Board meetings, in fact, were concerned with finances. During the years when enrollment was declining, severe budget cuts often were required, and while the administration made the actual decisions on what to trim, the Board kept a careful eye on the process. In some years, the Board approved the sale of assets in order to keep from borrowing to meet expenses.

Board minutes from the Gotcher years are filled with reports from the Oklahoma Christian College Investment Corporation. While this program began prior to Gotcher's term, it expanded considerably during his years. The reports tell of new property acquisitions, of a year when the Investment Corporation gave the college checks totaling $100,925,[28] and of some lean years as well.

The major step forward for the Investment Corporation during the Gotcher years was the decision to build a Christian care center, Tealridge Manor, on property adjacent to the Oklahoma Christian campus. The project is first mentioned in the minutes of November 2, 1984, with subsequent reports telling of the land acquisition and financing. Finally, the minutes record that the center opened on May 15, 1990.

During Gotcher's term as chair, a frequent topic was whether the college should sponsor a Christian high school. Some not associated with Oklahoma Christian had begun a Christian school in Oklahoma City called Living Word Academy that, after a time, fell into financial difficulty. Those operating the high school appealed to the college to take over the work and provide the finances. Such discussions began in 1985 and continued for several years. The majority of the Board thought the college should not embark on a high school project, but there was a vocal minority. A piece of property was left to the college with the understanding it would be used for the education of pre-college youth. When the Board decided not to pursue a high school, the college passed this property on to Living Word, but, through a series of legal tangles, had to make a payment of cash in addition to the transfer of the property. Some of the Board sessions on this topic brought strong differences, and the topic consumed a great amount of time.

The Board also spent considerable time discussing the operation of the ranches Judge Davisson had left the college. By 1987, it had become evident that the college would make a better return on these ranches to sell them and invest the money rather than to run a ranch operation, so the decision was made to sell them all by 1990.[29]

The most important single decision the Board made during the Gotcher years was its choice of a president to succeed Terry Johnson. On May 20, 1995, Johnson informed the Board he wanted to retire by the end of the year. The Board commissioned a presidential selection committee to recommend the best choices, and this committee reported on September 30, 1995. Board member Jack McGraw was chairman, and he, President Terry Johnson, and Dr. Howard Norton, faculty representative, reviewed for the Board the qualifications of each person they were presenting. Then Johnson and Norton withdrew from the meeting, leaving Board members alone for their discussion. By a secret ballot, they chose Kevin Jacobs as the next president of Oklahoma Christian University of Science and Arts.

Deryl Gotcher served the longest term of any Board chairman. He presided over a number of difficult meetings where Board members disagreed on issues, but he held the respect of all the members of the Board in a way that promoted unity. During his term, from 1980 through 1997, the operational budget of the university grew from $6,249,160 to $28,797,162, an indication both of the growth of the institution and the increase in its complexity. After the new president had been installed and had finished his first year, Gotcher decided it was time for a change in the Board chairmanship. The Gotcher Room in the Gaylord University Center is named in honor of this longtime chair.

Ralph Chain

On May 5, 1997, Ralph Chain became the eleventh chairman of the Oklahoma Christian Board of Trustees. Chain had been on the Board since 1977 and on the executive committee since 1989. His father, L. N. Chain, had served on the Board from 1959 to 1987. Ralph Chain owned several large ranch properties and had been very successful in managing them. His cowboys always performed well in the statewide rodeos held for working ranch hands, and he was an elder in the Church of

Ralph Chain

Christ in Canton.

Board officers serving with Chain were Dr. Charles Branch as vice chairman, Dr. Joe Stafford as secretary, and Lyle Harms as treasurer. Two others chosen to join these on the executive committee were Jack McGraw and Charles Floyd.[30]

Dr. Kevin Jacobs had been president at Oklahoma Christian for a year and a half when Chain took office. At that point, the financial situation was tight. In fact, the May 9, 1998, Board minutes reported that $5 million in university assets had been sold to help the cash flow problem.[31] There was, however, some good financial news. In 1997, Enterprise Square reported that it had balanced income and operating expenses for the first time.[32] In 1998, under the leadership of Dr. Lynn McMillon, the *Christian Chronicle* also reported that it had operated within its income.[33]

In view of the university's financial difficulties, the Board felt the need to exercise closer oversight of the budgeting process, and on January 30, 1999, passed a proposal from Don Millican, chair of the Board Finance Committee. This plan outlined a budgeting process for the administration which called for the Board, in its January/February meeting, to approve the basic assumptions for planning the budget starting the following July: number of students expected, anticipated tuition income, scholarship rate, room and board income, and similar key data. In April, the administration would submit to the Board its proposed budget, based on the approved assumptions. In September, the budget for the school year would be revised, based on updated enrollment and income data. In January, following the second-term enrollment, a final revision would be made.[34]

At the Board meeting of June 15, 2000, the Board continued to deal with financial matters. Vice Chairman Branch reported that in the 1999 fiscal year, operating expenses had been $2.7 million more than income, but this had improved for fiscal 2000, with an operating loss of $975,000. There had been, however, a gain of $1.1 million in assets including gifts.[35]

On February 23, 2001, the Board expressed confidence in President Jacob's leadership, saying it was "extremely pleased" with his performance. By the following month, however, on March 6, the Board had become more concerned about the situation and met to review the extent to which capital dollars were being used to pay overruns in operating expenses and other questions about Jacobs' leadership. President Jacobs, aware of the growing concerns, met with Chairman Chain on May 10 to give him a letter of resignation, effective immediately.[36]

At a May 11 conference-call meeting, the Board accepted Jacob's resignation. Dr. Charles Branch, vice chairman of the Board, resigned from the Board at this meeting because he knew his son, Alfred, current executive vice president, would likely be involved in filling the gap left by Jacobs' departure, and he wanted to avoid any appearance of a conflict of interest. At this meeting, in fact, the Board did ask Alfred Branch to serve as acting president until such time as a decision could be made about a new president. Also at this meeting, the Board began discussion of a search process. Chairman Chain advised the Board, "We do not want to be hasty in this process. This will be one of the most important things we do."[37]

The May 11 meeting also saw some changes in Board officers. With Vice Chairman Branch resigning, Don Millican was selected for that position. Terry Childers became secretary and David Seat was elected member-at-large on the executive committee.[38]

The Board met again on May 29 to discuss the selection process. Don Millican was asked to chair the committee, with Millie Roberson and Wayne Warren to be the other two Board members in the group. Paul Strasbaugh, who had for years been an Oklahoma City community leader, was also asked to serve. Ken Miller was chosen as faculty representative, Kyle Wray for the staff, and Kent Allen from the alumni.[39] The Board met almost monthly for a time.

At the June 29 Board meeting, a special time was spent in prayer. Fourteen different members of the Board led prayers on specific topics such as the health of some of its members, the presidential search process, Alfred Branch serving as acting president, the faculty, the students, and other areas of concern.[40]

On July 19, Branch reported to the Board that a staff and faculty reduction plan was being developed which would allow for some early retirements, thus reducing salary costs.[41] By the Board meeting on September 7, the search committee had developed a presidential profile and reported that forty-seven different persons had been recommended for consideration for the position of president.[42]

On December 10, 2001, the search committee presented three names to the Board for their consideration: Alfred Branch, the university's executive vice president and acting president, Dr. Phil Lewis, the current dean of the College of Business, and Dr. Mike O'Neal, vice-chancellor at Pepperdine University. They set January 16 and 17, 2002, as days for these three to go through a campus interview process, and on January 18, the Board met and made O'Neal their choice.[43]

With the selection process completed, Chain stepped out of the chairmanship on February 22, 2002, thus allowing the Board to select a new slate of officers to work with the new president. He had seen the Board and the university through some difficult times. Although enrollment was up and some new facilities graced the campus, there had been financial shortfalls and a difficult transition from one president to another. Chain provided important guidance through this period.[44]

Don Millican

Don Millican joined the OC Board of Trustees in 1996, became vice chair in 2001, and chaired the Board's search committee for Kevin Jacobs' replacement. When Ralph Chain stepped down on February 22, 2002, the Board chose Millican as the next chair. An elder of the Park Plaza Church of Christ in Tulsa, and with many years as national partner in a major accounting firm, he brought

Don Millican

extensive management experience to the role. To serve with him, the Board chose Jack McGraw as vice chair, Lyle Harms as treasurer, and Terry Childers as secretary.[45] A year later, Allison Garrett was named Board secretary.[46]

A review of Board minutes suggests Millican brought a new style of leadership to the Board. On July 20, 2002, for example, the Board adopted a twenty-four page policy manual that stated: "The Board's governing style will emphasize policy, a vision for the future, encouragement and acceptance of diversity in viewpoints, strategic leadership, clear distinctions between Board and staff roles, and pro-activity rather than reactivity."[47]

In this same manual, the Board adopted guidelines for campus construction: any new construction in excess of $1 million must be fully funded before begun and facilities in excess of $2 million must have a maintenance endowment at the time of construction.[48] The policy manual also continued the requirement that "all faculty and senior administrative staff shall be active members of the Churches of Christ."[49]

Even more than in previous periods, the work of the Board was done in committees: purpose, academic affairs, student affairs, finance, advancement/public relations, and resources. The Board developed many standards and projections which they expected the administration to use as guides. On July 18–19, 2003, for example, the Board set enrollment goals for the coming five years: the full-time equivalent goal for undergraduates was set at 1,800 to 2,000, with the graduate goal at 150 to 200. The minimum percentage of undergraduates from Churches of Christ was set at 70 percent and the percentage of undergraduates living on campus was also set at 70 percent. The goal for the average ACT score was set at 24, and the tuition discount rate was to be within the range of 35 to 40 percent. At the same meeting, financial goals were set: within three years, $15 million should be added to the endowment fund, tuition increases should be limited to no more than 2 percent above the increase in the Consumer Price Index, the operating budget should include a minimum contingency fund of 2 percent of its total amount, and spending from endowment funds would begin at 5 percent and gradually be reduced to 4 percent.[50] Setting such targets and policies was clearly a different approach for the Board. They were less involved in operational details and more involved in setting policy and direction. These goals gave the university administration clear guidance and measurable targets by which their work could be evaluated. Some of these targets have been adjusted over the years.

The Board also reviewed various foundation documents on which it operated. Revisions were made, for example, to the university's Articles of Incorporation. In an effort to clarify what was meant by the expression "Churches of Christ," used in the document, the Board ratified the following statement:

> "Churches of Christ" shall mean the individual and aggregate autonomous congregations of Christians whose creed and doctrine are the Word of God, comprised of the canon of the Old Testament and the New Testament without the apocryphal writings or other non-canonical writings. There is voluntary cooperation among most congregations, but no vertical human structure or hierarchy beyond the individual congregation. The Churches of Christ teach salvation through grace, which comes through faith in Jesus Christ as the Son of God and baptism by immersion for the forgiveness of sin. Sunday assemblies of the Churches of Christ are characterized by the Lord's Supper, proclamation of the Word of God, prayers, *a cappella* singing and the periodic collection of donations for the work of the church. The Churches of Christ in America trace their heritage from the establishment of the Church on the day of Pentecost as recorded in Acts 2, through the Restoration Movement of the 1800's, and are committed to the restoration of the Church as found in the inspired writings of the New Testament.[51]

The Board considered this clarifying statement to be necessary since their policies required all members of the Board and all faculty and major administrators to be members of the Church of Christ.

Millican also incorporated more prayer into Board meetings, which began with prayer as they always had, but now often started with devotionals and, on many occasions, involved prayers for specific topics with which the Board was dealing or prayers for specific people. At the meeting of February 21, 2003, Millican

> asked that each Trustee focus ongoing prayer efforts for their areas of responsibility. He encouraged Trustees and administrators to keep prayer an integral part of our institution. We cannot do all that is needed, but God can if we are willing to loosen our grip and allow God to be in control of our lives and this institution.[52]

On November 8, 2002, the Board initiated a new policy of "life trustees." As Board members reached a senior status, they would be appointed to the new position which invited them to all meetings and to participate in the sessions, but without voting privileges. This policy would allow older members to continue to be part of Board meetings but, at the same time, would allow for the addition of younger persons to the Board. Those first appointed to the new status were William Beeman, Karl Berg, Daryl Bond, Dr. Charles Branch, Joseph Hargis, Glenn Hetrick, Allen Reese, Dale Roberts, and Phillip Winn.[53]

On July 18–19, 2003, the Board adopted more goals, these related to student development: to "emphasize the essentiality of submitting every facet of life to the Lordship of Jesus Christ," "nurture a climate of excellence in every aspect of the university's work," "strengthen ties with and serve Churches of Christ," "nurture and mature the faith of all students, faculty, and staff," and "serve all students who seek to grow intellectually and spiritually—both those who are members of the Churches of Christ and those who are not."[54] The first academic goal listed was to "integrate faith and learning in every aspect of the university's work and champion the truths of Christianity while encouraging free and responsible investigation in scholarly pursuits, in accordance with the university's mission."[55]

As Millican continued to refocus the Board, he brought as a resource Dr. Robert Walker, vice president of development for Texas A&M University and a member of Pepperdine University's Board of Trustees. He addressed the Board at its November 7 meeting on "Why I am a Member of the Board at Oklahoma Christian." He spoke on various aspects of the work of Board members with an emphasis on the role of the Board in fundraising.[56]

In this meeting, the Board approved more goals for the administration: full-time faculty members should teach 80 percent of the courses, 70 to 75 percent of the faculty should hold terminal degrees, 40 to 45 percent of the budget should be allocated to instruction, and the racial/ethnic diversity should include 6 to 8 percent from minority groups.[57]

On November 7, 2003, the Board also approved the College of Biblical Studies to offer a Master of Divinity degree, endorsed the new statement called "The OC Covenant," which all students, faculty and staff were to observe, and agreed to a goal of $1 million for the Board to raise. At this meeting, Jack McGraw resigned because of ill health and Lyle Harms was chosen to replace him as vice chair; Todd Dobson replaced Harms as treasurer.[58]

At the next meeting, April 2, 2004, Millican reported for the Finance Committee that there "had been a $5 million dollar turnaround in the budget, showing a substantial improvement in the overall finances of the university."[59] He also reported that Cascade would have a "positive bottom line" for the year.[60] Obviously, President O'Neal and the Board were making important strides in the financial condition of the university. Because of this progress, the administration was able to propose, and the Board approved, a major new initiative in university housing for a total of $33,900,000. This amount would provide renovation of some existing residence halls, build a new major dormitory, and provide additional apartment units. For several years, the Board had been aware student housing needed to be both increased and improved. With the financial situation of the university much improved, they were able to take this major step. Most of the funds would be borrowed and then repaid with income from the housing facilities.

The October 29, 2004, meeting covered two major items. First, the Board adopted a new statement of purpose for themselves:

> The primary purpose of the Board of Trustees is to establish the spiritual and academic mission of the University and to ensure that the mission is effectively and efficiently accomplished. In fulfilling its role as guardian of the University mission, the Board of Trustees will conduct its business principally through the employment and empowerment of the chief executive officer, setting of broad board policy, and monitoring compliance with policy. In carrying out its duties, the Board of Trustees possesses all the powers of the corporation and is responsible to conduct all the business affairs of the corporation, including the establishment and operation of a non-profit institution for general education purposes in which the Holy Scriptures, arts, and sciences shall always be taught, together with such courses of instruction and such extracurricular programs as shall be deemed advisable by the Board of Trustees.[61]

Also at the October 29 meeting, David North presented a report from the Athletic Program Strategic Task Force, recommending the employment of a full-time athletic director, reinstating the baseball program, an increase in athletic scholarships, improvement in facilities, and a significant athletic fundraising program. Sherri Coale, OCC alumna and head women's basketball coach for the University of Oklahoma, was a member of the task force and spoke in support of the program. Dr. O'Neal indicated that the Strategic Vision Committee of the university had approved the plan and that it had his support. The Board expressed "its enthusiastic support of the general vision set forth in the report and encourages the Task Force to proceed with the furtherance of this vision, subject to the requirement of raising adequate resources principally from new sources and subject to the final plan and implementation thereof being approved through the appropriate University channels."[62]

In addition to approving the large housing initiative during the Millican years, the Board also approved a project to build a pavilion and tower as well as major landscaping improvements between the residence halls on the west and the Mabee Learning Center on the east. The total cost of this project, called Lawson Commons, completed in March 2008, was $2.2 million.[63]

At the October 28, 2005, meeting of the Board, the group amended its bylaws to allow Board membership to rise as high as fifty. Such a change would allow wider geographic representation and greater diversity of occupations, and it would also increase the amount of funds for the institution coming from members of the Board.[64] At the meeting on March 25, 2006, Board officers serving with Millican were changed to Dr. Mark Brewer as vice chair, Ken Parker as secretary, and Todd Dobson as treasurer.[65]

During the years Don Millican has served as Board chair, the Board has experienced a major change in operational pattern. They have come to operate primarily through setting goals and standards and then evaluating the extent to which these are being met. In addition, more of the details are handled through Board committees. Millican attends many campus events such as opening chapels, graduations, and special dinners where his presence has provided a useful tie between the campus and the Board of Trustees.

In the Spring 2007 issue of *Vision*, a publication for OC alumni and friends, Chairman Millican mentioned a study the Board had done to review institutions of higher education that had abandoned their Christian mission. He said six common factors had been identified: friction between Christian doctrine and academic freedom, trustees with more loyalty to the institution than to the Christian mission, putting the spiritual mission on the margin by the demise of chapel and separation of faith and learning in the classroom, presidential initiatives that compromised the mission, too many tenured faculty who were unsupportive of the mission, and breaking ties with the founding church and financial independence from them. As these factors played out over time, Millican wrote, the institutions left their original purposes. "If we are committed to continuing the Christian mission of Oklahoma Christian University, which we deeply are, then we must take these factors seriously and set policies to address them."[66]

Board Members of Special Note

In addition to those who have served as Board chairs, others deserve special mention.

Three Board members have come from the Maple family. From 1947 until 1961, John H. Maple of Cleveland, Kansas, served on the Board. A farmer and a deacon in the church at Kingman, Kansas, he had a strong interest in training Christian youth. In addition to serving on the Boards of Harper Christian College and Central

Christian College, in 1953, he started Silver Maple Camp on land his father homesteaded in 1877. His son, James S. ("Jim") Maple, came on the Board in 1951 and served until 1996. An elder of the church in Antlers, Oklahoma, Jim Maple owned an automobile dealership in partnership with his father-in-law, George O'Neal, Sr., the grandfather of OC president Mike O'Neal. Jim Maple's forty-five years on the Board is the record for the most

James S. Maple

years served. He was a generous donor to the university and his son, Dr. John Maple, has been on the history faculty at OC since 1977. S. Beach Maple of Wichita, Kansas, a nephew of John H. Maple, is the third Maple family member to serve on the OC Board of Trustees. The building inspection superintendent for the City of Wichita, Kansas, Beach Maple served on the Board from 1954 to 1961.[67]

Jesse G. Stratton

Jesse G. Stratton is another of those whose Board service spanned many years. A rancher "from the short grass country" of western Oklahoma, he came on the Board in 1955 and served until 1990, a total of thirty-five years. Stratton was secretary of the Board for a time and then served as vice chairman from 1968 to 1990. These twenty-two years in one office on the Board is the longest time of service in the same office for any Board member. The most frequent item in Board minutes connected with Stratton's name is a motion of appreciation for someone connected with the university. His son, J. G. Stratton, Jr, also served on the Board for five years, from 1985 to 1990.

Conclusion

The university owes a great debt to the 145 different persons who have served on the Oklahoma Christian University Board of Trustees. Some of these started the effort to locate a Christian college at Pryor in army surplus buildings after World War II. When that effort was abandoned, other Board members picked up the dream and led in getting a college started in Bartlesville. These Board members persevered under a very difficult financial situation to keep the college going, often digging deeply into their own pockets. This Board also agreed to move the college from Bartlesville to Oklahoma City—a difficult decision, but one that has proved to be wise. Later Board members have chosen presidents, set policies, approved construction of new facilities, dealt with numerous problems, and kept the spiritual aims foremost.

One of the key factors in the success of the Oklahoma Christian Board has been the long tenure of many of its members. As of 2007, a total of twenty-six Board members have served for twenty years or more. While many others have made very important contributions to the work of the Board, these deserve special note for their longevity. Even though some of these continued for an even longer period as life trustees, the list below provides the names and years of their regular membership on the Board.

James S. Maple (1951–1996)	45 years
Leon Lugar (1962–2001)	39 years
C. A. Buchanan (1964–1980; 1981–2004)	39 years
La Moine Neal (1966–2003)	37 years
J. E. Wright (1947–1984)	37 years
Dr. Jack Stephenson (1968–2004)	36 years
Jesse G. Stratton (1955–1990)	35 years
Henry Oldham (1954–1989)	35 years
Dr. John Sudbury (1969–2003)	34 years
Dr. Ralph Owens (1956–1989)	33 years
J. E. Novak (1947–1979)	32 years
Ralph Chain (1977–2008)	31 years
Dr. Joe Stafford (1966–1995)	29 years
Deryl Gotcher (1968–1997)	29 years
L. N. Chain (1959–1987)	28 years
Phil Winn (1968–1996)	28 years
Ralph Fails (1966–1993)	27 years
Lyle Harms (1981–present)	27 years
William Beeman ((1972–1995)	23 years
Vernon Newell (1962–1983; 1995–1997)	23 years
Joe Dodson (1981–2003)	22 years
Charles Floyd (1979–2001)	22 years
Glenn Durrill (1947–1968)	21 years
Allen Reese (1976–1996)	20 years
Glenn Alexander (1982–2002)	20 years
Riley Cavin (1969–1989)	20 years

Certainly the men and women who have served on the Oklahoma Christian University Board of Trustees have been a major factor in the origin, growth, and progress of the university. With little public acknowledgement, they have poured into the university their time, money, and spirit, and by their commitment have played a highly significant role in its success.

Chapter 5, Endnotes

[1]   Chester A Grimes, "The Beginning of Central Christian College," First Annual Central Christian College Lectureship, March 27, 1951, OC Archives.

[2]   L. R. Wilson, "Many Thanks to the Board of Directors," *Central Christian College Bulletin,* August 1954, OC Archives.

[3]   Minutes, Board of Trustees, July 31, 1947, OC Archives. Filed on January 22, 1948.

[4]   Minutes, Board of Trustees, March 31, 1959, OC Archives.

[5]   Ibid.

[6]   Minutes, Board of Trustees, April 19, 1959, OC Archives.

[7]   Minutes, Board of Trustees, Building Committee, June 7, 1960, OC Archives.

[8]   Minutes, Board of Trustees, June 14, 1961, OC Archives.

[9]   "New College Ready in Year, President Says," *Bartlesville Examiner-Enterprise,* August 31, 1949, Ruth Wilson Scrapbook, 2, OC Archives.

[10]   Minutes, Board of Trustees, October 28, 1955, OC Archives.

[11]   Minutes, Board of Trustees, October 17, 1959, OC Archives.

[12]   F. D. Moon, "Higher Education and Desegregation in Oklahoma," *Journal of Negro Education,* Summer, 1958, 300-301.

[13]   Minutes, Board of Trustees, March 31, 1960, OC Archives.

[14]   "Door Opens to Negroes," *Oklahoma City Times*, March 29, 1961, OC Archives.

[15]   John C. Stevens, *No Ordinary University* (Abilene, Texas: Abilene Christian University Press, 1998), 269-273.

[16]   Minutes, Board of Trustees, March 28, 1961, OC Archives.

[17]   *Aerie*, 1962, 72, OC Archives.

[18]   Minutes, Board of Trustees, October 27, 1961, OC Archives.

[19]   Minutes, Board of Trustees, February 11, 1964, OC Archives.

[20]   Minutes, Board of Trustees, February 9, 1965, OC Archives.

[21]   Minutes, Board of Trustees, February 8, 1967, OC Archives.

[22]   "G. A. Hale Dies; Headed Board of Trustees 5 Years," *Oklahoma Christian College Bulletin*, September 1967, OC Archives.

[23]   Minutes, Board of Trustees, March 2, 1967, OC Archives.

[24]   Minutes, Board of Trustees, June 1, 1967, OC Archives.

[25]   Minutes, Board of Trustees, April 18, 1967, OC Archives.

[26]   Minutes, Board of Trustees, Executive Committee, July 7, 1969, OC Archives.

[27]   Minutes, Board of Trustees, May 25, 1985, OC Archives.

[28]   Minutes, Board of Trustees, May 21, 1983, OC Archives.

[29]   Minutes, Board of Trustees, November 13, 1987, OC Archives.

[30]   Minutes, Board of Trustees, March 1, 1997, OC Archives.

[31]   Minutes, Board of Trustees, May 9, 1998, OC Archives.

[32]   Minutes, Board of Trustees, November 7, 1997, OC Archives.

[33]   Minutes, Board of Trustees, May 9, 1998, OC Archives.

[34]   Minutes, Board of Trustees, January 30, 1999, OC Archives.

[35]   Minutes, Board of Trustees, June 15, 2000, OC Archives.

[36]   Minutes, Board of Trustees, May 11, 2001, OC Archives.

[37]   Ibid.

[38]   Ibid.

[39]   Minutes, Board of Trustees, May 29, 2001, OC Archives.

[40]   Minutes, Board of Trustees, June 29, 2001, OC Archives.

[41]   Minutes, Board of Trustees, July 19, 2001, OC Archives.

[42]   Minutes, Board of Trustees, September 7, 2001, OC Archives.

[43]   Minutes, Board of Trustees, January 17-18, 2002, OC Archives.

[44]   Minutes, Board of Trustees, February 22-23, 2002, OC Archives.

[45]   Ibid.

[46]   Minutes, Board of Trustees, February 21, 2004, OC Archives.

[47]   Board of Trustees Policy Manual, Adopted July 20, 2002, 2, OC Archives.

[48]   Ibid., 19.

[49]   Ibid., 24.

[50] Minutes, Board of Trustees, July 18-19, 2003, OC Archives.
[51] Minutes, Board of Trustees, February 21, 2003, OC Archives.
[52] Ibid.
[53] Minutes, Board of Trustees, November 8, 2002, OC Archives.
[54] Minutes, Board of Trustees, July 18-19, 2003, OC Archives.
[55] Ibid.
[56] Minutes, Board of Trustees, November 7, 2003, OC Archives.
[57] Ibid.
[58] Ibid.
[59] Minutes, Board of Trustees, April 2, 2004, OC Archives.
[60] Ibid.
[61] Minutes, Board of Trustees, October 29, 2004, OC Archives.
[62] Ibid.
[63] Minutes, Board of Trustees, July 9, 2005, OC Archives.
[64] Minutes, Board of Trustees, October 28, 2005, OC Archives.
[65] Minutes, Board of Trustees, March 25, 2006, OC Archives.
[66] "Q & A with the Chairman," *Vision*, Spring 2007.
[67] Information from Dr. John Maple, January 15, 2007.

Chapter 6
THE KEY DECISIONS

In the history of Oklahoma Christian University, its leadership has made many key decisions, most of which are described in other chapters. Six very important decisions, however, because of their significance and complexity, deserve separate consideration: becoming a senior college, building the Learning Center, establishing the Oklahoma Christian Investment Corporation, building Enterprise Square, moving to university status, and adding Cascade College in Portland, Oregon.

The Expansion to Senior College

Although Central Christian College began in Bartlesville offering a two-year program, its goal was always to be a senior college. According to a report in the *Bartlesville Examiner-Enterprise*, President L. R. Wilson told a meeting of the Bartlesville Rotary Club in the summer of 1950:

> "Central Christian College is no junior college," although it is at first offering only two years of college work. The third and fourth year classes will be added as demand develops, he said. He expressed the hope that the additions might be made in three or four years, but said it might be "five or ten," because of the extensive laboratory and library facilities that would be demanded.[1]

Wilson's fourth number was right on target—in May of 1959, almost exactly ten years after Wilson's speech, the college made the following announcement:

> Beginning in September of 1960, Central Christian College will become a senior college, the Board of Trustees announced this week. The third year of college work will be added during the year of 1960–61 and the fourth year during the year of 1961–62. This means that the present freshman class and all those who enroll next year will be able to complete four years of work at Central Christian.[2]

The article in the *Central Christian College Bulletin* continued by giving three primary reasons for the change:

> Those interested in the college have, from the first, believed that the college would best serve the need for which it was created by offering four years of college work. A second important reason is that our enrollment is now increasing to the size that a senior college is becoming feasible. A third factor is that in many circles funds are available for senior colleges which are not available to junior colleges.[3]

The plan gave the administration and faculty the 1959–1960 year to prepare for the change, and the advance announcement allowed recruiting new freshmen on the basis of the coming four-year program.

The same May 1959 issue of the *Bulletin* also noted that starting in September 1959, the institution would change its name from Central Christian College to Oklahoma Christian College. The primary reason for this change was to avoid confusion with Central State College, located just three miles to the north.[4]

According to an article in the *Bulletin* of July, 1960,

Clarence Buller and helpers change the sign at Kelly and Memorial Road.

> During the entire school year just concluded, the Oklahoma Christian College faculty has given considerable thought to the preparation of the program to be offered as the school expands to senior college. Under the leadership of a steering committee composed of Mrs. Retta Scott Garrett, Harold Fletcher, Joseph Jones, Mrs. Oma Carter, and Stafford North, the faculty agreed upon graduation requirements and the fields of study to be offered.[5]

The article listed four bachelor's degree programs to be available: Bible, science, business, and education. The education programs included elementary education and six fields of secondary education. In developing the requirements, the faculty had consulted personnel directors of major business firms, Tinker Field, and the University of Oklahoma, had visited ten other colleges, and had reviewed many college catalogs.[6] Dr. James Fellows, dean of admissions and registrar at the University of Oklahoma, said OU would accept the third and fourth year classes, and would recommend the same action to others.[7] In July of 1961, just before adding the senior year, the State Department of Education agreed to certify OCC students finishing in May of 1962, even though the college had not yet received its official approval as a teacher training institution.[8]

On June 1, 1962, nineteen seniors became the first four-year graduates of Oklahoma Christian College. Nine received degrees in education, six in Bible, three in science, and one in business. Two of these would later return to teach at Oklahoma Christian: Gary Shreck and Gary Rayburn.[9]

The decision to move to senior college had immediate impact on enrollment. In 1958, the year just before the announcement, fall enrollment was 209, up only 18 from the previous year. In the fall of 1959, the beginning of the year spent in preparing, fall enrollment grew to 245. In 1960, when third-year courses were added, enrollment was 323, and the following year, when the first four-year graduates finished, the student numbers increased to 379. In the year after the first bachelor's degrees were bestowed, enrollment jumped to 481.[10]

Obviously, the administration and Board were right in their timing. The new campus in Oklahoma City provided facilities for expansion and students were interested. Since the college had built a good reputation in the educational community, its bachelor's degrees would be accepted. The consultation with others both broadened acceptability and provided good information from which to design quality programs.

The Learning Center

In 1958, when Central Christian College opened its new campus in Oklahoma City, the library occupied the 4,800 square feet in the eastern half of what later was named Cogswell-Alexander Hall, now the Registrar's Office. This library on the OCC campus was a great step forward from the cramped library facilities in Bartlesville, and the shelving and seating were all new. Starting in the new location with 7,500 volumes, the holdings grew rapidly. By 1962–1963, the number of books had risen to 20,000,[11] and student enrollment had grown from 209 to 481.[12] Clearly, the administration and librarian needed to begin planning for additional facilities.

As the need for more library space mounted, in August 1962, President James Baird attended a meeting for the Council for the Advancement of Small Colleges in Boston, sponsored by the Educational Facilities Division of the Ford Foundation. At this session, Dr. Baird made contact with Dr. Glenn Nimnich of the Ford Foundation staff, who soon came to speak at Oklahoma Christian. While on the campus, Nimnich mentioned that "one probable improvement of faculty efficiency could be achieved by the use of recorded materials with electronic access."[13]

These comments impressed Dr. Baird. He had been hearing dire predictions about the future of small, private colleges, and knew they would have to be innovative and creative to survive. Achieving greater efficiency in the learning process could certainly be a great help. Baird also knew that his chances of funding a new library facility would be enhanced if that building were more than just a conventional library.

About this same time, Baird and the OCC administrative team heard of other institutions who were installing carrels to provide students with individual study space, and in a few places, these carrels were being equipped with a dial system for access to pre-recorded audio learning materials.

Baird charged Business Manager W. O. Beeman and Dean of Instruction Stafford North to prepare a proposal he could submit to the Ford Foundation. Since the Foundation had helped instigate the idea, Baird thought that if OCC could be the first to present a proposal, they might fund it.[14]

By October 5, 1962, North and Beeman had written a three-page proposal to provide carrels in which students could listen to audiotapes, sometimes with many students listening to a tape at the same time, and, at other times, listening individually. The key ingredient, which no one had attempted before, was that every student enrolled in the college would have his or her own personal carrel. Thus, said the proposal, "For a student body of 1,000, there will be required 1,000 electronically equipped carrels. Each carrel will contain an electronic speaker, a set of earphones, and a three digit dial switching mechanism."[15]

This statement became the basis of an October 26, 1962, proposal to the Ford Foundation for funding, but no funding came. The germ, however, had been planted, and administrators continued to pursue the possibilities. To build a new facility utilizing the proposed concept, Dr. Baird secured a grant of $279,850 from the federal government's Educational Facilities Act,[16] and funds from several private donors, including $125,000 from the Mabee Foundation. The funding plan also included a loan to be repaid by a $30 a term carrel-use fee from each student.[17]

With the funding in hand, the work proceeded on two separate but related fronts. On November 11, 1963, the college awarded the contract for the building design to Caudill, Rowlett, and Scott, even though the decisions about the carrels and the dial system had not yet been finalized.[18] On the second front, Oklahoma Christian contacted major electronics companies such as RCA, International Telephone and Telegraph, Stromberg-Carlson, Webster Electric, and others to seek their assistance in designing a dialing system to meet the college's specifications.[19] After eighteen months of such investigation, W. O. Beeman, in a June 23, 1964, memo to Dr. Baird, said he and Dr. North had concluded that North Electric Company of Galion, Ohio, produced the best equipment for controlling the dial system, and they had estimated that the equipment for the Oklahoma Christian project would cost $250,000 plus the cost of installation and the cost of developing the specifications.[20] Beeman recommended that an Oklahoma City firm, C. H. Guernsey & Company, be employed to do the engineering work. They had proposed the best price, $11,500, and working with them to develop the specifications would be simpler because they were local.[21] Baird approved the Guernsey proposal and the company, working with Dr. North, prepared a twenty-five page document that became the basis of the bids for the electronic equipment.

Opening of the Learning Center

On September 4, 1964, Oklahoma Christian signed a contract with Barbour & Short of Norman, Oklahoma, to construct the 50,000 square foot, three-story Learning Center at a price of $543,621. On February 5, 1965, the college accepted the North Electric proposal to provide the switching system, audiotape decks, and related equipment for a total of $253,953. The final major piece was to purchase the 706 carrels for the existing student body. The Suttle Equipment Corporation of Lawrenceville, Illinois, won this contract for $70,600.[22] By the time new library stacks, tables and chairs, furnishings, a recording studio, and equipment for other parts of the facility were added, the total cost of the project was $1,056,432.[23]

The building was ready by the start of the fall term in 1965. On the first floor, the library moved into space for 50,000 books and a seating capacity of 110. The American Citizenship Center also had space on the first floor.

Students in the library

The electronic equipment and carrels, however, were a different matter. For one thing, there had been a delay in the delivery of the carrels. The first truck load had arrived with wooden legs instead of the specified steel, and North, not even letting the truck unload, sent them back to Suttle Equipment Corporation. Eventually the carrels arrived as specified.

Then the control panel for the switching system arrived from North Electric, composed of four pre-wired racks of equipment that could not be separated. The four connected racks were too large to be carried up the stairs to the third floor control room, so how could they be put in place? The contractor took out a window on the north end of the Learning Center's third floor and brought in a crane large enough handle a platform on which the racks could sit. The crane raised the platform slightly above the level of the third floor, and from that platform workers extended railroad ties from the platform slightly downward to the level of the third floor. Using pipes as rollers, they then

Equipment racks

pushed the racks down the railroad ties to the third floor where other workers were waiting to receive them. A hundred thousand dollars worth of equipment was at stake, but it worked.

John Morrison, an OCC physics teacher who had been employed to run the technical side of the Learning Center, worked with his crew of students to install the carrels and the wiring, much of it over the Christmas holidays of 1965. By the beginning of classes in January of 1966, all was in operation.[24]

Students installing carrels

The educational concept behind the Learning Center was that using audiotapes in various ways could both improve student learning and increase teacher efficiency. The Learning Center control center had 46 audiotape decks that could play up to 136 audio recordings at the same time. A daily published schedule told students when tapes for group listening would be played so a student in any carrel could dial the number at the designated time and hear that tape while others listened at the same time. Other recordings were available for individual dial-up at any time a student might wish. Thus, students could come to their individually assigned carrels, available from seven in the morning to eleven at night, and use that space for any type of study—reading, writing papers, and preparing assignments, as well as dialing audiotapes designated for students in a particular class to hear. Once the center was in full operation, the average number of calls was 3,500 a day.

The plan offered many benefits. First, students had a personal study space much more conducive for learning than a dorm room or even a table in the library with people walking by. The three-and-a-half by four foot carrel provided a desktop for work, a small side shelf for a typewriter, a lockable storage cabinet, and two acoustic side panels to give the student quiet and freedom from interruption. Second, students could use the audio materials prepared or selected by their teachers for supplemental learning. Third, in some cases, teachers provided exercises and lessons for

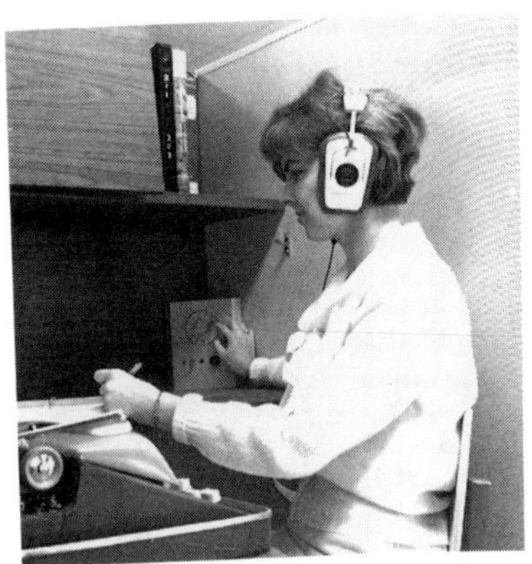

Student working in a carrel

students that replaced some class meeting times, thus allowing more efficiency for the teacher.

Student Alice Ann Conway wrote, "The Learning Center has helped me a great deal both socially and academically. It not only provides a student the opportunity to listen to lectures and such at his own convenience, it also speeds up the learning process by the student's hearing, seeing, and writing at the same time as he fills out worksheets accompanying tapes. This was especially helpful in many of my classes."[25]

Perhaps the most challenging part of the whole process, however, was getting faculty to prepare the materials for students to use. Faculty members typically like to teach their students using the methods by which they were taught. North, who had been appointed as director of the Learning Center in addition to his role as dean of instruction, developed the first course as a pilot program.

He made sixteen audiotapes of about forty-five minutes in length for use in the beginning speech class. Included were audio excerpts from great speakers to illustrate various techniques. Students could listen to these tapes and, at the same time, use worksheets for completing blanks, taking notes, seeing visuals, and completing exercises. Since the sixteen tapes covered all the basic content typically presented in class lectures, the number of class

John Morrison records Hugh McHenry

meetings per week was reduced from three to two with one day each week primarily for discussion and the other for student speeches.

Harold Fletcher developed audiotapes for listening to music in which he overlaid the music track with his comments on the techniques of the composer and the musicians. Jim Wilson traveled to Washington, D. C., to interview members of Congress and other government officials about their role in the political process, and made these audiotapes available to his government class. Raymond Kelcy made tapes to summarize the week's work in Greek so students could review it as often as needed. Hugo McCord placed lecture material on tape so students could listen while using worksheets. Other teachers provided tapes on foreign languages, math, shorthand dictation at various speeds, poets reading their own poetry, and recordings of plays so students could hear the performance while following the text. Freshman composition courses had tapes to instruct on elements of writing, education courses taught how to write instructional objectives and do statistics, and biology tapes provided information on mitosis and other topics. In all, some thirty-five courses were revised to a greater or lesser extent to use such methods.

A crucial part of the whole program was encouraging the faculty to participate. The college brought experts annually to work with faculty members, provided release time for teachers to develop materials, paid teachers for summer work on projects, offered funds for travel and consultation, and held a dinner each year for teachers working on projects so they could share with each other.[26]

The college also brought to campus those from other colleges and universities to tell of their work in similar activities. In addition, many faculty sessions offered the opportunity to discuss course design, writing objectives, and learning techniques. In a paper entitled "The Progression of OCC's Educational Philosophy," North wrote:

In the process of developing materials in a different format and in making changes in class meeting arrangements to utilize some recorded materials, something began happening to the whole academic structure at OCC. More flexibility had to be provided such as allowing teachers to develop completely different structures for their meetings with students. A three-hour class, which formerly met for three one-hour sessions per week, might meet only two hours a week with tape recordings being used to provide some of the instruction previously done in class. At the same time, another three-hour class might be meeting in one large group once a week and in several small groups once a week. As teachers began to see that many different arrangements could be useful in particular classes, a host of possibilities became evident. Not only were teachers' "eyes opened" to many scheduling possibilities, but as they were working on the uses of audiotapes for teaching, they also began to see possibilities in many other media they had not used before. Requests for films, overhead projectors, videotapes, programmed materials, and other media began to grow rapidly.

With a faculty and staff now willing to accept change and looking for better ways in which to teach, the next step came with the introduction of the systems approach to instruction. Just as the systems approach of setting specific goals and designing an exact program for reaching those goals has become an important technique in such areas as management, space exploration, research and other areas, it has also been introduced into education. While such an approach certainly did not originate at OCC, the OCC faculty and administration were at an appropriate stage to accept and utilize it. This systems approach in instruction means a much more exact statement of objectives and a more realistic measurement of the results of instruction. It means a more careful designing of learning experiences in order to assist students in reaching these objectives, and it means more adaptation to the individual needs of students.[27]

The Learning Center, with its private student carrels and dial-access to audiotapes, brought great attention to the OCC campus. Dr. Sam Baskin of Antioch College, one of America's leading colleges in innovation, wrote in an *Oklahoma City Times* article, "I consider this the boldest experiment in higher education I've seen in relation to the potential uses of media and technology combined with the individual study concept."[28] Dr. Benjamin Fine, in a nationally syndicated column of August 13, 1967, quoted Baskin's assessment and added, "Through this center, the college is revolutionizing the whole approach to teaching and learning."[29]

Almost immediately after the opening of the center, North was in demand as a speaker at many educational conferences such as a meeting of the Division of Audiovisual Instruction of the NEA at San Diego, the National Audiovisual-Programmed Instruction Conference at the University of Oklahoma, the Conference on Innovation in Higher Education at Magnolia, Massachusetts,[30] and the National Bookmakers Conference in Bermuda.

Stories about the OCC Learning Center appeared in a host of publications. The *National Observer* carried one of the first on February 14, 1966. Just a few days later, came an article in *Time* magazine of February 18, 1966, entitled "Happiness is Your own Carrel." The two-column story with a picture said, "This is 15-year old Oklahoma Christian College, a theologically conservative, Churches of Christ-run school, which, though academically obscure, has just opened the nation's first wholly electronic learning center." In May 1966, *College and University Business* published a four-page article with pictures. George Kiseda wrote an article with pictures appearing in *Parade* magazine, the nationwide Sunday supplement, entitled "Hello, Shakespeare, Are You There?" *College Management* carried a full-page story in October of 1968, in which Dr. North wrote that the key was "strategy, not equipment." North also wrote a four-page article in the September 1966 *Tennessee Teacher* entitled "Personalization by Mechanization." There was even a two-page spread in *Esquire*.

And there were more. North wrote a six-page article for the *American Journal of Pharmaceutical Education*, December of 1966, and in the *National Observer* for February 14, 1966. Other articles appeared in *The Speech Teacher* of September 1967, *Audiovisual Instruction* of May 1967, *International Science and Technology* of August, 1967, the *Christian Science Monitor* of June 1, 1968, and *Educational Technology* in December 1969. Newspapers all over the country carried wire service reports.

All of this attention brought many educators to the Oklahoma Christian campus to see the program firsthand. By 1970, five hundred colleges and universities had sent representatives to observe, and Oklahoma Christian had prepared a packet of written materials both for the visitors and for those making inquiries. The college also prepared an audiotape with a workbook called "The Sound of Learning," which utilized the tape-workbook method of instruction to teach the tape-workbook method of instruction. At $6 a set, the college sold 500 copies. North developed a fifteen-minute color-slide show with audiotape called "The College and the Leopard," which made the point that, while a leopard cannot change his spots, a college can change its methods. Fifty institutions requested this presentation.[31] College personnel were in frequent demand to speak at major educational gatherings.

Oklahoma Christian initiated studies on the effectiveness of its new patterns of instruction. The first study, made possible by a $70,000 grant from the U.S. Department of Education, compared the outcomes of two speech classes, one taught with the conventional three meetings a week and the other with two meetings a week plus North's forty-five minute audiotapes with worksheets played weekly. The results of this study showed "that students did equally well under either plan but the system using the tapes could make a teacher 60 percent more productive in the number of students taught. And students preferred the plan which combined tapes with fewer class meetings by 8 to 1."[32] Another study revealed "a 15 percent increase in student study time" and "a 40 percent increase in two-week library checkouts," when comparing OCC student practices before the Learning Center was built with those after.

Dr. Sidney G. Tickton, executive vice president of the Academy of Educational Development, Inc., did the major study on the Learning Center's effectiveness in learning outcomes. To assist with the study, Tickton engaged Dr. Jack Edling and members of his staff at Teaching Research, a Division of the Oregon State System of Higher Education. Funding for the study came from the Arthur Vining Davis Foundation, the Xerox Corporation, and the U.S. Steel Foundation.

In the summary of his findings, Tickton wrote that the study showed there was "no evidence that learning suffers and some very slight evidence it may have improved," that "the use of the audio-tape facility can result in increased instructional efficiency in terms of money," and that the OCC program "apparently also enables the student to obtain more personal feedback."[33]

In his letter to President Baird, Tickton wrote, "You are far ahead of other institutions which have installed dial-access systems." "The equipment is good and functioning; the technical skill to run and maintain the system is excellent; the students use the materials regularly and the faculty has prepared them carefully."[34]

In his letter, Edling said he had spent the last two school years visiting all fifty states to observe "innovative programs." He mentions a few places that had tried to "free things up," but had often met resistance. "The one exception that I have encountered is Oklahoma Christian College. The difference here is that it is not a piecemeal effort. When every student has an individual study carrel and is afforded the opportunity to complete a major portion of his work at a time and at a rate convenient to him, the effort is more than piecemeal. There is a dedication from the President of the institution and extending throughout the administrative and instructional staff to try to make a new system work. If they can succeed the model could be of considerable significance to higher education."[35]

Four major educational conferences were held on the OCC campus because of interest in the Learning Center. The first was a seminar sponsored by the college itself called, "What Are We Learning About Learning Centers?" On March 3, 1971, the conference brought more than 150 persons to hear some of America's leading educators: Dr. Earl J. McGrath, former U.S. commissioner of education; Dr. Harold B. Gores, president of the Educational Facilities Laboratories; and Dr. Wesley C. Meierhenry of the University of Nebraska. William F. May, president of the American Can Company also spoke, as did Dr. Stafford North and Dr. Marshall Gunselman from the college and Tom Glover, architect for the OCC Learning Center. The proceedings were published in a hardback book of a little over two hundred pages, made possible through a grant from the Esso Foundation.[36]

The second conference, in the 1972-1973 academic year, featured the former U.S. Commissioner of Education, Sterling McMurrin.[37] The theme for this conference was "The Human Dimension of Instructional Technology."

The NEA's Division of Audio-Visual Instruction brought the third conference. The three-day event, held in early August of 1974, brought more than a hundred specialists interested in improving learning through the use of various audio-visual methods. The conference, of course, offered a chance to display the Learning Center and its programs.

Oklahoma Christian also sponsored a conference on October 23, 1974, called "Teaching and Technology." The four speakers for the day were B. Lamar Johnson, professor at UCLA and executive director of the League for Innovation, who delivered the keynote address on teaching and technology; James T. Holderman, Jr., vice president for education at the Lilly Endowment, who spoke on "Foundations Respond to Teaching and Technology"; Pat Haggerty, chairman of the Board of Texas Instruments, who reviewed coming advances in technology for teaching; and Stafford North of Oklahoma Christian, who surveyed successful programs using technology.

In 1971, college officials decided it was time to expand the Learning Center building. Dr. Baird obtained a $552,000 grant from the Mabee foundation for the new addition, and the remaining $448,000 came from a drive among local businesses.[38] The new space added two-story wings on the east and west sides of the building. These wings allowed expansion of library space on the first floor, and, on the second floor, provided offices and classrooms for the English Department on the east side, and a television studio, photo studio, dial-system control room, and classrooms on the west side.

Several factors converged, however, to bring the dial access system and the private study carrels to an end. By the early eighties, the OCC dial equipment was outdated, making repairs and replacement very expensive. About this same time, computers were cheaper and more common as a learning tool. In addition, education at Oklahoma Christian was becoming more specialized in that students in art spent their time in art studios and not so much in carrels, students in science had specialized labs and research projects, and students in business worked in their department's computer lab. And, as the student body was growing, more space would have to be found to continue providing a carrel for each student. Finally, space the carrels occupied on the second and third floors of the Learning Center was needed for library expansion and other purposes.

While OC no longer has a dial system for audiotapes, still these innovations have left a residual effect. Oklahoma Christian has continued to be creative in its approach to learning through such methods as the use of simulations, practicums, the use of visuals in the classroom, providing a laptop for every student, and the work of the North Institute to assist teachers in finding new techniques for helping students learn. Thus, the focus continues to be on finding the best methods to promote student learning.

Oklahoma Christian College Investment Corporation

In 1969, President James Baird, working with Board member C. A. Buchanan, discussed the possibility of starting a corporation, separate from the college, that would seek to earn money in the regular marketplace so it could contribute from its profits to Oklahoma Christian. Since the college's American Citizenship Center gave strong support to the free enterprise market system, this venture would demonstrate that a college, in addition to seeking donors, could use the market system to produce money for itself.

In December 1969, seven men, five of whom were on the Board of Trustees of the college, formed a corporation called the Oklahoma Christian College Investment Corporation (OCCIC) primarily for the purpose of "aggressively acquiring properties to own and manage for the endowment of Oklahoma Christian."[39]   Roy V. Edwards, president of Wilson Foods, was the first chairman of the Board, and Terry Johnson, then OCC vice president, was the first president of the corporation. After receiving its charter on January 8, 1970, the corporation borrowed $450,000 through "good faith bonds" to acquire the capital needed to begin operation. Buchanan, at the time, was a vice president at T.G. &Y. Stores, and his role was to locate sites for new stores. The company did not wish to invest its capital in buildings, and so was interested in having another entity to own buildings they could lease. One of the early projects was constructing an 80,000 square foot shopping center in Atmore, Alabama, in which T.G. & Y., Piggly Wiggly Supermarket, B. C. Moore Department Store, and Revco Drugs would be the chief tenants. Other similar projects with T.G. & Y. included property at Alice, Texas; Tyler, Texas; Emporia, Kansas; and Elk City, Oklahoma. OCCIC developed another early project with a Winn-Dixie Supermarket in St. Augustine, Florida.[40] And there were similar connections with American Capital Mortgage Company, K-Mart Corporation, Major Video of Kansas, Inc., and Scrivner, Inc.[41]

By the early eighties, OCCIC also worked in ventures of other types. It developed Heritage Heights residential area on forty acres just to the east of the campus, Eagle Crest along Bryant south of Memorial Road, and University Park just across the street from the OCC entrance. In addition, the corporation developed Heritage Village Condominiums, with space for seventy-six units across Benson Road east of the OCC campus.[42]

The corporation also built a small shopping center and office complex on the corner of Benson Road and Memorial Road, and a shopping center on the corner of Bryant and Memorial Road, both near the campus. OCCIC made other investments in oil properties, short-term stock investments, ownership in an insurance company, and in a convenience store.[43]

By 1982, OCCIC reported it had benefited the college in the amount of $410,301. Of this $45,000 was in actual cash contributions. The remainder was in expenses on items for which the corporation had paid,

Tealridge Manor adjacent to the OC campus

such as the installation of a sewer line, the paving of roads adjacent to the campus, reductions on insurance premiums, the assumption of a bad debt, and $150,000 paid to OCC in overhead expenses for accounting services and rental of space.[44] As Oklahoma Christian College became Oklahoma Christian University in 1990, OCCIC became Oklahoma Christian Investment Corporation (OCIC).

OCIC's most significant undertaking was the development of Tealridge Manor, a six-story, 169-unit retirement center built on land adjacent to the Oklahoma Christian campus.[45] After several years of planning and negotiations, Dr. Kevin Jacobs, vice president of the Investment Corporation, was able to arrange "crucial financing for the project."[46] Construction began in 1989, and the $8 million center opened in May 1990. Tealridge has been highly successful since its beginning, with occupancy usually running above 95 percent. Occupants have individual apartments with one or two bedrooms, a bath, and a kitchenette. A complete meal service is available along with many activities. Each Sunday, members of the Memorial Road Church of Christ conduct afternoon services, and occupants are welcomed at sports and theatrical events on the OC campus next door. The OC Business Office reported in 2007 that Tealridge has a net income of over $1 million annually with $350,000 going toward the debt for its construction cost and another $750,000 flowing to OC as endowment income.[47]

Because of the Tealridge success, OCIC built a second retirement center, Meadow Lakes, in Ft. Worth, Texas. This center became operational in 1994 and was a financial success from its beginning. To meet the need for operational funding at the university, OCIC sold Meadow Lakes in 1999 at a net gain of $2.3 million.[48]

In 1998, Gary Fields prepared a report for President Terry Johnson that indicated OCIC had contributed $690,000 in cash, $210,750 in payment of overhead expenses, and other benefits bringing the total benefit to the college of more than a million dollars.[49] A report dated June 30, 1989, showed OCIC with equity in eighteen properties totaling $13,592,299.[50] Over time, some of these properties held their value well, while others experienced some decrease.[51]

By 2007, OCIC held property primarily near the OC campus: Eagle Crest Shopping Center, Heritage Village, Heritage Plaza, and raw land. These totaled in value $8 million with $7.3 million of debt. OCIC also owned Tealridge Manor worth a net of $6.7 million.[52]

In addition to providing a source of revenue, OCIC has given the university many intangible benefits: appropriate development of land near the campus, ties with many business interests, and goodwill to the university from the broader community, which has used the services of the Tealridge retirement center.

Enterprise Square, USA

Enterprise Square, USA, at a total cost of $15 million, was the single largest building project Oklahoma Christian has ever undertaken. Seven years in its planning and execution, the center brought widespread national publicity and, for several years, close to a thousand visitors a week to the campus.

The Conception

In 1971, Bob Rowland arrived to direct the American Citizenship Center, a corporation separate from the college but housed on its campus. He had been dean and president of Columbia Christian College in Portland, Oregon. His primary assignment at the Citizenship Center was to prepare materials and conduct seminars each year "for students, educators, and business-people."[53]

Rowland doubled the number of seminars, but by 1975, he still felt the Center was not reaching enough people. Rowland said, "I saw a complete revolution in the national business community, awakening to the need to educate young people about the system that has given them so much. And," he recalled, "business was ready to help do something about it."[54] "Instead of reaching out to 5,000 a year through structured programs," he thought, "why not have 250,000 a year come to OCC voluntarily, sponsor themselves and get the same message in a dramatic form."[55] The Cold War was at its height and Rowland believed there was a great need to educate young and old alike to appreciate the fundamentals of their own system as opposed to communism and socialism.

Bob Rowland

To put specifics to his dream, Rowland spread out butcher paper and began to conceptualize a pavilion to tell "the story of man's freedom to create and produce." The first floor of his "Center of American Heritage" would be a "museum" to showcase artifacts, replicas, pictures, and documents to trace the story of freedom and the free enterprise system. He envisioned a second floor to show slides and movies.[56] Rowland took his idea to Dr. Terry Johnson, president of Oklahoma Christian, who called in other administrators: Chancellor James Baird, Vice President for Development Guy Ross, and Executive Vice President Stafford North. "The administrative meetings began, followed by debate, comments, reviews and, finally, a decision to pursue the project."[57] "A $75,000 grant from the Noble foundation allowed the group to develop the concept and call in others."[58]

The college employed Dr. George Gallup "to conduct a nationwide poll to determine students' understanding of and appreciation for the free enterprise system." He reported "he had never studied where greater illiteracy existed than in the field of economics." Johnson then organized a national round table headed by William F. Martin, chairman of the Board of Phillips Petroleum and chief operating officer, to study the feasibility of developing a major exhibition center to teach economics.[59] With the need for better economic education clearly established, and with interest from major corporations, the college was ready to develop a more detailed plan for the center.

The Plan

First, the administrative team, now joined by Dr. Howard Leftwich, chair of the college's Division of Business, clarified the economic message to present. By January 1978, they had produced a book of 250 pages of text and appendices as an educational specification for the project to "establish a center which will provide an unforgettable educational experience for all ages in the area of economic understanding. By combining the very best in educational technique and effective entertainment, the facility would become a major attraction in the region to which teachers would bring classes on field trips, to which families would come for visits, and to which business and industry and labor would come for seminars and workshops."[60]

The document outlined principles the center would teach: great opportunity is still available under the American system; the consumer benefits from profits; the laborer, manager, and owner are partners in the business enterprise; the American system has provided a higher standard of living than any other; the law of supply and demand balances the goods supplied and demanded; competition is essential to the operation of a free market system; and government helps by preventing abuses.[61]

Rod Lopez-Fabrega

The team then sought a top exhibit designer with a reputation for creativity. They chose Rod Lopez-Fabrega, from Westport, Connecticut, who had developed outstanding major displays for many of the nation's largest corporations, and asked Wilson Martin of Glendale, California, a designer for Disney World, to assist him. After several months, Lopez-Fabrega came to Oklahoma City with a design for fifteen major exhibits to teach the concepts set out in the planning document. As Johnson's administrative team saw the exhibits unfold, they were overwhelmed with two thoughts: the proposal laid out the most imaginative learning strategies they had ever seen, and it was the most expensive. They had been stretching to consider raising a million dollars for their project, but this proposal would cost eight to ten million to develop and build, and additional funds to endow. Johnson, who would lead the funding effort, however, was enthralled with the plan, and believed it would be easier to raise many millions for such an exciting center than to raise less for largely static displays.

To check the economic message, the college engaged a

committee of Dr. Howard Leftwich of OCC; his brother, Dr. Richard Leftwich, economist from Oklahoma State University; Dr. Tom Johnson, economist from the American Enterprise Institute from Washington, D.C.; and Dr. Alvin Rabushka, economist from the Hoover Institute in Palo Alto, California. These had to approve the economic message as Lopez-Fabrega developed each exhibit.

President Johnson asked Dr. Stafford North, whose role as executive vice president included coordinating all building projects on the campus, to oversee construction of the building and the design and implementation of the exhibits for the proposed center. Compared to anything the college had previously done, the project was mammoth. Lopez-Fabraga in Connecticut produced the construction drawings for the exhibits, mostly built in Denver by the Condit Corporation who shipped them to Oklahoma City for installation. Mark Ritts of Short Hills, New Jersey, wrote scripts and produced the audio and video presentations for the exhibits. Daniel Wilcox of Los Angeles, a writer for *M*A*S*H*, assisted in writing scripts. Cy Poole of Atlantic Highlands, New Jersey, designed and installed the equipment to play the audio-visual presentations. David North, son of Stafford North and recent OCC graduate, led the on-campus team to develop six computerized video games and the Venture Game, which would be the climax of a visitor's tour. Don Leftwich, Bill Goad, Tom Stafford, Pen Woods, Ken Parker, and Darla Stucky were part of the on-campus team for these games and helped with other exhibits as well. Using this on-campus development team was much less expensive than contracting for these services from an outside company, and this saving allowed the total project to stay within budget.

As the project details were made public, the *Oklahoman* of April 1, 1979, commented editorially,

> Not in a long time has a project so exciting, so ingenious and yet so practical and necessary been presented as the Enterprise Square, USA, proposal just unveiled by Oklahoma Christian College.

> With the support of business leaders in Oklahoma City and elsewhere, the school has devised an intriguing way to put across one of the most urgent messages in this nation today, the message of how the American economic system works and why its continued health is vital to every citizen.[62]

Tom Glover and Ron Smith, of Oklahoma City's Glover, Smith, Nixon, and Bode, designed the 60,000 square foot building around the exhibits it was to hold. As details of the exhibits emerged, they had to make changes in walls, electrical service, and lighting. Ed Hughes, of Hughes Construction in Edmond, Oklahoma, was the general contractor. During the construction period, Stafford North held weekly meetings of the architects, builder, sub-contractors, and others involved in the process to enhance communication and solve problems.[63]

Fundraising and Construction

At a special meeting of the Oklahoma City Chamber of Commerce on March 30, 1979, William Martin launched a campaign to raise funds for Enterprise Square. Martin chaired the Enterprise Square Roundtable composed of a corporate "Who's Who" including Leonard Firestone, Dean McGee, John Pew, Sam Noble, and twenty-four more.[64] Martin reported that over $4 million of the $15 million needed had been raised. The Noble Foundation had provided the initial gift of $1.5 million. Phillips had pledged $2 million, and Edward L. Gaylord had promised $1 million.[65] Of course, OCC's president and vice president, Terry Johnson and Guy Ross, made most of the contacts for raising the money.

By Fall 1980, enough funds had been raised and plans were sufficiently developed to schedule the groundbreaking. Other major gifts had come from

Johnson and Ross

Ralph Harvey and his company, Marlin Oil, and from Eleanor Hamill, Garvey Enterprises, Mabee Petroleum Company, Texas Instruments, Conoco, Digital Equipment Corporation, the Williams Companies, Nowlin Construction Company, Exxon, Leonard Firestone, Getty Oil, Halliburton, Cities Service, Southwestern Roofing and Metal Company, Charles Floyd, Western Electric Company, Hughes Construction, AT&T, Carol Sutton, Quaker Oats, Justin Vogt, Leeway Motor Freight, and PepsiCo, Inc. Obviously, the Johnson-Ross team had been busy.

Groundbreaking and Grand Opening

The groundbreaking event on October 14, 1980, was quite impressive. A large speaker's platform was erected on the site so the crowd of fifteen hundred could see those making presentations. Former U.S. Secretary of Defense Melvin Laird, Senator David Boren, and Phillips

*Gaylord, Johnson, Laird, Martin,
and Boren break ground.*

Chairman William Martin all spoke. Martin publicly gave Terry Johnson a check for $2 million in payment of his pledge, there was a thundering flyover of four jets from Tinker Field, and 1,500 helium-filled balloons were released. Amidst patriotic music, the key figures wielded shovels and construction was officially underway.[66]

On November 19–20, 1982, seven years after discussions first began, Enterprise Square held its grand opening for the public. The building and exhibits were complete and operating, and William Martin reported that $15,000,254 had been raised.[67] The day began with a prayer breakfast at 7:30 a.m. At 10 a.m., a special chapel convocation featured Senator Don Nickles as speaker. Among his comments, he

Enterprise Square, USA

shared a message from President Ronald Reagan that read, "OCC's investment in Enterprise Square not only provides a new approach in the teaching of economics, but helps popularize free enterprise concepts that once were thought to be too complex for young people."[68] At noon, officials held a dedication luncheon under a huge tent on the Enterprise Square parking lot. Paul Thayer, chairman of LTV and chairman of the U.S. Chamber of Commerce, spoke to more than a thousand people,[69] and the OCC Band performed the Enterprise Square March, composed by Harold Fletcher of the college's Department of Music. After the luncheon came the ribbon cutting and tours of the center for the dignitaries. The public opening came the following day at 10 a.m., with Governor George Nigh giving the address. The opening ceremony also saw the sealing of a time capsule to be opened on November 20, 2032.[70]

A trip through Enterprise Square demonstrates both the message and the exciting style of presentation. After adults paid $3.50, high school students $2.50, or groups of twenty or more $2 each,[71] a cohort gathered in a darkened area where a Bob Hope video greeted them, saying they were about to see "the global economy we all grew up in—simplified a bit, shrunk some, and packed into this one building so you can take a

Bob Hope recording his message at his home in Hollywood

Bubbin and Zazzie in their space craft

look at it and see what it's about."[72] In the midst of his comments, Ed McMahan interrupted to say a UFO had just been sighted near Enterprise Square and, amidst a flash of light and noise, the saucer landed right beside the group, with two space creatures, Bubbin and Zazzie, emerging. Since the "thrombinator" on their space craft had been "snerked," they decided to explore the place where they had landed. Their journey through the center paralleled that of the guests.

The visitors then stepped into an elevator holding twenty who stood facing a glass wall. As they ascended slowly to the third floor, fifty-four screens, each three by four feet, came to life from rear projection. Sometimes using individual slides, sometimes with slides arranged in groups, these pictures with their soundtrack showed the multiplicity of ways everyone is involved in economic transactions every day: buying groceries, eating out, planning a wedding, renting an apartment, going to college, buying a car, losing a job, buying stocks. Economics is everywhere, the exhibit demonstrated, and we need to learn about it.

The visitors emerged on the third floor for the "Free To Choose" exhibit. Here each person could choose from one of ten occupations: president of the United States, airline pilot, crane operator, farmer, police officer, trucker, orchestra conductor, scientist, business executive, and surgeon. Since under free enterprise one is "free to choose" his or her own career, this exhibit illustrated that choice. After selecting an occupation, the visitor stepped before a blue background to allow his or her image to be "chromakeyed" into a prepared action clip.[73] With others in their party watching, people saw themselves among the actors in the clip as if they were actually performing in that occupation—doing surgery, flying an airplane, driving a police car, or standing behind the desk in the oval office.

Next came the "The Hall of Giants." Here visitors viewed sixteen-foot tall figures of six persons who have influenced the economic life of the world. As the visitor stepped in front of the head, an audiotape automatically began to describe the person and, using actual artifacts, told their story. Inside the Thomas Edison figure, visitors saw pictures of Edison at various stages of his life and a number of his actual inventions. The Sebastian Kresge figure presented the development of the wide-ranging Kresge

Heads of Kresge, Bell, Carver, and Edison

and then K-Mart stores, demonstrating that from small beginnings, one can make it big under free enterprise. George Washington Carver's figure contained samples of his work to broaden the uses for peanuts and sweet potatoes, and the economic impact of this work. Helena Rubinstein represented women who have excelled under free enterprise as she was shown building a huge cosmetics empire through knowledge, service, and imagination. The Henry Ford figure had an opening through which one could see an actual restored Model-T Ford while listening to an audio about Ford's life. One could look through the Alexander Graham Bell head to see a life-sized replica of his laboratory where he and his assistant were inventing the telephone.[74]

Visitors playing the supply and demand game

Next came the Donut Shop. Seated at a console, each visitor punched in to buy two, four, six, or eight donuts, depending on their price of ten cents, forty cents, or seventy cents. Of course, they always bought a lot at the lower price and not many at the higher price. Then the donut maker came out to say he wouldn't make any donuts to sell at ten cents because their cost was greater than that. He would make lots of donuts, however, at seventy cents, but then learns people wouldn't buy many at that price. The highly participatory exhibit demonstrated how supply and demand work together to set the price to the benefit of both supplier and customer.[75]

The Great American Marketplace told the story of the counter-balancing roles of the owner, the employee, and the consumer. Primarily through conversation and song, Franklin, Jefferson, Washington, and Hamilton, appearing through anamatronic heads from $1, $2, $5, and $10 bills, told of the freedom of the worker, the owner, and the consumer. By their free choices, they set necessary limits on each other.[76]

Four heads of great Americans move, speak, and sing.

Next came the Talking Face of Government. The large head with constantly changing pictures of different people in each of its nine screens showed that government is really all the people. The lips in this head began talking about the important role of government in providing laws and regulations to protect the people. As the audio moved along, however, government became more and more excited about devising more and more regulations, and finally it whirled out of control. The exhibit closed with the admonition for the people to "keep an eye on government as government keeps an eye on us."[77]

By this point, visitors had gradually moved downward on ramps between exhibits and were back on the first floor. They next entered the Economics Arcade, with eight different games to play, each available at four different stations. The games, each designed to teach economic principles, utilized an Apple II computer for their "brain." As an Oil Tycoon, a player started with $3 million and 500 days to make as much money as possible. The player determined how fast to drill, how deep, and where. In the Inflation game, players shot money at items to buy or invest, trying to balance their standard of life against the desire to make more money. The Lemonade Stand

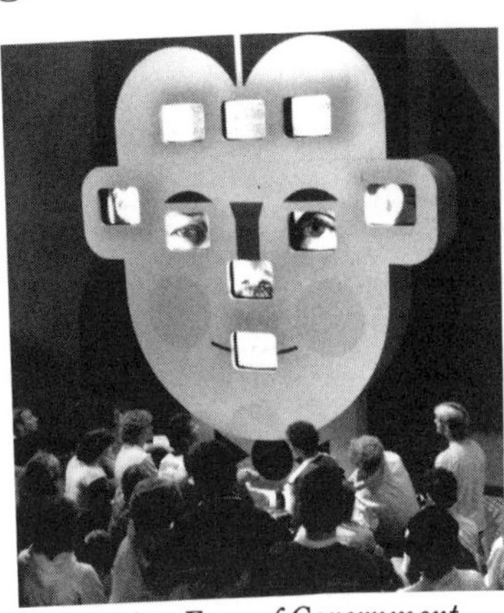

Talking Face of Government

let two players compete against each other by deciding how much lemonade to make, how many signs to put up, what to charge per glass, and how to assess the effect of the weather. Each player tried to make more than his or her opponent, recognizing that the costs lay in making the product and advertising, while sales provided income. In the Economy Machine, players tried to keep down "the misery index" seen as a combination of inflation, unemployment, and interest rates. To do this, they controlled taxes, government spending, the money supply, and government regulation. In the House Builder game, the player chose a lot on which to build, which crew to hire, and when to sell. Protect Your Rights let players

Playing Arcade games

shoot down invaders who were coming to take away their economic rights. The Lawnmower game gave players an opportunity to guide a lawnmower as quickly as possible around a yard since the more lawns mowed, the more money made. The player lost points, however, by skipping places in the yard or by running the mower over the shrubs. In Question and Answer, students answered twenty-five questions on economics as a review on what they had learned in Enterprise Square.[78]   The game area served three purposes: it taught lessons in economics, it utilized learning experiences that were fun, and it provided an opportunity for a crowd to build up for the next exhibit held in a theatre seating up to a hundred.

The Free Enterprise Theatre showed a twenty-six-minute story presented through the use of twenty-eight video and slide projectors.   The story line centered on the space creatures Bubbin and Zazzie, who had crash-landed during the Bob Hope presentation.   To fix their spaceship, they must have gleply (platinum), which on earth is very expensive. As a result of their visit through Enterprise Square, however, they have learned how the economic system works and so, to make enough blaffle (money) to buy the gleply, they will go into business. Since they wore antigravity shoes, and knew how to make them, this would be their product. As they went into business, they had to employ all the economic principles they had learned: supply and demand, how owners must work with employees and customers, dealing with competition, and problem solving. Their story, of course, summarized what each visitor also had learned.[79]

The last stop in Enterprise Square was the Venture Game, which provided an appropriate climax. Here the visitor sat at one of forty-seven computer terminals using the new "touch screen technology," and selected one of six professions: car maker, investor, oil producer, dress store owner, rancher, or trucker. The room around them started each morning at the year 1900, advancing year-by-year every six minutes to 1980. To begin, the player looked around the top of the circular room, containing a ten-foot wide, 365-degree screen. There the player found the current year and learned about it through pictures of events of major importance, sports, entertainment, and major figures of the time, all while listening to music of the era. As visitors played the game in their chosen occupation, they actually played in the context of what was happening in the world, and in their chosen career, at that particular year. So, if the investor was playing in 1929, he experienced the stock market crash. The oil producer played in light of the year's actual price of oil and other circumstances surrounding the drilling. The dress store owner played against the prices and inflation of her time. The rancher had to deal with the beef prices of the year as well as the price for hay, and the trucker competed with gasoline prices and the cost of his rigs during the year of play.

Venture Game. Player at lower left; at the top, pictures showing year of play

At the end of each year, players saw a summation of their year's performance and got appropriate video advice from an expert based on the decisions they made—good or bad. The development cost for the Venture Game would have been prohibitive had the game been farmed out to companies specializing in this work, but under the direction of David North, the OCC game crew collected all the data for this game, shot the "advice" footage, collected the pictures for the top of the room, and did all the programming to make the game work. Those who did especially well in the Venture game won prizes redeemable at the gift store as they left.

A great advantage of the Venture Game was that since it took a large computer to run it (a VAX from Digital Equipment Corporation), and since the computer mainframe had space for much more than the game, this computer enabled the college to take a huge leap forward in its campus computing ability. Business Office operations, for example, could be run on this computer, and after hours when Enterprise Square was closed, students were allowed to use the Venture Room as a computer lab.

Preparation for all the Enterprise Square exhibits required shooting "fifteen miles of film and video-tape on seventy-four locations and stage sets to develop over 240,000 images for the hungry battery of laser-disc units" which played the visuals.[80] In those days, laser-disc technology was so new that the master discs had to be made in Japan because no American companies could yet produce them.

When the center opened, Bob Rowland added directing Enterprise Square to his duties at the American Citizenship Center. Elenda Wise assisted him in his work, and Pen Woods did public relations.[81] Frank Irby served as technical director to keep all the exhibits running,[82] and many OCC students served as guides.

Enterprise Square, USA, attracted widespread attention and became a major attraction both for school trips and for tourists. The coverage on major networks included appearances on NBC's *Today* show and CBS's *World News Tonight*. Stories appeared in *Time* magazine, the *Wall Street Journal, Variety, Reader's Digest, U.S. News and World Report, Southern Living, Travelhost*, and many newspapers from New York to Dallas to Kyoto, Japan.[83] Paul Harvey included it in a column and mentioned the center in one of his broadcasts.[84] In 1983, Oklahoma City's phone book featured Enterprise Square on its cover. In 1984, Enterprise Square won the top award from the Freedoms Foundation in Valley Forge. Dr. Robert Miller, president of the Foundation, cited Enterprise Square as "An educational attraction, unique in the world, combining the magic of electronics and imaginative teaching concepts to present the American free enterprise system."[85]

One report said that, from its opening in November 1982 until July 1983, the center hosted 50,000 visitors,[86] while another estimated the number of guests at 100,000.[87] And, while later years did not hold the attendance of the opening year, the number of visitors in 1988 was 44,707, and just through October of 1989, they totaled 51,358.[88] Visitors came from every state and fifty foreign countries.[89]

The great interest in Enterprise Square, of course, enhanced the other efforts for the American Citizenship Center, which held teacher institutes, youth citizenship seminars, essay contests, and speech competition, and also distributed courses on various aspects of economics for use in schools.[90]

Pen Woods, John Wilguess, Bob Tucker, and Will Jones followed Bob Rowland as directors of Enterprise Square. As the Cold War wound down, there was some decreasing interest in the center's message, and about that time, some schools had to cut back on their number of field trips. Attendance at Enterprise Square began to decline while operating costs were rising. Some of the equipment began to be outdated and replacing it would be very costly. By 1999, the OC administration decided it was time to close the center.

For seventeen years Enterprise Square, USA, was among the top attractions in Oklahoma. By hosting more than 600,000 visitors, it educated many about the private enterprise economy and brought much goodwill to Oklahoma Christian. College administrators, of course, devoted a large amount of time and effort to Enterprise Square that might have been spent on other matters, but they believed that the eventual payoff in contacts made and publicity gained would make their investment worthwhile. Certainly, the center made friends who brought their support to the university itself, and the project led university officials to raise their sights about what the institution could accomplish. In 2007, the university announced plans for a $10 million renovation of the building for office, classroom, and exhibit space to be used primarily by university administrators and the College of Business. In this new use of the facility, however, they pledged to keep alive the message for which Enterprise Square was originally intended.

College to University

During the 1980's, many institutions of higher learning that had been "colleges" were changing to "universities." All of the Oklahoma regional colleges had made the transition and so had many of Oklahoma Christian College's sister institutions: Abilene Christian, Harding, Lubbock Christian, David Lipscomb, and Faulkner.[91] The reasons behind these changes were many. For one thing, most junior colleges had dropped the "junior" and now were just "colleges." And there were beauty colleges, vocational colleges, and business colleges, which made the name "college" less distinctive. Many colleges, having added specialized degrees and graduate studies, were more than the "liberal arts college" they had been and so had taken the name "university." International students typically looked for universities because to them "college" often meant secondary school. So Oklahoma Christian was faced with the decision as to whether it should make this change.

In 1985, the college launched its "With Wings As Eagles" fundraising campaign with the promise that if it were successful in reaching its goals, "the issue of university status would be opened for consideration."[92] The drive was successful, and by 1988, Oklahoma Christian had added a graduate program in Bible. Already the college was offering professional programs in fields such as education, business, and engineering, and its total enrollment had risen above sixteen hundred.

With all of this, it would seem that the time had come for Oklahoma Christian to make the move to university. The decision, however, had a complicating factor. To become Oklahoma Christian

University would carry the acronym of OCU, and there was already an OCU close by, Oklahoma City University. As the matter was under consideration, in fact, OCU officials notified they would sue OCC if the college used the same letters, causing people to confuse the two schools.

So the college faced a difficult dilemma. College administrators felt it was imperative that the institution become a university so as not to appear second rate among its peers. Was it worth it, however, if the college had to change its name and lose the years spent in developing the name recognition and related goodwill?

President Johnson appointed an eleven-member committee of administrators, faculty, staff, and alumni to consider the situation. After surveying students, alumni, faculty and staff, parents, and members of the college's Board of Development, it was clear that all elements of its constituency thought the time had come to make the change.[93] All on the committee agreed the college should move to university status, believing the college met the criteria. Some on the committee thought it best, in view of the OCU problem, to make a substantial change in the name, such as Baird University, in honor of the long-time president. Others opposed this change because they thought taking the word "Christian" out of the name would cause some to assume the college was changing its commitment to spiritual values. At first, those preferring the name Baird University had the majority, and a meeting concluded with that as the majority decision. In subsequent days, however, some had a change of heart, and decided that giving up the name "Oklahoma Christian" would be too costly, both in loss of the name equity and the message some would perceive.

Finally, the group settled on the name Oklahoma Christian University of Science and Arts. This would keep the familiar name and, by using the acronym OC, they could avoid the problem with OCU. The Board approved this decision, and the formal announcement came on March 28, 1990.

Activities for the day "included worship services, special ceremonies, addresses by George W. Bush, inauguration of a major capital fund drive, and presentation of honorary doctorates to friends of the University. The central event of the day was a chapel service followed by an address by Bush, general partner of the Texas Rangers and son of the president."[94] In his comments, Bush said universities

Johnson, Bush, Jullian, and Gotcher sing in chapel.

throughout the nation must teach the Bible's fundamental values and that universities must support fundamental rights such as economic freedom, political freedom, and religious freedom.[95] As part of the day's activities, Johnson and Board chair Deryl Gotcher bestowed honorary doctorates on Bush and long-time supporter Edward C. Joullian III.[96] No one expected that the speaker on that day would eventually become the president of the United States.

The April-May *Reporter* carried a large spread about the change to university. One article said, "Of great importance, the name allows the university to use its familiar name, Oklahoma Christian, and retain the equity that has been established in this respected name over the years. Its Board of Trustees, faculty and the majority of its students are members of the churches of Christ." The article added that OC was one of "a new class of university" that was smaller and still provided a liberal arts curriculum. It also was more concerned with teaching than with research.[97] President Johnson added, "Oklahoma Christian has served to fulfill the dreams and aspirations of many faithful Christians. As we move to university status, we are proud to reaffirm our commitment to value-centered, Christian education."[98]

As a result of the change, the academic departments were reorganized into five colleges: Bible, Business, Education, Liberal Arts, and Science and Engineering. In 2003, President O'Neal reduced the five colleges to three: Bible, Arts and Science, and Professional Studies. When Kevin Jacobs became president in 1996, the name became just Oklahoma Christian University with the acronym continuing to be OC.

Cascade College

Columbia Christian College had operated for thirty-seven years in Portland, Oregon, as a sister institution to Oklahoma Christian. In 1992, the Northwest States Association, however, withdrew accreditation from the college because of its weak financial picture, including not meeting salary obligations to faculty. "The loss of accreditation was a severe blow: It meant that credits would no longer transfer, that federal financial aid was no longer available for students attending there, and that the institution had no official standing."[99]

During the spring of 1992, the Columbia Board brought Don Gardner to serve as president to see if he could help them out of their troubles. Ninety students enrolled in the fall and many faculty and staff stayed with the institution, hoping for better days. Gardner and Sam Granberg, chairman of the Board, "began a campaign to keep Columbia."[100] They were determined to save Christian higher education in the northwestern United States. The pair contacted sister Christian universities to see if any would come to their aid. The plea fell on the sympathetic ears of President Terry Johnson who received approval from the OC Board of Trustees to investigate the matter. Johnson thought one possibility might be that OC could operate a two-year college in Portland to keep Christian education there while providing a feeder institution for Oklahoma Christian.

Cascade Campus

To investigate the possibilities in Portland, Johnson sent a three-person team: Stafford North, Kevin Jacobs, and Bailey McBride. The group met with administrators and students and, on a Saturday morning, with a hundred people who braved a ten-inch snow to state their case for keeping a Christian college there. Those in Portland hoped Oklahoma Christian would find a way to help, but made it clear that they did not want a two-year college since that would mean students from that area would go elsewhere to finish degrees and therefore be less likely to come back to the northwest to help the church. They wanted a four-year college in Portland.

When North, Jacobs, and McBride reported to President Johnson, he saw the need for the four-year school and set about to see how it might be accomplished. Eventually OC developed a plan and offered it to the Columbia Christian Board. Columbia would close for the 1993–1994 academic year to give a break between the former college and the new one. This would allow a new beginning for employing new faculty and staff. Oklahoma Christian would treat the new operation, to be called Cascade College, as a branch campus, thus allowing Oklahoma Christian's accreditation to be applied there. The Columbia Board would assume all financial obligations that had accumulated under the previous college operation, would contribute $450,000 a year toward recruitment and operational costs,[101] and would provide the existing Columbia campus without charge to the new institution. The new curriculum would offer four degrees: Bible, business, elementary education, and liberal arts. This limited curriculum would keep operating costs to a minimum. In 1993, both Boards approved the plan.

In August of 1993, Dr. Kevin Jacobs, who had been serving as vice president and general counsel at OC, moved to Portland to become the executive vice president of Cascade. On September

30, Oregon Governor Barbara Roberts signed a letter authorizing Oklahoma Christian to offer bachelor's degrees at Cascade,[102] and by mid-November, the North Central Association had approved the Oklahoma Christian request to extend its accreditation to the Cascade program.

By December, Jacobs had hired Dr. Arlis Wood, director of OC's Counseling Center, to be dean of student development, and brought Dr. Mickey Banister, assistant superintendent of schools in Stillwater, Oklahoma, to be the academic dean and chairman of teacher education. Jacobs also brought Brad Fisher to help him and Don Gardner raise funds for the program.[103] At that time, Jacobs also reported that the outstanding debts Columbia had owed, more than $1 million, had now been paid, and that he had $3 million in commitments.[104]

On Monday, August 29, 1994, Cascade College opened with President Terry Johnson and twenty-five OC Board members present on the campus. Through a fiber-optic link between Portland and Oklahoma City, the two campuses joined in the opening ceremony.[105] For this first year, Cascade had 119 students and hope had been restored for preserving collegiate education among Churches of Christ in the northwest. The number of students grew to about three hundred, a new residence hall was built, and the curriculum was expanded. Dennis Lynn replaced Kevin Jacobs, who moved back to Oklahoma City to be president of Oklahoma Christian. Then, in 2006, Dr. Bill Goad, long-time teacher and administrator at Oklahoma Christian, became president at Cascade.

The road has not always been smooth. For several years, the operation was a financial drain on Oklahoma Christian

Students at Cascade

mainly because enrollments at Cascade fell below expectations. In July of 2005, the operating deficit funded by Oklahoma Christian had risen to $2.2 million.[106] By 2007, however, through a key donation and other fundraising, the amount had been reduced to $1 million. In 2006, the Board of Columbia Christian deeded the campus, valued at $9 million, to Oklahoma Christian.[107]

While the financial aspect of the Cascade decision has not turned out as well as had been hoped, Oklahoma Christian's accepting the challenge of continuing Christian education on the former Columbia

Christian campus was an important step. It allowed students from homes among Churches of Christ in the region to be able to go to a college of their own and remain in the northwest where churches badly need them. It also demonstrated something about the character of Oklahoma Christian. Just as Harding College and Dr. George Benson had helped Central Christian when it needed help, so Oklahoma Christian came to the aid of another Christian college. Families and congregations among Churches of Christ in the northwest are certainly stronger because of this assistance.

Chapter 6, Endnotes

1 "Character Building Looms Large as Goal of College," *Bartlesville Examiner-Enterprise*, Ruth Wilson Scrapbook, 17, OC Archives.

2 "CCC to Become Senior College," *Central Christian College Bulletin*, May, 1959, OC Archives.

3 Ibid.

4 "College to Change Name in September," *Central Christian College Bulletin*, May, 1959, OC Archives.

5 "Senior College Program Given Approval," *Oklahoma Christian College Bulletin,* June, 1960, OC Archives.

6 Ibid.

7 Ibid.

8 Stafford North, "OCC Extends Work to Senior College Level, Offering Degrees in Four Different Fields," *Oklahoma Christian College Bulletin*, June, 1961, OC Archives.

9 "19 Seniors Earn Degrees for Commencement, June 1," *Oklahoma Christian College Bulletin*, May, 1962, OC Archives.

10 W. O. Beeman, *Oklahoma Christian College* (Delight, Arkansas: Gospel Light Publishing Company, 1970), 173.

11 *Report of a Self Study to the North Central Association*, May, 1965, 36, OC Archives.

12 Beeman, *Oklahoma Christian College*, 173.

13 Ibid., 106–7.

14 Ibid.

15 Stafford North, no title, October 5, 1962, Filed under Learning Center, OC Archives.

16 Beeman, *Oklahoma Christian College*, 124.

17 Stafford North, "Learning Center Gives Each Student a Study Carrel," *College and University Business*, May, 1966, Reprint in OC Archives.

18 Beeman, *Oklahoma Christian College*, 114.

19 Ibid., 110.

20 W. O. Beeman, Memo to Dr. Baird, June 23, 1964, OC Archives.

21 Ibid.

22 Beeman, *Oklahoma Christian College*, 114–115.

23 Ibid., 119.

24 Ibid., 115.

25 Alice Ann Conway, Unpublished essay under Learning Center in OC Archives.

26 Stafford North, "Dial Access Retrieval System at Oklahoma Christian College," Unpublished paper, n.d., Filed under Learning Center, OC Archives.

27 Stafford North, "The Progression of OCC's Educational Philosophy," Unpublished paper, n.d. OC Archives.

28 *Oklahoma City Times*, July 23, 1965, Reprint in OC Archives.

29 Benjamin Fine, Summary of Statements about the Learning Center, Learning Center File, OC Archives.

30 "International Attention Paid College's Learning Center," *Oklahoma Christian College Bulletin*, May, 1966, OC Archives.

31 North, "Dial Access."

32 Sidney G. Tickton, *Summary Report of An Evaluation of the Learning Center and Related Programs at Oklahoma Christian College*, September, 1970, Preface, OC Archives.

33 Ibid.

34 Ibid., Final letter from Sidney Tickton.

35 Ibid., Final letter from Jack Edling.

36 Marshall Gunselman (ed.), *What Are We Learning About Learning Centers?* (Oklahoma City: Eagle Media, 1971), *passim.*

37 *President's Report, November 9, 1973*, OC Archives.

38 "Vote of Confidence," *Oklahoma City Times*, December 18, 1971, Reprint in

OC Archives.

[39] Oklahoma Christian Investment Corporation: A Historical Abstract, Files of the Executive Vice President of OC under OCIC History.

[40] Brochure on Oklahoma Christian College Investment Corporation printed in 1981, Files of the Executive Vice President of OC under OCIC History.

[41] OCIC: A Historical Abstract.

[42] Ibid.; Brochure.

[43] OCCIC Business Plan Study, n.d., Files of the Executive Vice President of OC under OCIC History.

[44] Oklahoma Christian College Investment Corporation, Benefits to Oklahoma Christian College, June 30, 1982, Files of the Executive Vice President of OC under OCIC History.

[45] J. Terry Johnson, *Jubilee*, 2000, 122.

[46] Ibid.

[47] Report from the OC Business Office dated April 4, 2007.

[48] Terry Johnson in phone conversation with author on May 23, 2007.

[49] Files of Executive Vice President of OC under OCIC.

[50] Ibid.

[51] Report from the Business Office dated April 4, 2007.

[52] Ibid.

[53] "The Enterprising Mind Behind Enterprise Square," *Enterprise Square, USA News Brief*, Winter, 1982, OC Archives.

[54] Ibid.

[55] Ibid.

[56] Bob Rowland, Proposal to build a Center of American Heritage, Unpublished, OC Archives.

[57] "Enterprising Mind."

[58] Ibid.

[59] Enterprise Square, USA, OC Archives.

[60] "Enterprising Mind."

[61] Ibid., 5–13.

[62] "Dramatizing Free Enterprise," *Sunday Oklahoman*, April 1, 1979, quoted in *OCC Reporter*, April 1979, 2, OC Archives.

[63] "An Enterprise Square Who's Who," *Enterprise Square, USA News Brief*, Winter, 1982, OC Archives.

[64] Enterprise Square, USA, Booklet, OC Archives.

[65] "Building to be Constructed," *Talon*, March 30, 1979, 1, 9, OC Archives.

[66] "Ground Broken For Enterprise Square, USA; Dignitaries Keynote Ceremonies," *OC Reporter*, October 1980, OC Archives.

[67] "OCC Funds Pass Goal," *Daily Oklahoman*, November 14, 1982, report from NewsBank, Inc., OC Archives.

[68] "Dignitaries cut ribbon on Enterprise Square," *Daily Oklahoman*, November 19, 1982, Quoted in a release by Access World News, Files of the Office of the President of OC under Enterprise Square.

[69] "Enterprise Square, USA, Opens to Public Today." *Daily Oklahoman*, November 20, 1982, report from NewsBank, Inc., OC Archives.

[70] "ESUSA Grand Opening today, Nigh, donors dedicate center," *Talon*, November 19, 1982, B 1, OC Archives; "Enterprise Square, USA, Opens to Public Today," *Daily Oklahoman*, November 20, 1982, from NewsBank, Inc, OC Archives.

[71] "ESUSA Grand Opening."

[72] Script for Introductory Area, OC Archives.

[73] Script for Free to Choose, OC Archives.

[74] Script for Hall of Giants, OC Archives.

[75] Script for Donut Shop, OC Archives.

[76] Script for Great American Marketplace, OC Archives.

[77] Script for the Talking Face of Government, OC Archives.

[78] Scripts for the Arcade Games, OC Archives.

[79] Script for the Free Enterprise Theatre, OC Archives.

[80] "A/V Creative Chief Wipes Brow with Relief," Enterprise Square News Release, November 20, 1982, OC Archives.

81 "Rowland directs the staff," *Talon*, November 19, 1982, 3B, OC Archives.
82 "Mr. Fixit keeps the razzle-dazzle in Enterprise Square," *Oklahoma Today*, Winter, 1984, 8–12, OC Archives.
83 Who's Talking About Enterprise Square, USA, OC Archives.
84 "Paul Harvey spotlights ESUSA on radio, in syndicated column," *Enterprise Square, USA Insider*, Winter, 1994, OC Archives.
85 "Freedoms Foundation's Top Award Goes to Enterprise Square," *OCC Reporter*, April 1984, 1, OC Archives.
86 "Nets look at Enterprise Sq.," *TVNews*, July 17, 1983, OC Archives.
87 "Museum Enterprising Center," *Daily Oklahoman*, April 24, 1984, from Newsbank, Inc., OC Archives.
88 "Attendance Remains Up," Report from Enterprise Square, USA, Fall, 1989, OC Archives.
89 "Nations Represented by Visitors," OC Archives.
90 "Programs Emanating from Enterprise Square, USA," Associates of Enterprise Square, USA, OC Archives.
91 Minutes, Board of Trustees, February 25, 1989, OC Archives.
92 Johnson, *Jubilee*, 2000, 114.
93 "University Status," President's Report, 1988–89, OC Archives.
94 "Exciting Day Marks Change to University Status," *Oklahoma Christian Reporter*, April-May 1990, 1. OC Archives.
95 Ibid.
96 Ibid.
97 "Oklahoma's Newest University," *Oklahoma Christian Reporter*, April-May, 1990.
98 Ibid.
99 Bailey McBride, "Cascade College: strength out of weakness," *Christian Chronicle*, July, 1996, 21.
100 Ibid.
101 News Release to *Christian Chronicle*, April 21, 1993, Files of the Office of Executive Vice President of OC under Cascade.
102 "Cascade College Receives Approval to Operate from Oregon Governor," *Campus Community*, October 7, 1993.
103 Kevin Jacobs, Letter to Terry Johnson, December 17, 1993, Files in the Office of the Executive Vice President under Cascade College.
104 Ibid.
105 "Cascade/OC's 'wedding' celebrated in opening," *Christian Chronicle*, October, 1994, 1.
106 Minutes, Board of Trustees, July 9, 2005, OC Archives.
107 Records from the Office of Financial Affairs, OC.

Chapter 7
THE FACULTY AND STAFF

First Week Follies

Bob Lashley

It's 7 p.m. Thursday night, the first week of fall classes. Hardeman Auditorium's thirteen hundred seats are almost filled. Stage lights come up, the audience cheers, and Bob Lashley, organizer of the show, shouts, "Welcome to *First Week Follies.*"

Lashley, with his backup band, sings "Bridge Over Troubled Waters" and "Rocky Mt. High." Then Dr. Elmo Hall, in a tux as emcee for the evening, welcomes the audience and introduces three long-time OC professors as the Faculty Folksters: Dr. Harold Fletcher, on bass, and Dr. Darvin Keck and Dr. James Cail, both playing guitar, and all singing

Dr. Elmo Hall

"Uh Oh!," "Falling in Love," and "Honeycomb." Hall next introduces Dr. Kim Gaither, OC alum and professor in biology, singing "Because You Loved Me."

Hall: "And next, Harold Fletcher, directing the Faculty-Staff Men's Glee Club," who sing "Gaudeamus Igitur," "Take Me Out to the Ball Game," and their signature close, "Ruth rode

Dr. Kim Gaither

on my motorcycle, she rode in back of me; I hit a bump at sixty-five, and rode on Ruthlessly."

Hall : "Our next act features Dean Bob Smith singing the ever-romantic 'Feelings.'" Then, to everyone's shock, Smith begins singing the lovely ballad sounding exactly like Donald Duck.

Hall: "Now watch the screen for an original video: Germ Busters!!! featuring those intrepid searchers for germs, faculty members Ralph

Dr. John Thompson

Burcham, Dr. Lynn McMillon, and Dr. Max Dobson." Hall: "It's time for our sermon of the evening. Here's Dr. John Thompson preaching 'Green Eggs and Ham.'"

Hall: "Our next presentation comes from the unequalled Bible faculty of Oklahoma Christian University, scholars all, in 'Synchronized Swimming.'" And sure enough, the video begins with the Bible faculty all lined up along the edge of the OC pool, sequentially diving sideways into the water, followed by other choreographed maneuvers, much to the delight of the crowd.

Part of the cast from Spike Jones' Cocktails for Two: Mock, Bever, Leftwich, Dodd, Eggleston, and North directing.

Hall: "From our history faculty, rock-star Dr. Matt McCook singing parodies of 'Sweet Child of Mine' and 'Welcome to the Jungle.'" Hall: "And closing out the first act of our program tonight, it's that Spike Jones favorite, 'Cocktails for Two,'" and out come twenty faculty and staff members, weirdly dressed, to sing and make the strange noises.

Following intermission, Lashley and the band are back, this time with "I've Been Everywhere, Man." And, complete with pictures of places, Lashley, without missing a syllable, sings ever faster: "Nebraska, Alaska, Opalaka, Baraboo, Waterloo, Kansas City, Sioux City, Cedar City, Dodge City, What a pity, I've been everywhere."

Bob Rowley with Jim Wilson as Carnak

Hall: "Now for all the campus secrets, we turn to the Tattletales from Hee Haw." Out come the gossipy Polly Wiginton of the campus store, Marilyn Hankins from the Registrar's Office, and Gladys Burcham of the Library. Hall, with a swing of the arm: "And now ladies and gentlemen, here are the three tenors you have heard so much about." Enter Curt Niccum, Gary Bruce, and Chip Kooi to sing a parody of the Bohemian Rhapsody.

Hall: "Now for your amazement, First Week Follies presents Bob Rowley with his special guest for the evening." Rowley, with great flourish, brings on "Carnac, the Magnificent." Dr. Jim Wilson enters with a huge headpiece draped with pearls. Rowley hands Wilson the envelope, which he holds to his head and then gives the answer: "Arlis Wood, Pepe Le Pu, Saddam Hussein." Rowley repeats, "Arlis Wood, Pepe Le Pu, Saddam Hussein." Opening the envelope, Wilson now states the question, "Name a shrink, a stink, and the missing link."

Hall: "Now it's OC's own Sonny and Cher." And sounding a lot like them, Dr. Stafford North and Connie (McCormack) Penick, sing "The Beat Goes On" and "I Got You Babe." Hall: "Now the moment we've all been waiting for. It's J. Garth Johnson!!!" President Johnson enters, dressed like Garth Brooks, even to the attached microphone in front of his mouth, singing "The Dance" and "Friends in Low Places."

Hall: "To close our evening of entertainment, all our cast members return to join Bob Lashley and the band, singing a patriotic tribute to our great country. Watch the screens, and listen to 'God Bless the USA.'"[1]

President Johnson as Garth Brooks

First Week Follies is unique to Oklahoma Christian. Returning students look forward to the event and even alumni come back to see it. Since this show is how the faculty and staff have chosen to introduce each new academic year since 1979, it is an appropriate way to begin this chapter about them. While the above First Week Follies is a composite made from parts of programs since the event began, it demonstrates accurately a number of important qualities about Oklahoma Christian. The OC faculty and staff want to show themselves to the students as real people who are interested in students and willing to take off their "academic robes" for an evening of fun. As anyone who sees the program can attest, since the acts take a lot of time to learn and prepare, the participants are demonstrating their willingness to make a major investment in something to be fun for the students. The show also demonstrates that faculty and staff are talented in ways beyond their particular fields of work. While some of the skits and songs are foolishness, most of them take considerable performance skill. Both new and returning students come away from this performance with an enlightened view of faculty and staff.

OC Faculty Qualifications

One of the common observations among those connected with Oklahoma Christian University since its beginning in 1950 is that the institution has attracted a faculty of unusually high quality. The faculty sets high standards for students, and the professors are skilled in helping students reach these levels of performance. Student achievements, reported elsewhere in this history, attest to the faculty's success in preparing students for graduate training, employment, and service in the church.

Many other measures also indicate this high quality of the OC faculty. While in 1958 only 6 percent of the faculty held a doctor's degree, today 72 percent have doctorates or terminal degrees. These degrees have come from many outstanding institutions: Baylor University, Florida State University, Georgia Institute of Technology, Louisiana State University, Massachusetts Institute of Technology, Michigan State University, Notre Dame, Oxford University, Oklahoma State University, Purdue University, Texas A&M University, Texas Tech University, the University of Arkansas, the University of Edinburgh, the University of Florida, the University of Illinois, the University of Iowa, the University of Kansas, the University of Missouri, the University of North Dakota, the University of Oklahoma, the University of Tennessee, the University of Texas, Virginia Tech University, and many others. The number of faculty has grown from a full-time equivalent of 15 in 1958 to 103 in 2006. The student-faculty ratio has varied over the years from fourteen to one in 1958, to thirty-five to one in 1968, and then down to fifteen to one in 2006.[2]

Another indication of successful faculty at OC is the university's accreditation both for the institution and for individual departments. While Chapter 11 outlines these accreditation efforts in detail, the fact that Oklahoma Christian has gained these marks of approval not only with the North Central Association, but with specialized accrediting agencies in teacher training, engineering, music, and business, stands as another measure of faculty strength.

Many current and past faculty have taught at other universities, and many were employed in businesses or churches before coming to Oklahoma Christian. They clearly could make higher salaries elsewhere and have often found their students employed in jobs that paid what they were earning or more. Faculty could also have been in positions giving them greater standing in their professions. So why did they come and why did they stay?

Full-time faculty members and those in key administrative roles at Oklahoma Christian are required to be members of the Church of Christ, and their religious motivation is clearly a prime reason for their coming to an institution serving primarily families from these churches. They have wanted to see youth from these families attend college where they could advance in their faith while preparing for their careers. They have known of the many preachers and missionaries coming from Oklahoma Christian and wanted to have a part in continuing such education. In addition, they have known of many Christian doctors, lawyers, teachers, engineers, and those in business who have come from universities like Oklahoma Christian, and they want to help train more of these as well.

In addition, 60 percent of the 2006–2007 full-time faculty attended either Oklahoma Christian or a sister Christian institution for undergraduate or graduate training.[3] These came to help replicate for others the experience they received in their own education. The faculty members also come to OC because they like to teach in an institution where they have the opportunity for personal interaction with students, both inside and outside the classroom. Another factor in their coming to teach at OC is the desire to experience the camaraderie they can have with colleagues who share their faith and their standards. Even at a financial sacrifice and sometimes at a professional sacrifice as well, well-qualified faculty members have come all through the years to teach at Oklahoma Christian University.

The Faculty Role at OC

The faculty role at OC is multifaceted. Full-time faculty are expected to teach twelve semester hours during each fall and spring term. Until 1990, the standard load was fifteen-semester hours. The administration made the reduction for three primary reasons: to give faculty more time to make each class a better learning experience, to meet the common standard among universities of its type, and to satisfy accrediting associations, which frown on loads above twelve hours.

In addition to their responsibilities in teaching, however, OC faculty serve in other ways. For many years, they have been expected to be available at least ten hours each week in their offices for consultation with students. Students often drop by a professor's office to talk about classes and personal matters. In addition, professors are assigned students as advisees whom they assist with enrollment and other needs. Although not all make it each day, faculty members also are expected to attend daily chapel with students to take part with them in worship, to show their support for the required chapel policy, and to keep up with campus events. Many teachers also sponsor student clubs, attend student events, and have students to their homes for social occasions.

Each OC professor is expected to participate in the spiritual life of the campus. As stated in the OC Core Values, "The university integrates faith and learning and seeks to be and to be known nationally as an outstanding Christian learning community."[4] To help achieve this goal, faculty seek to combine faith and learning in their field, and receive in-service training in how to accomplish this goal. Many faculty members accompany students on mission trips to foreign countries or to do inner-city work in the United States. All OC faculty are expected to be active members of a local congregation of a Church of Christ.

Faculty members also take a leading role in governance of the institution. Until 2003 when the Faculty Association began, faculty participation in making university policies and decisions came primarily through their work on committees. Typically, these committees were composed of several faculty members, an administrator or two, and a student. The Academic Affairs Committee, for example, which has existed since the early days of the institution, approves degree requirements, determines courses for inclusion in the curriculum, and sets academic standards. Their recommendations typically go to the full faculty for approval, and usually then to the administration. Other major committees have been the Student Life Committee, which helps set student conduct standards and enforces them, the Spiritual Life Committee, which makes suggestions for improvement in the spiritual development of students, and the Rank and Tenure Committee, which recommends faculty for promotion and tenure to the president and Board of Trustees. The Teacher Education Council, another group primarily composed of faculty, sets standards for and admits students to teacher education and to student teaching. These and many other committees through the years have given faculty an opportunity to participate in governance of the institution.

Through the terms of Presidents Baird and Johnson, a faculty representative served along with administrators and the president of the Student Senate on the Administrative Council. This group worked primarily in matters of budget, enrollment procedures, campus event planning, general campus policies, and solving problems brought by members of the Council. The 1965 *Report to the North Central Association* stated,

> The administration is receptive to faculty thought and opinion and continuous attention is given to the procedure for expression of these ideas. The best method found so far for a direct flow of ideas from individual faculty members to the administration is for the faculty representative to poll the faculty for ideas in advance of the Administrative Council meeting. The faculty is then given a digest of the meetings.[5]

President Jacobs substituted for this plan a President's Advisory Council with several faculty representatives, and President O'Neal began the Strategic Vision Committee, composed of several administrators, the president of the Faculty Senate, the president-elect of the Faculty Senate, the dean of each college, and a faculty representative from each college. Staff representatives are also members of this body. Through each of these systems, faculty have been given a voice in administrative decisions, but the SVC plan gives faculty a stronger voice on major decisions than previous plans did.

When President O'Neal approved the Faculty Association, which began in 2003, the faculty for the first time met without administrators present to discuss any matters they wished to study and on which to make proposals. Under this system, faculty members elect a president and an executive committee, which appoint subcommittees to study issues of concern. The Faculty Association president calls meetings of the entire faculty as needed. Dr. Ken Adams was the first president of the Association in 2003, followed by Dr. Jim Baird in 2004, Dr. John Maple in 2005, Dr. Jim Cutbirth in 2007, and Don Leftwich in 2008.

The faculty has also occasionally assisted with fundraising, particularly the alumni callout. Especially through the 1980s and 1990s, faculty and staff members manned the telephones

This picture on a postcard alerted alumni that the callout was coming. From the left are Baxter, Dobson, Burcham, H. Leftwich, and Wilson.

for a blitz to ask alumni for funds. Typically, callers assembled in the "Board Room" of Cogswell-Alexander Hall, chose the cards of those they would contact, and began dialing. A friendly competition among the callers helped to keep everyone motivated and the process, extending over several nights, would usually bring in pledges well in excess of $300,000.

Academic Administrators

Many have played an important role in academic administration over the fifty-eight years of Oklahoma Christian's existence. Some of these are mentioned in other chapters of this history, but it is important to note here the vital role of those who have served long-term as deans and chairs. Their efforts have certainly made a major impact on the institution as they guided in developing policies and overseeing faculty.

Academic Deans and Vice Presidents

Dr. James Baird was the first academic dean, serving from 1950 through 1954, when he became president.[6] Highly qualified with a doctorate from George Peabody, as the first academic leader, he established a pattern for many policies, standards, and activities that continued for years. Following him, several served as academic dean for shorter periods: W. C. Whiteside in 1954–1956, Joseph Jones in 1956–1957, and Dr. Earle H. West, in 1957–1958. In 1958, President Baird chose Dr. Stafford North as dean of instruction. North, who had been on the faculty and was assistant to the president, filled this position until 1976, when Dr. Bailey McBride became academic dean. McBride, the first alumnus in the role, had been on the OCC faculty, held a doctorate from the University of Tennessee, and had taught at the University of New Mexico. He served until 1996 when President Jacobs selected Dr. Jeanine Varner, another alumnus, to become vice president for academic affairs. Varner had taught at OC since 1987, chaired the Division of Language and Literature, and served as dean of the College of Liberal Arts. She continued in this role of academic leadership until 2007. President O'Neal selected alumnus Dr. Allison Garrett as Varner's replacement. Garrett, with a law degree from the University of Tulsa and an L.L.M. from Georgetown University, had experience in business and had been teaching at the Faulkner University School of Law. She continues to serve in this academic leadership role.

As academic leaders, all of these deans and vice presidents have filled major roles in choosing new faculty members and helping faculty members increase their teaching effectiveness. They have been responsible for creating an atmosphere of academic excellence and providing the conditions under which faculty could do their best work. They led in accreditation efforts, participated in the development of academic facilities, and worked to integrate faith into the academic learning process. Sometimes they had to make the difficult decisions to terminate a teacher or drop courses or programs from the curriculum. Certainly their leadership has contributed significantly to the academic success of the institution.

Long-Time College Deans and Academic Chairs

While it is impossible in this history to mention all providing academic leadership as college deans and chairs of divisions and departments, those serving in such positions have filled a vital role in the work of Oklahoma Christian. These leaders, like the academic deans and vice presidents, have been involved in developing curriculum, improving instructional techniques, adding facilities, setting academic standards, gaining accreditation, overseeing the work of professors, and assisting students. In addition, they have been instrumental in decisions about employing new teachers. This section mentions those with long-time service in one or more roles of academic leadership.

Bob Smith came to OCC in 1968 as assistant dean for curriculum and records and, in 1970, became dean of admissions and records. He served in that and similar roles until he retired in February 1994.[7] During most of these twenty-six years, he was responsible for student recruitment, as well as the work of the registrar. Dr. Mickey Banister began serving in the role of registrar in 1996 and continues in that position.

Dr. Max Dobson

Dr. Max Dobson is the academic chair with the longest tenure. He first came to OCC in 1966 and began to lead the physical education program in 1972. He served for thirty-three years, retiring from that role in 2005, replaced by Curtis Janz. Dobson continues to teach in physical education.

Three long-term administrators have led the Bible program at Oklahoma Christian. Dr. Raymond Kelcy chaired the program from 1968 to the time of his death in 1986. At that time, Dr. Howard Norton became chair and served for ten years, from 1986 to 1996. Since then Dr. Lynn McMillon, an OCC graduate, has served as dean of the College of Biblical Studies.

Dr. Darvin Keck came to OCC in 1956 and from that time helped lead the science program. In 1968, he was officially designated as chair of the Division of Exact and Applied Science, and served in that role until 1978. Dr. Jim Baxter led in the science area for the next ten years, from 1978 to 1988. Others with long-time leadership in the science program include Dr. Michael Fowler, an OCC alumnus, who served as chair in natural sciences for four years and then as dean in the science area for another eight; Dr. Len Feuerhelm, who has been chair in the natural and physical sciences for fourteen years; and Don Leftwich, an OCC graduate, who has chaired in math and computer science for thirteen years.

Dr. O. B. Stamper joined the OCC faculty in 1961 to teach education as the college advanced to a four-year program. From 1964 through 1968, he served as associate dean of instruction and then, from 1968 to 1974, was chair of the Division of Education. He led in early efforts for approval of the teacher education program. Since that time, Dr. Gene Talbert, Dr. Lois Exendine, and Dr. Floyd Coppedge have all served for terms of six to eight years to guide the education program. Dr. Gary Shreck served many years as director of teacher education.

In business, Taylor Carter, who came to teach at Central Christian in 1953, served a leadership role until 1968 when Dr. Bernard Keys became chair. Keys served until he left in 1976, and then Dr. Howard Leftwich became chair and filled the role until 1992, a total of sixteen years. Dr. Jack Skaggs and then Dr. Phil Lewis have led the program since that time.

Dr. Ron Bever

Dr. Ron Bever came to OCC in 1964 to teach speech. In 1970, he was named chair of the Division of Speech and Fine Arts and continued in a role of administrative leadership in that area until 1990, a twenty-year period. Dr. Philip Patterson was chair in communications from 1990 to 2005, a total of fifteen years. Michael O'Keefe, who came to OCC in 1981, chaired seventeen years in the art and design program from 1990 to 2007. In music, Dr. Harold Fletcher, who was on the first faculty in 1950, led the program until 1983, when Dr. Ken Adams became chair. Adams and Dr. John Fletcher have alternatively led the music program since that time.

Dr. Jim Wilson is another with long tenure in a leadership role. From 1974 until 1998, twenty-four years, he was either a chair or a dean in the area of social science. Dr. John Maple, an OCC alumnus, has led in the social science area for the past ten years.

Joe McCormack, an OCC alumnus who returned to teach in 1967, has served in two periods of leadership in the language and literature program that together total ten years. Dr. Bailey McBride and Dr. Jeanine Varner have also led in this area and both moved on to become academic leaders of the institution.

All these and many others who have provided academic leadership over the years have played an important role in the success at Oklahoma Christian University. The chapters on Curriculum and Accreditations provide additional information on academic leadership.

The Oklahoma Christian University Teaching Hall of Fame

Six Oklahoma Christian professors have been elected to the university's Teaching Hall of Fame. Each of these faculty members was not only a great teacher, but also made a significant contribution to OC's academic success.

Dr. Harold Fletcher was a member of the very first faculty in Bartlesville in 1950 and continues to teach an occasional class even after his retirement in December 1992. His citation for the Hall of Fame reads in part:

> A true intellectual, Fletcher devoted his professional and personal life to the pursuit of knowledge and wisdom. An extraordinarily gifted musician, he was a talented composer, an outstanding director of the university's musical groups, and a beloved teacher of music theory and history. An avid reader and thinker, he loved introducing students to the great ideas of Western civilization.[8]

In the early years of Central Christian, Fletcher, through his work with the chorus and *Songs America Sings*, provided the premier window through which the public could view the quality of the institution. When he came to the college, he held a master's in music from Hardin Simmons University and, though generally regarded as one of the best informed members of the faculty, did not pursue a doctorate until later in his career, completing a Ph.D. at the University of Oklahoma in 1988. Fletcher was outstanding in motivating students to do their best work and took special satisfaction in helping them learn to think on their own. In 1978, Fletcher received the Gaylord Chair of Distinguished Teaching, and in

Dr. Fletcher with student
Scott LaMascus

2008 was elected to the Oklahoma Higher Education Hall of Fame. Because of his long tenure and outstanding service, Fletcher is clearly among those faculty members exerting the greatest impact on the institution.

Dr. Darvin Keck came to Central Christian College in 1956 from Wilburton, Oklahoma, where he preached and served on the faculty at Eastern State College. At OCC, he taught biology and, as chair of the college's science division, played a major role in laying the foundation for the development of the university's strong program in that area. With his warm smile and a pencil behind his ear, he formed close ties with students. Keck loved to show students the intricacies of God's creation in plants and animals through microscopes or in their natural habitat. For many years, he was a leader among the faculty in accreditation efforts and for improvements at the university. His citation for the Hall of Fame says:

> With the help of his family, Darvin worked sacrificially for the University and its students—raising funds, leading mission trips, coaching basketball, recruiting students, and, of course, teaching. He was known as a demanding teacher, and his teaching prepared generations of students well for graduate school and medical school.[9]

Dr. Darvin Keck

Keck completed his doctorate at Oklahoma State University in 1962, writing his dissertation on the subject of lichens. He received the Gaylord Chair of Distinguished Teaching in 1976 and retired from the university in 1988.

Raymond Vaughn came to Central Christian College in 1958, the year the college moved to Oklahoma City. A respected coach at Capitol Hill High School, Vaughn became the college's first athletic director, and so became the key figure in establishing the high standards of character and performance for the institution's athletic programs. Details of these achievements appear in the chapter on athletics, but Vaughn was much more than just a coach in basketball and track. Because of his deep Christian commitment, he had a strong spiritual impact on the campus, particularly on athletes. His wife Sue taught speech at the college for several years, and the

Ray Vaughn

Vaughns frequently entertained students in their home. A portion of his citation for the Teaching Hall of Fame states:

> His exceptionally rigorous training schedule each day for his track and field teams forced athletes to stretch their limits and to fulfill their potential. . . . Although he respected athletic ability and personal determination, he valued character and moral strength even more. His strong personal faith motivated and directed his whole life, and he mastered the art of helping young people understand the significance of spiritual realities.[10]

After serving more than twenty years, Vaughn died of a brain tumor in 1980.

Dr. Kelcy talking with student Suzie Harmon (Saffell)

Dr. Raymond Kelcy, another member of the OC Teaching Hall of Fame, was a long-time Bible teacher and head of the Bible Department. Kelcy drove from Tulsa to Bartlesville in the college's early days to teach part-time. Later, he attended Southwestern Baptist Theological Seminary for a doctor of theology degree and, in 1963, returned to OCC to teach full time. He showed an unusual combination of qualities: he was firm in the faith and yet showed an openness to learning new ideas; he was a scholar who wrote insightful commentaries on Scripture and yet was glad to take time to discuss with a student the simplest Bible question; he was serious in the pulpit and yet had a dry humor that enlivened his teaching, preaching, and personal relationships. In classes, he not only helped students learn the Scriptures, but helped them learn how to search for their meaning. Kelcy's citation for the Teaching Hall of Fame comments:

> His respect for the inspiration and infallibility of Scripture was the foundation of his teaching and preaching. His scholarship was apparent to his students and to an entire brotherhood. . . . He taught by example and by precept the importance of living with unresolved and unanswerable questions without losing faith in God's wisdom and purpose.[11]

Kelcy provided Oklahoma Christian a major link with the brotherhood of Churches of Christ with whom it is associated, resulting in a high level of trust in the institution's stance on spiritual matters. He died in 1986 of complications following heart surgery.

Dr. Jim Wilson, who taught at Oklahoma Christian from 1969 to 2002, is another member of the Oklahoma Christian Teaching Hall of Fame. His citation reads:

Dr. Jim Wilson

> Jim Wilson knew his students. He knew their names, their majors, their hometowns—and their hearts. He taught large lecture classes, yet he made it a point to know and love his students as individuals. And they loved him in return. He made American history come alive for thousands of students. . . . He had a delightful sense of humor, a winning smile, and an unfailingly kind spirit.[12]

Wilson, appreciated for his engaging teaching style, was known especially for his reenactment in class of the Hamilton-Burr duel and for his plaintive cry about "The Land, The Land." For many years, he taught large sections of required American Government and American History, thus impacting a high percentage of OC students. Wilson, who received his Ph.D. degree from the University of Oklahoma in 1973, served as chair of the History Department and as dean of the College of Liberal Arts. He retired in 2002 because of the onset of Parkinson's disease.

Dr. James Baxter

Dr. James Baxter came to Oklahoma Christian College in 1970 to teach primarily in chemistry. He held a bachelor's degree from David Lipscomb College and both a master's and doctorate from the University of Georgia. In the classroom Baxter was thorough and expected students to learn well, but coupled this with a patience that endeared him to his students. Baxter chaired the Division of Science from 1978 to 1988 and continued to play an important role in the sciences until his retirement in 2004. As an indication of his excellence in the classroom and laboratory, in 1981, Baxter was named to the Gaylord Chair of Distinguished Teaching. As a professor at OC for thirty-four years, Baxter influenced hundreds of students in his chemistry classes and his advising. He was especially helpful to those entering the medical professions.

His citation reads, in part:

> Dr. Baxter was admired for his quiet wisdom, his promotion of professional careers in health services, and his visionary leadership. At the heart of his service was his devotion to his students—his office door was always open and he spent many hours each week tutoring students who needed his help.[13]

Baxter led in expanding the curriculum in the sciences, taught his classes well, and always had time to help students individually.

Distinguished Professors

Five Oklahoma Christian University faculty members have been named to the rank of distinguished professor. This rank requires the professor to

> exceed the requirements of the professorial rank. To be a full Professor is to be recognized as an excellent scholar, teacher, and servant to church and community. The Distinguished Professor rank, therefore, is intended to recognize additional qualities or achievements which exceed the requirements of full Professor. This award is NOT primarily a means of recognizing longstanding service or longevity per se, but rather is an award for distinctive teaching, scholarship and Christian service."[14]

Attaining this rank requires both publishing and recognition in the field from beyond the campus

Dr. Robert McMillan was the first to be named a distinguished professor. McMillan came as a student to Central Christian in Bartlesville in 1957 and finished an associate degree in Oklahoma City in 1959. Returning to teach in 1966, just as the OCC Learning Center was beginning, he developed audiotapes in the teaching of mathematics that proved to be very effective. McMillan finished a doctorate in mathematics at Oklahoma State University in

Dr. Robert McMillan

1969. He was an outstanding teacher, a leader among the faculty, and achieved a high standing among his peers at other universities. McMillan was very active in the Mathematical Association of America, serving as Secretary-Treasurer of the Oklahoma/Arkansas region, a role in which he brought strong recognition to the OC mathematics department. One of his most interesting published articles was on "Babylonian Quadratics." In 1982, he was named to the Gaylord Chair for his outstanding teaching. McMillan was discovered to have cancer in 1999 and, although he was able to continue to teach for a time, the cancer took his life in 2001 after thirty-five years of teaching at OC.

Dr. Lynn McMillon was the second to receive the distinguished professor rank. Graduating from OCC in 1963, McMillon attended Harding Graduate School for the M.A. and M.Th. degrees before receiving his Ph.D. in religion from Baylor University. In 1966 he began teaching at OCC primarily in history, but gradually moved to teaching Bible. McMillon has published a number of articles, and his books include *The Church is Alive and Well on Planet Earth, Doctrines of Demons: A Christian Response to the Occult,* and *Restoration Roots.* For many years, McMillon has taught classes in marriage and family and is both a Licensed

Dr. Lynn McMillon

Professional Counselor and a Licensed Marriage and Family Therapist. He also teaches courses in New Testament books. In 1985, McMillon was awarded the Gaylord Chair of Distinguished Teaching. In 1988, he became chair of the Bible graduate program and, in 1996, dean of the College of Biblical Studies. He was named general manager of the *Christian Chronicle* in 1996 and editor in 2006.

Dr. North and his famous overhead projector

In 1994, Dr. Stafford North became the third recipient of the rank of distinguished professor. North came to Central Christian in 1952 primarily to teach speech, but also taught Bible, Greek, and tennis. Over several years in the late sixties and early seventies, he taught the first course for education majors called Instructional Strategies. For thirty years, 1964 to 1994, North was the primary instructor for freshman orientation from which students remembered his story on the "Bob-tailed Bull" and the "Six Shot Repeater Method." He was especially noted for using visuals: first with the overhead projector, and later using PowerPoint. For thirty-eight years, he served in administrative roles as the chief academic officer and, for twenty years, as executive vice president. During those years, he continued to teach, gradually moving to teach predominantly Bible courses. He was the first OCC professor to develop a course utilizing the audiotape system for the Learning Center and the first to develop a course on the Internet. When he retired from administration in 1994, he began teaching full-time in Bible. North has published many articles in educational and religious journals and written books such as *Handbook on Church Doctrines*, *Unlocking Revelation*, *Like a Thief in the Night*, and *Evangelizing Your Community*. Except for two years when he was away to complete a doctorate at the University of Florida, North has been with the university full-time since January of 1952, making him the person with the most years of full-time service in the university's history.

Dr. John Maple became the fourth OC Distinguished Professor in 1998. An OCC graduate of 1972, Maple returned to teach in 1977 after receiving his master's degree at the University of Virginia. In 1985, he completed his Ph.D. in medieval history at the University of Kansas. He served as the chair of the Behavioral and Social Sciences Department from 1997 to 2002 and then became chair of the History and Political Science Department. Maple has delivered papers and

Dr. John Maple

published articles on medieval Britain and on the British Churches of Christ in the nineteenth century. Maple's spiritual impact on campus is seen in his leading of fourteen campaigns to take students to do church work in England and Scotland between 1987 to 2001. He asks for a high level of performance from his students and many of his majors have been successful. His work with sponsoring the OC chapter of Phi Alpha Theta since 1985 has been outstanding, as that chapter has won numerous national "best chapter" awards. Maple received the Merrick Award for Teaching Excellence in 1980 and held the Gaylord Chair of Distinguished Teaching in 1991.

Dr. Philip Patterson became the fifth OC distinguished professor in 1999 after coming to teach communication at Oklahoma Christian in 1981. Patterson has a bachelor's degree from Lubbock Christian, a master's from Abilene Christian, and received his doctorate from the University of Oklahoma in 1987. He has

Dr. Philip Patterson

specialized in media ethics, writing a widely used textbook in that field with Lee Wilkins. The book was first published in 1991 and is now in its sixth edition. Other Patterson books include *Electronic Millstone: Christian Parenting in a Media Age, Redeeming the Time: The Christian Walk in a Hurried World; Stay Tuned: What Every Parent Should Know about the Media;* and *The Greatest Stories from the Bible.* Patterson has published more books than any other OC faculty member. Since 1997, he also has been the president of the National Christian Schools Association. Patterson has worked closely with students in developing their journalistic skills both in class and through his sponsoring the *Talon.* In 1988, he was awarded the Gaylord Chair.

Gaylord Chair of Distinguished Teaching

In 1973, Oklahoma Christian University established an annual award to be presented to one chosen by academic administrators as an outstanding professor. The award, at first with a $1,000 stipend, and later $2,000, is made possible by funds from the Gaylord family, long-time supporters of the university. The distinction places the professor among those considered to be among the university's best in classroom instruction. Following is a list of those receiving the award and the year of their honor: Don Dunn (1973, 1974), Max Dobson (1975), Darvin Keck (1976), Ralph Burcham (1977), Harold Fletcher (1978), Raymond Kelcy (1979), James Cail (1980), James Baxter (1981), Robert McMillan (1982), Howard Leftwich (1983), James Wilson (1984), Lynn McMillon (1985), Darryl Tippens (1986), John Vincent (1987), Philip Patterson (1988), Michael Fowler (1989), Jeanine Varner (1990), John Maple (1991), Howard Norton (1992), Joe McCormack (1993), Mel Stinnett (1994), Jerald Parker (1995), Paulette Shreck (1996), Loren Gieger (1997), John Thompson (1998), Elaine Kelly (1999), Penny Eubank (2000), Jim Baird (2001), Glenn Pemberton (2002), Scott LaMascus (2003), Kim Gaither (2004), Dwayne Cleveland (2005), David Crismon (2006), Curt Niccum (2007), and Ken Adams (2008).[15]

These professors all have made an important impact on the students of Oklahoma Christian, both by their excellence in the classroom and through their personal contact with students.

Other Faculty Awards

In 1990, the university began to give an award each year to recognize faculty members for their leadership activities with students and other faculty members. Those receiving this award must be exceptional in their classroom work and must demonstrate a positive influence on Oklahoma Christian. Those named for this award began receiving $1,000 but in 2008, the amount was increased to $2,000. Receiving this award over the last nineteen years are: Dr. Ron Bever, Dr. Lois Exendine, Ralph Burcham, Dr. Elmo Hall, Dr. Bill Jones, Dr. Jim Baxter, Dr. Jim Wilson, Dr. Bill Goad, Dr. Larry Jurney, Dr. Max Dobson, Dr. Dwayne Cleveland, Dr. Jack Skaggs, Joe McCormack, Dr. Ken Adams, Dr. Don Drew, Dr. Jim Baird, Dr. Phil Lewis, Dr. Floyd Coppedge, and Dr. Scott LaMascus.[16]

The Merrick Award is another faculty award that was provided most years between 1978 and 2004. Given by the Merrick Foundation to encourage faculty members to find ways to help students learn about free enterprise, the award carried a $1,000 stipend. Winners of the award include: Dr. Howard Leftwich; Dr. John Maple, Joe McCormack, Dr. Lois Exendine, Dr. Bill Goad, Steve Small, Dr. Mark Woodward, Gerry Nixon, Len Feuerhelm, Jim Carter, Dr. John Vincent, Dr. Ron Bever, Ralph DeBoard, Dr. Johannes Snyman, Dr. Jack Skaggs, Elaine Kelly, Jeanetta Sims, and Ken Miller.[17]

In 2008, Jack Rowe, long-time member of the OC Board of Trustees, established a fund to recognize a faculty member who demonstrates excellence in scholarship through published articles, papers, and books, patents, grants, performances, or consulting and related professional services. The winner is granted a $2,000 stipend and receives an additional $3,000 to use in pursuing further efforts in scholarship. Dr. Bill Luttrell was the first recipient in 2008.[18]

Faculty Teaching Twenty or More Years

For a university to have an effective faculty, many of its professors must remain with the institution for long periods of time. Through 2008, fifty-one of the Oklahoma Christian full-time faculty have taught for twenty years or more. The following list indicates the years in which teachers received their twenty-year recognition. Some had started at OC more than twenty years before but had been away for some period attending graduate school or on leave for other reasons. Many of these, of course, continued to teach additional years after their twenty-year mark.

1973 — Harold Fletcher
1974 — Stafford North
1976 — Hugo McCord
1978 — Darvin Keck, Ray Vaughn, Sr.
1980 — Ralph Burcham
1982 — William Jones

1983 — Darrel Alexander, Ron Bever, Bailey McBride*
1984 — Raymond Kelcy
1987 — James Cail,* Max Dobson
1988 — Elmo Hall, Lynn McMillon*
1989 — Howard Leftwich, Joe McCormack,*
         Robert McMillan,* Jim Wilson
1990 — James Baxter, Sandra Lockwood, Richard Mock
1991 — Lois Exendine, Gary Shreck,* Roland Schultz
1993 — Ken Adams,* Mike Gipson,* Geneva Hoover
1995 — Richard Greenhaw
1996 — Cherry Tredway,* Len Feuerhelm
1997 — Merle Gatewood, Randy Heath*
1999 — Peggy Gipson,* Don Leftwich,* Phil Reagan,
         Mark Woodward
2000 — John Maple,* Michael O'Keefe, Jack Skaggs,
         John Thompson,* John Vincent
2001 — Philip Patterson
2002 — Jim Cutbirth, Bill Goad*
2003 — Dan Hays
2004 — Ralph DeBoard,* Loren Gieger
2005 — Larry Jurney
2006 — Tamie Willis
2007 — Jim Elkins, John Fletcher*[19]

* OC Alumnus

Faculty Snapshots

A complete report of the more than six hundred different people who have taught one or more courses at Oklahoma Christian University since its beginning in Bartlesville in 1950 would be beyond the scope of this history.[20] Unfortunately, many who made a significant contribution through their years of teaching cannot be mentioned at all. Yet, all who have taught a class at the university have made an important impact for good on the twenty-five thousand students[21] who have attended during the university's fifty-eight years.

Students will recall certain images of teachers that can serve to summarize the vital effect of the faculty on their students and, through them, on the world. Here are "pictures" many will remember: Dr. Don Dunn enthusiastically filling the chalkboard several times during one lecture; Dr. Lynn McMillon and his genograms; Dr. Kim Gaither teaching almost until the day she died of cancer; Dr. Mike Gipson leading students around the campus to identify different types of foliage; Dr. Mike Fowler sharing with students about his work in St.

Anthony Hospital's laboratory; Dr. Jim Baxter patiently explaining again a formula in beginning chemistry; Dr. Howard Leftwich leading students through "supply and demand"; Dr. Raymond Kelcy, with his Texas drawl, diagramming a sentence on the board in Greek; Dr. Max Dobson helping his students work with handicapped children from Edmond; Dr. Hugo McCord saying, "Get out a half-a-sheet of paper"; Dr. James Cail and his matching test of a hundred psychological terms; Dr. Lois Exendine bringing food to students; Ralph Burcham remembering the names of all his students; Avon Malone and his sayings; Dr. John Thompson teaching his class by phone from a hospital bed; Dr. Stafford North balancing a fifteen-foot pole on his chin to amuse students in freshman orientation; Joe McCormack teaching the campus how to welcome Japanese exchange students with "konichiwa"; Dr. Cherry Tredway, in her early days at OCC, making costumes for *Songs America Sings*; and Dr. Gary Shreck sharing illustrations from his former students.

Dr. Bailey McBride making an insightful explanation of a Shakespearean metaphor; Dr. Loren Gieger commenting on a picture he took of a site in the Bible lands; Dr. Dudley Chancey helping a student find a job as a youth minister; Dr. Curt Niccum translating as he reads from the Greek text; Dr. Larry Jurney showing students how to use video equipment in the lab; Dr. Ken Adams insisting on the exact rhythm from the bass section; Dr. Darrel Alexander looking up from the sewing machine in the costume shop; Michael O'Keefe insisting that a student could do better work and then inviting him for a meal; Dr. Mark Woodward recruiting students for a Let's Start Talking Campaign; Randy Heath gathering the track team on the floor of the gym lobby before they go outside to run; Dr. Darryl Tippens encouraging the contemplative life by telling of the church fathers; Dr. John Vincent with a fake fly on his forehead to create class discussion; Dr. Jeanine Varner promoting lifelong learning by asking students about important discoveries in the last ten years; Howard Norton sharing stories from Brazil; and Mel Stinnett stimulating class discussion by posing questions for the class to consider.

Dr. Jerald Parker reviewing a senior project by telling how it could have been better and then commending its strengths; Dr. Paulette Shreck emphasizing to students that the grammar is important as well as the content; Elaine Kelly pleading for precision in an accounting paper; Penny Eubank singing with the Jazz Band; Dr. Glenn Pemberton insisting that since the Old Testament is three times longer than the New Testament it must be—well, you know; Dr. Dwayne Cleveland sharing the value of phonics with his class in teaching reading; David Crismon extolling the virtues of an abstract painting; Merle Gatewood explaining the requirements of certification to teach English; Dr. Peggy Gipson and Jane Austen; Arnie Anderson taking summer trips to find new places to paint; Dr. Ron Bever and I'm OK—You're OK; Dr. Elmo Hall explaining—at length—how to learn Christian truths from the young demon Wormwood; Dr. Roland Schultz extolling the virtues of Toastmasters; Dr. Len Feuerhelm's insistence that quantum physics is easier than calculus; Don Leftwich teaching the latest computer language; Phil Reagan reading Christmas poetry at *Cocoa and Carols*; Dr. Jack Skaggs sharing with students the latest theories in business management; Dr. John Fletcher preparing students for Vienna; Dr. Jim Cutbirth helping students build a car for the Baja competition; Ralph DeBoard recruiting students to work at Capitol Hill; Dr. Scott LaMascus giving individual attention to a student to encourage her to her best work; and Jim Baird's uproarious laughter at something funny in class.

Because of their courageous struggle with serious illness, five OC faculty members have held a special place in the hearts of their colleagues and their students. These five fought through difficulties with cancer or other debilitating illness and set for the entire campus an example of how Christians deal with such circumstances. Ray Vaughn, Dr. Robert McMillan, Dr. Kim Gaither, and Dr. Tony Alley all died of cancer, but all continued to teach as long as they were physically able to do so. These were much beloved and all demonstrated great courage in facing death. A fifth, John Thompson, suffers with diabetes, which eventually made it necessary for both feet to be amputated. He continues to teach from a wheelchair, and his courage has been inspirational to all who know him.

Librarians

Over the fifty-eight years of its history, six persons have served as directors of the OC Library. These faculty members have played a key role in designing and furnishing library facilities, in building the collection, and in keeping the library up–to-date. Winnie Clayton served as the first librarian from 1950 through 1953. Oma Belle Carter followed and served as head librarian from 1953 to 1964, a time that included the move of the library from Bartlesville to Oklahoma City. Clarice French came in 1964 and served until she retired in 1973. She oversaw both the move of the library into the Learning Center and the change from the Dewey Decimal System to the Library of Congress System. Les Lauen served from 1973 to 1979, and Dr. Brad Robison was the director who has served the longest, from 1979 through 1998. Tamie Willis replaced Robison

Geneva Hoover

and continues to lead in the library program. Malcom Hinckley was reference librarian from 1969 to 1980,[22] and Gladys Burcham served as circulation librarian from 1975 to 1991. Geneva Hoover is the librarian with the longest service—forty years from 1965 to 2005.

Faculty play a most important role in any educational institution, but at Oklahoma Christian, they have served well, not only to instruct students, but to encourage them, comfort them, correct them, and to model Christian living for them. Their personal interest in students' development has shown itself in many ways: individual conferences, course advisement, sponsoring student clubs, going on campaigns with students, attending student activities and performances, and having students in their homes.

Key Staff Members

As important as it is for a university to have an effective faculty, they cannot do their work well unless a good staff provides for them needed resources and facilities. Many have filled these staff roles well during the life of the university. Eldy Davis came in 1950 to oversee maintenance of the campus facilities in Bartlesville. Clarence Buller replaced him in 1957, oversaw the move to Oklahoma City, and continued as director of buildings and grounds until 1985. During many of these years, Lawrence Weber was director of maintenance. When Buller retired, after serving twenty-seven years, Jim Stephens came to oversee the campus plant and served until May 2007.[23] Having had only three men in this role over a span of fifty-six years is highly unusual. These men met emergency problems such as the campus being without electricity, water main breaks, sewer backups, malfunctions in the campus water pump, and even bomb threats. And they have overseen the day-to-day routine of keeping buildings clean, air conditioning and heating working properly, remodeling, repairs, and landscaping. Many have worked with them over the years with the following serving twenty years or more: Camey Johnson, Terry R. Johnson, Doug Bryant, Leland Parsons, Jacob Donnell, Ivan Stewart, and James Lauderdale, who has served as manager of the

Eldy Davis

Clarence Buller

Jim Stephens

apartments. These staff members, and those working with them, have made a most important contribution to the success of the university.[24] Maci Jackson has been the university's most productive volunteer, having come from Brownsville, Texas, in 1987 and serving in various roles but primarily, since 1998, in overseeing campus landscaping where her work has greatly beautified the campus.

From 1958 until 1977, Glenn Nance directed food service in the OCC Cafeteria. While sometimes stern on the exterior, Nance worked hard to serve, preparing many food boxes for students to take on special outings and providing many special dinners on campus. Kurt Hermanson, directing the work of the university's food service company, has filled this role well for twenty years.

Lou Phillips

Roberta Bachmann

Other long-term staff members represent those who have served well in roles of important service. Lou Phillips came in 1975 to be secretary to President Johnson and served throughout his term of office. She also worked in various capacities in the President's Office during the terms of Presidents Kevin Jacobs and Mike O'Neal. Roberta Bachmann came in 1962 as secretary to Dean North, then worked in various capacities in the Registrar's Office under Bob Smith and Mickey Banister, serving for thirty-eight years before retiring in 2000.[25]

Bryan Williams came in 1982 to head the college's computer services and, serving in various roles since that time, has helped in the advance from one computer on campus to thousands. Joyce Brownlie has served in the business office since 1977; Merle Neill and Janice Dodd worked in that area for more than twenty years, and so has Dorothy Whitley who continues there. David Owens served more than twenty years as director of public relations and Katherine Brown for more than twenty years as dormitory supervisor and dean of women. Polly Wiginton was director of the campus store for more than twenty years and Alice Merrell's work in the college-owned religious bookstore also exceeded twenty years.[26]

Several women have served as secretaries, administrative assistants, or other office roles for twenty years or more: Dot Maple in Admissions, Beverly Whiddon in Social Science, Wanda Neel in Business, Dea Fields in Physical Education, Mary Ann Sipes for the Oklahoma Christian Investment Corporation, Francis Sawyer in Language and Literature and the Office of Vice President for Academic

Affairs, Margaret Whaley in the Health and Counseling Center, Iola Gieger primarily in the Office of Vice President for Academic Affairs, Jane Neece in several administrative offices including Office of the President, and Julie Anderson in Education and Physical Education/ Athletics.[27]

Conclusion

More than buildings or curriculum, Oklahoma Christian University is people. Those faculty and staff who have come and stayed over a long period of time have made the major contribution to achieving the institution's goals for its students. Every day, faculty members contact students in their classrooms, helping them to grow intellectually and spiritually, and every day faculty members are also helping students develop through informal contact in the hallway, in their offices, directing a performing group, at a club meeting, or through a shared service experience. Staff members contribute too, not only by their work behind the scenes in providing necessary services, but by their contact with students who work with them or use their service. The faculty and staff of the university have come to the campus because they believe in the mission of Oklahoma Christian, and these have done their work to move students toward the goals the institution has for them.

Chapter 7, Endnotes

[1]   Records of First Week Follies, Office of Bob Lashley. Copy in the OC Archives.

[2]   Files of Vice President for Academic Affairs, OC Archives.

[3]   *Catalog, 2006–2007*, Oklahoma Christian University, 17–21.

[4]   "The Mission Documents of Oklahoma Christian University," available online at OC's homepage: About OC, Mission and Purpose, Mission Documents; *President's Report*, 1969.

[5]   *Report to the North Central Association*, May, 1965, 68, OC Archives.

[6]   Information on dates for this section is taken from OC Catalogs from 1950 to the present.

[7]   "Joe Watson appointed Vice President for Administration," *Campus Community*, January 6, 1994, OC Archives.

[8]   Citation for Harold Fletcher for the Oklahoma Christian University Teaching Hall of Fame, posted on the wall of the Gotcher Room in the Gaylord Center.

[9]   Citation for Darvin Keck for the Oklahoma Christian University Teaching Hall of Fame, posted on the wall of the Gotcher Room in the Gaylord Center.

[10]   Citation for Ray Vaughn for the Oklahoma Christian University Teaching Hall of Fame, posted on the wall of the Gotcher Room in the Gaylord Center.

[11]   Citation for Raymond Kelcy for the Oklahoma Christian University Teaching Hall of Fame, posted on the wall of the Gotcher Room in the Gaylord Center.

[12]   Citation for Jim Wilson for the Oklahoma Christian University Teaching Hall of Fame, posted on the wall of the Gotcher Room in the Gaylord Center.

[13]   Citation for James Baxter for the Oklahoma Christian University Teaching Hall of Fame, posted on the wall of the Gotcher Room in the Gaylord Center.

[14]   *OC Faculty Handbook*, 1998–99, 12.

[15]   From the Files of the Office of Vice President for Academic Affairs.

[16]   Ibid.

[17]   Ibid.

[18]   Ibid.

[19]   Ibid.

[20]   Estimate from Mickey Banister, Office of the Registrar.

[21]   Ibid.

[22]   "Hinckley Retires from Library Post after 11 Years of Service," *OCC Reporter*, June, 1980, OC Archives.

[23]   From the Files of the Office of Executive Vice President.

[24]   Ibid.

[25]   Ibid.

[26]   Ibid.

[27]   Ibid.

Chapter 8
THE STUDENTS

While presidents and administrators, faculty, staff, Board members, facilities, library, accreditation, and many other facets of a university are important, the students are the most important element, since everything else serves for their ultimate benefit. No history of Oklahoma Christian, therefore, would be complete without considering the students who have attended. Later chapters on Student Life, Athletics, Musicals and Theatre, Spiritual Life, and Missionary Spirit provide additional information on students and their activities. This chapter, however, focuses on demographic data about students, majors they have chosen, comparisons with students from other institutions, and student involvement in governance and campus publications.

Fifty-Eight Years of Students

According to Registrar Mickey Banister, some twenty-five thousand students have attended Oklahoma Christian during its fifty-eight years since 1950. Every state in the Union has been represented, with Oklahoma providing about 45 percent of the students, Texas usually sending about 15 percent, and Kansas about 5 percent. Colorado and Missouri stand next in line.[1] More than seventy-five foreign countries have been represented among OC students over the years, with Japan leading the list because of OC's exchange program with Ibaraki Christian University. Other countries having sent ten or more students are India, Canada, Brazil, Hong Kong, Kenya, Rwanda, United Kingdom, and Venezuela. A high point of international students came in 1991, when 101 students from outside the country represented 31 different nations. Again in 2007, the number reached 101, representing 35 countries.

Over the years, the number of men and women has been almost equal. In the earliest years, there were more men, then, a little later, women edged ahead. In 1987, the number was equal and from then to 2006, the men were usually one to three percentage points ahead. In 2006, however, the full-time women outnumbered the full-time men by a small number: 921 to 893, and in 2007, full-time women again outnumbered full-time men by 1040 to 1023.

As part of its mission, Oklahoma Christian has emphasized living on-campus so students can benefit from campus activities and dormitory life. With a requirement throughout the years for college-age, single students, living away from home to reside on campus, the percentage of full-time students in campus housing has remained relatively high. Once hovering around 90 percent, the number has gradually declined over the years as the student body has become more diverse. The age requirement has also been lowered a bit to allow a few more students to live off-campus. In 2001 through 2004, the percentage dropped into the high seventies, but with the opening of the new student residences, the number climbed back to 82 percent in both 2005 and 2006. In the fall of 2007, 78 percent of students lived in campus housing.

Religious preference of the students is another important factor. Since the university sees its mission to serve primarily those from Churches of Christ, it has drawn most of its students from this religious body. In the college's early years, the percentage of students from Churches of Christ exceeded 90 percent. From 1986 through 1995, the number ranged above 80 percent. From 1996 through 1998, the percentage fell slightly below the 80 percent mark, but from 1999 to 2004 was back in the 80s. In 2005, the percentage was 79, and in 2006 it was 77. In 2007, the percentage of undergraduate, full-time students from Churches of Christ students dropped to 73 percent, primarily because of an increase in international students and athletes. Baptists have averaged 4 to 7 percent of the student body, with the Christian Church, Methodist Church, Catholic Church, and community churches usually ranging from 1 to 5 percent.

Over the last twenty-five years, the racial mix among full-time students has changed modestly. In 1986, for example, Caucasian students composed 92 percent of the students, with Black students making up 5 percent and other races, 3 percent. By 2007, Caucasian students made up 81 percent, with Black students still at 5 percent, American Indian or Alaskan Native students at 4 percent, Hispanic students at 3 percent, and other ethnic groups making up the remaining 7 percent.

In terms of their readiness for college, as measured by the ACT test, students have shown marked improvement over the years. In 1985, for example, the composite score for OCC's entering freshmen was 18.8, compared with a 17.5 norm for Oklahoma and an 18.6 average nationwide. In that year, 30 percent of OCC's freshmen scored 15 or below on the ACT test. By 1993, OC's entering freshmen averaged 21.9 compared with 20.2 for Oklahoma and 20.7 nationally. The percentage at 15 or below had dropped to 26 percent. By 1998, the OC average had risen to 23.3 compared to a national average of 21.0. In the fall of 2007, the national average had risen to 21.2 and the Oklahoma average to 20.7, but the OC average had risen to 23.6. Since 1985, then, OC's average score on the ACT test increased 4.8 points, while the national average gained only 2.6 points and the Oklahoma average gained 2.2. Some of this increase was due to the start of engineering, honors, and other programs that draw students with higher ACT scores.

For many years, National Merit Finalists have chosen to attend OC. In the Fall of 1990, there were five in the student body. By 1993, the number had risen to twelve. In 1998, the number of finalists had risen to nineteen,[2] and the number has held near that with fifteen in the student body of 2006–2007.[3]

Student Accomplishments

A good measure of the quality of OC students and the programs in which they have taken part comes from their achievements over the years in activities that allow comparisons to students from other universities. A complete listing of such accomplishments would go far beyond the scope of this history, but the sampling below provides a window into the quality of work OC students have done when competing with those at other universities.

From the second year of Central Christian College in Bartlesville, 1951–52, through the mid-90's, students participated in intercollegiate debate and individual speaking contests. The activity was eventually dropped for several reasons: interest among incoming students had waned, no faculty member was interested in coaching the team, and tournaments began to be scheduled on Sundays, making it difficult for students and faculty to attend tournaments and still be faithful to their spiritual commitments.

Over the more than forty years of debate participation, Oklahoma Christian students consistently brought home speaking honors. In 1957, at the Oklahoma Junior College Tournament, for example, Stafford North coached debaters James Cail and Charles McCord to a first place finish and Barbara Anthony and Rose Mansur to second place and the team, as a whole, won the tournament. Cail and McCord won again in 1958. In 1959, the college again won the Oklahoma Junior College Tournament, their 124 total points far outpacing the 74

*Debaters James Cail
and Charles McCord*

points of their nearest competitor. Gary Rayburn, Leslie Kline, Linda Webb, Viola Thomas, Charles Floyd, and La Danta Fullington, all contributed to the success.

After moving to senior college status, OCC debaters continued to compete successfully. In 1979, for example, under the leadership of Coach Angela Laird (Brenton), the team garnered eighteen trophies, including a first-place trophy won by David Slaughter and Greg Watts at the Midwestern State University Tournament. Many on the team that year also placed in individual events.[4] By 1983, Roger Kelcy was coaching, and two OCC students, Allison Dabbs (Garrett) and James Hallmark, became the first from the college qualifying to compete at the National Forensic Tournament—both in two individual speaking events. The next year, the OCC team won thirty-seven trophies and qualified three students for nationals: Kelly King, Sharon Peugh (Simmons), and Brian Simmons. At nationals, Simmons had the fourth highest number of speaker points among all participants.[5] The next year, by December of 1984, the OCC team, still with Kelcy as coach, had risen to a third place ranking among all colleges and universities in the nation. UCLA and Weber State were first and second but OCC's third place ranked them above the Air Force Academy at fourteenth, the University of Florida at twenty-sixth, MIT at forty-forth, and the University of Oklahoma at fifty-sixth.[6] Six students participated on this squad: Simmons, Peugh,

*Coach Roger Kelcy, left, and the 1984 debate
team of Connie Dudgeon, Mark Melton,
Brian Simmons, Sharon Peugh (Simmons),
Kevin Landreth, and Piper Mills (John)*

Eddie Boren, Kevin Landreth, Piper Mills (John), and Mark Melton. The group ended the year ranked ninth nationally out of 282 colleges and universities and second in the South Central Region composed of Kansas, Oklahoma, Texas, Missouri, Arkansas, and Louisiana.[7]

OC students have also excelled in passing the CPA examination. For the past twenty years, OC officials have tracked the results to determine how well they were preparing students for this difficult test. In 1987, for example, the OCC pass rate was 23.3 percent, topped in the state only by the University of Oklahoma's 27.1 percent. In 1989, OCC ran away from other institutions with a pass rate of 38.2 while Oklahoma State came in second with 28.4. In 1993 and 1997, OC again had the highest pass rate.[8] Over a span of thirteen years, OC students topped all other Oklahoma universities eleven times.[9] In a different but related measure, in 2006–2007, three OC senior accounting majors won the first CPA Campus Competition over other Oklahoma universities in a program sponsored by the Oklahoma Society of CPAs.

OC business students have also shown success in their competition with students from other universities in business games and similar events. In 2006, for example, they won the nationwide competition to develop a marketing plan for a book by Ken Blanchard and Phil Hodges called *Lead Like Jesus.* As a reward, Dr. Blanchard came to Oklahoma City to speak at an event sponsored by the university.

Emory Team of 1970-1971. Front left to right, Shannon Jones, Larry Gould, Mike McDonald; standing Dr. Bernard Keys, Kerry Harvey, Ed Spencer, Dr. Howard Leftwich

OC's business students have won high honors in a wide variety of competition. In 2006, they took the first runner-up trophy in both Students in Free Enterprise and the International Collegiate Business Strategy Competition.[10] In 1983, the OCC team took first place nationally in parliamentary procedure[11] and continued to take that title for five more consecutive years.[12] In 1969 and again in 1971, OCC's business team took second place in the Emory University Intercollegiate Business Game. The *OCC Reporter* revealed that "Some 40 colleges and universities including The Citadel, Notre Dame, Vanderbilt, Wake Forrest and others competed in the hypothetical manufacturing and marketing of sports equipment." Dr. Howard Leftwich and Dr. Bernard Keys were faculty sponsors.[13]

OC students have also excelled in admission to medical schools. Just since 1992, seventy-nine OC students have been admitted to a medical school for training as a physician or dentist. Others have been admitted to programs in physical therapy, medical research, optometry, and other medical fields. According to Dr. Len Feuerhelm, who has kept records on these admissions, more than 90 percent of OC students who qualify to apply for medical school are admitted.

Engineering students from OC take the Fundamentals of Engineering examination, the national first exam for professional licensure. The pass rate for these students stands at 93 percent, another indicator of OC student success on outside standardized measures.

The Brass Ring Awards have been given since 1986 in a competition among university students in graphic arts. With entries from a six-state area, Oklahoma Christian students have won the "Best of Show" in nine out of twenty-one years. They have also brought home a number of other awards. In 2006, for example, students from fifteen universities entered 615 items, and of the 64 awards given, OC students won 18 of them.[14]

A student newspaper has been part of student activities since the university's very first year in Bartlesville. First called the *Tower* and later the *Talon*, this student newspaper has won high recognition. In 1985, for the first time, the Associated Collegiate Press named the paper as All-American, placing it among the top 5 percent of student newspapers. Dr. Philip Patterson, faculty sponsor, said the reason the paper received the high rating was "the outstanding look of the paper. Its style, its large number of pages, its use of syndicated and wire service material all combined to the winning of the honor."[15] Lora Postelwait was editor. In 1990, the *Talon* was not only named All-American but it also received one of three "Best of Show" awards for a four-year college at the National Conference of the College Press.[16] The *Talon* also won All-American for four more straight years, 1991–1994, and in 1994, was also named a "first place" newspaper by the American Scholastic Press Association.[17] While the *Talon* no longer enters this competition, the student paper is still of high quality and provides an excellent learning opportunity for students.

The trophy case in the Mabee Communications Building is filled with evidence that OC students have excelled in broadcast competitions. In 1993, Torrey Foster and David Jurney, for example, won "Best of Show" at the National Broadcasting Society/AERHO convention.[18] Since 1991, OC broadcasting students have won eleven first place awards from the Oklahoma Broadcast Education Association in such fields as radio documentary, TV and radio hard news, corporate video,

Trophy case for broadcasting awards

radio sports coverage, TV public service announcement, TV music video, radio feature news story, and radio entertainment. OC students also have captured seven first place awards from the National Broadcasting Society's regional awards in the Western National Competition. Former broadcasting students David Jurney and David Jones also have garnered seven Telly Awards for their work in video productions.

Joel Baxter, an electrical engineering graduate, received a $60,000 grant from the National Science Foundation for graduate study and chose to use it at Stanford University.[19] In 1993, Baxter and Tom Peterson won the Outstanding Engineering Achievement Awards from the Oklahoma Society of Professional Engineers.[20] In the same year, Paula Holcomb was accepted into the Summer Research Institution at NASA's Goddard Space Flight Center, and Thad McCraken went to Los Alamos National Laboratories for the Science and Engineering Research Semester.[21]

In music, OC students have also excelled. Five voice students won professional roles in Tulsa Opera Company's 1986 fall productions. Also in 1986, music student Robert Reed advanced to the finals of the National Association of Teachers of Singing Competition, being one of five out of 666 entrants from a three-state region to make the finals. He also won the district auditions of New York's Metropolitan Opera.[22] In 1993, Michael McLain won first in the Oklahoma Mozart Aria competition and, as a result, was offered a performing role with the Oklahoma Philharmonic's production of *The Marriage of Figaro*.[23]

An unusual measure of student quality comes from OC's Tau Sigma Chapter of Phi Alpha Theta, the National History Honor Society. This active group sponsors an annual history day for high school students in the area, and the OC students present research papers at regional and national conferences. This organization has won the national "Best Chapter Award" twelve times consecutively from 1996 through 2007.[24] They also publish a journal each year and enter it in a national competition. In 2003 they tied for first place and in 2007 placed third. Over the past twelve years, in the regional competition for research papers, students from OC have garnered seven firsts and seven seconds.[25]

In 2000, OC electrical engineering students Brandon Hombs and Jeremy Poole placed first in a contest with engineering students from fifteen other engineering schools in a contest to build a circuit from parts and instructions provided. In 2001, electrical engineering students from Oklahoma Christian placed second in a competition with major engineering schools to build a robot that could find its own way through a maze and then could remember the correct path and go through again making only correct turns. Amanda Bryan, Andrew Krebs, and Austin White designed and built the robot that won over universities from Oklahoma, Missouri, South Dakota, Illinois, Louisiana, and Arkansas.[26] Another electrical engineering student, James Klein, placed second in a regional contest among engineering students to write papers for submission to a journal. In 2007, engineering students Ben Johnson and Andrew Aston placed second in a contest to analyze a case involving engineering ethics.

OC's mechanical engineering students build a small car to compete with those constructed by students in many schools of engineering from all over the nation. One year, their car claimed fifth place in the engineering and design element, eighth in the maneuverability race, ninth in sales presentation, and thirty-ninth in the four-hour endurance race. Their overall finish was thirty-second out of eighty-seven entrants.

OC's entry in the mini-Baja competition in 1999

Another mark of student success has come on what has been called "the world's most difficult exam" given by the Mathematical Association of America. Usually a third of the students solve none of the twelve problems and a score of 30 out of 120 possible points is outstanding. In 2007, a typical year, 3753 students from 516 universities from the U.S. and Canada took the exam, including students from most of the major universities. Over the years, in the Oklahoma-Arkansas Section, three Oklahoma Christian students have taken the top honors in competition with students from the major universities in these two states: William Clinger in 1972, Don Leftwich in 1974, and Nicklaus Little in 2007.[27]

Alpha Chi is an organization for the top 10 percent of students in 300 colleges and universities around the nation. Its members are encouraged to participate in an essay contest for scholarships to graduate school and the top twelve are chosen each year. Recent OC student winners have been Lacey Turner in 2004 and Lauren Allison and Heather Meyer in 2006.

Oklahoma Christian's education majors, along with all the others in the state who want to be certified to teach, must take the Certification Examinations for Oklahoma Educators. From 2001 to 2006, OC's teacher education candidates had pass rates that placed the institution among the top three in four of the five years.[28]

These student achievements and awards are only illustrative. The list could be extended. Although many important awards are not included, these demonstrate that students from Oklahoma Christian fare well in a wide variety of fields in which they compete with students from other outstanding universities.

Student Majors

A look at undergraduate student majors at ten year intervals over the years in Oklahoma City demonstrates interesting trends. While exact matches on the numbers over this period are not possible because the categories of majors have varied through the years, the chart below gives a good overview of the number majoring in various fields.

Major	1965	1975	1985	1995	2005
Bible	58	130	107	114	126
Business	140	257	455	203	233
Art, Ad. Design, Interior Design	9	26	44	70	142
Speech and Mass Communication	21	71	87	86	125
Music	7	28	40	30	58
Elementary and Special Education	120	135	117	197	126
Secondary Education	89*				
Language and Literature	23	40	38	47	78
Physical Education	0	76	54	54	52
Natural Science, Pre-Med, & Related	68	151	114	197	178
Math and Computer Science	38	38	104	68	84
Pre-Engineering and Engineering	16	24	69	143	177
Pre-Nursing and Nursing	0	57	23	16	38
Behavioral and Social Science	47	140	143	147	194
Home Economics	24	62	19	0	0
Undecided and Liberal Studies	72	216	78	116	224
Part-time	58*				
Total Full Time and Part Time	790	1451	1492	1488	1835

*In 1965, the part-time students were not shown by majors and so are shown in the chart as a separate number; also in 1965, the secondary education majors were not shown by fields as in other years.

This data allows several observations. Some programs that once offered only the first two years have been expanded to baccalaureate programs: nursing, engineering, art, and music. The Bible majors have grown some in numbers over the years but are a decreasing percentage of the total enrollment. Business majors now are fewer than in some previous years, partly because such majors as computer science, while business related, are now classified in a different field. Education majors constitute a much smaller percentage of the whole than in previous years, reflecting both the availability of other options at OC and national trends. Natural science and pre-medical majors have grown to some extent, especially if coupled with the nursing program. Engineering has grown from 16 pre-engineering majors in 1965 to 177 in full degree programs in 2005. There has been strong growth in fields like advertising design and interior design, but there is no longer a program in home economics. Other majors such as speech and mass communications, music, language and literature, and behavioral sciences have grown in numbers as the total enrollment has grown. And as the university has added more specialized programs, a large number of students have moved into them.

Student Government

Andy Benton

Dusty Davis

Near the end of Oklahoma Christian's first year in Bartlesville, students elected Bill Gosnell as the first president of the student body. Since that time, the students have selected a successor each year. Fifty-five different persons, in fact, have served as presidents of the student government with two, Andy Benton (1972–1974) and Dusty Davis (1998–2000) serving two terms. Michelle Thompson (Stephens) (1988–1989) was the first female president, and she has been followed by three more: Jeanetta Sims (Davis) (1991–1992); Angel English (Holland) (1996–1997); and Jenny Davis (Vanover) (1997–1998).[29] The Davis family filled the role for three consecutive years with her brother, Dusty, following Jenny the next two years. Of those who have filled this role, thirteen have later served on the OC faculty or staff including long-term faculty members Gary Rayburn (1959-1969), Lynn McMillon (1961-1962), Ralph DeBoard (1967-1968), Kent Hartman (1976-1977), John Thompson (1977-1978), and Jeanetta Sims (1991-1992). Two have served on the Board

Michelle Thompson (Stephens)

of Trustees: Charles Floyd (1958–1959) and Michelle Thompson (Stephens) (1988–1989). Twelve went on to preach, and others have been successful in other fields.

Student government has filled an important role throughout the years. In addition to the president, students have chosen other officers and a council or senate for the student government. From their efforts have come recommendations to the administration about changes in policies, campus needs, and campus events. They have provided a means for students to express their views on many issues, and although university administrators have not always done as they requested, their voices have often led to the changes they sought. For many years, the student body president served on the Administrative Council where he or she took equal part with other members in making important decisions about a host of campus matters.

One of the most important functions of student government has been to provide members for many committees on campus. Over the years, most standing faculty-administrative committees such as the Academic Life Committee, the Spiritual Life Committee, the Student Activities Committee, and others have had student members. These students have provided useful insights for the work of these groups, and their participation has been a good learning experience.

Richard Mock, who served as advisor to student government for many years, recalls that when business major Ron Verner became president for 1975–1976, he initiated a program to train the student officers and representatives to make them more effective. Verner even worked with those chosen to serve on faculty committees to prepare them for their task. The training concept has continued through many years.[30]

OC student on Kite Day helping a student from Western Village

OC students have paid an activity fee or student senate dues that have provided funds for student government. The university allocates these funds to an account for student leaders to spend as they choose. In the 2006–2007 year, these funds amounted to $73,265.[31]

The student government has taken a major role in providing activities for students. They have brought movies, engaged performers for concerts, sponsored trips to Six Flags and local entertainment venues, and promoted school spirit with activities and prizes at ball games and chapel. Each year, the Senate sponsors a Christmas Banquet, continuing a tradition started in Bartlesville.

Throughout the history of Oklahoma Christian, the Student Senate has also encouraged students in service to the community and to the church. In many years, they have helped students financially to attend the World Mission Workshop, and since 2002, they have assisted the Campus Life Office in using students as mentors at the Western Village Elementary School. On some occasions, Student Senate has sponsored a fund drive among students to support special causes such as disaster relief and tragedies to individuals or families.

The student government has also been involved in many important campus events. They have overseen the selection of the Homecoming Court, including Homecoming Queen, and have sponsored activities and competition among clubs in Homecoming exhibits. For many years, they also coordinated the building of a Homecoming bonfire.

Gamma Rho Homecoming exhibit in 1979

They have helped orient new students to campus each fall, organized student retreats and picnics, and trained students who will occupy positions of leadership.

Student government at Oklahoma Christian, then, has been an important part of campus life since the beginning of the university. Through this channel, students have voiced their opinions and often affected policies and programs. Students themselves have brought their own entertainment and activities and have promoted service. Lurking behind the scenes, of course, is one of the major purposes of student government: an important learning experience for students.

Cheerleaders stir up the crowd at a homecoming bonfire in 1991

Student Publications

Student Newspaper

In the first year of its operation, Central Christian College students began a campus newspaper. Called the *Tower* after the imposing tower topping The Mansion, the publication began in October 1950.

The Tower of November 22, 1956

Published biweekly, the newspaper consisted of four pages, eight and a half by eleven inches in size. The first yearbook noted the following students as having part in gathering and writing the news: Gloria Fritzmeier, Barbara Minor, Mildred Webb, Ortell Armstrong, Gwen Hall, Lois Summers, Anne McPherson, Jo Anne Adams, and Sarah Parker.

As is typical of student publications, the *Tower* reported on campus events and personalities, announced coming activities, and expressed student opinions. The May 24, 1957, issue, for example, reported on some staff changes, told who would be the baccalaureate and commencement speakers, revealed who would edit the school paper and yearbook for the coming year, gave brief verbal snapshots of members of the sophomore class, reported on a faculty picnic, and provided sports news. Rita Payne (McGinnis) editorialized on the year by commending some activities, but criticizing other student groups for not being active enough during the year. "There were," she said, "just too few who have enough interest in the school at heart to carry out the responsibilities of the whole."[32]

In the 1957–1958 school year, the last in Bartlesville, Bailey McBride, the first student to return to teach, was faculty sponsor, while Charles Floyd and Francis Marbury were co-editors. The staff of twenty published the paper, which had grown to a page size of twelve by eighteen.

After Central Christian moved to Oklahoma City, the student newspaper changed its name from the *Tower*, which no longer fit, to the *Talon*, connecting it with the institutions' eagle mascot. The paper ran biweekly in tabloid size. By 1969, the *Aerie* reported that, under the editorship of Linda Butler (King), the *Talon* was "one of the best papers published by any college of comparable size," and "during the winter trimester the paper was published weekly."[33] The *Talon* has continued as a weekly publication since that time.

The Talon, January 12, 1968

For the Spring trimester of 1970, the paper became smaller in size, eight and a half by eleven, being called the *Mini Talon*, but the larger tabloid size returned in September. Starting in Fall 1971, however, the *Talon* used the smaller format for two regular school years. In September of 1971, editor Linda Thomas (Miller) explained: "By reducing the size of the paper to a magazine and emphasizing the interesting feature stories in college life rather than last week's news, that has already been hashed and rehashed in Chapel, I hope that my friend the *Talon* will become a part of the good times."[34] Sometimes during 1971–1972 and 1972–1973, the smaller *Talon* was in four pages in size, and sometimes it was eight.

Beginning in September of 1973, however, the *Talon* returned to the tabloid size and to the news format. In 1978–79, the paper grew to eight pages, and it continues with eight, tabloid-sized pages, through 2008.

Many faculty members have been sponsors of the *Talon*, but Dr. Philip Patterson has served the longest with twenty years. He considers the two primary purposes of the paper to be "a laboratory experience for students wanting to go into the field of journalism" and "a communication vehicle for and a service to the student body."[35]

One of the most memorable *Talon*s came on October 21, 1977, when the major headline on page one read, "Raw sewage floods men's B dorm." The story described a sewage backup that had caused eleven commodes to overflow.[36] The timing gave the story special impact: the next day was High School Day when many prospective students and their parents were coming to check out attending OC. By some strange turn of fate, no copies of the *Talon* were still in their stands on Saturday morning when the campus guests arrived.

The *Talon* has filled many purposes. It has been, of course, a major source of useful information about campus events, personalities, activities, and sports. Frequently it has been an important force in student morale, and has provided a laboratory where students learn the skills, ethics, and practice of journalism. In addition, the *Talon* offers the opportunity for a student voice on campus. While the university administration, through the faculty sponsor, has placed some boundaries, the *Talon* has provided students a means for expressing their support and sometimes their opposition to administrative policies. They also have sometimes agreed and sometimes disagreed with the Student Senate. Often the *Talon* has championed issues for student government to pursue, has called for greater campus security, and has called social service clubs to accountability.[37]

Over the fifty-eight years, then, the student newspaper has served a very important role in providing information, training, and influence on campus life.

Student Yearbook

La Quinta—Yearbook for 1951

Students at Central Christian published a yearbook the very first year of the college's operation, 1950–1951. They named it *La Quinta*, after the name of The Mansion. Mildred Webb was editor and Galen Groves the business manager. The publication, eight and a half by eleven in size, reviewed events of that first year in 58 pages, including 14 pages for advertisements. Each of the seven subsequent years in Bartlesville, students continued the yearbook and by the 1958 issue, it had grown to 116 pages, including 16 pages of ads. These yearbooks contained pictures of all the students, faculty, administration, and other campus workers. They also told much of the story of those early years through pictures of major events, the campus, the clubs, the chorus and other musical groups, plays, *Songs America Sings*, spiritual activities, intramurals, the basketball team, and campus favorites.

The Bartlesville yearbooks, as have those since, gave a pictorial record of the year to stimulate memories for students and faculty as they leafed through the pages at the time of publication and many years later, as well. They also provided an excellent record of the year for those who would later delve into the institution's history. The yearbooks have drawn people together as they looked back on events they shared, and have even helped people connect years later. In the hands of those reaching out to prospective students or prospective donors, the yearbooks offered a good tool to explain what the institution is like. And, in addition to these benefits, producing the yearbook offered students many excellent learning experiences.

When the college moved to Oklahoma City, students changed the yearbook name to *Focus*, since *La Quinta* no longer fit. The *Focus* of 1959 was 92 pages, including 12 pages of ads. Joe Eddie McCormack edited and Robert McMillan was business manager, both of whom eventually were long-term faculty members at the university. The style of this yearbook was clearly different from previous years. While still including many pictures, the yearbook used much more copy to tell the story of the year. The name *Focus*, however, lasted only two years.

In 1961, the yearbook name was changed to the *Aerie*. The staff explained: "Just as the name 'Aerie' suggests, OCC has become a 'dwelling on a height . . . an institution of higher learning dedicated to higher morals and ideals and thriving on a high regard for that which elevates the life of the individual."[38]   That year, the yearbook came with a larger size, nine by twelve, and had 140 pages of copy and pictures, including 12 pages of ads.

1967 Aerie

By 1968, the *Aerie* had grown to 300 pages including 30 for advertisements, and in 1974, had its first color pictures. Yearbooks continued generally in the same style and format until 1986.

For the 1986–1987 year, the *Aerie* came in two magazine-style publications, each of 60 pages. These still contained head shots of students, but were built primarily on feature stories about campus events and personalities. Those directing the yearbook thought a publication of this style would offer a better learning experience for journalism students than did the typical yearbook style. This format continued for two more years, growing to 85 pages an issue, filled with color graphics and interesting layouts.

In the 1989–1990 year, however, the yearbook returned to the more traditional style and had 210 pages. The *Aerie* staff wrote:

> After three years in a soft-cover, magazine format, *The Aerie* again changed its format this year, returning to a hard-cover.
>
> A 1988–89 yearbook task force found that most students and faculty were willing to pay more money for a hard-cover yearbook. The administrative council then approved the format change and the increase in student fees. . . .
>
> Whereas the soft-cover format was distributed twice during the school year, the new Aerie will be released each September, requiring books to be mailed to graduating seniors each fall.[39]

From this 1990 publication through 1995, the plan followed the typical yearbook style. Due to a variety of difficulties, however, no yearbooks were published in 1995–1996 or 1996–1997. For the 1997–1998 year, however, a student staff published a 256-page, hardcover yearbook covering all three years. It contained individual pictures of students and told of *Spring Sing*, athletics, clubs, and other student activities. The following year, 1998–1999, the yearbook was a normal publication covering just one year. The 1999–2000 and 2000–2001 years were combined into one publication of 184 pages.

Since 2002, the yearbook has been published annually, except for 2003–2005, when the two years were combined into one book. The style has been that of a typical yearbook but containing only about 130 pages.

Over the years since 1950–1951, OC students have published yearbooks representing each year of the institution's life. In a few cases, yearbooks have covered two or three years, and there have been variations in format and style. All of the publications, however, have sought to fulfill the general functions of building unity, providing memories, and offering training to the student staff. Those recalling their student days at OC and those reviewing the history of the university still find the yearbooks of great value.

Soundings

The OCC Creative Writing Club first published *Soundings* in 1972–1973 to give the opportunity for students to present their creative writing. English Professor Joe McCormack, the first sponsor, suggested the name which, he said, came from the story of how Sam Clemens found the name "Mark Twain." Clemens told of boats going down the Mississippi which made "soundings" to determine the water's depth, and from their cry "mark twain," he took his name. McCormack thought the name "soundings" provided an interesting connection with a great American writer and, at the same time, encouraged the concept of writings with depth.[40]

Senior English major Paul Varner edited the first issue of forty-five pages, which presented both poetry and prose OCC students had written. As has been the case with all issues of *Soundings*, a panel of judges decided what writings to include.

Starting with the second year, the OCC Department of Language and Literature has sponsored the publication, providing

Soundings *for 2002*

the faculty advisor and some of the funding. Other funds for printing the annual publication have come from faculty, alumni, the OCC student government, and others wanting to foster creative writing.

Each year, a well-known writer judges submissions to determine which items will be accepted for publication. In recent years, judges for the writing contests have included renowned poet Dr. Walt McDonald, award-winning writer and poet Diane Glancy, Rene Gutteridge, an Oklahoma City published writer of Christian fiction, and widely-read author Dr. Robert Pinsky. Dr. Peggy Gipson is the faculty advisor for *Soundings*. OC's Rho Mu chapter of Sigma Tau Delta, with Dr. Cami Agan serving as sponsor, collaborates in the publication.

For the 2007 edition of *Soundings*, co-editors Amy Hardin and Kate Long revamped the publication to encourage more students to submit creations in the medium that most interested them. This issue, subtitled "An Exhibition of Artistic Minds," presents seventy-four pages of poetry, prose, works of art, and photographs OC students have created. David Crismon of the OC Art and Design faculty judged the art work, while the LaChelle Shilling, an OC alumna with publications to her credit and a current visiting professor in the Department of Language and Literature, judged the written submissions.

This 2007-2008 year turned out to be the best for student writers and for *Soundings*. All ten students who submitted work for the national Sigma Tau Delta conference were accepted and presented their work in Louisville, Kentucky, in March 2008.[41] At this national meeting, *Soundings* won the top award as the Best Literary Journal coming from the 750 chapters of Sigma Tau Delta.[42]

Throughout its thirty-five years, *Soundings* has encouraged students to write creative poetry and prose and, in its later years, also to do paintings and photography. Since everything included has been juried, each publication offers some of the best creative work OC students are doing.

Conclusion

The students at Oklahoma Christian have come from all over the world and from widely diverse backgrounds, but the majority have been from families among Churches of Christ in Oklahoma, Texas, and Kansas. In the last decade, they have exceeded the average ACT scores for Oklahoma and for the nation. They have shown themselves highly capable through their successes in competition with students from other universities and through their relatively high scores on examinations in various fields. Being primarily residential, they have participated in all aspects of student life, particularly through student government and student publications and, thus, have made their own important contributions to the growth and development of the university.

Chapter 8, Endnotes

1   All student data in this chapter on enrollment and test scores comes from enrollment reports in the Registrar's Office. From 1988 through 1998, the Registrar's Office published an *Annual Institutional Data Report*, copies of which are in both the Registrar's Office and the OC Archives.

2   Annual Student Data Reports for 1993 and 1998.

3   Office of Financial Aid, OC.

4   "Debate Team Claims 18 Trophies," *OCC Reporter,* February 1979, 7, OC Archives.

5   "Forensic Team Takes Honors," *OCC Reporter,* June 1984, 11, OC Archives.

6   "OCC Debate Team Ranks Third Among Nation's Colleges," *OCC Reporter,* December 1984, 5, OC Archives.

7   "Debaters ranked ninth," *Talon,* April 12, 1985, 2, OC Archives.

8   Information on CPA pass rates taken from the Annual Institutional Data Reports for the years 1993 and 1998, OC Archives.

9   Information from Dr. Phil Lewis, Dean of Professional Studies, June 14, 2007.

10   Ibid.

11   "Forensics, Business Students Garner State, National Honors," *OCC Reporter,* April 1983, 10, OC Archives.

12   "Faculty and Student Accomplishments," *President's Report 1994–1995,* OC Archives.

13   "Business Team Places Second in National Meet," *Oklahoma Christian College Reporter,* March, 1971, OC Archives.

14   Report on Brass Ring Awards from the Art Department.

15   "*The Talon* wins All-American," *Talon,* February 15, 1985, 1, OC Archives.

16   "*Talon* Rates National Honors," *Aerie,* 1990, 61, OC Archives.

17   "Student Accomplishments," *President's Report 1993–1994,* OC Archives.

18   "Faculty and Student Accomplishments," *President's Report, 1992–93,* OC Archives.

19   "Student Accomplishments," *President's Report, 1991–92,* OC Archives.

20   *President's Report,* 1992–93.

21   Ibid.

22   "Faculty and Student Achievements," *President's Report,* 1987, OC Archives.

23   *President's Report,* 1992–93.

24   Information from chapter sponsor Dr. John Maple.

25   Ibid.

26   David Waldo, Email to the author on January 9, 2008.

27   Information from Don Leftwich.

28   Information from Dr. Floyd Coppedge.

29   All student body presidents and their dates of service are recorded on commemorative bricks at the kiosk between the Learning Center and Benson Administration Building.

30   Richard Mock, Telephone conversation with the author on July 26, 2007.

31   Records in Office of Budget Management, OC.

32   Rita Payne, "Tower Review '57–'58 Year," *Tower,* 2, OC Archives.

33   "Improved Talon Goes Weekly," *Aerie,* 1969, 181, OC Archives.

34   "Talon Talks," *Talon,* September 1971, 2, OC Archives.

35   Philip Patterson, Email to the author on September 12, 2007.

36   "Raw sewage floods men's B dorm," *Talon,* October 21, 1977, 1, OC Archives.

37   Patterson.

38   "Foreword," *Aerie,* 1961, 2, OC Archives.

39   "The Aerie Returns As A Hard Cover Yearbook," *Aerie,* 1990, 63, OC Archives.

40   Joe McCormack in conversation with the author, October 5, 2007.

41   Aaron Askew, "Students Recognized by National English Conference," Talon on line, March 7, 2008.

42   "Soundings wins national honor," OC News, OC Web site, March 12, 2008.

Chapter 9
THE DONORS

During its nearly sixty years, thousands of donors have contributed to Oklahoma Christian University. Their donations, of course, have been essential to what the University has achieved. Some have given a few dollars; others have given millions. Some have given once; others over decades. Most gave because they were strongly committed to the spiritual goals of the university, others because they believed the university produced good citizens and employees, some because they wanted to help a good private institution of higher education, and others because of friendship with those believing in what the university was doing.

Fundraising Methods

Stepping Stones / Oklahoma Christian Women's Association

The great majority of OC donors have given small amounts. As described in Chapter 2, one of President James Baird's early plans for raising funds was the dollar-a-month plan called Stepping Stones. The number of such donors eventually rose above five thousand.[1] Soon these donors, primarily women, gathered in chapters to support the institution. In addition to their monthly dues, the Stepping Stones, later the Oklahoma Christian Women's Association (OCWA), used a variety of fundraising methods to support projects. They held auctions, made and sold

Jessie Lee Cornwell, dressed in Gift Stars, gives Dr. Baird a $300 check for Learning Center carpet.

handcrafted items, offered meals, and sold afghans and blankets. They provided services and gave their wages to fund projects. They collected Gunn Brothers stamps and with them bought a bus for the college.[2] Under the leadership of Jessie Lee Cornwell, they also collected Gift Stars to buy two pianos for the Music Department.[3] OCWA's most famous fundraising project, which started in 1968, was a food booth at the Oklahoma State Fair. To operate the booth sixteen hours a day for over two weeks, they recruited a huge number of workers, including many OCC employees, from the president on down. The booth's profits eventually reached more than ten thousand dollars a year before the project was dropped because Fair regulations became too complex.

Four OCWA members ready the food booth for operation.

Over the years, OCWA has contributed more than two million dollars to operational funding and special projects aiding virtually every department at the university. They have furnished offices and dormitories, helped with campus beautification, and even paved parking lots. The *Reporter* for June 1979 indicated that there were then a thousand members in eighteen chapters.[4]

In the early 1960's, the college tapped Sue Vaughn, wife of athletic director Ray Vaughn, to coordinate Stepping Stone activities. She was followed in that role by Joy McMillon (1974–1979), Jo Anne Smith (1979–1989), Becky Durham (1989–2000), and Christine Meredith (2000–present). In addition to their fundraising, these women have also provided services to the university such as hosting recruiting parties, working registration tables at campus events, and providing personnel to conduct music contests. Although the numbers have declined since the peak years, the OCWA still serves as an important booster group for the university.

365 Club and Wills

Baird also initiated a plan for donating $135 to cover one day of the operational deficit. Those participating were designated as members of the "365 Club." By July 1957, these donors numbered 182, thus covering half of the amount the college spent above tuition income.[5] This amount, along with the Stepping Stones, provided a very significant portion of the operational money needed each year— and it came from a large number of small donors. In 1964, OCC's business manager, W. O. Beeman, estimated that "some 10,000 persons have contributed to OCC during its 14-year history for a total near $2,837,000."[6] During the years since that time, of course, both the number of donors and the amount given have risen to many times those figures.

Almost since the beginning, Oklahoma Christian has encouraged those interested in the university to make a bequest. Many issues of the *CCC Bulletin*, and later, the *Reporter,* encouraged giving through wills and estates, and several people, such as Ray Warlick, Byron Fullerton, Mack Curry, Dr. James Miller, Mickey Bowles, Brian Winger, and Stephen Eck have helped church members prepare wills and encouraged them to remember the university. As result of this effort, many have left sizable amounts to benefit the institution, and this approach continues to be one of the important functions of the development office.

Church Member Campaigns

When Central Christian College began raising funds for the move to Oklahoma City, it used a "campaign" approach. Dr. Ralph Owens, an Oklahoma City podiatrist and member of the Board of Trustees, led a "Victory Drive" that sought to contact every member of the Churches of Christ in Oklahoma. In January 1960, Owens announced that the goal of three hundred thousand dollars had been reached. An article in the *OCC Bulletin* said: "a committee of 1,000 Oklahoma members of the Church of Christ assisted in the solicitation of an estimated 60,000 individual fellow church members. One in four people contacted contributed an average gift of $100 payable over a two-year period."[7] Of course, not everyone of the sixty thousand were actually contacted, but the total number of contributors exceeded five thousand.[8] Bob Hunt, OCC's vice president for development, traveled fifty thousand miles in assisting with this campaign.[9] County chairmen worked with leaders from each congregation in their respective counties.

With this success, the college launched its next campaign in March 1961. Again Owens chaired the drive, called "The Progress Appeal," with one million dollars as the goal. Organized much as the Victory Drive had been, this campaign had district, county, and congregational chairs. In September 1961, college officials held a Labor Day Rally to climax the drive and create goodwill for the institution. They brought Pat Boone as the key attraction, along with Bobby Morrow, an Olympic gold medalist in track from Abilene Christian, and Norvel Young, president at Pepperdine. More than seven thousand attended the event.[10] Later, as a special feature of this drive, Dr. Baird brought Marshall Keeble, famous black preacher among Churches of Christ. The eighty-three year old Keeble spoke at six rallies in February 1962 to a total of eight thousand people. During this time, "Keeble addressed his largest audience in Oklahoma City, where about 4,000 persons gathered in the Municipal Auditorium. While in Oklahoma City, Keeble stayed in the OCC men's dormitory—at his request—and also spoke twice for the college's daily chapel service."[11] It is interesting to note that the college had just begun admitting black students the previous September.

As the drive got within $125,000 of its goal, Dr. Baird announced the Mabee Foundation had promised a $125,000 gift if the final amount were raised. The drive was designed to help the college meet the costs of moving from a junior to a senior college, but the last $125,000 of the drive along with the Mabee match would be applied to building the new learning center.[12] The final funds came in to put the drive over the top.

The next campaign started at OCC's annual Labor Day Rally in September 1964, when two thousand gathered on the campus. Dr. Owens, again the drive leader, "pledged an all out EVERY MEMBER CANVASS of Christian families throughout Oklahoma, southern Kansas and north and western Texas."[13] Called the "Matching Gift Campaign," the drive sought $750,000 among church members, and an additional $750,000 from Oklahoma City businesses to match funds from other sources.[14] The proceeds from this drive would provide "$400,000 for a new auditorium, $400,000 for a new field house, $300,000 in teaching improvements, $200,000 for equipping the new Learning Center, . . . [and] $200,000 in scholarships."[15] By March 1965, the $750,000 church member portion of the drive was completed,[16] and by June 1965, the second $750,000 had been raised, according to Phil Watson, vice president for development.[17] In the two phases, "some 2,000 people were actively engaged in raising funds."[18]

Vernon Newell, Board member and local roofing contractor, chaired the next campaign.[19] Called the "Youth Investment Campaign," this effort again sought $750,000 from church members.[20] These campaigns, now on a three-year cycle, used the same basic format: dividing the college's primary service area into ten to twelve districts with a chairman over each, using a chairman for every county in each district who, in turn, enlisted the help of a chairman in each congregation in his county. Funds from this drive were to aid "promising and deserving students, buy library books and science equipment, and provide new programs of instruction to serve more

James Duboise talks with students Phil Johnson and Gene Shoemake.

Christian young people."[21] This drive had two new features. Virgil Trout, minister at the Mayfair Church of Christ in Oklahoma City, led a speakers' bureau to provide speakers at congregations on behalf of the college. James DuBoise, of the development staff, led another new feature: a telephone effort to reach church members not contacted in person. Typically, a student would show a slide presentation about the college to a congregation following an evening service, and shortly thereafter, students would call the members of that church who had not already given.[22] In February 1970, Guy Ross, who was leading the drive as assistant to the president, announced the campaign had exceeded its goal by $150,000, raising a total of $900,000. In making this announcement, Ross highlighted the underlying purposes of these drives: to raise money, but also to keep the college close to its church constituency and dependent on church members for operating expenses, thus keeping "OCC firmly committed to the principle of its founders—that it will be deeply rooted in Christian faith and practice."[23]

Dr. Jack Stephenson, Oklahoma City physician and member of the Board, led the next campaign called "Decade of Progress," which sought a million dollars for operational costs: scholarships, faculty salaries, maintenance of campus buildings, and library books.[24] Again Guy Ross provided the administrative leadership, organizing the area into districts, counties, and congregations. Eight students were named "ambassadors," traveling over the state to tell "the story of OCC." Among these was Andy Benton, who later served as assistant to the president at OCC and eventually as president of Pepperdine University.[25] Other students made phone calls to those not seen in person.[26] In March 1973, Stephenson announced the successful completion of the campaign with a total of $1,001,817, commenting: "I'm impressed by the tremendous number of people who are willing to be involved in making the campaign

Guy Ross, Dr. Owens, and Dr. Stephenson view the tape showing the drive going over the top.

a success."[27] Ross emphasized the importance of church member support for operating expenses: "When we go to the Oklahoma City businessmen for assistance, they are always impressed by the support given us by members of the church."[28]

Dr. Terry Johnson became president in 1974 and continued the same general campaign approach President Baird had used. Vernon Newell chaired the next drive, "Building for Tomorrow," which raised a million dollars by April 1976. Newell said, "Some 1,700 individual members of the Churches of Christ throughout the state contributed to this important campaign."[29] Guy Ross, now vice president for development, said the funds would go for operational expenses.

Dr. Joe Stafford, Board member and surgeon from Enid, chaired the "Next Generation" campaign, launched in February 1978. Stafford pointed out that "[in] addition to providing for the operational expenses, the Next Generation Campaign is a catalyst in obtaining capital improvement funding from the corporate community and philanthropic foundations."[30] Stafford announced completion of the drive in February 1979, thanking the more than 150 volunteers who helped.[31] Different contributors totaled 1,040.[32]

The same three-year cycle continued with the "Today's Challenge" campaign in December 1980. Riley Cavin, Oklahoma City businessman and Board member, was general chairman. This drive sought $1,100,000 and, in February of 1982, Cavin announced that $1,107,000 had been pledged by more than 1,000 people over the state through the work of 300 volunteers.[33]

In January 1984, at the Preacher-Elder dinner of the Lectureship, Johnson and Ross launched the next campaign. Board Chair Deryl Gotcher, a lawyer from Tulsa, would lead the drive for $1,500,000 to be called "Horizons of Promise." The funds, again, would go for operations to complement the capital funding sought primarily from corporate donations and increases in endowment income flowing from wills and estates.[34] Guy Ross announced to the annual Preacher-Elder dinner at the 1985 Lectureship that the campaign had brought $1,615,367 in pledges, which he said was "a record amount of gift dollars pledged by Christians throughout the state and surrounding areas."[35]

The next church member campaign concluded at the 1988 Lectureship with the announcement to six hundred at the Preacher-Elder dinner that the "Bridges to Opportunity" campaign had topped the two million dollar mark. Chaired by Board member and cafeteria owner Joe Dodson, the campaign raised the most ever at OCC for an operational gift campaign,[36] and the total number of contributors for this campaign set a new record at 2,540.[37]

At the Preacher-Elder dinner of the 1990 Lectureship, Ralph Chain, Board member from Canton, Oklahoma, who chaired the next drive, announced the beginning of the "Vision for the 90s" campaign. This effort, directed by Alan Phillips, now vice president for development, sought $2,250,000, of which Chain announced $1,000,000 already had been pledged. The campaign followed the typical pattern, ten district chairs for Oklahoma with two more in Kansas and Texas. More than three hundred volunteers made calls to explain the OC story and asked for donations. College personnel in this campaign included Phillips; Andy Carpenter, field relations coordinator; Bob Lashley, director of alumni relations; David Duncan, field representative; and

Guy Ross, vice chancellor.[38] At the 1991 Lectureship, Chain announced that a total of $2,273,135 had been raised, a new record amount for such a drive. He commented that these gifts provided support for faculty salaries, maintenance of facilities, scholarships for students, curriculum, and library acquisitions. Phillips reported that more than 325 volunteers had worked to make the drive successful.[39]

To the five hundred attending the Preacher-Elder dinner at the 1993 Lectureship, Darrell Chabino, an Oklahoma City businessman and campaign chairman, announced a new drive for $2,300,000 under the campaign banner of "A Changeless Commitment." Alan Phillips, again, was the campus director of the campaign. In explaining the plan, Phillips commented, "It's important to note that the University does not accept contributions from churches. We will be contacting Christian families seeking their individual participation."[40] By the time of the 1994 Lectureship, Guy Ross, senior vice president, could announce that $2,367,000 had been raised.[41]

The 1993 church member campaign proved to be the last of this type of fund drive. Dr. Johnson did not start another such program before he resigned in 1995, and Dr. Jacobs chose not to use this type of fundraising when he became president in 1996. In all, eleven drives among church members spanning thirty-six years had raised pledges of more than $14,300,000. While not all pledges were actually paid, most were, and this campaign approach to fundraising had certainly been productive. In addition to the dollar amount produced, however, the approach had other benefits. It kept the university close to its church constituency, giving them a strong sense of ownership. Families both were more likely to send their children to the university they had helped fund and were more likely to attend its public events, such as lectureships, homecoming, and sports contests. In addition, from among these small donors, larger donors often came.

It took, of course, a large amount manpower to carry out drives of this magnitude, and some wondered whether the same amount of dollars might be raised with less effort. Others thought that the formula for district, county, and congregational chairs had run its course. The church member drives, starting in 1956 and lasting through 1993, however, played a very important part in the development of Oklahoma Christian University, both through the funds raised and in the sense of ownership the drives gave members of Churches of Christ in Oklahoma, Kansas, and Texas.

Alumni Callouts

Oklahoma Christian made its first formal effort at raising funds from alumni in 1966. Phil Watson, vice president for development, announced the effort to get individual alumni to give ten dollars a month with a total goal of fifteen thousand dollars annually. The new effort represented a shift in strategy. Watson said, "Much of the operational costs currently come from the brotherhood who make it possible for students to receive their degrees from OCC." He hoped, however, that someday all funds raised from major brotherhood drives would go into "capital expansion programs," since operational needs would be covered by endowment and alumni gifts.[42] While Watson's hopes have not totally come to fruition, alumni giving has become a major factor in Oklahoma Christian's financial picture.

By 1975, Bruce Kerr, of the development staff, had organized a callout that brought in $104,660 pledged over a three-year period. This was coupled with a matching gift of $75,000.[43] In 1979, the calls brought pledges of $145,850 from 750 alumni.[44] A dining room in the cafeteria had been outfitted with twenty telephones, and over several nights, forty different faculty, staff, alumni, and students made the calls. By 1982, Bob Lashley's first year to organize the event, the callout had moved into Cogswell-Alexander Hall where phones were set up around the large conference table. The callers, who spent a total of 259 hours on the phones, raised $225,000. In 1985, the pledged amount rose to $571,099 because two alumni, Allen Shepherd and Jim Eggleston, had each promised $100,000 if their amounts were matched.[45] In 1988, the fundraiser, held

Harold Fletcher, Alan Phillips, Don Dunn, Elmo Hall, and Jim Wilson calling alumni

between September 16 and October 3, topped $750,000, including a $250,000 matching gift from Allen Shepherd.[46]

In 1991, the callout goal was set at $300,000, not including any large gifts as inducement, and the total rose to $306,000. Bob Lashley coordinated this "Alumni Challenge '91," when 45 percent of the contacted alumni pledged financial support for the institution.[47] Three years later, in 1994, Lashley again directed the alumni callout with a goal of $350,000, and the response again went over the top with $360,000 pledged. More than 1,300 alumni were contacted by more than sixty faculty and staff callers, and 44 percent of those contacted made pledges.[48]

In 1998, the callout to alumni sought $200,000 for scholarships with nine nights set for calling between October 5 and 27. Alumni pledged a total of $104,622 on those nights, with a $10,000 gift coming in soon after. President Jacobs raised another $100,000 for a total of $214,622. Dr. Jim Wilson won the prize for the most raised with a total of $15,610.   Kinney Bryant reported that 50 percent of the contacted alumni made pledges.[49]

Just a year later, in October 1999, came the next callout. This time the goal was $50,000, since only a year had passed since the last set of calls. The calling extended over a two-week period and raised $80,000, with more than thirty faculty and staff making calls.[50]

After the callout in 1999, the pattern changed. Student workers have been employed since that time to call alumni on a continuing basis in a program that is now called the annual fund.

Comprehensive Campaigns

At the annual Spring Dinner in 1983, Guy Ross announced that over the last five years, a total of $25,000,000 had been raised through church drives and capital improvement campaigns that included Enterprise Square, the Harvey Business Building, and endowment gifts.[51]

On November 15, 1984, President Terry Johnson announced "the launching of a $50,000,000 campaign to strengthen and expand the institution over the next decade."[52] Ed Gaylord was general chairman of the drive, "the first comprehensive, private, fund-raising drive" in the college's history.[53]

Called "With Wings as Eagles," the new drive would include six "chapters," each of which addressed a particular college need: OCC Board member Deryl Gotcher chaired the effort to fund a new Biblical Studies Building; Ed Joullian, III, chaired the chapter seeking funds for the Department of Engineering; local business and civic leaders Richard D. Harrison and Lee Allen Smith co-chaired the Library and Academic Enrichment section; John Parsons, past president of Southwestern Bell of Oklahoma, led the drive for expansion of the gym into a Special Events Center; Robert Reece, local businessman, chaired the section on Endowment; and OCC Board member Ralph Harvey led the drive on Citizenship Education. Dr. Johnson, thus, sought to tie together the various facets of fundraising into a total package that would lift the sights of donors to a new level. These funds all would be in addition to operational funding that was then still being raised by church drives.

As a result of the "Wings" campaign:

> The library was remodeled, enlarged and enriched with new collections. New academic programs, such as engineering and finance were added. Innovative programs such as a semester abroad in Vienna and a master's degree in ministry followed. Highly qualified faculty were recruited and added to virtually every academic division of the University. New facilities

were added for engineering and Bible, while others were remodeled. New equipment was purchased for journalism and a host of other programs. And the entire campus was brightened by the addition of the Thelma Gaylord Forum.[54]

In reflecting on this drive, Johnson commented in the July-August *Reporter* that three factors had led to its success. The first he named as "the overriding providence of God." Second were those who dreamed the dream through brainstorming sessions and committees that developed the long-range plans, and third were those who embraced the dream and provided the financial backing.[55]

In 1998, President Jacobs developed the "Pillars of Strength" campaign, seeking to raise one hundred million dollars within a ten year period. This plan included more scholarships, another science building, Garvey Center expansion and renovation, endowed chairs, a new dormitory and upgrading of other dorms, increased library holdings, improvement of athletic facilities, and operating funds.[56] Jacobs' team was able to achieve some of these objectives before his resignation in 2001, and some others were completed during the administration of the next president, Dr. Mike O'Neal.

In 2004, President O'Neal and Vice President for Advancement John deSteiguer began working on a sixty million dollar comprehensive campaign called "Higher Learning—Higher Calling." This plan included funds for scholarships, a new science center, upgrades to the Biblical Studies Center and other classroom and laboratory spaces, a new university commons, a comprehensive student housing initiative, and enhanced athletic facilities.[57] By 2007, two new dormitories and three new apartment complexes had been completed and improvements made to a number of classroom spaces. The Lawson Commons, with its pavilion and tower, was completed in early 2008 and Dobson Field for baseball was ready for use in Spring 2008. During his first six years, O'Neal's team raised a total of $69,500,000 for all purposes.

Through this wide variety of methods, each adapted to its particular time and need, Oklahoma Christian has raised funds to carry out its work. Through large gifts and small, by paid staff and volunteers, and from its church constituency and others, the funding needs have been met.

Major Donors

A history of donors would be incomplete without mentioning those who have given the largest amounts over the years. While all who have given are important, the ones included in this section have, as of 2007, completed or will soon complete gifts of a million dollars or more to the operating expense, scholarship funds, endowment, or capital improvements of Oklahoma Christian.

The Gaylord Family

During the fifty-eight year history of Oklahoma Christian University, the Gaylord family has been its largest contributor. This family's relationship with Oklahoma Christian began when the college was considering a move from Bartlesville and deciding whether to choose Tulsa or Oklahoma City. E. K. Gaylord, editor and publisher of the *Daily Oklahoman* and very influential in Oklahoma City, wanted the college to relocate to Oklahoma City. He was well-impressed with Dr. Benson and his emphasis on Americanism and citizenship education at Harding, and he believed a college with a similar program would be good for Oklahoma City. Gaylord led the fundraising drive among Oklahoma City businesses to attract the college to Oklahoma City and participated in the selection of the site near Eastern and Memorial Road. Even before the college actually moved to Oklahoma City, then, E. K. Gaylord was a friend and supporter. Over the years, he gave generously to fund drives among the Oklahoma City corporate community, and after his and his wife's deaths, he left trusts to the institution that eventually brought $10,700,102 to the university.

While Benson had been the original contact, President James Baird become good friends with Gaylord and his family. Living to be 101 years old, Gaylord was active until the time of his death in 1974. His son, Edward L., who had begun to take over various elements of their business empire, and Edward's wife Thelma continued the family's friendship with Baird. When E. K. Gaylord died, Edward chose to have the funeral at OCC's Hardeman Auditorium and wanted Dr. Baird to be the principal speaker. Even though Baird was in the Far East on a mission trip, he quickly flew home to meet the family's request.

Edward Gaylord took a special interest in Oklahoma Christian, chairing fund drives among Oklahoma City businesses, giving generously himself, attending special events on campus, and enjoying a warm relationship with several people associated

Edward and Thelma Gaylord
(Photo courtesy Oklahoman Publishing Co.)

with the college. When Dr. Johnson became president, he and Gaylord also were good friends, often meeting at Johnnie's for a sandwich or coffee to discuss something about the college, and at these times Gaylord often passed along a check.

Three major locations on the Oklahoma Christian campus are named for the Gaylord family. One of the original four academic buildings is called Gaylord Hall. The garden area to the north of the Bible building is named the Thelma Gaylord Forum, and the student center is the Gaylord University Center. At the dedication of this expanded facility, when the building was named for Edward Gaylord, Ed saw the pool tables and joked, "Look, they named a pool hall for me."

Although interested in what the college was doing, Gaylord did not seek to control it. The presidents who worked with him kept him informed and on occasion asked his counsel, but he never sought to exert undue influence as one giving at his level might have done.

When Thelma Gaylord died, Edward used Hardeman Auditorium as the site for her funeral, as he had for his father. And again he asked the institution's president, this time Terry Johnson, to speak. When Edward L. Gaylord died on April 27, 2003, his funeral was at the Cowboy Hall of Fame, but Johnson spoke and presided at the services. The connection of the university with the three Gaylord funerals suggests the close personal relationships that had developed.

President Johnson recalls, "One of my all-time thrills as an administrator was receiving a telephone call from Ed Gaylord on April 3, 2000." The call informed Johnson that Gaylord was setting up a large Charitable Lead Trust that eventually would bring many millions to Oklahoma Christian University.[58] By the time this amount is received, the Gaylord family will have given in excess of fifty million dollars to Oklahoma Christian.

Richard and Pat Lawson

Richard Lawson graduated from Oklahoma Christian in 1966 with a degree in mathematics, and his wife, Pat, graduated a year later in elementary education. Both were involved in club activities. Pat was a cheerleader and homecoming queen, and Richard played on the tennis team and participated in the college's first international studies program to Europe. After OCC, Richard attended Purdue University for a master's in computer science, and Pat taught school while Richard finished his degree.

With his brother Bill and a friend, John Cerullo, Richard began a software company to do consulting with businesses needing computer services. Soon they started Lawson Software to offer customized

Richard and Pat Lawson

software packages. With careful management of their resources and expansion as the market grew, twenty-nine years later, the company had an international clientele and an annual revenue of $344 million. They were the first software company to provide business applications for the World Wide Web. In the early 1990s, Richard and his associates took the company to public ownership. With the company based in Minneapolis, the Lawsons spent many years there, but moved to Dallas in the 1980s and got reconnected with Oklahoma Christian. In 1994, Richard became a member of the university's Board of Trustees. Two sons, Ricky and Lance, have attended Oklahoma Christian.[59]

Between 2002 and 2004, the Lawsons gave Lawson Software stock to OC valued at more than thirty million dollars. Commenting on the gift, Richard said,

> We made these gifts in appreciation for the excellent academic and spiritual training we received at Oklahoma Christian and in hopes that it will encourage other alumni and friends to provide resources to help assure that Oklahoma Christian University strengthens its position as one of the finest private Christian universities in the country.[60]

To honor the Lawsons, in 2008 the university built the Lawson Commons, a beautiful and functional area between the Learning Center and the residence halls. The Commons features a soaring pavilion, named for Jack and Wanda McGraw, as a covering for outdoor activities and a one hundred foot Freede Centennial Tower. The tower, named to honor contributor Josephine Freede, celebrates Oklahoma's one-hundred years as a state. Inscriptions on the tower contain Scripture verses to indicate the university's commitment to its spiritual goals. The entire commons area is a fitting tribute to the couple who has provided the largest gift from alumni in the history of Oklahoma Christian.

William Guy and Reba Davisson

Judge William Guy and Reba Davisson of Ardmore, Oklahoma, are others whose contributions to Oklahoma Christian have had major significance. Although never actually a judge, Davisson's service as an attorney, including several appearances before the U.S. Supreme Court,[61] earned him the title from his constituents.

A native of West Virginia, Davisson moved to Oklahoma in 1914, where he practiced law and became a rancher. Eventually his ranches were one of the nation's largest producers of Black Angus cattle. Dr. George Benson, president of Harding College, made contact with Davisson as a prospective donor since Mrs. Davisson was a member of the Church of Christ. When Benson became chancellor of Oklahoma Christian in 1956, he turned the Davissons' interest in Christian education toward OCC.[62] Presidents James Baird and Terry Johnson continued the relationship through the years.

In 1968, the Davissons made their first major contribution, $500,000, toward the construction of the American Heritage Building. A second $500,000 gift in 1974 provided funds for the Reba Davisson Residence Hall.[63] Upon Judge Davisson's death in 1977, he left 13,000 acres of ranch land, 2,500 cattle, and $2,000,000 in cash to the college, an aggregate value of $6.8 million.[64] The Davisson legacy, thus, totaled nearly $8 million. Funds from the estate were placed

Judge Davisson with two students at the dedication of Davisson Dorm. Guy Ross watches from behind.

into the college's endowment.[65]

Davisson was attracted to Oklahoma Christian because of its citizenship program and stance on American values. He was the commencement speaker on May 27, 1966, when the exercises were held outside on the mall. The weather was hot and his speech was long, and those present have vivid recollections of the day.

Reba Davisson was an active member of the Oklahoma Christian Women's Association. As the *OCC Bulletin* recounts, "It was through Mrs. Davisson's efforts and the association with Oklahoma Christian College that Judge Davisson became a Christian. . . . Her Christian example was a strong factor in her husband's conversion in 1972."[66]

In 1973, Judge Davisson was elected to the Oklahoma Christian Board of Trustees, on which he served until his death at age ninety-five in 1977. Dr. Terry Johnson and Richard Black, minister of the Church of Christ in Ardmore, conducted the funeral service.

Vernon and Edna McNally

Vernon and Edna McNally were a Christian couple who lived on a farm not far from Waynoka, Oklahoma. They first learned about the university through a nephew, Stanley McNally, who attended Central

Christian in 1953 when the college was in Bartlesville. Later, OCC alumnus Duane Eggleston, who preached in Waynoka in his earlier years, continued to interest them in Oklahoma Christian. Bob Rowley and John deSteiguer continued the relationship.   The McNallys owned more than a thousand acres of farm land with mineral rights, and since they had no children, they sought a good use for what they had amassed.

For many years, Vernon, who farmed and participated in soil conservation efforts, taught the adult Bible class at the Elm and Murrow Church of Christ in Waynoka, and he was a careful Bible student. He strongly encouraged church members to be strong in their convictions and to stay with the Word. Edna, a career rural teacher, was also a person of great faith. They both held the work at Oklahoma Christian in high regard.

After Vernon's death in April 2002, Edna made the university the primary beneficiary of their estate. In an interesting sideline, Edna's brother, Dale Cropp, also owned a large farm and, with no other close relatives, willed what he had to his sister. In December 2005, Cropp died, leaving his farm to Edna. Only a month later, in January 2006, Edna died, leaving an estate gift

Vernon and Edna McNally

to Oklahoma Christian worth $2,600,000. Including lifetime support, the McNally family gave over $3,500,000 to OC. Phase V of OC's apartment complex is named in honor of the McNallys.

Ralph and Maxine Harvey

In 1980, Oklahoma Christian University was seeking funds for two major building projects: fifteen million dollars for Enterprise Square and three million dollars for a business building. Ralph Harvey had grown up in Oklahoma City, had attended Abilene Christian College, and now was successful in the oil business as president of Marlin Oil Company. The Harveys had given to the university since 1959 when they participated in a fund drive to build the new campus. Over the years, Ralph both donated to and made solicitation calls for church campaigns.[67]

Vice President Guy Ross took Harvey to lunch at the Beacon Club in downtown Oklahoma City and shared with him the case for both Enterprise Square and the business building, urging him to make a major contribution. While a student in ACC, years before, Harvey had determined to make a major contribution to a Christian college like the people he heard about there in chapel. Now, Harvey decided the time had come and called Ross that afternoon to say he had discussed the matter with his wife, and he would give one million dollars to each of the two projects, as well as continuing his sizable

Ralph and Maxine Harvey break ground for the new business building.

commitment for operational funding. Harvey's gifts came at a critical time in the funding process for both projects, helping to lift them to a level that made completing the funding much more likely. Ross returned to campus, called Johnson out of a meeting, and broke the news in phases. Ross said, "Ralph will continue his $35,000 a year in operational funding." Johnson said, "That's good." "But," said Ross, "that's not all. He will also give a million to Enterprise Square." Now Johnson was really excited and said, "That's great." Ross continued, "But that's not all. He is also going to give a million to the business building." At which time Johnson lay on the floor and said, "Pour it over me man."[68] Because of this timely gift, the OCC Business Building was named in honor of the Harveys.

Ralph became a member of the college's Board of Trustees in 1980 and served until 1989; Maxine was active in the OCWA. In commenting on their donation, Harvey said, "Young people have always been uppermost in my mind and my life. I feel they get a better background for life at a college where spiritual values are represented as well as academic achievement."[69]

Ralph and Maurine Fails

Ralph and Maurine Fails lived in Sayre, Oklahoma, where Ralph was a successful rancher. Maurine served as a teacher and school administrator for forty-one years, spending many of those years as registrar at Sayre Junior College. In 1966, Ralph became a member of the Oklahoma Christian Board of Trustees and served in that capacity until 1993, a term of almost thirty years. They were active members of the Church of Christ and were interested in the university almost from its beginning. Both the Fails were frequent

Maurine Fails

visitors to the campus, often coming to Lectureship, dinners, and other public events. For their generosity over the years, a men's residence hall was named in their honor. Their estate gift to Oklahoma Christian, with land and mineral rights, brought their total contribution to well over the million dollar mark. Ralph died in 1993 and Maurine in 2003.

Tom and Ada Beam

When Central Christian College moved to Oklahoma City in 1958, Tom Beam was building a successful company in manufacturing automobile seat covers. Soon the company expanded into seat belts, and today, Beam's Industries serves a worldwide market. The Beams were members of the Church of Christ and very interested in mission work. For several years, they aided an inner city work in Oklahoma City called West Main Mission. Their adopted son, Gerd Fecht, attended OCC, where he met his wife, Lucky, who worked for several years in the OCC library. For more than four decades, the Beams supported Oklahoma Christian, particularly in funding scholarships. Tom died in 1994 and Ada in 2004. President Jacobs worked with them on their estate planning, which left a legacy to Oklahoma Christian. In honor of their contributions in excess of a million dollars, the university designated the university's library as the Tom and Ada Beam Library. The plaque there reads, in part, "They shared a passion for young people and their generous spirit assisted the University as well as other organizations in their desire to spread the good news of the gospel of Christ."

Tom and Ada Beam

Edgar and Della Bullard

Edgar and Della Bullard

Edgar and Della Bullard, a Christian couple from Tyler, Texas, owned a feed and seed store and got to know Oklahoma Christian primarily through the efforts of Terry and Marty Johnson. Their interest in helping students receive a Christian education led them to establish scholarship funds at several institutions supported by members of the Churches of Christ. When Edgar died in 2005, Dr. Terry Johnson and Dr. Jay Lockhart presided at the funeral. Three Christian university presidents attended: Dr. Milton Sewell from Freed Hardeman, Dr. Cliff Ganus from Harding, and Dr. Mike O'Neal from Oklahoma Christian.[70] The Bullard's contributions to Oklahoma Christian also have exceeded a million dollars.

Dr. and Mrs Henry J. Freede

Jose Freede

Dr. Henry Freede was an orthopedic surgeon who also developed holdings in oil and gas. Freede and his wife Josephine have been important to many good causes in Oklahoma City, both through donations and volunteer services. Jose started a local chapter of the Freedoms Foundation, in which several women from the Oklahoma Christian family were involved. Lou Phillips, long-time secretary and administrative assistant to presidents at OC, was one of those, and she and Jose have worked together in many activities over the years. Jose has strong dedication to citizenship and patriotism and was involved with Enterprise Square, USA. She has been a generous supporter of many projects at Oklahoma Christian, her donations exceeding a million dollars. In 1995, Oklahoma Christian recognized her many civic and philanthropic efforts by awarding her an honorary doctor of humanities degree. In her honor, the one hundred foot tower standing on the OC campus as part of Lawson Commons, is named Freede Centennial Tower.

Olive White Garvey

Mrs. Olive Garvey, chair of Garvey Enterprises in Wichita, Kansas, became interested in Oklahoma Christian primarily because of its American Citizenship Center, and she spoke several times in its seminars. She had given to two previous capital campaigns but contributed $500,000 at a key time in raising funds for the arts and communication wings added to Hardeman Auditorium in 1978. The entire complex, therefore, was named the Garvey Center. Later she contributed a million dollars to Enterprise Square. Of the university, she said, "I consider Oklahoma

Dr. Johnson shows Olive Garvey and Don Moyers of the Mabee Foundation how to imprint their hands in wet concrete.

Christian one of a select few institutions which, along with their academic subjects, teach sound economic principles, moral and spiritual values, and motivate their scholars to become active, productive citizens."[71] Mrs. Garvey died in 1993.

Stanley and Dorothy Kresge

To an earlier generation, the Kresge name was familiar as a widespread "five and ten" store, known today as Kmart—"[f]ounded by Sebastian S. Kresge, these stores were precursors to the modern discount 'superstores' we know today."[72] Kresge left much of his fortune in a foundation primarily to help higher education. Stanley Kresge, son of Sebastian, became a foundation trustee and made a number of donations to Oklahoma Christian, including a million dollar grant for Enterprise Square. In addition, Stanley and his wife, Dorothy, made a personal gift to the fine arts wing of the Garvey Center built in 1978. This gift was to honor their friend, Minnesota Congressman Dr. Walter H. Judd, who previously had been a missionary in China, and who spoke often at seminars of the American Citizenship Center. In recognition of this gift, the university designated the theatre in the Garvey Center as Judd Theatre.

Bill and Bonnie McIntosh

Bill McIntosh was an executive with the Eli Lilly Pharmaceutical Company. He and Bonnie lived in Oklahoma City and attended the

Bill and Bonnie McIntosh with scholarship recipients

Mayfair Church of Christ. They came to appreciate Oklahoma Christian and what it stood for and were frequent visitors to campus. They donated a large scholarship fund to help students attend the university, and enjoyed associating with those students at dinners designed to connect donors with students. When a fire destroyed much of the Garvey Center in 1997, Bill and Bonnie made a major donation to help with the rebuilding and expansion of that center. Because of this, the beautiful conservatory in the new center, a location for weddings, receptions, displays, dinners, concerts, and many other events, was named in their honor. Their contributions over the years exceeded a million dollars. Bill died in December 2005.[73]

Don and Donna Millican

Don and Donna Millican became well-acquainted with Oklahoma Christian when they lived in Edmond and were often part of campus activities. Don's work as a partner in the Ernst and Young accounting firm took him to Tulsa where, in time, he became an elder in the Park Plaza Church of Christ. Later he became Chief Financial

Don and Donna Millican

Officer of Kaiser-Francis Oil Company. The Millicans sent two children, Kate and Eric, to Oklahoma Christian. In 1996, Don joined the OC Board of Trustees, and in 2002, became Board chair. In that role, he is often at campus events. Both teach Bible classes in their congregation. In 2005, Don and Donna established at Oklahoma Christian an endowed chair in accounting to honor Don's father, JJ Millican. This and other gifts to the university, totaling in excess of a million dollars, have demonstrated their continuing interest and generosity.

Bobby and Millie Roberson

Bobby and Millie Roberson

In 1995, when Oklahoma was adding its new engineering program, Millie Prince came forward with a gift in honor of her recently deceased husband, Darryll, founder and president of Prince Valve Company. This important contribution was a key factor in constructing the Prince Engineering Center. Later, Millie married Bobby Roberson, another friend of Oklahoma Christian. Four of Bobby's grandchildren have attended OC: Natalie, Amberly, Leslie, and T. J. Together, the Robersons have continued to make important contributions to the university, and their combined contributions now exceed a million dollars. Since 1994, Millie Roberson has served on the Board of Trustees.[74]

Leo and Mable Scott

Leo and Mable Scott lived in Thackerville, Oklahoma, not far from the Red River. Their 2,600 acre ranch was not only valuable for agricultural purposes but also had a valuable mineral interest for the sand and gravel it provided. Leo was a rancher and Mable a registered nurse. Dr. Darvin Keck, long-time Oklahoma Christian faculty member, along with Guy Ross, built a friendship with the Scott family and, in 1977, the Scotts generously provided a $666,667 endowment annuity. Their total contributions to OC eventually rose above a million dollars. The Scotts attended a Church of Christ in Gainesville, Texas.[75] Scott Chapel, on the second floor of the Williams-

Branch Biblical Studies Center, is named for the Scotts and is the frequent location for weddings, lectures, special small group chapel occasions, and classes.

Allen and Stephanie Shepherd

Allen Shepherd

Allen Shepherd attended Oklahoma Christian and was active in student affairs. He especially remembers working in the new Learning Center to install carrels. After graduating in 1966, he joined the U.S. Air Force and served as a pilot during the Vietnam War. He was shot down over the Ho Chi Minh Trail and spent a night in enemy territory before being rescued. He later flew missions as a B-52 pilot. After military service, Shepherd settled in Columbus, Ohio, where he entered the construction business, specializing in excavation. His company is now one of the state's largest in providing this service. He and his wife, Stephanie, are members of the Church of Christ, and he has served on the Board of Development and the Board of Governors for the university. Over the years, Vice President Guy Ross made numerous trips to Columbus to keep the Shepherds informed of developments at OC.[76] The Shepherds have contributed well over a million dollars to many alumni fund drives and various other projects, as well as for endowment to benefit the university.

Dr. Charles, Jr., and Lesa Branch

Charles Branch, Jr., and Lesa Williams met as students on the Oklahoma Christian campus. After their marriage and graduation, he received a medical degree from Southwestern Medical School of the University of Texas in Dallas, and then specialized in neurosurgery at Wake Forest University. After completing his training, he joined the faculty at Wake Forest in 1988, and in 2001, was named as the chair of neurosurgery.

In 2004, Charles and Lesa pledged $1,500,000 to Oklahoma Christian for upgrading the Biblical Studies Center and for university endowment. The building was named the Williams-Branch Center for Biblical Studies in honor of Lesa's parents, Charles and Joyce Williams, and his parents, Dr.

Charles and Lesa Branch

Charles and Sylvia Branch.[77] Charles Williams is a long-time minister, who, along with Joyce, has served many Churches of Christ. Dr. Branch, also a neurosurgeon, served for many years on the OC Board and as an elder of the MacArthur Park Church of Christ in San Antonio. Sylvia is on the Board of the *Christian Chronicle.*

Charles and Lesa live in Advance, North Carolina, where he is a deacon in the local Church of Christ and participates in medical missions. Their son Daniel is a graduate of Oklahoma Christian.

Mark and Beth Brewer

Mark and Beth Brewer live in Edmond, Oklahoma, and are among those who have given more than a million dollars to Oklahoma Christian University. Mark and Beth are both graduates of Oklahoma State University with degrees in electrical engineering and elementary education respectively. Mark has served on the OC Board of Trustees and is a senior vice president and chief information officer for a high-tech firm. Mark and Beth, together

Mark and Beth Brewer

with their children, have also lived in Chicago and in Singapore. They have had an important impact on Oklahoma Christian through both their generosity and their service to the institution.

Loyce L. Youngblood

Loyce Youngblood

For twenty-five years, Loyce worked with her husband, Laurence, in the oil business and after his death in 1965, she continued to operate the L. S. Youngblood Company for another forty-two years until her death in 2007. She assisted many Oklahoma institutions and at Oklahoma Christian University she helped make a new dormitory possible. The Loyce L. and Laurence S. Youngblood Scholarship Endowment was created to honor this outstanding couple and in 1988, Oklahoma Christian awarded her an honorary doctorate of humanities to recognize her community service.

Foundations

Many foundations have given generously to projects at Oklahoma Christian, usually for construction, but sometimes for scholarships, research, library books, citizenship efforts, or faculty development. Three foundations have given more than a million dollars over the years. The Mabee Foundation has given since 1965 to help construct the Learning Center that bears its name, to fund the communications building that also bears its name, to construct the science building, and to other projects. The Noble Foundation has given since 1979 to help expand the science facilities, to assist with corporate campaigns, and to build Enterprise Square and fund the American Citizenship Center. The Freuhoff Foundation gave its first gift to the university in 1980 and has helped with the Learning Center, the Garvey Center remodeling, the Harvey Business Building, Enterprise Square, and an endowment for faculty development.

Other foundations have also contributed significant amounts. The Pfeiffer Foundation has helped primarily with projects involving science facilities. The Hatton W. Sumners Foundation has given especially for the university's efforts toward citizenship education. The Arthur Vining Davis Foundation has given primarily on capital projects, and the Tulsa Christian Foundation has supported scholarships for Bible students. The McCasland Foundation has given to OC's citizenship work and the Kirkpatrick Foundation toward capital projects and a lecture series.

Corporate Donors

When Central Christian College was investigating the possibility of moving from Bartlesville to a larger city in Oklahoma, the corporate community in Oklahoma City showed a strong interest in having the college come to their city. Under the leadership of E. K. Gaylord, fifty Oklahoma City business leaders agreed to help raise $200,000, which the college sought as a demonstration of the city's interest. Those helping with the campaign included B. D. Eddie, president of Superior Feed Mills; H. B. Groh, general manager of Southwestern Bell; D. W. Hogan, Sr., president of City National Bank; Don Kennedy, president of OG&E; Roland V. Rodman, president of Anderson-Prichard Oil Corporation; John Kirkpatrick, president of Kirkpatrick Oil Company; Cecil Webb, district vice president of Oklahoma Natural Gas; C. A. Vose, president of the First National Bank; and many others. Such backing allowed the college to move into Oklahoma City with good support and interest from the local business community.[78] These same businesses and others have provided continuing support.

Since that time, the university frequently has asked for funds from the Oklahoma City corporate community, always receiving a good response. The drives were typically for buildings and other capital expenditures. An important selling point, in fact, with local leaders has been that since OC's church constituency and endowment have provided the funds for operational support, the local community should be willing to provide for capital expansion.

Corporate drives have been held periodically, usually every five years, and have grown to provide several million dollars each time. Supplementing these drives, of course, have been the personal contributions from local leaders such as the Gaylords, W. T. Payne, Ed Joullian, Dr. and Mrs. Henry Freede, C. A. Vose, and many others. The largest single corporate donation to Oklahoma Christian came from Phillips Petroleum Company of Bartlesville when they made the two million dollar lead gift to Enterprise Square.

Clearly the university's American Citizenship Center, with its programs of seminars, speakers, publications, and Enterprise Square, has drawn the interest of corporate leaders. A twenty-page brochure prepared for the 1956–1957 campaign, when the college was moving to Oklahoma City, gives two pages to the fact that Central Christian would have a citizenship program patterned after the one at Harding, and Dr. George Benson's connection with both institutions was featured prominently.[79] The university has continued this strong support of the American political and economic system through the years, now focusing that work in its Academy for Leadership and Liberty housed in the Enterprise Square building.

Oklahoma Christian's list of donors ranges from individuals who have given much to those who have given small amounts and, in addition, includes many corporations and foundations that have given generously over the years. The university has sought in many ways to recognize these donors, both to show appreciation and as a way to encourage others to give. Since the university has no government support and since raising student tuition to an amount equaling its cost of operation would price the university out of the market, donor support is both required and appreciated.

Recent Fundraising

In recent years, President Mike O'Neal and Vice President for Advancement John deSteiguer have developed a team in fundraising and public relations to complement their efforts. This fundraising team includes Bob Rowley, Stephen Eck, John Michener, Michael Mitchell, Mike Johns, Brian Bush, Jo Griffin, and Kent Allen working in diverse areas such as church relations, major gifts, planned gifts, annual fund, and foundation and corporate relations. On the public relations side, Ron Frost and Stephen Bell have responsibilities in communications and web design. The broad sweep of these activities show both the diversity and the complexity of the university's current program. While there is no longer a church drive or a faculty-staff alumni callout, the development staff calls prospects almost every day of the year.

Since the 2002-2003 year, Dr. O'Neal's first year as president, the university's fundraising results have shown remarkable progress. From his inaugural year through 2007-2008, the number of donors increased from 1,450 to 2,770, an increase of over 90 percent. Additionally, not including the extraordinary Gaylord and Lawson gifts, giving has increased in virtually every measure—endowment, capital, unrestricted, and restricted giving. Counting all categories, annual giving has increased from $1.7 million in 2002-2003 to $8.8 million in 2007-2008.[80]

Conclusion

In looking at Oklahoma Christian and its donors over the years since fund solicitation began in 1948, four observations stand out. First, those charged with raising funds have acquainted prospective donors with the purposes of the institution so they know what their giving will support so their contribution can come from a commitment to the university's purposes. Second, those charged with raising funds have developed sincere personal relationships with donors, as with the Gaylords, the Lawsons, the Davissons, the Fails, the McIntoshes, the McNallys, and many others, and these donors have become a part of the OC family. Third, the university recognizes the generosity of its donors. Whether a Spring Dinner honoring the OCWA, the annual Associates Dinner, naming a building in honor of a donor, or in some other way, those charged with raising funds salute donors to give honor where honor is due. They have regarded this notice as important, not just to bring recognition to the donor, but to give the campus family an opportunity to say "Thank you." Fourth, the university has sought small as well as large gifts, knowing that all who give become part of the fabric of the institution.

Private collegiate institutions must attract donors, and over the years, Oklahoma Christian has been fortunate in finding those who support the mission of the university and who, in turn, have received satisfaction from doing so.

Chapter 9, Endnotes

[1]   "Drive for 10,000 Stepping Stones Begun," *Central Christian College Bulletin*, September 1957, OC Archives.

[2]   "Stepping Stones Renew Activity," *Oklahoma Christian College Bulletin*, January 1966, OC Archives.

[3]   Caption of picture, *Oklahoma Christian College Bulletin*, May 1967, OC Archives.

[4]   "OCCWA Provides Important Assistance," *OCC Reporter*, June 1979, 3, OC Archives.

[5]   "'365 Club' Grows Under Direction of Associate Board," *Central Christian College Bulletin*, July 1957, OC Archives.

[6]   "10,000 Persons Aid OCC During 14-Year History," *Daily Oklahoman*, November 24, 1964, N7.

[7]   "Statewide Drive Ends Successfully, Announces Dr. Owens, Chairman," *Oklahoma Christian College Bulletin*, January 1960, OC Archives.

[8]   "$300,000 Drive Nears Goal as 5,000 Give," *Central Christian College Bulletin*, July 1959, OC Archives.

[9]   "Statewide Drive."

[10] W. O. Beeman, *Oklahoma Christian College: From Dream to Reality* (Delight, Arkansas: Gospel Light Publishing Company, 1970), 64.

[11] "Marshall Keeble Praises Christian Education in Statewide Rally Series," *Oklahoma Christian College Bulletin*, March 1962, OC Archives.

[12] "Progress Appeal Climbs As Deadline Nears," *Oklahoma Christian College Bulletin*, July 1962, OC Archives.

[13] "Workers to Launch Every Member Canvass," *Oklahoma Christian College Bulletin*, September 1964, OC Archives.

[14] "Campaign Continues Momentum Gained in Rally," *Oklahoma Christian College Bulletin*, September 1964, OC Archives.

[15] "Matching Fund Campaign Continues Toward Its Goal," *Oklahoma Christian College Bulletin*, October 1964, OC Archives.

[16] "Oklahoma City Launches Campaign's Second Phase," *Oklahoma Christian College Bulletin*, March 1965, OC Archives.

[17] "Campaign's Second Phase Matches Success of First," *Oklahoma Christian College Bulletin*, June 1965, OC Archives.

[18] Ibid.

[19] "Brotherhood Exceeds Goal by $150,000," *Oklahoma Christian College Bulletin*, February 1970, OC Archives.

[20] "Newell, Owens Will Direct Youth Investment Campaign," *Oklahoma Christian University Bulletin*, March 1968, OC Archives.

[21] "College Plans $2 Million Expansion, *Oklahoma Christian College Bulletin*, March 1968, OC Archives.

[22] "Operation Saturation Gets Good Reception," *Oklahoma Christian College Bulletin*, April 1969, OC Archives.

[23] "Brotherhood Exceeds."

[24] "Brotherhood Pledges $1 Million in Decade of Progress Campaign," *Oklahoma Christian College Reporter,* March 1973, OC Archives.

[25] "Ambassadors to Aid Campaign," *Oklahoma Christian College Reporter,* March 1972, OC Archives.

[26] "Report to the President from the Assistant to the President," *President's Report*, November 10, 1972, OC Archives.

[27] "Brotherhood Pledges"; "Report to the President from the Assistant to the President," *President's Report*, November 9, 1973, OC Archives.

[28] Ibid.

[29] "$1 Million Raised in Campaign," *Oklahoma Christian College Reporter*, April 1976, OC Archives.

[30] "$1 Million Next Generation Campaign Launched, Drive Leaders Selected," *OCC Reporter*, February 1978, OC Archives.

[31] "Drive Raises $1 Million," *OCC Reporter*, February 1979, OC Archives.

32 "'Vision for the 90's' $2.25 Million Campaign Marks Successful Start," *OCC Reporter*, February 1990, 1, OC Archives.

33 "Today's Challenge Campaign Exceeds Goal," *OCC Reporter*, February 1982, 1, OC Archives.

34 "Massive Operational Campaign Announced," *OCC Reporter*, February 1984, 1, OC Archives.

35 "Horizons of Promise tops goal," *OCC Reporter*, February-March, 1985, 1, OC Archives.

36 "Highlights of 1987–88," *Report from the President, 1987–88*, OC Archives.

37 "Vision for the 90s."

38 Ibid.

39 Ibid.

40 "'A Changeless Commitment' Theme of $2.3 Million Drive," *Oklahoma Christian Reporter*, January-February, 1993, 1, OC Archives.

41 "'A Changeless Commitment' Exceeds $2.3 Million Goal," *Oklahoma Christian Reporter*, February-March, 1994, 1, OC Archives.

42 "College's Alumni Announce Drive Aimed at $15,000 In First Year," *OCC Bulletin*, September 1966, OC Archives.

43 "People doing their jobs well," *President's Report*, 1976, OC Archives; "Alumni Callout Exceeds Goal," *Oklahoma Christian College Reporter*, December 1975, OC Archives.

44 "Alumni Callout Tops Goal: $145,850 Pledged," *OCC Reporter*, October 1979, 3, OC Archives.

45 Minutes, Board of Trustees, November 16, 1985, OC Archives; *President's Report, 1986*. OC Archives.

46 Minutes, Board of Trustees, November 5, 1988, OC Archives.

47 "Alumni Challenge '91 Goal Exceeded," *Oklahoma Christian Reporter*, November-December, 1991, 1, OC Archives.

48 "Alumni Challenge '94 Exceeds $350,000 Callout Pledge Goal," *Oklahoma Christian Reporter*, December 1994, 1, OC Archives.

49 "Alumni Callout Report," *Campus Community*, November 19, 1988, OC Archives.

50 "Alumni Callout Surpasses Goal!" *Campus Community*, November 11, 1999, OC Archives.

51 "$25 Million Raised by College," *OCC Reporter*, April 1983, 1, OC Archives.

52 "College's Largest Campaign Launched," *OCC Reporter*, December, 1984, 1, OC Archives.

53 "With Wings as Eagles, A Retrospective," April 26, 1991, 1, filed as the President's report for 1991, OC Archives.

54 Ibid., 2–3.

55 "Johnson Charts University's Future After 'Wings' Success," *Oklahoma Christian Reporter*, July-August, 1991, 2, OC Archives.

56 "Pillars of Strength, Oklahoma Christian University Strategic Plan," September 1998, OC Archives.

57 "Higher Learning—Higher Calling" campaign brochure, OC Archives.

58 Terry Johnson, Videotaped interview with author, June 16, 2006, OC Archives.

59 "Meet the Lawsons," *Vision*, Spring 2005, 5–7, OC Archives.

60 Ibid., 7.

61 "William Guy Davisson—1882–1977," *Oklahoma Christian College Reporter*, June 1977, OC Archives.

62 "Fifth Annual Spring Dinner Set for March 31," *OCC Reporter*, February 1978, OC Archives.

63 Ibid.

64 "Davisson Bequeaths OCC $6 Million," *Oklahoma Christian College Reporter*, October 1977, OC Archives.

65 Ibid.

66 "William Guy Davisson."

67 "Mr. and Mrs. Ralph L. Harvey Pledge $2 Million to Okla. Christian College," *OC Reporter*, April 1980, 1, OC Archives.

[68]   As Dr. Johnson has recounted the story.
[69]   Ibid.
[70]   Terry Johnson, Email to the author, December 5, 2007.
[71]   "Gold Eagle Circle," *OC Associates Foundations of Strength*, March 29, 2007, 10, OC Archives.
[72]   Ibid., 12.
[73]   Ibid., 13.
[74]   Ibid., 16.
[75]   "College Shares $1 Million Gift," *OCC Reporter*, June 1977, 1, OC Archives.
[76]   Johnson, Email.
[77]   "Couple pledge $1.5 million to OC in honor of parents," *Daily Oklahoman*, September 6, 2004. Files of the Office of the President.
[78]   "Oklahoma City Drive in Progress," *Bulletin Central Christian College*, January 1957, OC Archives.
[79]   "'Upon These Broad Shoulders Rests The Future of America,'" campaign brochure, OC Archives.
[80]   From the Office of John deSteiguer.

Chapter 10
THE CURRICULUM

1950–1959

The Articles of Incorporation for Central Christian College set the parameters for its curriculum, stating that the purpose of the college is "for the advancement of education in which the arts, sciences, languages and Holy Scriptures shall always be taught, together with such courses of instruction as shall be deemed advisable by the Board of Directors."[1] Those who opened Central Christian College at Bartlesville in 1950 developed a curriculum based on that statement and their philosophy for how it should be carried out. This review of the university's curriculum through the years starts with a look at those beginnings.

Bartlesville

The first Central Christian College catalog stated that the college:

> was founded primarily for the purpose of providing a school where young people may continue their education under Christian environment and influence. . . . The greatest service [the college] can render is that of strengthening young people in character and preparing them for Christian service, regardless of their calling in life.[2]

Each student was required to take a Bible course each term because "no system of education or philosophy can compare with the Bible in its influence for good on the lives of young people."[3] The Bible classes from which students could choose were primarily studies in the text of Scripture because those planning the program believed the most useful long-range impact on students would come through their knowledge of the Bible itself.

In its early years, CCC offered a two-year program leading either to an associate degree or a junior college certificate, with sixty-four hours required for both.[4] The first catalog listed 119 courses divided into fourteen departments: Art, Bible, Business, Education and Psychology, Physical Education, English, Industrial Arts, Home Economics, Languages, Mathematics, Music, Natural Science, Social Science, and Speech.[5]

While some classes listed were never offered, a review of courses and degree requirements reveals much about the educational philosophy of the new college. The curriculum was built on three fundamental elements. First, all degree programs required twelve hours of Bible, almost 20 percent of the total. Second, students took courses in basic liberal arts: twelve hours in English composition and literature, and six hours in American history and government. Two hours were required in physical education. As a third element, students were required to take at least twelve hours in a major. Twenty hours in electives could be used to strengthen any of these three elements to bring the total to sixty-four hours. At this point there was no science requirement all had to meet, but many students used elective hours for courses in biology and chemistry and some majors required hours in science.

Students, then, completed a foundation in Bible and the liberal arts, and on that base began career preparation in such fields as business, secretarial science, education, home economics, music, science, and social science. Those planning the initial curriculum believed courses in Bible, literature, history, writing, and science would train the mind to think and communicate as well as furnish the mind with a good understanding of the world and the Scriptures. Unlike some liberal arts colleges, however, Central Christian also saw its mission to include specific career preparation. This plan of developing the spirit and the mind through courses in Bible and the liberal arts while also preparing students for a career has characterized the institution's educational philosophy throughout its years. Since Dr. James Baird was the first academic dean, he was a major influence in developing the early curriculum.

Dr. James Baird

In the second year, the catalog showed courses divided into seven academic divisions: Bible and Related Subjects, Business Education, Fine and Applied Arts, Language and Literature, Mathematics and Natural Science, Social Science, and Physical Education-Psychology.[6]   The physical education requirement had been raised to four hours, and a one-hour course in freshman orientation had been added. The courses listed remained much the same except the four courses in industrial arts had been dropped.

The catalog for 1953–54 showed a major change in degree requirements. The Bible requirement had been dropped from twelve to eight and English from twelve to six, while the other general requirements remained unchanged. These reductions allowed students to take additional courses in their major fields of study. Twenty-one different curricula were listed, eight called terminal and thirteen listed as college continuation curricula.[7] By the last year in Bartlesville, 1957–1958, the number of courses listed was 125, about the same as the first year, and the requirements for graduation remained much as they were in the 1953–1954 catalog.[8]

Oklahoma City

The first catalog for Central Christian on its Oklahoma City campus reflected major changes. The general education requirements for all the two-year programs had been increased to forty-six hours, with each student taking an additional eighteen to twenty-eight hours in a major and electives. The Bible requirement remained at eight hours, two hours per term enrolled, but the social science requirement had grown to nine, and speech was now required along with a second course chosen from English, speech, or mathematics. A music or art appreciation course was also required as well as eight hours in science. Eight different programs were available for a major: Bible and Greek; Business Administration or Secretarial Science, General Liberal Arts to serve those wishing to major in teaching or communications, Pre-Agriculture, Music, Pre-Engineering or Mathematics and Physical Science, Pre-Medical, and Home Economics.[9] The program still reflected the three basic elements of Bible and liberal arts along with career preparation. The number of courses in the catalog remained relatively unchanged, with 124 being listed.

An interesting feature of the 1958–1959 catalog is an explanation for each of the general education requirements. The eight hours in Bible, for example, was intended "to increase the student's knowledge and appreciation of God and his understanding of the Scriptures, and to develop in him a desire for truth. They also prepare him for mature self-direction based on a commitment to the teachings of Jesus."[10] The nine hours in social science was intended to "prepare the student for the responsibilities of family and community life in our democratic, private enterprise society

Dr. Stafford North

and assist him in acquiring an appreciation for his cultural heritage."[11]   The thirteen hours in communication was designed to "cultivate the student's ability to think and communicate more effectively, and assist in developing qualities of leadership."[12]   By this time, Dr. Stafford North was dean of instruction and was working with faculty committees on matters pertaining to the curriculum.

1960–1962

Four-year Degrees and Name Change

By 1960, the Central Christian College Board of Trustees had made two important decisions: changing the name to Oklahoma Christian College, and expanding the program from two years to four. The July 1960 *Bulletin* explained:

> During the entire school year just concluded, the Oklahoma Christian College faculty has given considerable thought to the preparation of the program to be offered as the school expands into a senior college. Under the leadership of a steering committee composed of Mrs. Retta Scott Garrett, Harold Fletcher, Joseph Jones, Mrs. Oma Carter, and Stafford North, the faculty agreed upon graduation requirements and the fields of study to be offered.[13]

The committee had consulted personnel directors of major corporations, visited ten other colleges and universities, and consulted many college catalogs. Particularly they had visited with Dr. James Fellows, registrar at the University of Oklahoma, whose approval would keep them with the important "A rating" in the publication of the American Association of Collegiate Registrars and Admissions Officers.[14]

Through the work of the OCC faculty, the college had decided to offer bachelor's degrees in Bible, business, science, and education. Students were required to complete 126 hours for the degree, including sixty-four hours in general education and not less than twenty-four hours in a major.[15]

The sixty-four hours in general education covered both the Bible and the liberal arts foundation begun in Bartlesville. Students were required to take sixteen hours in Bible through a combination of two- and three-hour courses. The policy continued the requirement for full-time students to take a Bible class each term.[16] In this requirement, Oklahoma Christian had sought something of a middle ground among its sister Christian colleges. Some, like David Lipscomb, for example, required students to attend a Bible class every day but gave them only two hours of credit for the five-day–a-week class. Others, like Abilene Christian, required fifteen hours of Bible credit, with students attending class three days a week for three hours of credit, normally completed in five semesters. The Oklahoma Christian plan, on the other hand, required all students to take a Bible class each term, thus keeping them always in a Bible class throughout their four years, but they did not have to meet the class every day and a wide range of two-hour courses were available.

In the liberal arts segment of the new four-year plan, students were required to take twelve hours in social science, including a survey course in civilization, two courses in American history, and a course in American government. Students also took two courses in science and one in math. In communication, students had to complete six hours in English composition and three hours in speech. In addition, they were required to have a course in improvement of reading unless exempt by testing at an acceptable level of speed and comprehension. In humanities, students took nine hours—an English literature course, an art or music appreciation course, and a third course in literature, music, or art. For graduation, students also had to have three physical education activity courses, a course in health education, and an orientation to college class taken as an entering freshman.[17]

In these first baccalaureate degrees, the number of hours required in the major varied among the four degrees. Bible required thirty-two hours; business and secretarial science required thirty; science required thirty; and education required twenty-four in professional education courses, plus about thirty hours in the teaching field. The education curriculum included courses to prepare students to teach business, bookkeeping and clerical practice, language arts, mathematics, science, and social studies.[18]

In addition to its four-year degree programs, Oklahoma Christian also offered seven two-year pre-professional programs students could transfer toward degrees at other institutions: home economics, journalism, music, pre-agriculture, pre-engineering, pre-law, and pre-medical or pre-dentistry. These programs were built on a base of the same three elements: Bible, liberal arts, and career preparation.[19] The courses listed in the catalog had grown to 184 to serve the students now in a four-year program.

By the spring of 1962, nineteen students had met requirements to graduate under this plan, thus constituting the first bachelor's degree students finishing at Oklahoma Christian.

1962–1972

Changes in the Bible Requirement and Expansion of Majors

From 1962 to 1972, the OCC curriculum remained much the same. One interesting change, however, came in the Bible requirement. While continuing the policy for a student to take a Bible class each term, thus, in effect, requiring sixteen hours in Bible for graduation, the catalog for 1962 reduced the stated Bible requirement to ten hours.[20] The reason for this change was obviously not to reduce the number of Bible courses students would take, but was rather an effort to make the requirement easier to administer for transfer students who came with no Bible hours. Under this requirement, a person transferring in as a junior, for example, would have to meet the ten hour requirement during their four remaining terms. Students attending OCC for four years would still be taking sixteen hours in Bible.

The 1962 catalog also showed a significant increase of the fields in which degrees were offered. Now a student could receive a bachelor of arts degree in English, History, Speech, or Bible. For a bachelor of science degree, the student could major in Bible, Business Administration, Secretarial Science, Science, Biology, Mathematics, or History. To receive a bachelor of science in education, the student could specialize in Elementary Education or in any of six fields of secondary education: Bookkeeping and Clerical Practice, Business Education, Language Arts, Science, Social Studies, or Speech.[21]

Summer School

The first summer school program at Oklahoma Christian came in 1964. From June 8 to July 31, students could earn up to nine hours of credit by choosing from courses in art, Bible, business, education, English, history, mathematics, physical education, secretarial science, speech, and science. At the end of the summer classes, students had the option of earning additional credit from a twelve-day tour to the World's Fair in New York City.[22] In addition to serving student needs, the summer program also offered additional employment opportunities for faculty, thus supplementing their salaries.

First Overseas Study Program

Another important curriculum development came in 1965, when eleven OCC students became the first to participate in an overseas study program. All traveled to Europe by ship. Some stayed in Florence, some in Heidelberg, and others near Stuttgart. These

*First OCC international students looking at their European destination.
Note Mike O'Neal is at the right end of the front row, and on the back
row, second from the right is future Board member Richard Lawson.*

students took a course in European culture through OCC by writing papers on their experiences in Europe through reading, attending concerts, and visiting museums. They also took a Bible course by studying the churches they visited and talking with missionaries with whom they were to work while abroad. For other courses, the students either worked through independent study with an OCC teacher or enrolled in a course in a European university. Faculty member James Parker directed the program. The first students in this program, including future Oklahoma Christian president Mike O'Neal and future major donor Richard Lawson, encouraged the college to continue it and made suggestions for improvements such as better student preparation in language, closer supervision, and requiring fewer courses.[23] This beginning would eventually blossom into far more extensive overseas opportunities.

Trimester Calendar

September 1967 brought another significant change in the OCC curriculum with the introduction of the trimester calendar. Instead of the typical college year composed of two semesters of fifteen weeks of classes plus time for enrollment, breaks, and final exams followed by a nine week summer session, the trimester plan offered three equal four month periods. Such a plan allowed fourteen weeks of classes, one less than in the semester system, plus registration, finals, and breaks. The plan's disadvantage, of course, was one week less of class time for students to achieve the same learning as in the longer semesters. The OCC administration and faculty, however, thought the plan's advantages more than offset this disadvantage. Students could now have a full length term over the summer months, thus allowing students wishing to attend year-round to finish in two years and seven months. Also, under the semester plan, students had returned from Christmas vacation for three more weeks of the first term. The trimester plan allowed for a more natural rhythm, as the space between terms fell at the same time as Christmas break, allowing students returning from the break to start in a new set of classes. Today, most colleges and universities have moved their fall starting date earlier to provide this same advantage, but that was not typical in 1967. Other advantages were the possibility of year-round use of campus facilities and faculty and a full four months over the summer break for students who wanted to work or faculty who wished the time off for research, writing, or rest.[24]

While the third trimester at Oklahoma Christian has never had the same number of students as the other two, the faculty and administration have considered the overall advantages to be sufficient to continue this system to the present.

1972–1980

New General Education Requirements and More Majors

The 1972–1974 catalog announced that the faculty had developed a new set of requirements for a degree at Oklahoma Christian. The general education portion was a revised package of sixty hours. The catalog explained:

> The new degree requirements provide many advantages: they allow more choice by students; they are more flexible; they provide more interdisciplinary experiences; they allow students who are either ahead or behind as they enter college to move at a speed suited to their individual needs; they provide a wider range of experiences; and the new plan is more geared to the interests of today's college students.[25]

The new general education requirements provided six basic, one-hour courses to provide a "flexible entering point for all students." Except for the freshman orientation class, these courses offered a pre-test, and based on this evaluation, students were either placed in the basic course or given credit for it and moved into the next course in that field. Those required to take any of the five courses—Bible, English, history, math, and humanities—might take all the units of the class, might test out of some of the units, or might spend longer on some units if necessary. Many of these courses utilized the dial-access system in the Learning Center, which had become available in 1967.

Beyond these introductory courses, students took a four-hour composition course, a three-hour speech course, and three hours in physical education activities. All students had to have nine hours in Bible courses for graduation but were still required to take a Bible course each term they were enrolled. This meant that students used seven of their elective hours for Bible courses beyond the nine required hours, making a total of sixteen. Students took four hours in biology and four in physical science, three hours in American government, four hours in American history, and a three-hour aesthetics course. To complete the sixty hours in general education, students could choose three courses from social science, human behavior, and humanities. Then they chose two more courses from among these same three areas plus science.

By 1972, the college had added more majors from which students could choose. For a bachelor of arts degree, students could now major in Art, Bible, History, Mass Communications, Missions, Music, Sociology, and Psychology. For a bachelor of science degree, students could now major in Accounting, Business Management, Chemistry, Home Economics, Medical Sciences, Pre-professional Social Work, and Religious Education. The bachelor of science in education had added majors in the following fields of secondary education: Art, French, Home Economics, Mathematics, Music, and Physical Education. To accommodate these additional programs, the number of courses in the catalog had grown to 450.

Campus Radio Station

KOCC studios in the Learning Center

In September 1973, the mass communications department took a major step forward when a campus radio station, KOCC, began broadcasting. Having a station on campus provided important experience for students wishing to prepare for careers in broadcasting. It afforded them practical experience in management, announcing, and technical operation of a radio station. At this beginning point, the station could be heard on campus with transmitters in all the dormitories and it also could be heard a short distance off-campus. The station gave students in broadcasting an opportunity to cover sporting events and campus news, and to provide musical programming as well.

The KOCC studio was located on the west side of the second floor of the Learning Center.[26] Dr. Ron Bever supervised the station's operation, John Morrison was technical director, and Randy Foshee was the student manager.[27] On November 3, 1980, the campus radio station expanded its coverage with an FM transmission that carried more than twenty-five miles from its facilities, now in the Mabee Communications Building built in 1978.[28] Dr. David Lowry supervised the station from 1980 to 1985, and in 1985, Dr. Larry Jurney became the faculty advisor and has served since that time.

Dr. David Lowry supervises a student in the new KOCC studios.

Ties with Ibaraki Christian College

Another major step forward in OCC's curriculum came when the college developed an exchange program with Ibaraki Christian College in Japan. President James Baird had traveled to Japan in 1974 and was instrumental in working out the arrangements.[29] OCC alumnus Jim Batten taught at Ibaraki and was another major player in establishing the program. The first exchange of students came in the summer of 1975 when twenty-one Ibaraki students came to the OCC campus. Tim Denton and Jeff Haseltine spent that summer at Ibaraki, thus being the first OCC students to participate in the program.[30] In the summer of 1976, eight OCC students went to Japan from April to August, with seventeen Ibaraki students coming to Oklahoma for the month of July.[31] The *OCC Reporter* said, "The exchange program is a mutual effort designed to strengthen relations between American and Japanese Christians as well as give both groups a better understanding of each other's culture."[32] The OCC students took a full term of work, completing sixteen hours in cross-cultural evangelism, cross-cultural communication, Japanese travel experiences, and a textual Bible course.[33] Joe McCormack of the English faculty was one of the early leaders in this program, even spending from April 1979 to March 1980 at Ibaraki Christian College as a visiting professor.[34]

Joe McCormack

Oklahoma Christian students participated in this summer program through 1996. After the first three years, they always had an OCC faculty member with them as the sponsor. Five times, Joe McCormack, sometimes with his wife,

Lottie, served in this role; three times it was Head Librarian Brad Robison; also three times, Dr. John and Marcia Vincent accompanied the group; twice Dr. Ryan Newell went. During these years, the Japanese students continued to come for a month, usually during the spring term.

In 1997, Oklahoma Christian expanded the exchange program to include visits to other locations in the Far East. Now called the Pacific Rim Program, students go during the fall term and, while spending six weeks at Ibaraki Christian College, they visit such places as China, Singapore, Australia, New Zealand, and Hawaii. Joe and Lottie McCormack led the first group on this program, which usually takes about twenty-five students.

OC Pacific Rim students at the Great Wall of China

The Ibaraki Exchange program, in addition, now allows the opportunity for both OC and IC students to spend a full year at the other institution.

In a related move, in 1976 the degree for Teaching English as a Foreign Language first appeared in the catalog. [35] This degree, along with the Ibaraki Christian exchange program, has led many Oklahoma Christian students to go to Japan to teach English. Along with their teaching, many of these OC alumni also work with churches there.

1980–1985

Changes in General Education

The 1980 OCC catalog announced changes in the college's general education program. While the total of fifty-eight hours was the same, some courses had been dropped, others changed, and some added. The one-hour leveling courses were gone except for Bible and the freshman orientation course, called Ed 1111, Introduction to College. Two three-hour freshman English courses were now required and students had to take a two-hour course in economics called "The Free Enterprise System." Business students were exempt because of economics courses they took in their major. The physical education requirement was down to one hour. The Bible requirement remained at nine hours, but full-time students still had to take a Bible course each term and that would normally total sixteen.[36]

Additional Majors

The number of degree programs had also increased. The Division of Bible offered six: a B.S. and a B.A. in Bible, Missions, Preaching, Religious Education, and Youth Ministry. The Division of Business had ten: Accounting, Business Administration, Management, Management Science, Marketing, Office Management, Executive Secretarial Administration, and two in teacher preparation—Business Education and Bookkeeping and Clerical Practice. The Division of Communication and Fine Arts offered thirteen: two degrees in Art, Drawing and Painting, and Commercial Art, Mass Communications, Music, Speech Communication, Speech/Pre-Law, Speech Pathology and four in teacher preparation—Art, Music, Speech Communication, and Speech Pathology. The speech pathology program required taking some courses at Central State University.

The Division of Education and Psychology offered five different degree programs: both a B.S. and a B.A. in Psychology, Elementary Education, Special Education/Elementary Education, and Early Childhood/Elementary Education. They also worked with other departments for degrees in specialized areas for teaching both in secondary schools and in kindergarten through twelfth grade.

The Division of Language and Literature had three degrees: English, Teaching English as a Foreign Language, and a teacher preparation degree in Language Arts. The Division of Physical Education offered two degrees: Physical Education and a teacher preparation degree in Physical Education.

The Division of Science listed twelve degree programs: Biochemistry, Biology, Biology-Chemistry, Chemistry, Computer Science, Home Economics, Mathematics, Math-Computer Science, Medical Technology, and teacher preparation degrees in Mathematics, Home Economics, and Science. The Division of Social Science offered seven degree programs: both a B.A. and B.S. in American Studies, History, Human Behavior, Social Work, Sociology, and a teacher preparation degree in Social Studies.

These majors totaled fifty-one in all. While the differences between some of the degrees in a division were small, the college believed that having a breadth of degrees improved its appeal to students who were sometimes looking for a very specific degree program. By 1980, the college listed 599 courses in its catalog. Dr. Bailey McBride, who became academic dean in 1976, worked with the faculty on curricular changes during this period of time.

Dr. Bailey McBride

In 1984, OCC added a degree in Family Life. Led by Dr. Marge Jennings, "the degree is the first of its kind among Christian colleges."[37] The degree combined courses from the departments of "Christian Family, communication, psychology, sociology, economics, Bible, and others."[38]

1985–1990

Changes in General Education

The 1985 catalog shows more changes in the general education program. These courses now were grouped under six headings, with most of the requirements as they were, but with a few changes. Under a heading of Personal Development, students still took Introduction to College and one hour in physical education activity. Under Communication and Logic, students continued to take six hours of English composition, plus speech and mathematics. Under Religion and Values, students still took a minimum of nine hours in Bible but continued with at least one course each term, and they took the capstone course in Topics in Philosophy. In Political, Economic, and Social Backgrounds, students took one course in American history, one in American Government, and one in economics. Now, however, students were required to take the beginning course in either psychology or sociology. The humanities requirement was also different, with students now taking one course in literature, one in art, music, or theatre appreciation, and one in Western Civilization. The requirement in science had been reduced from eight to seven hours including one course each in biological and physical sciences. The total number of hours had fallen from fifty-eight to fifty-three, although the student attending for eight terms would take sixteen hours in Bible, seven more than the nine hour requirement, and thus would take a total of sixty hours in general education.

The 1985 catalog is the first to indicate that the college expected all students to become competent in the use of computers. "Recognizing the impact that computers are having on society," the statement reads, "OCC provides computer access for every student. OCC's General Education program incorporates numerous opportunities for each student to become familiar with the three basic areas of computer application: Word processing, databases, and spreadsheets."[39] While it would be another twelve years before each student had his or her own laptop, even before that time, the college provided computer laboratories to encourage students to develop computer skills.

Changes in Majors Offered

The 1985 catalog also shows some changes in the majors OCC offered. The former Division of Social Science had been renamed the Division of Behavioral and Social Science. The Department of Psychology had moved there from the Division of Education, and Home Economics had moved there from the Division of Science. In Behavioral Science, a new degree was added in Interior Design. The field of home economics was changing and colleges were dropping courses in cooking and sewing. OCC would, therefore, soon drop its degree in home economics as students showed more interest in interior design.

The Division of Business had dropped the major in Management Science, but still had a degree in Management. They had also dropped the teaching major in Bookkeeping and Clerical Practice, but retained the degree in Business Education. In keeping with the rising interest in the use of computers, the 1985 catalog listed a degree in Computer Information Systems that had been added to the program in 1983.

From 1980 to 1985, the Division of Communication and Fine Arts had made several changes. Mass Communications now offered degrees in four areas of specialization: Journalism, Photojournalism, Radio-Television, and Public Relations/Advertising. The Art Department was also moving in a new direction. While continuing to offer the more traditional degrees in drawing and painting, the 1993 catalog showed the addition of a degree in Advertising Design. This degree would eventually attract more students than any other program in the department. The Division of Language had added a degree in English/Writing.

Engineering

Jim Cutbirth

The biggest news in the 1985 catalog, however, was the addition of two degrees in engineering. The process began in 1993 when Jim Cutbirth, an engineer who came to teach pre-engineering and engineering physics courses, Jim Baxter, chairman of the Division of Science,

Jim Baxter

and Len Feuerhelm, physics professor, developed a proposal for the administration to consider.

They had visited other colleges, studied catalogs, and projected

Len Feuerhelm

the costs.[40] Since engineering was a growing field attracting many from Churches of Christ, and since none of the colleges serving this constituency offered degrees in engineering, the faculty and administration concluded that Oklahoma Christian should be the one to meet that need.[41] The cost of adding such a program would be $7,000,000, including $3,000,000 for a building, $1,000,000 for equipment, and $3,000,000 for endowment to keep the program going.[42] In addition to raising the funds and building a facility, the college also would have to attract qualified teachers for the program, which would be difficult because industry salaries would be far ahead of what the college could pay teachers in engineering.

At a press luncheon in the Skirvin Plaza Hotel on August 8, 1984, President Terry Johnson announced that OC would start an engineering program the following year. Johnson said that "the move will result in OCC's being the only college operated by members of the Churches of Christ offering bachelor degrees in the engineering field. OCC will also be the

Dr. Terry Johnson announces OCC's Engineering program at a press luncheon.

only college in Oklahoma County and the first liberal arts college in Oklahoma to develop an engineering program."[43] Others at the luncheon offered their endorsement: Edward L. Gaylord, publisher of the *Daily Oklahoman*; Walt Beam, vice president of engineering at Conoco; Dr. Jerald Parker, professor of engineering at Oklahoma State University, who had served as a consultant to develop the program; and Dr. William Banowsky, president of the University of Oklahoma.[44] Banowsky commented, "What will be especially appealing is the opportunity for quality engineering education within the Christian college atmosphere. In the six years that I have been at the University of Oklahoma, I have heard nothing but respect and praise for the quality and integrity of Oklahoma Christian College. I am not surprised that OCC is the first in the brotherhood to initiate an ambitious program that will offer a Bachelor of Science degree in

Engineering. This is an idea whose time has come."[45]

Troy Pemberton

Lynn Nored

In the fall of 1985, fifty students enrolled in the first engineering courses. In 1986, two joined Jim Cutbirth on the engineering faculty: Dr. Troy Pemberton, who came from Phillips Petroleum Company to head the program, and Lynn Nored, who brought more than twenty years of experience in engineering. The first engineering graduates finished in April of 1989 when four received their degrees. By the fall of 2007, students enrolled as engineering majors numbered 212.

Vienna Program

In 1986, Oklahoma Christian announced that its overseas offering would include a semester-long program based in Vienna. After considering several possible European sites, OCC faculty and administration selected Vienna because of its central location, its own unique ties with European history and culture, and because church connections there offered good opportunities. Ralph and Gladys Burcham were the first faculty sponsors for the program.

OC Vienna Studies students visiting the Roman Coliseum

In this program, students typically leave in late August and, after spending a week in England and a few days in France, arrive in Vienna in early September. They take classes with the sponsoring OCC faculty member, study German under a teacher in Vienna, and take other courses by independent study or via the Internet.

From Vienna, they visit sites in Italy, Greece, Germany, and other European locations. The students return in early December. Dr. Ken and Lindy Adams have sponsored the group three times and so have Dr. John and Cynthia Fletcher. Dr. John and Connie Maple have travelled with the group twice, as have Dr. Mickey and Jane

Banister, and Dr. Shawn and Nancy Jones from Cascade. Typically, thirty students are selected for this program, and because of the large number wishing to participate, a shorter summer version, which began in 2000, typically takes twenty students. In 2007, a Latin American summer program began with six students travelling to study Spanish as well as the Mayan, Incan, and Aztec cultures. These students also do church work, particularly in Honduras. Along with the PAC Rim program, the university now offers three overseas study programs.

Degree Changes

Other changes came with the 1988–1990 catalog: OCC's Division of Business now presented a degree in Information Management but no longer offered Executive Secretarial Administration, and the Interior Design program had been moved to the Department of Art. The Department of Communications had also added a degree in Organizational Communication, and Engineering had added a degree in Engineering Physics.[46] The number of courses listed in the catalog had grown to 721, with courses in engineering and growth in other fields accounting for the increase.

Graduate Program in Bible

The most significant change in the 1988 year was the addition of the first graduate program at Oklahoma Christian, a master of arts in Bible. The Bible faculty had engaged in a careful study of other master's degree programs and had met with preachers and elders to learn what courses should be offered to make the new program provide a combination of scholarship and practical training. The result was a degree requiring thirty-six graduate hours. Sixteen students enrolled for the first year, and by 1990, a total of forty-eight were enrolled.

1990–1998

Move to University

In 1990, Oklahoma Christian College announced its move to university status. It was offering graduate work in Bible, strong professional preparation in many fields, and its enrollment was at 1,673—as large as many universities. Since many of its peer institutions had already made the move, the OCC administration believed the time was right to make the change. The subsequent academic reorganization, first appearing in the 1992–1994 catalog, showed the previous eight academic divisions now combined into five colleges: Biblical Studies, Business, Education, Liberal Arts, and Science and Engineering. In this change, the Division of Physical Education was placed in the College of Education, and the Divisions of Communication and Fine Arts, Language and Literature, and Behavioral and Social Science were combined to make the College of Fine Arts.

Changes in General Education and Majors

The 1992 catalog also showed the next change in general education requirements, although the change was more in wording than in substance. That year, the catalog raised the requirement in Religion and Values from twelve to nineteen. The Bible requirement no longer was listed at nine hours along with a statement that required students to take a Bible course each term. Now the requirement was shown as sixteen hours, the number of hours all but transfer students had already been required to take. An accompanying chart indicated how many hours in Bible each transfer student would be required to take based on the number of hours being transferred. The minimum number for those transferring eighty or more hours, for example, was six.[47] Under the new requirement, freshmen and sophomores still would take a Bible class each term, but other students were allowed some flexibility as to when they took their Bible classes. This move was partly due to the fact that more students were taking longer than eight terms to finish their degrees, and to require them to take additional Bible classes beyond sixteen hours would be more than the faculty thought necessary.

In the 1992 catalog, the College of Business dropped its degree in pre-law, and in 1994, they dropped the degree in Business Education. Also in 1994, they dropped the degree in Computer Information Systems, but the Department of Mathematics and Computer Science simultaneously was adding a degree in Information Systems. In 1996, Business dropped the degree in Finance.

Other changes in majors also came during this period. In 1992, Language and Literature added a degree in Spanish. In 1994, Behavioral Science dropped the degree in Social Work, and in 1996, dropped the degree in Sociology.

By the 1997–1998 catalog, the number of courses at OC had grown to 769.

Vocational Ministry Degree

The 1994–1996 catalog shows, for the first time, a degree in Vocational Ministry. This program, developed by the College of Biblical Studies, allowed a student majoring in another field to take thirty-three hours in Bible courses to constitute a second major.[48] Since students must take sixteen hours in Bible to meet the general requirements, to receive this second degree, they only took seventeen additional hours from other courses in Biblical Studies. With such a degree, the Bible faculty hoped to encourage students to take the additional courses in Bible to prepare themselves more thoroughly for work in churches while they were earning their living through their first major. These courses would better prepare them to be Bible teachers, deacons, elders, and missionaries.

The number of those taking the vocational ministry program has varied but sometimes has been as high as 145.

Honors Program

One of OC's most significant curriculum developments came in 1996 with the addition of an Honors Program. The catalog stated:

> in an effort to challenge those students who are highly motivated to excel academically, OC provides an Honors Program to replace a significant portion of the general education core curriculum. Assuming a mastery of any discipline's fundamentals, the professors of honors courses encourage a high level of participation, foster considerable independent research, and mentor their students in writing papers that demonstrate mature, scholarly thinking.[49]

The honors program provides four, four-hour courses: two dealing with Western thought and expression, and one each with the Bible and literature and the Bible, science, and human values. A three-hour course studies Christ and the quest for meaning and another considers race, class, and gender in American thought. These courses, all interdisciplinary and team-taught, along with selected other courses, carry honors students through their first two years. In addition, three symposiums of one-hour each are required for honors students in their junior and senior years, along with a three-hour research project. [50] Dr. Bailey McBride has been the key figure in developing the program and in administering it through the years. This program has attracted many students to OC with outstanding academic credentials, including National Merit Scholars.

1998–2008

The 1998 OC catalog brought the next major change to the general education program. Under the leadership of Dr. Jeanine Varner, who became vice president for academic affairs in 1996, a faculty committee developed a completely new statement of the goals of the general education program. Now called "Core Curriculum Requirements," the statement used as its foundation the university's mission statement of educating "students for purposeful lives of leadership and service." A triangle illustrated the new plan, with "Faith" in the

Dr. Jeanine Varner

center of the triangle and the words "Think," "Act," and "Communicate" around the sides. The catalog emphasized that "faith is, therefore, the central concept in our core curriculum model. All of the specific objectives listed in each category are built on this central concept."[51] One goal of the program was to develop a student's "cognitive ability to think critically and creatively using appropriate methods of study, research, reasoning, and problem solving."[52] Another goal of this core curriculum was for each student to "communicate ideas effectively to others, including those of cultures and faiths different from his or her own, and receive ideas efficiently from others."[53] The third broad goal of the curriculum said the student would actively exhibit a personal faith and be a good citizen through understanding of "American history and the political and economic issues faced by American society."[54]

The curricular requirements for this new statement of goals totaled sixty hours and included four fundamental elements. The first, Basic Skills, included the freshman orientation class for one hour, six hours in English composition and research, three hours in oral communication, a one-hour course in fitness and wellness, and three hours in mathematics.

Illustration of the "Core Curriculum" adopted in 1998

The second element, Bible, required sixteen hours, with four two-hour courses required for the first two years: Matthew and Acts for freshman, and Story of the Old Testament and Story of the New Testament for sophomores. A new two-hour course, Senior Bible Seminar, designed as a capstone for the Bible classes, was required in either the junior or senior year. For the other six hours, students were allowed to choose from a list of six textual and six non-textual courses.[55]

The third element of the new core curriculum, Basic Perspectives, called for twenty-seven hours: six in American Political Economy and Turning Points in U.S. history, six in literature and fine arts, six from either biological science or physical science, and six hours in global civilization, including three in Western civilization and three in non-Western civilization. The fourth element in the new core curriculum was a continuation of the general education capstone course called the Senior Seminar. This general education plan remains the requirement in the 2007–2008 year.

M.B.A. Program

A very significant step in the OC curriculum began to develop in 1998–1999, when faculty members of the College of Business along with members of the Business Advisory Council considered whether the time had come to offer a master's degree in business. They recommended the addition of an M.B.A. to the curriculum, and the OC faculty and administration gave approval. Dr. Phil Lewis came as dean of the College of Business in the fall of 1999 with the charge to initiate the program. Graduate business classes began in the fall of 2000 with twenty-seven students. Dr. Don Drew was the first to direct the program, and after two years, Dr. Ken Johnson came to fill that role.[56]

The M.B.A. program is built around cohorts of students who start at six different points during the year. Those wishing to complete the degree in one year meet for classes two nights a week, while those wanting to finish in two years come one night a week. Students may take a general business program by choosing courses from a variety of fields, or they may specialize in any of the following: accounting, leadership, health services management, e-business, engineering and technology, or finance. Those coming with an undergraduate business degree must complete thirty-six hours, while those without such a degree must take an additional four leveling courses. The students come primarily from local businesses, with about half of the students receiving part or all of their expenses from their employers. The program appeals primarily to working adults, and the average age of the students is thirty-two. Members of the OC business faculty teach about half the courses with the other half taught by qualified adjunct faculty members. [57]

OC's M.B.A. program has been highly successful. By October 2007, 227 students were enrolled for graduate study in business.[58]

Three Colleges

Dr. Lynn McMillon

Dr. Larry Jurney

Dr. Phil Lewis

Dr. David Lowry

Starting with the 2003–2004 year, Oklahoma Christian University, in an effort to reduce administrative costs and achieve certain other economies, reorganized its colleges by reducing them from five to three. The College of Bible remained as it was, with Dr. Lynn McMillon continuing as dean. All other OC programs were arranged into two other colleges. The programs in business, engineering, and education were consolidated into the College of Professional Studies, with Dr. Phil Lewis as dean. The three units within this college were the School of Business, the School of Education including Physical Education, and the School of Engineering, which had within it the Department of Mathematics and Computer and Information Services, the Department of Electrical and Computer Engineering, and the Department of Mechanical Engineering.

All other programs were consolidated into the College of Arts and Sciences, with Dr. Larry Jurney serving as interim dean until Dr. David Lowry came in 2005. Within this college were the Department of Art and Design, the Department of Biological Sciences and Physical Sciences, the Department of Communication, the Department of History and Political Science, the Department of Language and Literature, the Department of Music, and the Department of Psychology and Family Studies.

Nursing

For many years, Oklahoma Christian has offered pre-nursing. Sometimes formal connections with other universities provided transfer opportunities that allowed OC students to complete their nurse's training. Occasionally, these agreements even involved a specified number of places reserved for OC students. By 2006, however, it was apparent that these various arrangements were no longer going to serve satisfactorily, primarily because the demand for nurses had grown to the point that other universities were having more applicants for their own programs than they could admit. Those completing OC's pre-nursing program, therefore, had limited opportunities to finish elsewhere.

During the spring of 2006, Jeanine Varner, vice president for academic affairs, Lisa McWhirter, chair of the Department of Biology, and Jan Link, a nurse educator consultant, developed a plan for offering a bachelor's degree in nursing at Oklahoma Christian. With faculty approval and the approval of the Oklahoma Board of Nursing, OC began recruiting students to start the program in the fall of 2006, when seventeen were admitted to the nursing program with fifty-two others in pre-nursing.[59] By the fall of 2007, the nursing program had grown to thirty-one freshmen, thirty-eight sophomores, twenty-three juniors, and seventeen seniors for a total of 109. To provide instruction for those students, OC had employed Linda Fly as the director of Nursing, as well as three full-time teachers: Kay Elder, Beth Scott, and Shawna Hood. Seven others served as adjunct faculty for the program.[60] The university also had remodeled some classroom space for nursing and obtained for their use a 1,640 square foot modular building.[61]

Linda Fly

Other Changes

Several other changes in majors also came during between 1998 and 2008. Business Education was dropped in 1999. In 2000, Behavioral and Social Sciences added a degree in Governmental and Legal Studies for those interested in political science. By 2000, the Mass Communications degree had new specialized areas: Interactive Multimedia, Corporate Media, Broadcast Management, and Broadcast Journalism. In 2001, Engineering added a degree in Computer Engineering. In 2003, Education dropped Special Education and Art Education as majors. In 2004, the Art Department added a degree in New Media Design. Also in 2004, the College of Biblical Studies added a master of divinity degree.

Several changes came in 2005: Communications added a degree in Theater Performance, Business added back a degree in Finance, and Communications dropped the degree in Communications Studies Education. In 2007, Education added a degree in Sport and Wellness. In Spring 2008, a master's degree program in engineering was announced.

Dr. Allison Garrett

The Oklahoma Christian catalog for 2007–2008 listed 854 undergraduate courses. In addition, there were sixty-seven graduate classes listed in Bible and thirty-four in Business. Together, these total 955 courses now available on the OC campus. Dr. Allison Dabbs Garrett, an OC graduate of 1984, began serving as vice president for academic affairs in August 2007 and now works with faculty in development of curriculum.

Conclusion

Since 1950, the curriculum at Oklahoma Christian University has grown from a two-year program providing only an associate's degree to a broad-based offering of sixty-six different bachelor's degrees plus master's degree programs in Bible and business and engineering. In the fall of 1950, students could choose from among thirty-seven courses on the schedule, while in the fall of 2007, they chose from an offering of 370.

In spite of this great expansion, however, the basic elements of the curriculum remain unchanged. Students still typically take a two-hour Bible course in each of eight terms, in every major they still must complete a strong liberal arts base of courses in communication, humanities, science, and social science, and they still focus on a career path in a major. While the particular requirements in these areas have varied through the years, the foundations on which they have been built remain the same.

Since the curriculum of the university is a good indicator of its philosophy, in staying with these basic elements, the university faculty and administration have shown their intent to continue in the path begun so many years before.

Chapter 10, Endnotes

1   Articles of Incorporation, dated January 22, 1948, Office of President, Oklahoma Christian University.

2   *Central Christian College Catalog*, 1950, 11, OC Archives.

3   Ibid., 11.

4   Ibid.,10.

5   Ibid., 11–21.

6   *Central Christian College Catalog*, 1951–52, 25, OC Archives.

7   *Central Christian College Catalog*, 1953–54, 24–33, OC Archives.

8   *Central Christian College Catalog*, 1957–1958, 46–64, OC Archives.

9   *Central Christian College Catalog*, 1958–1959, 36–49, OC Archives.

10   Ibid., 36.

11   Ibid.

12   Ibid., 37.

13   "Senior College Program Given Approval," *Oklahoma Christian College Bulletin*, July, 1960, 1, OC Archives.

14   Ibid., 1–2.

15   *Oklahoma Christian College Catalog*, 1960–1962, 37.

16   Ibid., 37.

17   Ibid., 37–38.

18   Ibid., 39–50.

19   Ibid., 51–54.

20   *Oklahoma Christian College Catalog*, 1962–64, 42, OC Archives.

21   Ibid., 40, 63–64.

22   "Oklahoma Christian Announces First Summer School Session for June, July," *Oklahoma Christian College Bulletin*, February 1964, 1, OC Archives.

23   "First Overseas Students Report Success," *Oklahoma Christian College Bulletin*, July, 1966, OC Archives.

24   *Oklahoma Christian College Catalog*, 1968–1970, 46, OC Archives.

25   *Oklahoma Christian College Catalog*, 1972–1974, 45, OC Archives.

26   "KOCC Broadcasting," *Oklahoma Christian College Reporter*, October, 1973, OC Archives.

27   Ibid.

28   "KOCC Airs Nov. 3," *OCC Reporter,* October, 1980, 6, OC Archives.

29   "Japanese Students To Study at OCC," *OCC Reporter*, May 1975, OC Archives.

30   Ibid.

31   "OCC, Ibaraki Students Participate in Cross-Cultural Exchange Program," *OCC Reporter*, June, 1976, 1, OC Archives.

32   Ibid.

33   Ibid.

34   Joe McCormack, Email to the author on October 10, 2007.

35   *Oklahoma Christian College Catalog*, 1976–1978, 92, OC Archives.

36   *Oklahoma Christian College Catalog*, 1980–1982, 38, OC Archives.

37   "New Family Life Degree Program Offered," *OCC Reporter*, October, 1984, 5, OC Archives.

38   Ibid.

39   *Oklahoma Christian College Catalog*, 1985–86, 24, OC Archives.

40   Jim Cutbirth, Conversation with the author, October 2, 2007.

41   Ibid.

42   "$7 Million Engineering Department Established," *OCC Reporter*, 1, August, 1984, OC Archives.

43   Ibid.

44   Ibid.

45   Ibid.

46   *Oklahoma Christian College Catalog*, 1988–1990, 55, 65, OC Archives.

47   *Oklahoma Christian University Catalog,* 1992–1994, 34, OC Archives.

48   *Oklahoma Christian University Catalog*, 1994–1996, 43, OC Archives.

49   *Oklahoma Christian University Catalog*, 1996–1997, 35, OC Archives.

[50] Ibid.
[51] *Oklahoma Christian University Catalog*, 1998–99, 41, OC Archives.
[52] Ibid., 42.
[53] Ibid.
[54] Ibid.
[55] Ibid., 43.
[56] Phil Lewis, Conversation with the author on October 3, 2007.
[57] Ibid.
[58] Ibid.
[59] Report of a Self Study, Fall 2007, 2.
[60] Ibid., 5.
[61] Ibid., 25.

Chapter 11
THE ACCREDITATIONS

Introduction

From its very conception, those founding Central Christian College desired a college in good standing with other colleges and universities, whose credits would be acceptable in transfer. Other colleges among Churches of Christ held this status, and Central Christian had to have this acceptability to fulfill its mission. Even before classes began, President L. R. Wilson and Dean James O. Baird made contact with the Oklahoma State Regents for Higher Education about approval so credits could transfer.[1] An article in the *Bartlesville Examiner-Enterprise*, prior to the start of classes in September of 1950, stated that Dr. C. E. Lewis, member of the Oklahoma Regents, visited the campus and said, "'Central Christian College will be dealt with on its merits.'" The article summarizes Lewis's comments: "If students transfer to other institutions, they will be accepted conditionally. If they are able to do acceptable work in such colleges, then they will be given credit for their work at Central Christian."[2] Before the end of the first semester, Dr. Mel Nash, chancellor for the Regents, wrote indicating that, based on a visit by Dr. Loren Brown, courses at Central Christian would be accepted in transfer.

This initial approval was not all the accreditation the college needed, but it was a good start and a clear indication that the college would seek inclusion in accredited higher education. Regular contact with the Regents and with Dr. J. E. Fellows, registrar and dean of admissions at the University of Oklahoma, allowed credits to continue to transfer to other institutions until the college gained a higher accreditation.

North Central Association Accreditation

From its earliest years, administrators at Central Christian in Bartlesville were pointing toward accreditation by the North Central Association of Colleges and Schools. Such accreditation, although called "regional," actually meant acceptability nationwide. In a letter dated April 22, 1966, to Norman Burns, executive secretary of the North Central Association, Dr. James Baird wrote: "I was Dean of Instruction of Oklahoma Christian College when our College began in 1950. I distinctly remember at our first faculty meeting that one of the matters discussed was our hope that the College might continue to develop its capacity for wholesome introspection and improvement so that eventually the College might be accredited by the North Central Association."[3] By March of 1954, the college's fourth year, Baird and President L. R. Wilson attended a meeting of the Association in Chicago.[4]

In 1955–1956, the Central Christian faculty conducted their first self study after the style required for application to the North Central Association. They did another one in 1956–1957.[5] On July 4, 1957, President Baird sent to campus administrators and faculty a thirteen-page statement on "Suggestions for North Central Accreditation." This document used major points in the accreditation manual to give suggestions about how to improve the report the faculty had written and about changes the college should make in each area.[6] The college also brought several educational specialists for advice.[7] Among these was Dr. E. T. Dunlap, then president of Eastern Oklahoma State College at Wilburton, Oklahoma. Since his college had recently been through the accreditation process, he knew the procedures and expectations well and gave useful advice. The connection with Dunlap was also fortunate because he was later chosen to fill the role of chancellor of the Oklahoma State Regents for Higher Education, and these early contacts with him later proved helpful.

1960 Application

After moving to its new campus in Oklahoma City, the Central Christian faculty completed a self study in 1958–1959 and another in 1959–1960, prepared with Dr. Dunlap's assistance.[8] This last study became the basis for Central Christian's first formal application for membership in the North Central Association, submitted in September 1960. The report followed the standard format of that time, focusing on eight questions: (1) Is the educational task clearly defined? (2) Are the necessary resources available? (3) Is the institution well-organized? (4) Are the curriculum and instructional programs adapted to the goals? (5) Are the conditions of faculty service likely to promote high morale?   (6) Is student life well-balanced and educationally meaningful?   (7) Is the level of achievement of students consistent with the goal?   (8) What are the future plans?[9] Study committees chaired by James Baird, Stafford North, Don Beck, Harold Fletcher, Kay Ragan, Joseph Jones, and Floyd Reeves prepared the college's answer to each of these questions.[10]

The report indicates there were twenty faculty members, ten full-time, with six others as full-time administrators, librarians, or coaches who taught as part of their load, and four more as part-time instructors. Of the twenty, three (or fifteen percent) held a doctorate, and eighty-eight percent of the remainder had a master's degree.[11] The library reported over 10,000 volumes and 120 periodical subscriptions[12] to serve the student body of 323. An appendix provided the results of a study of eighty-four students who had transferred to Abilene Christian College, David Lipscomb College, and the University of Oklahoma. On the whole, students going to the three institutions had a higher grade point average at the transferring institution than at Oklahoma Christian. This information was offered as evidence that academic work at the college was at a standard college level, and that students who transferred were well-prepared.

At the time the college submitted this self study, however, the situation was quite unusual. The information had been gathered during the 1959–60 school year while the college was offering two years of collegiate work, and thus while the school was a junior college. By the time the self study was submitted in September 1960, however, the college was already adding the third year of instruction and would add the fourth year in September 1961. The application, then, was for membership as a junior college even though the college was already expanding to a senior college. The Association said Oklahoma Christian could still submit the request for membership as a junior college,[13] so they did.

The four-person evaluation team from the North Central Association visited on December 12–14, 1960. The visiting committee listed nineteen strengths of the institution, such as the preparation of the faculty, the physical plant, financial condition, administrative leadership, future planning, organization of student government, and faculty morale. They also listed fourteen needs, which included weak library facilities, low salaries, few opportunities for students to elect courses, and the need for better retirement benefits.[14] Their report stated, however, that they found it difficult to evaluate the institution as a junior college when it was already becoming a senior college.

After a visiting team filed its report, it was customary for representatives of the institution next to meet with a different group, called the Committee by Type, to review the findings of the visiting team, to invite comments from the institutional representatives, and to

Dr. Baird and Dr. North

allow the committee to ask questions. The time set for those from Oklahoma Christian to meet with the committee was on Sunday morning, March 19, 1961. President Baird and Dean North were scheduled to appear, but the time of the meeting put them in a dilemma. Should they miss attending church services on Sunday morning, which was not in harmony with the type of institution they served, or should they take a chance on offending someone in the North Central Association by asking for a change of time? In a letter dated January 5, 1961, President Baird wrote:

> I would like to make a request of you which may sound a bit unusual but which is altogether in harmony with the faith of the religious group with which our college is identified. Would it be at all possible for you to set this meeting of the Committee at some other hour? I have checked with the Churches of Christ in the Chicago area and find their services are at 11:00 a.m. Unless prevented by an emergency or illness, our people make a great effort to attend church services and, if it could be arranged, Dean North and I would appreciate tremendously your consideration in this matter.[15]

The committee granted the request, changing the meeting to 2 p.m. While seemingly a small matter, this incident indicates the determination of these men to hold to their religious principles even at some risk.

A few days before this important meeting in Chicago, Dr. Baird received word from the Association indicating that one of the institution's history faculty had written a letter of protest to the Association. He had been not been re-employed for the following year and claimed this action had been taken because he did not always agree with the conservative political stance that college leaders publicly took. He quoted a newspaper statement from Dr. Benson, who had said the college would "teach respect for the American system of private enterprise," "the competitive market," "the profit incentive," "constitutional government," and "people's faith in God and a willingness to abide in Christian principles." While admitting that "Dr. Baird has never interfered with my teaching," he said, "what he wants in the classroom is plain enough." The teacher charged that he was not re-employed for a fourth year, which would have granted tenure, because of his political views.[16]

At the meeting on March 19, the Committee asked about the letter. North had prepared in advance a response should the point be raised. He said:

> Although his knowledge of his field is adequate, we received numerous complaints from students that they were dissatisfied with his courses. Some refused to take a class under him, indicating they would take the classes which he teaches in summer school at another college. In general his grades have reflected that his students have not been sufficiently motivated.

> Although we were aware that some of his personal political views were not in complete agreement with those held by some others on the staff, this was not the basis for not re-employing him. He has held and has expressed freely his views from the beginning of his employment with the college and has never been told what to say or what not to say in the classroom. If this were to be the basis of dismissal it would have been done after the first year and not after he had taught for three.[17]

The Committee apparently was satisfied with this response because the matter did not surface again.

Even though the Association had indicated Oklahoma Christian could apply as a junior college while moving to senior college status, in the final analysis, the Association did not proceed with such an action. The net outcome of this application in 1960 was that the North Central did not accredit the college at the junior college level but did grant "candidate for membership" status as a senior college.[18] In many ways, this was better. Instead of accreditation as a junior college, it received the first level of approval as a senior college, which now it was. The Association also suggested Dr. E. M. Gerritz, dean of admissions of Kansas State University, as a consultant, and he proved to be "of great service in stimulating the college to improvement as it worked toward full membership in the Association."[19]

1964 Application

By June of 1964, Oklahoma Christian believed it was ready to apply for full accreditation and submitted a self study prepared during the 1963–1964 academic year. This study was organized around the same questions as before, and Ralph Burcham, Darvin Keck, Leonard Johnson, O. B. Stamper, James Parker, W. E. Kirk, Harold Fletcher, and Stafford North chaired committees. The North Central

Association responded that they were "unable to decide whether or not an examination of your institution is advisable."[20] The letter continued, "the uncertainty of the Board is due to the weaknesses in the self study report concerning the stability of income, the library resources and facilities, and conditions of faculty employment."[21] They said if the institution requested consideration under these circumstances and was turned down, it could not apply for three more years. While the college wanted North Central Accreditation to bolster its standing in the collegiate community and acceptability of its academic work, the implications were clear. No accreditation this time. So college officials withdrew the application, planning to resubmit it after another year, during which they would make improvements in the areas suggested.

1965 Application

Faculty committees updated the 1964 self study with new information and submitted it in May 1965. This report followed the same organizational structure as had the report of 1960. The section on the "educational task" of the institution contained this revealing statement:

> Oklahoma Christian College joins other collegiate institutions throughout the state and nation in seeking to provide both general and vocational education beyond the high school. The college finds its special "reason for being," however, in the spiritual goals which undergird all its activities.

Both these academic and spiritual purposes, the report continued, sprang from the constituency who founded and supported the college, for they established the college to provide higher education within a distinctively Christian context. In keeping with this intention, the college has developed a program of general education and career training, with each rooted in a spiritual soil.[22]

By the time of the 1965 report, the number of students had grown to 644, and the faculty numbered twenty-eight with 29 percent holding a doctorate and all but one of the remainder a master's. Since 1960, the total number of library books had more than doubled to 25,000. As this report was submitted, the new library building was under construction and to be finished in the fall of 1965. This would be

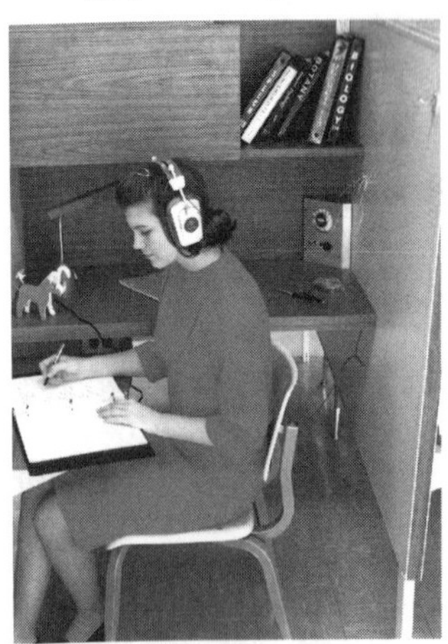

Learning Center Carrel

the three-story Mabee Learning Center that would not only provide greatly expanded space for the library collection, but also would contain a private study carrel for each student from which the student could dial tape recordings prepared by the faculty.

Certainly Oklahoma Christian College had made many improvements since its admission to candidacy for membership in 1960. It had more students, more faculty, more facilities, more books, and a stronger financial base. With all of this came great hope of full membership in the North Central Association.

A visiting committee of two came to the campus on December 15 and 16, 1965. In its exit interview with the president, the team said, "[W]e were pleasantly surprised." They commented that the Bible program was strong, the faculty seemed devoted, dedicated, and loyal, and the facilities were good. They said the students were "refreshing" and "class discussions are lively." They added, however, that foreign language, women's physical education, and some social science areas needed strengthening. They cautioned that "it will take active involvement in leadership to keep the Learning Center usage from deteriorating into high school type busy work."[23]

While the Committee could not reveal its recommendation, there were enough positive comments to create an expectation that approval would come with this application. The Association set March 28, 1966, in the Palmer House in Chicago as the date and place for college officials to meet with the Committee by Type. At this meeting, the college would respond to the visiting committee report and present updated information as well as answer questions. This committee would, in turn, make a recommendation to the Commission as a whole.[24] President Baird and Dean North would represent the college.

All was not well, however. About three weeks before the meeting, Dr. Baird received a call from someone inside the North Central Association to inform him that negative comments were making their way around high places in the Association about the American Citizenship Center the college sponsored. The center conducted seminars and provided materials for both high school students and teachers relating to the free enterprise system, constitutional government, and faith in God as foundations of American life. The approach was anticommunist, antisocialist, and pro-conservative. The message to Dr. Baird was that college sponsorship of this program would hinder accreditation. A second related issue was Dr. George Benson's role as chancellor of Oklahoma Christian. Benson was concurrently president of Harding College in Searcy, Arkansas, and there he had pioneered a citizenship program along conservative political and economic lines after which the one at Oklahoma Christian had been modeled. It was widely thought that Dr. Benson's positions and the citizenship education program at Harding had delayed its admission to the North Central Association. Now, it appeared the same issue might hinder accreditation for Oklahoma Christian.

Time between receiving this word and the date for appearing before the review committee was just a matter of days. Could anything be done to lessen the potential problem? Dr. Baird and Dr. Benson decided on a course of action. First, they would separate the American Citizenship Center from the college by establishing it as a separate corporation with its own board. While the program would continue to be housed on the campus, it would have no organic connection with the institution. In a meeting on March 24, 1966, just four days before the scheduled meeting with the review committee, the Executive Committee of the Oklahoma Christian Board of Trustees made this action official.

In a second action they thought would be helpful, they announced that Dr. Benson, then sixty-eight, would retire as chancellor in the near future. They agreed that if the present arrangement would "prevent the College from receiving accreditation, he will resign immediately."[25] While they preferred time to phase out Dr. Benson's role, he would step out immediately if required.

Dr. E. T. Dunlap, chancellor of the Oklahoma State Regents for Higher Education, who had strong ties with the North Central Association, wanted to be of help. In earlier years, he had been a consultant to Oklahoma Christian on its accreditation efforts and, through the years, had maintained close ties with the institution. Although he originally had not intended to attend the North Central meeting that year, he decided he would go to speak on behalf of Oklahoma Christian wherever his word might have weight.

When Baird and North met with the Committee by Type on March 28, Dr. Baird made a brief presentation updating some of the data in the original report and spoke about improvements in areas the visiting committee had noted as weaknesses. He mentioned the start of construction on a new 1,300-seat auditorium, authorization to build a new field house, and improvements in the average student ACT score. Of greatest significance, however, was an improvement in faculty salaries, with an average faculty increase of $1,300 and increases averaging $2,468 for professors and $2,449 for associate professors.[26]

After these initial comments, it was time for the committee to raise questions. The committee's first question was about the American Citizenship Center. Baird and North responded that this center was no longer part of the operation of the college, now being a separate corporation with its own board. Committee members were taken by surprise and spent the remainder of the time probing this issue, as well as Benson's role as chancellor. The separation had been made, however, and it was now difficult for anyone to substantiate a major objection to accrediting the college on this point.

The Committee by Type would now report to the entire Commission on Colleges and Universities, which would make the final decision on March 30. Dr. William Hale, president of Langston University, located about thirty miles north of Oklahoma Christian, was one of the members of the Commission. Through the natural associations in higher education in Oklahoma, Hale knew both Baird and North well and was present in the meeting of the Commission for the discussion of Oklahoma Christian. When they made the decision in favor of accreditation, he feigned a coughing spell so he could leave the meeting to bring the good news to his friends from Oklahoma Christian.

Official word of the accreditation came in a letter from Norman Burns, dated April 8, 1966. In the letter, he wrote, "It is a pleasure to inform you officially that the Commission on Colleges and Universities of the North Central Association at its meeting on March 30 voted to accredit Oklahoma Christian College as a bachelor's degree-granting institution." He went on to say,

> In making this decision, the Commission took into account the action taken by the College providing for the separating of the "Oklahoma Christian College Letter" from Oklahoma Christian College and for the phasing out of the position of chancellor in the near future. Would you please file with our office a copy of the document separating the College from the "Oklahoma Christian College Letter," as well as the plan for phasing out the position of chancellor.[27]

Why Burns spoke of the Citizenship Center as the "letter" is not clear, but from this statement it is obvious that the two matters of the Citizenship Center and Benson's role as chancellor were crucial questions in considering the accreditation. In a letter dated April 22, Dr. Baird responded to Burns, expressing "appreciation for your kind and encouraging words regarding this" and "enclosing a copy of the resolution passed by the Executive Committee separating the Citizenship Center from the College and a copy of the Articles of Incorporation of the separate organization."[28] He also assured Burns that Dr. Benson's retirement would proceed, although there would be a period of transition.

This first full accreditation by the North Central Association was a highly significant step forward for Oklahoma Christian College. It meant easier transfer of credits, a higher standing in the collegiate scene, and later, the opportunity to participate in federal grant programs for students. It was also important because it laid a foundation for specialized accreditations.

1975 Application

Since the North Central Association had granted accreditation for ten years, the next self study report was filed December 1, 1975. The plan for self studies had changed, so the new report was divided into seven chapters. The chapters and committee chairs were: Purposes and Objectives, Dr. William Jones; Instruction, Dr. Bailey McBride; Student Activities, Dr. Max Dobson; Student Services, Dr. Gary Rayburn; Management, Dr. Howard Leftwich; Physical Plant, Dr. Gene Talbert; and Financing, Guy Ross.[29]

During the previous ten years, many changes had taken place. The college had grown to 1,451 students from forty-five states and six foreign countries.[30] In 1969, the college had done an extensive long-range planning effort called the *Design for Progress Study*. There were now thirty-seven faculty members, 62 percent of whom had doctorates,[31] and the Library housed 80,000 volumes.[32] The State Department of Education had approved thirteen areas of teacher education, and in 1972, NCATE had accredited all the college's teacher education programs. Several new majors had been approved, and a new design for the general education program went into effect in 1974.[33] Also in 1974, Dr. Terry Johnson had replaced Dr. James Baird as president.

A three-person North Central team came February 22-25, 1976. They noted several strengths: "faculty members and students are loyal to the institution," "the quality of preparation of the faculty has greatly improved," "the physical plant is well conceived and well maintained," and "the financial status is excellent." They also, however, pointed to concerns: "The faculty members are over burdened with many preparations and a large number of advisees," "there are many very large classes," "the policy on termination of continuous employment has strong elements of arbitrariness," and "there is excessive reliance on part-time faculty members."[34]

Their report concluded with a recommendation that Oklahoma Christian "be continued with accreditation for offering a Bachelor's degree."[35] This time, there were no surprises from Chicago: the Commission on Colleges and Universities approved accreditation for another ten years.

1985 Application

By the reaccreditation review in 1985, the format for the self study had changed considerably, reflecting a new emphasis on assessment. Standards for accreditation were now arranged around four evaluative criteria: a clear statement of purposes, adequate resources for achieving the purposes, a substantiated record of achieving the purposes, and the capacity for continuing to achieve the purposes. President Terry Johnson chaired an eighteen-person steering committee and Executive Vice President Stafford North chaired the six-person Executive Committee. The sixteen subcommittees and their chairs were: Athletics, Dr. Ron Bever; Auxiliary Enterprises, Bruce Kerr; Budget, Dr. Richard Greenhaw; Conditions, Dr. Howard Leftwich; Curriculum, Dr. Robert McMillan; Development, Dr. James Cail; Governance, Dr. Jack Skaggs; Imagination, Andy Benton; Instruction, Dr. Gary Shreck; Library, Dr. Jim Baxter; Physical Plant, Dr. Jim Wilson; Purpose, Dr. Lynn McMillon; Recruitment and Retention, Dr. Darryl Tippens; Spiritual Life, Dr. James Baird; Student Activities, Dr. Mike Gipson; and Student Services, Phil Heffington. Each committee had faculty, administration, and students, and in addition, some had Board members and alumni.[36]

The four-member North Central visiting team came on October 21–23, 1985. Their report listed a number of commendations for such things as growth in the endowment from two million dollars in 1975 to sixteen million dollars in 1985,[37] a balanced budget,[38] a shared sense of mission on the campus,[39] students enjoying a high quality of collegiate life,[40] and good long-range planning.[41]

Among the areas for improvement, they recommended providing a special fund for faculty development,[42] funding for depreciation on physical facilities,[43] additional opportunities for women in athletics,[44] additional compensation for those in higher faculty ranks,[45] reduction in faculty loads because of a 1:24 student-faculty ratio,[46] increase in library holdings,[47] more computer services,[48] and more exposure of students to non-Western cultures.[49] The visiting committee recommended reaccreditation for another ten years, and that was the decision of the Association.

1995 Application

Dr. Stafford North, while dean of instruction, dean of the college, and executive vice president, had led in the accreditation efforts of 1960, 1964–65, 1975, and 1985. When time came for the 1995 study, Dr. Bailey McBride, provost, chaired the Steering Committee and gave general direction to the study. The North Central Association had added a fifth criterion to the previous four, "The institution demonstrates integrity in its practices and relationships." McBride established a committee for each of the five criteria, and these were chaired by Dr. Jack Skaggs, Dr. Jeanine Varner, Dr. John Vincent, Dr. Gary Shreck, and Dr. Don Vinzant.

Dr. Bailey McBride

The report noted a number of changes since the report of 1985.

The North Central Association had approved both a master of arts in ministry in a focused visit in 1988 and an arrangement by which Ohio Valley College could offer a bachelor's degree through a distance learning arrangement with Oklahoma Christian. The Association had also approved opening Cascade College as a branch campus in Portland.[50] Since the Association's last visit, OCC had added degrees in electrical and mechanical engineering, and these had received accreditation by the Accreditation Board for Engineering and Technology in 1991. The computer science degree had been moved from Business to the Department of Math/Computer Science, and the university had added degree programs in finance and Spanish. The music program had been accredited by the National Association of Schools of Music in 1992, and the College of Business had been accredited by the Association of Collegiate Business Schools and Programs in 1994.[51]

The report also noted that library space had been almost doubled by a remodeling of the Learning Center and that the card catalog had been replaced with an automated system. Three facilities had been built: Allison Biblical Studies Center, Prince Engineering Center, and an expansion of Payne Physical Education Center. Major additions had also been made to campus computing opportunities, with new computer laboratories and additional personnel.[52]

The 1995 North Central report also noted a number of improvements in the academic program: faculty holding doctorates had risen to 68 percent, the college had begun a trimester abroad program centered in Vienna and another in Latin America, more funds had been set aside for faculty development, all full-time faculty now operated on a twelve-hour assignment rather than the fifteen-hour load of ten years before, and the student-faculty ratio had fallen to 14:1.[53]

A visiting team of six members came on September 25–27. Their report commended the institution's strong international commitment,[54] the increase in endowment from $16 million in 1985 to $37 million in 1995 (although they thought $32.5 million more accurately represented the actual number),[55] good progress toward gender equity in intercollegiate sports,[56] an attractive physical plant,[57] commitment to mission,[58] and the fact that the students held the faculty in high regard.[59]

As concerns, the visiting committees indicated that retention required more attention, better financial records should be kept in some areas and better financial forecasting would help, library holdings were weak, and the curriculum needed more of a multicultural perspective.[60] They also suggested that the university do more to support underprepared students.[61]

The committee recommended and the Association approved

another ten year accreditation period. This time, however, by December of 1998, there were to be three interim reports on retention, institutional long-range planning, and finances. These reports were filed and accepted.

2005 Application

As time came for the preparation of the 2005 report, several administrative changes had taken place. Dr. Jeanine Varner was now vice president for academic affairs, and she and Dr. Don Drew co-chaired the study. Varner brought to the work over fifteen years of service as an evaluator with the North Central Association, and she had been very involved in previous OC self studies. Drew, a member of the business faculty, contributed through his special skills in data collection and analysis. After 2001, the division of the North Central Association working with colleges and universities was known as the Higher Learning Commission, and the plan for the self study had been changed to put still more emphasis on assessment. There were now five criteria: (1) the institution "operates with integrity to ensure the fulfillment of its mission through structures and processes that involve the board, administration, faculty, staff, and students"; (2) the "allocation of resources" and "processes for evaluation and planning"; (3) "the organization provides evidence of student learning and teaching effectiveness"; (4) the institution "promotes a life of learning for its faculty, administration, staff, and students"; and (5) "as called for by its mission, the organization identifies its constituencies and serves them in ways both value."[62]

Dr. Jeanine Varner

On the Steering Committee with Varner and Drew were Dr. Mike O'Neal, Dr. Bill Goad, Dr. Lawrence Murray, Dr. Johann Snyman, Dr. Burt Smith, Dr. Tony Alley, Dr. Lisa McWhirter, Dr. Phil Lewis, Dr. Kathy Thompson, Dr. Molly Hill, Dr. Robyn Miller, and Dr. Chip Kooi. There were subgroups to work on each of the criteria.

In preparation for the examination and to enhance its own work, the university had established a strong program to assess its effectiveness. Each college of the university had developed a plan for evaluating its work and had been collecting data and information as part of that plan for several years. During the week following the spring term each year, faculty meetings gave special attention to assessment of the academic program and to determining what changes in the program should come as result of that information.

The report of the self study was an impressive 131-page document published in book form with color pictures, charts, and highlights.

Parenthetical citations provided references to documents available to the visiting committee in a resource room for their use. The six-person team came on March 6–8, 2006, to evaluate the institution. Two of the team members also visited OC's branch campus, Cascade College in Portland, Oregon.

The team commented, "The self-study report is a clearly organized and well-written document, speaking specifically to the five criteria, and presents a self-critical account of the university's mission, current operations and structure, and potential for continuing success. Concerns of the previous teams were adequately addressed."[63]

The team spoke favorably about recent improvements in the university's financial condition, the new housing being constructed, and the "comprehensive planning from the Strategic Vision Committee and the administration."[64] The team also spoke favorably of the institution's assessment efforts:

> Annual assessment reports confirm that OC has created a culture of assessment across all departments, using multiple and varied tools to assess student learning at designated intervals in the student's program of studies. The annual spring assessment workshop provided faculty with time and support to review data, make recommendations, and determine specific goals and action steps for future improvement.[65]

The evaluators also were pleased with the 7 percent improvement in the retention rate of first year students,[66] "excellent learning support services,"[67] and support for faculty development.[68] They also commented favorably on the formation of the Faculty Association, on providing a laptop for each student, and on the increased opportunities for students to have contact with non-Western cultures.[69]

The visiting team also praised the university's connection with its outside constituencies. They spoke of contact with churches, hospitals, and schools, and of the use of advisory groups. They also liked the student service projects at places like Western Village Elementary School. The team thought the university was also connecting well with its church constituency, mentioning particularly preacher's luncheons on campus, the *Christian Chronicle*, the online eBibleStudy materials, mission trips, and the participation of faculty and staff in local Churches of Christ.[70]

The team made some suggestions, but fewer than in previous years. They thought the advancement office was "understaffed" and were concerned that Cascade College was creating a cash flow problem.[71] They commented that "advising, especially for undeclared, nontraditional, or double major students, was uneven, and that still more improvements should be sought in retention.[72] While the team recognized "incremental advancement toward increasing its [library] collection and creating an environment that is more suitable for this generation of learners, ongoing assessment of, and planning for, increasing the collection, fiscal allocations, and staffing will be necessary for this essential academic support to serve all OC constituents."[73]

The visiting team from the Higher Learning Commission recommended another ten years of accreditation with no intermediate reports. The report's closing comment reflected Oklahoma Christian's great progress since its first accreditation as a senior college in 1966: "The visiting team has verified that the Commission's Five Criteria for Accreditation are met and is confident that Oklahoma Christian University, as a mature institution of higher learning, will continue to satisfy these Criteria until the next Comprehensive visit."[74] The university hardly could have hoped for a more favorable report and the additional ten-year accreditation was confirmed by the Commission.

North Central Association accreditation has been of great benefit to Oklahoma Christian. Coming in 1966, when the institution was only four years into being a senior college, the approval helped in recruiting students and faculty, enabled students to transfer to other colleges and universities with their courses recognized, allowed the college to participate as a full-fledged member of the higher education community, permitted students to participate in federal funding programs, and laid a foundation for accreditation in specialized areas. The process, also, had required the institution to take a good look at itself and to find those areas needing improvement and to work on them.

All in all, while the process has often been arduous, Oklahoma Christian's contact with the North Central Association has been very beneficial, both for its standing in the educational community and for the improvements resulting from the self studies.

National Council for Accreditation of Teacher Education

State Department of Education Approval

When Oklahoma Christian College decided to move from junior college to senior college status in 1960, education was one of the four degree programs first offered. Since many of its students were service-oriented, college officials believed that training teachers could be one of its best programs. In the spring of 1963, for example, 111 of the college's 397 full-time students listed

Dr. O. B. Stamper

teaching as their career objective.[75]

Dr. O. B. Stamper, who had long experience as a teacher and administrator in Oklahoma secondary schools, as well as in college level teaching, led in the early efforts in developing the education degrees and in seeking their approval at the state level. A 1963 report to the Commission on Teacher Education recounted:

> With a large number of students interested in entering the teaching profession and with the Board and clientele definitely behind the move, OCC began working toward approval from the State Department of Education to train teachers. With the help of the State Department, initial programs leading in the direction of certification were developed and in November, 1961, a preliminary examining committee visited the college to assist in setting up the program. A special arrangement for the certification of 1962 graduates was made and of the twelve students completing these programs that year, nine applied for and received certificates from the State Department.[76]

On September 24, 1962, the State Board of Education gave Oklahoma Christian official recognition as a Teacher Training Institution.[77]

In the spring of 1963, less than a year after graduating its first students with bachelor's degrees in education, Oklahoma Christian applied to the Oklahoma Commission on Teacher Education and Professional Standards to certify students in seven areas: elementary education, and six fields in secondary education.[78] The Teacher Education Committee was composed of O. B. Stamper, chair; Oma Carter, librarian; Ralph Burcham, business education; Leonard Johnson, elementary education; Darvin Keck, science; Hugh McHenry, mathematics; James Parker, language arts; Don Green, social studies; and Stafford North, speech. They prepared a 172-page document outlining the requirements for the degree in each of these fields, explaining the steps by which one could move to graduation and recommendation for certification, and providing an analysis on various points of quality for each program.

The visiting committee commended the Oklahoma Christian program in education for the good climate for teacher education, the facilities, "a dedicated faculty, a harmonious staff, and a Christian atmosphere."[79] They also commented favorably on the "excellent pre-visitation self-study," the curricula, and the organization of the teacher training program.[80] For the length of time the college had been working on the programs, they commended the library on a good start and they considered the faculty well-qualified for their teaching roles.[81] They found the handbook outlining various policies regarding the faculty "worthy of special commendation."[82]

The Committee, however, thought there was a need for more science equipment and they were quite critical of "the very low salary structure" and the "heavy teaching loads."[83] They had other suggestions too: some of the areas of certification needed more faculty members so the students would have a broader experience, in some areas they wanted a specific methods course, and they suggested a classroom specifically for elementary methods classes.

All in all, however, the Committee was satisfied with the quality of the program and recommended approval for a three-year period and a re-evaluation at that time.[84] With nearly a third of its student body interested in preparing to be teachers, it was very important for these students to receive state certification upon graduation from OCC. This approval by the State Department of Education has continued until the present time.

As important as state level approval was, however, it was not the final goal. While Oklahoma had reciprocal agreements with some states to honor each other's certification, graduation from an institution holding accreditation from the National Council for Accreditation of Teacher Education carried more weight with those making employment decisions and with those determining admission to graduate schools. So, college administrators began making plans to apply for NCATE accreditation.

1970 Application

Dr. Marshall Gunselman

In September of 1970, the college submitted its first application to NCATE. Many on campus were responsible for the preparation of this document of more than a hundred pages. Dr. Marshall Gunselman, dean of learning resources, chaired the study. Others wrote particular chapters: Dr. Stafford North, dean of the college; Dr. Raymond Vick, education faculty; and Dr. O. B. Stamper, director of teacher education and chairman of the Division of Education and Psychology. Others gathered material for particular curricula: Dr. Leonard Hall, Dr. Max Dobson, Dr. Faye Dillingham, Dr. Robert McMillan, Dr. Darvin Keck, Ralph Burcham, Oliver Howard, and Dr. Ronald Bever. The report asked for approval of the following programs: elementary education, secondary education programs in business education, language arts, social studies, mathematics, science, and speech, and a K-12 program in physical education.

The NCATE application showed that those seeking to enter the teacher education program had higher ACT scores than the average

OCC student, and it also detailed the extensive process students were required to follow for admission to teacher education. The report further included complete information on each teacher involved in teacher education programs and showed that of all those teaching in professional education programs, 69 percent had doctorates, and of those teaching in the Division of Education and Psychology, 88 percent held doctorates. These figures compared with 59 percent of the faculty as a whole. The report included full details on the requirements for each of the programs being submitted, a description of the physical facilities used in teacher training, and information on library holdings in education. Since about half of the OCC graduates were then being certified to teach,[85] NCATE accreditation was very important.

The visiting team came in November, and on May 20, 1971, the Council reviewed the team's report. In a June 3 letter to President James Baird, Rolf Larson, director of NCATE, stated that the request for accreditation had been "deferred" until October 1972,[86] and at that time, they would deny accreditation unless the college "could demonstrate that the decision was faulty."[87] The NCATE criticisms were: insufficient time allotted for the director of teacher education to do his work, a process of admission to teacher education that did not sufficiently screen out unlikely candidates, an overloaded teacher education faculty, and a plan for student teaching that needed revision.

If they chose to do so, the additional sixteen months would allow the college time to make improvements and to respond to questions and comments the Council had raised. Having worked for almost ten years with the State Department of Education toward meeting their standards, the NCATE response was quite disappointing.

"Immediately the faculty and administration began studying the weaknesses outlined in the report. It was apparent that the initial report had failed to communicate sufficiently the qualities of the program. Also the College was already shaping changes which addressed many of the key issues."[88] In February 1972, the college filed a supplemental report to inform the Council of improvements made, and to explain items that they thought had been misunderstood. Dr. Oscar K. Oksol, who had chaired the visiting team, returned to the campus for a three-day review of the matters covered in the supplemental report. On October 28, 1972, Dr. Stafford North, dean of the college, met with the review committee in Washington, D. C., and on the basis of the improvements, the additional information, and the interview, the Council reversed its original decision and approved Oklahoma Christian College for an initial accreditation of five years.[89]

1977 Application

In 1977, the five-year accreditation term was up for review, so Oklahoma Christian filed an application for renewal. Academic Dean Bailey McBride chaired the Steering Committee for this report with six others on the committee: Dr. Max Dobson, Dr. Stafford North, Gail Robertson (student), Dr. Gary Shreck, Dr. O. B. Stamper, and Dr. Gene Talbert. McBride, North, Shreck, and Talbert chaired subcommittees for the report. By this time, home economics, music, and art had been added.

The report showed that since 1972, the college's total enrollment had grown from 1,149, to 1,463 and the faculty had increased from forty-one to sixty.[90] In the 1975–1976 year, a total of ninety students had been admitted to the teacher education program.[91] The report carefully laid out the procedure for application to the teacher education program and for student teaching, and it reported that during the 1975–1976 year, twelve students had been denied admission to the program with two of those later being admitted. Twenty-two had been denied permission for student teaching, with eighteen of those later qualifying.[92] The report provided information on all those who taught courses connected with teacher education and indicated teachers holding a doctorate taught 80 percent of the courses in the teacher education curriculum.[93] A section of the report described each of the elementary and secondary curricula for which approval was being sought.

The visiting team from NCATE came on March 7–9, 1977, and this time, there was no delay. On October 7, 1977, Rolf Larson notified Oklahoma Christian that accreditation was renewed for ten years.[94]

1985 Application

By the time for the 1985 application for renewal, the process had grown more complex. The report now took two volumes containing a total of 373 pages. Part 1 dealt with Accreditation Standards, and Part 2 described Faculty and Programs. Certification in special education for the mentally handicapped had been added. Enrollment had not grown much over the ten-year period, with the college's headcount only increasing from 1,463 to 1,522.[95] The topics presented in the report were quite similar to that of the previous study, but greater detail was given.

The report of visiting team was a little more critical this time than in 1976, and so Dean Bailey McBride prepared a "rejoinder," which he submitted on April 25, 1986. This document provided answers to some of the criticisms by demonstrating that the faculty had extensive experience in teaching in elementary and secondary school, that those who did not hold a doctorate had extensive post-master's degree work, and that the library holdings for education were stronger than the visiting team had suggested.[96]

With the submission of the additional information, NCATE continued the accreditation, but they were now on a seven year-cycle of reaccreditation.

1993 Application

Dr. Floyd Coppedge

The next NCATE application was submitted in January 1993, and the visit would serve for both NCATE and the Oklahoma State Department of Education. On April 4, 1993, a team of nine examiners arrived, five representing the Council and four representing the State of Oklahoma. Dr. Floyd Coppedge, dean of the College of Education, chaired the team preparing the 259-page report.

This time the report and the examination covered five major areas: Knowledge Bases for Professional Education, Relationship to the World of Practice, Students, Faculty, and Governance and Resources. Under these five areas fell eighteen standards with ninety-four criteria divided among them. The report spoke to each of these items and, in addition, provided information on the curriculum of each of the certificate areas and a section containing faculty vita.

By 1993, with the expansion of the Oklahoma Christian curriculum, education majors were now at 11 percent of the student body rather than half, as they had earlier been. In that year, though, there were fifty-three education graduates.[97]

After its four-day visit, the committee determined that the OC program met all the criteria, and thus, NCATE renewed the accreditation.

1999 Application

Dr. Dwayne Cleveland

The education faculty, now led by Dean Dwayne Cleveland, began in the fall of 1997 to prepare for the next NCATE visit, set for 1999, as the preparation process was quite lengthy. By this time, OC offered eleven teacher education programs: early childhood; elementary education; special education; secondary education in English, social studies, mathematics, science, and communication; and PK-12 in art, music, and physical education. The education faculty now had made technology a priority, and they practiced a more rigorous program of evaluation. The curriculum was operating now from a "competency based" approach.[98]

The Board of Examiners visited the campus November 14–17, 1999, and at this visit, found the university in compliance with all the criteria. They cited a weakness, however, in the recruitment of minority students.[99] Cleveland filed a rejoinder in February of 2000 to correct some factual errors in the examining committee's report and to speak to weaknesses noted. A letter from Arthur E. Wise to President Kevin Jacobs, dated April 7, 2000, indicated that NCATE accreditation had been extended.[100]

2005 Application

NCATE made some changes in its pattern of examinations and slated a visit to OC in Fall 2004. Dr. Jeanine Varner, in a letter on October 8, 2002, asked that the time be changed to a fall visit in 2005 to allow more space between this visit and the previous one. NCATE granted the request. Dr. Floyd Coppedge again chaired the committee preparing the report, this time numbering ninety-seven pages. The Board of Examiners came November 12–16, 2005. In their report, these examiners gave OC a very good rating with only minor weaknesses, noting that Oklahoma Christian met all of the standards. On April 13, 2006, Arthur E. Wise wrote President Mike O'Neal that NCATE accreditation was renewed with the next examination in 2112.[101]

Observations

Governor Frank Keating watches as Dr. Floyd Coppedge accepts the position of secretary of education.

Since the preparation of teachers is one of its primary areas of service to its religious constituency, Oklahoma Christian University has offered programs in teacher education since its awarding of its first bachelor's degrees in 1962. In the more than forty years since that time, the university has maintained a good relationship with the Oklahoma State Department of Education, meeting its criteria for approval, supplying members for various committees and examining teams, and participating in various studies. In fact, Oklahoma Governor Frank Keating selected Dr. Floyd Coppedge, dean of the Oklahoma Christian University's College of Education, to be his secretary of education during the years of 1995 to 2002.

OC's NCATE accreditation has been a key factor in its overall success in supplying well-prepared students for the education profession, and many of them have served well both as teachers and administrators in public and private schools.

Accreditation Board for Engineering and Technology

In 1984, after a lengthy investigative process, Oklahoma Christian College announced that starting in 1985, it would begin to offer programs leading to bachelor's degrees in electrical and mechanical engineering. The step was certainly a bold one: no other college or university among OCC's sister institutions offered these programs, and only three large universities in the State of Oklahoma had them. Yet the college decided there was clearly a need for engineering education in Oklahoma that combined job preparation with a liberal arts curriculum and spiritual training such as Bible courses, chapel, and a Christian college atmosphere.[102]

1990

As the faculty developed the engineering program, they planned eventually to apply for approval from the Accreditation Board for Engineering and Technology (ABET).[103] This accreditation was the standard for engineering programs throughout the nation and they felt it essential that the OC program achieve this recognition. Although the engineering faculty wanted this accreditation as soon as possible, they knew that applying before the likelihood of approval would not be in the best interests of the program. After careful consideration, they decided to apply in 1990, after the program had been operating five years. Knowing that even some major universities had not been accepted on their first try, the engineering faculty realized that for a program at a small university to be approved on their first application would be most unusual.

Dr. Troy Pemberton, chairman of the Engineering Department, took primary

Dr. Troy Pemberton

Joe Watson

responsibility for the process with Joe Watson, professor of Electrical Engineering, leading in drafting the report. Dr. Jim Cutbirth led in preparing the information for mechanical engineering, while Lynn Nored led in preparing the electrical engineering material.

The completed document was in two volumes with a total of 211 pages. The report laid a foundation by describing the work of outside consultants the department had used, called its Engineering Advisory Council, noting that this group assisted in planning and developing the program.[104] The report also described the engineering program as "strong hands-on, engineering workplace oriented education."[105] The self study demonstrated the college's commitment to the engineering program by reporting that four million dollars had been invested in facilities and equipment, plus a three million dollar endowment raised, prior to the enrollment of the first engineering freshman.[106] The self study also reported 128 engineering majors from over half the states in the nation and ten faculty members, "bringing more than 200 years of engineering practice and engineering education experience."[107] The ABET report included a lengthy vita of each professor and a complete description of each engineering and engineering-related course.

The visiting committee's report observed that the faculty had made "excellent preparation" for their coming[108] and commented favorably on the facilities.[109] They expressed, however, two primary concerns: the lack of time for faculty development activities and the low salary structure.[110] On August 28, 1991, Leslie F. Benmark wrote to President Terry Johnson that both the electrical and mechanical engineering programs had been accredited for the normal term.[111] The news brought great satisfaction to the campus, especially to the engineering faculty who had worked so hard both to develop the program and prepare the study.

1996

Dr. James Cutbirth

In 1996, the time came to apply for reaccreditation. Dr. James Cutbirth chaired this study with Dr. Lynn Tyler, heading the work for mechanical engineering, and Lynn Nored, leading the effort in electrical engineering. The two-volume report, 207 pages in length, stated, "From that first class through the capstone senior engineering design course, the student is challenged, led, and taught by seasoned engineers who have practiced their professional, moral, and ethical values."[112]

The ABET report noted that the number of engineering students had grown to 143, and that the university had introduced its laptop program for every faculty member and student and had a wireless campus. This, the faculty said, had been a great help to the engineering program.[113] They also stated that since the last visit, the university had spent forty thousand dollars to upgrade the engineering collection in the library.[114]

Lynn Nored

The four-person visiting committee came on October 28 and 29, 1996, and reported the faculty was well-qualified and that the curriculum met the ABET standards. They called the faculty "extremely dedicated to teaching at the undergraduate level" and said they "bring valuable experience to their classrooms and laboratories."[115] Again, however, the committee commented on the heavy loads the faculty carried.[116] On September 5, 1997, Stanley I. Proctor wrote President Kevin Jacobs that the electrical and mechanical engineering programs had been reaccredited.[117]

Dr. Lynn Tyler

2002

On June 14, 2002, the engineering faculty submitted another self study to ABET, this one totaling 399 pages. Dr. David Cassel led the mechanical engineering study while Dr. Jeff Bigelow led the electrical engineering section. The results were essentially the same—good marks on the faculty, the program, and the

Dr. Jeff Bigelow

Dr. David Cassel

facilities, but concerns about faculty load and salaries. A letter dated August 15, 2003, brought the news to Dean Phil Lewis that the two programs had been accredited until 2009.

2004

In 2004, the School of Engineering applied for ABET accreditation in a third area: computer engineering. While the electrical engineering program had included substantial work in computers, those wanting employment as computer engineers would benefit from more specialized training. A total of twenty-six students were enrolled in this degree program.

Under the leadership of Dr. Bigelow, chair of Electrical and Computer Engineering, the faculty prepared a self study on the computer engineering program. This report stated that the university president had initiated a program that would allow salaries at OC to be increased in those fields where faculty at other institutions were paid at higher levels. This change in policy, according to the report, would help raise the low OC engineering salaries often noted in prior ABET reports.[118]

The study also noted another change. A survey had revealed that students were hitting a "downturn in attitude towards the program in the junior year." To remedy this situation, the faculty had created more opportunities for faculty to meet with students in informal settings, provided more mentoring opportunities, and adjusted the timing when certain projects and exams would be due. As a result of these changes, the interest level of students had improved from a 2.29 in 2001 to 3.81 in 2002 and to 3.30 in 2003.[119]

The team exit interview on September 28, 2004, indicated several strengths in the program. For one, the team found, "The student body is enthusiastic and lavish in praise for the program. This is partly due to the unique cultural environment of a Christian institution."[120] The team also said, "The computer engineering laboratories are first class."[121] As result of this review, on August 8, 2005, ABET sent word that the computer engineering program had been granted accreditation, retroactive to October 1, 2002.

For the engineering program at Oklahoma Christian to receive ABET accreditation on its first attempt, after only five years of offering the program, was an outstanding achievement, and to maintain it since that time shows a strong commitment of the faculty and the administration to maintaining excellence in this program.

National Association of Schools of Music

1989

In 1988, the Oklahoma Christian Department of Music, under the leadership of Department Chair Ken Adams, believed the time had come to seek specialized accreditation from the National Association of Schools of Music. While music classes and programs had been offered from the institution's earliest days in Bartlesville, and while the department shared in the North Central accreditation of the institution as a whole, the

Dr. Ken Adams

music faculty believed achieving NASM accreditation would benefit recruitment of good students and help in placement of graduates.

In preparation for the report, the department brought George Umberson of Arizona State University to consult on June 10 and 11, 1988. A year later, on June 13, 1989, the department submitted a self study to NASM seeking membership. This study mentioned several strengths, such as a "highly competent faculty," "excellent facilities," and "reasonable budgets, but could use improvement."[122] The self study also noted weaknesses: "low retention rate of music majors," "music executive's load too heavy," "faculty loads too heavy," and "library holdings very inadequate."[123]

A two-person NASM team came on October 3 and 4, 1989. Their observations noted such strengths as the "dedicated and hard-working full-time faculty," "bright and talented students who are responsive, enthusiastic and committed to their department and OCC," "excellent facilities," and "location in a metropolitan area, with proximity to major universities, many resources, and community involvement."[124] The committee also observed some weaknesses: "library is minimally adequate and needs systematic acquisition policy as well as consolidation and proper classification of scores and recordings," "no music education specialist," "need budget to adequately support programs and NASM standards."[125]

On June 29, Samuel Hope, for the Association, sent word that the decision on accreditation had been "deferred."[126] While accreditation was not granted, the institution did have the opportunity to make improvements and submit further information. On May 25, 1992, Adams responded to concerns NASM had expressed in June 1990. He told of improvements in the curriculum, a plan for piano maintenance, budget plans for providing new pianos and band instruments, and improvements in auditions now being conducted for every entering music major. He also noted that a music education specialist would be hired in 1993–1994.[127]

On June 30, 1992, NASM responded that the application again had been deferred. After additional information was submitted, however, NASM wrote in November of 1992 granting membership to the Department of Music, thus providing the specialized accreditation it had sought.

1998

In granting accreditation, NASM had asked the OC Department of Music to apply for reaccreditation in the 1997–1998 year, but in the fall of 1997, a fire destroyed most of the Music Department's facilities. The Department requested and NASM granted a year's delay for their application. Prior to submitting its next self study, the

Department of Music employed the services of another consultant, Robert W. Thayer of Bowling Green State University, who came on October 1 and 2, 1997, to help assess strengths and weaknesses and to assist in planning for the self study.[128]

The department filed the application for reaccreditation on March 11, 1999. In it, they reported that their library budget had received a special ten thousand dollar allocation for 1998–1999 to upgrade their library holdings, but they also had to report that the department was still understaffed.[129] A two-person visitation team came on April 11–13, and after their report and the meeting of the Association, Samuel Hope wrote, in a letter of December 20, 1999, that the Department had "an excellent self study" and had been approved for renewal of membership. He added, "Upper administration is also commended for its tremendous understanding and support for the Department, especially in light of the devastating fire that gutted the music facilities in November of 1997."[130] While the fire, indeed, had been devastating, requiring music activities to be moved to another campus facility while remodeling was underway, the net result was that the music facilities were now much better than before, with better office space and classrooms, and a beautiful new recital hall.

Hope asked for a progress report to be filed by October 1, 2002, on such items as the library and student experiences in the practicum and student teaching. On that date, Dr. John Fletcher, department chair, filed the supplemental report on the concerns expressed in 1999. As with other specialized accreditations, NASM approval has led the Department of Music through a process

Dr. John Fletcher

of introspection which has brought improvements and the resulting accreditation has given the Department added standing in recruitment of students and placement of graduates.

Association of Collegiate Business Schools and Programs

1993

Oklahoma Christian University had taught classes and offered degrees in business since its very beginning in Bartlesville but never sought specialized accreditation for this field until 1993. Dr. James Rix coordinated the business faculty in a self study report for the Association of Collegiate Business Schools and Programs, presented on

Dr. James Rix

December 15, 1993. The report first answered twenty-one questions about the nature of the program and policies of operation. Next, the report provided information about the extent to which the program met standards regarding the content of courses, faculty, equipment, facilities, and curriculum. A three-member team came for an on-site visit on February 2, 1994, and on June 6, 1994, word came that the Association had granted "conditional accreditation." On June 20, 1994, the College of Business received its certificate at the Annual ACBSP Conference in Minneapolis.

Dr. Jack Skaggs

The conditions, to be satisfied by no later than June 1997, dealt with such matters as assurance that adequate coverage of specified topics would be provided in certain courses, that faculty with doctorates taught at least 40 percent of the credit hours, that the program was fully in compliance with outcomes assessment and making continuous improvement, and that there were more scholarly and professional activities. On July 18, 1996, Dr. Jack Skaggs filed a report indicating that all the conditions had been met.[131] This report satisfied the Association, which granted full accreditation and advised the university to advertise that, through its College of Business, it "is nationally accredited by the Association of Collegiate Business Schools and Programs (ACBSP) for the offering of the following degree programs: the Bachelor of Business Administration (BBA) in Accounting, Finance, General Business, Management, and Marketing."

2003

Dr. Phil Lewis

On July 1, 2003, the Oklahoma Christian College of Business, now led by Dean Phil Lewis, filed a reaffirmation self study covering the 2002–2003 academic year. Skaggs coordinated the study, which reported that during the year, the College had 250 undergraduate and 80 graduate students. This study was built around standards and criteria on the following topics: leadership, strategic planning, student and stakeholder focus, information and analysis, human resources development and management, and educational and business process management.

The study reported that the pass rate on the CPA exam for OC students over the ten-year period of 1992–2002 was 28 percent, compared with an average of 18 percent for all Oklahoma colleges and universities. It also indicated that OC's institutional average for undergraduate performance on the MFT since 1992 was at the 79th percentile, and for MBA graduates it was at the 62nd percentile, both exceeding the national average.[132]

There was, however, still a problem on the percentage of credit hours taught by doctorally qualified faculty. The report showed the level at 36 percent, below the 40 percent minimum, but four faculty were currently in doctoral programs and another would soon be enrolled.[133]

The self study reported that the campus was wireless and each student and faculty member was provided a laptop computer. Teachers also had assistance to help make good use of these computer resources.[134] A team from ACBSP began a three-day visit on September 29 and found "the College of Business extremely committed to the high quality standards of ACBSP."[135] On November 11, 2003, Ron C. DeYoung wrote that the Association had "granted reaffirmation of accreditation of your business programs."[136] The School of Business Administration was asked to file reports on progress on the "doctoral coverage in undergraduate programs" and "the faculty load at the graduate level and part time faculty teaching 18 credit hours."[137] Accreditation was extended through 2014.

Conclusion

From its very beginning in 1950, the administration and faculty of Oklahoma Christian University aspired to excel both academically and spiritually. Their aim always was to offer a collegiate program meeting rigorous standards and to be well-accepted among the ranks of colleges and universities. To achieve these ends, they knew they would need to meet the standards of various accrediting agencies. Unlike some private, religious institutions, neither they nor their clientele feared the accreditation process. They believed they could build on high academic standards, thus meeting the demands of accreditation, without compromising their spiritual values. With this philosophy, Oklahoma Christian has found success in achieving the approval of demanding accrediting agencies, while still maintaining its commitment to the spiritual purposes for which it was founded.

Chapter 11, Endnotes

1 James O. Baird, Interview on audiotape with author on November 1, 1989, and subsequent days, Tape 1, OC Archives.

2 "State Board Will Accept CCC Credits," *Bartlesville Examiner-Enterprise*, Ruth Wilson Scrapbook, 19, OC Archives.

3 James Baird in a letter to Norman Burns, April 22, 1966, Files of the Office of the President under North Central Association.

4 "Wilson, Baird Attend North Central Session," *Tower*, April 6, 1954, OC Archives.

5 *Report of a Self Study, Oklahoma Christian College, September 1960*, Preface, OC Archives; "Summary Report from Oklahoma Christian College Presented to the Board of Review, Commission on Colleges and Universities, March 19, 1961," Files of the Office of the President under North Central Association.

6 James O. Baird, "Suggestions for North Central Accreditation," Files of the Office of the President under North Central Association.

7 *Report of a Self Study*, Preface.

8 W. O. Beeman, *Oklahoma Christian College: Dream to Reality* (Delight, Arkansas: Gospel Light Publishing Company, 1970), 121.

9 Ibid.

10 Ibid.

11 Ibid., 20–21.

12 Ibid., 27.

13 *Summary Report from Oklahoma Christian College*, March 19, 1961.

14 *Report of An Accrediting Examination, December 12–14, 1960, of Oklahoma Christian College*, 34, 35, OC Archives.

15 James O. Baird, Letter to David Madsen, January 5, 1961, Files of Office of the President under North Central Association.

16 William Morrow, Letter to Dr. Milo Bail, March 7, 1961, Files of the Office of the President under North Central Association.

17 Ibid.; Typed note attached to copy of William Morrow letter.

18 *Report of a Self Study*, Oklahoma Christian College, June, 1964, vi, OC Archives.

19 Ibid., vii.

20 Richard. H. Davis, Letter to James O. Baird, August 7, 1964, Files of the Office of the President under North Central Association.

21 Ibid.

22 *Report of a Self Study*, May, 1965, 1, OC Archives.

23 Memorandum on Comments from the North Central Examining Team, Files of the Office of the President under North Central Association.

24 Joseph J. Semrow, Letter to James O. Baird, January 19, 1966, Files of the Office of the President under North Central Association.

25 Memorandum to the Committee by Type from James O. Baird, March 28, 1966, 8, Files of the Office of the President under North Central Association.

26 Memorandum to the Committee By Type, March 28, 1966, 2, 5, Files of the Office of the President under North Central Association.

27 Norman Burns, Letter to James of Baird, April 8, 1966, Files of the Office of President under North Central Association.

28 James O. Baird, Letter to Norman Burns, April 22, 1966, Files of the Office of the President under North Central Association.

29 *A Self Study Report from Oklahoma Christian University*, December 1, 1975, v, vi, OC Archives.

30 Ibid., i.

31 Ibid., 51.

32 Ibid., i.

33 Ibid., 23.

34 *Report of a Visit to Oklahoma Christian College, February 22–25, 1975, 12–13*, Files of the Office of the President under North Central Association.

35 Ibid., 13.

36 *Report to the North Central Association, August 1, 1985*, 6–8, OC Archives.
37 *Report of a Visit to Oklahoma Christian College, October 21–23, 1985*, Files of the Office of the President under North Central Association, 12.
38 Ibid.
39 Ibid., 26.
40 Ibid.
41 Ibid., 27.
42 Ibid., 3.
43 Ibid.
44 Ibid.
45 Ibid., 11.
46 Ibid.
47 Ibid., 15.
48 Ibid., 23.
49 Ibid., 25.
50 *A Self Study Report to the North Central Association of Colleges and Schools, September, 1995*, 3, OC Archives.
51 Ibid., 3.
52 Ibid., 4–5.
53 Ibid., 5–6,
54 *Report of Visit to Oklahoma Christian University, September 25–27, 1995*, 6, Files of the Vice President for Academic Affairs under North Central Association.
55 Ibid., 23.
56 Ibid., 42.
57 Ibid., 48.
58 Ibid., 47.
59 Ibid.
60 Ibid.
61 Ibid., 48.
62 *Self Study Report for Continued Accreditation, Spring, 2006*, Oklahoma Christian University, 1, 31, 65, 87, 117, OC Archives.
63 *Report of a Comprehensive Evaluation Visit to Oklahoma Christian University, March 6–8, 2006*, 4, Files of the Vice President for Academic Affairs under North Central Association.
64 Ibid., 7.
65 Ibid., 9.
66 Ibid.
67 Ibid.
68 Ibid.
69 Ibid., 9–11.
70 Ibid., 13–14.
71 Ibid., 8.
72 Ibid., 10–11.
73 Ibid., 12.
74 Ibid., 17.
75 *Report to Visitation Committee of Oklahoma Commission on Teacher Education and Professional Standards, March 13, 1963*, 13, OC Archives.
76 Ibid., 2.
77 Ibid., 3.
78 Ibid., Table of Contents.
79 *Report on Oklahoma Christian College Teacher Certificate Programs, March 13–15, 1963*, 1, OC Archives.
80 Ibid.
81 Ibid., 2, 4.
82 Ibid., 3.
83 Ibid., 3–4.
84 Ibid., 14.
85 *A Report to the National Council for Accreditation of Teacher Education, September, 1970*, ii, OC Archives.

86   *A Supplemental Report to the National Council for Accreditation of Teacher Education, February, 1972, Preview*, Files of the Vice President for Academic Affairs under NCATE.

87   *A Report to the National Council for Accreditation of Teacher Education, 1985–86*, Part 1, 5, OC Archives.

88   Ibid.

89   Ibid.

90   *A Report to the National Council for Accreditation of Teacher Education, March 7–9, 1977*, 8, OC Archives.

91   Ibid., 37.

92   Ibid., 41.

93   Ibid., 20.

94   *NCATE Report, 1985–86*, Part 1, 5–6.

95   Ibid, 13.

96   *Rejoinder for 1986 Visiting Team Report, April 25, 1986*, Files of the Vice President for Academic Affairs under NCATE.

97   *Board of Examiners Report, November 14–19*, 4, Files of the Vice President for Academic Affairs under NCATE.

98   Ibid.

99   Ibid., 16.

100   Letter to Kevin Jacobs from Arthur E. Wise, April 7, 2000, Files of the Vice President for Academic Affairs under NCATE.

101   Letter to Mike O'Neal from Arthur E. Wise, April 13, 2006, Files of the Vice President for Academic Affairs under NCATE.

102   *Self Study Questionnaire for Review of Engineering Programs, May 30, 1990*, I, 1–2, Files of the Vice President for Academic Affairs under ABET.

103   Ibid.

104   Ibid.

105   Ibid., I–9.

106   Ibid., I–10.

107   Ibid.

108   Final Statement, 1991, 1, Files of the Vice President for Academic Affairs under ABET.

109   Ibid., 3.

110   Ibid.

111   Leslie F. Benmack, Letter to President Terry Johnson, August 28, 1991, Files of the Vice President for Academic Affairs under ABET.

112   ABET Self Study, 1996, I, 11, Files of the Vice President for Academic Affairs under ABET.

113   Ibid., II, 10.

114   Ibid., II, 75.

115   Ibid., II, 5.

116   Ibid., II, 4.

117   Letter to Kevin Jacobs from Stanley I. Proctor, September 5, 1997, Files of the Vice President for Academic Affairs under ABET.

118   *Computer Engineering Self Study Report, June 4, 2004*, 4–5, Files of the Vice President for Academic Affairs under ABET.

119   Ibid.

120   Exit Interview, ABET team, September 28, 2004, 3, Files of the Vice President for Academic Affairs under ABET.

121   Ibid.

122   *Music Department Self Study, June 13, 1989*, 3, Files of the Vice President for Academic Affairs under NASM.

123   Ibid.

124   *Visitor Report, National Association of Schools of Music, October 3 and 4, 1989*, 9, Files of the Vice President for Academic Affairs under NASM.

125   Ibid., 9–10.

126   Samuel Hope, Letter to Department of Music, June 29, 1990, Files of the Vice President for Academic Affairs under NASM.

127 "Response, May 25, 1992," Files of the Vice President for Academic Affairs under NASM.

128 *Consultant's Report from visit by Robert W. Thayer on October 1–2, 1997,* Files of the Vice President for Academic Affairs under NASM.

129 *Self Study for NASM, March 11, 1999,* Files of the Vice President for Academic Affairs under NASM.

130 Samuel Hope, Letter to Department of Music, Files of the Vice President for Academic Affairs under NASM.

131 *Report to ACBSP on July 18, 1996,* Files of the Vice President for Academic Affairs under ACBSP.

132 *Reaffirmation Self Study for the Association of Collegiate Business Schools and Programs, July 1, 2003,* I, 19, OC Archives.

133 Ibid., 23.

134 Ibid., 54.

135 *Report of a Visit, September 29–October 1, 2003,* Files of College of Business under ACBSP.

136 Ron C. DeYoung, Letter to Dr. Mike E. O'Neal, Files of the Dean of the College of Professional Studies under ACBSP.

137 Ibid.

Chapter 12
THE FACILITIES

Winston Churchill once commented that "we shape our buildings and then they shape us." While many through the years have emphasized that Oklahoma Christian is people and not buildings, the buildings on the campus have played a major role in what the university has become.

1950

When Central Christian College started in Bartlesville in 1950, its facilities were limited but adequate for a beginning. The primary building was The Mansion. Its first floor housed administrative offices, the cafeteria, the library, and the main reception area where the vending machine provided a coke for a nickel. The second floor provided three rooms for up to twenty-four men and a supervisor's apartment. A basement room served as the biology classroom, and connected buildings housed a chemistry lab, home economics classroom, and studios for music and art. A few feet from the elegant mansion, a white frame building housed an auditorium with about two hundred folding chairs for chapel and other assemblies. This building also provided eight small rooms for classes and faculty offices. The campus had a women's dormitory for up to seventy women and there was a small bookstore building. In 1955, the college obtained an army barracks building and remodeled it to house twenty-two men. These facilities did not present a unified architectural design, but they did meet most of the basic needs of the young college. Though they had no facility for indoor athletics, the college did have a tennis court, a grassy area for intramural football, and a rather rocky softball field.

There were plans for more buildings in Bartlesville, but President Baird thought that before moving toward expansion plans for an auditorium, gymnasium, and cafeteria, the Board should take a look at whether the college would stay permanently in that location. Once the decision was made to move, of course, all the attention was focused on developing the new campus in Oklahoma City.

1958

As mentioned in Chapter 3 on the move to Oklahoma City, the plan for the new campus provided a "zoning" concept: a housing area on the west, a classroom area on the east, and an activity area between for facilities students would access from both sides—a cafeteria, a gym, a library, and parking.   This design placed buildings with like purposes close to each other, and allowed for traffic-free pedestrian access from one end of the campus to the other.

The first seven buildings on a barren campus of two hundred acres. The academic area is in the foreground, next the activity area, and to the far west, the housing.

The new campus opened with seven buildings: an administration building and a library-auditorium on the south side of the mall, two split-level classroom buildings on the north side of the mall, a student center-cafeteria in the activity zone, and two dormitories on the west. The student center and two residence halls were financed by $600,000 in self-liquidating government bonds.[1] Lippert Brothers Construction Company built all seven of these first buildings.

Three observations about the new campus are of special note: there was a consistent style of architectural design, red brick with a white band at the top; the buildings were modular in construction, which allowed for internal relocation of walls; and buildings were all placed in an overall campus design that allowed an orderly arrangement of buildings far into the future.

1960s

Basketball in The Barn

In 1960, the college added "The Barn," as everyone called it, a metal building just outside the loop road on the west side of the campus. This facility provided a basketball court and bleachers and, with folding chairs on the court area, could also be used for large public events. Although the facility was not up to the standard of other campus buildings, it provided a much-needed site for varsity basketball games on campus, for student intramural basketball and volleyball, and for physical education classes. The Barn continued to serve these needs until 1970 when the college built a gymnasium, but it continues to be used heavily for athletic activities even to the present time.

By 1961, increased enrollment brought a need for more student housing. Over the next four years, the college added four more residence halls, two for men and two for women. Wynn Construction Company built Wilson East Hall, with space for eighty-eight men in 1961. Commander Construction Company built Tinius Hall to house eighty-two women in 1963. Smithco Construction Company erected Fails Hall for seventy-three men in 1965. Each of these cost near $275,000.[2] Also in 1965, J. J. Cook Construction Company built Gunn-Henderson West for 116 women at a cost of $506,357. Because these facilities were income-producing, it was possible to build them with government loans to be repaid by student housing fees.[3]

Student devotional in the courtyard of the Student Center

With more students came the need for a larger student center. In 1962, the college doubled the size of the original building by adding more seating space for food service, a larger recreation area, and a larger school store. The remodeled facility was built in the shape of a "U," which allowed for a courtyard furnished with benches and plants.

In 1965, at a cost of $1,056,432 for construction and equipment, the college added the Mabee Learning Center with 50,000 square feet for the academic program. The library occupied the first floor, supplying a major increase in space both for the book collection and for study. The second and third floors contained study carrels for students and office space for faculty. More details of this project are found in Chapter 6, "Key Decisions."

An activity in Cogswell-Alexander Auditorium

By 1964, the student body had grown to 644, requiring four different chapel sessions each day in Cogswell-Alexander Auditorium. Public events attracting large numbers, such as evening sessions of the Lectureship and Commencement, were held in The Barn. Accommodating the number attending *Songs America Sings* in this small auditorium required nine performances. Clearly, the college needed a large auditorium.

President James Baird employed the architectural firm of Hudgins, Thompson, Ball to begin planning for the facility, and Tom Glover became their architect assigned to the project. He eventually designed more of the campus buildings than anyone else. The auditorium would have full stage facilities and would seat thirteen hundred. The front half of the seating area, holding about 750, would

Chapel in Hardeman South

accommodate chapel and many other assemblies. Since there were no large classrooms in any existing buildings, President Baird and Dean North decided that this facility should also provide for that need. Large motorized walls would divide the auditorium's back half from the front and also divide the back half into two classrooms, each side seating about 325 each. These two back portions each had a built-in teacher's desk containing controls for lighting and the room's own speaker system. Also, from the desk, the professor could lower a large motorized screen from the ceiling either to show a movie or to use an overhead projector.

Baird, a graduate of Freed-Hardeman College, approached the Hardeman family about having a facility on the Oklahoma Christian campus to bear the name of N. B. Hardeman, a famous preacher among Churches of Christ and the long-time president of Freed-Hardeman College. The family agreed to make a contribution and others gave in Hardeman's honor. The facility, as a result, bore Hardeman's name and contained a room off the lobby to replicate his office as of the day he died, complete with the desk and items that were on it, pictures, clothing, and other furnishings.

Another portion of the funding came from the U.S. Office of Education. Since the back half of the auditorium was designed primarily for classrooms, and since the federal government, at that time, had a program for helping colleges build facilities to accommodate growing student enrollments fueled by the baby boom, the college applied for a federal grant to help fund the two classrooms. From this source, the college received $67,000[4] to assist with the total construction cost of $604,420.

Hardeman Auditorium, completed for use by the fall of 1966, was a major step forward in facilities, and the space quickly became a workhorse. The entire student body gathered for chapel daily at 10 a.m. in the front portion, called Hardeman South. During other hours of the day, students met in the two back sections, Hardeman East and West, for class sessions in Bible, history, political science, and other subjects having larger classes. In the evenings, the auditorium was filled with the sounds of rehearsals for plays and musicals, and, of course, it was the primary location for Lectureship addresses, Commencement, and other special events.

One postscript. As the student body grew, chapel expanded into the back half of the auditorium, as planned, by retracting the movable walls. Someone from off-campus, whose identity was never known, reported to the U.S. Office of Education that a facility constructed with federal funds was being used for worship purposes, which, of course, was true. While college officials had shown that the back half of the building could be incorporated into the auditorium for larger assemblies, the matter of using it for chapel services had never arisen. Government officials contacted President Baird about the matter, asking him to come to Washington to discuss it. He and Dean North made the trip to meet with a representative from the government who wanted to find a solution to the problem. He asked what the daily chapel program was like. Baird and North replied that it was a daily devotional period usually followed by announcements of campus interest and sometimes a secular speaker or performance. The government official made a proposal: if the college would agree that there would always be a secular portion of the program so that the event would never be entirely religious, they could keep the money. After pondering this proposal, however, the two decided that such would be a limitation on chapel they did not want to live with. So they returned the government's $67,000, and Baird had to raise the money elsewhere.

In 1968, the college opened two new residence halls, Warlick Hall[5] for 130 men, at a

Men's halls from upper left are Fails, Warlick, Wilson West, and Wilson East; women's halls from lower left are Gunn-Henderson West and East, and Tinius West and East. Note the trailers beside Tinius East, used in the early 1970s for an overflow of women.

cost of $418,182, and another for 116 women, Gunn-Henderson East, at a cost of $520,267. The two buildings were funded through the Oklahoma Industrial Trust Authority.[6] These additions gave a total of four residence halls each for men and for women.

1970s

Enrollment was growing rapidly. By the 1968–69 year, Oklahoma Christian had 1,132 students, more than double the number of only six years earlier.[7] With more growth anticipated, the administration saw an urgent need for additional classroom space. The U.S. government had expanded its program for assisting colleges and universities to build additional academic facilities. While the federal plan only paid a part of the cost, their portion could be of substantial help and offer an incentive for donors to provide the remainder. These federal funds were administered at the state level, and the Oklahoma State Regents for Higher Education publicized their plan for deciding who would receive the money: Their funding formula included such factors as the percentage of increase the new space would add to the institution's instructional space, and the percentage of the total cost the requested federal funds would supply. Thus, the lower the percentage of the cost the government would pay and the greater the percentage of increase the space would provide, the greater the chance of receiving money.

Baird and North decided to seek the federal funds. In order to make the best case, and in order to meet the needs of the campus, they decided to build three new buildings: a second science building, a building for education and social science, and a new gymnasium. Working with architect Tom Glover, they designed the three facilities that, with their combined 72,460 square feet,[8] would certainly provide a large percentage increase in the college's total amount of instructional space. With the application in the hands of the State Regents, college officials waited for the word, hoping they would be among those receiving funding.

On the day before the decision was to be made, Baird received a call from the State Regents Office saying the college's request was not among those set to receive funding, but it was close. If he wished to reduce the percentage of funding being requested, he could retrieve the proposal, make the change, and resubmit it. With this challenge before them, Baird and North went to the Regents' Office in the State Capitol Building, and pulled their request. They found a private place and discussed what to do. The burden, of course, was on Baird,

The OCC campus in 1970 showing Hardeman Auditorium, the Learning Center, Davisson American Heritage, the new gym, Herold Science Hall, and four dorms each for men and for women. The Barn is at the upper left.

because to lower the percentage requested would place on him the responsibility of raising more money from other sources. After some deliberation, the two submitted a revised request asking for a smaller percentage of the construction cost from the government.

Within a few days, the announcement came that the federal government had accepted their proposal and would provide $1,270,000 toward the total cost, which turned out to be $1,782,220 for the three buildings and their basic equipment.[9] Baird got a major gift of nearly $500,000 from Judge Guy Davisson[10] and named the education and

Davisson American Heritage Building

social science building for him. From the Pfeiffer Foundation, Baird obtained a substantial gift and named the science building in honor of one of their board members, Matthew Gering Herold. The Mabee Foundation and others contributed sufficient funds to complete the project, and the addition of these three facilities in the 1970–1971 year provided a tremendous boost to campus capacity and appearance. Buildings were no longer just along the east-west mall, and as a result, the campus had the feel of a much larger institution. The American Heritage Building had an auditorium on the first floor with arena seating for two hundred. This auditorium also could be divided by a motorized wall into two separate classrooms of a hundred each, thus providing flexibility. The American Citizenship Center and a printing facility occupied the remainder of the first floor. The building's second floor had two classrooms—each of which could be divided by movable walls into two smaller rooms—and also had two seminar rooms, faculty offices, and space for dial-access carrels for students majoring in education and social science.

Herold Science Hall provided additional science laboratories in both chemistry and biology, as well as classrooms and faculty offices. The gymnasium had a playing court for physical education classes, intercollegiate athletics, and intramural sports, with a second floor housing faculty offices and classrooms.

Adding three major buildings at one time was a substantial undertaking, both for fundraising and for those on campus involved in planning and overseeing construction, but expansion of facilities for the growing college was crucial.

As enrollment continued to increase at Oklahoma Christian, the number of married students was also growing. These students had to live away from campus, thus making it harder for them to be part of campus life. In 1972, the college added its first married student apartments. At a cost of $504,822, the new facility provided forty-eight apartment units including one or two bedrooms, a living room, a bath, and a kitchen.

In 1973, two-story wings were added on each side of the Learning Center at a cost of $1,281,663. This addition increased library capacity and provided office space for the English Department, more classrooms, and studios for audio and video recording. The second and third floors continued to be primarily occupied with carrels for students.

Dr. Terry Johnson became president in 1974. Johnson's first major building project, in 1975, was the fifth women's residence hall, named for Reba Davisson, Judge Davisson's wife, since he contributed $500,000 to its construction.[11] This dorm, built at a cost of $835,000 and housing ninety-four, provided larger rooms and nicer facilities, including a kitchen for student use, laundry facilities, and a large lounge area. The rooms were arranged in suites with a shared bath facility.

The next major building project added 20,000 square feet to the Student Center. The growth of the student body to 1,280 required more room for food service, and the new addition provided that and more space for recreation, a snack bar, a student lounge, and the bookstore. The 1976 addition, at a cost of $1,281,663, also included space for the health center and two guest rooms.[12]

As enrollment continued to grow, the administration addressed the need for more places for students to live. In 1976–1977, the college completed the second phase of apartments for married students, another forty-eight units at a cost of $813,760.

By 1978, enrollment had reached 1,431, and the college needed still more academic space. The primary concerns were in fine arts and communications, and new rooms for these departments would free up for others the space they had been using. The Music Department needed more classrooms, studios for faculty who taught private lessons, more student practice rooms, larger and specialized spaces for band and chorus rehearsal, and an auditorium accommodating performances intended for smaller numbers than Hardeman Auditorium was designed to serve. The Art Department needed rooms especially designed for instruction in drawing and painting with "north light" and a room for teaching pottery. The Communications Department needed facilities for a campus radio station and classrooms for teaching speech and other communications courses.

Married Student Apartments

*Helicopter bringing
the air handling unit
to Kresge Fine Arts*

To meet these requirements, Tom Glover, with help from faculty and administrators, designed two new buildings connecting with Hardeman Auditorium, thus forming a three building complex.

Johnson got the lead gift of $500,000 for this expansion from Olive Garvey, a business woman from Wichita, Kansas, and so named the building complex the Garvey Center. Other major donors were the Kresge Foundation, the Mabee Foundation, Carrie Lou Little, and the Merrill Trust. The names of these remain with handprints in concrete hexagons along the walk into Hardeman Auditorium. The new fine arts wing was named Kresge Fine Arts Center and the communications wing became Mabee Communications Center. Total cost for construction of the two new buildings was $1,351,612.

Aerial photo showing the three buildings of the Garvey Center at the left, Harvey Business Center at the upper right, and Enterprise Square at the lower right

The new small auditorium, called Judd Theatre in honor of Dr. Walter Judd, a U.S. Congressman who had spoken several times on OCC's citizenship programs, seated 278 and was designed to be used both as a small auditorium and a large classroom. For productions, the stage was highly flexible with a large area in front of the curtain, thus allowing full shows to be performed on a "thrust" stage. If directors preferred, they could do a show behind the proscenium arch, or they could combine the two.

Also in 1977–1978, the college added, at a cost of $845,295, the third apartment unit, this one with forty-eight apartments for upper-

Judd Theatre

class men. This facility allowed men the opportunity for apartment life during their last two years of college rather than spending all four years in the dormitory setting. The same year, the 4,500 square foot Nowlin Center opened as a "student center" for students living in the apartments. Named for Kent Nowlin, a member of the OCC Board, and his wife Kathryn, who donated funds to meet the $100,000 cost, this center provided a gathering place for students and offices for apartment management.[13] A year later, at a cost of $1,431,802, the college added forty-eight apartments for junior and senior women, thus completing a four-phase set of apartment units.

1980s

The next major facilities challenge was to meet the needs of the Division of Business. While students in this field constituted 27 percent of the college's enrollment, this program had no building of its own. Johnson and his team determined to remedy this problem

Students celebrating the opening of the new Harvey Business Center

and, again with Tom Glover, designed a split-level building with the upper floor providing rooms of various sizes for business and secretarial science classes and offices for professors. The building's lower portion would house the college's central computer and related services.

Vice President Guy Ross solicited Ralph Harvey, a local member of the Church of Christ with a thriving oil business, to assist with the project, and Harvey agreed to contribute a million dollars. Other donors assisted with funds to cover the total cost of $1,627,175. The building, called Harvey Business Center, opened in the fall of 1980.

In 1981, the campus saw the addition of a twenty-five meter swimming pool to the physical education building. Since W. T. Payne contributed the major portion of the funds for this $601,004 addition, the entire building was named the Payne Physical Education Building. While swimming classes had been part of the curriculum since Bartlesville days, the college had never had a pool of its own. Students and employees alike praised this addition of a heated pool with two diving boards, lane lines when needed, and dressing facilities, because it served both classes and recreational needs.

Enterprise Square, USA, opened in 1982 and, of course, occupied the attention of both the OCC development team and those on campus working with construction. The story of this facility is told in Chapter 6, "The Key Decisions."

In 1986, college officials saw the need to modify the Learning Center. The dial system equipment was becoming outmoded and would cost too much to change, and the concept of a carrel for every student was being replaced by special laboratories and other facilities for specific majors. They determined, therefore, to remodel the Learning Center at a cost of $1,140,613, putting the space previously used for carrels to other use. The south end of the second floor became offices for President Johnson and Executive Vice President North. The second floor also provided space for other offices, the audio-visual services for the campus, and more classrooms. The third floor allowed a major expansion for library space, particularly for periodicals and specialized collections.

The next need for facilities was in the Bible Department. Even though students took at least sixteen hours in Bible, the Bible Department had no location of its own, Bible classes and offices of Bible teachers being spread around the campus. President Johnson decided it was time to remedy this situation and to give this vital academic department a home of its own.

The first decision was where to locate the building. Following the overall master plan would likely place the Bible facility in the academic zone along an extension of the mall to the east, thus giving it an entrance from Benson Road. Carrie Lou Little, a member of the OCC Board and whose family had a thriving oil business, agreed to pay for the architectural plans and recommended Bill Culver as the architect, one with whom she had worked on other projects. She also suggested that the building be located in the center of the campus near the entrance off Memorial Road. After much discussion, college administrators agreed to place the building there, where all entering the campus would see it. Such a location would make it easily accessible to all students and would demonstrate the important place of Bible instruction in the college's curriculum. This location would have another advantage: it would place the building in the middle of what had been a parking lot, thus spreading out the parking, and locating an attractive building where a heavy concentration of unattractive parking had been.

Culver, along with college officials, developed the plans for the building with eight classrooms of various sizes, a library room, and offices to occupy the first floor, and a three hundred seat chapel on the second level. The building's tower would house the bell alumni had saved from the Christian college in Cordell, Oklahoma, that had closed in 1931. On the north side of the building, the planners located a "forum" area to be used for informal gatherings, small group meetings, devotionals, and outdoor performances and gatherings. It would also provide a major walkway as students crossed the campus from the Student Center to Hardeman Auditorium and other academic buildings. To plan this outdoor area, the college engaged Tommy Roberts, a local but nationally known landscape architect and a member of the Mayfair Church of Christ. Roberts, who had done work for the college since its move to Oklahoma City, designed the park-like area, which was named for Thelma Gaylord, wife of Ed Gaylord, who had given generously to the college.

Bible Building and Forum

Next came funding. Mrs. Little agreed to provide a substantial portion of the funding for the facility. The year, however, was 1986, the year the oil boom went bust, and the Little family was not able to provide the funding. President Johnson found another donor in Barry Tapp, who asked that the building be named in honor of his wife's family, the Allisons, so the building was named the Allison Biblical Studies Center. Other funding came from Leo and Mabel Scott of Thackerville, Oklahoma, for whom the chapel would be named. In all, "twenty-six founding donors contributed."[14]

By September of 1987, the building and forum, which had cost a total of $3,005,176, was ready for use, so the new school year began with the Bible classes and faculty now operating from a central point on the campus. Unfortunately, Tapp also had financial setbacks, and was not able to provide funding. Most of the construction costs, therefore, had to be carried as long-term debt for the university, requiring substantial payment of interest. In 2005, the remaining debt on this building, along with other debts, was consolidated, with an annual amount set aside in the regular operational budget to retire the obligation.[15] In 2006, alumni Dr. Charlie and Lesa Branch committed $1.5 million dollars toward the Biblical Studies Center for upgrading the building and operation of the program, and it was renamed for their parents, Dr. Charles and Sylvia Branch and Charles and Joyce Williams.

The decision to add an engineering program in 1985–1986 obviously brought with it the need for the specialized space required for laboratories, as well as a need for more classrooms and offices. The architectural firm of Benham and Blair offered the winning bid for designing the building, and the faculty and administration worked with them through 1985–1986 to design the 30,000 square foot building, which was completed in the summer of 1988. The college named the new engineering facility Prince Engineering Center in

Engineering Building from the southwest

honor of Darryll Prince, who had died in a swimming accident in Cancun. His wife, Millie, made a substantial contribution toward the $2,826,027 cost of the building and equipment. Other large contributors were Edward and Tish Joullian, Riley Sheets, Lyle and Mary Harms, The Kresge Foundation, the Mabee Foundation, and the Noble Foundation.[16] The two-level building, with a connecting enclosed walkway to Herold Science Hall, had twenty-two faculty offices, a student lounge, and four classrooms, including one with arena-style seating for 124 and another for 56. Because of the nature of the classes in engineering and computer science, the building provided laboratory space for physics, fluid dynamics, systems design, solid mechanics, machine design, heat transfer, four rooms for student computer use, and three research rooms. Unfortunately, some of the funding pledges for this building did not materialize, and a substantial amount of the cost of construction and equipment had to be carried as debt along with that on the Bible building. This debt payment was made part of the operational budget in 2005.[17]

The new center, along with the remodeling of Herold Science Hall, provided an excellent facility for the new engineering program, and the equipment was first rate. Soon after the addition of the Computer Aided Design lab, a group of OCC engineering students toured the Boeing facility in Wichita and came to their new computer aided design lab. The person there was to demonstrate their latest computer addition, but couldn't get it to work properly. One of the OCC students said, "Let me show you how to do that," and promptly solved the problem.

1990s

By 1988, it was evident that the current field house was not going to meet the growing needs in athletics and physical education. Dr. Johnson employed a firm that had designed multiuse gymnasiums to see if such a facility could provide both a basketball playing court with a large seating area and a facility for large gatherings such as commencement and lectureship. After the study was done, however, it was apparent that the expense of such a building was more than Oklahoma Christian could afford. Still, the need for more facilities remained. In 1990, again with Tom Glover as architect, planning began for an expansion of the existing field house. The added space would allow a second playing court, thus meeting needs in physical education classes, intramurals, and varsity sports. The expansion also increased the spectator capacity for varsity basketball by adding more seating on the north side, including seats with backs instead of standard bleachers. The third area of the expansion provided a fitness center for students, athletes, and employees. The new facility opened in the fall of 1992 at a cost of $1,007,711 for construction, $76,109 for fitness equipment, and $126,592 for new gymnasium seating. The expanded facility was ready for use in the fall of 1992.

Lady Eagles play; the crowd in new seating watches.

Dining in the remodeled University Center

After Kevin Jacobs became president in 1996, he decided to locate his office in the Student Center as demonstration of his desire to be close to students. He also believed it was time for another expansion of the building, both to accommodate continuing growth of the student body and to upgrade the quality of the facility. In this remodel, Jacob's office would occupy the northeast corner. Along the building's east side would be a coffee shop, student government offices, a luxurious private dining room for special events, and a larger second private dining room. The plan, designed by Tom Glover, also expanded space for general student dining and provided it with new carpeting, paneled walls, coffered ceilings, and movable walls to allow various configurations of the seating space. This remodeling also provided both a new entrance with a covered drive and more parking, while expanding the campus health center.

This expansion and remodel, at a cost of $3,734,820, marked a significant step forward in the appearance of campus buildings. The upscale carpeting, paneling, and lighting provided a new degree of elegance and made a good impression on those visiting the campus for special events. The majority of the costs were covered by donations, but about $500,000 was added to campus debt.[18] The official opening of the expanded Gaylord University Center came on October 1, 1997, with Governor Frank Keating as the principal speaker.[19]

On Sunday, November 30, 1997, at 9:44 a.m., worshippers at the Memorial Road Church of Christ were momentarily distracted by the wailing of sirens from emergency vehicles speeding east on Memorial Road. What they didn't know was that just ten minutes earlier, Matt Manamey and Marie Otte, working the morning shift on the campus radio station, KOCC, were startled by smoke coming through the air vents. The two students had rushed out of the radio station into a hallway filled with smoke and groped their way to the exit and out of the building.[20] Within four minutes after the call at 9:40, the fire department arrived and began extinguishing the blaze.

Clint Brumit of Campus Security observed freshman student James Hopper among those watching. Knowing that he had been questioned about a $5,000 fire at the Student Center on September 22, and hearing his comments about the fire in progress, Brumit detained Hopper, who soon confessed to starting both fires.[21] On October 16, 1998, he was sentenced to seven years in prison, seven years probation, and a $10,000 fine for setting the two fires.[22]

Hopper had started the fire in a sofa in the music wing's student lounge, and the flames had spread quickly to other portions of the building, with smoke filling Hardeman Auditorium, the art and music sections of the Kresge Fine Arts Building, and the Mabee Communications Building.[23] These damaged buildings were closed for the remainder of the fall term, with all classes in art, music, and mass communication relocated elsewhere. Chapel met in the Payne Field House for the remaining two weeks.

McIntosh Conservatory

With the start of the new trimester on Monday, January 12, Hardeman Auditorium and Mabee Communications were usable, having been cleaned and freed from the smoke odor, but the art and music areas were still closed for a major renovation.[24] Eighteen art classes, thirty seven music classes, and offices for music and art faculty had to be moved to other locations spread over the campus.[25] Darrel Alexander reported that the insurance company paid for sending over ten thousand items from the costume shop to Wichita for special cleaning to get rid of the smell of smoke.

Joe Watson, vice president for operations, took the lead in planning for the cleanup, remodeling, and new construction, working with architect Tom Glover. By the end of the spring term, on April 24, President Jacobs announced the new plans. The new Garvey

Center would be much more than just a renovation of what it had been. As difficult as the fire was, college officials wanted to use it an opportunity to upgrade the facility. Working with faculty, they had decided, in addition to remodeling and cleaning existing areas, to add five major new elements. To enlarge the Hardeman lobby space, they planned a hundred foot by eighty foot conservatory with skylights, to give it an open feeling. This area would improve access to the auditorium and would be an attractive space for dinners, weddings, displays, performances, and socializing. Since W. E. and Bonnie McIntosh contributed a million dollars to the new construction, this space was named the McIntosh Conservatory.

Recital Hall

Adjoining the conservatory to the north, the plan provided an elegant new recital hall for smaller music presentations, chorus rehearsal, and gatherings of up to two hundred. A computer laboratory for graphic arts would finish the space, filling the open "U" that previously had separated the fine arts and communication wings. The art department would get a new gallery for displaying the work of students outside artists along with a redesign of its existing space to fit current needs. The final addition would be a new entrance to Hardeman Auditorium from the west side, complete with a circle drive for the convenience of those coming to events in the building.

The cost of the cleaning, remodeling, and new construction would eventually come to $4,830,037. Of this, $2 million would be paid by insurance and the rest by donations. Unfortunately, the fundraising fell about $1.4 million below the required amount and was added to the long-term debt to be repaid.[26] The new facilities were largely ready for the start of classes in September of 1998.

Like the remodeled Gaylord Student Center, the new Garvey Center continued the higher quality look in buildings on the OC campus. This new center not only has been a great boost to the departments of music, art, and communication, but also many from off-campus have chosen this center as a site for events they wished to hold. The wide variety of spaces, from a 1300-seat auditorium to an intimate recital hall to an art gallery, classrooms, and even the music practice area, named for Mayola Tippens Kerr, form an excellent, well-coordinated center.

By 1998, then, the academic and activity areas of the campus had grown from the original five buildings to twelve, plus Enterprise Square. And, of course, the new buildings were much larger. The original Student Center had been expanded four times and the original Learning Center had been expanded twice. These new facilities have given the academic program superior facilities with well-equipped classrooms and specialized laboratories.

In addition to the buildings added, however, someone who last saw the campus in 1958 and returned in 2007 would be struck by the vast improvement in campus landscaping. In leveling the land for the original buildings, nearly all of the topsoil was lost, leaving the campus grounds primarily hard clay. It took years of work to get even a stand of grass.[27] In 1971, the college engaged the nationally known landscape firm of Sasaki-Dawson-DeMay and Associates to lay out a master plan for the campus landscaping. Their report suggested concentrating the trees and other planting to the interior zones of the campus while the "periphery remains reminiscent of the Oklahoma prairie."[28] Generally, those in charge of the campus have followed this plan. Particularly with Macie Jackson's work over the past ten years, the campus has color with sculpted shrubs, flowers, well-manicured lawns, and trees that have grown substantially. The once barren 200-acre field has been transformed with buildings, trees, and plants into an attractive and beautiful environment for academic learning.

2000s

Aerial view of the academic zone of the OC campus today,
plus the University Center in the lower left

In the 2003–2004 school year, President O'Neal and Executive Vice President Branch decided that the next major step in facilities had to be student housing. The university had a capacity of 1,254 beds almost filled to capacity.[29] In addition to the need for more space, they believed that the lack of higher quality housing was holding back enrollment. No new housing had been built since 1979.[30] Prospective students were accustomed to nicer homes, but housing at the university had not kept pace. They decided, therefore, to embark on the largest single building project in the history of the university.

The new plan involved leaving some rooms unchanged, remodeling others, and building new ones. Dormitory rooms with a capacity of 545, and apartments with a capacity of 414 would remain basically unchanged. College officials considered these rooms adequate and would continue using them as lower cost housing. Dorms with a total of 250 beds, however, would be renovated, as would rooms with 12 beds in the apartments. The final step in the plan would add rooms for 206 new dormitory occupants in University House and space for 378 new apartment occupants in the new buildings. Believing the upgraded housing would have a beneficial effect on enrollment, the administrators borrowed the nearly $35 million the project required.[31]

Of this amount, renovation of Fails Hall for men cost $2,064,181, renovation for Warlick Hall for men cost $638,716, and renovation of Tinius Hall for women cost $3,210,602. The new University House, the north portion of which initially would house men and the south portion of which initially would house women, cost $10,435,621. Trammell Crow Company managed the construction and development, while DalMac Construction served as the general contractor.[32] The new dormitory would have a fitness center, laundry rooms, study rooms, a room for meetings and classes, and, of course, the entire building, like the rest of the campus, would be equipped with wireless internet.

To serve all the residence halls, plus other buildings on campus such as the Student Center and the Mabee Learning Center, the university built, as part of this project, a new central heating and cooling plant at a cost of $4,708,860.[33] In the long term, this efficient system would more than save in utility bills what it cost to build.

The new apartment units called Phase V would cost $3,655,190, and Phase VI, another $10,190,000. Other miscellaneous expenditures would bring the

New apartment units for upper-class and married students

total housing project to $34,903,170.[34] Put into service during the 2005–2006 year, the new housing opportunities proved to be very attractive to students and the actual income from them exceeded the projections.

As Dr. O'Neal said at the dedication of University House, "Because we take a holistic approach to education, we believe that residential life and co-curricular activity is a critical part of [a student's] education…. We are purposefully a residential campus with 80 percent or more of our students living on campus."[35] O'Neal told how administrators had obtained input from students about what they wanted in their residences and called the new housing "a quantum leap forward in the students' holistic education experience."[36]

The final piece in campus facilities came with the Lawson Commons. For many years, the space between the Learning Center and the residence halls had

Lawson Commons from the west with the Freede Centennial Tower in the foreground and the McGraw Pavillion behind.

little beautification. Lawson Commons changed that with the addition of the eighty by one hundred foot Jack and Wanda McGraw Pavillion that has the feel of the outdoors while still being protected from the elements. In addition, the hundred-foot tall Freede Centennial Tower signifies both the Oklahoma centennial and the history and vision of Oklahoma Christian. The $2 million project also included extensive landscaping to beautify the entire area and make it a focal point on campus.

Conclusion

To look at each building on the Oklahoma Christian campus really means thinking of the people who made it possible. The faculty and administrators who conceived of it and developed the general plan, architects who took these concepts and provided the final design, builders who brought the plan to life, advancement personnel who raised the necessary funds, and donors whose contributions were essential. All of these deserve credit for the thirty-six buildings that now grace the campus.

OC's facilities have an order and common motif that give a sense of harmony to life on campus. Their practical and efficient design allows faculty and students to do their work well. The spots of beauty in the McIntosh Conservatory, the Thelma Gaylord Forum, the Lawson Commons, and other places on campus provide a sense of relief to those who need a respite from the pressures of the day. The quality of the buildings calls those who occupy them to quality in their work. The OC campus, with its buildings and landscaping, is a testament to the combination of elements that have made the university what it has come to be: strong administrative leadership, active faculty participation, and outstanding donors who have provided the means to bring dreams to reality.

Ducks on the pond at the campus entrance, with the
Williams Branch Center in the background

Chapter 12, Endnotes

1 W. O. Beeman, *Oklahoma Christian College: Dream to Reality* (Delight, Arkansas: Gospel Light Publishing Company, 1970), 124.

2 All data in this chapter on the cost of buildings and the date of their construction, except as noted, is from the Records of the Business Office, Oklahoma Christian University.

3 Beeman, 124.

4 Ibid, 125.

5 Names of some residence halls were added after they were constructed but are here referred to by their current names. Initially they were called by the letters A, B, C, and D.

6 Ibid.

7 Enrollment data in this chapter is from the Registrar's Office, Oklahoma Christian University.

8 "President's Report," 1970, OC Archives.

9 Minutes, Board of Trustees, April 1, 1969, and Minutes of the Executive Committee of the Board of Trustees, July 7, 1969, OC Archives.

10 "Davissons Give $400,000 for New Heritage Building," *Oklahoma Christian College Bulletin*, November 1968, OC Archives. Other sources indicate the gift was nearer $500,000.

11 "Judge William G. Davisson Donates $500,000 for Women's Residence Hall," *Oklahoma Christian College Reporter,* April 1974, OC Archives.

12 "Construction of Student Activity Center Underway," *Oklahoma Christian College Reporter*, December 1975, OC Archives.

13 "Nowlins Provide Funds for Recreation Center," *OCC Reporter*, April 1978, 1, OC Archives.

14 "Institutional Advancements," *Report from the President 1986–87,* OC Archives.

15 Conversation with Jeff Bingham, Vice President for Finance at OC, April 23, 2007.

16 "President's Report," 1988, OC Archives.

17 Ibid.

18 Ibid.

19 Heather Burgland, "Governor Keating addresses crowd at University Center grand opening," *Talon*, October 3, 1997, 1.

20 Wes McKenzie, "Picking Up the Pieces," *Talon*, December 5, 1997, 5.

21 "Student Confesses to Campus Fire," *Daily Oklahoman*, December 1, 1997, 1; Luke Hartman, "Campus Cops Helped Detain Arson Suspect," *Talon*, December 9, 1997, 1.

22 "University Arsonist Gets 7-Year Term," *Daily Oklahoman*, October 17, 1998, 1.

23 "Former Freshman at OC to Stand Trial in Arsons," *Daily Oklahoman*, April 10, 1998, 24.

24 "Auditorium Opens for Chapel," *Daily Oklahoman*, January 13, 1998, 3.

25 Erin Engelke, "Fire Results Linger for Some," *Talon*, January 16, 1998, 2.

26 Jeff Bingham, Conversation with the author.

27 Beeman, 130.

28 "President's Report," November 20, 1971, OC Archives.

29 "Student Housing Initiative," Files of the Executive Vice President, OC.

30 Mike O'Neal, University House Dedication, December 5, 2005, Files of the Office of Public Relations, OC.

31 "Student Housing Initiative."

32 "Oklahoma Christian Dedicates New 'Signature' Student Housing," News Release of December 5, 2005, Office of Public Relations, OC.

33 "Student Housing Initiative."

34 Ibid.

35 O'Neal, "University House Dedication."

36 Ibid.

Chapter 13
THE SPIRITUAL LIFE

From its very first days in Bartlesville through its years in Oklahoma City, Oklahoma Christian has remained focused on its fundamental purpose: encouraging spiritual growth among its students. In harmony with this principle, as the university has chosen personnel, no Board member, administrator, faculty, or staff member has been considered without weighing his or her potential impact on the spiritual life of OC students. This criterion has provided the university with those who believe in its spiritual goals and make personal and institutional decisions in harmony with them. These have provided leadership and examples to accomplish the statement written in the first Central Christian College Catalog: the college was "founded primarily for the purpose of providing a school where young people may continue their education under Christian environment and influence. . . . The greatest service [the college] can render is that of strengthening young people in character and preparing them for Christian service, regardless of their calling in life."[1]

In addition to selecting people who share in its spiritual goals, Oklahoma Christian has worked to enhance the spiritual life of students through high standards of conduct, required Bible classes and daily chapel attendance, evening devotionals, student religious clubs, personal contact between faculty and students, connecting with a local congregation, and student involvement in Christian service opportunities locally, nationally, and internationally.

Earlier chapters have spoken of OC's spiritual life as related to the Board, presidents, curriculum, faculty, staff, and students. This chapter discusses the impact of out-of-class activities on student spiritual growth, and the following chapter adds more by describing OC's missionary spirit.

Chapel

The story of Oklahoma Christian University would be incomplete without telling of required daily chapel that has characterized the university since the first day of classes in September 1950. Over its fifty-eight years, there have been nearly nine thousand days of chapel. While these assemblies have provided an important means for communication about campus events, opportunities to build school spirit, a time for students to see friends, and a venue for secular speakers and programs after the devotional, chapel's great constant has been daily worship by the campus family. Chapel has been a time for singing together, for Bible reading, for prayer, and for talks on religious themes. While many students do not recognize chapel's impact on them until they look back on their college experience, the some five hundred times a student goes to chapel during four years at OC make their mark. That the campus sets a daily time when students, faculty, and administrators gather for worship plants a deep impression in the minds of students. And, while students may not recall many specific chapel devotionals or talks during their time at OC, the cumulative effect has proven to be a significant spiritual factor. Studies of colleges founded for religious purposes show that dropping the daily chapel requirement marks a point when institutions tend to leave their spiritual moorings.[2] OC Board Chair Don Millican shared this truth in a 2007 article in *Vision*. He wrote of a Board study indicating "the demise of chapel" was one of the factors leading colleges away from their Christian purpose and promising the Board's commitment to "continuing chapel as a daily reminder of the centrality of faith to our mission."[3]

Chapel at Oklahoma Christian has been much the same over the years: a twenty-five minute period when there are no classes, laboratories, or other campus activities so students and faculty can gather to sing, pray, and consider a biblical topic. A student from any era of the university's history would feel at home in a chapel of any other era. The style of songs chosen might be different and the dress of those leading might vary, but the activities would be familiar.

For about the first forty years, each chapel service was typically planned and led by administrators and faculty. During this time, students would sometimes be invited to

Chapel in Bartlesville in 1952

lead, and occasionally a student group would plan and conduct a week in chapel. In more recent years, however, while an administrator has selected themes and speakers, chapel has been primarily a student-led event. With this change, contemporary praise songs are more common than traditional hymns, and instead of hymnals, the words are projected on two screens. The singing, however, remains robust, with most students participating in the singing and giving attention to the readings, speakers, and prayers. Visitors from other religious colleges with required chapel comment on the relatively good student conduct.

Don Beck conducting chapel in Cogwell-Alexander Auditorium in 1960

The first chapel services were held in the assembly hall in the classroom building in Bartlesville. When the college moved to Oklahoma City, chapel met in the auditorium of Cogswell-Alexander Hall which seated a few more than the two hundred in Bartlesville. Since enrollment passed six hundred before a larger auditorium was built, sometimes chapel was held as many as four times a day. Occasionally on Mondays, chapel would meet in The Barn so everyone could worship together. Since 1966, when Hardeman Auditorium was built, chapel has been conducted there. On occasion, Judd Theatre has served as an overflow location to accommodate more students. Those in Judd sometimes have had an alternative program, while on other occasions, they participated in Hardeman chapel via television. In 1978 and again in 1982, there were two chapel services in Hardeman, with the students about equally divided between the two sessions, one at 10 a.m. and the other at 11 a.m.[4]

Often there have been small concurrent chapels for various individual groups, usually meeting one day a week. Some academic departments have had their own devotionals, and these occasional alternative meetings have also included services in Spanish and French, chapels focused on missions, a "seekers

Chapel in Hardeman Auditorium

chapel," chapels led for and by women, and meetings of religious groups such as Harvesters for men and Gleaners for women.

Over the years, OC's administrators have found various ways of checking chapel attendance to enforce the required chapel. At the beginning, students were assigned seats, and checkers walked the aisles to mark empty seats. For a time, attendance was checked by taking pictures from the back of Hardeman Auditorium to identify the empty seats. In more recent years, students scan their ID cards.

Over the years students have been allowed different numbers of absences during a term (usually about fifteen), and various methods have been assessed for making up excessive absences: listening to sermons on audiotape, completing service projects, writing papers, and attending alternate events. Occasionally, students have been denied re-admission the following term because their excessive chapel absences showed they were not in harmony with the university's spiritual goals. Most students, however, have attended chapel consistently, and the common experience both binds them together and gives them a beneficial spiritual experience.

Some chapel traditions have been longstanding. Since Harold Fletcher led "I'm Not Ashamed to Own My Lord," at the first chapel in Bartlesville in 1950, that hymn has been led at the opening chapel every year. For over fifty years, Fletcher continued to lead the song. In an appropriate continuation, his son, John Fletcher, who followed his father in teaching music at OC, now leads the traditional opening hymn. Another tradition connected with the opening chapel is the reading of the beatitudes. For many years, Hugo McCord read this scripture. Now Lynn McMillon, dean of the College of Biblical Studies reads the passage. Since the early sixties, chapel each Monday has started with the recitation of the pledge of allegiance to the U.S. flag followed by the singing of the OC alma mater.

Those making lists of the most memorable chapels would recall different occasions with special meaning to them. One of the most powerful chapels in recent years was the day Dr. Tony Alley spoke to a hushed student body about his brain cancer, which he knew would take his life in a few months. He told them that one of his early thoughts upon learning he had a serious problem was that he would find a way to use this circumstance to glorify God. His lesson that day certainly fulfilled that goal as he allowed all to witness a Christian facing death with great hope. On another occasion, alumnus Ben Langford spoke in chapel a few days after his brother Adam had been killed while serving with him as a missionary in Uganda. His thoughts helped students realize that the focus of one's life is far more important than the length of it.

Batsell Barrett Baxter spoke to students on the first day of the first Lectureship in Hardeman Auditorium on "The Power of a Greater Love," and Willie Franklin has spoken about "What a Dedicated Life Looks Like." One of the most striking chapel occasions happened when Jeff Bennett returned from the Olympics. He had missed the bronze medal in the decathlon by only ten points with unfortunate circumstances making the difference. After giving him a great welcome home, the chapel audience was moved by his great spirit in saying that he had been proud to represent his country and that overall, he had a great experience. His lack of bitterness about the circumstances blessed everyone who heard him.

Joe Malone came to chapel with his drawings for Christ, and Mike Lewis has been four times to draw a large picture of Christ while the audience sings hymns and listens to Bible passages. Ronnie White brought meaningful lessons on sexual restraint, and Ray Vaughn, Sr., spoke on endurance. Each Friday, in recent years, Kent Hartman has presented a "mission minute" to highlight some missionary effort. This weekly reminder seeks to encourage students to consider how they might become involved in mission work. The most repeated chapel talks have been Dr. North's "submarine" series in which he urges students not to have air-tight compartments for sins in their lives.

In addition to the overtly religious parts of the services, chapel has hosted many outstanding speakers—governors, senators, congressmen, mayors, and George W. Bush, a future U.S. president. Many leaders in business have spoken. On the day Judge and Reba Davisson gave half a million dollars for the Davisson American Heritage building, he spoke in chapel and then students and faculty assembled to see the couple plant a maple tree in front of the facility.

One of the continuing chapel events has been fun over football rivalries. Dr. Don Dunn and Jack McElroy had a "bet" each year on whether OU or OSU would win their annual football game. The loser had to humble himself by kissing a pig or engaging in some other ignoble activity. Jim Wilson later replaced McElroy as the OU representative. In more recent times, the football rivalry has revived with Al Branch boosting the University of Texas and Neil Arter favoring the University of Oklahoma. The loser has to show up in chapel with hair dyed in the opponent's color and afterward take a swim in the pond.

Dedicated primarily to spiritual matters, but also to other enriching and unifying experiences, the daily chapel certainly ranks high in its overall, long-term impact on the spiritual lives of students and faculty. Alumni often reflect on the powerful influence chapel had on them.

Student Religious Groups

Student religious groups have been another important spiritual influence throughout the fifty-eight years at Oklahoma Christian. In the Bartlesville years, there was a preacher's club, a women's

Gleaners in 1967

training class, a men's training class, a group of Future Christian Homemakers, and a meeting for mission study. Through the years, similar groups have continued. In the first year in Oklahoma City, fourteen preaching students composed the Harvesters Club, twenty-seven young ladies met in Worthy Women, and thirty-six women were members of the Future Christian Homemakers. In 1965, Worthy Women became Gleaners, a club for women interested in developing spiritually and in serving skills. By that time, the Future Christian Homemakers was no longer functioning.

Morris Thurman with Harvesters preparing a youth forum in 1973

Harvesters and Gleaners continued for many years. Often the Harvesters conducted youth forums and gospel meetings, both to serve and to learn.[5] In the 1972–1973 year, for example, they planned and spoke at thirty rallies in five states. A *Talon* story says, "Almost 400 people have responded, including 100 who were baptized."[6] In many of these activities, the Gleaners also participated. In 1984–1985, the Harvesters sponsored an on-campus seminar on the theme, "Where Do I Fit In?" and brought speakers to campus to give lectures and teach classes to help students think about how they could serve in the Lord's kingdom. That same year, the Gleaners, meeting during the Friday chapel time, conducted their own worship and, for a service project, adopted grandparents at an Edmond nursing home.[7] Early in the 1990s, Harvesters stopped meeting, and in 1994, the Gleaners changed their name to College Women for Christ. This group continued to meet until 2001.[8] Outreach, featured in the next chapter, was playing a larger role, and interest in the other two groups waned.

Over the fifty-eight years, religious clubs have provided opportunities for students to learn, to develop their skills in ministry, to be encouraged for work in the church, and to develop close bonds with those who share their interests.

Youth Forum

Beginning in Spring 1959, the first school year in Oklahoma City, OCC students, under the leadership of the student government and a faculty advisor, began a program that lasted more than twenty years. Called "Youth Forum," this event brought hundreds of high school students to campus to hear OCC students give lectures and participate in discussion groups led by students, ministers, and some high school

Youth Forum with speaker and panel in 1961

students. In the first year, 750 high school students and sponsors came for the three-day event, most of them housed overnight on the campus.[9]

With this outstanding success, the event continued, and by 1962, more than a thousand high school students were attending. OCC students still gave the lectures, and the Saturday program featured more than thirty classes and panels from which to choose. Topics for these sessions included lessons against drinking, gambling, smoking, dancing, and divorce, while other sessions dealt with evangelism, Christian courtship and marriage, Christian evidences, and opportunities for young Christians to serve.[10]

In 1972, Youth Forum was scheduled with Spring Sing, then in its fourth year, so the two events could share the same weekend. This combination brought increased numbers to both events and continued for many years.[11] In 1981, however, students did not continue Youth Forum,[12] but it had blessed the lives of the thousands who attended, and many of the student speakers on the program went on to become outstanding preachers and teachers in Christian higher education.

Student Devotionals

Another major spiritual activity on the Oklahoma Christian campus has been student-led, voluntary devotionals. In various forms and in a variety of places, these devotionals have played an important part in student spiritual life.

Beginning the first year in Bartlesville, the weekly devotionals met either around the fountain in the circular drive or on the western terrace. They were student-led, but faculty members often attended. Roy Lanier, Sr., often came and when a student read a scripture, Lanier would usually quote the next verse or two.

Student devotional in a dorm lounge in 1960

In Oklahoma City, the devotionals continued, meeting on the mall, in the "U" formed by an addition to the student center, in the outside area north of Hardeman Auditorium, in a park area west of the dormitories, in the auditorium of the Davisson American Heritage Building, and in the Thelma Gaylord Forum. More recently, View 63, a weekly devotional activity, has met in the Hall of Giants at Enterprise Square. Attendance at these informal times of songs, prayer, Bible reading, and sometimes short talks has varied from fairly small numbers to several hundred, depending on the time of the year and the publicity given them. Regardless of size, they have offered comfort and enrichment and thus are a vital element among the opportunities for student spiritual development.

Participation in Local Congregations

Many students have pointed to their attendance at local congregations and participation in their programs as being a major part of their spiritual growth while at Oklahoma Christian. Several congregations of Churches of Christ in Oklahoma City have well-developed ministries for college students including not only classes and fellowship, but also opportunities for students to serve. Through these congregations, students have taught children's and teen's Bible classes, participated in service projects to assist the needy, done inner city work at West

Main Mission and later at Capitol Hill Church of Christ, helped with door-to-door evangelistic campaigns, participated in benevolent work, helped lead the public worship, and gone on campaigns to foreign lands. Some students have chosen to go to small congregations where they fill special needs.

While the work of these congregations is separate from Oklahoma Christian, the university encourages students to connect with local congregations and gives those working with college students an opportunity to speak in chapel and advertise their efforts on campus. In these congregations, students often see faculty and staff taking an active part in church work, allowing students to see these OC employees in a different and favorable light. Attending these congregations also gives students an opportunity to see effective congregations at work, giving them useful insights about how to work with the church after they leave Oklahoma Christian.

Other Service Opportunities

From its beginning, OC has encouraged students to serve others as a means of growing spiritually. Taking seriously Jesus' statement, "I came not to be ministered unto but to minister" (Matthew 20:28), OC has intentionally created opportunities to serve in almost every phase of campus life. While other chapters describe many specific service activities, it is important to note their place in the spiritual life of the campus.

Some teachers make service projects one of their course requirements. The Student Senate has encouraged service through such programs as serving at Western Village Elementary School and other ministries to help the needy. Student clubs often collect Christmas toys, sing at rest homes, visit children in the hospital, and help with needs on the campus. On student campaigns over fall, spring, and summer breaks, students often serve in building church buildings and homes and working at orphanages, as well as in teaching the gospel message. Students have gone to help people meet disasters such as the Oklahoma City bombing, a serious grass fire across the street from the Bartlesville campus, and many natural disasters. Regular blood drives at OC get a good response as students donate blood to help people they will never see.

One of the most interesting opportunities for students to serve comes through the class Dr. Max Dobson teaches in physical education for handicapped children. In 1976, a woman in the community called Dobson asking if OCC had a program allowing children with disabilities to play with college students. He had to tell her "No," but that was not the answer for very long. He was captivated by the

OC student helps a disabled child. Dobson stands in the background.

idea and soon developed a program to bring handicapped children to the campus to put them in contact with college students who would play with them. Since then, more than 1,200 students have taken classes in which they work hands-on each week with children having special needs. The class draws children from five Edmond elementary schools, and OC students from many different majors take Dobson's class. In this activity, students give their service, but they receive so much in return that develops in them a spirit of serving.[13]

At OC, developing a heart to serve is part of the plan for spiritual growth, and students have many opportunities to learn through these activities.

Spiritual Impact of Faculty and Staff

The relationship between faculty and students on the Oklahoma Christian campus has always been special. Many faculty members encourage close ties with an open door policy to their offices, by inviting students to their homes, sponsoring clubs, attending student events, coaching or directing student activities, and having contact with students at church. By requiring all faculty and administrators to be active members of a local congregation of a Church of Christ, the university seeks to be sure that many on campus can play this role.

One of the most important ways faculty encourage students spiritually is through their classes. They teach to enhance students' faith as well as to help them learn their discipline. Since all full-time faculty are practicing Christians, they lead students not only to learn the essentials of their academic field, but to understand them in harmony with a Christian worldview. Both by their examples and their teaching, then, faculty members often make a strong spiritual impact on students.

Administrators and other staff members also play their part in the spiritual development of students. They often have contact with students who work in their areas and with those who come to them for services. Like the faculty, staff members make an important impact by sponsoring clubs, having students in their homes, treating students with respect and compassion, and setting Christian examples.

One of the strongest spiritual influences faculty and staff have on students is by leading groups of them on mission trips. On these campaigns, students and their mentors work closely together to teach and serve. While these activities are detailed in the chapter on "The Missionary Spirit," they are an important part of the OC strategy for developing students spiritually.

With few exceptions, both faculty and staff have served well as a major force in the spiritual development of students. They have led them by their actions, by their teaching, by sharing with them in activities of service, and by personal relationships they have developed with them.

Examples of Student Spiritual Growth

Stories of individual students illustrate how various elements of the OC experience work together to bring a positive spiritual effect in the lives of many.

Mel Latorre came in 1962 from Brazil to the United States to study chemical engineering at the University of Oklahoma. OU, however, said his English was not good enough and suggested he attend an English school in Michigan. Latorre had an uncle in Oklahoma City, and one night the two of them met a "Persian man" who told them he had attended Oklahoma Christian College. The next day, at the grocery store where Mel had a job, another employee, James Freed, mentioned he was going to attend Oklahoma Christian. Freed's father took Latorre to the OCC campus to meet with President James Baird, who offered him a tuition scholarship provided by a group of women in Texas. So Latorre enrolled at OCC, planning to attend two years and then transfer to OU. He

Mel Latorre

knew nothing of the Church of Christ when he came but, being impressed with the Christian environment, the Bible classes, and the good examples on campus, he was baptized in January. He decided to stay at OCC where he could study the Bible along with majoring in math education. After graduation, he got a job at Cedar Vale, Kansas, and became a member of the Overland Park Church of Christ. Some from that congregation preached at smaller congregations in the area, and Latorre joined in doing that. Eventually the church in Olathe, Kansas, invited him to preach for them full-time. In 1971, the Southwest Church of Christ in Ft. Worth sent Latorre back to his native Brazil as a missionary, a role in which he served for nine years.

During that time, he married Marly, and they had two boys. In 1980, the Latorres came back to Olathe for two years and then returned to be missionaries in Brazil, supported by the Quail Springs Church of Christ. In 1992, Mel came to Olathe again to preach while his two sons attended Oklahoma Christian. In 2003, Mel and Marly returned to Brazil again to serve as missionaries, this time sponsored by the Memorial Road Church of Christ, their primary work to be holding seminars to strengthen preachers and churches throughout that nation. After coming to OCC as a second choice, and that through a providential set of circumstances, Latorre has now been preaching and serving as a missionary for forty years.

Jeff Bennett

Jeff Bennett came to Oklahoma Christian in 1966 from Vinita, Oklahoma. Coach Ray Vaughn had seen athletic potential in him that other coaches had missed. Before coming to OCC, Bennett had a loose connection with a church but had not attended recently. When he arrived at OCC, he began to attend church "because everybody else did." He saw in the teachers, especially in Coach Vaughn, the example of Christ, and from classes and chapel he could see that following the Scriptures was important. In his sophomore year, his suitemate paid special attention to him and, one day, had a long discussion with him about the biblical plan of salvation. Bennett decided it was time to make a commitment, and the following Sunday at the College Church, he confessed Christ, and Phil Watson, the preacher that day, baptized him. Since then, Bennett has been faithful as a Christian, setting an excellent Christian example as a student, an athlete, and in his roles in education. After working for many years in public schools, in 2003, Bennett came back to OC as assistant dean of campus life, dealing mainly with student discipline, and helping coach track.[14]

Joyce Ashlock Redd

Joyce Ashlock grew up in Philadelphia. Her grandmother encouraged her to read the Bible, but she found it hard to comprehend and prayed God would help her understand it. She attended Northeastern Christian Junior College near Philadelphia for her freshman year, and at the end of that year decided to become a Christian. In 1970, Dean Lawrence Rhodes visited Northeastern to recruit for OCC, and with some scholarship encouragement, Ashlock decided to come. Still young in the faith, at Oklahoma Christian she found many positive spiritual influences. She remembers the impact of chapel, devotionals, Bible classes, and many teachers.

Dr. Clyde Muse took a special interest in her, as did Dr. Jim Wilson. As a student, she worked at West Main Mission, an inner-city work of Churches of Christ, and she went to Belize on two campaigns. All of these opportunities for spiritual growth she considers an answer to her childhood prayer. While at OCC, a friend set her up to meet one of the college's best baseball players, Harold Redd, who was studying to become a preacher. Although she never anticipated being a preacher's wife, after a time, she and Harold were married. Following graduation, she taught in elementary school and helped her husband in working with a church in West Memphis and then at the Mid-Town Church of Christ in Memphis, a large congregation serving primarily African Americans. She has had six children of her own, and the couple has adopted two more and raised a ninth, the child of Harold's late sister. In addition to her work as a wife and mother, Joyce has taught Bible classes for children and women and has spoken often at ladies' day events in Arkansas, Mississippi, and Tennessee. Two of Redd's children have attended Oklahoma Christian.

Chuck White grew up in Oklahoma City and was religiously active but was uncomfortable because his church was moving worship toward entertainment. During the summer baseball season after his 1971 high school graduation, an umpire recommended he contact Coach Dobson about playing at Oklahoma Christian. Since Dobson, however, had already used up his scholarships, White enrolled at the University of Oklahoma to walk-on for baseball. He didn't make the team, however, and was dissatisfied with the environment. During the summer of 1972, White competed against the OCC team in

Chuck White

summer league play, and again made contact with Dobson. This time Dobson could offer him a scholarship, and White came to OCC where he was an outstanding baseball player. He remembers his first chapel service when he heard the student body singing unaccompanied; he thought, "This is the right thing." He had Bible courses under Hugo McCord, Raymond Kelcy, and Bill Jones and had conversations with Coach Dobson about spiritual topics when the Dobsons invited him for dinner. During his senior year, White married Marti Bell, a member of the Church of Christ. Dobson helped him get a job at Mid-Del Schools where he coached baseball and softball, and in 1977, about a year after graduating from OCC, White decided to be baptized. From then until 2004, he attended the Eastside Church of Christ in Midwest City, where he served as a deacon and later as an elder. In 2004, White returned to

OC, where he now serves as director of athletic operations and coach of the newly revived Eagle baseball team. He is active in the Edmond Church of Christ.[15]

Jennifer Jackson

Jennifer Jackson enrolled in Oklahoma Christian in 1974, coming from a farming family in southwestern Oklahoma. The family was strong in the church and, although the parents had not attended college, they sent all five of their children to Oklahoma Christian. The devotionals, Bible classes, and mission activities put Jennifer in contact with OCC faculty who had a profound impact on her life. Dr. Howard Norton fueled her desire for missions, and she went on two campaigns with Dr. Ron Bever and Dr. Elmo Hall as they took students to Belize and Trinidad. Fellow students who later became full-time missionaries also had an impact on her spiritual growth: Mark and Paul Brazle, Dale and Kent Hartman, and Nancy Price (Hartman). Jackson completed a bachelor's degree in nursing through a cooperative program between OCC and Central State University, and then spent twenty months out of the next two and a half years with a Christian Mobile Clinic in Cameroon, West Africa. In 1980, after working for eight months as OCC's school nurse, she married OCC alumnus Randy Gray. After spending time in Duncan, Oklahoma, and St. Louis, Missouri, they moved to Arlington, Texas. Both have been active in teaching Bible classes, drawing on what they learned in Bible classes at OCC. Randy, now an elder, has become the stateside coordinator for the Chimala Mission in Tanzania, Africa. In both 2003 and 2005, Jennifer sponsored teams of high school and college students to campaigns in Chimala. Jackson completed both a master's degree and a doctorate in nursing and teaches at the University of Texas in Arlington.

Daniel Langdon came to OC in 1992 as a junior, not because he had a particular plan, but because his brothers had come to OC and he "didn't know what else to do." At OC he came in contact with Dr. John Maple, who took student campaigns each summer to the British Isles. He met Kathy Smith, whom he later married, and they went on a campaign together in 1993. Through this experience and further contact with Maple and others at OC, the Langdons decided after graduation to go to Japan to spend a year teaching English in public schools and working with the church as they could. Once there, they decided to stay a second year. During this time they laid a foundation for the English Bible Schools now in Mito and Hitachi-taga. Four months after returning from Japan, the Langdons decided to go back to Scotland where they had been on campaigns, and spent eight years there working full time with two congregations and bringing to maturity a Christian camp with which Maple and others had worked. After their years in the mission field, the Langdons returned to the U.S., where Daniel now serves as a minister in Broken Arrow, Oklahoma. Langdon said, "OC is not just my alma mater, it's part of who I am for my Lord."[16]

When Jason Snethen's time for college came in 1994, he had to make a difficult choice between two universities where he had been

Jason Snethen

accepted: Harvard and Oklahoma Christian. He decided that a Christian school was more important than what Harvard had to offer, and does not regret that choice.[17] Offered a scholarship in Bible, he became a Bible major, but to pursue his interest in international politics, he also studied History/Pre-Law. During his second year, Snethen began to become more deeply involved in fulfilling his spiritual reasons for coming to OC. Dorm devotionals with his hall director, Tim Lewis, and preparation for a summer campaign to England with Dr. John Maple inspired him.

Snethen still had no intention of entering full-time ministry, but OC influences were at work. He continued to go on summer campaigns to Scotland and England and considered the possibility of becoming a worker for two years in Helpers in Missions (HIM). In his junior year, Snethen was asked to speak in chapel. This talk led to his being asked to serve as chaplain of Alpha Gamma Omega, his social service club, and he coordinated their weekly devotionals held in Scott Chapel. In this role, he also had the opportunity to "minister to individual needs," and that service was having an effect on him, as well.[18] After graduation in 1998, Snethen went to Bristol, England, as a HIM worker with the Bedminster Church of Christ. At the end of his term, he returned to Oklahoma to serve at the Westside Church of Christ in Norman, Oklahoma, and taught social studies in Spencer, Oklahoma. His heart, however, was still in Bristol, and in 2001 he returned there with U.S. support to serve as a full-time minister. In 2003, Snethen married Heidi Holder, a British Christian, and continues to work for the church in Bristol.

Conclusion

Stories about students whose years at Oklahoma Christian have given them spiritual growth could be multiplied a hundred-fold, but these cases demonstrate the wide variety of ways the influences at Oklahoma Christian contribute to the spiritual growth of its students. Over its first fifty-eight years, Oklahoma Christian has, indeed, provided "a school where young people may continue their education under Christian environment and influence" and has strengthened "young people in character," preparing "them for Christian service, regardless of their calling in life."[19]

Chapter 13, Endnotes

1   *Central Christian College Catalog*, 1950, 6, OC Archives.
2   George M. Marsden and Bradly J. Longfield, *The Secularization of the Academy* (New York: Oxford Press, 1992), 158.
3   "Q & A with the Chairman," *Vision*, Spring 2007, 3–4.
4   "Chapel Change," *OCC Reporter*, October, 1982, OC Archives.
5   *Aerie*, 1967–68, 156–157.
6   "Young Preachers Reach Out In Week-End Rallies," *Oklahoma Christian College Reporter*, January, 1973.
7   Tina Wiggs, "Harvesters and Gleaners Provide Christian Leadership and Spiritual Unity For All Campus Residents," *Aerie*, 1984–85, 186, OC Archives.
8   Tricia Clarkson, "College Women for Christ," *Aerie*, 1995, 97; Tamie Willis, Email to the author on June 19, 2008.
9   "First Youth Forum Huge Success," *Oklahoma Christian College Bulletin*, May, 1959, OC Archives.
10 "Youth Forum," *Oklahoma Christian College Bulletin*, February, 1962, OC Archives.
11 "Youth Forum To Feature Stop, Look And Go Theme," *Oklahoma Christian College Reporter*, January, 1972, OC Archives.
12 *OCC Reporter*, December, 1980, 7, OC Archives.
13 "Making a Child's Life Better One Hour at a Time," *Vision*, Summer 2004, 5–6.
14 Jeff Bennett, Conversation with the author, April 17, 2008.
15 Chuck White, Interview with the author, May 19, 2008.
16 Daniel Langdon, Email to the author, April 21, 2008.
17 Jason Snethen, Email to the author, May 13, 2008.
18 Ibid.
19 *Catalog*, 1950.

Chapter 14
THE MISSIONARY SPIRIT

Oklahoma Christian is "a college with the map of the world imprinted on its heart." Dr. Jerry Rushford, an OCC graduate of 1965 and long-time professor at Pepperdine, used these words as he spoke at the OCC Lectureship on January 25, 1988. His comments pictured well the strong missionary spirit so pervasive on the Oklahoma Christian campus that its dedicated alumni are quite literally all over the world.

From its beginning, the university has had a missions thrust, leading many to commit themselves to spreading the gospel to all nations. There is a world map in the Biblical Studies Center that designates by numbered pins the more than two hundred former OC students who have served as missionaries and the regions in which they have worked. This chapter details the activities and people that have stirred the missionary zeal leading so many from Oklahoma Christian to become missionaries and tells a few of their stories.

The Beginnings in Bartlesville

From its earliest days in Bartlesville, Central Christian College promoted missions. Missionaries spoke in chapel and at a weekly missions meeting. Zelma Lawyer, English teacher and dormitory supervisor who had spent four years in Africa, encouraged students to consider missions, as did Roy Lanier, head of the Bible Department, and Dr. James Baird, the first dean and the second president of CCC. Baird and his family, in fact, were packed and ready to go to Nigeria when President Wilson resigned and the Board of Trustees selected Baird as president. From those eight years in Bartlesville and with a small student body came twenty-three students who became long-term missionaries in places like Italy, Sweden, Brazil, China, Nigeria, Cameroon, and Nhowe Mission. So by the time the college moved to Oklahoma City, the spirit of missions was already strong on the Central Christian College campus.

Mission Study and Outreach

Taylor Carter

The interest in missions continued once the college moved to Oklahoma City. In 1958, sixteen were in the Mission Study club with business faculty member Taylor Carter as sponsor. They communicated with missionaries to learn about their work and created missions interest among students. This missions group brought as campus speakers Jordan Wen from Formosa and Otis Gatewood, missionary to Germany.[1] The next year, missionaries from Sweden, Australia, and Switzerland spoke.[2]

By 1964, Mission Study often had a hundred people at their meetings. Their goal was to "stimulate interest in evangelizing the world, to teach methods of evangelism, and to point out great opportunities for evangelism."[3] The group held a Mission Study Workshop on the campus and brought missionaries Otis Gatewood and Maurice Hall as speakers. Ivan Stewart also spoke to the mission study group about conducting small campaigns, and they held several door-knocking efforts in the area. Leonard Johnson was sponsor that year.[4] Dr. Ron Bever became sponsor in 1965 and continued in that role until 1974. In 1968, the group changed its name to Outreach but continued with the same mission.

Dr. Ron Bever

Bever and Outreach officers had a well-defined strategy for increasing attendance at the meetings and, thus, promoting interest in missions. They encouraged campus leaders such as Student Senate members and club officers to be part of Outreach so, through their involvement, others would attend. They also held an All-School Retreat each third week in September. All OCC

All-School Retreat, Fall of 1974

students were invited, but the event was primarily for missions recruitment. They brought an inspiring missionary as the speaker and introduced the various locations to which missions campaigns would be going that year. Using this strategy, by 1969–1970, three hundred students a week often attended the Monday Outreach meetings. From these students, they built attendance for the World Mission Workshop in October, and by November, they had groups well established for the coming year of campaigns.[5]

In 1968, Outreach did three door-knocking campaigns and conducted a spring break campaign at the University of New Mexico, where OCC students contacted students on the campus to engage them in conversations about religious questions and to invite them to visit the Church of Christ Student Center.[6] In 1970, the group took

Spring Break Campaign to the University of New Mexico

a hundred OCC students to the World Mission Workshop held at Northeastern Christian College in Pennsylvania. They also did campaigns on three university campuses: Oklahoma State University, the University of New Mexico, and Kansas State University.[7]

When Bever stepped out of his work with Outreach in 1974 because of other responsibilities, Ralph Burcham became sponsor and served through 1992. Bill Goad sponsored the group in 1993, and after that, Gary Shreck was sponsor from 1994 until 2005, when Bob Carpenter took that role.[8]

Throughout OC's history, then, a group of students interested in missions has met weekly to study about the work of missionaries, to hear from those returning from the field, to design activities on the campus to promote a missionary spirit, and to plan for mission campaigns. Under student leadership, with assistance from a faculty sponsor, this group has played a major role in promoting missions at Oklahoma Christian.

Professors Returning from the Mission Field

Through the years, one of the most important factors in developing a strong interest in missions at Oklahoma Christian has been the presence on the faculty of those who have returned from the mission field. Zelma Lawyer filled that role at Bartlesville, and others have done the same since the move to Oklahoma City. Howard Horton, a missionary in Nigeria and Japan, came in 1966 to teach Bible and serve as dean of students. In 1977, Howard Norton, who had previously been a visiting missionary, came as a member of the faculty. Norton had served for sixteen years as part of a missionary team in Brazil. At Oklahoma Christian, he not only taught Bible but also served for ten years as chair of the Bible department. Two others from the same Brazil team also taught Bible: Don Vinzant from 1989 to 1997 and John Pennisi from 1981 to 1996. Bob Carpenter, another missionary to Brazil, joined the faculty in 1998 and continues to teach at OC. Dr. John Harrison came to OC in 2000, having served for six years as a missionary to Northern Ireland and Scotland. In addition to these, Dr. Alan Martin, from South Africa, Dr. Jim Baird, who preached in England while studying at Oxford, and Dr. Harold Shank, who was a domestic missionary in Wisconsin, have each brought an important missions perspective.

Dr. Mark Woodward

Also of importance has been the presence of returning missionaries who have taught in departments other than Bible. In 1979, Dr. Mark Woodward came to teach English after he and his wife Sherrylee had spent eight years in Germany. During his years at OCC, Woodward developed the concept of helping people learn English while using the Bible as their reading material and topic of conversation. This plan allowed English-speakers to provide a service to those in other countries wanting to learn English, while at the same time giving them the opportunity to learn about the Bible. The first to use this method were two groups of OCC students of five each who went to Germany in the summer of 1981. This plan, called "Let's Start Talking," became so large that Woodward left OC in 2002 to give full-time management to this program. In 2006 alone, LST sent 430 Christians to 29 countries.[9] Over the years, LST has trained and sent over five thousand people to sixty-five different countries, with over five hundred of these being students from Oklahoma Christian.[10] Other returning missionaries include Gail Nash, who taught English after three years in Portugal and seven years in Germany, and Ralph Burcham, who took leave from OCC in 1966 to serve two years in Vietnam.

These missionaries who have taught at Oklahoma Christian after their mission work abroad have helped build the mission spirit at Oklahoma Christian. As "real life" examples of people who have gone abroad, they have stirred interest through their contact with students, encouraged missions, and often taken groups abroad on campaigns.

Teachers and Administrators from Outside the Bible Faculty

Almost everyone who analyzes the unusual success at Oklahoma Christian in producing missionaries mentions the strong support for missions not only from Bible teachers, but from other faculty and administrators, as well. In addition to Lawyer, Woodward, and Nash, all of whom taught English, and Burcham who taught business, there have been others: Elmo Hall in English, John Maple in history, Gary Shreck in education, and Ron Bever in communications. James Baird, while president, Stafford North, while dean of the college, Bailey McBride while academic dean, Bob Smith while dean of admissions and registrar, and Katherine Brown while dean of women, all led or helped with campaigns. Head Librarian Tamie Willis has been on fifteen spring break campaigns to Mexico.

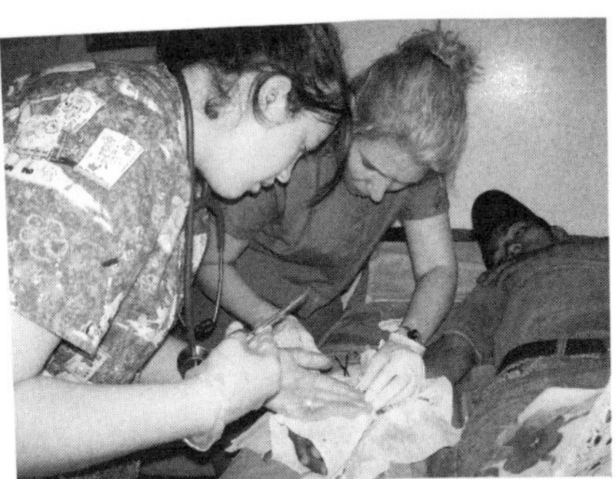

In Honduras, OC nursing student Rebecca McGonagill sutures a wound while Linda Fly assists.

Two departments at Oklahoma Christian have connected campaigns to the particular skills they teach students. Dr. Ben Hutchison in engineering began a program of taking engineering students to Honduras to work on water systems to provide assistance and bring goodwill to the church. In nursing, Linda Fly has initiated a program that takes nursing students to Honduras to do medical missions, both to help students' skills and to create in them an interest in missions.

Of these faculty, Mark Woodward said:

> Probably the most unique trait of the spirit of missions that has been a part of OCC for a long time, was that this spirit flowed not just out of the Bible or Missions Departments, but was equally apparent in faculty and staff across the entire campus. . . . The Administration never saw this as a distraction from, but rather an enhancement of Oklahoma Christian's core purpose.[11]

Upon Ralph Burcham's retirement in 1992, Dr. Howard Norton said, "Mission work permeates . . . Oklahoma Christian because it has emanated from other departments. Today you can look at every one of our departments and find people vitally interested in missions."[12]

World Mission Workshop

In 1961, colleges among Churches of Christ began a joint annual meeting to encourage students in missions, and Oklahoma Christian was among the early participants. This annual World Mission Workshop brings many leaders among Churches of Christ to deliver informative messages about missions around the world and provide stories of inspiration about spreading the gospel.

Ralph Burcham

Oklahoma Christian hosted the workshop in 1963, its third year, and the students planning the program and preparing materials needed help with printing. Since Ralph Burcham, of the OCC business faculty, was doing much of the printing for the college at that time, they turned to him for help. The students also insisted that, since he had helped them so much with getting things ready, he should attend the workshop. So the Burchams came, and by the end of the workshop, they had made a commitment to become active in missions themselves.[13] Three years later, Burcham and his family met this obligation by going to Vietnam for two years. The war there was at its height, and they were sometimes in danger as they carried out their work to lead people to Christ. He has detailed his story in a book called *Vietnam—Triumphs and Tragedies*, published in 2007.

In 1970, OCC again hosted the Workshop. Ron Bever was sponsor and Ralph Burcham, cosponsor. Since the expected crowd was too large for Hardeman Auditorium, the final session was held at the Civic Center Music Hall in downtown Oklahoma City. At this last session, with some 2,000 present, 200 people committed themselves to enter mission work, 112 of these from OCC.[14]

Flag Ceremony at the World Mission Workshop

The World Mission Workshop has been held on the Oklahoma Christian campus a total of seven times: 1963, 1970, 1977, 1984, 1992, 1999, and 2007. These have all been banner years for a missions emphasis as students, along with faculty sponsors, work for many months to plan the sessions, market the event, prepare the campus for hundreds of visitors, and get speakers to come from all over the world.

In the years when Oklahoma Christian has not been hosting the conference, a large number of students have attended. Often, OC has taken the most students of any Christian college to the workshop, testifying to the strong campus interest in missions. This annual program has been a major factor in helping OC to continue a high level of student interest in missions.

Campaigns

One of the strongest forces moving Oklahoma Christian students toward an interest in missions has been the campaigns in which groups of students, typically under the leadership of faculty members, have gone to work with churches either in other states or overseas. While campaign expenses were borne by the individuals, usually with help from congregations, the students and sponsors were typically from the campus. In the summer of 1962, for example, Keith Marshall, OCC's baseball coach, took a group to Wyoming, and Roy Lanier, Jr., a minister in Norman, took six students to Canada. Individuals also went to Germany and Scotland.[15]

Another early type of campaign was for OCC students to spend their spring break at state university campuses to invite those students to attend activities at congregations near the campuses. Such campaigns grew in size over the years so that by 1973, when Dr. Lynn McMillon took a group to the University of New Mexico campus in Albuquerque, the number going reached seventy-six.[16]

Although OCC students had been going on campaigns to various places in the United States since the early sixties, and some students had been going to international destinations on their own, the first overseas campaign from the OCC campus came in 1967. The 12th and Drexel Church of Christ in Oklahoma City sponsored missionary Lloyd Collier in Wiesbaden, Germany, and decided to send a group to assist him. A total of sixteen made the trip, including ten students. These campaigns to Germany continued almost every year thereafter. Dean Bob Smith took the group in 1976, and Ralph Burcham began sponsoring the campaign in 1978, eventually leading nine groups over the following years.[17]

These campaigns to Germany had a significant effect as students who had gone returned to the campus to tell how they had spread the gospel message in another country, and to share the positive spiritual benefits they received.[18] In 1971, Dr. Ron Bever took twenty students on a campaign to British Honduras, establishing a new congregation there. Bever led campaigns to the same location three more years, with the number rising to forty-three the last year with still more congregations established and

Dr. Elmo Hall

existing ones strengthened.[19] Dr. Elmo Hall went on the last three of these campaigns to British Honduras (known as Belize after 1973) and then led ten campaigns to Trinidad, where students made contact with people who would study with them. From these studies also came baptisms and new congregations. Dr. Darvin Keck went with Hall to assist with four of these campaigns.

In 1980, while Hall was in Trinidad with seventeen students, they were confronted by a group of local radicals called Rastas who sat in the outdoor tent meetings to frighten people away and confronted Hall with questions. During the night, the Rastas cut tent ropes and poured gasoline on the tent and burned about a twenty by twenty hole in it before the fire could be doused. Hall reported, "The conduct of the campaigners and the local Christians made a strong impact on the townspeople. The Christians' patience and lack of vindictiveness were a great testimony to the non-Christians. Many townspeople came and apologized for the incidents." Despite the opposition, Hall reported that fourteen were baptized.[20]

In 1976, sixteen different groups from Oklahoma Christian went on campaigns either abroad or to the northeastern United States. Some of these went over spring break, but most went during the summer, usually for a month or six weeks. In that year, 103 OCC students went to Australia, Belgium, Brazil, Canada, Germany, Japan (two groups), Ireland, Scotland, Trinidad, Yugoslavia, and the northeastern United States. Student Roger Massey led the Yugoslavia campaign, which marked the first time OCC students went behind the Iron Curtain. Individual students also went to Sweden and Switzerland.

When Howard Norton joined the OCC faculty in 1977, he began to encourage campaigns to Brazil, and with the participation of other faculty who had been missionaries to Brazil, Don Vinzant, Johnny Pennisi, and Bob Carpenter, OC has sent a campaign or a Let's Start Talking group to Brazil every year since that time.

By 1981, the total number of OCC students going on campaigns had risen to 317, the largest number to that point, and this from a student body of 1,488. Some of these groups went over the fall and spring breaks and some in the summer. In 1984, Dr. Gary Shreck led his first group to Hungary and followed that with sixteen other trips, the last in 2002. Dr. John Maple took campaigns to Oxford, England, in 1987 and 1988, and Dr. Loren Gieger took the group there in 1989. Maple resumed taking a campaign to the British Isles in 1990, going twelve

Dr. Gary Shreck

Dr. John Maple

more times with the focus on Loughborough, England, and Dundee, Scotland. For ten years in the 1980s and 1990s, John and Katherine Brown led campaigns to London, England, where they established a congregation in the Wimbledon YMCA.

From 1990 through 2003, Clyde and Gwen Antwine took campaigns to Germany, with the total number of students going during those years at 198. Dr. Dudley Chancey, who joined the OC Bible faculty in 1998, has had a major impact on student campaigns. He has led many groups to Honduras and helped arrange for others. Since his coming, campaigns have gone there every year. Kent and Nancy Hartman came to serve as missionaries-in-residence in 2002 and have taken campaigns to Australia each summer since they arrived.

OC student with children in Mexico

Over the years, many other OC faculty and staff have been active in campaigns. Carolyn Castleman took groups to France, Lynn and Joy McMillon led campaigns to Australia, Joe McCormack to Japan, Phil Heffington to Belize, Phil Parmer to Germany, Brad Robison to Korea, John Thompson to the Bahamas, Curt Niccum to Germany, Lois Exendine to Japan, Jack Skaggs to the Northeastern United States, Darrel Alexander to Japan, Lynda Sheehan to Venezuela, David North to Germany, David Cassel to Peru, Darin Martin to Albania, John Harrison to Northern Ireland, Alex Humphrey to points in Asia, Ralph DeBoard to Australia, Richard Poe to Ethiopia, Bryan Hixson to Rwanda, and Jeff McMillon to the Village of Hope in Ghana. Undoubtedly there are others, but these examples suggest both the wide range of countries receiving campaigns and the wide spread of those on campus leading them.[21]

The number going on campaigns continues to be impressive. In 2007–2008, for example, the number involved in fall and spring break, as well as summer campaigns, totaled more than four hundred. Local congregations such as Memorial Road, Quail Springs, Britton Road, and Edmond have been major players in continuing the interest in campaigns with their financial support and assistance with campaigns each year. Local reporter John Williams, for example, wrote in the *Daily Oklahoman* about the spring break campaign sponsored by the Edmond Church of Christ, "Right now, 24 white vans from the Edmond Church of Christ are taking more than 200 college students

OC students work to build a
church building in Mexico.

to Mexico for the next 10 days. There they will travel to villages near Aquiles Serdan, improving homes, laying pipelines to bring potable water to the villages and constructing church buildings and a camp. This is the church's 19th annual mission to the mountains of Mexico."[22] In addition, the group also held a medical clinic, taught individual Bible classes, and held a VBS.

Campaign groups engage in a wide range of activities. In some cases, students study the Bible one-on-one with those wanting to learn from the Scriptures. Sometimes they use the LST program for English conversation through using the Bible. In other cases, they work to interest local people in attending special lectures or meetings by singing on street corners, passing out leaflets, or engaging strangers in conversations. Sometimes they build or repair church buildings, build homes for church members, teach VBS programs, assist with medical clinics, or even play sports with young people to attract them for a Bible lesson.

While the major purpose of these campaigns is to strengthen Christians and churches abroad, they also make an impact on the campaigners, who return stronger in the Lord. And many of those who go on campaigns later become full-time missionaries.

The HIM Program

In 1974, the College Church of Christ (now Memorial Road), adjacent to the OCC campus, decided to encourage recent graduates to do mission work for one or two years before embarking on their careers. Marilyn Hankins suggested the name HIM, for "Helpers in Missions."[23] The plan encouraged the graduates to go where missionaries were already working to accomplish three goals: to provide assistance for the missionaries, thus strengthening churches around the world; to provide an experience for graduating students to strengthen them spiritually and create in them a lifelong interest in missions; and to provide an experience that would lead some to decide to become long-term missionaries. Memorial Road normally pays about 40 percent of the salary of the HIM workers, who raise the remainder for salary and expenses from other churches or individuals.

Dr. Bob and Donna Carpenter

The first two students going abroad as HIM workers were Donna Buchanan and Glenda Pope, who went to Brazil. In an interesting turn of events, while there Buchanan met Bob Carpenter, who was in Brazil on a research project. Later the two were married and served a decade as full-time missionaries in Brazil. Now Bob Carpenter teaches missions at OC and is sponsor of Outreach.

In the early years, only one or two people went as HIM workers, but after Clyde Antwine and later Kent Hartman came to serve as OC missionaries-in-residence, the numbers grew to as many as fifteen a year. By 2007–2008, ninety-seven had served either one or two years as HIM workers, and of these, nineteen either stayed longer than their terms or returned later to work as missionaries. OC graduates going on the HIM program have worked in Africa, South America, Central America, North America, Australia and New Zealand, the Asian nations of Malaysia and Indonesia, and six nations in Europe.

Jonathan Hanegan, for example, went in 2006 to Caracas, Venezuela, as a two-year HIM worker already fluent in Spanish. He has had great success in preaching, working with youth programs, and encouraging Christians both in Caracas and in other locations. He continued there after his term ended. Laurie Norton went in 1980 as a HIM worker to Guatemala. Later she married Allen Diles, and they

Jonathan Hanegan in Caracas

worked for many years in the Czeck Republic. Amber Foster went to Honduras in 2004 on a two-year term but has stayed to continue her work, particularly with children and youth, and she helps with campaigns that come there.

The Antwines and Hartmans oversee the HIM program, not only recruiting students to accept the challenge but helping train them as well. Since students are graduates of OC, they already have had at least sixteen college hours in Bible courses. The training, therefore, concentrates on how to function in a different culture, how to join in the work with their supervising missionaries, and how to make regular reports. Typically they begin training in November and meet weekly through the end of the school year. After the HIM workers are on the field, Clyde and Gwen Antwine usually visit them at least once a year at their field location.[24]

The HIM program has been highly successful in getting OC graduates to spend two years soon after graduation on a mission field where they can assist an established church. Working closely with missionaries on the field, they extend the capacity of those missionaries by working with youth, teaching, assisting in worship services, and helping the churches to be better known among the locals. In this way, the HIM program is having a positive influence in missions all over the world.

Ibaraki Christian College Exchange Program

OC student and friends in Japan

In 1975, President James Baird sought to broaden the experience of Oklahoma Christian students by initiating an exchange program with Ibaraki Christian College in Japan. He believed that bringing a group of ICC students to Oklahoma Christian and sending a group of OCC students to Japan not only would offer mutual cultural enrichment, but also would help Japanese students have a greater appreciation for the church worldwide while creating in the OCC students an interest in returning to Japan to help churches there.

A look at the map in the Biblical Studies Center confirms the effectiveness of this program. The heavy concentration of pins on Japan shows the large number of students who have returned to Japan, particularly to teach English. After having been there with the Ibaraki program or the university's Pacific Rim semester abroad, many students return to teach English and to help the church there. Long-time OC English professor Joe McCormack has been instrumental in building interest in Japan in many ways: sponsoring campaign groups to Japan, initiating the major in Teaching English as a Foreign Language, spending a year as an exchange professor at Ibaraki Christian College, and encouraging students to go there to work.

International Study Programs

The first Oklahoma Christian overseas study program began in 1965 when eleven students traveled to various places in Europe, somewhat on their own. In 1986, OCC began its Vienna Studies Program, which offered students a much more structured program for travel and study in Europe. In this program, students and faculty sponsors connect with churches there to participate with them in their activities. The students sometimes work with the youth, do individual studies, and assist in spreading information about events the church is having.

In 1997, OC expanded its Ibaraki Exchange Program to include visits to other locations in the Far East. Now called the Pacific Rim Program, students not only visit Japan, but also China, Singapore, Australia, and New Zealand. More recently, OC has also established an international studies program in Central America. Most of the students in these international study programs develop long-term interest in the places where they have been and in the churches there, sometimes leading to their return as missionaries.

An excellent example of how this connection can blossom into later mission work is seen in the team of four couples, all OC graduates, who moved to Vienna in 2007. All of them had been on the Vienna Studies Program and/or overseas campaigns, and those experiences had planted seeds for them to return to serve as missionaries.

Visiting Missionaries

After Ralph Burcham returned from Vietnam, he was inclined to leave college teaching to serve full time on the mission field. He and President James Baird discussed several times ways in which Oklahoma Christian could increase its influence in missions. These sessions led Burcham to decide he could do more "mission work" by staying to encourage and train missionaries on the OCC campus than by returning to the mission field. Among the conclusions Baird and Burcham reached was for OCC to have a faculty member who especially gave his or her time to encouraging mission activities. Since the school could not afford that, Baird suggested they seek a congregation that would continue its support of a missionary while letting him come back to the U.S. to spend a term at Oklahoma Christian. The missionary could teach some Bible classes and, in addition, promote missionary activities among the students.

Howard Norton was the first missionary contacted about coming to fill such a role and he came in the spring of 1971 and returned again in 1973 and 1975. Norton created so much campus interest in missions, the college decided to continue the visiting missionary program. Two others came in 1980, and since the spring of 1987, OC has had a visiting missionary every year, except

Howard Norton

for 1997–1998 and 2001–2002. A total of twenty-eight have served in this role, sometimes staying for one term, sometimes for the entire school year, and some more than once. These missionaries have come from all over the world: Europe, Australia and New Zealand, South America, Central America, both the Near East and the Far East, Africa, and locations in the United States.

These Christians have taught classes, provided excellent role models, formed campaign groups, recruited missionaries to work with them when they returned, and generally promoted spiritual growth on the campus.

Missionaries in Residence

Clyde and Gwen Antwine

The first permanent missionary-in-residence at Oklahoma Christian came in January 1988, when Clyde Antwine arrived along with his wife, Gwen. The Antwines had been missionaries in Germany and Switzerland for twenty years and had decided their best way now to serve was to work on a Christian college campus, recruiting and training students to be missionaries. They chose to come to Oklahoma Christian at the urging of Dr. Howard Norton, then chair of the Bible department, and Board member Dr. John Sudbury, and also because Clyde knew of OCC's strong missions spirit. The congregation in Del City, along with individuals who had been supporting them, continued to provide for the couple as they moved into this new role, thus allowing them to serve both OCC and missions around the world. Later, the Memorial Road Church of Christ joined in this support to allow Antwine time to direct the HIM program.[25]

As a missionary-in-residence, Antwine teaches one class each term, including such courses as mission preparation, mission methods, and the local church and missions, as well as courses in various biblical topics. In his work, he has encouraged many to be missionaries in various places throughout the world. He was, for example, primarily responsible for recruiting and training a mission team for Dresden, in formerly Soviet-occupied Germany, composed of six students from Oklahoma Christian: Randy and Brianna Carroll, Robert and Brenda Stolte, and Steve and Kristi Martin.

In 2002, Kent and Nancy Hartman, both OCC alumni returning from seventeen years of mission work in Australia, came to be the university's second couple as missionaries-in-residence. They both teach classes and make regular contacts with students, encouraging them to go on campaigns, take part in the HIM program, and work as long-term missionaries. Each Friday in chapel, Kent presents a "missionary minute," in which he reminds students of the importance of missions and ways they can take

Kent and Nancy Hartman

part by giving a quick look at something happening on the mission field. Nancy also promotes missions and teaches a popular course called "Women in Missions."

Missions Courses and Missions Major

In 1972, the Oklahoma Christian Bible Department began to offer both courses in missions and a missions major. That year saw the addition of courses in Biblical Mission Methods and Missionary Preparation. These two courses, along with World Religions and a missionary practicum, then constituted the specific missions curriculum. Of course, students also took both textual and nontextual Bible courses and often gained practical experience on campaigns.

By 2008, OC was offering forty-two hours in missions and missions-related courses, and the missions degree called for students to take nineteen hours in missions courses along with other work in Bible and religious education.

Conclusion

All through its fifty-eight years, the Oklahoma Christian administration, faculty, and staff have held a high interest in missions. From its earliest beginnings in Bartlesville through its fifty years in Oklahoma City, the missionary spirit has always been strong. From the work of many faculty and student leaders, the Outreach program has stimulated interest in missions and a large number of students have participated in campaigns and the HIM program. Bible faculty and professors in other departments have motivated students toward involvement in some type of missionary activity and have participated in these activities with them. Sometimes the mission work has been in the U.S., but more often it has taken place in nations abroad. The missionaries-in-residence and visiting missionaries have, likewise, stimulated interest and participation in various kinds of mission work, and local congregations have also played an important part. OC's missions major has also contributed by helping prepare students for their work as missionaries.

The story of one of the many mission teams that have formed at Oklahoma Christian illustrates how the range of factors at OC work together to lead students toward missions. Between 1994 and 1996, eight students came to Oklahoma Christian, not knowing each other, and only one of these had any intention of being a missionary: Terry Fischer, Kelli Bryan, David Duncan, Barbara Dulohery, Rick Sandoval, Monika Harrison, Taylor Cave, and Connie Hanks. These students all attended Outreach, they all had former missionaries as teachers, they all participated in overseas experiences like the foreign study programs and campaigns, they attended World Mission Workshops, they came in contact with visiting missionaries—and, in the process, they became four married couples with the common purpose of establishing a congregation in Brazil.

Left to right standing—the Caves, the Fischers, the Sandovals, and the Duncans

Under the guidance of professors like Howard Norton and John Pennisi they developed into a missionary team. Three of the men continued at OC to receive a master of ministry degree. In 1992, the four couples left the U.S. for Vitoria, Brazil, where they stayed from seven to twelve years, learning the language and customs, meeting people, holding Bible studies, working with children and youth, helping the needy, and conducting worship services. And they raised money in the United States to help their work. By the time they had all come home to find other ways to serve the Lord, they left a congregation of a hundred in an excellent building free of debt. Teston and Jo Gilpatrick, OC alumni from earlier years who have spent most of their lives in Brazil, came to work with the congregation as the four couples were leaving.

The missions environment at OC had done its work, and these four couples carried the gospel message to a distant land. All those who know this team mourn for Rick Sandoval, who died in a private plane crash in 2007. The work of this team lives on the lives of those Brazilians they influenced for the Lord, and their experience there serves them well as they now work in churches in the United States.

Adam Langford

Another OC alumnus who chose to serve as a missionary also died in 2007. Adam Langford, class of 2001, was killed in a highway accident as he was serving in Uganda. The campus was stunned and sorrowful that this young man and his family suffered such a tragedy. His brother, Ben, also a missionary in Uganda, told those at the funeral that on the day following his death, Adam was scheduled to see the king of Uganda "to speak of missions." The last text message Ben received from his brother contained these words, "I'm going to see the King tomorrow." While the reference was to an earthly king, the statement came true about a heavenly king. Neil Arter, OC's dean of students commented: "He died doing what he wanted to do, and that was serving the Lord he loved."[26]

The sentiment of doing what they wanted to do, serving the Lord they loved, could be said of many OC students and alumni who have imbibed the missionary spirit of Oklahoma Christian and gone throughout the world to serve. Indeed, Oklahoma Christian does have "the imprint of the world on its heart," and the forces that have created this imprint are still strong on the OC campus.

Chapter 14, Endnotes

[1]   "Mission Study for Students," *Focus*, 1959, 46, OC Archives.
[2]   *Focus*, 1960, 38, OC Archives.
[3]   *Aerie*, 1964, 110, OC Archives.
[4]   Ibid.
[5]   Ron Bever, Phone conversation with the author, May 27, 2008.
[6]   *Aerie*, 1969, 175, OC Archives.
[7]   *Aerie*, 1970, 219, OC Archives.
[8]   Gary Shreck, Conversation with the author on May 27, 2008.
[9]   Erik Tryggestad, "Let's Start Talking: Ministry asks churches to send 10,000 workers," *Christian Chronicle*, November, 2007, 1, 16.
[10] Mark Woodward, Email to the author on May 26, 2008.
[11] Ibid.
[12] "Burcham was 'Pivotal,'" *Oklahoma Christian Reporter*, July-August, 1992, 4, OC Archives.
[13] Ralph Burcham, Interview with the author on May 26, 2008.
[14] Ron Bever, "Workshop Results in 200 Mission Work Commitments," *Oklahoma Christian College Bulletin*, October, 1970, OC Archives.
[15] "Students Scatter to Mission Fields," *Oklahoma Christian College Bulletin*, July, 1962, OC Archives.
[16] "Campus Evangelism Travels to Albuquerque Once More," *Talon*, Feb. 2, 1973.
[17] Ibid.
[18] Burcham.
[19] Bever, Interview.
[20] Lindy Adams, "Dr. Elmo Hall Has Brush With Political Radicals During Caribbean Campaign," *OCC Reporter*, August, 1980, 4, OC Archives.
[21] "Students and Staff Plan Mission Efforts for Summer," *OCC Reporter*, February, 1982, 2, OC Archives; "Where Campaigners From OCC Will Go This Summer," *OCC Reporter*, April-May, 1985, 12, OC Archives; "Where Campaigners From OCC Will Go This Summer," *OCC Reporter,*, February, 1983, 12, OC Archives.
[22] John A. Williams, "Mission trips help teens to be involved in volunteerism," *Daily Oklahoman*, March 13, 2008, Edmond section, 1.
[23] Ralph Burcham, Email to the author, June 6, 2008.
[24] Clyde Antwine, Interview with the author on May 19, 2008.
[25] Ibid.
[26] Rachel Chisholm, "University remembers Adam Langford," *Talon* online, January 26, 2007.

Chapter 15
THE STUDENT LIFE

From its beginning, Oklahoma Christian University has provided opportunities for students to participate in a wide array of campus activities.   Believing they learn valuable lessons through such involvement, the university has encouraged students to join in these activities by requiring single students away from home to live on campus. Until 1985, more than 90 percent of students lived in campus housing and, while the number since then has varied somewhat, the number is still above 80 percent.

While other chapters describe facets of student life such as the spiritual life, mission activities, athletics, music and theatre, student publications, and student government, this chapter focuses on six other areas of student life: how new freshmen have been introduced to the campus, life in the residence halls, campus standards and expectations, social life, social service clubs, and the student productions of Spring Sing and Freshman Fanfare.

Freshman Orientation

Since its early years in Bartlesville, Oklahoma Christian has always used a one-semester-hour course to introduce new students to college life. This course has focused on their opportunities, the expectations they are to meet, academic requirements, and study skills. At first, Mrs. Oma Belle Carter, librarian, and the current academic dean taught the course, which lasted through the fall term.[1]

After moving to Oklahoma City, several staff members collaborated to teach this one-hour course to help freshmen students get started well. The content of the course continued to be similar to the one taught in Bartlesville.

Not connected with the course, but starting after CCC moved to Oklahoma City and running through the early 70s, incoming freshmen experienced Fish Week. These days were a time when upperclassmen subjected freshmen to various indignities with the general intention of helping them feel accepted. One day of the week, for example, freshmen had to wear an onion around their necks and dress in outlandish garb. Another day they had to dress up. They were also subject to carrying out requests from upperclassmen such as standing on a table in the cafeteria and singing the alma mater or carrying books.

Fish Week Fun

While it was intended all in good fun, after a time it was discontinued because it was too much like "hazing," which was going out of style.

In September 1966, the *Oklahoma Christian College Bulletin* carried a story headed "New Course Battles Dropout Rate."[2] The article says Dean Stafford North, department heads, and off-campus consultants helped design the new plan, which was "three years in the making." The course taught students about graduation requirements, related the students' goals to those of the college, and presented the philosophy of higher education "as it relates to liberal arts, general education, career training, religious development, support of colleges and values in attending college."[3] The course also included information on the history and traditions of the college, academic policies, and information on study skills, including use of the library. Teaching methods for the course included lectures, films, textbooks, and listening to audiotapes in the college's new learning center.[4] Teachers tested the students over the content and asked students for reports on activities they were to complete. It was a substantial one-hour college course.

"Doc" Bailey McBride talks with a group of students during Neat Week '73.

The next major change in the freshman orientation program came in 1973. That year, the college administration began offering orientation for incoming freshmen as a week-long course to take either June 4 through 8 or the week before the start of classes in September. This orientation course, a slightly slimmed down version of the previous one, allowed time both for students to take CLEP exams to test out of some introductory courses and to complete enrollment for fall. The week included a large number of get-acquainted activities, and those attending got a taste of dorm life and eating in the cafeteria. Incoming freshmen taking the course during the week before the start of the fall term got the same content, except the CLEP tests were not part of the scheduled events. To increase the week's "sales appeal," college administrators called the five-day session "Neat Week." Student response was positive with seventy-five incoming freshmen attending the first year.[5] As the number coming increased, the college added a second Neat Week in July, and over the years, those attending these early two sessions grew to near three hundred.[6]

At first, Dr. Stafford North, dean of the college, Dr. Bailey McBride, academic dean, and Dr. Lawrence Rhodes, dean of campus life, shared instructional sessions during Neat Week, while many others worked on various aspects of the week's program.[7] Most of the sessions were lectures with the opportunity for questions, but the week also offered some smaller group meetings. When Dr. Richard Mock became dean of students, he shared in the presentations, and there was always a session with librarians like Clarice French, Geneva Hoover, and Malcom Hinckley.

One of the interesting features of Neat Week was the Thursday night dinner when faculty members served as waiters. They brought plates to the tables, refilled water and tea glasses, and removed plates as students finished their meal. When students were through eating, the waiters became the Men's Faculty Glee Club to provide entertainment. This event was fun for everyone, and sent a message to students that the faculty really was interested in serving them.

Some of the speakers during the week referenced biblical principles and spoke of moral standards students were expected to follow. Devotionals during the week also gave students a taste of spiritual life on the campus.

Dr. North teaching at Neat Week in the Davisson American Heritage Auditorium

Two things many Neat Week students remember are "The Six-Shot Repeater Method" and "The Bob-Tailed Bull." These were devices North developed to help students with study skills. "The Six-Shot Repeater Method" provided a plan for study when classes used textbook assignments:

(1) look back at the chapter previously read, (2) scan the chapter to read next and then (3) read it, (4) preview the following chapter, (5) study the chapter again after taking notes in class, and then (6) review the chapter prior to the next test. In this way, students used "spaced repetition," covering each chapter six times—thus "The Six-Shot Repeater Method."[8]

Through "The Bob-Tailed Bull" story, North emphasized the importance of doing assignments on time. He told it like this:

> "An old rancher in Texas had a beautiful daughter many young men wanted to court, but without much success. Finally, one young man won her favor, and on a moon-lit night he pulled his Ford pick-up under a spreading mesquite tree and asked for her hand in marriage. She accepted, but on the condition he would gain her father's approval. 'Oh,' said the young man, 'for you I would swim the deepest river, cross the widest ocean, or climb the highest mountain. So I will certainly ask your father.'

> "He found the father in the ranch house living room, reading the newspaper. The young man entered, cleared his throat several times, and finally the father looked over the paper and said, 'Yeah, what do you want, boy.' The young man said, 'Sir, uh sir, you may have noticed that your daughter and I have been spending a lot of time with each other, and, well, we've fallen in love and want to get married. I'd like to ask for your permission.' The old rancher paused for a moment and drawled, 'Well, son, I've got a little test for you to see if you're fit to marry my daughter. Let's go out to the corral.'

> "In the pen, the rancher had thirteen bulls of different sizes and breeds. He told the young man, 'I'll get on m'pony, cut out each of these bulls and send 'em, one at a time, down the chute to the next corral. You stand there near the end of the chute, and all you have to do to get my permission is to grab any one of the bulls by the tail.'

> "The young man thought, 'This won't be so hard. I can do this.' But the first bull was rather large, so the young man let him go by, thinking another one would be safer. The second one was even bigger, so the young man thought, 'Surely there's a smaller one.' So he let that one go by. Next was a Brahma bull looking pretty mean, so he didn't try that one. Then came a Texas Longhorn with really long horns, so he let that one pass. And so it went until the young man was down

to the thirteenth and final bull. As this one came down the chute, the young suitor thought he had made a really good decision; this bull was not big or mean-looking at all. So as this bull passed by, he made a lunge for the tail, but—that bull was bob-tailed. No tail at all. And the old rancher had found out what he wanted to know. The young man had a character flaw; he put things off instead of using his opportunities well. And so the rancher said, 'Sorry, son, but you failed the test, and you can't marry my daughter.'"

Then North made the point. "Like thirteen bulls," he said, "a trimester has thirteen weeks of classes. If you let your papers and assignments wait, thinking I'll have more time later, or I've still got plenty of time, you will always find that the last week is 'bob-tailed,' and you won't get it all done. So do each week's work as that week comes along."[9]

Parents participating in their orientation

In 1990, Bob Lashley began a program of orientation for parents. These sessions, usually on the last day of student orientation, provided important information about the OC philosophy, academic programs, housing, health care, regulations, financial expectations, and other beneficial topics. Basically, the program, which continues to be offered, prepared parents to be good participants with their children in the OC experience.

In 1994, Dr. North retired from administration to become a full-time faculty member and so no longer did the orientation program. For twenty-eight years, Oklahoma Christian had passed all its incoming freshmen through the program developed in 1966, and for the last twenty-one years of that time, most of the university's students had attended the Neat Week program to complete the course and their fall registration during the summer. The other students took the course in the week prior to the opening of classes in the fall. Since the Neat Week experience was the first time for these incoming freshmen to live in the dorms, eat in the cafeteria, meet other incoming students, and take a college class, it became one of their strongest memories of college life.

Dr. Jim Wilson

Starting in the summer of 1995, college administrators selected Dr. Jim Wilson as the key person in orientation programs. A popular teacher who made an excellent connection with students, Wilson led most of the sessions during the Neat Weeks in June and July and in the August orientation week. These sessions continued with instruction on academic skills, but there was less testing and more emphasis on establishing relationships. Team-building games helped students develop connections with each other and with the college. Devotionals and the faculty-served dinner continued as important elements. Penny Eubank, then serving as registrar, led in the enrollment portions of the week. To acquaint students with the OC campus, they were given a passport and toured the campus to locate something in many of the buildings.

In 1996, Dr. Kevin Jacobs became president, and he selected Dr. Jeanine Varner to be vice president for academic affairs and Dr. Arlis Wood to be vice president for student life. Varner and Wood thus became responsible for overseeing the orientation of new students.

*Neil Arter at his usual post
for a campus cookout*

In 1998, Neil Arter became the director of freshman experience. In that year, new students came to an orientation session in June, July, or August for a Friday through Sunday program directed primarily at acquainting students with their major area and getting them enrolled. In 1999, the Student Life Office began "Earn Your Wings." Held during the week before classes began, the new program centered on developing relationships among the students. The activities included small group sessions and many get-acquainted activities. Evening activities included ice skating and a movie. Fall 1999 also brought a new course called Freshman Seminar. With classes meeting twice a week during the first five weeks of the fall term, this one-hour course encouraged good study habits, gave the students a good overview of the academic program, and helped them understand the spiritual life on campus.[10]

In 2002, Neil Arter was promoted to be dean of students, and Amy Janzen became director of freshman experience in 2003. In these roles, Arter and Janzen took the primary responsibility for orienting new students.

Amy Janzen

In 2003, administrators modified the orientation program. First, both freshmen and transfer students had a one-day session in May, June, or August for two purposes: to give the students their own laptops and to get them enrolled. Second, these students all came to campus the week before classes began for Earn Your Wings. This session, conducted primarily by students with guidance from the Student Life Office, started on Tuesday and ran through Saturday. Those not yet enrolled came on Tuesday to arrange their classes. Activities for everyone began Tuesday night with a welcome from President Mike O'Neal and a devotional speaker. During Earn Your Wings, students divided into "hub groups" that allowed about twenty incoming students to have small group time with three or four returning students. These groups met every day to help new students develop close friendships and to allow upper-class students to answer questions, rather than an administrator or faculty member.[11]

Since 2004, Earn Your Wings has provided two days of orientation on campus, Tuesday and Wednesday; then Thursday after lunch, all incoming students along with those working with the program, about 675 in all, travel to Dry Gulch. Located about forty miles northeast of Tulsa, this former movie set of a western town has been transformed into a retreat center. Students sleep in "bunk houses," eat in the "mess hall," and meet in the "town hall" for larger sessions. [12]

OC students ride to Dry Gulch in twelve charter busses. On the trip there and back they watch DVDs about OC, and group leaders on the bus make this time useful. Once at Dry Gulch, students have large group meetings for instruction, hear speakers on spiritual topics, and share in a candlelight devotional. They also meet in their hub groups to provide the opportunity for a small group atmosphere and discussion. Games, sports, and movies provide opportunities for fun and developing relationships. The students even swim in nearby

Candlelight Devotional at Dry Gulch

Lake Hudson wearing shorts and T-shirts. The rustic setting helps break the ice, and since everyone is dressed pretty much the same, the situation tends to level the playing field. Students cannot take their laptops, so they focus more on getting acquainted. They return Saturday at noon. [13]

The third element of the program is the Freshman Seminar, a class in which incoming freshmen study "the nature of a Christian liberal arts education," consider "the university's mission and its relation to their own personal mission and goals," and prepare to "succeed at Oklahoma Christian University."[14] Some OC colleges and departments have developed their own Freshman Seminar classes to help students who share the same major begin to get acquainted and to learn about that particular discipline, as well as study the specific topics covered in other sections of the class.

Since its earliest days Oklahoma Christian has provided incoming students with an introduction to college and to OC through a one-hour orientation course. This program has typically introduced the academic curricula, developed study skills, provided opportunities to develop relationships, prepared students to meet the moral standards and other regulations of the college, and given opportunities for spiritual development. Students who have experienced the program, whatever its form, recall this first introduction to OC as useful and fun.

Residence Hall Life

From its inception, Oklahoma Christian has provided students the opportunity to live in student housing. In those early years, eight men sometimes lived in one large room, and two-person dormitory rooms were small. The move to Oklahoma City brought better student housing with improved bath facilities, more lounge space for visiting, and more attractive design. Over time, however, students and parents came to expect even more: larger rooms, laundry facilities, microwaves, and access to

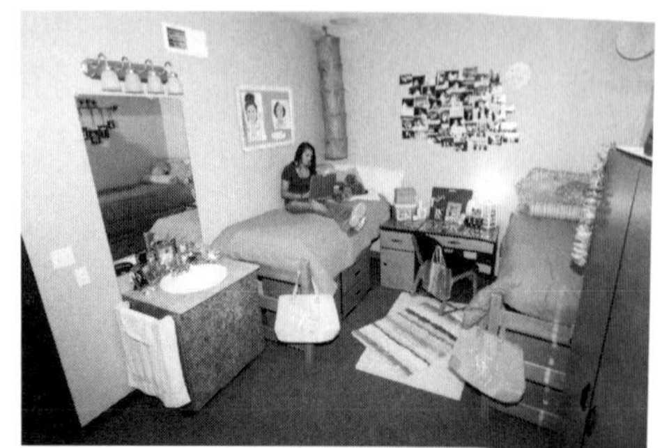

A student room in University House

exercise equipment. With its thirty-five million dollar housing initiative begun in 2005, OC was able both to improve existing residence halls and build new facilities. The new University House accommodates 206 students, and six new apartment buildings can serve another 385 students. Including some additional beds provided by space added to existing dormitories, the housing initiative allowed the college to add more than six hundred spaces for students. And these residences now offered the upscale conveniences many wanted.

Over the years, 80 to 90 percent of OC students have experienced living together in residence halls. They have learned both the joys and the challenges of roommates and they have participated in dormitory councils to deal with issues and problems.

The university has seen itself as a bridge between the home life of the adolescent and independent

Remodeled Tinius East Dormitory for women

adulthood, and an important part of crossing that bridge has been living with others in a residence hall. Students have learned to cope with close quarters and limits on activities, and they have had to learn to solve problems within their "families." All of these experiences are designed to be part of personal growth during the college years. These shared experiences have brought many lifetime friends, and students look back on their late-night conversations with fondness.

Living on campus has, of course, had other advantages. It has allowed students to participate in evening activities such as club meetings, intramurals, student government, student publications, plays, musicals, and athletics. And these experiences, in turn, have improved their skills in relationships and leadership.

Campus Standards of Conduct

Oklahoma Christian has been primarily residential and regards campus living as part of its total learning experience. Since the university seeks to help students live by Christian standards and since the conduct of one student often affects the conduct of others, OC has always had guidelines for students to follow.

1950–1958

Comparing student regulations of the early 1950s with those in 2008 gives the impression that rules were quite restrictive in those early years. The standards of conduct at Central Christian College in

Bartlesville, however, did not differ markedly from those of that time in other colleges among Churches of Christ. These institutions saw themselves as acting in the place of the parents, and parents held them accountable for such a role.

The 1953 *Student Handbook* provides several rules about conduct. "All boarding students are expected to attend church services both morning and evening on Sunday, and on Wednesday night." "Date night is designated as Friday night from 7:00–10:30." "After evening church services, students are to return immediately to their dorms, but may visit in the parlors until 10 p.m." "All associations between boys and girls after dinner are confined to dormitory parlors or patio if lighted." The dormitory host or hostess had to give permission for all off-campus dates, and on leaving the campus, "a couple must be accompanied by a chaperone or another couple." "Boys and girls, in their relationships one with another, must keep well within wholesome limits, refraining from any familiarities which might bring reproach upon themselves, the church, their home, or the College." Any student engaging in premarital sex, of course, would be dismissed, although this was not explicitly spelled out. The *Handbook* also stated, "Students of Central Christian College do not attend Sunday shows." Smoking was not permitted on campus, and while drinking alcohol would lead to dismissal, the latter policy was assumed since it is not mentioned in the *Handbook*.[15]

In the women's dormitory, lights had to be turned off at 10:30, with no "playing radios, no turning on faucets, using typewriters, or visiting from room to room." Any time women left the campus, they had to secure permission from the hostess, check out, and indicate when they would return. The women were to be in their rooms by 7 p.m. but could check out to the library or evening campus events. When they arrived at their campus destination, they were checked in and upon leaving were given a slip to take back to the dorm telling what time they left. Women wore skirts and dresses with slacks and blue jeans allowed only for active sports.[16]

The men had similar dormitory regulations, but they had until 11 p.m. before lights out. They were to be in their rooms by 7:15, fifteen minutes after the women to give them time to walk their girl friends to the women's dorm by 7:00 and return to their own dorm.[17]

An interesting note in the *Handbook*: "The library is not a rendezvous for courting couples. Please do not make the mistake of attempting to use it as such."[18]

By 1955, students were allowed to stay out until 9:30 p.m. after church on Wednesday nights and until 10:00 p.m. on Sunday nights. First semester freshmen still had to double date, but other couples could go by themselves. Saturday night had been added to Friday for a date night but only until 9:30 p.m.[19] In 1956, the *Handbook* still

*Student Handbook
1957*

required first semester students to double date but said, "If a dating couple cannot find another couple with whom to double-date, they must have a girl to escort them, not a boy."[20]

The 1957 *Handbook* was much improved in appearance and contained a wide range of useful information, including the year's calendar of important dates and twenty-two pages of material about the aims of the college, the objectives of the academic program, information on student counseling, academic regulations, scholarships, the library, and the religious life on campus.

The rules, which occupied only five pages, had been rewritten and were accompanied by explanations to help students understand the reasons for the rules. This handbook is the first specifically to prohibit gambling, drinking of alcoholic beverages, and attending dances.[21]

Following the regulations came another seven pages of useful information about student health, student government, and extracurricular activities. College administrators were seeking to put the regulations in a broader context of Christian conduct and to communicate information on many topics more clearly to students. The *Handbook* also contained a helpful list of whom to see on campus for various needs.[22]

1958–1966

When Central Christian College moved to Oklahoma City in 1958, the first *Student Handbook* was much like the previous one. It, too, framed regulations with a philosophy and provided helpful information along with the rules. Now in a larger metropolitan area, the curfew on Friday night dates had been extended to 11:00 p.m., but double dating was now required for all students. A couple still could take a girl, but not a boy, with them, or they could request special permission to go alone.[23]

All students were to be in their dorm rooms or the library or at a campus activity from 7:00 to 8:45 p.m. on Monday, Tuesday, and Thursday evenings. They could go to the Student Center for the next hour but were to be back in the dorm by 9:45 on every evening except Friday. "Bedtime is 11 p.m. except on Friday nights when lights must be out by 11:30."[24] Students still had to sign out of the dorms after 7 p.m. or anytime they left campus, noting where they were going, with whom, and when they expected to return.[25] An additional rule about leaving campus was that students could go into Edmond at their own discretion, but were permitted to go into Oklahoma City only "once each week with the consent of the dormitory supervisor."[26] Students also had to have special permission to leave town, although their parents could give a standing permission for them to come home.[27]

The 1958 *Handbook* changed the rule about smoking. Prior to this time, it had been entirely forbidden on the campus. Now, however, men were permitted to smoke in their dormitory rooms. Women were not permitted to smoke at all.[28]

The 1959 *Handbook* shows several changes to policies about dating. On-campus dates were permitted Saturday nights from 6:30 to 9:45, and double-dating applied only to first semester freshmen. The *Handbook* also stated that parents must give permission for a student to date someone other than an OCC student.[29] Women students still were not allowed to wear slacks or blue jeans, except when playing sports.[30]

By 1960, students had two date nights—Friday night from 6:30 to 11 p.m. and Saturday night from 6:30 to 10 p.m.[31] Students were to be in the dorms by 10 p.m. on weeknights, but lights-out had been extended to 11:30 p.m.[32] Other regulations remained about the same. This *Handbook* was also the first to feature a cartoon-like character which appeared in many OCC publications. His name was "Ocie C," and he became an easily recognized logo to create humor and continuity.

Ocie C.

The 1962 *Handbook* was the first to mention special privileges for upperclassmen. In the evenings, they were allowed to go to the library at Central State College (now, the University of Central Oklahoma). Juniors could have one extra date night a month, and seniors could have two.[33] This handbook was more specific about drinking intoxicants, indicating that the "purchase, drinking, or bringing on campus of any alcoholic beverages such as beer, wine or whiskey is forbidden. Students found to be using or in possession of such intoxicants are subject to dismissal."[34]

1966–1975

By Fall 1966, the Friday night curfew had been extended to midnight and Saturday night to 11 p.m. On other evenings, students were to be in the dormitory by 11 p.m. with lights out by 11:30. The 1967 *Handbook* continued the same curfew hours, but no longer had a requirement for lights to be out by a specific time. By 1967, the limitation for only one trip a week to Oklahoma City had been removed.

In 1968, after the *Handbook* was printed, the college published a supplement that contained an interpretation of a rule about "careful grooming." It stated, "This rule is interpreted to mean a regular haircut for men such as is worn by the majority of adults in Oklahoma. Beards are not permitted except for the one month of the year designated by the Campus Life Committee for the Western Day beard contest."[35] Long hair and beards, in those years, were associated with "rebellion" among youth around the country, and the college sought to separate itself from such attitudes. Another new rule also reflected the times: "As relating to women's skirts, they must be modest and reach at least to the knee."[36] Knowing church families expected the campus to show more modesty than the cultural norms, OCC provided these guidelines for dress and hairstyles to be more in keeping with what its constituency desired.

Also as a recognition of the times, this supplement described legitimate ways for students to communicate with administrators about campus issues but declared that "picketing, 'sit-ins,' rioting, and any form of disruption of legitimate activity [is] forbidden as a means of communication." Those who engaged in such activities were "subject to suspension."[37] In March of 1969, some students staged a sit-in in the administration building and, as described in Chapter 4 on "The Presidents," were suspended.

This supplement also recognized that because of the growth in enrollment, the college was not able to provide housing for all students. It had, therefore, loosened the requirement that single students living away from home must live in a dormitory, which allowed some upper-class students to live off-campus.[38]

The *Handbook* published in 1969 defines places of entertainment that are off-limits. "Students must not attend dances or frequent places of entertainment, or other places the nature or reputation of which might bring discredit to the college."[39] Dr. Lawrence Rhodes, dean of students from 1969 to 1975, was charged with enforcing this regulation. One day, a student reported he had seen another student's car parked at a bar a few miles from the campus. Rhodes decided he should check the matter out and went to the bar to see whether any students were there. As he walked down a row of booths, an OCC student saw him and said, "Dean Rhodes, what are you doing in a place like this?"

Dr. Lawrence Rhodes

The 1969 *Handbook* was the first to specify the types of disciplinary actions the college might take when students broke the rules: reprimand, unrecorded disciplinary probation, recorded disciplinary probation, suspension, dismissal, request to withdraw, and withdrawal of privilege. Using such procedures was not new, of course, but this *Handbook* was the first to list them explicitly.[40]

In 1971, for the first time, women were allowed to wear "dress slacks" anywhere on campus after 6:30 p.m. and all day on Saturday. When the college was having a major public event, however, women were not to wear them, and wearing slacks on Sundays was still prohibited.[41] This handbook was the first to mention that use or possession of any "illegal drug" made the student subject to dismissal.[42] No doubt a sign of the times.

By 1972, the curfew on Monday through Thursday nights was extended to 11 p.m. for women and 11:30 p.m. for men. Friday and Saturday nights, both men and women were to be in by midnight, and Sunday nights, women were to be in by 11 p.m. and men by 11:30 p.m.[43] This year, there was also a change in the sign-out regulations: students had to sign out only when leaving the campus, both in the day and in the evening.[44]

The dress and grooming code also had a major change in 1972. Women could wear "pant suits or slacks with tunic tops" to class but were instructed to wear dresses to church since, at that time, women did not wear pants to church. After 5 p.m. and on Saturdays, women could "dress in more casual wear including non-tunic tops," but they were not to wear "faded, frayed, or patched pants" anywhere.[45] For men, the hair policy was much more explicit: sideburns should not go below the bottom of the earlobe, hair should not overlap the ear, and hair in the back could not go below the collar of a dress shirt. Mustaches were allowed but could not extend below the lower lip. Beards still were not permitted except during the month prior to Western Day.[46] Since college officials were trying to avoid having students who appeared as "hippies" or "rebellious," they forbade long hair, but they had found the regulation needed to be specific in order to be enforceable.

1975–1984

By Fall 1975, the curfew policy was modified a bit in view of federal regulations about equal treatment of men and women. Sunday through Thursday, both men and women were to be in their residence halls by 11:15 p.m. For both, Friday night curfew was 12:30 a.m., and Saturday was midnight.[47]

In 1976, the *Handbook* had the first explicit statement about dismissal for "sexual immorality." While the practice always had been to dismiss anyone, male or female, found to have engaged in premarital or extramarital sex, the *Handbook* now stated: "Sexual immorality is defined as premarital sexual relations and homosexuality. Any student engaging in or encouraging sexual immorality will be dismissed."[48] The 1978 *Handbook* was the first to state that any student "who has an abortion will be dismissed immediately."[49]

The 1980 *Handbook* came with distinctive change in format—it was a calendar. With a page for each month of the year, the calendar listed all major events for the year, including holidays, sporting events, musicals, plays, concerts, and special visitors coming to the campus. Information about student life, as well as the rules and regulations, showed at the top of the opening with the monthly calendar at the bottom. While there were no substantial changes in regulations for students,

STUDENT HANDBOOK   1980
AND CALENDAR   1981

Student Handbook as a calendar—1980

administrators hoped the format would keep the *Handbook* more available, thus encouraging students to be better acquainted with the information provided.

By 1981, students were no longer required to sign out of the dormitory unless they were to be gone overnight, but curfew hours remained the same.[50] By 1982, the policy against beards had been removed from the *Handbook*, but there were still limits on men's hair length.[51]

1984–1996

In 1984, the *Student Handbook* brought three significant changes. First, those using or possessing alcoholic beverages were still subject to dismissal, but, for the first time, an exception was provided. Students found to be drinking could stay at OCC if their previous records of conduct and their attitudes were good, and if the circumstances and amount of their drinking were not considered too unfavorable. Those meeting these criteria could stay at OCC by participating regularly in an alcohol education program the college conducted.[52]

A second change was in the dress code. For many years, handbooks had stated that dresses must be no shorter than three inches above the knee, and shorts of any kind had been forbidden except for athletic activities. Now the *Handbook* said, "Knee length walking shorts are acceptable" for general campus attire. Now that stylish shorts were longer than dresses and often were actually more modest, the administration changed the policy to allow the shorts.[53]

The third change dealt with hair styles. The detailed description about men's hair had been replaced with a new statement: "Students should keep their hair neatly groomed and not in an extreme style which calls undue attention to itself."[54]

In 1985, the curfew for Sunday through Thursday nights was extended from 11:15 p.m. to midnight for those living in the apartments. The curfew for all students remained at 12:30 a.m. on Friday night and at midnight on Saturday.[55]

In 1988, the dress code was modified. Dresses now had to be a little longer, no more than two inches above the knee, and "for classes, chapel, offices, and all public events," students were not allowed to wear shorts of any type, and any "pant type wear" had to be at least mid-calf. At the Student Center, at sporting events, and at picnics and retreats, however, students could wear "near knee-length shorts."[56] The next year, this rule was modified a bit. "Knee-length shorts may, however, be worn on campus after 4:30 PM, on Saturdays and after 1 PM on Sundays with the exception of night classes and events to which the public is invited."[57]

The 1991 *Handbook* extended the shorts rule a bit. "Dress shorts which are near knee-length are permitted generally for campus wear. However, they are not considered appropriate for class, chapel and some campus jobs."[58] That handbook continued the rule about men's hair being "well-groomed" and not calling "undue attention," but added, "Extremes in color or pony-tails for men, for example, would not be in compliance with this standard."[59]

The 1992 *Handbook* again extended curfew rules. Freshmen and sophomores in the residence halls still had to be in by 11:15 p.m., but juniors and seniors in the dormitories had until midnight. All students who were twenty-one and younger, wherever they lived, also had the midnight curfew. On Fridays, all students had to be in their residences by 12:30 a.m. and on Saturdays by midnight. Those living in the apartments had a midnight curfew every night except Fridays when, like others, 12:30 a.m. was the limit.[60]

In 1995, curfews remained the same, but senior students, those with ninety-six or more hours, could apply for a curfew waiver.[61] Another new feature in 1995 was "open house." For the first time, under specified circumstances, men could visit in women's rooms and women in the men's rooms. Men could visit one night a month in women's rooms from 7 to 10 p.m. and on one Sunday afternoon each month. In the single-student apartments, visitation was allowed on two Friday nights a month from 6:30 p.m. to midnight.[62] Students visiting during these hours had to sign in at the registration desk, and the door of the room or apartment and/or the window blinds had to remain open. All the other regulations about drinking, drugs, and sexual misconduct remained as they had been.

1996–2007

In 1996 Kevin Jacobs became president and sought to make Oklahoma Christian more "user friendly" for students. The rules about major moral issues such as sexual misconduct or the use of alcohol and/

or drugs remained the same. Jacobs, however, did initiate changes in other matters. "Shorts and skirts are permitted for campus wear including class and chapel, but must always be at least mid-thigh in length."[63] The rule against long hair for men was dropped, and curfew was set at midnight for Sunday through Thursday and at 12:30 a.m. on Friday and Saturday.[64] Students in the apartments, however, could request a permanent curfew waiver.[65]

By 1999, the dress code simply stated, "Shirts, shorts, blouses or skirts should not be too short, too tight or too revealing. Tank tops, shirts with more than the sleeve cut out and spaghetti straps are prohibited."[66]

The *Student Handbook* for 2001 was the first to be distributed by the OC Web site. By this time, the curfew for those living in the dormitories was midnight on Monday through Thursday, 1 a.m. on Friday, and 12:30 a.m. on Saturday. Those living in the apartments had no curfew at all unless they were placed on disciplinary probation.[67]

This handbook also stated that students who "voluntarily confess an addictive lifestyle issue (including alcohol, drugs, sexual, pornography and eating disorders) to the dean of students or the vice president of student services will be eligible for a range of non-disciplinary options, including counseling or medical treatment."[68] They were required, however, to start this process before they were found to be violating the rules. This same handbook also contained a statement on appropriate dress: shirts, shorts, blouses or skirts should not be "too short, too tight, too revealing, or provocative." Shirts and blouses were to be at least waist length thus covering the stomach and back, while shorts should be approximately midthigh or longer. . . . Hair, jewelry, and attire should not call undue attention to the wearer.[69]

By 2005, the *Student Handbook* was 111 pages long. It contained information about OC's core values, spiritual life, judicial procedures, academic policies, library, computer services, security, and privacy rights, as well as information on student conduct.

The modesty policy asked students to remember that what they wear should honor God and be a positive Christian influence. Specific prohibitions included tube tops, showing cleavage, clothing that was too tight or too low, and transparent clothing. Shorts and skirts were to be at least midthigh in length.[70] The same policy on alcohol and drugs continued, with students having the possibility of a counseling program.[71] The prohibition of sexual relations outside of marriage continued, including a prohibition of homosexuality. Specific penalties for violation of the sexual behavior policies, however, were not stated.[72] Reflecting federal policy and the times, the *Handbook* had six pages about sexual harassment and assault.

A change in 2005 stated that only freshmen living in residence halls were subject to any curfew regulations, which for them was midnight on Sunday through Thursday, 1 a.m. on Friday, and 12:30 a.m. on Saturday.[73] Another change came in the apartment visitation policy. Students could visit in apartments from 5 p.m. to midnight on every day except Wednesdays and Sundays. Students visiting in apartments had to sign in and out at the reception desk, and could only visit in the living area of the apartment, not in the bedroom. During visitation times, students had to leave blinds open so a supervisor could see into the room. Also by 2005, students in the dorms only had to sign out when leaving campus overnight.[74]

This story of the standards of conduct is quite revealing. The basic moral expectations remain much the same: students are not to drink intoxicants or use illegal drugs, they are not to engage in sexual relations outside of marriage, and they are not to engage in or promote homosexual behavior. Gone, however, are most of the earlier policies that sought to limit when and where students could go as an attempt to reduce their temptation to misbehave. The institution no longer sees its role as that of a parent, but still maintains the standards believed necessary while giving students more responsibility for their own conduct Many of these changes, of course, have come as customs and attitudes in the culture have changed generally and among church members in particular.

No data exists to determine whether the loosening of the regulations has increased the type of behavior the university wants students to avoid. So many factors in the culture are different that comparisons would be difficult. The current regulations still, of course, would be different in many respects from typical state institutions, which have even fewer restrictions on conduct.

Social Life

Students visiting on campus

Christian colleges always have had the goal of creating an environment where students could develop social skills along with the opportunity to meet prospects for a lifetime mate. From its earliest days, therefore, Oklahoma Christian has promoted social activities among its students. Receptions, banquets, picnics, retreats, trips, chapel, intramurals, club meetings, classes, and all other student activities are venues for student interaction. At the beginning of the school term each fall, the institution has held get-acquainted events where students could meet. Chapel speakers have even promoted dating.

Student clubs have provided some of the best opportunities for social life. Whether social-service clubs, departmental clubs, geographic groups, or those with a spiritual interest, these have provided opportunities for students to meet and work together, and in addition, the clubs have sponsored banquets, picnics, parties, and retreats. Student government, also, has planned many events that allow for social contact.

Through all of these gatherings, many students have found their mates. In a recent survey of a random one-hundred alumni, sixty-eight responded. Of these, 71 percent said they met their mates at Oklahoma Christian.[75]

Christmas Banquet in 1952

The university's long-term impact may be as great here as in anything else it does. For a student with Christian convictions to find a mate who shares those convictions certainly increases the likelihood that these two will be faithful to that commitment. Their children, likewise, are likely to grow up in the Christian faith. While the "mating game" on the OC campus is carried out through informal and even random activities, it is, nonetheless, a significant part of student life.

Social-Service Clubs

Student organizations, such as religious groups, geographic clubs, academic clubs, and service groups, have been part of the fabric of Oklahoma Christian since its early days. In 1957-1958, however, clubs of a new type arrived on the scene. Developed after a plan from Harding, these clubs offered an opportunity for social activities, club competition in sports and forensics, and an opportunity for another arena in which students could develop leadership and relational skills.[76] College administrators decided to permit only coed clubs to reduce the risk of undesirable behavior they thought more likely if clubs had only men or women. The groups were called social-service clubs, rather than fraternities and sororities, to reduce the likelihood of the conduct often associated with the latter, and to assure no connection with such groups on other campuses. The clubs had names from Greek city-states rather than Greek letters, thus giving a slight nod to the Greek system. Four clubs began operation that year: the Spartans, Dorians, Trojans, and Olympians.

After the move to Oklahoma City in 1958, the same four clubs continued. They competed in intramural sports and the annual speech tournament, and they sponsored social events and service projects. That first year, the Dorians had twenty-eight members, the Olympians fifty-four, the Spartans forty-six, and the Trojans twenty-nine.[77]

Dorians sing at a rest home in 1963

By 1961–1962, two new clubs had started, the Bereans and the Athenians, both still coed. The following year, the Ionians began. The clubs that year were all involved in Homecoming activities and began the tradition of club breakfasts with returning alumni. By this time, clubs not only competed in various contests through the year, but had begun vying for a sweepstakes trophy awarded to the club scoring the most points from a wide range of activities. That year, the Dorians won for the third year in a row.[78]

The 1962–1963 year offers a good sample of club service activities. The Athenians had projects for beautifying the campus, the Bereans held devotionals at the County Girls Home, the Dorians conducted devotionals at a home for the elderly, the Ionians supported mission work in Canada, the Olympians planted grass on the baseball field and provided a garden on campus, the Spartans developed a bulletin board in the Student Center for campus announcements, and the Trojans worked on improving Trojan Park between the dorms and the Barn. While all clubs had events to fulfill their "social" side, they were equally active in service.[79]

The 1966–67 year brought something new. The Spartans decided to become an all-men's club with the Greek letters of Sigma Epsilon.[80] This change, approved by the college administration, represented the first substantial change in club structure since they began in the fall of 1957 and began a trend that continued over the years. The following year, another all-men's club, Beta Chi, had its beginning.[81] The 1968–1969 year brought two new developments: Alpha Chi Omega became the first coed club with a Greek letter name,[82] and Theta Theta Theta became the first all-women's club.[83] That year, the Bereans had seventy-five members.[84] The spring of 1969 was especially significant for clubs because that was the first year for Spring Sing, the topic of a later section of this chapter.

By 1970–1971, there were seven clubs: two for men only, Beta Chi and Kappa Sigma; two for women only, Kappa Phi Delta and

Theta Theta Theta; and three coed clubs, the Athenians, Bereans, and Dorians.[85] By 1972–1973, only the Bereans, with 110 members, was left of the coed clubs, but there were two new clubs: Delta Tau Omega for women and Delta Gamma Sigma for men.[86] In 1973, a new coed club began, Omega Nu Epsilon, and in 1974 came Alpha Sigma Phi for women. Now there were nine clubs, two of which were coed.[87] The trend for single-sex clubs continued in 1975–1976 with the addition of two more: Chi Lambda Chi for women and Alpha Gamma Omega for men.[88]

By the 1977–1978 year, the Bereans were gone, but new clubs were on the scene: Shantih for women, Chapter 10 for men, Sigma Zeta Chi for men, and Lambda Chi, a coed club primarily composed of African American students.[89] In 1978 came Gamma Rho for women. By 1980–1981, the club picture had changed considerably. Beta Beta Sigma for women was new that year, and Zeta Rho Chi was a new men's club, as was Phi Gamma Delta. Lambda Chi was the only coed club still operating.[90]

An article in the Campus Preview section of the *OCC Reporter* for October of 1981 urged incoming freshmen to join a club. The article indicated that 1,039 students out of a student body of 1,613 held club membership—64 percent. The article quotes Phil Johnson, dean of men: "Any student at OCC who wants to join a social-service club is guaranteed a place. Some students get in the club they choose, but because of demand, membership in a particular club can't be guaranteed." The article urged incoming students to consider club membership by reporting, "Authorities on adjusting to college life stress that joining a club generally helps a student become involved in college activities and feel a part of the campus much sooner."[91]

By 1985, the number of clubs had grown to thirteen, with six for men only and seven for women only; no more coed clubs existed, although Sigma Chi Eta for women and Zeta Rho Chi for men joined their forces for their Spring Sing show.[92] By 1990, the club picture had not changed much. Some new clubs such as Alpha Gamma Omega, Ko Jo Kai, Omega Tau Xi, Sigma Chi Sigma, and Sub T-13 were on the scene, but the number of clubs had been rather constant: six for women and eight for men.[93]

In March of 1995, Tracey Inman wrote a *Talon* story about shrinking club sizes. She said, "Almost everywhere you go and almost everyone you see has some connection with social-service clubs," but she reported that Nancy Inman, student activities and conference director, had found that only 47 percent of students were in a club.[94] She indicated that while the percentage had once been above 60 percent, that number gradually had been going down. In 1987–1988, the number had been 51 percent. In the next two years, it had risen to 56 percent and in 1991–1992 reached 57 percent. Since then, however, the percentage had declined to the present 47 percent. Activities Director Inman attributed the decline to a policy from the Student Life Office, which had placed a limit on club sizes, dropping the number allowed in a given club from over a hundred to eighty for women's clubs and seventy-five for men's. The plan was designed to create more clubs but had not been entirely successful.[95]

By fall of 2005, there were twelve clubs, and more changes had been initiated. Membership in clubs was no longer guaranteed to all who applied, and freshmen were no longer admitted to clubs. The Campus Life Office now believed that freshmen would do better with more association within their class, reserving club membership for the sophomore year. Bob Lashley now directed an early fall show, Freshman Fanfare, in which freshmen worked together, and freshmen had their own teams in intramurals and their own show in Spring Sing. Those working with freshmen believed this arrangement promoted better freshman retention at the university. Without freshmen in clubs, of course, the percentage of students in clubs became considerably lower than before with 32 percent of those eligible to be in a club participating, and 23 percent of the total student body in a club.[96]

In 2007, the 13 clubs had 716 members, 36 percent of the full-time student body. The seven clubs for women and their membership numbers were: Beta Beta Sigma, 34; Delta Tau Omega, 16; Gamma Rho, 108; Iota Kappa Phi, 41; Lambda Chi Zeta, 70; Pi Zeta Phi, 69; Theta Theta Theta, 43. The six clubs for men and their memberships were: Alpha Gamma Omega, 68; Chi Lambda Phi, 74; Delta Gamma Sigma, 50; Kappa Sigma Tau, 88; Omega Psi Omicron, 26; Sigma Chi Sigma, 29.

The club system has played a major part in student life at Oklahoma Christian University. It has given thousands of students the opportunity to create stronger relationships, develop socially, engage in meaningful spiritual activities in club retreats and devotionals, build talents through stage appearances, and gain a sense of responsibility and experience in leadership.

One of the great benefits to students from the club experience has been participating in service projects. Every club over the years has had a service element in its program. Clubs have worked with the handicapped, with those in homes for the

Phi Beta Nu students visit in the children's hospital.

elderly, and in providing Christmas gifts for the underprivileged. They have helped with missionary activities and assisted fellow students facing particular crises. They have carried out projects to benefit the university by paving parking lots, assisting with campus landscaping, and picking up trash. Clubs have added to school spirit by bouncing a basketball from the OC campus to the location of a game with a rival school and by forming cheering sections at games. They have often served to greet campus guests by serving as hosts, ushers at public events, and greeters to incoming students. Clubs have added an important element to Homecoming with their window decorations, parade, and other displays. Certainly one of the many benefits club life has offered is promoting the spirit of service among students.

The social-service club structure has also been the basis of intramural athletic competition over the years. While some teams

Powder-puff football

have come from independents or other groups, the primary source of the athletic teams has been social-service clubs. Intramurals have involved a wide range of sporting contests: flag football, basketball, softball, ping pong, bowling, volleyball, track, and occasionally wrestling. In many years, there have been competitions in three or four levels to allow those in clubs who were not outstanding in the sport still to participate in the competition.

Social interaction, of course, has been one of the primary values from club membership. Clubs have hosted banquets, receptions, breakfasts, retreats, and picnics. These provide many venues in which to develop social skills. Club membership has given many students a chance to make friends on campus, and some of these relationships have continued through lifetimes. Club loyalty is strong, and this club loyalty is also often a factor in a continuing loyalty to the university.

The clubs, of course, have also had a downside. Some students spend time in club activities to the detriment of their grades. Clubs have, occasionally, had problems over hazing and

Men's basketball

other issues of conduct and not only have been reprimanded, put on probation, or been suspended, but have been a bad influence on their members. Sometimes a spirit of competition in intramurals or Spring

Sing has led to bad attitudes between students. Officials responsible for club activities have sought to counter such possibilities by training club officers, providing guidelines for activities, and requiring faculty or staff club sponsors.

On the whole, club life has been and remains an important and beneficial part of student life at Oklahoma Christian. Although the percentage of those in clubs has decreased in recent years, the clubs remain a vital part of the campus and continue to provide a useful means of student development.

Spring Sing

One of the most important functions of Oklahoma Christian's student government over the last forty years has been their production of Spring Sing, an annual musical show. Years ago, student Ken Adams visited a friend at Oklahoma State University and while there, saw their student clubs present a musical show. Adams thought this type of activity would be good for OCC and brought the idea to the Student Senate at their retreat in the fall of 1968. Other OCC students had seen a similar program, Sing Song, at Abilene Christian College. The Senate liked the concept and decided to start such a program at OCC in the spring of 1969.[97]

Unlike similar shows at many other universities, Spring Sing at OCC began and continues entirely as a student-produced show. The Student Senate selects the theme and chooses a master and mistress of ceremonies. They select a student director and pass along to the social-service clubs the framework in which they are to operate. Clubs develop their own shows, rehearse them on their own, and finally, students put the program together. A member of the OC staff—Bob Lashley since 1999—works with clubs to review lyrics and choreography and props to help the students be sure that nothing planned is inappropriate for a Christian college presentation. At first, only a piano accompanied the songs, but since 1972, a pit band has worked with the show, particularly accompanying the host and hostess.

When Spring Sing began in 1969, there were nine social service clubs, three for men, one for women, and the others were coed. These participated in the first show with Beta Chi, a men's club, winning first. The second year, the theme was "Salute to America," and Beta Chi again was announced as the winner. The next week, however, a recount of the judges' ballots revealed that actually Theta Theta Theta had the most points. Those in charge decided to declare the two clubs as co-winners.[98] In an interesting twist, Bruce Kerr, who directed the show for Beta Chi, and Sherril Day, who directed Theta's

Chi Lambda Phi closing their winning show in 2006

show, had married the previous year.

The records for the 1971 show are quite complete. Nadine Stephens, who chaired the Spring Sing Committee, submitted a twelve-page, handwritten report to help the person filling the role for the next year. She listed all the roles to be filled: stage technician; light technician; sound technician; stage crew of ten to fifteen; lighting crew of five; publicity chair for poster, program, and ticket design; a second publicity chair for TV, radio, and shopping centers; two ballot counters; a person to get five judges and coordinate their work; eight ushers; someone to direct the preparation of the master and mistress of ceremonies; and a secretary. She gave a number of suggestions for the following year, such as not letting clubs drop out once they have committed to the show, making the "dress rehearsal" a time when everyone does everything they will do in the show, and choosing the chair and the committee at least three months in advance.[99]

Theta's winning show in 1986

Over the years, the quality of the production has improved and so has the attendance. By 2007, the show ran four times to a total audience of more than 4,500. Chi Lambda Phi has the longest winning streak, six years from 2001 through 2007. Theta Theta Theta has the second longest win streak, with five in a row from 1970 to 1974.

Student competition between the clubs is keen, sometimes even engendering rather strong feelings. Students who have participated in Spring Sing, however, look back on those shows as definite highlights of their times at OC. The practices develop strong ties, and being in the show with several hundred other students gives a sense of camaraderie, even when one's club does not win a prize. The many hours of practice take time away from study for some, but on the other hand, students are having a learning experience of a different kind. Spring Sing continues to be one of the major events of the year.

Freshman Fanfare

In September, 1988, Bob Lashley began a new campus activity to give incoming freshman students an opportunity to perform on stage and, along with that, to get to know each other and build unity by working together. Called Freshman Fanfare, the show allows any freshman to participate. Auditions give Lashley the chance to select some for solos or small groups, but large group acts give all the opportunity to perform. Freshmen also play in the band and do all the backstage work. After the show is done, the freshmen do all the clean-up.

Freshman Fanfare in 2006

In the early years, 30 to 40 students performed, but the show has grown, and by 2007 the number had risen to 250. By 2007, two or three upperclassmen were assisting Lashley in preparing the students for the show, which now draws an audience of more than a thousand for each of the two performances.

Lashley placed the show at the end of September for several reasons. That is the date for the first fall visit, so it provides a draw for prospective students and an opportunity to showcase student talent. Being about a month after the beginning of school also means it is a good weekend for parents to visit, not too close to the opening of school, but soon enough to make them glad to have an opportunity to see their children who have just started at OC.

Near the start of the school year, Lashley invites all interested freshmen to meet so they can start making plans for the show. They choose a theme and work together to develop the acts. Freshmen even write new lyrics for some popular songs to sing. Rehearsals begin about three weeks before the show but last only an hour and a half until about two days before performance.

Freshman Fanfare has served as an excellent way to get new

freshmen acquainted and working together. They develop strong bonds and sometimes even start dating someone they met while doing the show. Lashley knows this can happen–because it happened to his son, Andy, and Andy's wife, Summer.

Conclusion

Every collegiate institution has its own personality. Some give intellectual pursuits the highest priority, others are a "football" school, some are known for "partying," still others are famous for the beauty of their location, and some are best known for their focus on spiritual things.

Oklahoma Christian's personality comes from a mixture of what it believes is important, and the university has developed an interesting balance of these. Certainly the spiritual development of its students comes first, and along with that, even enhancing that, is a high academic expectation from its students. However, the school also prizes wide student participation in the extracurricular life of the campus, which develops students' social, personal, and leadership skills. Because the university places importance on these campus activities, they are invested with quality, and there are enough activities for every student to find a place in them. This chapter, along with the chapters on spiritual life, athletics, musicals and theatre, and students, tells the story of this side of Oklahoma Christian's personality.

Chapter 15, Endnotes

1   Schedules referenced are in the OC Archives under Registrar.
2   "New Course Battles Dropout Rate," *Oklahoma Christian College Bulletin*, September 1966, OC Archives.
3   Ibid.
4   Ibid.
5   "Neat Week Appears to be Fine Success," *Campus Community*, June 7, 1973, OC Archives.
6   *Annual Institutional Data Report*, 1997, 14, OC Archives.
7   "Neat Week Offers Many Opportunities," Talon, May 31, 1974, OC Archives.
8   Stafford North, personal records.
9   Ibid.
10   Amy Janzen and Neil Arter, Conversation with the author, November 8, 2007.
11   Ibid.
12   Ibid.
13   Ibid.
14   Syllabus, Freshman Seminar, Fall 2004.
15   *Central Christian College Handbook*, 1953–54, 3–4, OC Archives.
16   Ibid., 3, 6–7.
17   Ibid., 9.
18   Ibid., 13.
19   *Central Christian College Handbook*, 1955–56, 2–3, OC Archives.
20   *Central Christian College Handbook*, 1956–57, 3, OC Archives.
21   *Central Christian College Handbook*, 1957–58, 30, OC Archives.
22   Ibid., passim.
23   *Central Christian College Handbook*, 1958–59, 6–7, OC Archives.
24   Ibid., 7.
25   Ibid., 9.
26   Ibid.
27   Ibid.
28   Ibid., 9.
29   *Oklahoma Christian College Handbook*, 1959–60, 7–8, OC Archives.
30   Ibid., 13.
31   *Oklahoma Christian College Student Handbook*, 1960–62, 13, OC Archives.
32   Ibid., 15.
33   *Oklahoma Christian College Student Handbook*, 1962–1963, 18, OC Archives.
34   Ibid, 28.
35   *Supplement to Student Handbook*, 1968–69, 1, OC Archives.
36   Ibid.
37   Ibid., 6–7.
38   Ibid., 3–4.
39   *Oklahoma Christian College Student Handbook*, 69–71, 16, OC Archives.
40   Ibid., 17–18.
41   *Oklahoma Christian College Student Handbook*, 1971–73, 14–15, OC Archives.
42   Ibid., 13.
43   *Oklahoma Christian College Student Handbook*, 1972–73, 21, OC Archives.
44   Ibid., 18.
45   Ibid., 26.
46   Ibid., 27–28.
47   *Oklahoma Christian College Student Handbook*, 1975–76, 19, OC Archives.
48   *Oklahoma Christian College Student Handbook*, 1976–77, 19, OC Archives.
49   *Oklahoma Christian College Student Handbook*, 1978–79, 21, OC Archives.
50   *Oklahoma Christian College Student Handbook*, 1981–82, 11, OC Archives.
51   *Oklahoma Christian College Student Handbook*, 1982–83, 18, OC Archives.
52   *Oklahoma Christian College Student Handbook*, 1984–85, 23, OC Archives.
53   Ibid., 24.
54   Ibid.

55 *Oklahoma Christian College Student Handbook*, 1985–86, 24, OC Archives.
56 *Oklahoma Christian College Student Handbook*, 1988–89, 12, OC Archives.
57 *Oklahoma Christian College Student Handbook*, 1989–90, 14, OC Archives.
58 *Oklahoma Christian University Student Handbook*, 1991–92, 14, OC Archives.
59 Ibid.
60 *Oklahoma Christian University Student Handbook*, 1992–93, 12, OC Archives.
61 *Oklahoma Christian University Student Handbook*, 1995–96, 11, OC Archives.
62 Ibid., 10.
63 *Oklahoma Christian University Student Handbook* 1998–99, 9, OC Archives.
64 Ibid., 22; Tonna Condict, "Hair, Curfew Changes Approved by Jacobs," *Talon*, March 1, 1966, 1, OC Archives.
65 Ibid., 23.
66 *Oklahoma Christian University Student Handbook*, 1999–2000, 35.
67 "Curfew for Residence Halls," Oklahoma Christian University Student Handbook on Intranet; "Curfew in Apartments," *Oklahoma Christian University Student Handbook* on Intranet.
68 "Code of Conduct and Discipline," *Student Handbook* 2001–02, 2, OC Archives.
69 Ibid, 6.
70 *Oklahoma Christian University Student Handbook*, 2005, 30–31, OC Archives.
71 Ibid., 33.
72 Ibid., 39.
73 Ibid., 65.
74 Ibid., 66–67.
75 Michael Mitchell, director of alumni, December 4, 2007.
76 "Harding Plan Is Explained," *Tower*, April 13, 1956, OC Archives.
77 "Dorians Sponsor College Sweaters," *Focus*, 1959, OC Archives.
78 Aerie, 1963, 80–86.
79 Ibid.
80 "Sig Ep's first all men's club on campus," *Aerie*, 1967, 116, OC Archives.
81 "Beta Chi Bounces Basketball, Boosts Spirit," *Aerie*, 1968, 102, OC Archives.
82 "Alpha XI Omega Deviates from Rigidity," *Aerie*, 1969, 190, OC Archives.
83 "Theta Theta Theta For Women Only," *Aerie*, 1969, 202, OC Archives.
84 "Bereans Is Largest Social-Service Club," *Aerie*, 1969, 194, OC Archives.
85 *Aerie*, 1971, 114–126, OC Archives.
86 *Aerie*, 1973, 128–141, OC Archives.
87 *Aerie*, 1975, 136–153, OC Archives.
88 *Aerie*, 1976, 154–155, OC Archives.
89 *Aerie*, 1978, 211–222, OC Archives.
90 *Aerie*, 1981, 96–111, OC Archives.
91 "Membership Guaranteed to all OCC Students," *OCC Reporter*, October 1981, 6, OC Archives.
92 *Aerie*, 1986, 100–125, OC Archives.
93 *Aerie*, 1991, OC Archives.
94 Tracey Inman, "Club sizes shrink for fourth straight year," *Talon*, March 10, 1995, OC Archives.
95 Ibid.
96 "2006 Fall Rush Statistics," Report from the Campus Life Office.
97 Ken Adams, Conversation with the author, July 10, 2007.
98 Ken Adams, Email to the author, July 12, 2007, OC Archives.
99 Nadine Stephens, handwritten report for Spring Sing 1971, OC Archives.

Year	Show Director(s)	Show Theme	Hosts & Hostesses	Winners
1969	(information unavailable)	(information unavailable)	Sherril Kerr Eddie Rogers	1st: Beta Chi
1970	Nadine (Bruce) Stephens	Salute to America	Dan Deaver Becky Walker	Co-winners: Theta Theta Theta; Beta Chi
1971	Nadine Stephens	Through the Eyes of Children	Bernard Lassiter Sherril Kerr	1st: Theta Theta Theta 2nd: Kappa Phi
1972	Andy Benton	Sign of the Times	Eddie Howard Janice (Winkelman) Ward	1st: Theta Theta Theta
1973	Andy Benton	I Believe in Music	Connie Hannah Bob Lashley	1st: Theta Theta Theta 2nd: Kappa Sigma Tau
1974	(information unavailable)	American Pie	Marcia (Adams) Lightsey Phillip Prosser	1st: Theta Theta Theta 2nd: Bereans
1975	Darla Dean	Time for Living	Connie Hannah Johnny Henderson	1st: Kappa Phi 2nd: Delta Tau Omega
1976	Ron Verner	Wings of Dreams	Phillip Prosser Vicki McElroy	1st: Theta Theta Theta; 2nd: Alpha Gamma Omega
1977	Jim Eggleston	Singing to the World	Rory Rosenbalm Vickie McElroy	1st: Theta Theta Theta 2nd: Kappa Sigma Tau
1978	Dan Benton	Riders to the Stars	Gary Smith Amy Webb	1st: Theta Theta Theta 2nd: Beta Chi Omega
1979	David Estes	Miracles of Music	Karen Killion Eddie Keener	1st: Theta Theta Theta 2nd: Kappa Sigma Tau
1980	Kim Ott	Lights of Broadway	Eddy Query Lisa Terry	1st: Kappa Sigma Tau 2nd: Theta Theta Theta
1981	Terri Ross	Celebrate America	Terry Taylor Sherrie Musgrove Susan Laningham	1st: Kappa Sigma Tau 2nd: Beta Chi Omega
1982	Tim Marlatt Terri Ross	Hey There, Good Times	Tom Norwood Laura Rucker Matt Thomas Carrie Loughman	1st: Theta Theta Theta 2nd: Delta Gamma Sigma
1983	Mark Hayes Laura Rucker	Remember When	Johnny Brown Heather Weber	1st: Kappa Sigma Tau 2nd: Beta Chi Omega
1984	Alfred Branch	Through the Looking Glass	Ron Cole Rexann West Brian Dickerson	1st: Delta Gamma Sigma 2nd: Gamma Rho
1985	Stuart Graham Kelly Holman	College Life	J. D. Beard Leslie Hill Angela Roper Brian Thacker	1st: Delta Gamma Sigma 2nd: Theta Theta Theta

Year	Show Director(s)	Show Theme	Hosts & Hostesses	Winners
1986	Stuart Graham Brian Thacker	Reach	Brandon Boswell Stan Shelton Gwendaline Hatfield Connie McCormack Penny Stafford	1st: Theta Theta Theta 2nd: Kappa Sigma Tau
1987	Mark Parker Stan Shelton	We've Got the Answer	Darryl Oliver Lori Linn	1st: Theta Theta Theta 2nd: Gamma Rho
1988	Greg Cohn Angi Roper	Putting It Together	Vanessa Jackson Robert Orr Ivey Bacani Lisa Shinnerer	1st: Kappa Sigma Tau 2nd: Theta Theta Theta
1989	Cami Agan	Colours	Melinda Fuchs Lane Fields Jennifer Grady Daren Harris	1st: Kappa Sigma Tau 2nd: Alpha Gamma Omega
1990	Todd Brooks Dawn Stanley	A Time to Sing	Robert Orr Kristi Grady Pete Wutzke Vanessa Jackson	1st: Alpha Gamma Omega 2nd: Kappa Sigma Tau
1991	Clair Stevenson Jennifer Glover	Steppin' Out	Chris Floyd Bryce Gage Missy Wood Felisha Chase	1st: Alpha Gamma Omega 2nd: Kappa Sigma Tau
1992	Lane Fields Leslie Owen	It's Your Move	Doug Lalli Dan Langdon Kristi Grady Shannan Branscum	1st: Alpha Gamma Omega 2nd: Kappa Sigma Tau
1993	Kenne Whitson Mary Ford	Pathways	Stephanie McDonald Lee Keele Scott Haagensen	1st: Gamma Rho 2nd: Theta Theta Theta
1994	Aimee Lynn Cox Sara Sampson	Dreamers Wake the Nation	Amy Ginnings Scott Lovett Corey Whaley Stacey Owen	1st: Alpha Gamma Omega 2nd: Kappa Sigma Tau
1995	James Nored Carie Keas	Into the Night	Steve Schinnerer Adrian J. Engram Patti Neuhold Tracey Inman	1st: Kappa Sigma Tau 2nd: Alpha Gamma Omega
1996	Stacey Parker Mindy Cail	Reaching Higher	Angel English Heath Wiederstein Jennifer Childers Steve Martin	1st: Alpha Gamma Omega 2nd: Gamma Rho

Year	Show Director(s)	Show Theme	Hosts & Hostesses	Winners
1997	Tara Winn Kyle Lankford	Shining Through	Jennifer Childers Jason Carroll Lisa Curl	1st: Alpha Gamma Omega 2nd: Beta Beta Sigma
1998	Kyle Lankford Seth Hoe Anna Heffington	Right Here, Right Now	Kevin Arter Jason Carroll Lafe Coldwater Lisa Curl Shawna Robinson	1st: Kappa Sigma Tau 2nd: Alpha Gamma Omega
1999	Co-directors: Jenny Frank Kevin Arter Rob Carpenter	Believe	Erick Alexander Jason Carroll Lafe Coldwater Aimee McBroom Jayna Perry Tatricia Randle Dewayne Winrow	1st: Kappa Sigma Tau 2nd: Lambda Chi Zeta
2000	Jason Carroll Julie Knox Seth Hoe	Once In A Lifetime	Lisa Curl Tatrica Randle Erin Cooper Matt Quirey Erick Alexander Benji Peck	1st: Alpha Gamma Omega 2nd: Chi Lambda Phi
2001	Justin Hatfield Angela Risley	Generations	Linnita Thomas Katierose Krause Llon Clendenen Larry Inman	1st: Alpha Gamma Omega 2nd: Chi Lambda Phi
2002	Summer Billings Lori Ford	Up In Lights	David Burch Morgandi Whitehead Devon Bohanan Nkere Reed	1st: Chi Lambda Phi 2nd: Gamma Rho
2003	Anna Jane Forrester Rose Langham	Hardrock Café	Dave Burch Lacy Eddy Penny Roberts Joe Downs	1st: Chi Lambda Phi 2nd: Kappa Sigma Tau
2004	Rose Langham Kelsey Rogstad Anna Rawlins	Rewind	Derek Hurst Kelsey Larr Joe Downs Jake Jarrell	1st: Chi Lambda Phi 2nd: Gamma Rho
2005	Amy Barker Kelsey Larr Nathan Porter	One Hit Wonders	Annalisa Balerio Kevin Peters Derek Hurst Lindsey Vanhooser	1st: Chi Lambda Phi 2nd: Gamma Rho

Year	Show Director(s)	Show Theme	Hosts & Hostesses	Winners
2006	Anne Rawlins Leah Sherman	Premier	Raymond Mobley Logan Rosenbalm Halie Swan Addi Herndon	1st: Chi Lambda Phi 2nd: Kappa Sigma Tau
2007	Amy Hubble Chrissie Carter	The Big Show	Caleb Foster Abby Phillips CAST: Justin Brown Melodi Bailey James Simmons Whitney Riggs	1st: Chi Lambda Phi 2nd: Gamma Rho
2008	Josh Bouye Allison Harmon	Debut	Halie Swan David Bowden Meagan Martin Bryson Holley Lacey Thomas Raymond Mobley	1st: Gamma Rho 2nd: Kappa Sigma Tau

Chapter 16
THE ATHLETICS

From its beginning in Bartlesville, athletics has played a vital role at Oklahoma Christian University. Sports have created school spirit, developed Christian character, built friendships, and gained recognition for the university. Whether attending, participating, or associating with players, students remember athletics as an important part of their OC experience. Stan Green, OC's long-time sports information director, wrote, "Fifty years of athletics at Oklahoma Christian University have established a rich tradition of quality and success—in the competitive arena, in the classroom and in the support and commitment of alumni and friends of the University."[1] The fact that currently 20 percent of OC's full-time, undergraduate students participate in intercollegiate athletics bears testimony to its importance at the university.

This chapter will look at each sport at Oklahoma Christian University, generally in their order of beginning, reporting its start, its coaches, its successes, its most outstanding players, and a few of the most important moments in that sport.

Men's Basketball

The Bartlesville Years

Men's basketball was the first sport CCC students played against others. In the college's first year, they played company teams in a YMCA league. History professor Joe Spaulding coached the eight players, winning five out of nine games. Biology teacher Gerald McCoy, for the next four years, coached the team against the same competition.

In 1955–1956, for the first time, McCoy's team played other junior colleges on an "experimental basis," winning two out of four games. The next year, the college officially moved into intercollegiate competition. Unfortunately, in the first semester, the eight-man squad lost its first four games, and the rest of the season was cancelled because four of the eight players became academically ineligible.[2] In 1957–1958, Central Christian's last year in Bartlesville, with biology teacher Darvin Keck coaching, the team won four out of fourteen.

The Ray Vaughn Years

The move to Oklahoma City brought a major step forward in athletics. President James Baird brought Ray Vaughn to direct CCC's young athletic program. Vaughn, a highly successful and well-respected coach at Oklahoma City's Capitol Hill High School, brought his experience in coaching plus his strong reputation to begin a new era in athletics. In Vaughn's first year, 1958–1959, the Eagles won fifteen of twenty-three games, including victories over Central State, Oklahoma Baptist, and St. Gregory's.[3] With no gym on campus, the eleven-member squad practiced and played home games at a local high school facility.

Ray Vaughn, Sr.

The next year, Vaughn's team won twelve and lost seven, placing third in the Oklahoma Junior College Athletic Conference. John Kelly's average of eighteen points a game placed him third in OCC's region of the National Junior College Athletic Association.[4]

The 1960–1961 year brought "The Barn," Oklahoma Christian's first gymnasium. A metal building with bleacher seating for about six hundred, it provided a good playing court and a big increase in campus interest. That year, Vaughn's team went twenty-four and two. In this transitional year to a senior college, they still played junior colleges and teams from air force and army bases. Jim Miller set a single-game scoring record of thirty-six. The other four starters were Dennis McMasters, Robert Watson, and two transfers, brothers James and Frank Davis.[5]

Frank Davis, in a published memoir, tells how he and his brother came to OCC. James had played a year at Arkansas Tech, and Frank had committed to play there, as well. During the summer, however, Ray Vaughn visited, explaining, as Davis recalled, "that life was a lot more than sports and that most likely we would marry someone that we went to college with. He reasoned that our chances of finding someone who held similar views about family and God would be greatly increased if we came there."[6] The Davis brothers were also impressed that Vaughn urged them to "do something significant" by helping a young Christian college do well at the senior college level.[7]

This report reveals much about Vaughn's recruiting techniques, and apparently he was convincing because the Davis brothers wanted to come. They boarded a bus for Oklahoma City, but at Ft. Smith, the Arkansas Tech coach and their brother Wilburn were waiting. Since they had not notified the coach of their change in plans, he intercepted them to enforce their previous commitment. The Davis brothers stayed at Arkansas Tech that year,[8] but the next year, transferred to help Vaughn's team reach the twenty-four and two mark.

Frank Davis

In 1961–1962, Vaughn and his thirteen-member squad began playing senior colleges and went thirteen and nine. The most exciting games were with Abilene Christian. The OCC campus was excited for their small, young college to play the older and better-known sister college from Texas. The first game in Abilene, to the surprise of many, was very close, with the Eagles ahead late in the game. A final surge, however, gave the Wildcats the victory 68 to 66.[9]

A few weeks later, the teams met in The Barn. With ten seconds left, OCC led 61 to 58, with ACC ready to inbound the ball. There was then no three-point shot, so Coach Vaughn called time and told the team the only way they could lose the game was if they fouled. Then he said, "Just go on the court and stand there. Let them bring the ball down and score their two points. Then we'll have the ball and time will run out." The team did just as instructed, the Wildcats scored their two points, and the Eagles ran out the clock, winning 61 to 60.

It was a great win and showed Eagle athletics had risen quickly to be competitive with their older, sister Christian colleges. What seemed like the beginning of a great rivalry, however, was short-lived. Abilene Christian would never again schedule another regular season game with the Eagles.

In just four years, Vaughn had led the basketball program of a school with only 379 students to be

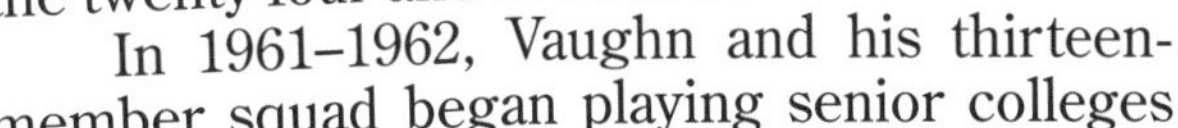

The OCC Eagles and ACC Wildcats play in The Barn.

competitive with much larger colleges. More than that, however, Vaughn was laying the foundation for an athletic program that reflected his own deep spiritual commitment and high character. He recruited players who would be a credit to the institution, and he took a real interest in each player, not only in their athletic skills but also in their personal development. Often he and his wife, Sue, invited players to their home, and encouraged their spiritual lives. The 1960 yearbook described Vaughn well: "Even though he wants to win in the events, he considers honesty, fair play, and true Christian behavior more important. He is concerned with each individual boy and hopes that participation in athletics in a Christian atmosphere will build strong character."[10] Vaughn's four-year record was sixty-four wins against twenty-four losses, a truly outstanding record for a small school just getting started in intercollegiate play.

The Haskell Sinclair Years

As the athletic program grew, Vaughn decided to bring someone else to coach basketball, and in 1962, Haskell Sinclair became OCC's second head basketball coach. An Abilene Christian graduate, he brought the experience of five seasons as a high school coach and two as freshman coach at ACC.[11] His first-year record was seventeen and five.[12] Frank Davis was the leading scorer, with an average of twenty-six points per game.[13] In Sinclair's second year, the team went seven and thirteen. Mike Gipson, who later taught biology for many years at Oklahoma Christian, was the leading scorer that year, averaging twenty-three points per game.[14] Sinclair resigned after his second year.

Haskell Sinclair

The Frank Davis Years

In 1964, the college brought Frank Davis back to coach basketball. Only a year after his graduation, Davis returned to lead a team that included several with whom he had played. While still a student, Davis had married Judy Watson, a girl he met at OCC, just as Coach Vaughn had predicted. Davis was drafted by the St. Louis Hawks but didn't make the cut.[15] In his year away, he taught in Ponca City, and at age twenty-two, became the college's third basketball coach.

Mike Gipson

In Davis's first two years, Mike Gipson continued as the leading scorer and still ranks nineteenth on the career scoring list. David Smith scored the most points the following two years, Ancil Johnson the next year, and Charles Smith the year after that.[16] The two Smith brothers and Johnson made the NAIA All-American list as honorable mentions, OCC's first All-Americans in basketball.

Eagle players and fans hoist Coach Davis on their shoulders after a great win in 1967.

In 1966–1967, OCC's first year in the NAIA, the team, with a twenty and five record, qualified for the NAIA state play-offs but lost to OBU.[17] The following year, the Eagles had another outstanding season, going seventeen and five. To make the NAIA regional play-offs, they had to win over Oral Roberts, who earlier had beaten them 116 to 95. The Eagles took the rematch 89 to 78, putting them in regional competition against Southwestern State, with whom they had split during the year. Playing before 3,000, they led at half-time 41 to 38, but with seven minutes to go, they were down by 4. With no shot-clock then, Southwestern went into a delay game. Billy Brooks stole the ball and scored on a layup. Eagles down by 2. Another steal and J. D. Moomaw poured in a twenty-foot jumper to tie the score. Over the final minutes, led by Benny Price and David Smith, the Eagles outscored the Bulldogs to win 79–71. Now the Eagles faced a best 2-out-of-3 regional finals against Northeastern State, the NAIA's top-ranked team. OCC won the first game at Northeastern 80 to 70. The second game, OCC's home game, was played at Central State's gym because The Barn was too small to meet NAIA standards. Northeastern won 74–72. Tied at one game each, the Eagles returned to Northeastern's home court, but won 74 to 69 to gain OCC's first trip ever to the national tournament in Kansas City.

At nationals, the Eagles played Fairmont State from West Virginia and fell behind by 13 with just six minutes to play. "Thanks to the ball-hawking of Billy Brooks," the team came back to tie the score at 71. In overtime, however, they lost 78–75.[18] Fairmont eventually took second in the tournament.

David Smith

While the loss was a heartbreaker, the season had been a great success, with twenty wins and eight losses, the first NAIA Regional Championship, the first visit to the NAIA National Championships, and a very respectable showing on the national scene.

Frank Davis resigned after the next season to coach at Georgia State University.[19] During his six years, Davis had a record of ninety-seven wins and forty-four losses. He had led the Eagles to their most successful season ever, building on foundations Coach Vaughn had laid. In 1966, Davis also "started the first overnight and weeklong basketball camps in the state."[20] He was elected to the OC Athletic Hall of Fame in 1991.

The Bill Villines Years

Bill Villines, who had coached at Abilene High School, came to OCC in 1970. His first game is memorable because the Eagles beat Sam Houston State at Homecoming, and it was the first game in OCC's new 2,500 seat Payne Field House. Having played home games for ten years in The Barn, the new facilities represented a major step forward. The far larger seating capacity meant the home crowd could be a much more important factor.[21]

Bill Villines

Villines resigned after his fifth year with a record of seventy-three wins and sixty-eight losses. Reed Johnson, honorable mention All-American in both 1972 and 1973, was the most outstanding player during the Villines years with an average of twenty-five points a game in 1971–1972.

The Jerry Jobe Years

In 1975, Jerry Jobe became OCC's head basketball coach. With eleven years at Southwestern Oklahoma State, Jobe was well-prepared.[22] In his first year, the team won fourteen and lost sixteen, but in each of the next seven years they had a winning record. In 1978, Jobe brought OCC to its first national number one ranking, and his overall win-loss record was 211 to 56. In each of his last seven years, Jobe took the Eagles to the NAIA District IX playoffs, and in 1982, they made it to the NAIA Nationals where they lost by one point in the first round. That year, OCC was thirty-three and three.

Jobe's second year brought one of the most memorable moments in Oklahoma Christian sports history. On January 18, 1977, the Eagles played cross-town rivals, the Bethany Nazarene Redskins, in the Myriad before a crowd of 3,100.[23] The Eagles were number three in the NAIA, with the Redskins number five.

Chuck Johnson scores against BNC in the Myriad.

The game had been close throughout as Chuck Johnson, Bob Williams, Steve Green, Ed Pipes, Keith Pigg, Nate King, and the Holloway brothers, Duffy and Greg, led the way for OCC. With sixteen seconds to play, however, Bethany led by five and was inbounding the ball. The game seemed out of reach. The Eagles played tight defense on the inbounds pass and Ed Pipes drew a foul, sending him to the line for two shots. He made the first, missed the second, but got the rebound and scored two more. OCC down by 2! Bethany brought the ball down the court, but the Eagles got a steal, moved quickly toward their goal—and Duffy Holloway got a tap-in just as the clock ran out. Score tied! Overtime! Each team scored eight in the first overtime, forcing a second overtime. In this final five minutes, the Eagles outscored the Redskins by four to win 84–80.[24] This thriller was one of thirty wins against three losses that year for Coach Jobe's Eagles, but the great comeback win over Bethany, against seemingly impossible odds, was the game everyone remembered.

Another great achievement during the Jobe years came in December of 1979 on an early road trip. That year's team included four who ended the season on the Sooner Athletic Conference All-Conference roster: Rob Mayberry, Kenneth Orange, Brent Marquardt, and freshman Kelly Jobe.[25] Coach Jobe scheduled three tough teams on a swing through Tennessee. In the first game against sister Christian college David Lipscomb, the Eagles topped the Bison 91–79. Next the Eagles took on NCAA Division I power Memphis State, a recent winner over the University of Arkansas. With three players on their team later taken in the NBA draft, obviously the MSU Tigers expected to trounce the small college from Oklahoma. A huge crowd of 8,151 attended, certainly the largest crowd to that point in OCC basketball history. The Eagles built an early lead, then for the final thirty minutes played a four-corners offense, not, Jobe said, to run out the clock but to use the best offense for slowing the game's tempo to the Eagles' advantage. The plan allowed Kelly Jobe, over and over, to penetrate the middle to score on driving layups or on foul shots, giving him a game-high thirty-two points. Teammate Rob Mayberry poured in nineteen, and Dwayne Williams fifteen. Final score: Eagles 90, Tigers 76. With less than a minute to play and the outcome certain, Coach Jobe called time-out to tell his players not to be overly enthusiastic after the game but to walk off the court "with class."[26] In a third game on the road trip, the Eagles played Freed-Hardeman, another sister school with a strong basketball tradition. The Eagles again came out on top, but this time by the close score of 46–44.

For the entire 1979–1980 season, the Eagles were twenty-five and nine, beating USAO (the University of Science and Arts of Oklahoma) in their first playoff game 67–60, but losing to East Central 53–48. From that year's team came three leaders in career scoring at OC: Kelly Jobe at number five, Kenneth Orange at number seven, and Dwayne Williams at number twelve. Kelly Jobe still holds the OC record for both season and career assists.

During the Jobe years from 1975 to 1983, five players were named NAIA All-American: Kevin Jones, honorable mention in 1978; Kelly Jobe, honorable mention in 1980; Kenneth Orange, honorable mention in 1981, and first team in 1983; Norvell Brown, first team in 1982; and Ron Webb, second team in both 1982 and 1983.

L to R—Kelly Jobe, Kenneth Orange, Coach Jobe, Ron Webb, and Norvell Brown

During his eight years as OCC's head basketball coach, Jobe's winning percentage of .790 was the highest of any among Oklahoma Christian's six basketball coaches. He won Texoma Conference Coach of the Year in 1977 and 1978, was Sooner Athletic Conference Coach of the Year in 1982, and three times was named coach of the year for his NAIA district. Jobe is a member of the Oklahoma Basketball Coaches Hall of Fame and, in 2007, was named to Oklahoma Christian's Athletic Hall of Fame. His OCC years were also noted for the summer basketball camps which drew large numbers to the campus.

Unfortunately, during Jobe's tenure came the most difficult problem in Oklahoma Christian athletics. Over the Christmas break in 1982, the men's basketball team and supporters traveled to Hawaii where the team played two games. Following this trip, allegations arose regarding the conduct of one of the players and, while investigating this matter, other charges developed about the basketball program: grade tampering, use of alcohol, and players receiving gifts from outside sources. To review all of these questions, President Terry Johnson chaired a committee including Deryl Gotcher, chairman of the Board; Stafford North, executive vice president; Guy Ross, vice president; Richard Greenhaw, faculty representative; and Joel McKenzie, president of the Student Senate.[27]

This committee spent more than thirty hours interviewing over fifty individuals and reviewing written documents. They determined that charges about grade changes or teachers treating athletes differently than other students were not true.[28]

The committee found that some athletes had been involved in rules violations, particularly in the use of alcohol. The student whose behavior in Hawaii brought other matters to light, in fact, had already been dismissed for drinking. The committee did not find, however, that athletes had been treated differently than other students in such matters. While the drinking among athletes was a concern, the committee found that coaches had discouraged such conduct.[29]

On the final charge, the committee found that off-campus supporters had, in fact, provided money and other benefits to players on several occasions to assist them with personal expenses. While coaches had both warned athletes against receiving gifts and sent a newsletter to boosters explaining that such was not allowed, the practice had continued.[30]

Since giving student athletes money beyond what they received through the institution violated NAIA rules, the OCC administration believed the honest course was to submit its findings to the NAIA and withdraw itself from the national tournament for which it had already qualified. While Coach Jobe had not been found to be at fault in the matters investigated, some believed it would be better to have different personnel in the basketball program to demonstrate a clear break with the past. After discussion with President Johnson, Coach Jobe submitted his resignation.

The matter had been painful on many fronts. The college had publicly released its findings and the actions taken. The campus was sorry that a great team with a thirty-one and four record and with national title aspirations had been withdrawn from competition. And many individuals had been seriously affected by the process. In the end, however, the college sought to demonstrate the principles in which it believed.

In the *Edmond Sun*, editor Ed Livermore wrote about OCC's demonstration of "ethics and integrity." "This writer grows slightly cynical on the subject of college athletics," he said, "and didn't believe there was a school in the country that would undertake this type of internal investigation, penalize itself severely and make a full report to its accrediting association. But Oklahoma Christian College did it."[31]

The Dan Hays Years

In 1983, Dan Hays began as OCC's head basketball coach. He had worked as assistant for three years at Southeastern Oklahoma State, and led the basketball program at Northwestern Oklahoma State for five seasons.

Dan Hays

In his first year, the Eagles went ten and twenty-four, but in Hays' next twenty-three seasons, the team had a winning record twenty times. Six times they have been Sooner Athletic Conference Champions, and in six of his twenty-five years, Hays has taken his team to the NAIA national tournament, advancing to the "sweet sixteen" five times. His twenty-four year record includes 513 wins and 271 losses, for a winning percentage of .654. The Hays years have included eight of the ten OC career scoring leaders and fifteen different players who have been selected as NAIA All-Americans.

Jay Mauck

Under Hays, two players were named NAIA Player of the Year. Jay Mauck, from Calera, Oklahoma, came in 1996. A five foot eight guard, Mauck was both ball-handler and shooter. His freshman year he shot .913 percent from the free-throw line sinking 84 out of 92 attempts, a record that still stands. His career free-throw percentage was .875, at one point making 65 consecutively. He also holds the record for 3-point shots, having made 378 in his career, with 11 in one game against Athens State. His career scoring average also tops the OC charts at over twenty points per game. In Mauck's junior year, OC started the season with twenty-one straight wins and was ranked number one in the NAIA. In game twenty-one, however, Mauck went down with a torn ACL, and without him, the team struggled, losing six of their last eleven to finish twenty-six and six. Mauck had knee surgery and came back his senior year, but he hurt the knee again and did not finish the year. He was a two-time All-American and NAIA Player of the Year in 1999.[32]

Jarred Merrill came to OC from Abilene, Texas, in 2001. A six foot, nine inch forward, Merrill was a two-time first team NAIA All-American who holds the men's OC record for the most points scored in a career

Jarred Merrill

at 2,189. In his senior year, he was second in the NAIA in scoring, with twenty-four points a game, and also second in rebounding, with ten and a half per game. In 2005, Merrill was named the NAIA Player of the Year and led the Eagles to the second round of the NAIA championships in Kansas City.

Cory Cole was another outstanding player for Coach Hays, being named NAIA first team All-American in 1984. Cole is third on the all-time scoring list with 1,916 points. Cole was OC's assistant women's basketball coach for ten years and was named to the OC Athletic Hall of Fame in 2000.

Hays remembers several games as especially exciting. In 1986, Oklahoma City University was in its first year in the Sooner Athletic Conference. OC already had beaten the Chiefs by one at the Eagles' Nest, and now met them in Fredrickson Field House. With 2,500 watching, the game was tied 80 to 80, with fifty-six seconds on the clock. The Eagles had the ball for a last shot and, with eight seconds left, Doug Bradley's try was in and out, and going after the rebound, he fouled the Chiefs' Chip Zumer. Now it seemed hopeless. Zumer hit the first, putting OCU up by one, but missed the second. Collis Clark quickly brought the ball down and let fly a thirty-footer which zipped through the cords at the buzzer. OC 82, OCU 81.[33]

The 1994–1995 season finished with several outstanding games. The Eagles met OCU, ranked NAIA number two, and won 100 to 95, with Eric Weins, Greg Brown, and Fred Garcia combining for 79 points. In the SAC play-offs, they first met Wayland Baptist. OC led 73–64 with 2:40 left, but Wayland closed the gap to one with forty-nine seconds remaining. Eric Wiens sank two free throws, but Wayland got a three to tie with only twenty-two seconds left on the clock. Fred Garcia got a bucket to give the Eagles the lead by two, but Wayland scored with one second left to tie at 86–86. After the first overtime, the score was still tied, but in the second, OC led by one with thirty-seven seconds left and the Eagles with the ball. Wayland fouled Weins with six seconds on the clock. He made the first, missed the second, but Wayland could not get off a shot before the buzzer. OC 99, Wayland 97, with Weins scoring a career-high 40 points. [34]

The next game was at OBU, a team that had beaten the Eagles twice in the regular season. The game turned out to be what Coach Hays called "the best game" of his first twelve years at OC. Before a packed house of 2,200, the Eagles got off to a 16–2 lead and, at the half, still led 43–34. Behind Greg Brown's 37 points, including 18 of 20 from the charity stripe, the Eagles won 108 to 85. OC shot 58 percent from the field and 79.6 percent from the line.[35] Although the team lost to OCU in the SAC tournament finals, they went to the NAIA Nationals at the Oral Roberts field house and defeated Southern University of New Orleans by 87–70.[36] In their second game at the

Nationals, OC met the eventual tournament winner, Birmingham-Southern, and lost 69–41, but it had been a great run.[37]

Two of the most exciting games of the Hay's era came back to back in February 2008. The Eagles played at OBU, ranked nationally at number twenty, and the game was close throughout. With 29.1 seconds left, the score was tied at 66 and OC had the ball. With 2.5 seconds remaining, an inbounds pass to Kyle Tefft allowed him to get off a quick 3-point shot which bounced off the rim. Jason Taylor grabbed the rebound and put it in at the buzzer for the win.[38]

Just two days later in the Eagle's Nest came another nail biter. OC led St. Gregory's through most of the game, but the score was tied at 44 when, with 3.3 seconds to play, St. Gregory's scored 2 to lead 46–44. The Eagles inbounded the ball only to be fouled almost immediately and, not being in the bonus, OC had to inbound the ball on the backside of the half-court line with only 1.8 seconds left. During a time out, Coach Hays drew the play and the Eagles executed. They inbounded to freshman Jeff Crocker just inside the half-court line, he moved toward the goal, dribbled once, and from thirty-three feet, he let fly—and "nothing but net" as he sank a three for the win. His heroics left him at the bottom of a huge pile of appreciative players and fans.[39]

Along with excellence on the court, Hays has emphasized good academic work and high character. More than 90 percent of of those staying until their senior year have completed their degrees. During his years, fourteen different players have been named as NAIA Scholar Athletes. Sports information directors have named two Hays players, Dillon Ripley and Brady Page, to receive their CoSIDA Academic All-District VI honors, and one, Cary Manek, was named to the second team of CoSIDA Academic All-Americans. In 2005, Kory Allen was selected for the NAIA Champions of Character Award.

Hays not only has taught his own players the game of basketball but has instructed thousands of youth over the years in his outstanding basketball camps. In 1998, he helped coach the USA team to a gold medal in the Junior World Championships and, in 1991, he served as the assistant coach for the gold-medal winning USA team at the World Championships for Junior Men.

Five times while at OC, Hays has been chosen Sooner Athletic Conference Coach of the Year, and twice he has won NAIA District IX Coach of the Year. He served as president of the NAIA Coaches Association from 1991 to 1993 and was elected to the NAIA Hall of Fame in 1998 and the OC Athletic Hall of Fame in 2002.

As its first intercollegiate sport and as its largest spectator sport, the OC men's basketball program has been a very important part in student life at Oklahoma Christian. Men's basketball has been one of the major windows through which the public has observed the university, and to the credit of coaches and players alike, the program has shown them to be young men of Christian character who make good grades and represent the institution well both on and off the court.

Track and Field

Men's Track and Field

The OC track and field program began in 1958–1959, the year Coach Ray Vaughn came to the college, and under his leadership, it made a strong beginning. The second year, he had twelve on the squad, including Lynn McMillon and James Moore running the mile; Alan Ritchie, Ben Stephens, John Doughty, and Tom Heinen in the sprints; Duane Robinson, Wade Sumpter, Artie Lee, and Don Sigmon in the quarter mile; and Eddie Davidson and Hickory Starr in field events.[40] This team established a number of OCC firsts: the Oklahoma Junior College Conference Championship, the NAIA Regional Championship, and participation in the nationals.[41] Remarkable achievements for only the second year in competition!

The track program took a huge leap forward in 1962–1963 with the completion of the new OCC track, provided largely through the efforts of the Booster Club.[42] The squad now had its own practice facility and hosted its first meet, bringing teams from Missouri, Kansas, Texas, Arkansas, and Oklahoma.[43] Now in senior college competition, the Eagles took third place in the Memphis Indoor Relays. [44] This same year also saw the beginning of the cross country team.

Dickie Gray in a winning jump

The 1964–1965 year brought OCC track to a new level of achievement. The eighteen-member squad won first in five events at the University of Oklahoma meet, matching the five firsts from the host school. At the Memphis Relays, the team took first place in the college division, with Olten McDade winning four firsts, Dickie Gray and Ed Harless winning one each, and the team taking three relay firsts.[45] The next year, Gray jumped 24'9," and Hal Ballou sped to a victory in the 330 yard hurdles, both new meet records.[46] Gray became the college's first All-American in track and, in fact, the first in any sport.

With Vaughn still coach, the 1966–1967 year was remarkable in several ways. OCC took first in the mile relay and second in the two-mile relay at the Kansas State meet. And the

800 meter relay of Gray, Roscoe Cogburn, Larry Rehl, and Ballou set an OCC record at 1:25:24, a record that still stands. In that same year, Rehl, Cogburn, Ballou, and Jim Butler ran the 1,600 relay at 3:11:32, another enduring OCC record. In addition, a new freshman made his mark: Jeff Bennett took first in the pole vault at Dallas and first in the 440 hurdles at East Texas State.[47]

In 1967–1968, Jeff Bennett became OCC's second All-American in track, winning first nationally in the 440 hurdles with a time of 51.44. Because he excelled in so many events—including the pole vault, hurdles, and other running events—Bennett entered Olympic training in the decathlon. The next year, Vaughn turned over the cross country program to Randy Heath but continued to coach indoor and outdoor track.

Jeff Bennett clears the bar at over 15' in the pole vault.

At the Kansas Relays in 1970, Bennett took first in the decathlon and Gary Hill third, and at the Drake Relays—one of the largest meets in the nation—the same outcome. At Drake, Bennett scored 8,072 points, the third highest in U.S. history and an OC record that still stands. Following his graduation in 1970, Bennett continued training for the 1972 Olympics held in Munich, where his fourth place finish was the best showing of any American. He missed the bronze medal by only ten points, and that because another runner bumped him in the hurdles. Bennett won All-American honors in the hurdles, pole vault, and decathlon, and some dubbed him "the world's greatest athlete, pound for pound." In 1976, Bennett was inducted into the NAIA Hall of Fame and into the OC Athletic Hall of Fame in 1991.

The 1972 track and field team took fourth out of 123 colleges in the National NAIA meet, the best finish to that point on the national level, with Gary Hill finishing first in the decathlon, Jim Neugent first in the hammer throw and discus, and a second place finish by Dale Paas in the two-mile race-walk.[48] Neugent still holds the best performance in university history in shot put, discus, and hammer.

In 1976 came the first All-American in cross country when Bobby Boswell took eleventh nationally, and Tom Story followed with All-American in 1977 with a twenty-third place finish. In that year, OCC posted its highest finish in the national cross country meet, winning fifth place out of the forty-nine schools that qualified.

The years from 1976 through 1980 were outstanding in OCC track. In 1977, at the NAIA National Meet, the distance medley relay team finished first, Ron Stangeland took second in the 1000-yard run, and the two-mile relay team finished third. These achievements gave the team a tie for second place, the highest finish ever for OC in a national track meet. Many of the records set in those years still stand: Wayne Long in the outdoor 400 meters; Steve Wolf in the outdoor 1,500 meters and the indoor 3,000 meters; Mike Herndon for both the indoor and outdoor 5,000 meters and for the steeplechase; Bob Bayless for the indoor 55 meter hurdles and the outdoor 110 hurdles; and Bobby Smith, Pat Becher, Ron Stangeland, Wayne Long, Gary Tatum, Steve Wolf and Milt Gilliam combining for many relay records both indoor and outdoor.

Mike Herndon in the steeplechase

In those years, OCC also won many championships. In 1978, the Eagles took the Texoma Conference and District IX Championships and All-American honors went to five athletes: Ron Love, Bobby Smith, Tom Story, Gary Tatum, and Danny Neugent.[49] In 1979, the Eagles had another good year, winning their fifth straight District IX Championship. Also that year, the cross country team again did well, finishing ninth place at the national level. Mike Herndon led the way, with the highest individual finish any OC runner has ever attained at the national cross country meet, coming in sixth. While Herndon came to OC to play basketball, Coach Jobe soon recognized he would be better in track and passed him to Coach Heath and Coach Vaughn. Herndon not only won All-American honors for his sixth place finish, but he also took three other All-American awards, two for indoor and one outdoor in the mile and the steeplechase.

Ray Vaughn in a familiar pose

After 1979, Vaughn decided to step out of coaching track but continued as athletic director. In 1973, he had coached the U.S. indoor team in a dual meet against the Russian team, and he had worked with U.S. decathlon athletes for two summers prior to the 1972 Olympics. During his twenty-one years of coaching at OCC, he developed fifty-six athletes who became All-Americans. In 1969, he was inducted into the NAIA Hall of Fame[50] and was the first inductee into the OC Athletic Hall of Fame in 1991.

On September 14, 1980, after a year-long struggle, Ray Vaughn died at sixty-three of a brain tumor. As successful as he had been in training athletes, his character and spirituality were most remembered. President Terry Johnson wrote:

Coach Vaughn was loved by faculty, students, and friends because he kept the athletic program at OCC in perspective with the ultimate mission of a Christian college. More than forty young men were led to Christ as a direct result of Coach Vaughn's Bible teaching, and many others were doubtless converted through his Christian example.[51]

In a statement to faculty and staff, Stafford North wrote, "When the history of OCC is written, few people will deserve a more prominent place than Ray Vaughn."[52]

Coach Randy Heath

After Coach Vaughn resigned, Randy Heath, who had been coaching cross country for eleven years, became head track coach as well. Heath recalls the 1985 team as outstanding. That year, the Eagle cross country team took the District IX Championship and placed twenty-fifth out of thirty-eight teams at nationals. In the indoor season, seven athletes took All-American honors; also, the OCC two-mile relay team placed third and the distance medley relay team second at the NAIA national meet, with seven OCC runners taking All-American honors: five in running events and two others in pole vault. In the outdoor season, four won first in the District IX meet. The highlight of the year, however, came at the Drake Relays. In the 3,200 relay, usually called 4 x 800, OCC was running against the best college-level teams in the nation. After the carries by Brett McKnight, Joe Alexander, and Paul Davies, the Eagles were in seventh place, but as Brent Fowler ran the closing 800 meters in 1:50.2, he passed six runners, coming in first. It was OCC's third relay win at Drake, having previously won in the two-mile relay in 1977 and in the distance medley in 1983.[53]

Brent Fowler anchors the Eagles to first place.

In 1991, Erich Momberger placed second at the NAIA in the decathlon, thus winning All-American honors. In the 1992 Olympics, he represented his country, Papua New Guinea, in that event, placing twenty-fifth out of thirty-six who competed in the Olympic decathlon.[54]

In more recent years, Jordan Powell has been outstanding, setting OC indoor marks in both the 800 meters at 1:53.8 and in the mile at 4:09.9. He was named All-American in 2007, when he helped OC to a fifth place finish in the outdoor 4 x 800 meter relay.

Bobby Smith has collected more All-American honors than any other OC track and field athlete. From 1977 through 1979, he ranked fifth nationally in the 1,500 meters and ran on five NAIA first place relay teams, as well as two other relay teams that took second and third. Ten members of the OC track and field team have been elected into the OC Athletic Hall of Fame: Bob Bayless, Jeff Bennett, Dick Gray, Mike Herndon, Gary Hill, Jim Neugent, Kurt Siebold, Bobby Smith, Tom Story, and Wayne Strohman.

Men's track also has had its share of academic honors. Twenty-two have been NAIA Scholar-Athletes and four have been CoSIDA Academic All-Americans: Damon Sims, third team; and Kenneth Bowling, third team; Blake Blackwell, first and second teams and Luke Anderson on the first team twice. Anderson, also a four-time All-American in the hurdles, received three of the NAIA's most prestigious awards: in 2001, the Dr. Leroy Walker Sportsmanship Award recognizing scholarship, character, and sportsmanship; the A. O. Duer Award recognizing athletic achievement, character, and scholarship, also in 2001; and in 2002 the Woody Hays Scholar Athlete award, being chosen for excellence in academics, athletics, and community service above more than 45,000 NAIA athletes.

Including his time with both cross country and track, Randy Heath has coached for thirty-nine years at OC, giving him the longest tenure of any coach in OC history. Ten times, he has won Coach of the Year awards from NAIA District IX and the Sooner Athletic Conference, and he has coached 61 different athletes to 122 All-American awards. In 1997, he was inducted into the OC Athletic Hall of Fame, and in 2003, he was elected to the NAIA Hall of Fame.

In 2007, OC alumnus and five-time All-American in track Wayne Strohman began coaching cross country both for men and women.

Women's Track and Field

In 1987, OC added a women's track and field and cross country. Randy Heath coached the new women's program as well as continuing with the men. In the twenty years of the women's program, many athletes have done well. Their best team finish in the NAIA national cross country meet is fourteenth, achieved in 2005. Four women have gained All-American honors in cross country: Peggy Murphy, Tara Collins, Kate Hudgens, and Sylvia Chirchir.

Peggy Murphy

In track and field, the women have also excelled. Murphy, who came to OC because her husband was transferred to Tinker Field, took first nationally in the marathon in both 1991 and 1993. She holds OC outdoor records in the 1,500 meters, 3,000 meters, 10,000 meters, and the marathon. Indoors, she has the best OC times in the one mile run and the 3,000 meters.

Kathy Nelson, who came to OC through the efforts of former OC track star Gary Hill, was second in the indoor 400 meters in 1998. She holds school outdoor records in the 100 meters, 200 meters, and 400 meters. Indoors, she has the records in the 100 meters, 400 meters, and 600 meters.

Alicia Gunter took third in the marathon in 1999. Rachel Krause, who ran long distances but had never run a full marathon, entered that race at the NAIA Nationals in 2001. She led for all the last half of the race only to be overtaken about 300 meters from the end. Taking second in her first marathon and at the national level, however, was an outstanding achievement. Krause holds the OC outdoor record in the 5,000 meters. Crystalyn Starks (Filmore) holds multiple OC records in the hurdles: indoors at 55 meters, and outdoors in the 100 and 400 meters. After graduating from OC, she entered the military and did a tour of duty in Iraq.

Women's relay teams have finished at the national meet in fifth and sixth, and twice in eighth. Seven have made All-American and sixteen have been named NAIA Scholar-Athletes. Kathy Nelson was also named CoSIDA second team Academic All-American.

Baseball

After CCC moved to Oklahoma City and Ray Vaughn arrived as athletic director, sports blossomed at the college. In Vaughn's first year, OCC fielded teams in basketball and track, and the next year, 1959–1960, baseball began. In that first year, Leonard Hall coached, and the team played on a new field provided by the Eagle Booster Club.[55] For the next six years, baseball had five coaches: Darvin Keck, Keith Marshall, Haskell Sinclair, Steve Small, and Ralph Samples.

In 1966–1967, Max Dobson came to coach baseball, and during his tenure, he gave the program continuity and made the Eagles

Coach Max Dobson

highly competitive. With OCC on a trimester system, most team members took classes in the second and third terms, thus allowing Dobson to have a collegiate season in the spring and a semi-pro season through the summer. The summer games allowed the team to play in excellent competition and garner valuable experience.

OCC baseball's two greatest years were the collegiate seasons of 1972 and 1973. In 1972, the team won NAIA District IX and the regional championship as well, advancing them to the NAIA World Series in Phoenix. In their first game, Eagle ace Morris Karnes lost 1–0 to Frostburg from Maryland, putting the team in the loser's bracket. Next the Eagles played Winona State (Iowa). OCC was ahead 5–3 in the ninth, but Winona loaded the bases with two outs. Dobson brought in Karnes to face one of Winona's top hitters and, with three curve balls, he struck him out and guaranteed an OCC win. Then the team played St. Francis (Illinois), ranked number one in the nation. The Eagles were behind 2–4 coming into the seventh when OCC tied the game. The score stayed at 4–4 through the ninth and on into the bottom of the twelfth. Then Tom McLemore walked and David White hit a fastball into the alley off ace pitcher Tom Brennan to score McLemore, giving OCC the win. The team lost the next game to David Lipscomb, but they had gained a tie for third place nationally. Karnes was named first team All-American and Johnny Inman was honorable mention.[56] The third place national finish was the highest ranking any Eagle sport had to that time.

The next year, 1973, also brought strong recognition to OCC baseball. The University of Oklahoma, ranked in the top five in the NCAA, scheduled the Eagles for an early season contest and sent to the mound their ace, Jackson Todd, who later played for the New York Mets. OU had a thirty-three home game winning streak. Coach Dobson called on Karnes to pitch. Scoreless through eight, the Eagles came to bat in the top of the ninth. Mike Baker singled and Dobson sent speedster Jeff Whitehead in as a pinch runner. A bunt advanced him to second, and when Chuck White singled, Whitehead came home with the winning run. Karnes retired the side in the bottom of the ninth for the four-hit victory. The Eagles had taken a thriller from one of the best collegiate teams in the nation. The next year, with Brad Jones pitching, OCC beat OU again, this time 5 to 3.[57]

Besides Karnes and Inman, Dobson coached four other All-Americans: Ken Hope, first team; Gary Noske, honorable mention; Speedy Faith, honorable mention; and Alan Hoffhines, honorable mention.

Dobson gave up coaching baseball in 1980 after amassing a record of 461 wins against 288 losses. He was elected to the OC Athletic Hall of Fame in 1995 and into the NAIA Hall of Fame in 1996.

Tommy Heath coached baseball for a year (23–26), Kerry Tremain for a year (19–24), then Tim Smith for a year (8–33). Tremain returned for three more years. In 1984, the team won 20 and lost 27, and the following year, they went 28 and 13, taking third in the District IX play-offs, with Tremain winning District IX coach of the year. The next year, under Tremain, the Eagles went 24–24.

Johnny Inman

In 1987, Johnny Inman, who played for Dobson in the seventies, began as baseball coach and filled that role until 2001. During his fifteen years, the Eagles had five thirty-win seasons, and Inman's overall record was 389–386. He coached four All-Americans: Mark Jackson, first team; Eric Armstrong, second team; Manny Bones, honorable mention; and Clint Vaughn, second team. Vaughn, grandson of Coach Ray Vaughn, was Sooner Athletic Conference Player of the Year in 1997, hitting .477, a school record that still stands. That year, he had eighteen homeruns. After graduation, Vaughn was drafted by the Cincinnati Reds and played in the advanced rookie Pioneer League, where he made the All-Star team. In 1993, when the Eagles went 30–20, Inman was chosen as both SAC Coach of the Year and District IX Coach of the Year.

After the 2001 season, the OC administration decided to drop baseball. The university was in a transition between presidents and was experiencing financial strains that required belt tightening in many areas. Many were sorry to see baseball go and hoped it would someday return.

At the meeting of the OC Board of Trustees on October 29, 2004, David North reported for the Athletic Program Strategic Taskforce, recommending the employment of a full-time athletic director and the reinstatement of baseball. The Board approved the recommendation and DeWayne Hall was employed to direct athletic programs. He embarked on a major fundraising drive to build a baseball stadium at the cost of $800,000. With more than 60 percent of the donations coming from former baseball players, he raised the amount required, and construction started on the new field, which was ready for the 2008 season. The new baseball venue was named Dobson Field, in honor of Max and Ramona Dobson. He had coached the baseball program for fourteen years, including its highest ranking ever, and Ramona had been a team player in his work.

On February 9, 2008, baseball returned to OC. With former player Chuck White coaching, the Eagles took the field for the first time in seven years. In a close and well-played game, OC beat Peru State (Nebraska) 5–4. A large turnout on a beautiful February day clearly indicated that the campus was glad to have baseball back.

Tennis

Men's Tennis

Men's tennis began at OCC in 1960–1961 with six players on the squad. In the early years, they played other Oklahoma colleges and out of state Abilene Christian, Hardin Simmons, and John Brown. Bill Kirk, dean of students, coached in 1963, followed by business faculty member Steve Small who coached the team to eleven wins, seven losses, and one tie, including victories over Central State, Phillips, Oklahoma Baptist, and John Brown. Richard Lawson, who later served on the OC Board of Trustees and became one of OC's major donors, played that year.

When Frank Davis came to coach basketball in 1964–1965, he also coached tennis. Others coaching tennis during those early years were Kenny Kaaiohelo, former player Tom Lashley, Tom Heath, Gary Call, and Jan Handley. Ray Vaughn, Jr., later an OC Board member and member of the Oklahoma House of Representatives, played four years, 1967 through 1970. In 1984, Dan Hays became the tennis coach, along with his basketball duties. Kris Miller, who later coached tennis, played from 1982 through 1986.

There were no tennis scholarships in those years, but often players had academic scholarships that provided some tuition assistance. When the tennis coaches were also coaching other sports, their primary role for tennis was arranging games and overseeing travel.

In 1987, Kris Miller became tennis coach and began a new era. In 1989, for the first time, the coach had scholarships—an amount equaling the tuition, room, and board for two students to distribute among players. These grants allowed Miller to draw players from a new level. By 1995, the tennis team was ranked twenty-fifth in the NAIA, and in 1996, Miller took the team to the national tournament for the first time. This team of Sam Winterbothom, Srdan Kalajdzic, Alex Fernandez, Dan Nelson, John Blackburn, Charles Meave, and Eddie Dacuyan finished that tournament ranked thirteenth in the nation, a new mark for tennis at OC.[58]

Miller was able to recruit players from outside the United States because he had long been around the tennis world and knew tennis coaches at several major universities. Through them he learned of coaches from other countries who told him of players who would come to play on partial scholarships.[59] Eventually the scholarships were increased to four, which gave Miller more opportunity to draw outstanding prospects.

After their first visit to nationals in 1996, Miller took his men's team back for the next six years, usually winning in the first round but being defeated in the second. Then came 2003! Miller had already decided this would be his last year to coach tennis because the university was having to trim the budget, which included a reduction in tennis scholarships. He considered that year's team not necessarily his most talented, but he was impressed with their hard practice. With the help of funds saved from the previous year, this team was able to travel to more tournaments than in past years, and in fact, early in the season, they flew to Georgia for a three-day tournament. There they beat the NAIA's number four, number three, and number two, proving to Miller and the team that this year could be something special. Throughout the season, they continued to win, only losing once and that to the University of West Florida, ranked number two in NCAA Division II.[60]

The team won the Sooner Conference Championship and made it into the national finals for the eighth year in a row. Because of their number two ranking, they received a first-round bye, thus automatically advancing them to the second round. In the second round, they beat Indiana Wesleyan 5–0, and in the third round they won over Cumberland, Kentucky, 5–0. In the semifinals they played against Georgia Southwestern, a team they had beaten earlier in the year 6–3, but at that time one of its best players was out with an injury.[61]

After the three doubles matches and the first five singles matches, the score was tied 4–4, so the outcome would turn on the last match, which pitted each team's number two player against the other. OC freshman Ondrej Fukala would meet a player from Georgia Southwestern who had not lost all year. They split the first two sets, bringing the match—and a chance to go into the finals—down to the third set. After eight games, Fukala trailed 3–5 and was down 40-love. Game, set, and match point! Fukala made an outstanding running shot to get the ball back over the net, but set up the opportunity for a smash which could close out the match. But, a miss, and the game was still on. With that success, the inspired Fukala won the next five match points to bring the game score to 4–5. To win, he would have to take three more games from his opponent, and he did exactly that, winning the match 7–5 and putting OC into the national finals.[62]

In the game for the national championship, OC met Azusa Pacific, ranked number one all year. Miller had worked the players hard all season, conditioning them through weights, sprints, and agility drills. The team also had worked every day on fundamentals such as having to hit a hundred straight good forehand and backhand shots down the line. And for the three weeks before the tournament, OC's players had been out of school, spending four hours a day on the court along with an hour and a half working out in the gym.[63]

All of this prepared them for their final match. By a score of 5 to 1, OC crushed Azusa Pacific to win the NAIA National Championship.

A team of five freshmen and one junior had brought OC its first and only national championship. In that great 2003 year, six men took All-American honors: Ivan Angulo, Eduardo Autran, Alfonso Bacalja, Ondrej Fukala, Lee Gregg, Daniel Omana.

Unfortunately, after this great success, five of the six players transferred to other universities because of OC's cutback in scholarships, which left Chris Young, the next coach, with a rebuilding year in which the team went 11–5. Lisa Johnson, an OC alumna, coached the four following years with record of 38–37. In both 2006 and 2008, the men won the conference championship, and in the fall of both 2006 and 2007, they won the ITA Regional Championship. In 2008, the team also went to the NAIA Nationals. During the Johnson years, Bruno Andrade, Luis Arguello, and Juraj Sekera all were two time All-Americans.

While OC tennis teams go back to 1960, their greatest success has been in more recent years. Since 1995, twenty-four different men have been named All-Americans, ten being first team selections. Sam

Sam Winterbothom

Winterbothom was named All-American all four of his OC years, with two first place honors and two second place. Dante Magnoni won three first place selections; Alfonso Bacalja, two firsts and a second; and Ondrej Kebrle, two firsts. Ten have been named NAIA Scholar Athletes, and John Riehs was three times a GTE/Verizon/ESPN Academic All-American. For coaching the men, Kris Miller was named three times as District IX Coach of the Year, once as Southwest Region Coach of the Year, once Sooner Athletic Conference Coach of the Year and, in the year OC became NAIA Champions, National Coach of the Year by the NAIA and the ITA. Lisa Johnson was named NAIA Region VI Coach of the Year for 2006.

Women's Tennis

The women had a tennis team as early as 1977, but there has not been one every year. Nevertheless, the women's program has had many successful years. In 1997, Kris Miller became the women's coach, along with coaching the men, and directed the women's program until 2002. The team first went to the national tournament in 1988 and qualified again for nationals in each of the next four years. The best year for the women came in 2000, when

Gabriela Lancman

they placed third nationally.[64] That year they were fifteen and seven and placed Gabriela Lancman and Natalya Nikitina as first team All-American and Monica Ribero on the second team. Since 1998, the women have had eleven different players receive All-American honors, with many gaining the honor in more than one year. In all, they have had thirteen on the first team and six on the second.

Lancman won recognition as an NAIA Scholar Athlete all four years at OC, took the GTE/Verizon/ESPN award for Academic All-Americans twice and, in 2001, won Tennis Magazine's Arthur Ashe Award for Sportsmanship and Leadership, an honor Jennifer Le also won in 2007. Eight other Lady Eagles have been named NAIA Scholar Athletes. As a group, in 2006, the women's tennis team had a collective grade point average of 3.67, which earned them the number two rank in the nation for NAIA Scholar Teams.

In 2003–2004 and 2004–2005, Chris Young (24–14) coached the women, taking them to the national tournament both years. From 2005 through 2008, Lisa Johnson (50–30) coached the women, leading them to the national tournament in 2006 and 2007. Jennifer Le was the most outstanding women's player during the Johnson years, being All-American for three years. In 2006, the women placed number two in the nation as an NAIA Scholar Team.

In the fall of 2008, Kris Miller returned to coach both the men and the women in tennis. With restored scholarships, he hopes to take the Eagles back to national prominence.

Women's Volleyball

Women's volleyball got its beginning at OCC as an extramural sport in the fall of 1973.[65] At this level, the women primarily participated in tournaments with teams from other colleges within the state. When Jerry Jobe came to coach basketball in 1975, his wife, Laura Beth, coached volleyball.

By 1978–1979, the team had progressed to playing a regular season of intercollegiate matches and finished with a record of thirteen and eleven and a second place finish in the Oklahoma Association of Intercollegiate Athletics for Women.[66] The next year, the team had a sixteen and fourteen record, including a first place at the Central State Tournament.[67] The next two years, Terri Stewart coached the team, and in her second year (1981–1982), the team

Denise Whittaker blocks a shot.

finished third in the NAIA District IX State Tournament.[68] In 1982–83, Laura Beth Jobe returned as coach, but the program was clearly in decline, and the ladies won only two games that year.[69] The next year, Pete Brazle and Kerry Tremain coached the women's volleyball team in what turned out to be its final year at OCC. Interest was waning, and other schools were dropping the sport, so the college's administration and athletic department decided not to continue with volleyball.[70]

With the recent expansion of OC athletic programs, volleyball is set to return in 2009.

Golf

Intercollegiate golf at Oklahoma Christian began in 1975–1976 as a nonscholarship program.[71] Jerry Jobe, who came the previous year to coach basketball, began coaching the golf team in 1976–1977.[72] Under Jobe in 1980, the team had its most successful year to that point, winning second in the Sooner Conference.[73] Golf continued to serve those who wanted to play but did not offer scholarships. The 1986 *Aerie* included the following note:

> The Eagle tennis and golf squads struggled through another tough spring season, while trying to hold their heads high in honor of the sports which they love. Both sports have been under budgeted and neglected for many years, but those who are dedicated to these two outdoor sports always manage to come out and make the best of the spring weather and the satisfaction of being a part of the Eagle's varsity athletic program in spite of the sometimes discouraging situations.[74]

By 1991, the Athletic Department had dropped the golf program but, the *Aerie* reported, "four OC men came together to form the Eagle Golf Club," saying they were committed to "keep golf alive at OC by organizing their own team."[75]

Bob Lashley

In May 1996, Bob Lashley was raising money for OC and approached a man who said the only gift he would make was $100,000 to start a golf scholarship fund if the university would resume its golf program. Lashley visited with Kevin Jacobs, who had been named president but had not yet taken office. Jacobs accepted the offer and named Lashley to coach the team. With two full scholarships to divide among the players, the new coach immediately started the search for golfers.

His greatest find fell into his lap when Richard Guzzo from Australia learned about the program and asked to come.[76]

The promised $100,000 never actually came, but its prospect had triggered the revival of golf at OC. The team did not win any tournaments in the first year, but Guzzo tied for first at the Sooner Athletic Conference championship. In the second year, the team played in a collegiate tournament at David Lipscomb, and in a sudden death play-off against the reigning NAIA champion, Berry College of Georgia, won their first tournament. Later that year they were, at one point, ranked third in the NAIA. In the national tournament, the golf team finished thirteenth and the following year took twelfth.[77]

Richard Guzzo

In 1999–2000, OC alumnus David Lynn became coach and continued to build the program. That year, the team finished third at nationals, and Richard Guzzo, Nick Hartzler, and Michael Martin became the first OC All-Americans in golf. In the next eight years, OC finished each year in the top four in the National Tournament and had nine additional All-American selections, most of them receiving the honor for multiple years.

David Lynn

One of OC's most acclaimed golfer has been Juan Lizarralde from Uruguay. He made NAIA All-American four years, was first team Ping All-American twice, and made the NAIA All-Tournament Team in 2004 and 2005. Another golfer taking top honors was Bruno Buccolo from Argentina who has been NAIA first team All-American four times, Ping first team All-American, NAIA Scholar Athlete, NAIA All-Tournament team, and GTE/Verison/ESPN Academic All-District VI. In 2008, Buccolo was one of three NAIA golfers named by the Golf Coaches Association of America to the All-Nicklaus team. Rhein Gibson has also chalked up four first team All-American awards and won the Oklahoma State Amateur Championship in 2008.

Juan Lizarralde

Under Coach Lynn, the OC golf team has developed a strong international flavor. The 2007–2008 team of thirteen

Bruno Buccolo

members had five from the U.S., two from Scotland, two from Bolivia, and one each from Argentina, England, Australia, and Germany.

The three national second place wins in 2001, 2005, and 2008 rank as three of the five times the Eagles have finished with a national first or second in all sports. With strong showings in recent years, golf has certainly established itself as one of OC's most successful programs.

In Summer 2008, Coach Lynn resigned as the OC golf coach and was replaced by Kelsey Cline, an outstanding golfer for the University of Oklahoma, graduating in 2001.

Women's Basketball

Julie Ross

As Title IX was encouraging more women's sports, in 1977 OCC added women's basketball, with Dr. Max Dobson as coach. While a women's team had played other colleges in extramural basketball since 1975, Dobson fielded the first team actually at the intercollegiate level. With ten freshmen, one sophomore, and one senior on the team, Dobson got the program off to an excellent start with a season of fourteen wins and eleven losses.[78] The team even beat Oklahoma State University and, later in the year, Beth Malone scored thirty-nine points against Langston. In 1980, with a record of twenty-three and twelve, the team won the AIAW State Championship, beating Southwestern Oklahoma State, Oklahoma Baptist, Langston, and Northwestern Oklahoma State. Quite an accomplishment for a team in only its third year of competition!

Dobson continued as coach for another five winning seasons, capturing the Sooner Athletic Conference Championship in both 1984 and 1985. Dobson's eight-year record was 173 wins to 80 losses. During those years, Julie Ross was the most outstanding player, being chosen as second team All-American once and earning an honorable

Dobson and Coale

mention in three other years. She was also SAC Player of the Year and NAIA Scholar-Athlete in 1985. Dobson's best-known player, whom he coached for her first two years at OCC, is Sherri (Buben) Coale, now the very successful head women's basketball coach at the University of Oklahoma.

Stephanie Findley, who played guard for Dobson from 1979 to 1982, and served as his assistant for three years after her graduation, became the head women's coach in 1985 when Dobson retired from the job. Findley now has coached the Lady Eagles for twenty-three seasons.

Stephanie Findley

In her first year, Findley led the team to twenty-three victories against eight losses, winning the District IX Championship and reaching the quarterfinals of the NAIA National Tournament. During her years, she has amassed a winning percentage of .638, taking her team to the nationals twelve times, twice reaching the top eight.

During the Findley era, four women have been named first team NAIA All-Americans: Pam Kelly (1988), Sarah Reese (2002), Lauren Decker (2006), and Rachel Martin (2007). Thirteen others have been second team, third team, or honorable mention, some of them in multiple years. Also, April Clowdus (Kaaiohelo) in 1995 and Rachel Martin in 2007 have been named as first team Kodak All-Americans.

One of Findley's strongest points of emphasis has been her team's academic work. Twenty-three of her players have been named as NAIA Scholar-Athletes, many of them in more than one year, and Kim Golden was CoSIDA Academic All-American, first team in 1991. Findley's 2007 team compiled the highest team grade point average (3.56) of any athletic team in the Sooner Athletic Conference and achieved the number three NAIA ranking on the Women's Basketball Coaches Association Honor Roll. The 2006–2007 team also won the NAIA Champions of Character award for their numerous community initiatives, particularly with Washington Irving Elementary School and Habitat for Humanity.

The Lady Eagles have had their share of exciting games. One of Findley's best memories comes from 1987 in her first year as head coach. The Lady Eagles were twenty-four and seven going against Cameron, nationally ranked at number eight, contending for the District IX title. Playing at Cameron, OCC had one of those nights when all the shots fell. They led by twenty at the half and won 92–68, shooting 79.6 percent from the field, an NAIA record that still stands. They only missed ten field goals in the entire game. Next they beat St. Mary's of the Plains in a regional playoff game and then took Wisconsin Green Bay 78–48 in the first round of the national tournament before falling to Georgia Southwestern.

In 1994, the Lady Eagles trailed OBU by eleven with less than two minutes to play. Coach Findley told her players to foul as soon as OBU had the ball and, fortunately for OC, OBU was missing free throws.

With ten seconds left, OC trailed by two and got the rebound from a missed foul shot. Findley called time-out to set the play. Nicole Sanders got the inbounds pass and drove toward the basket. Having pulled the defense toward her, she was to pass back to April Clowdus for the three-point attempt. Clowdus, however, was covered, so Sanders passed to Missy McClure who sank a three to win at the buzzer.

April Clowdus

Another exciting finish came in 2006, when the Lady Eagles played nearby University of Central Oklahoma. Trailing 34–30 at half-time, OC came back to lead by one in the final minute. With 11.8 seconds to go, however, UCO had regained a one-point lead, but the Lady Eagles had the ball. Kailan DeCamp scored on a driving layup to give the Lady Eagles a one-point win.

Julie Ross, who played from 1981 to 1985, still holds the record for the most points in an OC basketball career with 2,565. Pam Kelly (1984–1988) with 2,558 points is second, and Beth Malone (1977–1981) with 2,219 points is third. April Clowdus (Kaaiohelo) holds the records for most points in a game (43) and highest rebound average (12.5).

Over the span of thirty-one years, the Lady Eagles have had only two head coaches: Max Dobson for eight years and Stephanie Findley for twenty-three. Over those years, the team has a win-loss record of 619 to 333. Dobson won SAC Coach of the Year for women's basketball in 1981, 1984, and 1985, and he is in both the OC and NAIA Halls of Fame.

Findley has been president of the NAIA Women's Basketball Coaches Association three times, SAC Coach of the Year four times, and NAIA District Coach of the Year twice. She also has served as the NAIA representative on the USA Women's Collegiate Committee since 2001. In 2004, she was inducted into the Oklahoma Christian Athletic Hall of Fame.

Soccer

Men's Soccer

As interest in soccer was growing throughout the nation, and with more high schools fielding teams, OCC added men's soccer in 1986.[79] Bob Whidden coached that year, and since they were just getting started, the team won only one game, beating Friends in overtime. The next year, Nathan Shotts began his seven-year coaching stint, and the team improved to 8 wins, 11 losses, and 1 tie, making it into the NAIA District IX semifinals. Again in 1992, Shotts took the team to the District IX playoffs, beating Oklahoma City University 2–1 before losing to Northeastern 1–2. In 1992, OC had its first soccer All-Americans: Kevin Arledge on the second team and Chris Smith as honorable mention. Overall, Shotts' record was 69 wins against 64 losses and 9 ties.

Jon Goad became men's coach in 1994 and that year led the Eagles to the District IX Playoffs. There the team beat Southern Nazarene 3–0 and OCU 3–2 to advance to the NAIA Southwest Regional, where they lost to Belhaven (Mississippi) 1–2. In 1995, the team advanced to the NAIA Sectional Semifinal, where they lost to Phillips 0–1. In Goad's last year, 1998, the Eagles won the SAC Tournament with a two-overtime win over St. Gregory's 3–2 and a 2–1 win over USAO. In the Southwest Regional, they lost to William Carey (Mississippi) 0–2. That year, OC got its third soccer All-American: Sam Winterbothom as honorable mention. From 1995 through 1999, goalie Coal Burgman set the record for the most saves with 513. Goad's five-year record was 49 wins, 46 losses, and 3 ties.

In 1999, OC alumnus and former soccer player Eric Thornhill became coach only two years after his graduation. In Thornhill's three years, OC men's soccer had a record of 36 wins, 22 losses, and 2 ties. In 1999, the team made the NAIA North Zone Playoffs and in 2001 beat John Brown and St.

Thornhill and Odhiambo

Gregory's to win Region VI and then won over Aliant International (California) in the first round of the national tournament in a tight game ending 1–0. Although they lost in the second round, making it into the final tournament and winning in the first round gave OC its highest finish ever. That year, Tom Odhiambo became OC's first and only first team soccer All-American. Also in 2001, Andres Rota was named to the second team All-American and Chris Lemons to the third team, after he was honorable mention the two previous years. The successful 2001 season brought Thornhill the award for NAIA Region VI Coach of the Year.

Another OC alumnus, Adam Basic, coached from 2002 through 2005. His four-year record was 37 wins against 26 losses and 9 ties. Matt Clark was the most outstanding player during these years, being honorable mention All-American three times and getting his fourth honorable mention under Basic's successor. Clark holds the OC record for the most goals scored in a season at twenty-three and the most scored in a career at seventy-one. Clark also holds the record for the most points, which combines goals and assists.

For the 2006 and 2007 seasons, David Scott was the coach. In his first year, Scott took the Eagles to the NAIA National Tournament, beating Embry-Riddle (Florida) 2–1 and losing in the quarterfinals to Webber International (Florida) by a score of 2–3. Scott's two-year record was 20, 12, and 4.

Since 1992, a total of fifteen OC players have received All-American honors, and twelve players have won NAIA Scholar Athlete awards. Two, Austin Taylor and Adam Barnes, have been named GTE/Verizon/ESPN Academic All-Americans.

When Adam Langford, who lettered four years in soccer during his OC years, was killed in a January 2007 truck accident in Uganda where he was serving as a missionary, friends and relatives established a soccer scholarship endowment in his honor because his hard-working and friendly spirit typified the best in what OC soccer seeks to be.

Women's Soccer

Women's soccer began at OC in 1993. Nathan Shotts, men's coach, also coached the women. The first year was very successful, with a record of 10 and 6 and a bid to the NAIA District IX playoffs, where the women lost to Southern Nazarene 2–0. Jon Goad began coaching both men's and women's soccer in 1994 and stayed for five years. During his time, the women had a total record of 35 wins against 66 losses and 2 ties.

Elizabeth Brewer (Mullins) kicks hard

In 1999, Adam Basic came in as the new coach. Six of the seven years under Coach Basic brought winning seasons, and Basic's overall record was 79 wins, 59 losses, and 9 ties. In two of Basic's first three years, the women went to the NAIA regional playoffs and, in 2002, women's soccer had its best year to that point. They beat Northwestern 1–0 in the Sooner Athletic Conference Playoffs but lost to OCU in the finals 0–1. Their record, however, got them an invitation to the NAIA Regionals, where they beat Southern Nazarene 2–0 and then faced OCU again. This time they beat OCU after a 0–0 tie by winning on penalty kicks 4–3. This win put them in the national tournament, where they lost to Lindenwood (Missouri) 1–4.

In 2004, the women had another great year, beating OCU 1–0 in the SAC Playoffs, and beating them again 2–0 in regionals. In the regional finals they met Northwestern and played to a 1–1 tie but took the victory on penalty kicks 4–3. Again in the nationals, they lost in the first round to William Jewel (Missouri).

Five different women took All-American honorable mention honors during Basic's years: Piper Coalson three times, Julie Crosley three times, Megan Childers twice, and Chelsee Truesdell and Kristin Brown once each.

In 2006, for the first time, the women had a coach who was not also coaching the men at the same time. Sean O'Connor, an All-American at Lindenwood College who had played four years of professional soccer in Sweden, coached the women to an outstanding record in his first year. They went seventeen and two, with two ties. In the NAIA regional tournament, they beat OCU 3–2 but lost to College of the Southwest (New Mexico) 0–1. Still, they got a bid to the national tournament where they lost in the first round to Concordia (Oregon). Two women made honorable mention All-American in 2006: Taryn Caylor and Stephanie Duncan. O'Conner's two year record is 25, 11, and 4.

In Fall 2008, Randall Robison came from Westmore High School to coach women's soccer.

Women's Softball

In 1995, OC added softball as another sport for women. Tom Heath, who had been directing intramurals and filling various other roles at OC since 1973, took the coaching responsibilities and has served since that time. An OC alumnus who lettered in baseball, Heath's record over thirteen years is 390 to 280, with 1 tie. The Lady Eagles play their home games at a field on the OC campus.

Twice Heath's team has earned a berth in the NAIA World Series. The first came in 2002 when the Lady Eagles were ranked seventh nationally. In the SAC Tournament, the team beat USAO 3–2 and OBU 1–0 but then lost to OCU 0–4, and to OBU 0–5. They still received a bid to the NAIA Region VI Tournament, where they beat Northwood (Texas) by 7–1 but then lost to OBU 0–1. They then beat Houston Baptist 1–0 but lost to St. Gregory's 1–2. With their good record, however, they were invited to the national tournament, where they beat Biola (California) 3–0, lost to OCU 1–3, and beat Ohio Dominican 1–0, before losing to Pt. Loma Nazarene (California) 0–3.

The next year, 2003, the Lady Eagles had another great year. In the SAC tournament, they beat St. Gregory's and lost to OCU but still got a bid to the regionals. There, they beat OBU 4–0 but lost to Houston Baptist and USAO. Still they were invited to the national tournament. Ranked eleventh in the final poll, OC first met fifth-seeded Thomas (Georgia). Stephanie Gault pitched a three-hit shut-out and back-to-back doubles by Shawna Lenz and Ginny Herndon brought in the winning run. In the second game, the Lady Eagles met Houston Baptist, which had beaten them before. In this game, Gault allowed only five hits and struck out ten. Lenz singled, stole second, and scored on Lacy Botchlet's second hit of the game. The second 1–0 game in a row! Although they lost the next two games, they tied for fifth nationally, their best finish ever.

Ten Lady Eagles have taken All-American Honors. Rebecca Robinett was the first in 1988, listed on the second team. Amy Vanderpool (Truesdell) has a first and two seconds, while Leah Carrell has a first and a second. Shawna Lenz won first team honors with her great hitting in 2003. Amber Moser and Lindsey Lawson have been on the second team, while Stephanie Gault, Tiffany Willis, and Tracy Washam have all been honorable mention.

Amy Vanderpool has the highest season batting average at .470 and the highest career average at .403. In March 2007, in a game against Southern Nazarene, Angie Plowman hit three home runs, the most any player has

Leah Carrell

had in a single game. In that game, she also had nine runs batted in. Rebecca Robinett (Cobb) has the most career home runs at thirty-two. Leah Carrell holds the most records as a pitcher: 20 strikeouts in one game and 698 strikeouts in her career; best winning percentage at .782; lowest earned run average at 1.02; and most wins in an OC career at 86.

As in many other OC sports, softball players have also excelled in the classroom. Over the team's thirteen years, 99 percent of those reaching their senior year at OC have completed their degrees. Twenty-two Lady Eagles have been named as NAIA Scholar-Athletes, and ten have been named to the list of GTE/Verizon/ESPN Academic All District VI. In 2004, the players had an overall grade point average of 3.549, and the softball team was ranked fourth on the National Fastpitch Coaches Association Academic Teams list.

Others Involved in OC Sports

Sports at Oklahoma Christian involves much more than the contest on the field or the court. Student athletes also excel in academics as shown by their success in 2008 when a school record six students were named to the ESPN Academic All-American list, "the most of any NAIA Division I institution."[80] Adam Barnes (3.97), Kristin Brown (4.0) and Cassie Tyoer (4.0) played soccer, while Bruno Buccolo (3.82) played golf, and Patrick Grewe (4.0) and Charlotte Heron (4.0) ran track. Also in 2008, OC ranked eighth out of all NAIA school with twelve of its sports teams earning a grade point average of 3.0 or above.[81]

Roderick Green running in Australia

Another interesting sports story has been the achievements of Roderick Green who won three medals in the Sydney Paralymics in 2001. With his right leg replaced with a prosthesis, Green won a silver and two bronze in running and jumping events.[82]

OC's Sports Information Department has also been outstanding. Jack McElroy, Ralph Turner, Steve Dodd, Curtis Janz, Stan Green, and Wes McKenzie have led the program, which has received numerous awards for its outstanding publications. In 2008, for example, the NAIA Sports Information Directors of America awarded OC first place for its men's and women's basketball guide, and they won the top two places in the "Multi-Sports Brochure category for the spring and fall sports guides."[83]

Another important element of OC sports is its cheerleading squad. Every year since intercollegiate sports began in 1956, these students have worked hard to lead cheers, perform acrobatics, and do routines. Through the years they have helped stir the crowd at men's and women's basketball games. For many years, also, the "Nine Noises" added their antics to enliven the crowd.

And then there are the fans. Over the years, thousands of OC fans have cheered their teams and, compared with the number of fans at OC's competing schools, the numbers are large. This fan support led the *Daily Oklahoman* to name the Eagle's Nest as the number one venue for NAIA basketball in the state.

Conclusion

From playing basketball in a YMCA in its first year through 2008 when baseball got a new start, athletics has been an important part of Oklahoma Christian University. Teams have been successful in winning games, conference titles, and national awards. Sports for both men and women have attracted many students to Oklahoma Christian, and the teams have made a major contribution to school spirit through the years. Athletics has brought the university important recognition, not only with wins but also in appreciation of the sportsmanship and service of the athletes. In the minds of the coaches and participants, however, OC athletics has made its greatest contribution by being an important formative agent in building the character of those who have participated. That was the goal of Coach Vaughn, who laid the foundation, and it has been the goal of all the coaches who have followed. While in the short-term, everyone wants to win, in the long-term, providing an avenue through which athletes learn to be better people, better citizens, and better Christians is the true goal of the programs.

Chapter 16, Endnotes

1   Stan Green, "Fifty Years of Athletics," OC Archives.
2   "CCC Cancels Basketball," *Tower*, February 8, 1957, OC Archives.
3   *Focus*, 1958–59, 73–74, OC Archives.
4   *Focus*, 1960, 71, OC Archives.
5   "Emerging Cage Power Eagles March to 24–2 Record," *Aerie*, 1961, 51, OC Archives.
6   Frank Davis, *From Hopper to Here*, privately published, 2005, 36.
7   Ibid.
8   Ibid.
9   *Aerie*, 1962, 101, OC Archives.
10   *Focus* 1960, 68, OC Archives.
11   "Haskell Sinclair Takes Over as Head Basketball Coach," *Oklahoma Christian College Bulletin*, March, 1962, 4, OC Archives.
12   *Aerie*, 1963, 108–110, OC Archives.
13   Davis, 41.
14   *Aerie*, 1964, 131, OC Archives.
15   Davis, 41.
16   Data on players, scoring averages, OC records, All-Americans, information on coaches, OC Hall of Fame, and similar statistics throughout this chapter not otherwise attributed is taken from the OC Media Guides for 2007 and 2008, prepared primarily by Stan Green and Wes McKenzie. The author expresses his debt to and appreciation for these outstanding compilations of information on OC sports.
17   *Aerie*, 1967, 186, 195, OC Archives.
18   *Aerie*, 1968, 185, OC Archives.
19   Davis, 48.
20   Ibid., 49.
21   "Major Assembly To Kick-Off Homecoming," *Oklahoma Christian College Bulletin*, October, 1970, OC Archives; "Eagle Rally Stuns Sam Houston in Homecoming Victory," *Aerie*, 1971, 174, OC Archives.
22   Bob Colon, "OSSAA's Jobe Was a Winner Wherever He Coached," *Daily Oklahoman*, June 8, 1996.
23   "OCC Does It in 2 OT's," *Daily Oklahoman*, January 19, 1977, 21.
24   "Green Hero For Eagles," *Bethany Tribune Review*, January 20, 1977, 9.
25   "Team wins Sooner Conference for fourth year," *Aerie*, 1980, 256–257, OC Archives.
26   "Eagles win over Memphis State, David Lipscomb, Freed-Hardeman," *Talon*, December 7, 1979, 16, OC Archives; Jerry Jobe, phone conversation with the author on January 24, 2008.
Note: In 1994, Memphis State University changed its name to the University of Memphis.
27   Minutes, Board of Trustees, February 16, 1983, Exhibit A, OC Archives.
28   Ibid.
29   Ibid.
30   Ibid.
31   Ed Livermore, Jr., "In Pursuit of Integrity," *Edmond Evening Sun*, March 4, 1983, reprinted in the *OCC Reporter*, April 83, 2, OC Archives.
32   *Basketball Guide*, 2007–2008, 26–27.
33   Volney Meece, "Prayer Shot Lifts OCC Over OCU," *Daily Oklahoman*, February 11, 1986.
34   Christy Robinson, "Weins scores career high in double OT win," *Talon*, March 3, 1995, OC Archives.
35   Murray Evans, "OC Advances to SAC Final," *Daily Oklahoman*, March 5, 1995, 7, Newsbank.
36   Christy Robinson, "Eagles advance to NAIA Sweet 16," *Talon*, March 17, 1995, 6, OC Archives.

37 Christy Robinson, "Eagles fall to Birmingham-Southern," *Talon*, March 31, 1995, 6, OC Archives.
38 "Taylor's buzzer shot beats Bison," OC Web site, Athletics, February 7, 2008.
39 "Eagles win in buzzer-beating fashion, again," OC Web site, Athletics, February 9, 2008.
40 *Focus*, 1960, 61–62, OC Archives.
41 *Aerie*, 1961, 58, OC Archives.
42 *Aerie*, 1962, 112, OC Archives.
43 *Aerie*, 1963, 118, OC Archives.
44 Ibid.
45 *Aerie*, 1965, 155, OC Archives.
46 *Aerie*, 1966, 164, OC Archives.
47 *Aerie*, 1967, 198, OC Archives.
48 "Eagles are Number 1," *Oklahoma Christian College Reporter*, August, 1972, OC Archives.
49 "Track Team Claims Texoma Championship," Aerie, 1978, 232, OC Archives.
50 "Ray Vaughn Wraps Up 40-Year Coaching Career," *OCC Reporter*, April, 1979, OC Archives.
51 J. Terry Johnson, "In Memory of Coach Ray Vaughn," *OCC Reporter*, October, 1980, OC Archives.
52 "Campus Mourns Loss of Coach Vaughn, *OCC Reporter*, October, 1980, OC Archives.
53 "Tracksters Place in Prestigious Meets Across Region," *OCC Reporter*, April-May, 1985, OC Archives.
54 Randy Heath, Conversation with the author, August 5, 2008.
55 "Baseball Team Makes Good Showing," *Focus*, 1960, 64, OC Archives.
56 Max Dobson, Interview with the author, February 8, 2008.
57 Ibid.
58 Kris Miller, Interview with the author, February 18, 2008.
59 Ibid.
60 Ibid.
61 Ibid.
62 Ibid.
63 Ibid.
64 Ibid.
65 Ron Spotts, "Extramural Volleyball Commences," *Talon*, December 7, 1973, 4, OC Archives.
66 "Volleyball team wins second place in OAIAW," *Aerie*, 1979, 134.
67 "Young Team Does Superb Job," *Aerie*, 1980, 252, OC Archives.
68 *Aerie*, 1982, 185, OC Archives.
69 *Aerie*, 1983, 144, OC Archives.
70 "Volleyball Team Gives Their All During Final Season," *Aerie*, 1984, 169, OC Archives.
71 "Eagle golfers set future foundation," *Aerie*, 1977, 233, OC Archives.
72 "Tennis and Golf teams enjoy competitive seasons," *Aerie*, 1980, 271, OC Archives.
73 Ibid.
74 "Striving to Survive," *Aerie,* 1986, 148, OC Archives.
75 "Golf and Tennis Teams Struggle to Get Some Support," *Aerie*, 1991, 80, OC Archives.
76 Bob Lashley, Conversation with the author, February 15, 2008.
77 Ibid.
78 Max Dobson, Interview with the author, February 6, 2008.
79 "Soccer Craze Hits OCC," *Aerie*, 1986, 151, OC Archives.
80 "OC Leads in Academic All-Americans," OC Web site, June 26, 2008.
81 "OC eighth in NAIA with 12 scholar teams," OC Sports Update, July 23, 2008.
82 "Bionic Man," *Vision*, Spring, 2001.
83 "OC Wins Top Honors in NAIA Contest," OC Web site, June 30, 2008.

Chapter 17
THE MUSIC AND THEATRE ACTIVITIES

Music and theatre activities have been part of student life at Oklahoma Christian from the beginning. The very first year in Bartlesville, 1950, Harold Fletcher directed a one-act opera called *Down in the Valley*, and in the second year, he and Stafford North directed the students in *Amahl and the Night Visitors* and *The Telephone*. In the fall of 1952, they wrote and directed the first production of *Songs America Sings*. From those beginnings, described in Chapter 2, music and drama activities have grown to the annual production of a Broadway show, an opera every year, the annual Cocoa and Carols program, the annual Valentine Cabaret, and several drama productions each year. Spring Sing is another important annual presentation and, as part of club life, is covered in Chapter 15 on "Student Activities."

Musical and theatrical productions fill an important place at Oklahoma Christian. They are an integral part of the curriculum for students with degrees in music and drama, providing important training in performance, technical theater, and directing. But they are much more than this. Most of the students appearing in these shows are not music or drama majors. For them, the musicals and plays offer purely an opportunity for artistic expression, development of their talents, a broadening of their understanding of the arts, and a challenging experience. The shows also provide the campus and the university's clientele with entertainment opportunities and give the public a window through which to view the high quality of the university.

This chapter will look at the facilities students and faculty have used for their productions, survey the musical and theatrical shows and concerts presented, review the directors who have had the greatest influence in these activities and, finally, mention some students who have found their professions in music and drama.

The Facilities

When Central Christian College began in Bartlesville, it had virtually no stage facilities. The only auditorium on campus was a large room with space for two hundred folding chairs. At one end of the room,

Harold Fletcher rehearses the chorus on the Bartlesville stage.

the speaker's platform was elevated nine inches above the floor to serve as a stage. There was no curtain, although sometimes one was improvised by hanging a wire along the ceiling. Here students performed one-act plays and provided other entertainment.

On the west side of The Mansion, a seventy foot wide terrace, four steps above ground level, was often used as a stage, both for productions and for public events such as graduations. By placing folding chairs on a grassy area facing the terrace, an audience of up to three hundred could view a production. The performers in one-act plays and operas had to speak and sing loudly in this outside setting because sound systems were not available. For *Songs America Sings*, a show designed for larger audiences, the directors rented the Central High School Auditorium. Students built sets for shows in the basement of The Mansion, being sure not to make something too large to move out through the door.

When Central Christian College opened in Oklahoma City, much better production facilities were available on the campus. Now there was an auditorium, the west half of Cogswell-Alexander Hall, which could seat some 250 when extra folding chairs were added along the steps on the sides. The stage had both a front curtain and a cyclorama but was small, measuring only eighteen feet deep and thirty-two feet wide. There was no space behind the cyclorama and only a few feet available behind the curtain on either side. The nine foot wooden ceiling meant very limited special effects and difficulty in designing and changing sets.

Stafford North developed a plan for using backdrops in this limited space by designing six aluminum frames on wheels, each standing eight feet tall, and with three equal sides. With two hooks at the top of each of the three sides, stage crews could mount three different painted panels of fiber board, one on each of the three sides of the towers. By placing the frames close together along the back wall, a show could open with one background visable, and then, by rotating all the towers one-third to the right, another background would appear. By turning the frames another third, still another would show. At intermission, the first three could be removed and others added. This system allowed a quick change of "sets" and made the most of the limited space available. There were stage lights in the ceiling, controlled from a six-slide dimming panel in the projection room behind the audience.

Songs America Sings, *1959, in Cogswell-Alexander Auditorium*

In 1966, Hardeman Auditorium opened, seating about thirteen hundred and giving directors and students an entirely new world in which to operate. A thirty-six foot wide stage, with a ten foot apron in front of the curtain and twenty-five feet of playing space behind it, gave plenty of room to work with. A fly loft allowed scenery to be "flown" in and out and gave additional opportunity for changing sets and providing special effects. Restrooms beside the stage and a basement area served as dressing rooms, and a "green room" supplied makeup facilities. A lighting board provided manual dimming control of both house lights and stage lights. Pre-set lighting had not yet come, but with two well-coordinated people at the board, the forty-two large control handles could be adjusted to provide a wide variety of lighting possibilities. A light bridge offered a location for spotlights, as did a projection room above the audience at the rear. Set construction took place in a large space behind the stage, connected to the stage by a twenty-by-twenty foot "garage door." Thus, sets could be wheeled from the construction area to the stage even during a show.

One of the challenges in designing this auditorium was to make the stage area work well for actors as well for speakers in chapel and special events. For musicals, it was important to have an orchestra pit in front of the stage, but placing speakers on the stage with a large gaping hole separating them from their audience did not promote a good speaker-audience relationship. So the college staff and architects provided an orchestra pit, but developed a plan for three large rolling platforms to fill it when it was not needed. These formed a lower stage in front of the stage proper, where a speaker could stand quite close to the audience. The lower level also could be used as additional space during a play or musical when the orchestra pit was not needed. The flexibility of this arrangement has served well through the years.

While Hardeman Auditorium was suitable for productions with large audiences, it was not a good venue for smaller, more intimate shows. In 1978, when two additional buildings were added as wings for Hardeman Auditorium to make the Garvey Center, the new space included a smaller theatre. Seating 278, the new Judd Theatre allowed performances in either a semi-thrust or full proscenium stage. Thus, twenty-four feet was available in front of the curtain to allow intimate productions, with almost no space between players and audience, or the show could take place entirely behind the curtain line on a stage twenty feet deep, or a show could combine the two. To provide for an orchestra pit, a section of the stage floor near the front was removable. In later years, this orchestra pit was covered over and no longer used, orchestras typically being placed behind the actors. An electronic control board permitted an entire lighting plan to be pre-programmed, and, with the touch of a button, the lighting would advance to a new setting. Judd Theatre has been used for plays, operas, smaller musical performances, and recitals.

In 1998, when the Garvey Center was remodeled following the fire (described in Chapter 12), the Music Department added another small auditorium called the Recital Hall. This facility seats two hundred in an elegantly decorated room with a twenty-one by forty-two foot stage. There is no front curtain, but the small theatre has been used often for small scale musical shows and concerts. It also serves as a rehearsal hall for the Chorale and, as the name suggests, recitals by the music students.

Plays and Musicals

In 1958, when Central Christian College moved from Bartlesville to open the new campus in Oklahoma City, the crunch of starting in a new location precluded the possibility of any shows during that year, but in the fall of 1959, *Songs America Sings* returned as a feature at Homecoming. Cogswell-Alexander Auditorium, although small, gave new opportunities. That year Elizabeth Ross joined the writing team of Harold Fletcher and Stafford North, and starting in the summer, they created three acts that presented a trip to the moon, a set of familiar songs all starting from a posed picture inside a large picture frame, and a Greek scene about problems between Mac the Knife (Phillip of Macedon) and his wife.[1] In a subplot, one of the Athenians bought a vase on credit and so "owed on a Grecian urn." To pay his debt, he wrote a poem, and thus "earned on a Grecian ode." As usual, Fletcher directed the music and North the acting and staging. Mary Helon Fletcher, as in all the early *SAS* productions, joined her husband to provide the piano accompaniment. The 1959 version played to an audience of 3,100 in seven performances on the campus and one in Tulsa.[2] The drama critic for the *Daily Oklahoman* reviewed the show, commenting, "Act III takes the prize for originality, literary quality, timeliness, cleverness and college-grade performance . . . the by-play and asides and dialogue are rare."[3]

In 1960, *Songs America Sings,* featuring a murder mystery and a scene with King Arthuritus and his round table,[4] saw eleven performances, eight on campus and one each in Tulsa, Wichita, and Dallas,[5] with a total viewing audience of over five thousand. In 1961, the final act showed American life through an uprising in the South American country of Tamale where a female army was highly successful because "no Tamale man would shoot a Tamale woman." That year, the cast of sixty-five students did nine shows on campus and played on the road in Tulsa, Dallas, and Wichita to a total audience of 5,500.[6]

By 1962, Darrel Alexander had arrived to lead theatre activities, and he directed the college's first full-length play, *A Connecticut Yankee in King Arthur's Court.* Mary Fern Stansberry and James Watson had leading roles. While there had been several one-act plays

OCC's first three-act play: A Connecticut Yankee in King Arthur's Court

before, this major drama production moved the college into new territory. In 1963, *Songs America Sings* returned. James Cail, a star performer in the show at Bartlesville now on the OCC staff, joined the Fletcher-North-Ross writing team. Alexander led in preparing the sets. This year's show featured a parody of a western movie and a political satire about the current national scene.[7] Senator Saltwater was running for president, campaigning with the song "Saline, saline, over the bounding main; many a stormy wind shall blow ere Jack gets in again." John Kennedy was not a character in the act, but his brother Bobby was. The show began its run a week before Homecoming, already having done six performances when tragedy struck on the first day of the Homecoming celebration. On Friday, November 22, at 12:30 p.m., President Kennedy was shot, and later in the afternoon was pronounced dead. The campus, like the rest of the nation, was in shock and mourning. An immediate decision had to be made about the show, scheduled for 4 and 8 p.m. the next day. Should the show go on, and if so, what about the part that involved the Kennedy family? There was no good option, but Fletcher and North decided that, since many alumni were already on campus or en route to Homecoming, they should proceed with the show.

Guy Ross as Saltwater

They would, however, rewrite the last act to take all references to the Kennedys out of the script. Students had to learn new lines quickly and, in fact, were still being given changes as they walked on the stage.[8] At the beginning of the show, North announced that they had struggled with the decision but had decided that it would bring no disrespect to the fallen President to continue with the Homecoming activities, and he mentioned that the script had been revised to remove any references to Kennedy. One thing the writers had forgotten was that in the western scene, one of the cowboys bragged that he was known all the way from Dallas to Fort Worth. When the word "Dallas" was spoken, a sudden hush came over the audience.

After 1963, *Songs America Sings* moved to "an every third year" schedule, with major drama productions providing the Homecoming show in the intervening years. In 1964, Alexander directed *The Little Foxes,* with Donna Butz and Robert Stalcup in leading roles. In Fall 1965 came *The Silver Cord* and 1966 the *Diary of Anne Frank*

Western Scene–1963

in which Dessain Terry, who played in many productions, had a leading role.

The Little Foxes *in 1964*

In 1966, *Songs America Sings* was back at Homecoming with a show that featured the Johnson family, then in the White House. Lyndon Johnson became Lord Byrde while his wife was still Lady Byrde. Lord Byrde, secretly, was also Robin Hood, robbing from the rich to give to the poor. Bruce Henderson, who played Lord Byrde, was on stage by himself one afternoon a day or two before the show was to open. While practicing his Robin Hood swing through the trees on a rope suspended from above the stage, he fell, breaking his arm. Although he could still play the part, a double had to swing through the trees. This 1966 version of *Songs America Sings* was the first major production in the new Hardeman Auditorium and was part of the grand opening of the building.[9]

In 1967, Alexander directed *Look Homeward Angel* for Homecoming, and in 1968 came another first.[10] Al Lewis, choral director, directed the college's first Broadway musical, *Brigadoon,* with Sheril Day (Kerr) and Paige Pfeiffer in leading roles. In 1969 it was *SAS* again, with alumni providing the first act with songs they had performed in earlier shows. A Roman scene featured the Emperor Zero with his son Zerox, an exact copy of his dad.[11] Al Lewis directed

Brigadoon *in 1968*

the music, and George Mastick did sets and costumes.[12] That was the year a cloud dropping Pam Shipman (Harris) and Lynne Hearn (Rowley) from the sky got stuck and they had to be rescued.

For the next three years, Alexander directed the Homecoming play: *Blithe Spirit* in 1970, *The Miracle Worker* in 1971, and *I Never Sang for My Father* in 1972.

In 1973, *Songs America Sings* revived, with North and Cail as the authors, Ken Adams as the music director, and Alexander the technical director.[13] This show told the story of a trip to the moon, from the preparation, through the trip, and to the landing.[14] The names of the characters were a special feature: an entertainer named Eileen Back, a plumber named John LeSeuer, a cook named Ashley Baker Burns, and the astronaut A. O. Kaye.

In the 1973 fall play, *The Glass Menangerie*, the lead actor wrenched his back the day before the play opened and Alexander replaced the ailing actor with Curtis Michener, who did the final dress rehearsal with script in hand and, on opening night, discarded the script by the second act and completed the run of the show without it.

In Fall 1974, Alexander directed *You Can't Take It with You*, and the following spring did *The Mad Woman of Chaillot* with Sue Ott (Rowlands) in the leading role. For Homecoming in 1975, it was *Stories of America* and in 1976, *Songs America Sings* returned with a patriotic show. Fletcher, North, and Cail again combined for the writing, with Alexander doing sets and costumes, and music faculty members Warren Casey and Steve Smith directing the music. The opening act paid tribute to the American Revolution, followed by an act of folk songs through American history, and finally, "A Funny Thing

Happened on the Way to the White House," to highlight election-year politics.[15]   In 1977, Steve Smith directed a musical for Homecoming: *Fiddler on the Roof* starring Jim Baird as Tevye. In 1978, Smith did *The Music Man* with Rod Arndt and Amy Webb carrying the leads.

Dan Branch as King Tut

In 1979, for the fifteenth and last time, came *Songs America Sings.* Fletcher, North, and Cail wrote the show, and North led in the staging. Casey and Smith again directed the music, Alexander did costumes and makeup, Phil Reagan did sets and lighting, and Rodney Brown helped with choreography. Act 1 showcased favorite American songs from marches to love ballads to westerns. The political satire moved the Washington scene to ancient Egypt, complete with Jimmy Pharaoh and his family, along with parodies of other well-known politicians. Over seventy were in the cast, sixteen in the orchestra, and another seventy on the crews. It had become a giant undertaking.[16] By this time, however, the college was able to do well with Broadway musicals and full-length plays, and Spring Sing, which began in 1969, was giving students a good theatrical experience. So *Songs America Sings,* having filled its special role well, was replaced by other theatrical activities.

Since 1980, there has always been a Broadway musical for Homecoming. In 1983, for example, Laura Rucker (Coale) and Robert Reed played the leads in the *Sound of Music,* and in 1989, Scott Langdon starred as Fagin in *Oliver.* In 1991, *Camelot* featured Jennifer Lewis, Scott Langdon, and Lane Fields, and in 1993, Chad Anderson and Celeste Dvorak carried the leads in *Guys and Dolls.*

Of the musicals, some have played more than once: *Fiddler on the Roof* has run three times (1977, 1988, and 2004), and several have played twice: *Brigadoon* in 1968 and 1985, *Man of LaMancha* in 1981 and 1998, *Into the Woods* in 1996 and 2005, *Oklahoma* in 1984 and 2002, and *West Side Story* in 1983 and 2007. Other shows have included *Carousel* (1979), *Shenandoah* (1982), *The Unsinkable Molly Brown* (1987), and *My Fair Lady* (1990).

The performance of *Titanic* in November of 2000 was a highlight among the Broadway shows. This presentation was the first Oklahoma production of *Titanic* and was done soon after the show ended its run on Broadway. The total cost for the performance rose to $24,000,[17] well above the usual cost. The cast of sixty-eight included forty-six students, two people from the local community, and twenty alumni, most of whom had starred in musicals when they were students: Jim Baird, Lottie McCormack, Stan Shelton, Lane Fields, Angi Roper

Titanic *in Hardeman*

Lovejoy, Laura Rucker Coale, T. J. Lauxman, La Nita Davis Lough, Melinda Flanery, Scott Hall, Peggy Stickler Hoshall, Amanda Kenney, Dan Lovejoy, Jeanise Wynn Morton, Robyn Plummer, Connie McCormack Penick, Jason Snethen, Terry Taylor, and Corey Whaley. Vince Leseney, from the faculty at Oklahoma City University, directed the show, with Dr. Ken Adams serving as musical director and conductor of a large orchestra of students and professionals. Phil Reagan, who had come in 1979, was producer and Darrel Alexander, costumer.[18] *Titanic* lived up to its name, being the biggest Broadway show in OC history.

Another special occasion involving OC alumni came April 1, 2000, as part of the year-long celebration of the university's fifty years. This particular show, performed in Hardeman Auditorium, was composed entirely of songs from previous campus musicals using the original student performers. John Fletcher reprised "The Impossible Dream" from his performance in *The Man of La Mancha*, Laura Coale gave her rendition of "The Sound of Music," Jim Baird played Tevye again, singing "If I Were a Rich Man," and Sherril Day Kerr did "Almost Like Being in Love" from *Brigadoon*. Chad Anderson sang "Where in the World" from *The Secret Garden*, Scott Langdon sang "Reviewing the Situation" from *Oliver*, and James Hallmark performed "Meditation I" from Shenandoah, while a group sang the *Songs America Sings* theme, and James Cail sang, also from an *SAS* show, "All the Things You Are." The alumni performed twenty-four acts, and it was a grand evening of music and remembrance.[19]

During these years of Broadway musicals for homecoming, the Drama Department typically has staged major drama productions in both the fall and the spring. In 1980, for example, Alexander directed *Purlie Victorious* in the fall, with Troy Smith in the leading role, and *Beyond the Horizon* in the spring. In 1986, Alexander directed *Our Town* in the fall, and Phil Reagan did *Crimes of the Heart* the following spring.

In October 1988, Alexander decided to make use of the recently completed Thelma Gaylord Forum to present an outdoor production of *Romeo and Juliet*. The first performance went well, with patrons sitting on blankets on the lawn and in seating areas around the walls. The next day, however, a cold front dropped the temperature into the low fifties, and the second performance was rained out. The day after that, the temperature dropped into the mid-forties, and the cast and audience shivered their way through the performance with one of the actresses almost fainting from hypothermia. With the improvement of the weather over the weekend, Alexander added a performance on Monday evening that was well attended. The show closed, however, with Alexander resolving never again to do a show outdoors in the fall or early spring, weather being so unpredictable.

In 1992, when Reagan did *Charlotte's Web* in the fall, Cheney Luke, who was playing a goose, tripped over a piece of scenery and injured her foot, requiring immediate first aid. Alexander ran backstage, picked up the injured "goose" and carried her to the infirmary for treatment. Meanwhile the other members of the cast ad libbed their way through the remainder of the performance sans goose.

In 1998-1999, Phil Reagan did *Alice in Wonderland* in the fall and in the spring Alexander directed *The Miser* with Barrett Huddleston in the role of Harpagon. Students Ann Longfellow and Anna Reyher Wilcox also directed plays that year.

The high quality of plays at Oklahoma Christian has been demonstrated in many ways, one of the most important being reviews by outside critics. When Darrel Alexander directed *The Importance of Being Earnest* in 1988, with James Mace in the title role, for example, the drama critic for the *Oklahoma Gazette* commented that "Phil Reagan's set designs are impressive and the whole production, with brilliant directing and good acting, is exquisite."[20] Bob Smith, critic for the *Edmond Sun*, saw the OCC outdoor production of *Romeo and Juliet* and commented: "Director Darrel Alexander expertly brought the production to life in the outdoor Thelma Gaylord Forum. Alexander does a fine job of leading his players through the production, allowing the audience to see the emotions that run so high in youth."[21] Cliff Warren of the *Edmond Sun* saw Phil Reagan's production of *Ten Little Indians* and said, "Oklahoma Christian College thespians turned up the energy, polished the charm and demeanor and delivered a delectable version of 'Ten Little Indians.'"[22] Still another critic, Doug Bentin (*Oklahoma Gazette*), wrote about the 1995 production of the *Diary of Anne Frank*: "But what makes this production so memorable is the acting." He went on to say, "The OCUSA Theater Department continues to be the best-kept secret of our theater scene. The work there is solid, and the faculty is excellent."[23]

Operas

The Oklahoma Christian Music Department also has produced many operas over the years. The first ones on the Oklahoma City campus came in 1965, when Sam Haynes directed two one-act

The Merry Widow *in Hardeman Auditorium*

operas: *The Telephone* and *Madame Butterfly*. In 1978, Steve Smith directed OCC's first full-length opera, *Cosi Fan Tutte*, performed in Judd Theatre. Students Gary Smith and Amy Webb had major roles. An interesting sidelight about this opera is that Smith brought Chris Merritt from Oklahoma City University to perform the lead tenor role. Since that time, Merritt has done extremely well professionally, being the first American ever to sing in an opening night opera at La Scala in Milan, Italy.

In 1980, Smith directed *New Moon*, and in 1981 and 1982, selected scenes from operas. In 1984, Smith directed *Dialogue of the Carmelites*; in 1985, *Cavalleria Rusticana*; in 1986, *Werther*; and in 1987, two one-act operas, *Gianni Schicchi* and *Sister Angelica*. Alexander costumed many of Smith's productions, with Phil Reagan doing the sets. Almost every year since 1980, OC students have performed either an opera or scenes from opera. Vince Leseney, currently on the faculty at the University of Oklahoma, has provided direction for ten of these productions. Students have performed many well-known operas such as *The Magic Flute, The Barber of Seville, Don Giovanni, Marriage of Figaro, Die Fledermaus, The Merry Widow*, and *Hansel and Gretel*.

Ken Adams has pointed to three primary values for students at Oklahoma Christian who perform in operas. First, he says, is the educational value of learning about opera. Most students, either music majors or other students, have not had much contact with this genre, and to be able to perform opera broadens their musical understanding. Second, the operas give serious students the experience of participating in one of the most challenging forms of musical performance, thus providing a "culminating experience."

Third, Adams says, those students who go on to graduate school or to teach music have an impressive opera performance as part of their resume.[24] Their success in competing for operatic roles in graduate schools testifies to the educational and professional benefit of this experience.

Another interesting opera performance at Oklahoma Christian, although it did not involve students, came in the summer of 1994. The college produced the first professional opera performance in Oklahoma in more than twenty years when *La Traviata* came to the Hardeman stage. With a budget of $100,000 raised from outside sources, under the auspices of the Opera Festival of Oklahoma, and with Dr. Adams as General Director, opera lovers came to the campus for an outstanding evening.

Cocoa and Carols

In 1976, Adams decided that OCC music students needed an additional performance opportunity, particularly one involving both orchestra and chorus. He selected December for the event, placing it after the Homecoming musical and before Spring Sing and the spring opera. This date also gave the performance a connection with the Christmas season.

Dr. Ken Adams conducting Cocoa and Carols

In the beginning, the Chamber Singers, a smaller group of singers taken from the larger Chorale, performed the first half of the show. The second half presented a major choral work with orchestral accompaniment. At first, the choir was composed of alumni who had sung in the chorus and a few faculty members. Over the years, student singers were added and, by 1991, the chorus was made up entirely of students. The orchestra has involved both students and professional musicians, and Adams conducts both chorus and orchestra. Over the span of thirty years, Adams has chosen works by such composers as Bach, Beethoven, Mozart, Hayden, Puccini, and Stravinsky. In 2000, the group did Handel's *Messiah*. In 1987, other student performing groups began joining the Chamber Singers for the lighter section of the show.

In 2001, the twenty-fifth year for Cocoa and Carols, sixty alumni joined the choral group to perform selections from previous years. Cocoa is served at the intermission. Attendance usually runs between six and seven hundred.

Valentine Cabaret

Chase Cob, Noah in Two by Two, *peers out of the ark.*

In the fall of 1988, Dr. Ken Adams decided that a good activity for the Chorale, both for the experience of the students and as a fundraising opportunity, would be to host a dinner theatre for Valentine's Day. For entertainment after the meal, the students would present songs from familiar Broadway musicals. The first Cabaret presentation came in 1989, when the students did excerpts from *Les Miserables, South Pacific*, and *Phantom of the Opera*. The next year, 1990, the group presented a reduced version of *My Fair Lady*. In the years since, most of the shows have focused on excerpts from a single musical such as *Oklahoma, Carousel, Pirates of Penzance, You're a Good Man Charlie Brown, The Fantasticks, Two by Two*, and *Les Miserables*. Patrons come for a meal, served by the students, and then enjoy the music to follow. Valentine Cabaret has become very popular, with many looking forward to sharing with their mates an evening out with good food and entertainment. Adams has now produced this show for eighteen years.

Chorale

The Chorale, primarily an *a cappella* singing group ranging from about thirty voices in the beginning in 1950 to its largest group of one hundred in 1994, has served as one of the most active musical groups on the campus. Harold Fletcher conducted the Chorale from 1950 until 1964. Through the years, the chorus not only has served to provide students with an outstanding learning experience and to offer entertainment on campus, but also has acted as one of the primary public relations tools for the college. Each year the group takes an extended tour,

The Chorus in 1952

sometimes in the major service area of the college and sometimes to distant states. These tours seek to attract both prospective students and donors to the college. The quality of the group, as noted elsewhere, has been outstanding.

Sam Haynes conducted the chorus from 1964 to 1967 and Margaret Paas during the 1967–1968 year. Al Lewis led the group from 1968 through 1970 and Ken Helterbrand from 1970–1972.

Ken Adams has conducted the Chorale since 1972 except for one year, 1976–1977, when Steve Smith directed. Thus, Fletcher with his fourteen years and Adams with his thirty-five have been the primary conductors for the group. During the Adams years, the group has sung with the Oklahoma City Symphony and taken trips to Europe in addition to their regular performances at churches, schools, public events, campus events, and extended tours.

For students, singing in the choral group has often been one of the highlights among their OC experiences. They have not only found the choral opportunity satisfying artistically, but have formed close friendships and had the opportunity for travel. Their repertoire has always included hymns and spirituals as well as special choral arrangements of a wide range of religious numbers. Their secular selections have covered the humorous to the classical. In a few years, there were two choral groups and, for a short time, a chorus for women.

In addition to the Chorale, smaller vocal groups have also been part of the Oklahoma Christian musical scene. In the beginning there were quartets and sextets, and the Madrigal Singers. By the mid-sixties, other groups came, like The Windstormers, the Windy Hill Minstrels, the Pacesetters, Studio One, and the Chamber Singers. The Summer Singers began in 1971–1972 under the auspices of the Admissions Department to help with recruiting students. Many students, over the years, have had additional musical experiences in these smaller groups.

Instrumental Groups

While vocal groups were first at OCC, instrumental groups have long been a very important part of the musical life of the institution. Student instrumentalists were in *Songs America Sings* in Bartlesville, but the first permanent organized instrumental group came in the first year at Oklahoma City. In 1958, Harold Fletcher organized a Pep Band to play at basketball games. The sixteen-member group had four trumpets, three clarinets, two trombones, one flute, one bass horn, one saxophone, one guitar, and one banjo. The *Talon* reported, "It began as a student idea."[25]

By 1963–1964, there was a concert band of twenty members and a stage band of thirteen that played at many functions during the year. Fletcher directed both. After Sam Haynes came to direct the chorus in 1964, Fletcher concentrated on the instrumental groups. The band grew larger and gave spring and winter concerts, as well as performing on an annual tour. The Pep Band continued, and in 1966–67, a new instrumental group arrived on the scene: the Enchilada Brass. This ten-member ensemble, fashioned after Herb Alpert's Tijuana Brass, performed for high schools in the area, on television, and for many OCC events. Ken Adams played trombone in the group.

In 1970–1971, Ken Helterbrand replaced Fletcher as band director and remained for two years. The number of players had grown to forty. Former band member Ken Adams, who received a master's degree in music from North Texas State University,

Dr. John Fletcher conducts the Symphonic Band.

returned in 1972 and conducted the band until 1976 when he left for additional graduate work. Warren Casey directed the band from 1976 to 1982, Brian Shepherd from 1982 to 1986, and John Fletcher, another former band member, from 1987 to 1994. When Fletcher left OC to direct the music program at Cascade, Mike Aston took on the conducting. Fletcher returned to direct in the fall of 1997, and continues to conduct the group, now called the Symphonic Band. These performers take an annual tour to various parts of the United States, give several concerts each year on campus, and play for other special events. Players from the band also often participate in the pit band for musicals and operas.

The Jazz Band began in 1977–1978 under Warren Casey. Those directing the concert band often have also conducted the Jazz Band with John Fletcher having served the longest term of ten years in that position. In 2000, Heath Jones became director for the Jazz Band and continues in that role. Dr. Kathy Thompson has worked with many different string ensembles since her coming in 1993, these groups playing especially for campus events.

A major orchestra of seventy members, the Oklahoma City

Community Orchestra, is also part of the broader music program at OC. This group began in 1984 and soon began to use the facilities on the OCC campus for its rehearsals and programs. In 1987, the group officially became the university's orchestra in residence. The players are primarily adults from the community, but OC students and faculty as well as local alumni perform with the group. In 2005, the orchestra selected Dr. John Fletcher as its conductor.

The Directors

Dr. Harold Fletcher

Harold Fletcher conducting from the orchestra pit

At Oklahoma Christian University, Dr. Harold Fletcher holds many special distinctions among directors of choral, instrumental, and stage groups. He began the chorus in 1950, in 1951 was the first to direct an opera, in 1952 was the first to direct a musical show, and began the band program in 1958. For many years, he *was* the Music Department.

Involved in both vocal and instrumental activities as a student at Abilene Christian College, Fletcher was an outstanding performer on piano and string bass as well as an excellent conductor. Showing his versatility, he conducted the chorus and related singing groups for fourteen years and directed the band for seven. He was on the team of writers and directors of *Songs America Sings* for fourteen of its fifteen performances.

During the years of his work, Fletcher led many students to greater musical skills and to appreciation of the artistic merit in pieces they performed. He taught two who would later play a major role in musical activities at OC: Ken Adams, and his own son, John Fletcher.

Dr. Stafford North

Dr. Stafford North joined the faculty of Central Christian College in January of 1952. As a student at Abilene Christian College he had performed small roles in plays and operas, and did backstage work on many productions. He had also studied directing in his master's work

North at a rehearsal

in speech at Louisiana State University. He was stage director for two one-act operas in his first term at OCC, and in other years at Bartlesville, he directed several one-act plays. In the fall of 1952, he and Harold Fletcher began *Songs America Sings*, and North shared in the writing and served as stage director for the show in thirteen of its fifteen years.

Dr. Darrel Alexander

Darrel Alexander

Dr. Darrel Alexander joined the OCC faculty in 1962 to teach speech and direct the drama program. He had a bachelor's degree from Harding and a master's degree from the University of Denver, and at both institutions, received training in drama. He later completed a doctorate with a drama emphasis at Louisiana State University.

Since his arrival, Alexander has directed sixty-one plays. In only four out of his forty-five years has he not directed some production, and in many of those years he did two and sometimes more. For many of his plays, he chose from well-known classics such as *The Importance of Being Earnest* (1964, 1988), *The Glass Menagerie* (1965, 1973), *The Diary of Anne Frank* (1966, 1995), *Our Town* (1967, 1986), *The Miracle Worker* (1971), *Arms and the Man* (1973), *Pygmalion* (1977), *Frankenstein* (1978), *A Midsummer Night's Dream* (1979), *Arsenic and Old Lace* (1979), *Beyond the Horizon* (1981), *Romeo and Juliet* (1988), *Father of the Bride* (1997), and *The Barretts of Wimpole Street* (2003). In more recent years, he has directed plays for children such as *Cinderella* (1997), *Raggedy Ann and Andy* (1999), *Aladdin and the Magic Lamp* (2001), and *The Secret Garden* (2006). On October 22, 1998, Oklahoma Governor Frank Keating presented Dr. Alexander the Governor's Award for Excellence in the Arts.

In addition to his work as director, Alexander has also costumed many shows, raising the number of productions on which he has made a major contribution to more than a hundred. Although Alexander officially retired in 1996, he continues to assist with some productions. Having been a major player in the OC theatre over so many years, Alexander has certainly been key in developing the program's excellence.

Dr. Ken Adams

Dr. Ken Adams joined the OCC music faculty in 1972 and has served since that time, except for a year away for doctoral study in choral conducting at the University of Iowa. He came to OCC as a sophomore

Ken Adams conducting the Band in 1973

student in 1966, having spent his first college year at Southwestern Oklahoma State College, where he played trombone in the band. At OCC, Adams continued to be active in instrumental activities, being in both the band and the Enchilada Brass. Taking courses both at OCC and Central State University, Adams graduated from CSU in 1970 with a Bachelor of Music Education degree. After receiving a Master of Music degree in 1972 from North Texas State University, Adams returned to OCC to teach music.

Adams conducted the OCC band for the four years from 1972 through 1976 and, during those same years, also directed the OCC Chorale. After completing his doctoral work from the University of Iowa, he focused on the vocal side, and he has conducted the Chorale since 1977. His four years with the band plus thirty-five years conducting the Chorale give him the most years of conducting musical groups of any person in OC history. In addition to conducting these two groups, Adams also has directed the combined orchestra and chorus for Cocoa and Carols, produced the Valentine Cabaret, and conducted the orchestra for more than fifty-five musicals and operas. Among the shows for which he has served as musical director have been *Fiddler on the Roof* (1977), *The Music Man* (1978), *Oklahoma* (1991), *Carousel* (1992), *Titanic* (2000), and *West Side Story* (1986, 2007). In addition, he has directed opera productions such as *Cosi Fan Tutte* (2004), *The Marriage of Figaro* (1992), *Don Giovanni* (1995), and *Carmen* (2002). Beyond the OC campus, Adams has directed at the Pollard Theatre and the Oklahoma Civic Opera. Adams certainly has been a major contributor to the development of the OC Music Department and to the musical understanding of the host of students under his baton.

Steve Smith

Steve Smith came to OCC in 1976 to teach music, instruct in voice, and share in directing musical productions. Smith graduated from Harding College, where he was outstanding in vocal performance, and he also had a master of music degree from the University of Arkansas. During his eleven years at OCC, he completed a master of

Steve Smith

performing arts at Oklahoma City University, specializing in opera.

Smith directed the college's first full-length opera in the winter of 1978, *Cosi Fan Tutte*. During his years at OCC, Smith directed twelve major productions of opera and Broadway musicals, including *The Music Man, Carousel, Dialogue of the Carmelites, Cavalleria Rusticana, Brigadoon,* and *Sister Angelica*. While on the faculty at Oklahoma Christian, Smith had leading roles in shows at the Lyric Theatre and sang in other venues. He left OCC after the 1986–1987 year. Since 1998, Smith has been on the voice faculty of the highly respected Juilliard School of Music in New York, and in 2007, Oxford Press published his book called *The Naked Voice: A Holistic Approach to Singing*.[26]

Warren Casey

Also in 1976, Warren Casey joined the OCC music faculty, coming from Harding, where he was active in instrumental groups and excelled on the clarinet. While at OCC, he finished a master's degree at the University of Oklahoma. Casey directed the band program from 1976 to 1982, conducting both the Concert Band and the Jazz Band. After the 1981–82 year, he returned to Harding, where he continues to teach.

Warren Casey

Phil Reagan

Phil Reagan

Phil Reagan joined the Drama Department in 1979 with a bachelor's degree from Harding and a master's degree from Memphis State University. Reagan has directed eleven musicals and twenty-two plays. His shows have run the gamut from comedy to tragedy and from Shakespeare to relatively unknown authors. Reagan directed his first play at OCC in 1982, *The Crucible*, and in 1983, he did *The Real Inspector Hound*. Since then he has directed such plays as *Arms and the Man* (1986), *Ten Little Indians* (1987), *Esther* (1990), *Taming of the Shrew* (1994), *Beauty and the Beast* (1994), *The Lion, the Witch, and the Wardrobe* (1996), *The Miracle Worker* (1998), *Charlie's Aunt* (2003), *As You Like It* (2004), *Bus Stop* (2005), and *Charlie and the Chocolate Factory* (2005).

Reagan has served as stage director for twelve musicals, including *Man of La Mancha* (1981), *Sound of Music* (1983), *West Side Story* (1986), *Fiddler on the Roof* (1988), *Oliver* (1989), *Camelot* (1991),

Guys and Dolls (1993), and *How to Succeed in Business Without Really Trying* (2001).

Over his twenty-nine years at OC, Reagan has led a host of students to a deeper appreciation of the theatre through his teaching and directing, and has brought many hours of entertainment to the campus.

Dr. John Fletcher

John Fletcher joined the OCC faculty in the fall of 1987 to direct the band program and teach music classes. Fletcher, son of long-time professor Harold Fletcher, grew up as part of the OCC community. He did his first two years of college at OCC, transferred to the University of Oklahoma for two years, and then returned to OCC to graduate in 1982. He completed a master of music degree at the University of Missouri—Kansas City and, in 2002, a Ph.D. in conducting at the University of Oklahoma. While a student at

John Fletcher conducting

OCC, Fletcher sang in the Chorale, played in the band, and performed the lead in OCC's production of *Man of La Mancha*.

At the university, Fletcher has directed the Symphonic Band and Jazz Band. Although OCC had a band to play at basketball games before, in 1987 Fletcher began a new tradition with a pep group called "The Sweat Band." He has also served as musical director for several of OC's Homecoming musicals: *Unsinkable Molly Brown* (1987), *My Fair Lady* (1990), *Camelot* (1991), *Man of La Mancha* (1998), *Crazy for You* (1999), *Oklahoma* (2002), and *Fiddler on the Roof* (2004). Since 2005, he has conducted the Oklahoma Community Orchestra. His conducting skills and knowledge of the Oklahoma Christian scene have enabled him to serve the students and the campus with distinction.

Student Directors

OC students have directed many plays over the years, including both one-act and three-act plays. Offering students the opportunity to learn from directing, especially full-length plays, in fact, has been one of the distinctive features of the OC Drama Department. In 1975, Sue Ott became the first student to present a full-length show, directing *Sticks and Bones*. Since 1979, students have directed one or two shows virtually every year, not only giving student directing experience, but also providing additional opportunities for students to perform and to work in technical theatre.

The Graduates and Other Former Students

While the music and theatre activities are available to all students, most of whom have no plans to enter these areas as careers, OC programs have prepared some for careers in these fields. Among those who have worked professionally is Karen (Killion) Bender (1979), who recently won three New York State Association Merit Awards, one for directing *Jekyll and Hyde*, one for an acting role, and another for her work with an ensemble. Kerry Kelly (1985) has performed for fifteen years at the opera and music theatre Volkstheater Rostock in Rostock, Germany. Bob Orwig (1979) had roles in Oliver Stone's *Platoon* and *JFK*, Anna Heffington Klein (1998) has recently acted in an Off Broadway show. Raymond A. Bailey (2001) had the starring role in the feature film *11:59*, an official selection of the Montreal International Film Festival, and was featured in a television pilot. Barrett Huddleston, an alumnus of 2001 who returned to teach drama at OC in the fall of 2007, won awards for his studies in drama at Oklahoma State University and has received his doctorate in theatre from the University of Minnesota.

Lane Fields (1995) was a member of the professional repertory company of the Pollard Theater, performing many lead roles. Oklahoma's "evolution rock" band, the Matt Stansberry Band Stansberry Band [guitarist Matt Stansberry (2004), bassist Denver Greene (2003), and drummer Ben Tinius 2003)], was nominated, was nominated for "Best Group with Vocal" at the 2007 LA Music Awards. Tara Flynn of ABC Television called them, "The best new band I've seen this year."

Chad Anderson (1998) had the lead in *Oklahoma* at Discoveryland, USA, and Kari McFarland Hatfield (2000) had a lead in shows at the Busch Gardens Theme Park in Virginia and in *Texas* in a theatre in Canyon, Texas. Scott Langdon (1992) performed regularly with the Lyric Theatre in Oklahoma City and earned a principal role in *The Sound of Music* in the Philadelphia Music Theatre. Carrie Seat Gotcher (2003) has performed as a singer with the Oklahoma City Philharmonic's *Yuletide Festival*. Bart Varner (2000) is music director, instrumentalist, and stage performer for the Pollard Theater. Angela Wallace Richards (1996) holds the second trumpet chair with the Ft. Smith Symphony Orchestra. Danny Vaughn (1996) is a professional guitarist in Oklahoma City, having performed with the Oklahoma Symphony Orchestra, the Oklahoma City Philharmonic Orchestra, Ballet Oklahoma, and Lyric Theatre. He also teaches jazz guitar at the University of Central Oklahoma. Nelson Eubank (1987) plays electric bass for recording sessions in Oklahoma City. Craig White (1997), professor at Rose State College, is a guitarist, educator, and recording store owner and engineer. As an award-winning songwriter, he has had compositions appear in film and on television in such shows as *Another World, As the World Turns, E! True Hollywood Story,* and *Access Hollywood.* Gena Shoemake Alexander (2001) is a private teacher and professional violinist in Oklahoma City.

Heidi Jones (1986) performed with the Houston Opera Studio and the Houston Grand Opera. Jim Elliot (1978) is the Production Manager for the Amarillo Civic Center and Globe News Center for the Performing Arts. Eddie Keener (1983) has performed and directed onboard productions for Holland America Cruise Lines. Robert Reed (1987) sings professionally in St. Louis. Sue Ott Rowland (1975) has done a one-woman show both nationally and internationally and is now dean of the College of Arts and Science at Virginia Tech.[27] Many others have performed in community theaters, opera choruses, community orchestras, bands, and choirs, have sung professionally as soloists, and have taught music and drama in high school and college.

In addition, three alumni are now OC music professors and, in addition, fill professional roles outside their campus work: Dr. John Fletcher (1982) conducting the Oklahoma Community Orchestra, Dr. Ken Adams (1969) conducting the pit band at the Pollard Theater, and Dr. Heath Jones (1994) performing with the Oklahoma Philharmonic Orchestra.

Theatre Organizations

In the 1952–53 school year, cosponsors Stafford North and Sarajane Brandon formed the first club for those interested in theatre. Called La Quinta Players, after the name of The Mansion on the Bartlesville campus, the group had forty members. The club had initiation ceremonies and a banquet and worked together on student plays.[28] The group continued throughout the Bartlesville years.

After moving to Oklahoma City, the first revival of a theatre organization came in 1962–1963 with the beginning of the Thalian Players. Darrel Alexander started the group in his first year at OCC. The twelve members' first project was to record books for the blind. The next year, Alexander began a chapter of Alpha Psi Omega, the honorary society for theater on college campuses, which continues to the present.

Conclusion

From the school's earliest days, music and theatre productions have been a very important part of the campus scene at Oklahoma Christian. In the beginning, shows like *Songs America Sings* used nearly every student to serve as cast and crew members, drawing students together in a common activity and providing an important growth experience in responsibility and appreciation of the arts. In later years, the percentage of students participating in any one show was less, but the number of opportunities increased. With Spring Sing included in the mix along with Broadway musicals, operas, Valentine Cabaret, and Cocoa and Carols, over the years probably half the Oklahoma Christian students have had some experience in participating in stage productions, thus receiving the many benefits that such activities provide.

Also from the beginning, the Chorale, other vocal groups, the band, and other instrumental groups have been a vibrant part of campus life, touching the lives of many students. Such activities have added to the total package of experiences Oklahoma Christian has provided for its students and have contributed in a major way to public events both on and off the campus.

The directors have been skilled in making these experiences beneficial. In addition, the public performances have demonstrated to the public the high quality of work OC teachers and students can produce. These activities, too, have brought students closer to each other.

Clearly, then, the Departments of Music and Drama have played a vital role in making Oklahoma Christian what it has been over the years. They not only train their majors for later roles in teaching and performance but give the student body as a whole an excellent opportunity for development, and many from off-campus have gained a greater appreciation of the university through their performances.

Chapter 17, Endnotes

[1]   *Aerie*, 1960, 28–31, OC Archives.
[2]   "3,000 Applaud 'Songs America Sings'—1959," *Oklahoma Christian College Bulletin*, January 1960, OC Archives.
[3]   Ibid.
[4]   *Aerie*, 1961, 86–87, OC Archives.
[5]   "OCC Prepares for homecoming, SAS," *Oklahoma Christian College Bulletin*, November 1960, OC Archives.
[6]   *Aerie*, 1962, 91–93, OC Archives.
[7]   *Aerie*, 1964, 60–61, OC Archives.
[8]   "OCC Presents 'Songs America Sings' Musical Comedy, Political Parody," *Daily Oklahoman*, November 11, 1966, 24, OC Archives.
[9]   *Aerie*, 1967, 162, OC Archives.
[10] Information about dates and directors of both drama and music productions is taken from Dr. Darrel Alexander's list posted on the OC Web site under Arts, Theatre, History.
[11] *Aerie*, 1970, 30–31, OC Archives.
[12] *Songs America Sings* Program, 1969, OC Archives.
[13] "SAS: Return to Tradition," *Talon*, November 9, 1973, 1, OC Archives.
[14] "SAS Features Moon Landing," *Oklahoma Christian College Reporter*, October, 1973, OC Archives.
[15] *Songs America Sings* Program, 1976, OC Archives.
[16] *Songs America Sings* Program, 1979, OC Archives.
[17] Jonathan Barr and Morgan Thomas, "'Titanic' marks Homecoming," *Talon*, November 3, 2000, 1, OC Archives.
[18] *Titanic* Program, OC Archives.
[19] Program from *Thanks for the Memories*, Alumni Musical Revue, April 1, 2001, OC Archives.
[20] J. Landis Fleming, "Wilde's wit still highlights 'Earnest,'" *Oklahoma Gazette*, February 10, 1988, 47.
[21] Bob Smith, "Romeo, Juliet Come to Life in OCC Show," *Edmond Evening Sun*, October 14, 1988, Files of OC Theatre.
[22] Cliff Warren, "OCC Cast, Crew Add 'Thrill' to 'Ten Little Indians,'" *Edmond Sun*, October 16, 1987, Files of OC Theatre.
[23] Doug Bentin, "OCUSA's 'Diary of Anne Frank' a not-to-be-missed production," *Oklahoma Gazette*, February 23, 1995, Files of OC Theatre.
[24] Ken Adams, Conversation with the author on June 21, 2007.
[25] "Pep Band Organized," *Talon*, December 1958. A framed copy of this issue hangs on the wall of the student lounge in the Mass Communications Building.
[26] Web site, Julliard School of Music, Faculty.
[27] Most information about alumni is from the OC Web site under Arts, Theatre, Alumni.
[28] *La Quinta*, 1953, OC Archives.

Chapter 18
THE OUTCOMES

Those who struggled four hard years to found Central Christian College in Bartlesville, those who have supported the institution financially over the past 58 years, those 145 who have served on the Board of Trustees, the more than 1,000 who have taught or served on the staff, the parents of some 25,000 who have attended, and OC students themselves have a right to ask, "Is Oklahoma Christian University what they hoped it would be?" Has the university been the force for good to which they have devoted their lives and their fortunes? Has it cultivated good citizens? Has it trained effective employees? Has it nurtured faithful and active Christians? Does the university actually "transform lives for Christian faith, scholarship and service," as its mission statement declares?

The underlying philosophy on which Oklahoma Christian has operated throughout its existence is that bringing young people from Christian homes into a collegiate environment designed by and for Christians will produce adults who will be faithful to their Christian commitment and make an impact for good on their professions, communities, and churches. Oklahoma Christian and others have made attempts over the years to measure the extent to which this belief is true and such measures are helpful. This data, however, does not tell the whole story because OC alumni are scattered around the world and some of these desired outcomes are difficult to quantify.

This chapter presents some recent data about OC alumni and their spiritual lives but, primarily, it tells of alumni who illustrate OC's positive effects on its students. Earlier chapters, of course, have included many such cases, but these additional examples declare that Oklahoma Christian has produced alumni with the wide-ranging influence for which its founders hoped and for which many since that time have given their dedicated efforts.

Data on Spiritual Impact

Dr. Flavil Yeakley of the Harding Center for Church Growth Studies published in 2008 the results of research he had done about students and alumni of colleges and universities among Churches of Christ. The specific information he found about Oklahoma Christian University speaks to its spiritual influence. From a sample of 208 current students, Yeakley found that 86.1 percent of those who considered themselves members of the Church of Christ had a congregation where they regularly attended. Another 11.5 percent attended services regularly but did not connect with any specific congregation. Only 3.4 percent said they did not attend church at all.[1] Of these students, 64.4 percent said they attended two or three times a week, another 28.4 percent said they attended at least once a week.[2] These numbers suggest that the circumstances at OC encourage its students to faithful church attendance along with the attendant long-term benefits such attendance brings. As Yeakley suggests, "the highest retention rate [in continued church attendance after college] is with those young people who attend a Christian college or university _and also_ stay involved with a local congregation."[3]

Another section of Yeakley's study found that among OC alumni, 77.3 percent said they were members of a congregation of the Church of Christ, and 72.7 percent of these were in a leadership or service role in the congregation.[4] Since one of OC's aims is to produce graduates who will serve actively in Churches of Christ, these numbers indicate success in this effort.

Another way in which OC seeks to attain its long-term goal is to offer the opportunity for Christian youth to meet those with whom they may build Christian families. As noted earlier in Chapter 15, out of a recent survey of 100 random alumni, 68 replied, and of these, 71 percent said they met their mate at OC.[5] These numbers suggest that the majority of students who attend OC do meet their mate while at the university and, thus, marry someone likely to share their Christian faith.

Although these studies are not extensive, they do indicate that OC makes a positive long-term spiritual difference in its students' lives.

Impact on Churches of Christ

Missions

While there are no specific measures for the total effect Oklahoma Christian has had on Churches of Christ through its fifty-eight years, there are clear indicators. From its earliest days, the university has

Jim Batten

emphasized foreign mission work as a calling, and a large number of its students have chosen this work. Typically these students have become missionaries because they were inspired by OC teachers, some of whom have spent years in the mission field; by attending Outreach and the World Mission Workshop; by meeting missionaries who visit the campus; by going on campaigns to distant places to work at mission points; or by going on one of the OC overseas study programs.

OC has produced many long-term missionaries, such as Loy and Donna Mitchell (1954), who served for forty years in Zimbabwe, and Jim Batten (1970), who has served almost that long in Japan. John Beckloff (1953) and his wife Dottie (1953) spent forty years working with Nigerian missions. Ken Beckloff (1966) and his wife Pat (1968) were missionaries in Sierra Leone, West Africa, for ten years and in Kenya for eleven years and, after returning to the U.S., have gone back to Kenya about three months of each year to teach in the Great Commission School in Nairobi and work with the church in Mombasa. Dale Hartman (1974) spent eleven years in Australia as a missionary and after returning in 1990 has returned each year to preach, encourage churches, and teach in the Macquarie School of Biblical Studies. Allen Dutton, who received a Bible master's degree from OC in 1992, and his wife Robin Tomes Dutton (1992) have served with great success for many years as missionaries in Campinas, Brazil. Michael Mazzalongo (1984) and his

Ken and Pat Beckloff

wife Lise came to OCC from Montreal, Canada, and after several years of preaching in the U.S., they returned there to work with the church. Mazzalongo has been especially successful in using television as an outreach tool.

OC has produced more than two hundred and fifty people who have gone to live in either foreign or domestic mission fields to help send the biblical message around the world.

A recent example illustrates how the OC experience helps create in its students the desire to serve God in missions. In July 2007, four alumni couples left the United States to embark on a mission project to establish a new congregation of the Church of Christ in Vienna, Austria. Jake Haskew (2000) majored in Electrical Engineering and had a good job as an engineer. His wife, Amanda (1999), had majored in Early Childhood Education. Josh Hensal (2003) had majored in Information Systems with a second major in Vocational Ministry and worked for a major oil company.

Vienna Team. Left to right adults: Hensals,
Rushers, Lockwoods, and Haskews

His wife Kim (2002) received her degree in Advertising Design. Ira Lockwood (2003) had a double major at OC in Mechanical Engineering and in Bible and Ministry and was employed as an engineer. Kari (2001), his wife, finished a degree in Liberal Arts, completed a master's in family life at UCO, and was working at the Oklahoma Department of Human Services. Brian Rusher (2002), who had majored in English/Writing with a Bible minor, had a job with a major U.S. corporation. His wife, Alisha (2002), who got her degree in Information Systems, had completed an MBA at OC and was working at a major oil company. These students all met their mates at OC and all participated in campaigns or overseas studies as part of their OC education. After graduation, the four couples all attended Memorial Road Church of Christ, near the campus.

A few years out of college, these four couples were moving forward with careers and two of the four couples had children. Only one among these had been a Bible major, and he had carried that along with a major in engineering, and another had vocational ministry as a second major. When Mission Resources Network held an information meeting during the 2004 OC Lectureship, the Hensals and Lockwoods attended. MRN was seeking to find a mission team for Vienna, and OC professor Dr. Curt Niccum started prayer sessions about such a team forming. The Henshals and Lockwoods attended the prayer sessions and were later joined by the Rushers. By May, these six decided they were the ones God was preparing for Vienna, and their friends the Haskews soon joined them. The OC experience, the OC Lectureship, and an OC professor had worked in their hearts. After three years of preparation, including some in the group doing Bible graduate work at OC, they gained their support, gave up good jobs, and left family and friends. Now they live in a new culture, are learning a new language, and are beginning their work of spreading the gospel in Vienna.

Preaching

Oklahoma Christian alumni who serve as ministers of the church number in the hundreds. Some have preached among Churches of

Christ in congregations of more than a thousand in membership, such as Kent Allen (1979) in Oklahoma City, Chuck Monan (1986, 2001) in Little Rock, Harold Shank (1972) in Memphis, Noel Whitlock (1986) in Searcy, Ronnie White (1976) in Midland, and Mark Taylor (1984) in Oklahoma City. Many more have served in congregations of less than a thousand members. A sampling of these shows the wide geographic range in which they have served: Wayland Whitlow (1964) in Clearwater, Kansas; Shon Smith (1991) in Tuscaloosa, Alabama; Steve Bailey (1976) in Mesquite, Texas; Pat Peters (1976, 1990) in Clinton, Oklahoma; Jimmie Keas (1963) in Salina, Kansas; Randy Woodfin (1992, 1995) in Denver, Colorado; Tim Lewis (1994) in Oklahoma City; David Duncan (1989) in Houston, Texas; Shawn Fowler (1997, 2000) in Del City, Oklahoma; Tim Lewis (1994) in Oklahoma City; Dr. Harold Redd (1975) in Memphis; Dr. Phil Sanders (1974) in Franklin, Tennessee; Dean Bryce (1970) in Stillwater, Oklahoma; David Deffenbaugh (1983,1991) in Tahlequah, Oklahoma; James Waugh (1982) in Nashville, Tennessee; Art Hinley (2003) in Bartlesville, Oklahoma; Dr. Dan Owen (1975) in Paducah, Kentucky; Bud Ross (1965) in Ada, Oklahoma; Jack English (1971) in Fayetteville, Arkansas; Everette Dunn (1964) in Checotah, Oklahoma; Bill Mays (1973) in Sherman, Texas; Leon Dennis (1963) in Norman, Oklahoma; Monty Ginnings (1967) in Lawton, Oklahoma; Allen Hahn (1966) in Rosenberg, Texas; and Robert Hamm (1955) in Dewey, Oklahoma. Then there are the four Brazle brothers, Mike (1974), Mark (1975), Paul (1979), and Pete (1980), all of whom have served in ministry and/or foreign missions roles since their graduation. And there are many more.

Richard Shough (1987) has served twenty years as a youth minister and church life minister in Sherman, Texas, and San Antonio, Texas. In addition, Shough began Camp Inpact for fourth through sixth graders on the OC campus in 1992 and this became the stimulus for other summer camps such as Camp Cornerstone for middle school and Camp Zenith for high school.[6] These and other summer camps for youth, which bring hundreds to the OC campus each summer, constitute another element of OC's impact on the church.

All these preachers have received their training, and often their inspiration to become ministers, through their classes and activities at Oklahoma Christian. While, as stated in early documents, the university had no intention of making the preparation of ministers its primary goal, certainly the large number of OC graduates who have devoted their lives in a variety of roles in ministry is an important measure of the university's success.

Other Work for the Church

Beyond these working full-time in church work, there are thousands of OC alumni serving in their churches who teach Bible classes, do prison work, help in benevolence ministries, work with internationals, engage in personal evangelism, go on campaigns, serve as elders and deacons, and work in a host of other ways. Six will illustrate how so many serve. Barbara (Butler) Houck (1962) is the wife of an elder and teaches Bible classes, including seminars for women. Joy (Cole) McMillon (1963), also the wife of an elder, has had a variety of important roles with the *Christian*

Joy McMillon

Chronicle, has done extensive work in teaching Bible classes for women and, with her husband Lynn, has conducted many marriage seminars. In 2003, she received the Distinguished Christian Service Award from Pepperdine University.[7]

Many OC alumni serve as elders in their local congregations. Four among these are Max Pope (1971), successful in the roofing business, who gives a substantial portion of his time to work as an elder in the Memorial Road Church of Christ and in leading campaigns to Mexico; Gaylen Rawlins (1980) in Hutchinson, Kansas; Darrell Gingerich (1976) at Blackwell, Oklahoma; and Dr. Richard Blankenship (1959), a veterinarian, who serves as an elder in the Edmond (Oklahoma) Church of Christ.

These are but a few of the host of OC alumni who are faithful in their service to God as full-time ministers or missionaries or who are making a substantial contribution to their congregations through volunteer service. The many OC alumni serving in a wide variety of ways in churches all over the world testify to the success of Oklahoma Christian University.

Alumni in Education

OC alumni often have excelled in educational roles. Many, for example, have fulfilled vital positions in Christian universities and schools of preaching. Dr. Earl Edwards (1953) was on the Bible faculty at Freed Hardeman University for twenty-six years, much of that time as chair of the graduate program, while his fellow missionary to Italy, Dr. Don Shackleford (1953), has been a long-time Director of International Campaigns and Dean of International Studies as well as a Bible professor at Harding University.[8] OC alumnus Andy Benton (1974) is president at Pepperdine, and their provost, Dr. Darryl Tippens (1968), is also an OC graduate. Dr. Jeanine Varner (1973) is the dean of the College of Arts and Science at Abilene Christian University. Dr. Bill Goad (1979) is president at Cascade College in Portland. ZoaAnn Williams Turner (1969) is vice president for academic affairs at Southwestern Christian College. Dr. Jerry Rushford (1965) has taught at Pepperdine for thirty years and has published many useful books and articles. Dr. Bob Young (1970, 1990) served on the Bible faculty and as executive vice president at Ohio Valley University. Mark Hanstein (1975) is the dean of the Bear Valley School of Preaching in Denver. Dr. Jim Beyer (1962) taught psychology at Lubbock Christian University for twenty-six years. Dr. David Holmes (1986) is currently a professor at Pepperdine University who has also preached during the years since his graduation. He holds a Ph.D. from the University of Southern California and has written a number of articles for scholarly journals.

Since OC began in 1950, ninety-eight alumni have become regular members of the OC faculty, and still others have served on the staff and administration. The last three presidents have been alumni, as have the last three chief academic officers. Almost half of the university's Board of Trustees are now alumni of the institution. These returning alumni have brought their expertise to the university but have, as well, brought their own loyalty and insights to assist in the work the university does.

Dr. John Thompson

Among these alumni serving in education, Dr. John Thompson (1978) serves as a notable example. He completed a master's degree at the University of Oklahoma and a doctorate at Purdue University. He first returned to his alma mater in 1980 to teach history and has been an outstanding favorite among the students. As noted in Chapter 7, when suffering from illness, as unfortunately often has been the case, he sometimes taught classes via telephone from his hospital bed and continues to teach, even after both feet have been amputated. Thompson's great spirit, dedication to the university, and determination always to do his best at his work personify Oklahoma Christian University's goal to produce graduates who provide exceptional service in their chosen fields.

The education program was among the first offerings when OCC became a senior college, and more than 2,290 graduates now have finished with degrees in education.[9] While not all of these have gone into teaching, those graduating with other degrees have often chosen that profession.

OC's best-known graduate in education is Sherri Coale (1987), who graduated with an English major and was a star player on the women's basketball team. Coale coached at Norman High School and then was chosen as the head women's basketball coach at the University of Oklahoma. Taking over a program on the verge of elimination, Coale has built the program into a national powerhouse, regularly qualifying for the NCAA national tournament.

Coach Sherri Coale

Her Christian example and effective work have brought to her and her alma mater important recognition.

Other educators from Oklahoma Christian also have done well in their profession. In 1994, Dr. Fred Rhodes (1976) was named both Oklahoma Administrator of the Year and the National Distinguished Principal by the U.S. Department of Education, and Dr. Bill Pink (1990) serves as state director of program accreditation for the Oklahoma Commission for Teacher Preparation. Lynne Hearn Rowley (1971) is executive director of elementary education for Edmond Public Schools. Dr. Renee Axtell (1984) is special services director at the Mid-Del Schools. Dr. Sue Ott Rowlands (1975) is dean of the College of Liberal Arts and Human Sciences at Virginia Tech.[10] Dr. Walter Daugherity (1967) made a perfect score on the mathematics area of the Graduate Record Examination, one of two in the nation that year to do so. For this, he was selected for a special program at Harvard University from which he eventually received an Ed. D. degree. He is currently on the faculty at Texas A&M teaching artificial intelligence. Dr. Ron Wright (1969) is president of Cincinnati State Technical and Community College. Dr. James Lankford (1964) has served as the dean of the College of Health and Human Sciences at Northern Illinois University.[11]

These and a host of other OC graduates have made a strong contribution to the education profession both at the collegiate and elementary/secondary levels and in both public and private schools.

Medicine

Medicine is another field attracting a large number of OC graduates. Just since 1992, seventy-nine have entered programs to become physicians or dentists, and when taking into account the school's forty-two previous years, the number entering these professions rises to well above a hundred. These physicians and dentists have served their patients throughout the world, with many being involved not only in their own practice but in medical missions, as well.

Dr. Dan Miller finished two years at OCC in Bartlesville in 1956 and later received his M.D. degree from the University of Oklahoma. Miller, a surgeon, practiced in Tulsa for twenty-three years and in recent years has been particularly active in boosting activities among OCC alumni from Bartlesville. Dr. Danny Minor graduated from Oklahoma Christian in 1961 with an associate's degree and then attended the University of Oklahoma for both his bachelor's degree and his M.D. After two years in the U.S. Navy, he has served for thirty years as a general surgeon in Tahlequah, Oklahoma. An elder in the church there for twenty-three years, he has been involved in medical missions in Kenya, Nigeria, Guatemala, Ukraine, and Zimbabwe.

Dr. Mike Herndon (1980) received his D.O. degree from OSU Medical Center in Tulsa. He worked for many years in family practice, often has served as a physician in the OC Health Center, and is now employed by the State of Oklahoma. A deacon in the Memorial Road Church of Christ, Herndon has done medical missions in Guatemala and Mexico and has provided volunteer services at the Hope Center in Edmond, Oklahoma, and at the Lighthouse Medical Clinic in Oklahoma City's inner city. Dr. Charles Branch, Jr., (1977) received his medical degree at University of Texas Southwestern Medical School and completed a specialty in neurosurgery at Wake Forest, where he stayed on and now is chair of neurosurgery. Branch, known internationally for surgery techniques and equipment he has developed for spinal operations, has been on medical missions to Nigeria, Guyana, and Haiti and is a deacon in his church. Dr. Russ Hanan (1969) is a surgeon in Oklahoma City who serves as an elder and has worked with internationals at the Memorial Road Church of Christ for twenty-five years. He also has volunteered at the Lighthouse Medical Clinic.

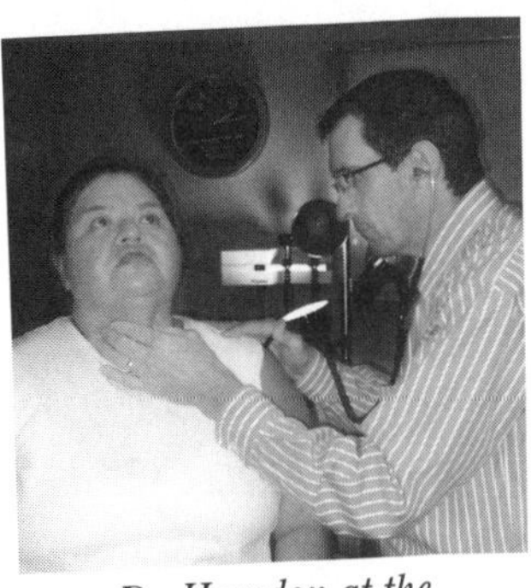

Dr. Herndon at the Lighthouse Medical Clinic

Dr. Lynn Mitchell (1978), daughter of Coach Ray Vaughn, has for fifteen years been the director of medicare for the State of Oklahoma and oversees the expenditure of more than four billion dollars a year. She, along with her husband Barry (who is also a physician), have worked for medical missions in Honduras and have volunteered at the Lighthouse Medical Clinic. Dr. Nicquel Gordon (1995) is another OC alumna who serves well in the medical field. An obstetrician/gynecologist in Hot Springs, Arkansas, Gordon has now delivered more than two thousand babies in her medical career and credits her time at OC as starting her down the medical career path.[12] Dr. Brad

Britton (1983) has a medical degree from the University of Oklahoma where he specialized in ophthalmology. He has developed the largest ophthalmology practice in Oklahoma, with fifty-one locations, and has been named three times as one of the top fifty LASIK surgeons in North America. Britton has been on medical missions to Guatemala and has developed Vision for Humanity to provide cataract surgery for those who cannot afford it.[13] Dr. David Keck (1976), son of long-time OC teacher Dr. Darvin Keck, has been practicing dentistry for twenty-eight years and has gone on medical missions to Honduras and Mexico. Dr. Warren Branch (1977), son of long-time Board member Dr. Charles Branch, is another alumnus in dentistry. In addition to his practice, he has taught in dental schools and been to Guyana on a medical mission.

These doctors and dentists, as well as those who have entered other medical fields such as optometry, nursing, and pharmacy, have served their communities, but in an even larger sense, they have provided both the medical and the spiritual needs of people around the world.

Government Service

Ray Vaughn, Jr.

Some OC alumni have entered politics. John Nance (1955) has served in the Oklahoma House of Representatives, as has Raymond Vaughn, Jr. (1970), who is now a county commissioner in Oklahoma County. Dan Branch (1980) is a member of the Texas House of Representatives, and Charles Portwood (1985) serves in the House of Representatives in Missouri. Nancy Carol (Moore) Riley (1979) from Tulsa has served in the Oklahoma State Senate.[14]

Diana Kniffin had wanted to work at NASA since she was eight. She enrolled at OC in computer science, and following her junior year, she was 1 of 36 out of 5,000 applicants selected for a summer internship with NASA. Following her OC graduation in 2003, she earned a master's degree from Florida Institute of Technology and then got her dream job in the IT Security Office at NASA. Her boss, Henry Yu, says, "the quality of her work is exceptional" and "she performs like a seasoned veteran."[15]

Diana Kniffin at NASA

Dr, Randy Hatfield (1985) is another OC graduate filling an important government post. After majoring at OC in American Studies with minors in Spanish and political science, Hatfield completed a master's degree from American University and a doctorate in social policy and administration from the London School of Economics and Political

Dr. Randy Hatfield in Pakistan

Science. For the last twenty years he has worked in Pakistan, at first with foundations, and then as the director of the education office for USAID. He recalls that Ralph Burcham inspired him to travel and he went on mission trips while at OCC. Hatfield says, "the trips I took during the summers of my college days provided an excellent platform for my later service abroad."[16] Kevin Ward (1979) works with the Upper Nicola Indian Band and Scw'exmx Child and Family Services in British Columbia.[17]

These alumni demonstrate the OC values of participation in the democratic process and of making their communities and their world a better place.

Military Service

Many former OC students have served in the military. One of those who has excelled is Marine Major General John Admire. Admire attended OC two years, 1960–1962, playing on the basketball team and being involved in student government. After two years, he transferred to the University of Oklahoma to complete a degree in journalism. While there, he also received a master's degree. A few weeks after graduation, Admire joined the Marine Corps and soon was serving as a combat platoon leader in Vietnam. He chose

General John Admire speaking at OC

to stay in the Marines and advanced through the ranks to Major General before his retirement in 1998. Admire was stationed all around the world: Asia, Europe, Persian Gulf, Australia, Hawaii, and other locations. Two of his most significant assignments were serving on the staff of General Colin Powell in the Pentagon and his position as a Senior Military Social Aide to the White House during the Jimmy Carter administration.[18] Allen Shepherd, mentioned in

Chapter 9, "The Donors," served as a pilot in Vietnam and, after being shot down, had to be rescued from enemy territory.

Sgt. Kyle Seitsinger

Marine sergeant Kyle Seitsinger was called to active duty from his senior year at OC in November of 2003. On January 29, 2004, word came that he had been killed while serving in Afghanistan.[19] Crystalyn Starks Filmore, All-American in track at OC, after graduating from OC in 2002, joined the U.S. Army and has attained the rank of captain.[20] Jared Kite (2003) also holds the rank of captain in the U.S. Army and has done two tours of duty in Iraq.

A more recent OC graduate, Tony Weedn (2004), came to OC wanting to become a pilot in the U.S. Air Force. He has achieved this dream, and did so well in his own pilot training he was assigned as a flying instructor. In that role, he not only trains pilots but says his "goal is to be the best Christlike example I can be and bring as many people to heaven with me as possible."[21]

Lt. Tony Weedn

Some OC students have prepared for military service through OC's cooperative ROTC programs with the University of Central Oklahoma and the University of Oklahoma, thus allowing students to graduate with commissions in the U.S. Army or the U.S Air Force. OC counts as one measure of its success those alumni who have entered the military service and who have, by so doing, protected the United States.

Business

OC has produced many who have excelled in the world of business. Richard Lawson (1966), also mentioned in Chapter 9 on "The Donors," has developed a major computer software company. Mark Jackson (1978) has served as president and CEO of the Noble Corporation of Houston, Texas. Ken Parker (1983) is co-head of Managed Services, RiskMetrics of Norman, Oklahoma, and is on the OC Board. David Smith (1968) is the owner of one of the largest trophy companies in the world, located in Midwest City, Oklahoma.

Mark Stansberry (1977) is chairman of GTD Group, which comprises several companies, primarily in the oil business. In 2007, he received the Fund for American Studies Service Award during

Jeff Dimick

the Fund's 40th Anniversary Celebration in Washington, D.C.[22] Jeff Dimick (1983), another OC graduate excelling in his profession, is a rocket scientist who is a manager with Boeing in Los Angeles. On the side, he works with One World, a digital editing company that prepares material for television. He is also active in church work in El Segundo, California, and serves on the OC Board.[23]

Greg Christison graduated with an engineering degree specializing in computers. He completed a master's degree in communications from Purdue and, after several years of working with the U.S. Air Force, moved to Texas Instruments. In 2004, he joined WiQuest Communications as vice president of engineering to develop silicon solutions for Ultra-Wide Band products. He is now Chief Technical Officer for WiQuest. As of 2007, he held eleven U.S. patents and has more pending. He is active in church, and he and his wife Paige provide a home for foster children.[24]

And there are many more. David Seat (1973) is a regional president of BancFirst, and Todd Dobson (1985) is the chief financial officer and executive vice president for Midland Financial Corporation. Both of these serve on the OC Board. Mike Carroll (1975) is president and CEO of Heritage Trust, a financial planning company; and Janice Toldan Guymer (1983) is manager of payroll and human resources at Devon Energy. Aaron Sales (1972) is operations manager for Intel Corporation.[25] Patrice Dills Douglas (1983) was named as one of "50 Women Making a Difference" by the *Oklahoma Journal Record*. She has served as vice president and general counsel for ACP Sheet Metal Co., Inc. & Air Spiral Manufacturing Co.[26] Dr. Allison Garrett was employed at Wal-mart as vice president of benefits compliance and planning and then as vice president and general counsel of the Corporate Division before returning to OC as vice president for academic affairs.[27]

In communications, several have gone from Oklahoma Christian to become television reporters and anchors: Ray Vaughn, Jr. (1970), Barrett Vanlandingham (1987), Erin McLemore (2005), and Tamara Pratt (1990), who won an Emmy in her first year on the job. Megan Johnson Harris (2002) is a producer for the evening news for a station in Dallas and has won an Emmy and a regional Edward R. Murrow award. David Jurney (1994) and David Jones (1994) have won awards for videos they have produced. Mike Brown (1993) has served as lead operator/master control supervisor at the Ohio News Network; also, he and his wife, Aleshire (1992), have been foster parents to eight children.[28] Bobby Ross (1993) has been a journalist with major newspapers and with the Associated Press, and now he is the managing editor for the *Christian Chronicle*. Murray Evans (1989) reports for the Associated Press; Steve Lackmeyer (1990) often writes by-lined articles for the *Daily Oklahoman*, and so does Mike Baldwin (1978).

Jennifer Ma

From the OCC program in advertising design, Scott Horton (1986) is in charge of the Web site for the *Daily Oklahoman*, and Daniel Streety (1992) is creative director for Saatchi and Saatchi, one of the largest and most creative design shops in the world. Jennifer Ma (1993) offices in New York City and served as the chief designer of the highly acclaimed visual and special effects for the 2008 Olympics in China. She also has had works exhibited in the Guggenheim Museum and the Museum of Modern Art in New York, the Tate Modern in London, and the Centre Pompidou in Paris. She attributes much of her success to the foundations laid at OC with professors Michael O'Keefe and David Crismon.[29]

Legal Profession

Many OC alumni have completed law school and gone on to success in their field. Ray Don Jackson (1962) has been both a district attorney and a judge, Gayland Gieger (1994) has been an assistant district attorney in Oklahoma County, sometimes prosecuting high profile cases, and Sandra Howard Rinehart (1981) has served in the Oklahoma Office of the Attorney General since 1986, advancing to senior assistant attorney general. Andrea Poteet Johnson (1987), after serving in the Oklahoma Attorney General's Office, has been senior counsel for the Oklahoma Corporation Commission. Jay Tabor (1986), after receiving a law degree from Harvard, is now partner in an international law firm. Many others have successful law practices, such as Eric (1970) and Linda King (1969), Dewey Leggett (1986), Daryl Lidia (1985), Matthew Winton (1996), and Tyson Schwerdtfeger (1999).

Service to the Community and Beyond

Many Oklahoma Christian alumni have found their own unique ways of making the world a better place. Whether meeting a need in their own communities or moving in broader circles, these former students have shown concern for improving the conditions of others. Some particular examples well illustrate the heart of helping others found in many OC graduates.

Vernetta Hardin Wallace

Vernetta Hardin Wallace (1968) lives in Anchorage, Alaska, where she has found a special way to help others. In 1972, she and her husband, David, began taking foster children into their home, and by 1994, they had helped 107. The first child was deaf, and others have been born addicted to drugs, physically or sexually abused, or abandoned. In 1994, she was named one of twenty recipients of the First Lady's Volunteer Award given by the wife of the governor of Alaska. She also was chosen to attend the 1980 Conference on Families at the White House.[30]

Molefi Kete Asante, whom OCC students will remember as Arthur Smith (1964), was the first African American student to graduate from Oklahoma Christian. Asante has published sixty-five books, and the last, *The History of Africa* (2007), is used all over the world. Asante calls his time at OC "valuable and productive" and "the incubator of many thoughts and ideas that have led to my achievements." "[31]

After graduating from OCC in 1981, Steve Hassman moved to New York City to work with a financial firm. While there, he became active in the Manhattan Church of Christ and was drawn to work with the underprivileged. In 1994, he became the executive director of Camp Shiloh, which provides a new kind of experience for children from poor families, and he served in that role until 1999.[32] Bill Hamrick (1953) has served for twenty-nine years with Hope Harbor home for children near Tulsa, including fifteen years as Executive Director.

In the Philippines, Salvador Cariaga (1983) preaches and operates an orphanage for children. After a recent disaster in Leyte, he took in fifteen children, many of whose families were buried in a mudslide. The children attend a Christian school in Butuan City and are active in the church.[33] Cariaga's father, Roman, also a preacher, attended OC, and his son, Peter, is now attending in preparation for the ministry.

Conclusion

Many other alumni might have been mentioned and other categories might have been explored for success stories. These samples, however, represent the wide diversity of fields in which Oklahoma Christian graduates have served and demonstrate they have done so with distinction. The university's alumni have excelled in spiritual ministry, with a large number serving as missionaries around the world, as pulpit ministers, and in other ministry roles, and thousands fill volunteer roles in their churches. They have been successful in careers in education, medicine, law, business, government, the military, communications, and other fields. In addition, they have served their communities in important ways.

Oklahoma Christian University has been recognized by *U.S. News & World Report* as one of the most outstanding institutions in the nation among its peer institutions, ranking in the top ten among colleges and universities of its type in the western states. The John Templeton Foundation has placed the school among the nation's best character-building colleges.[34] The Princeton Review also listed OC as a "Best Western College."

This history of Oklahoma Christian University has told the story of those who began efforts to establish a Christian college in Oklahoma in 1946 and of those who have followed in their steps. From its very small beginning in Bartlesville with fewer than a hundred students and only a two-year curriculum, OC has developed into an internationally known university with 2,500 students a year earning both baccalaureate and graduate degrees. It has a campus of fourteen academic buildings and twenty-two buildings for campus housing and food service. These facilities have a fair market value in excess of $100 million. The university has an endowment of $69.8 million, and an annual operational budget of $31 million for its Oklahoma City campus. Most importantly, though, it has positively influenced some twenty-five thousand students who have served well in their professions, their communities, and their churches.

A favorite scripture on the OC campus is Isaiah 40:31: "but those who hope in the LORD will renew their strength. They will soar on wings like eagles; they will run and not grow weary, they will walk and not be faint" (NIV). This passage carries additional meaning for the school since OC's athletic teams are "The Eagles," and its words are inscribed both in the Biblical Studies Center and the Centennial Tower.

Oklahoma Christian University has indeed "soared on wings like eagles."

Chapter 18, Endnotes

1   Flavil Yeakley, Results of Student and Almuni Surveys at Oklahoma Christian University, 1, April 8, 2008, Files of the Office of the President of OC.

2   Ibid., 2.

3   Ibid., 46.

4   Ibid., 9–10. A total of twenty-three OC alumni responded to this survey, but the results are similar among those attending all the Christian universities surveyed, a total number of 1,873. This information is from Yeakley's Preliminary Report, 23–24, Files of the Office of the President of OC.

5   Survey done by the Alumni Office at Oklahoma Christian University in 2007.

6   Allison Shumate, "Shough Named Distinguished Alumnus," *Vision*, Fall 2007, 2–3.

7   "Milestones," *Vision*, Fall 2003, 9.

8   "Milestones, *Vision,* Spring 2008, 16.

9   Count of education graduates from commencement programs from 1992 through April of 2008.

10   Rachel Yeakley, "Sue Ott Rowlands," *Vision*, Fall 2007, 19.

11   "Milestones," *Vision*, Spring 2001, 9.

12   Rachel Yeakley, "Gordon Named Distinguished Young Alumna," *Vision*, Fall 2007, 5.

13   Brad Britton, Email to the author, June 16, 2008.

14   "Milestones," *Vision*, Spring 2001, 10.

15   Allison Shumate, "Reaching for the Stars," *Vision*, Spring 2008, 6–7.

16   Dawn Shelton, "Across the World: Hatfield Leads U.S. Education Project in Pakistan," *Vision*, Spring 2008, 4.

17   "Milestones," *Vision*, Fall 2007, 23.

18   John Admire, Conversation with the author, November 8, 2007.

19   Kyle Seitsinger, Internet entry from Wentworth Military Academy.

20   Alumni Direcctory, Oklahoma Christian University, 2006, 81.

21   Michael Mitchell, "Flying by the Seat of His Pants," *Vision*, Fall 2007, 16–17.

22   Ibid., 22–23.

23   Dawn Shelton, "Jeff of All Trades," *Vision*, Fall 2007, 18.

24   Greg Christison, Email to Joe Watson, October 1, 2007.

25   "Milestones," *Vision*, Fall 2003.

26   "Milestones," *Vision*, Spring 2004, 11.

27   Allison Garrett, Email to the author, June 16, 2008.

28   "Milestones," *Vision,* Spring 2001, 13.

29   Wes McKenzie, "Creative Renaissance," *Vision*, Spring 2008, 9.

30   "Alumni profile: Vernetta Hardin Wallace," *President's Report, 1993–1994*, OC Archives.

31   Molefi Kete Asante, Email to the author, October 18, 2007.

32   Sarah Thornburg-Horton, "Camp Shiloh," *Vision*, Spring 1999, 5–6.

33   Salvador B. Cariaga, Email to the author, June 12, 2008.

34   *President's Report, 1993–1994*, OC Archives; *President's Report, 1994–1995*, OC Archives.

INDEX